Problems of Democratic Transition and Consolidation

PROBLEMS OF DEMOCRATIC TRANSITION AND CONSOLIDATION

Southern Europe, South America, and Post-Communist Europe

Juan J. Linz and Alfred Stepan

The Johns Hopkins University Press

Baltimore and London

© 1996 The Johns Hopkins University Press
All rights reserved. Published 1996
Printed in the United States of America on acid-free paper
6 8 9 7 5

The Johns Hopkins University Press
2715 North Charles Street
Baltimore, Maryland 21218-4363
www.press.jhu.edu

Library of Congress Cataloging-in-Publication Data
will be found at the end of this book.
A catalog record for this book is available from the British Library.

ISBN 0-8018-5157-2   ISBN 0-8018-5158-0 (pbk.)

Contents

Figures, Tables, and Exhibits

EXHIBITS

Preface and Acknowledgments

In the penultimate paragraph of the preface to the multivolume work we edited, *The Breakdown of Democratic Regimes,* we wrote that "high priority for further work along these lines should now be given to the analysis of the conditions that lead to the breakdown of authoritarian regimes, to the process of *transition* from authoritarian to democratic regimes, and especially to the political dynamics of the *consolidation* of postauthoritarian democracies."[1] The book in your hands represents our effort to contribute to that research agenda.

A caveat about the title of the book is first in order. As comparativists we are painfully aware that most political transformations away from a once-stable nondemocratic regime do not end in "completed democratic transitions." Fewer still become consolidated democracies.[2] And, as our 1978 volume makes clear, even once-consolidated democracies can break down.[3]

Yet, precisely because we believe completed democratic transitions are an empirical minority of all major political transformations and because we adhere to the normative position that completed democratic transitions and democratic consolidations are desirable, this book is explicitly devoted to the analysis of the conditions and practices that make such outcomes possible. Completed democratic transitions, and consolidated democracies, are the key dependent variables of this book. While we try to call attention in the book to "possibilist" strategies,

1. Juan J. Linz and Alfred Stepan, eds., *The Breakdown of Democratic Regimes* (Baltimore: Johns Hopkins University Press, 1978), ix–x. Emphasis added.

2. Indeed, much of our work has been devoted to the analysis of political transformations that do not result in completed democratic transitions. A prominent group of such countries includes Iran after the fall of the Shah, Haiti after the fall of "Papa Doc," and Nicaragua after the fall of Somoza. In all these countries, a sultanistic form of what Weber would call extreme "patrimonialism" was present. These cases will be analyzed separately in a volume on sultanistic regimes and their legacies being edited by H. E. Chehabi and Juan J. Linz. A related, but analytically distinct, problem of noncompleted democratic transitions emerges when a nondemocratic regime breaks down or is overthrown and an "emergency interim regime" created, which postpones democratic elections *sine die,* in order to make fundamental changes. See Yossi Shain and Juan J. Linz, *Between States: Interim Governments and Democratic Transitions* (New York: Cambridge University Press, 1995). Alfred Stepan, as a member of the human rights group *American Watch,* constantly had to urge U.S. government administration officials not to debase the word *democratization* by equating it with the mere *electoralism* found in countries such as El Salvador, Guatemala, and Honduras, where the military exercised their large undemocratic prerogatives even after elections.

3. An extensive discussion of our definitions of *completed democratic transitions* and *consolidated democracies* will be found in chapter 1.

we will also call attention to problems and to how successful outcomes are heavily conditioned—and in some cases precluded—by socioeconomic factors or even the crisis or absence of a state.

Our book develops the following line of exploration and argumentation. Part 1 is devoted to general theoretical considerations, which while of direct relevance for the rest of the book, can be read as a set of freestanding theoretical arguments. In chapter 1 we begin by defining and discussing our two dependent variables, *completed democratic transitions* and *consolidated democracies.* We then develop an argument as to why and how democracies need five interacting arenas to become consolidated. These arenas, which interact with and reinforce each other, are: a lively civil society, a relatively autonomous political society, a rule of law, a usable state, and an economic society (note, *not* just a capitalist market).[4] In the remainder of part 1 we explore seven independent generic variables that we argue are particularly important for analyzing processes of democratic transition and consolidation, and we advance propositions concerning these variables.[5] Two of our variables are so important that we will call them *macro variables* and give them chapter-length status.

In chapter 2 we discuss our first macro independent variable, one that has to date been seriously underanalyzed in the literature on democratic transition and consolidation, namely the complex relationship between state, nation(s), and democratization. We call this variable *stateness.* We show why the existence of a sovereign state is a prerequisite for democracy, and indeed citizenship. We then assess the implications for democracy of different strategies of state-building and nation-building when state and nation do not coincide, or indeed when the nation-state and democracy have conflicting logics, as they all too often have.

In chapters 3 and 4 we discuss our other macro variable, namely the character of the prior regime type. Since we argue for a modified "path-dependent" approach to democracy, it seemed to us important to reanalyze the major types of modern nondemocratic regimes from which different transition attempts begin. To do so, in chapter 3, we first create a revised typology of modern nondemocratic regimes: totalitarian, post-totalitarian, authoritarian, and sultanistic. In chapter 4, we then attempt to make as explicit as possible what *paths* to democratic transition are available, or unavailable, from each of these four regime types. We also discuss what predictable *tasks* must be accomplished within each of the five are-

4. While we argue in support of a definition of democracy that includes these minimalist requirements of a consolidated democracy, we do not have a teleological end-state in mind because a quite distinctive interplay of the five arenas inevitably emerges in each consolidated democracy. Even consolidated democracies can differ significantly as to their quality and the degree to which they do, or do not, deepen to include greater equality and more intense participation.

5. For better or worse we will not restrict ourselves to the procrustean bed of this framework. The specificities of history are also important, and thus we will discuss the contributions, where appropriate, of some variables (such as *leadership* and *timing*), that do not lend themselves to generic propositions but are critical to the historical analysis of any particular case.

nas of a consolidated democracy, before a polity, starting from a position approximating one of these four ideal type regimes, could possibly become a consolidated democracy.

In chapter 5 we discuss our five remaining independent variables. Two are actor-centered and three are context-centered. The two actor-centered variables concern the question of the specific leadership base of the prior nondemocratic regime and the question of who initiates and controls the transition. The three context variables relate to international influences, the political-economy of legitimacy and coercion, and constitution-making environments.

In parts 2, 3, and 4 we apply the framework developed in part 1 to fourteen countries, using both *cross-regional* and *intra-regional* analysis. In the process of our research for this book, one or both of us made multiple visits to each of the thirteen countries (not including successor states) considered. One or both of us also studied extensively a number of relevant countries that we do not include, such as South Korea, Peru, Bolivia, and Indonesia. Why so many countries? Why the exclusion of potentially relevant cases? Why a single authorial voice instead of an edited volume, with country specialists who inevitably would know much more than we about particular countries? Our response to all of these valid questions is that, at this stage of the development of knowledge about democratic (and nondemocratic) politics, one of the critical tasks is to explore, using a fairly rigorous cross-regional comparative analysis, major differences and similarities between democratization problems in various regions of the world. We believe this is best done from a single authorial perspective. Moreover, we also believe that contextualized, *intra-regional* comparative analysis will allow us to call attention to, and hopefully explain, major differences that might have been overlooked in the single-country monographic literature.

To combine the advantages of cross-regional and intraregional analysis, we decided to select and directly observe countries that belong to three distinctive regions in the world. This makes sense only if *most of the region had made a recent and significant effort at democratic transition.* This limited the possible range of regions.[6] We chose southern Europe, which in the 1970s had been on the periphery of the democratic core of the European Community; we chose the southern cone of South America, capitalist and part of the West ideologically, but not sociologically, politically, or economically a part of the advanced democratic market community; and finally, we chose post-Communist Europe, until recently under a system that was not ideologically part of the West and where, we assumed, "real

6. In the early 1990s these criteria excluded African and Islamic regions. South Korea and Taiwan would have made an interesting small set. However, the region would have had to include countries such as North Korea and China that are not even liberalizing, much less democratizing. We believe that the South Korean and Taiwanese transitions could have been studied using our framework, notwithstanding their Confucian legacy. One of the most important problems for South Korea and especially Taiwan was in fact one of our macro-variables, *stateness.*

existing socialism" produced a persisting legacy of interests in tension with the newly expressed goals of a democratic market future.

Within these three different regions we decided to work with entire *sets* of countries, so that we did not select countries that would privilege or prejudge certain conclusions. The easiest set to choose was Southern Europe. Only three southern European countries began a transition in the last thirty years—Spain, Portugal, and Greece—so we included all of them.

In South America, a regional set was chosen for us by modern history and modern scholarship. Four relatively developed countries—Brazil, Argentina, Chile, and Uruguay—all had democratic breakdowns in the 1960s and early 1970s and, in Guillermo O'Donnell's famous analysis, had all established "bureaucratic authoritarian regimes." These regimes demobilized popular organizations, repressed civil societies, were (unlike the countries in Southern Europe) led by hierarchical military regimes, and were "presidential" instead of "parliamentary" in their institutional and cultural legacies.[7] As late as 1987 the outcome in three of these four countries was highly uncertain, so we had the chance to observe directly possible transitions and possible failures.[8]

In post-Communist Europe we decided to include all the countries that were a clear part of the Soviet subsystem in that they belonged to the Warsaw Pact security zone and the COMECON economic zone. Our set, therefore, includes the former Union of Soviet Socialist Republics (USSR), Poland, Hungary, Czechoslovakia, Romania, and Bulgaria.[9] The task for a comparativist is to iden-

7. See Guillermo O'Donnell, *Modernization and Bureaucratic Authoritarianism: Studies in South American Politics* (Berkeley: Institute of International Studies, Politics of Modernization Series, 1973) and David Collier, ed., *The New Authoritarianism in Latin America* (Princeton: Princeton University Press, 1979). To have chosen the more than thirty countries in Latin America and the Caribbean as one set would have made little analytical sense and in any case would have been unmanageable. We acknowledge that at least three different sets in the region could have been chosen, each one with a slightly different socioeconomic, political, and geopolitical mix. These are an Andean regional set, which would have been less developed socioeconomically and would have introduced a strong component of indigenous cultures; a Central American regional set, where civil wars and U.S. involvement would have been more prominent; or the Caribbean microstates that were formerly British colonies and most of which are long-standing parliamentary democracies.

8. In 1987, Chile was in the midst of an economic boom, the hierarchically led military were united behind Pinochet, and the democratic opposition was divided. In Argentina, democracy in 1989 looked extremely perilous as the first democratically elected president, Raúl Alfonsín, had been subject to five uprisings led by junior officers and twelve general strikes since his inauguration, the economy was experiencing a hyperinflation, and Alfonsín was forced to leave office early due to the chaos. In 1989 in Brazil, a country with one of the most unequal distributions of income in the world, the hierarchically led military were still influential, a direct presidential election had still not been held, and a populist presidential candidate with virtually no organized party behind him was on the horizon. Brazil as of this writing is still not close to full democratic consolidation.

9. The only country that met this criterion that we excluded was East Germany, which, due to its situation of "two states, one nation," voted to subsume itself into the ready-made democratic state of the Federal Republic of Germany; thus, East Germany is not really a case of sovereign democratic state transition except for the period of March 18 to October 3, 1990. In some ways the loss of East Germany to the book is especially unfortunate because Linz was born in Germany and spent 1990–91 at the Wissenschaftskolleg zu Berlin. We will refer to East Germany in passing when we discuss the stateness problem, cases of regime

tify and evaluate elements of commonality and diversity. Only by so doing can we evaluate some problems that all the European post-Communist countries we explore share because for so long they were the targets of the effort of the former Soviet Union to impose a common political, economic, and ideological system on them. But, despite this shared legacy, there was, and is, great diversity in the region. In the process of analyzing and explaining these elements of commonality and diversity, we hope to contribute to the task of incorporating post-Communist politics into comparative politics, so we end the book by trying to put the great problems and diversity of post-Communist Europe into a full comparative and theoretical perspective.[10] In the process we were forced to recast and rethink much of the transition and consolidation literature that we have been so involved with since the mid-1970s. This explains our dangerous, and seemingly illogical, choice of making the post-Communist part of the book (the area where our expertise and linguistic ability is weakest) the longest. Even if not for all the readers, at least for the authors the journey has been worthwhile.

As befits a book of this scope, we employ a variety of methods: typological analysis, survey analysis, content analysis, neo-institutional and path-dependent analysis; some game theory; and extensive interviews with key actors, to name the most prominent. We believe that this is the first conceptually oriented, empirical, cross-regional and intra-regional study of modern democratization, written with a single authorial voice. Precisely because of this, as we put the volume to press, we are acutely conscious of its inherent limitations. There is no doubt that it would be a *better* book if we had five more years to study and think about post-Communist Europe and to read the fundamental historical studies that are only now in progress. However, as scholars who are committed to interactive research in our broad international community, we believe that this book will probably be more *useful* if released now, so that the new generation of social scientists, historians, and political thinkers and activists, who in many cases are writing their first monographs, can have access to our tentative arguments. We hope our successors will refine and, if necessary, refute our arguments in the interest of a better understanding of one of the most exciting and difficult processes in modern history.

Let us acknowledge another limitation of this book. The type of social science

---

"collapse," and what we call the *informer-lustration* syndrome. By our criteria, Yugoslavia had to be left out. But Yugoslavia analytically shares some important features with the USSR, such as the sequence of liberalization without democratization, an extreme federal constitution that took on a new life after contested multiparty elections were held in the republics before they were held in the center, and the subsequent disintegration of the state and (with the major exception of Slovenia) the emergence of ethnocracies. As an extension of our analysis of the USSR, we explore the consequences of this form of state disintegration for Russia and the successor states of Estonia and Latvia, where issues of citizenship and nationalizing states versus homeland states became a central problem. Albania is left out because, not only was it not in the Warsaw Pact or COMECON, but also it did not start a democratic transition until much of our research was complete.

10. The theoretical framework we explicate in part 1, especially our typology of modern nondemocratic regimes, provides a new analytic perspective on the variance in post-Communist Europe.

in which we are engaged, and which excites us, will, a century from now, be material for historians and might not be very relevant to a theory of democracy or democratization. This is perhaps unfortunate for those who dream of social physics or of models of social change like that offered in economic theory by the students of capitalist market economies. But, we surmise that these models will also become historicized. That is the fate of social science. The events we are studying took place in historical time, in particular social spaces, and in particular states and nations that we know are not eternal. We gladly accept this inherent limitation of our effort. We believe, however, that to gain some understanding now of the events between the 1970s and the twenty-first century is a worthwhile and exciting goal. Whatever our success or failure, to try to analyze the events in thirteen countries, in three different regions, in which at least 500 million people live (and in one of which one of the authors is a citizen) is a worthwhile endeavor for social scientists.[11]

A book such as this not only has many limitations but also incurs extremely high debts of gratitude. There is hardly a country or a problem we write about that one of our former or current students at Yale University (where, shortly after writing the 1978 preface to *The Breakdown of Democracy*, we created and occasionally co-taught what may have been the first course on democratic transition and consolidation), Columbia University, the Juan March Institute, or the Central European University has not informed us about and helpfully criticized our earlier analysis. We are grateful to our student-colleagues from around the world who read the classic works on democracy with us and shared their critical insights not only on Southern Europe and South America, but also on what they saw as the potential for major transformative changes, the final direction of which was of course never fully certain, in such countries as South Korea, the Philippines, Iran, and Poland. A few of the many to whom we owe gratitude are Nancy Bermeo, H. E. Chehabi, Paloma Aguilar, Ed Gibson, Robert Fishman, Daniel V. Friedheim, Charles Gillespie, Jan T. Gross, Luis Eduardo González, Jonathan Hartlyn, Mimi Keck, Robert Martínez, Guillermo O'Donnell, Vello Pettie, Oleg Protsyk, Cindy Skach, Brian Smith, Hector Shamis, Evelyn Huber Stevens, John Stevens, and Mark Thompson. They have enriched our work and our lives.

We want to thank the Wissenschaftskolleg zu Berlin, where Linz had a fellowship in 1990–91 and which hosted a small international conference on an early draft of the book. Early work leading to the book was also encouraged by the in-

11. An unfortunate, but we believe necessary, limitation of the book is that, to fit our analysis into the compass of one book, we greatly compressed the "democratic transition phase" of southern Europe and South America because, as our notes to each chapter make clear, we and other scholars have published extensive monographs on these topics elsewhere. We also under-report and indeed underanalyze some arguments that have been central to our scholarly production in the last twenty years, such as timing, leadership, religion, and corporatism. We do, of course, integrate our approaches to these themes into this book.

vitation to Linz to be Max Weber Visiting Professor at Heidelberg University. Both authors are also happy to acknowledge their fellowships at the Juan March Institute of Advanced Social Science in Madrid. Our temerity to write such a wide-ranging book was encouraged by the colleagueship and advice we received as participants in the multivolume project *Politics of Democratic Consolidation in Southern Europe,* edited by Richard Gunther, P. Nikiforos Diamandouros, and Hans Jürgen Puhle, and the multivolume project Linz co-edited with Larry Diamond and Seymour Martin Lipset, *Democracy in Developing Countries.* Stepan wants to thank his colleagues in two multiyear, multivolume projects, one on East-West transformation coordinated by Adam Przeworski, published as *Sustainable Democracy,* and the other a project edited by Guillermo O'Donnell, Philippe C. Schmitter, and Laurence Whitehead, which resulted in their *Transitions from Authoritarian Rule.*

Alfred Stepan also wants to thank St. Antony's College, Oxford, where he was a Senior Associate Member, for its hospitality in 1993 and Timothy Garton Ash, Archie Brown, and Alex Pravda, who gave us the benefit of close readings of early drafts of this book. Other readers from around the world who helped us greatly were Yitzhak M. Brudny, László Bruszt, Richard Gunther, János Kis, Wiktor Osiatynski, Paulo Sergio Pinheiro, Anna Seleny, and Samuel Valenzuela.

Richard Rose deserves our special thanks for having produced with the Paul Lazarsfeld Society of Vienna a unique database for the study of political and economic change and public response to those changes in the former Communist countries. Our analysis relies heavily on those surveys—although the responsibility for their interpretation is only ours—from which he gracefully has allowed us to quote extensively. The same is true for the data made available to us by Hans-Dieter Klingemann on the Baltic countries and those from surveys in other countries whose authors are acknowledged in different chapters. We are especially grateful to Marta Lagos for making available to us the pre-publication data of the first ever Latino Barometer. Public opinion research in our view is essential to the study of democracies, and we acknowledge here the importance of the work in this area for efforts like ours and our hope that we might have in the future a World-Barometer of Democracy.

Numerous presidents, prime ministers, ministers, and opposition leaders and hundreds of key opponents and proponents of democratic transition submitted to long interviews, for which we are grateful. These included opposition labor leaders who became presidents or presidential candidates of their countries, such as Lech Walesa of Poland and Luís Ignácio da Silva ("Lula") of Brazil; members of the ruling nomenklatura or the ruling military who advocated and designed the initial liberalization of their countries, such as Aleksandr Yakovlev of the former Soviet Union and General Golbery do Couto e Silva of Brazil; political leaders who crafted historic pacts, such as the former prime minister of Spain, Adolfo Suárez, and the president of Uruguay, Julio María Sanguinetti; major scholars who became theoreticians of civil society opposition and eventually political leaders in the new democracies, such as Bronislaw Geremek of Poland and Fernando Henrique Cardoso of Brazil; and leaders who tried to settle democratically the legacy of the past by holding trials, such as those of the military responsible for the "disappeared," organized by the former president of Argentina, Raúl Alfonsín. Where appropriate and authorized we acknowledge the particulars of these and other interviews specifically in the text of the book.

Alfred Stepan would very much like to thank the Ford Foundation and the Carnegie Corporation of New York, whose generous research grants allowed him to carry out extensive field research in all three regions, especially in post-communist Europe, in 1991–93. He would also like to thank Columbia University and the Central European University, which encouraged him to teach, research, and write while carrying out major university administrative duties. Once again we are fortunate to be working with Henry Tom of the Johns Hopkins University Press. We thank Ken Eaton for his painstaking index.

The writing and rewriting of the book involved long days and especially nights of work together in Berlin, Brasília, Budapest, New Haven, New York, Madrid, Taipei, and Warsaw.

We dedicate this book to Rocío de Terán and Nancy Leys Stepan, colleagues and collaborators in intellectual and other adventures.

Part I

Theoretical Overview

1

Democracy and Its Arenas

IN PART 1, we explore how the character of different nondemocratic regimes affects, or does not affect, the paths that can be taken to complete a transition to a democratic regime. We also explore what implications prior nondemocratic regime types have for the probable tasks that must be undertaken before such fledgling democratic regimes could be considered consolidated.

Having structured our question thus, our argument cries out for definitions of *completed democratic transition* and *consolidated democracy.* In this book, whenever we attempt to establish how far any given country has gone toward completing a transition to democracy, the definitional standard we will use is the following:

A democratic transition is complete when sufficient agreement has been reached about political procedures to produce an elected government, when a government comes to power that is the direct result of a free and popular vote, when this government *de facto* has the authority to generate new policies, and when the executive, legislative and judicial power generated by the new democracy does not have to share power with other bodies *de jure.*

With this working definition, it should be clear why democratic activists and theorists insist on distinguishing between *liberalization* and *democratization.* In a nondemocratic setting, *liberalization* may entail a mix of policy and social changes, such as less censorship of the media, somewhat greater space for the organization of autonomous working-class activities, the introduction of some legal safeguards for individuals such as *habeas corpus,* the releasing of most political prisoners, the return of exiles, perhaps measures for improving the distribution of income, and most important, the toleration of opposition.

Democratization entails liberalization but is a wider and more specifically political concept. Democratization requires open contestation over the right to win control of the government, and this in turn requires free competitive elections, the results of which determine who governs. Using these definitions, it is obvious that there can be liberalization without democratization.[1]

---

1. Much of the conceptual confusion about what Gorbachev was and was not doing with glasnost and perestroika could have been avoided by a clearer understanding of these two concepts. The above discussion of the difference between liberalization and democratization is drawn from Alfred Stepan, *Rethinking Military Politics: Brazil and the Southern Cone* (Princeton: Princeton University Press, 1988), chap. 1. Also see Guillermo O' Donnell and Philippe C. Schmitter, *Transitions from Authoritarian Rule: Tentative Con-*

Our discussion of what constitutes a completed democratic transition helps highlight two further issues. First, transitions may begin that are never completed, even though a new authoritarian regime does not assume power. Our definition helps guard against the "electoralist fallacy," that is, that a necessary condition of democracy, free elections, is seen as a sufficient condition of democracy.[2] Some of the most common examples of electoralist nontransitions are found in those cases where a previously ruling military (e.g., in Guatemala in the 1980s), though relinquishing direct control of government, retains such extensive prerogatives that the democratically elected government is not even *de jure* sovereign. Second, by including in our definition the need to reach an agreement on the specific institutional arrangement for producing democratic government, we are alerted to decision-making within the democratic political arena. Disagreements *among democrats* over such issues as a unitary versus a federal state, a monarchical or republican form of government, or the type of electoral system may create questions about the legitimacy of the emerging democratic government, the decision-making process, and indeed the future of the political system. Such institutional indeterminacy about core procedures necessary for producing democracy may not only leave the transition incomplete, but also postpone any consolidation of democracy. We do not mean that there cannot be disagreement about the most desirable democratic institutions early in the transition and in the constitution-making process. Such disagreement is normal. But a deep and continuous confrontation and ambivalence about democratic institutions among the political elites and the majority of the population, with no sign of accommodation to the enacted institutions, is certainly not conducive to consolidation. It is, therefore, disagreement not only about the value of democracy but also about the specific institutions of a democracy that might make consolidation difficult.

There is a further political and intellectual advantage to being clear about what is required before a *transition* can be considered complete. Nondemocratic power holders frequently argue that certain liberalizing changes they have introduced are sufficient in themselves for democracy. Introducing a clear standard of what is actually necessary for a completed transition makes it easier for the democratic

---

clusions about Uncertain Democracies (Baltimore: Johns Hopkins University Press, 1986), 7–11, Adam Przeworski, *Democracy and the Market: Political and Economic Reforms in Eastern Europe and Latin America* (New York: Cambridge University Press, 1991), chap. 2, Guiseppe di Palma, *To Craft Democracies: An Essay on Democratic Transitions* (Berkeley: University of California Press, 1990), esp. 81–89, and Samuel P. Huntington, *The Third Wave: Democratization in the Late Twentieth Century* (Norman: University of Oklahoma Press, 1991), 9.

2. "Electoralism," or what we call the "electoralist fallacy," figured prominently in recent debates about Central America. See Terry Karl, "Imposing Consent? Electoralism vs. Democratization in El Salvador," in Paul W. Drake and Eduardo Silva, eds., *Elections and Democratization in Latin America, 1980–1985* (San Diego: Center for Iberian and Latin American Studies, University of California, San Diego, 1986), 9–36. See also Abraham F. Lowenthal, ed., *Exporting Democracy: The United States and Latin America* (Baltimore: Johns Hopkins University Press, 1991) and Thomas Carothers, *In the Name of Democracy: U.S. Policy toward Latin America in the Reagan Years* (Berkeley: University of California Press, 1991).

opposition to point out (to their national and international allies as well as to the nondemocratic regime) what additional, if any, indispensable changes remain to be done. Such a standard is also extremely useful in circumstances where the old nondemocratic regime has collapsed or been overthrown and an interim government is in power. Such moments are normally replete with elation, sweeping reforms, and decrees. However, unless there is a rapid commitment to completing all the steps required for a democratic transition, the "temporary" interim government may become permanent.[3]

In most cases after a democratic transition has been completed, there are still many tasks that need to be accomplished, conditions that must be established, and attitudes and habits that must be cultivated before democracy could be considered consolidated. What then are the characteristics of a consolidated democracy? Many scholars, in advancing definitions of consolidated democracy, enumerate all the regime characteristics that would improve the *overall quality* of democracy. We favor, instead, a narrower definition of democratic consolidation, but one that nonetheless combines behavioral, attitudinal, and constitutional dimensions. Essentially, we mean by a consolidated democracy a political situation in which, in a phrase, democracy has become "the only game in town."[4]

Behaviorally, democracy becomes the only game in town when no significant political groups seriously attempt to overthrow the democratic regime or secede from the state. When this situation obtains, the behavior of the newly elected government that has emerged from the democratic transition is no longer dominated by the problem of how to avoid democratic breakdown. Attitudinally, democracy becomes the only game in town when, even in the face of severe political and economic crises, the overwhelming majority of the people believe that any further political change must emerge from within the parameters of democratic formulas. Constitutionally, democracy becomes the only game in town when all the actors in the polity become habituated to the fact that political conflict will be resolved according to the established norms and that violations of these norms are likely to be both ineffective and costly. In short, with consolidation, democracy becomes routinized and deeply internalized in social, institutional, and even psychological life, as well as in calculations for achieving success.

Our working definition of a consolidated democracy then follows:

---

3. We discuss interim governments in more detail in chapter 5. For an extensive discussion of such governments, see Yossi Shain and Juan J. Linz, *Between States: Interim Governments and Democratic Transitions* (New York: Cambridge University Press, 1995), esp. 28–40.

4. For other discussions about the concept of democratic consolidation, see Scott Mainwaring, Guillermo O'Donnell, and J. Samuel Valenzuela, eds., *Issues in Democratic Consolidation: The New South American Democracies in Comparative Perspective* (Notre Dame, Ind.: University of Notre Dame Press, 1992). For an especially rigorous discussion of the concept, see in that volume J. Samuel Valenzuela, "Democratic Consolidation in Post-Transitional Settings: Notion, Process, and Facilitating Conditions," 57–104. Also see di Palma, *To Craft Democracies*, 137–55. We owe the telling expression "only game in town" to Guiseppe di Palma.

— Behaviorally, a democratic regime in a territory is consolidated when no significant national, social, economic, political, or institutional actors spend significant resources attempting to achieve their objectives by creating a nondemocratic regime or turning to violence or foreign intervention to secede from the state.

— Attitudinally, a democratic regime is consolidated when a strong majority of public opinion holds the belief that democratic procedures and institutions are the most appropriate way to govern collective life in a society such as theirs and when the support for antisystem alternatives is quite small or more or less isolated from the pro-democratic forces.

— Constitutionally, a democratic regime is consolidated when governmental and nongovernmental forces alike, throughout the territory of the state, become subjected to, and habituated to, the resolution of conflict within the specific laws, procedures, and institutions sanctioned by the new democratic process.

Two important caveats. First, when we say a regime is a consolidated democracy, we do not preclude the possibility that at some future time it could break down. But we do mean to assert that such a breakdown would not be related to weaknesses or problems specific to the historic process of democratic consolidation per se, but to a *new* dynamic in which the democratic regime cannot solve a set of problems, a nondemocratic alternative gains significant supporters, and former democratic regime loyalists begin to behave in a constitutionally disloyal or semiloyal manner.[5]

Our second caveat is that we obviously do not want to imply that there is only one type of consolidated democracy. An exciting new area of research is precisely on the variety of consolidated democracies. We also do not want to imply that consolidated democracies could not continue to improve their quality by raising the minimal economic plateau upon which all citizens stand and by deepening political and social participation in the life of the country. Within the category of consolidated democracies there is a continuum from low to high quality democracies; an urgent political and intellectual task is to think about how to improve the quality of most consolidated democracies. Our goal in this book is related but distinct. Since we are living in a period in which an unprecedented number of countries have completed democratic transitions and are attempting to consolidate democracies, it is politically and conceptually important that the specific tasks of crafting democratic consolidation be understood. Unfortunately, too

5. In essence this means that the literature on democratic breakdown, such as that found in John J. Linz and Alfred Stepan, eds., *The Breakdown of Democratic Regimes* (Baltimore: Johns Hopkins University Press, 1978), would be much more directly relevant to analyzing such a phenomenon than this current book or other books on democratic transition and consolidation. We obviously do not mean this as a criticism of the transition literature. Rather, our point is that the democratic transition and democratic breakdown literatures need to be integrated into the overall literature on modern democratic theory. From the perspective of such an integrated theory, the "breakdown of a consolidated democracy" is not an oxymoron.

much of the popular and ideological discussion of the current "wave" of democratization is dominated by electoralism per se and/or the assumed democratizing potential of market mechanisms per se. But democratic consolidation requires much more than elections and markets.

The Five Arenas of a Consolidated Democracy

We believe that consolidated democracies need to have in place five interacting arenas to reinforce one another in order for such consolidation to exist. There is an additional factor involved.

Democracy is a form of governance of a state. Thus, no modern polity can become democratically consolidated unless it is first a state. Therefore, the inexistence of a state or such an intense lack of identification with the state that large groups of individuals in the territory want to join a different state or create an independent state raises fundamental and often unsolvable problems. Because such "stateness" problems are so basic, and so underanalyzed, we devote the next chapter to examining this topic. For our argument here, however, it is enough to say that, without the existence of a state, there cannot be a consolidated modern democratic regime.

If a functioning state exists, five other interconnected and mutually reinforcing conditions must also exist or be crafted for a democracy to be consolidated. First, the conditions must exist for the development of a free and lively civil society. Second, there must be a relatively autonomous and valued political society. Third, there must be a rule of law to ensure legal guarantees for citizens' freedoms and independent associational life. Fourth, there must be a state bureaucracy that is usable by the new democratic government. Fifth, there must be an institutionalized economic society. Let us explicate what is involved in crafting this interrelated set of arenas.

By *civil society* we refer to that arena of the polity where self-organizing groups, movements, and individuals, relatively autonomous from the state, attempt to articulate values, create associations and solidarities, and advance their interests. Civil society can include manifold social movements (women's groups, neighborhood associations, religious groupings, and intellectual organizations) and civic associations from all social strata (such as trade unions, entrepreneurial groups, journalists, or lawyers). The idea of civil society, as a normative aspiration and as a style of organization, had great capacity to mobilize the opposition to the military-led bureaucratic-authoritarian regimes in South America, most notably in Brazil, and was crucial in Eastern Europe as a vehicle for asserting the autonomy of those who wanted to act "as if they were free," especially in Poland.

In addition to the whole range of organizations, such as illegal or alegal trade unions, religious communities, bar associations, associations of students and professors, which constitute the complex web of civil society, we should not forget another part of society: ordinary citizens who are not a part of any organization. Such citizens are often of critical importance in shifting the regime/opposition balance because they turn up in the streets in protest marches, heckle the police and the authorities, express their opposition first to specific measures, support broader demands, and ultimately challenge the regime. Normally they are initially small in numbers and later more numerous and can, in some cases, overwhelm the representatives of the regime, forcing them to consider a growing liberalization and ultimately a regime change. However important, numerous, and heroic such relatively unorganized groups may be, they would not be able to overthrow the regime *and* establish a democratic regime if there were not the processes we focus upon in this book. The fact that none of the regimes included in our work, in the transition periods we analyze, was ready to use massive force, to give orders to shoot on the crowds and thus provoke a massacre, as in Tiananmen Square, has led us to give relatively little attention to the possibility that these nondemocratic regimes could have been maintained by force. There is evidence that some leaders considered that possibility. They occasionally alerted their security forces for combat readiness (e.g., in Berlin the day after the wall was breached). Ultimately, however, such repression did not happen. The cost of that scale of repression was too high, and the belief in the legitimacy of such a response too weak. Nondemocratic regimes, at least in southern Europe, the southern cone of South America, and most of Communist Europe, did not enjoy that kind of legitimacy, and many ordinary, unorganized people in civil society often discovered it, almost before the rulers themselves. The most dramatic area where this was so was in parts of Communist Europe, such as East Germany and Czechoslovakia.

By *political society* in a democratizing setting we mean that arena in which the polity specifically arranges itself to contest the legitimate right to exercise control over public power and the state apparatus. At best, civil society can destroy a nondemocratic regime. However, a full democratic transition, and especially democratic consolidation, must involve political society. The composition and consolidation of a democratic polity must entail serious thought and action concerning the development of a normatively positive appreciation of those core institutions of a democratic political society—political parties, elections, electoral rules, political leadership, interparty alliances, and legislatures—by which society constitutes itself politically to select and monitor democratic government.[6]

For modern democratic theory, especially for questions about how to consolidate democracy, it is important to stress not only the *distinctiveness* of civil society and political society, but also their *complementarity*. This complementarity is

---

6. For an earlier discussion of the need to distinguish between the civil society arena and the political society arena, see Stepan, *Rethinking Military Politics*, chap. 1. For an adroit use of the concepts in a concrete historical analysis, see Paolo Farneti, "Social Conflict, Parliamentary Fragmentation, Institutional Shift, and the Rise of Fascism: Italy," in Linz and Stepan, eds., *The Breakdown of Democratic Regimes*, 3–33.

not always recognized. As we document throughout the book, one of these two dimensions is frequently neglected in favor of the other. Worse, within the democratic community, champions of either civil or political society all too often adopt a discourse and a set of practices that are implicitly inimical to the normal development of the other. Since this opposition is seldom explicit, let us discuss the forms this implicit opposition may take and how and why such discourse and practice impede democratic consolidation.

In the recent struggles against the nondemocratic regimes of Eastern Europe and Latin America, a discourse was constructed that emphasized "civil society versus the state." This dichotomy, of course, has a long philosophical genealogy.[7] More importantly for our purposes, this philosophical tradition was politically useful to those democratic movements that emerged in recent contexts where explicitly political organizations were forbidden or extremely weak. A conception of a civil society in opposition to the state was also politically useful as the opposition attempted to isolate the nondemocratic regime and its state by creating an "us" versus "them" ethical politics. Civil society in many countries was rightly considered the celebrity of democratic resistance and transition.

The problem arises at the moment of democratic transition. Quite often democratic leaders of political society argue that civil society, having played its historic role, should be demobilized so as to allow for the development of normal democratic politics.[8] Such an argument is bad democratic theory and bad democratic politics. A robust civil society, with the capacity to generate political alternatives and to monitor government and state can help transitions get started, help resist reversals, help push transitions to their completion, help consolidate, and help deepen democracy. At all stages of the democratization process, therefore, a lively and independent civil society is invaluable.

But we should also consider how to recognize conceptually, and thus help overcome, the false contradictions some set up between civil society and political society. The danger that democratic groups primarily located in civil society

7. For the contemporary revival of civil society (especially in Eastern Europe and South America), see the chapter by that name in Jean Cohen and Andrew Arato, *Civil Society and Political Theory* (Cambridge: MIT Press, 1992), 29–82. This invaluable book adroitly combines political philosophy with comparative political analysis. Also see the introduction to John Keane, ed., *Civil Society and the State: New European Perspectives* (London: Verso, 1988), 1–31. The Cohen-Arato book is also valuable because it does not subsume political society into civil society. János Kis, an important political philosopher, dissident, and former president of the Free Democrats of Hungary, was one of the first thinker-activists to discuss the distinctive arenas of civil and political society. See Kis, *Politics in Hungary: For a Democratic Alternative* (Boulder, Colo.: Social Science Monographs, 1989).

8. In some transitions the apparent crisis of civil society merely reflects the fact that some of the movements called *civil society* had, to a great extent, been created and directed by previously illegal political parties. When these political parties were able to participate legally in politics, they shifted their efforts away from the mobilization of civil society and, in some cases, consciously demobilized society. This phenomenon was particularly noticeable in Spain concerning those civil society organizations controlled by the Communist Party. Many civil society movements in Chile were analogously controlled by Christian Democratic or Socialist Party leaders.

might occasionally present for the development of political society is that normative preferences and styles of organization, perfectly appropriate to civil society,
might be taken to be desirable or, indeed, the only legitimate style of organization
for political society. For example, many civil society leaders view with moral
antipathy "internal conflict" and "division" within the democratic forces. Institutional routinization, intermediaries, and compromise within politics are often
spoken of pejoratively.[9] But each of the above terms refers to an indispensable
practice of political society in a consolidated democracy. Democratic consolidation requires parties, one of whose primary tasks is precisely to aggregate and represent *differences* between democrats. Consolidation requires that habituation to
the norms and procedures of democratic *conflict* regulation be developed. A high
degree of *institutional routinization* is a key part of such a process. *Intermediation*
between the state and civil society and the structuring of *compromise* are likewise
legitimate and necessary tasks of political society. In short, political society,
informed, pressured, and periodically renewed by civil society, must somehow
achieve a workable agreement on the myriad ways in which democratic power
will be crafted and exercised.

To achieve a consolidated democracy, the necessary degree of autonomy and
independence of civil and political society must further be embedded in and supported by the rule of law, our third arena. All significant actors—especially the
democratic government and the state—must respect and uphold the rule of law.
For the types of civil society and political society we have just described, a rule of
law embodied in a spirit of constitutionalism is an indispensible condition. A
spirit of constitutionalism requires more than rule by majoritarianism. It entails
a relatively strong consensus over the constitution and especially a commitment
to "self-binding" procedures of governance that require exceptional majorities to
change. It also requires a clear hierarchy of laws, interpreted by an independent
judicial system and supported by a strong legal culture in civil society.[10]

The above three conditions—a lively and independent civil society, a political
society with sufficient autonomy and a working consensus about procedures of
governance, and constitutionalism and a rule of law—are virtually definitional
prerequisites of a consolidated democracy. However, these conditions are much
more likely to be satisfied if a bureaucracy usable by democratic leaders and an
institutionalized economic society exist.

Democracy is a form of governance of life in a polis in which citizens have

9. We discuss at length the question of antipolitics in our chapter on Poland and in our discussion of
Czechoslovakia. For an example of how the language of "ethical civil society" and "normal political society"
can at times emerge as normative opposites, see our chapter on Poland and especially table 15.1. Antipolitics
also created problems in post-transition Brazil.

10. For an excellent volume that discusses the relationships between constitutionalism, democracy, legal
culture, and "self-bindingness," see Jon Elster and Rune Slagstad, eds., *Constitutionalism and Democracy*
(Cambridge: Cambridge University Press, 1988), esp. 1–18.

rights that are guaranteed and protected. To protect the rights of its citizens and to deliver the other basic services that citizens demand, a democratic government needs to be able to exercise effectively its claim to the monopoly of the legitimate use of force in the territory. Even if the state had no other functions than these, it would have to tax compulsorily in order to pay for police, judges, and basic services. Modern democracy, therefore, needs the effective capacity to command, regulate, and extract. For this it needs a functioning state and a state bureaucracy considered usable by the new democratic government. As we shall see in chapter 2, there are many reasons why in many territories of the world no such state exists. In this book the question of state disintegration is particularly important in parts of the former Soviet Union. But, insufficient state taxing capacity or a weak normative and bureaucratic presence in much of the territory, such that citizens cannot effectively demand that their rights be respected or receive any basic entitlements, is a great problem in many countries in Latin America, such as Brazil. The question of the usability of the state bureaucracy by the new democratic regime also emerges in countries where the outgoing, nondemocratic regime has given tenure (as in Chile) to many key members of the state bureaucracy carrying out politically sensitive functions in justice and education. Important questions about the usability of the state bureaucracy by new democrats inevitably emerge in cases (as in much of post-Communist Europe) where the distinction between the party and the state had been virtually obliterated and the party went out of power, disintegrated, or was delegitimized.

The final supportive condition for a consolidated democracy concerns the economy, or rather an arena we believe should be called *economic society*. We use the phrase "economic society" to call attention to two claims that we believe are theoretically and empirically sound. First, there has never been and there cannot be a non-wartime consolidated democracy in a command economy. Second, there has never been and almost certainly there never will be a modern consolidated democracy in a pure market economy. If both of these claims are demonstrated to be sound, modern consolidated democracies require a set of socio-politically crafted and sociopolitically accepted norms, institutions, and regulations, which we call *economic society*, that mediates between state and market.

Empirically, no evidence has ever been adduced to indicate that a polity that would meet our definition of a consolidated democracy has ever existed in a command economy. But the question persists. Is there a theoretical reason to explain such a universal empirical outcome? We think so. On theoretical grounds, our assumption is that at least a nontrivial degree of market autonomy and ownership diversity in the economy is necessary to produce the independence and liveliness of civil society so that it can make its contribution to a democracy. Likewise, if all property is in the hands of the state and all price, labor, supply, and distributional decisions are the exclusive purview of the state in control of the command economy, the relative autonomy of political society required in a consolidated democracy could not exist.[11]

But why do completely free markets not coexist with modern consolidated democracies? Empirically, serious studies of modern polities again and again verify the existence of significant degrees of market intervention and state ownership in all consolidated democracies.[12] Theoretically, there are at least three reasons why this should be so. First, notwithstanding the ideologically extreme but surprisingly prevalent and influential neoliberal claims about the self-sufficiency of the market, pure market economies could neither come into being nor be maintained without a degree of state regulation. Markets require corporation laws; the regulation of stock markets; regulated standards for weight, measurement, and ingredients; and the protection of property, both public and private. All of these require a role for the state in the economy. Second, even the best of markets have market failures that must be corrected if the market is to function well.[13] No less an advocate of the "invisible hand" of the market than Adam Smith acknowledged that the state is necessary to perform certain functions. In fact, in a neglected but important passage in *The Wealth of Nations*, Adam Smith assigned three indispensable tasks to the modern state.

First, the duty of protecting the society from the violence and invasion of other independent societies; secondly, the duty of protecting, as far as possible, every member of the society from the injustice or oppression of every other member of it, or the duty of establishing an exact administration of justice; and, thirdly, the duty of erecting and maintaining certain public works and certain public institutions which it can never be for the interest of any individual, or small number of individuals, to erect and maintain; because the profit could never repay the expense to any individual or small number of individuals, though it may frequently do much more than repay it to a great society.[14]

The third reason for market intervention in consolidated democracies is that democracy entails free public contestation concerning governmental priorities and policies. If a democracy never produced policies that generated government-mandated public goods in the areas of education, health, and transportation,

---

11. Robert A. Dahl in a similar argument talks about two arrows of causation that produce this result. Concerning the political arrow of causation (e.g., in the case of Leninism in power), the party-state's ideology goes explicitly against the autonomy of civil society and political society. Or, in the case of a state controlled command economy, the economic arrow of causation goes against certain material needs of a consolidated democracy, such as freedom of the press, because paper and printing materials could be denied. See Dahl, "Why All Democratic Countries Have Mixed Economies," in John Chapman and Ian Shapiro, eds., *Democratic Community* (New York: New York University Press, 1993), 35:259–82.

12. See, for example, the ample documentation concerning fourteen advanced democracies contained in John R. Freeman, *Democracies and Market: The Politics of Mixed Economies* (Ithaca, N. Y.: Cornell University Press, 1989).

13. For an excellent analysis of inevitable market failures, see Peter Murrell, "Can Neoclassical Economics Underpin the Reform of Centrally Planned Economies?" *Journal of Economic Perspectives* 5, no. 4 (1991): 59–76.

14. Adam Smith, *The Wealth of Nations* (London: J. M. Dent and Sons, Everyman's Library Edition, 1910), 2:180–81.

some safety net for its citizens hurt by major market swings, and some alleviation of gross inequality, democracy would not be sustainable.[15] Theoretically, of course, it would be antidemocratic to rule such public policies off the agenda of legitimate public contestation. Thus, even in the extreme hypothetical case of a democracy that began with a pure market economy, the very working of a modern democracy (and a modern advanced capitalist economy) would lead to the transformation of that pure market economy into a mixed economy, or a set of norms, regulations, policies, and institutions we have called an *economic society.*[16]

Any way we analyze the problem, democratic consolidation requires the institutionalization of a socially and politically regulated market. This requires an economic society, which in turn requires an effective state. Even such a neoliberal goal as narrowing the scope of public ownership (privatization) in an orderly and legal way is almost certainly carried out more effectively by a stronger state (in terms of capacity) than by a weaker state. A severe breakdown of the existing levels of the economy because of state incapacity to carry out any regulatory functions greatly compounds the problems of economic reform and of democratization.[17]

In summary, a modern consolidated democracy can be conceived of as being composed of five major inter-relating arenas, each of which, to function properly, has its own primary organizing principle. Properly understood, democracy is more than a regime; it is an interacting system. No single arena in such a system can function properly without some support from one, or often all, of the other

15. The working of a modern democracy will normally also result in the legal exclusion of some activities from the market, such as the sale of human organs and the sale of children for sexual services.

16. Robert Dahl's line of reasoning follows a similar development. "Democracy would almost certainly lead to the destruction of certain economic orders [including] not only a capitalist command economy but also a strictly free market economy. . . . If people who are harmed by the market have the freedom, power, and opportunity to do so they will attempt to regulate the market so as to eliminate, or at least limit, the damage they perceive . . . Political competition provides elected leaders with incentives for responding to the views and votes of any organized or unorganized aggregate of people. . . . One way or the other, then, over time the victims of free markets are likely to influence the government—or *some* government, whether local, state, provincial, or regional—to adopt interventionist policies intended to mitigate the harm. . . . The upshot is, then, that every democratic country has rejected the practice, if not always the ideology, of unregulated competitive markets. Although it is true that a market economy exists in all democratic countries, it is also true that what exists in every democratic country is a market economy modified by government intervention." See his "Why All Democratic Countries Have Mixed Economies," 259–82.

17. In post-Communist Europe, the Czech Republic and Hungary are well on the way to becoming institutionalized economic societies. In sharp contrast, in the Ukraine and Russia the writ of the state does not extend far enough for us to speak of an economic society. The consequences of the lack of an economic society are manifest everywhere. For example Russia, with a population fifteen times larger than Hungary's and with vastly more raw materials, received only 3.6 billion dollars of direct foreign investment in 1992–93, whereas Hungary received 9 billion dollars of direct foreign investment in the same two years. Much of the explanation for this variance was that Hungary had a strong economic society in the area of a law, contracts, and regulatory regime, whereas Russia had virtually no economic society and its command economy had ceased to exist. The direct foreign investment figures are from the *Wall Street Journal* publication, *Central European Economic Review* (Summer 1994), 6. The most cited example of market success, the Czech Republic, is in fact one of the clearest examples of the political crafting of a new economic society. Indeed, Stephen Holmes argues that "Prime Minister Václav Klaus, far from being the antistatist he pretends to be, is the most talented state-builder of postcommunist Europe." See Holmes, "The Politics of Economics in the Czech Republic," *East European Constitutional Review* 4, no. 2 (1995): 52–55, quote from p. 52.

Table 1.1. The Five Major Arenas of a Modern Consolidated Democracy: Inter-related Principles and Mediating Fields

Arena	Primary Organizing Principle	Necessary Support from other Arenas	Primary Mediation upon other Arenas
Civil society	Freedom of association and communication	Rule of law which establishes legal guarantees State apparatus to enforce rights of civil society to organize if these rights are violated Economic society with sufficient pluralism to support the necessary degree of autonomy and liveliness of civil society	Interests and values of civil society are the major generators of political society Civil society generates ideas and helps monitor the state apparatus and economic society
Political society	Free and inclusive electoral contestation	Needs legitimacy in eyes of civil society Needs legal guarantees anchored in rule of law and maintained by impartial state apparatus	Crafts constitution and major laws Manages state apparatus Produces overall regulatory framework for economic society
Rule of law	Constitutionalism	A legal culture with strong roots in civil society and respected by political society and the state apparatus	Establishes a hierarchy of norms that make actions by, and upon, other arenas legitimate and predictable
State apparatus	Rational-legal bureaucratic norms	Normative support from civil society for rational-legal authority and its attendant monopoly of legitimate force Monetary support levied by political society and produced and rendered to the state by a functioning economic society, which has produced a sufficient taxable surplus	Imperative enforcement on civil, political, and economic societies of democratically sanctioned laws and procedures established by political society
Economic society	Institutionalized market	Legal and regulatory framework produced by political society, respected by civil society, and enforced by the state apparatus	Produces the indispensable surplus to allow the state to carry out its collective good functions and provides a material base for the pluralism and autonomy of civil and political societies

arenas. For example, civil society in a democracy needs the support of a rule of law that guarantees the right of association and needs the support of a state apparatus that will effectively impose legal sanctions on those who would attempt to use illegal means to stop groups from exercising their democratic right to organize. Furthermore, each arena in the democratic system has an effect on other arenas. For example, political society crafts the constitution and major laws, manages the state apparatus, and produces the overall regulatory framework for economic society. In a consolidated democracy, therefore, there are constant mediations between the arenas, each of which is correctly in the "field" of forces emanating from the other arenas (table 1.1).

2

"Stateness," Nationalism, and Democratization

In this chapter we turn to the issue of stateness, a variable so undertheorized but so critical to democracy as to require a full analysis before we proceed. Our focus is on the relationship between state, nation(s), and democracy.[1] A modern democratic state is based on the participation of the demos (the population), and nationalism provides one possible definition of the demos, which may or may not coincide with the demos of the state. A number of the problems we shall analyze derive from this.

When thinking about transitions to democracy, many people tend to assume that what is challenged is the nondemocratic regime and that with democracy a new legitimate system is established. However, in many countries the crisis of the nondemocratic regime is also intermixed with profound differences about what should actually constitute the polity (or political community) and which demos or demoi (population or populations) should be members of that political community. When there are profound differences about the territorial boundaries of the political community's state and profound differences as to who has the right of citizenship in that state, there is what we call a "stateness" problem. Aspirant modern democracies can vary immensely on this variable from those polities that have no stateness problems to those where democracy is impossible until the stateness problem is resolved.

The original and now classic work on democratic transitions did not give much thought or attention to "stateness" problems because most of that literature focused on transitions in Southern Europe and Latin America, where the challenge of competing nationalisms within one territorial state, or the question of who was a citizen of the new democratic polity, was on the whole not a salient issue.[2] Even

1. Our point about undertheorization concerns in particular the triadic inter-relationship between the modern state, modern nationalism, and modern democracy. There have, of course, been some excellent recent works on the history of the state. See, in particular, Michael Mann, *The Sources of Social Power,* Vol. Two: *The Rise of Classes and Nation-States, 1760–1914* (New York: Cambridge University Press, 1993).

2. For example, the most influential study of democratic transitions is the four-volume work edited by Guillermo O'Donnell, Phillipe C. Schmitter, and Laurence Whitehead, *Transitions from Authoritarian Rule* (Baltimore: Johns Hopkins University Press, 1986), which is devoted to southern Europe and Latin America and which contains virtually no discussion of stateness problems or even of nationalism.

the competing Catalan and Basque nationalisms in Spain barely entered the theoretical literature because the legitimacy of Spanish stateness was managed with reasonable success. What follows is our effort to incorporate a systematic approach to stateness into the theory of democratic transition and consolidation. We will approach our task by exploring three different questions. Why is the existence of a sovereign state a prerequisite for a modern democracy? Why are state-building and nation-building conceptually and historically different processes? And, most importantly, when are nation-states and democracy complementary or conflicting logics, and what can be done to craft democracy if they are conflicting logics?

A Sovereign State as a Prerequisite to Democracy

Democracy is a form of governance of a modern state. Thus, without a state, no modern democracy is possible.[3] These assertions hold true both theoretically and empirically. Let us look at some of the basic definitions of the state to see why this is so. Max Weber provides a classic and clearly focused discussion of the central attributes of the state in modern societies.

The primary formal characteristics of the modern state are as follows: It possesses an administrative and legal order subject to change by legislation, to which the organized corporate activity of the administrative staff, which is also regulated by legislation, is oriented. This system of order claims binding authority, not only over the members of the state, the citizens, most of whom have obtained membership by birth, but also to a very large extent, over all action taking place in the area of its jurisdiction. It is thus a compulsory association with a territorial basis. Furthermore, today, the use of force is regarded as legitimate only so far as it is either permitted by the state or prescribed by it. . . . The claim of the modern state to monopolize the use of force is as essential to it as its character of compulsory jurisdiction and of continuous organization.[4]

Charles Tilly offers a more recent formulation, which also calls attention to the state's ability to control the population in the territory. For Tilly, "an organization which controls the population occupying a definite territory is a state in so far as (1) it is differentiated from other organizations operating in the same territory; (2) it is autonomous [and] (3) its divisions are formally coordinated with one another."[5]

3. To be sure, other forms of social organization than a modern state, including prestate (or even stateless) forms of political organizations, might—as anthropologists have correctly noted—use democratic procedures to reach decisions. Such forms of decision making are, however, fundamentally different from our use of the term *political democracy* as a form of authority creation in a modern state.

4. Max Weber, "The Fundamental Concepts of Sociology," in Talcott Parsons, ed., *The Theory of Social and Economic Organization* (New York: Free Press, 1964), 156.

5. Charles Tilly, "Reflections on the History of European Statemaking," in Charles Tilly, ed., *The Formation of National States in Western Europe* (Princeton: Princeton University Press, 1975), 70. In the same definition, Tilly also says that states should be "centralized." We omit this so as not to introduce confusion about federal states, which, as long as they are "formally coordinated," in Tilly's sense, can of course be

Unless an organization with these statelike attributes exists in a territory, a government (even if "democratically elected") could not effectively exercise its claim to the monopoly of the legitimate use of force in the territory, could not collect taxes (and thus provide any public services), and could not implement a judicial system. As our discussion of the five arenas of a consolidated democracy made clear, without these capacities there can be no democratic governance. Logically and empirically, therefore, the argument leads to the same conclusion, that the absence of an organization with the attributes of a modern state (as in Somalia in 1992–94) precludes democratic governance over the whole territory of the state, although it might not preclude areas of segmented political authority.

If one accepts (as we do) Weber's injunction about an organization needing to claim binding authority successfully in a territory before it is a state and Tilly's requirement that a state be "autonomous," it should also be clear that these are severe (and we believe insurmountable) limits to democracy unless the territorial entity is recognized as a sovereign state. We will develop this argument via an excursus on Hong Kong. The basic agreement between the United Kingdom and the People's Republic of China (PRC) in 1984 accords fundamental constitutional prerogatives to the People's Republic of China; until the latter becomes democratic or cedes independence to Hong Kong, Hong Kong cannot become a democracy, despite the growing scope and strength of democratic movements there.

The initial 1984 formulation, "One Country, Two Systems," and the agreement promising the preservation of the existing legal, economic, social and political systems of Hong Kong for fifty years from July 1, 1997, illustrate very well the limits of democratization without statehood. If we substitute the expression "one country" by "one state," it becomes evident that the decision about what kind of political system should prevail is ultimately in the hands of that state. The People's Republic, for its own reasons, particularly its plans for the reunification of Macao and above all Taiwan with the PRC, might be willing to grant more or less autonomy and self-government to the special administrative region of Hong Kong. But that decision will ultimately be in the hands of the Chinese government. Only those institutions guaranteed by the agreement between the United Kingdom (UK) and China would have some likelihood of persisting as part of an international treaty, and that is the reason why the government in Beijing has consistently rejected any institutional reforms that would even approach what we would call political democracy in Hong Kong.[6]

---

states. For an excellent short analysis of the emergence of the modern state, see the historically and conceptually well-grounded book by Gianfranco Poggi, *The Developement of the Modern State: A Sociological Introduction* (Stanford: Stanford University Press, 1978).

6. For example, a careful reader of the proposed constitutional structure after 1997 will note that the political system in Hong Kong, as presently envisioned by the 1984 agreement, would not meet our criteria for a democracy because the government of Hong Kong would not be elected but would be appointed by Beijing from a list of three people jointly proposed by representatives of Hong Kong and the People's Republic of China.

The case of Hong Kong illustrates a problem not discussed in the literature on democratization. Is it possible to create and have a functioning democratic political subsystem within a nondemocratic state? Can a democratic political subsystem exist within the overall framework of a totalitarian or post-totalitarian state? Politically, probably not—because of the example that it would provide for the citizens of the larger unit to see one region enjoying freedoms to which they would not have access. This dissonance would generate a persistent temptation for the sovereign state to subvert those democratic institutions. But there is a more serious and principled constitutional difficulty. The state would still have the right to modify the political status of any component unit. Certainly, to do so might generate a serious political conflict, and a Dahlian calculus of the cost of repression, compared to the cost of toleration, might incline the sovereign state to tolerate democratic institutions in part of the country. Even so, the delimitation of areas of decision-making reserved to what we would call a federal subunit, and other areas of decision-making to the nondemocratic central government would leave important decisions totally outside of democratic control. In any democratic federal state, the citizens of a subunit obviously have their share in the decision-making process in the center through democratic participation in the federal representative bodies. But in a system that is nondemocratic at the center, they would have no share, and the nondemocratic system would make the most important decisions. Thus, a Hong Kong–like unit would not meet either of Robert A. Dahl's two necessary criteria for a democratic federation, his requirement that "in a federal system a national majority cannot prevail over a minority that happens to constitute a majority in one of the local units that is constitutionally privileged" (because Hong Kong has no constitutionally guaranteed privileged status) or his requirement that all units in the federation must be democratic and thus that all political rights of individual citizens must be respected.[7]

In a nondemocratic system, like the colonial rule of Britain over India, there may be extremely important democratic developments and there may be some form of power sharing and significant consultation with democratic elected representatives, but any such system, by our definition of political democracy, could not have been a democracy in view of the reserved powers held by Westminster until the United Kingdom recognized the independence of India. Democracy requires statehood. Without a sovereign state, there can be no secure democracy.[8]

7. For Dahl's short but classic discussion of democratic federalism and the inherent (but acceptable) limits that a federal system implies for some categories of democratic decisions by some of the citizens of the state, see Robert A. Dahl, *Democracy, Liberty, and Equality* (Oslo: Norwegian University Press, 1986), 114–26. Quote from 115.

8. Divided but independent and sovereign states such as North and South Korea and Taiwan and the People's Republic of China can produce democracy in one component, but elite perceptions of security threats may privilege military or intelligence organizations and add special complications to the process of democratization. For example, democratization in Taiwan was gravely complicated by the legal fiction that the Republic of China (controlling *de facto* only Taiwan and some nearby islands) claimed to represent all

STATES AND STATE-BUILDING, NATIONS AND NATION-BUILDING

Having established the indispensability of a modern state for democracy, we next examine why state-building and nation-building are two overlapping but conceptually and historically different processes. To the extent that state-building and nation-building are not tightly overlapping and largely inseparable processes—and we show they often are not—the interaction of the two processes can produce problems for both stateness and democratization.

State-building accelerated with the crisis of feudalism and the development of the Renaissance and the Reformation.[9] It was the result of the crisis of the Christian empire and the rivalries between emerging monarchies in Western and later Northern Europe. The state, as the great historian Burckhardt noted, was a "work of art" and since its beginnings has had an artificial quality.[10] It is no accident that, in describing that process, architectonic images were invoked. The state-building process did not have the connotations of an organic growth that would prevail in the later discussions of nationalism. The state was not associated with the idea of nature, of organic birth, but with the ideas of creation and craft.

The state-building process went on for several centuries before the idea of the nation—and especially the "nation-state"—fired the imaginations of intellectuals and the people. In fact, the state-building process contributed decisively to the slow reduction of the hundreds of political entities on the historical map of Europe in 1500 to only about 25 by 1900.[11] Until the French Revolution, the support by the French Republic of republican independence in its periphery, and later the support by Napoleon of some nationalist movements, and the nationalist response to Napoleonic domination, the state-building process went on without being based on a national sentiment, identity, or consciousness.[12] States as they

---

Chinese people and that therefore seats were reserved for "representatives" from the mainland who were not continuously subject to election. They had "prolonged mandates," and after their deaths substitutes were appointed. Furthermore, to argue for separate statehood for Taiwan was illegal. The fiction of return to China was one of the rationales for continued authoritarian rule. Significantly, the transition to democracy in progress in Taiwan has led to the abandonment of the reserved seats and the prolonged mandates and to an open debate about independence for Taiwan. For the recent changes in Taiwan, see Chia-lung Lin, "Political Elites and Democratic Consolidation in Taiwan: Institutional Connection in a Divided Society" (paper presented at the First Annual Taiwan Studies Conference in North America, Yale University, June 2–4, 1995).

9. For a more detailed and documented discussion (from which we will draw heavily), see Juan J. Linz, "State Building and Nation Building," *European Review* 1 (1993): 355–69. We are grateful to the publishers of *European Review* for giving us permission to draw from that article in this chapter. Also see Juan J. Linz, "Plurinazionalismo e democrazia," *Revista Italiana di scienza politica* 25, no. 1 (1995): 21–50.

10. J. Burckhardt, *Die Kultur der Renaissance in Italien* (Bern: Hallwag, 1943). The book opens with a section entitled "Der Staat als Kunstwerk," 11–144. The book was first published in 1860 and remains a key text.

11. See, for example, the map depicting the 300 small petty states and free cities in existence in 1648 in what is now the single state of Germany in Geoffry Barraclough, *The Times Concise Atlas of World History* (London: Times Books, 1982), 79.

12. Often the literature on nationalism explicitly or implicitly draws a strong line of causal connection between the French Revolution and nationalism. Historically and conceptually, the relationship was much

emerged after the fifteenth century did not require intense identification of their subjects with territorial boundaries, history, culture, or language. Indeed, state identification and loyalty were often expected to be *transferable* merely by virtue of dynastic marriages. That is, loyalty belonged to the dynasty, not to the nation (which in many cases had not yet been "invented").

However, there can be little doubt that the identification with a state by the subjects or the loyalty to a common king of people living in the different units making up the modern monarchies was accompanied by a protonational sentiment.[13] Sooner or later, in many of the states, the state generated a *state nation–building* process and eventually, with democratization, a nation-building process. This brings us to the difficult terms of nation and nation-state.[14]

For Weber the concept of nation belongs to the sphere of values; it "means above all that it is proper to expect from certain groups a specific sentiment of solidarity in the face of other groups."[15] As Weber also notes, there is no agreement on how these groups should be delimited or about what concerted action should result from such solidarity. In ordinary language, a nation is not necessarily identical with the people of the state, that is, with the membership in a given polity. This does not mean that it cannot be identical, but it does not have to be. The situation before the recent German unification illustrates the difference quite clearly. There were two states, although there was a claim shared by many people, finally expressed in the breakdown of the German Democratic Republic (GDR) and in the expression *Wir sind ein Volk*, that there was a German nation divided between two states.[16]

---

more complex. The French Revolution did not export nationalism, since the republics it created in Batavia and Helvetia were an instrument of exploitative armies and the French occupation. If there is a relation between nationalism and the French Revolution, it is the arousal of counter-revolutionary popular responses sometime after the failure of the dynastic rulers, politicians, and diplomats to defend the people, who then took sovereignty into their own hands (as in the Spanish resistance to Napoleon). Nor was the aim of gaining the French "natural borders" in any way based on modern conceptions of the nation but rather on the interests of the French state. Napoleon I, in redrawing the map of Europe, did not endeavor to create nation-states to be ruled by his brothers and generals, but assigned to them old states—kingdoms—like Spain and Naples or created states, like Westphalia.

13. See the important work by Liah Greenfeld, *Nationalism: Five Roads to Modernity* (Cambridge: Harvard University Press, 1992).

14. Although we speak of the United Nations of the world, we are really dealing with the united states of the world. The UN, if the trademark US had not been pre-empted by the United States of America, should have been called the US.

15. For his discussion of nationalism, see Max Weber, "Political Communities," in Guenther Roth and Klaus Wittich, eds., *Economy and Society* (New York: Bedminster Press, 1968), 11: 921–26.

16. M. Rainer Lepsius, "Ethnos and Demos," in *Interessen, Ideen und Institutionen* (Opladen: Westdeutscher Verlag, 1990), 250–51, 232–46. The constituent assembly in Austria in 1919, in article 1 of their draft constitution, voted, with only one dissenting vote, to merge with Germany, but the merger was forbidden, for geopolitical reasons, by the victors of World War I. This left a legacy of stateness problems that weakened democracy in both interwar Austria and Germany. See Walter B. Simon, "Democracy in the Shadow of Imposed Sovereignty: The First Republic of Austria," in Juan J. Linz and Alfred Stepan, eds., *The Breakdown of Democratic Regimes: Europe* (Baltimore: Johns Hopkins University Press, 1978), 80–121; for the vote see 83.

Let us now turn to some of the more significant differences between states and nations. A nation does not have officials, and there are no defined leadership roles, although there are individuals who act as carriers, in the Weberian sense of Träger, of the national sentiment in movements or nationalistic organizations. There are no clear rules about membership in a nation and no defined rights and duties that can be legitimately enforced (although nationalists often attempt to enforce behavior on the part of those who identify with the nation or who they claim should identify with it). However, without control of the state, the desired behaviors cannot be legally or even legitimately enforced. A nation and nationalist leaders in its name do not have resources like coercive powers or taxes to demand obedience; only a state can provide those resources to achieve national goals in a binding way.

The nation as such, therefore, does not have any organizational characteristics comparable with those of the state. It has no autonomy, no agents, no rules, but only the resources derived from the psychological identification of the people who constitute it. Whereas a state can exist on the basis of external conformity with its rules, a nation requires some internal identification. Benedict Anderson is quite right. Without "imagined communities" there are no nations.[17]

It can, of course, be argued that a nation crystallizing out of a nationalist movement, even when it does not control a state, can exercise power, use violence, or exact contributions without having yet gained statehood. But in a world system of states this means that the movement is taking over some of the functions of another state, subverting its order, so that a state is breaking down in the process. Nationalists can create private armies to enforce their aspirations and challenge the authority of the state, which in some cases can lose control over a territory. In that case we are talking of the development of a civil war or a national liberation struggle, which might end in the creation of a new state.

Whereas we date the emergence of the modern state to the fifteenth century, modern ideas of the nation and modern nationalism did not emerge until the late eighteenth century, and nation-states became major forces only in the second half of the nineteenth century.[18] But although historically "nations" started appearing in the nineteenth century, mostly in the second half of the nineteenth century,

17. See his excellent book, *Imagined Communities: Reflections on the Origin and Spread of Nationalism* (London: Verso, 1991), revised and expanded edition, 141.

18. For somewhat different reasons, Benedict Anderson and Ernest Gellner concurred in 1983, when their major books on nationalism were both first published, that nationalism as we define it emerged in the late eighteenth century. For Anderson, "nationality . . . as well as nationalism, are cultural artifacts of a particular kind. . . . I will be trying to argue that the creation of these artifacts towards the end of the eighteenth century was the spontaneous distillation of a complex 'crossing' of discrete historical forces." Anderson, *Imagined Communities*, 4. He gives particular attention to the diffusion of print-language: "Print-language is what invents nationalism, not a particular language per se." Ibid., 134. His analysis of the emergence of nationalism, *before* industrialization, and where language differences were not important, in North and South America, is original and convincing. Ibid., 47–66. For Gellner it was the emergence of industrialization that required a high and literate culture, a division of labor, and especially a complex educational system to socialize people beyond their immediate locales. For Gellner, "the imperatives of exo-socialization

only a few of them served as a basis for state-building processes; they included Italy, Germany, Greece, and, in a unique way, Hungary within the dual monarchy. Belgium is a particularly interesting case: a state gaining independence from the Netherlands in 1830 (although with a political distinctiveness since the sixteenth century) might, at some point, have seemed to engage in a nation-state–building process, but in the twentieth century, challenged by Flemish nationalism, it created political institutions and practices that made it a democratic *multinational* state. Hungarian nationalism was among the strongest of the nineteenth century, but the crown of St. Stephen extended its authority over a multinational state. Historians of Italy disagree to what extent the Risorgimento and unification were more a process of state-building under the leadership of Cavour than of nation-building led by Mazzini and Garibaldi.[19] Although in Germany there was a strong nationalist movement behind the unification process, the German Reich was more the product of state-building by Bismarck than by the nationalists.

The peace treaties after World War I represented a high point of nation-building, with the proclamation by Wilson of the principle of self-determination. But the new states that emerged after 1918 were *not* in fact all nation-states. In Czechoslovakia, Czechs and Slovaks accounted for 64.8 percent of the population in the new republic, the Germans 23.6 percent, Ruthenians 3.5 percent, Jews 1.4 percent and "other" 6.7 percent. In Poland, the Poles were 69.2 percent, the Ukrainians 14.3 percent, the Jews 7.8 percent, the Germans 3.9 percent and the Russians 3.9 percent. In Latvia, the "titular nationality" was 73.4 percent, in Lithuania 80.1 percent, in Estonia 87.6 percent. The disintegration of three empires into a number of new states and the redrawing of boundaries between states were not directly the result of the efforts of nation-building movements. Of the new states emerging from the Paris peace treaties or those whose territories were expanded, it is difficult to argue that most were nation-states for significant parts of their population were not part of the dominant nationality. Listing some of the states makes it obvious: Yugoslavia, Czechoslovakia, Poland, the enlarged Romania, Lithuania, and Latvia.

The dominant "nations" (or populations) in those new states, namely Serbs, Czechs, Poles, Lithuanians or Latvians, could feel "liberated," but not those peoples

---

is the main clue to why state and culture *must* now be linked, whereas in the past their connection was thin, fortuitous, varied, loose, and often minimal. Now it is unavoidable. That is what nationalism is about, and why we live in an age of nationalism." See Ernest Gellner, *Nations and Nationalism* (Ithaca: Cornell University Press, 1983), 38.

For an important analysis that acknowledges that most modern scholarship dates nationalism as a movement and ideology of the late eighteenth century but argues for the vitality of "greater continuity between pre-modern *ethnies* and ethnocentrism and more modern nations and nationalism," see Anthony D. Smith, *National Identity* (London: Penguin Books, 1991), 43–70. Quotation from 52. Also see the previously cited book by Liah Greenfeld, *Nationalism: Five Roads to Modernity.* For a pioneering theoretical and empirical work on nationalism in Europe, see Guy Hermet, *Les nationalismes en Europe* (Paris: Editions du Seuil, 1996).

19. H. Ullrich, "Bürgertum und Nationale Bewegung im Italien des Risorgimentos," in O. Dann, ed., *Nationalismus und Sozialer Wandel* (Hamburg: Hoffman und Cape, 1978).

subjected to them, if they had or later developed a separate national consciousness, like the Croats and Slovenians in Yugoslavia, Sudeten Germans in Czechoslovakia, Germans and Ukrainians in Poland, or even the different minorities in
the Baltic countries. The degree of respect for or repression of the minorities varied
in the different states. The idea of multinational states was sometimes advocated,
although rarely implemented, due to the appeal of the idea of "nation-building."
Indeed, the difficulty faced by the new states was that of successful state-building.
One could historically analyze how, in a number of cases, the priority given to
nation-building in the state contributed to democratic instability, crisis, and
sometimes demise in later decades of the state itself. Of the eight new states
formed in Europe after World War I, only three—Finland, Czechoslovakia and
Ireland—were stable democracies. In contrast, of the fifteen older states, nine remained stable democracies. *None* of the successor states of the defeated Ottoman
or Romanov empires, with the exception of Finland, became a stable democracy.[20]

This rather sad record of the link between the emergence of modern nation-
building states and consolidated democracy leads us to our central concern in this
chapter. Neither of the two brilliant books by the most influential scholars of
modern nationalism, Ernest Gellner or Benedict Anderson, is centrally concerned
with the links among nationalism, states, and democracy.[21] The rest of this chapter will be devoted to this subject.

NATION-STATES AND DEMOCRATIZATION: INCONVENIENT FACTS

Under what empirical conditions do "nation-states" and "democratization" form
complementary logics? Under what conditions do they form conflicting logics? If
they form conflicting logics, what types of practices and institutions will make
democratic consolidation most or least likely?

Many political thinkers and activists assume that Weberian states, nation-
states, and democracy cohere as part of the very grammar of modern polities. And

20. See J. Linz, "La crisis de las democracias," in Mercedes Cabrera et al., eds., *Europa en crisis, 1919–1939* (Madrid: Editorial Pablo Iglesias, 1991), 231–80. For our purposes Finland is especially interesting. Finland was close to being a homogeneous nation-state. However, Finland had a Swedish-speaking minority. In the successful effort to craft state loyalty, Finland made Swedish one of the two national languages and granted broad citizenship rights. In this context the Swedish minority easily developed loyalty to the democratic state of Finland while retaining important Swedish cultural institutions, which were recognized as legiti-mate by the Finnish state.

21. Indeed, neither even mentions democracy in his extensive index. Gellner, in some of his other works, most particularly, *Conditions of Liberty: Civil Society and Its Rivals* (London: Hamish Hamilton, 1994), is concerned with democratic practices. However, his central intellectual preoccupation in *Nations and Na-tionalism* is with the emergence of industrialization and nationalism. In the overall corpus of his work, he sees nationalism (and democracy) as complicated offshoots of industrialization. We believe that Gellner's explanation, especially for an empirically based analysis of the actual emergence and variety of democra-cies in the world, is excessively functionalist. It neglects among other things the international diffusion ef-fect of democracy to polities such as India or many countries in the British Caribbean that subsequently became long-standing democracies without undergoing extensive industrialization.

in a world where France, Germany, Portugal, Greece, Japan, and Sweden are all Weberian states, nation-states, and democracies, such an assumption may seem justified. Yet in many countries that are not yet consolidated democracies, a nation-state policy often has a different logic than a democratic policy. By a nation-state policy we mean one in which the leaders of the state pursue what Rogers Brubaker calls "nationalizing state policies" aimed at increasing cultural homogeneity. Consciously or unconsciously, the leaders send messages that the state should be "of and for" the nation.[22] In the constitutions they write, therefore, and in the politics they practice, the dominant nation's language becomes the only official language and occasionally the only acceptable language for state business and for public (and possibly private) schooling, the religion of the nation is privileged (even if it is not necessarily made the official religion), and the cultural symbols of the dominant nation are also privileged in all state symbols (such as the flag, the national anthem, and even eligibility for some types of military service) and in all of the state-controlled means of socialization such as radio, television and textbooks. By contrast, democratic policies in the state-making process are those that emphasize a broad and inclusive citizenship where all citizens are accorded equal individual rights.

Under what empirical conditions are the logics of state policies aimed at nation-building and the logics of state policies aimed at crafting democracy congruent? Conflicts between these different policies are reduced when empirically almost all the residents of a state identify with one subjective idea of the nation, and that nation is virtually contiguous with the state. These conditions are met only if there is no significant irredenta outside the state's boundaries, if there is only one nation existing (or awakened) in the state, and if there is low cultural diversity within the state. Virtually *only* in these circumstances can leaders of the government simultaneously pursue democratization policies and nation-state policies. Such congruence between the polity and the demos would facilitate the creation of a democratic nation-state. This congruence empirically eliminates most stateness problems and thus should be considered supportive conditions for democratic consolidation. However, under modern circumstances, very few states that are nondemocratic will begin a possible democratic transition with a very high degree of nation-state homogeneity.[23] This inconvenient fact for nation-state proponents is insufficiently recognized and/or taken into serious consideration and tends to exacerbate problems of stateness.

22. See Rogers Brubaker, "National Minorities, Nationalizing States, and External Homelands in the New Europe: Notes toward a Relational Analysis" (May 1994, unpublished manuscript), which we received after completing an earlier draft of this chapter.

23. For example, of the set of states we consider in this book, only Portugal, Greece, Poland, Chile, Uruguay, and Argentina began their transitions anywhere near to the position of ideal typical "nation-state" homogeneity. The former USSR, Yugoslavia, and Czechoslovakia now constitute 22 states. In Spain, Romania, and Bulgaria, more than one nation resided in the state. In Hungary many Hungarian "nationals" live beyond the border of the state in Romania, Slovakia and Serbia. Brazil is a special case, given its great racial and socioeconomic diversity.

Very often, the nationalist aspirations of political leaders are incongruent with the empirical realities of the *demoi* (populations) in their state. There are many sorts of polis/demos incongruence, and all of them create problems for democratic consolidation unless carefully addressed. There are in fact many states (not merely governments) whose legitimacy is questioned. One of the main reasons for questioning the legitimacy of a state is when there are nationality groups that claim the right of national self-determination and where dominant or (to use the Soviet phrase) "titular nationality" groups deny the de facto, multinational character of the state, reject any compromise with other groups, and exclude them from full citizenship. Another reason to question the state is when a large majority of citizens of one state want to join another state, normally because—like Austrians in 1919 or East Germans in 1989—they consider themselves a part of that state, a state that is conceived of as embodying the nation-state.

A further complication for democracy and occasionally even for interstate peace arises when a large minority in a country is, or could be, considered by a neighboring state as an irredenta. The potential for exacerbation of this latent conflict is increased if the leaders of the titular nation try to pursue an aggressive nation-building policy that alienates the minorities, who then turn to the neighboring country for support. Such a nation-building policy in turn may fan extremist nationalism in the neighboring country, which in a vicious cycle could delegitimize the government for not defending the interests of their "co-nationals" or for not militantly pursuing an irredentist policy. However it starts, when irredentist politics become dominant they represent a serious strain on democracy in both the external "homeland" of the minority and the neighboring nation-building state.[24]

The neglect in the literature on democratic transition and consolidation of the question of the legitimacy of the state is unfortunate because this variable, while not always of great importance for nondemocratic polities, is of fundamental theoretical and political importance for democracy. In fact, agreements about stateness are logically *prior to the creation of* democratic institutions. The classic statement of this problem is by Robert A. Dahl: "We cannot solve the problems of the proper scope and domain of democratic units from within democratic theory. Like the majority principle, the democratic process presupposes a unit. *The criteria of the democratic process presuppose the rightfulness of the unit itself.* If the unit itself is not [considered] proper or rightful—if its scope or domain is not justifiable—then it cannot be made rightful simply by democratic procedures."[25]

24. This sets into motion a contested field of forces between the triad of "nationalizing states, national minorities and external homelands" so well discussed in the previously cited article by Rogers Brubaker. For example, the Armenian irredenta in Nagorno-Karabagh gravely complicated the democratization process in Armenia. If Yasir Arafat convinces the Palestine Liberation Organization (PLO) to democratize Gaza and Jericho as the nucleus of a Palestinian state, he will face the challenge of those who consider the West Bank an irredenta.

25. See Robert A. Dahl, *Democracy and Its Critics* (New Haven: Yale University Press, 1989), 207. Emphasis in the original. After a visit to the Soviet Union, Dahl amplified his thoughts on this theme in "Democracy, Majority Rule, and Gorbachev's Referendum," *Dissent,* (Fall 1991): 491–96.

We do not believe that Dahl's important observation would mean that stateness problems are always unsolvable. Rather, complex negotiations, pacts, and possibly territorial realignments and consociational agreements are often necessary before the majority formula will be accepted as legitimately binding. But, as Dahl argues, simple insistence on the majority formula per se will not do anything until the appropriateness of the unit is established.

Here democratic regimes contrast particularly sharply with any nondemocratic regime whether it is "authoritarian," "sultanistic," "totalitarian," or "post-totalitarian."[26] Agreements about the territorial domain of the state are not necessarily prior for a nondemocratic regime. A nondemocratic regime may be able to impose acquiescence over large groups of people for a long period of time without threatening the coherence of the state. In a nondemocratic regime, the fact that central authority is not derived and maintained by free electoral competition means that separatist or irredentist aspirations, if they exist, are not routinely appealed to in the course of normal politics and can possibly be simply suppressed.

In sharp contrast, the very definition of a democracy involves agreement by the citizens of a territory, however specified, on the procedures to be used to generate a government that can make legitimate claims on their obedience. Therefore, if a significant group of people does not accept claims on its obedience as legitimate, because the people do not want to be a part of the political unit, however democratically it is constituted, this presents a serious problem for democratic transition and even more serious problems for democratic consolidation.[27]

The degree to which inhabitants accept the domain and scope of a territorial unit as an appropriate entity to make legitimate decisions about its possible future restructuring is thus a key variable for democratic theory. A hypothesis that derives from this therefore is that the greater the percentage of people in a given territory who feel that they do not want to be members of that territorial unit, however it may be reconstituted, the more difficult it will be to consolidate a single democracy within that unit.

Agreements about the citizenship in the state are also not necessarily essential in a nondemocratic regime. A national majority—linguistic, religious, ethnic, or cultural—often imposes its rule or conception of the state on minorities. The government, "claiming to represent the people," cannot be challenged through potentially authoritative and binding institutional channels (e.g., courts and open and free elections) because in a nondemocracy such appeal channels do not exist. The problems of "exclusion" of minorities from the electoral franchise or the

26. Each of these nondemocratic regime types is defined and analyzed in chapter 3.

27. In fact, even in democratic regimes, when faced with a majority or a significant minority that questions the legitimacy of the state, the response of the central democratic government has often been the suppression of democratic process in the territory, the establishment of nondemocratic direct rule, and sometimes serious violations of civil liberties and even human rights. We only have to mention Northern Ireland or Kashmir to make this point.

rights of full citizenship are also less politically salient in the nondemocratic context because *everyone* is normally excluded from such rights.

But in a democratic transition, two potentially explosive questions are unavoidable: Who is a citizen in the state? And how are the rules of citizenship defined? A democracy requires a definition of the *demos*. Already the notion of demos as "the people" raises a question: Who are the people? The German word for people, *Volk,* makes obvious that the definition of the demos presents problems. We would feel easier if we could say that the demos is the citizens—with its individualistic connotation—rather than the collectivistic people, *Volk,* or Nation. But it is only a partial solution, since we must then ask: Who defines citizenship, and how? Traditionally two main principles have been used: *ius sanguinis* (citizenship by descent) or *ius soli* (citizenship by the singular virtue of having been born in the country). There is also a third principle, which involves the doubly voluntaristic acts of asking for and being granted citizenship. Citizenship in any of these three ways relates to the state: *descent* normally refers to descent from citizens of the state, sometimes for generations immemorial, without asking questions about language, religion, race, or subjective identity. The relation to the state is even more obvious in the case of the *ius soli,* to be born within the territorial limits of a state. Citizenship based on petition is of course the most closely linked to the state because those who want to be citizens have to be granted it, by law or concession, by the state.

This brings us back to our basic affirmation: modern democratic governance is inevitably linked to stateness. Without a state, there can be no citizenship; without citizenship, there can be no democracy. This assertion is not to be confused with the Hobbesian notion that no form of organized society can exist without a state. As anthropologists have repeatedly shown, many kinds of belonging, of membership, in a community do not entail formal citizenship. Our contention, however, is that there can be no complex modern democracy without voting, no voting without citizenship, and no official membership in the community of citizens without a state to certify membership. In the Latin American and Southern European transitions, questions about the definition of citizenship in the state did not arise. Citizenship had been defined by the citizenship (nationality) laws before the emergence of nondemocratic rule, maintained under authoritarian rule (except for some *cassados* who were deprived of their political rights under the Brazilian dictatorship), and did not change fundamentally in the process of democratization. Even in Spain, where some extreme nationalists in the Basque country and Catalonia denied legitimacy to the state, the question of *demos,* of who was a citizen in the Spanish state, never became for the Spanish state an issue. The legal status of being a Spanish citizen was never denied to any Basque or Catalan armed militant or separatist. Unlike the USSR, there never was a place for nationality on the identification card of the Spanish state. Any Spanish citizen, whatever his or her language, national self-identification, or area of birth had and has equal political and civil rights in all territorial units of the Spanish state.

The starting situation in some of the states of Eastern Europe and the former Soviet Union was radically different, however. The twentieth-century history of the demise of the Austro-Hungarian and Soviet empires, the ebb and flow of Nazi and Soviet expansionism, the attendant brutal expulsions and marches of peoples, and the massive redrawing of borders have made the question of stateness and nation especially problematic. Many individuals in this part of the world have been citizens or subjects of three or more states in the course of their lifetimes without ever moving from their birthplaces. Post-Communist Europe therefore is a region where, for reasons of recent history and not merely "primordial sentiments," there are disagreements about who is the demos, what is the polis, and, most of all, what, in Robert Dahl's sense, are the proper units for decision-making and state sovereignty. Let us quote again another of Robert A. Dahl's sobering reflections:

It is particularly important that the domain—the persons who comprise the unit—be clearly bounded. This is doubtless one reason why territorial boundaries, although not strictly essential, are so often used to specify the domain of a unit, particularly if they reflect obvious historical or geophysical factors. Conversely, *the more indeterminate the domain and scope, the more likely that the unit would, if established, become embroiled in jurisdictional squabbles or even civil wars.*[28]

Democracy is characterized not by subjects but by citizens, so a democratic transition often puts the polis/demos questions at the center of politics. From all that has been said thus far, three assertions can be made:

1. The more the population of the territory of the state is composed of plurinational, lingual, religious, or cultural societies, the more complex politics becomes because an agreement on the fundamentals of a democracy will be more difficult.

2. Although this does not mean that democracy cannot be consolidated in multinational or multicultural states, it does mean that considerable political crafting of democratic norms, practices, and institutions must take place.

3. Some ways of dealing with the problems of stateness are inherently incompatible with democracy.[29]

Probably the first thing clear thinking demands on this subject is that we deliberately problematize some facile assumptions. One of the most dangerous

---

28. Dahl, *Democracy and Its Critics*, 207. Emphasis added.

29. Obviously, for purposes of this book, the problems confronted by Eastern Europe and especially the former Soviet Union and Yugoslavia were understandably much greater than the political problems of any of the Southern European, South American, or even Central European cases we consider.

ideas for democracy can be summed in the maxim that "every state should strive to become a nation-state and every nation should become a state." In fact, in our judgment it is probably impossible that half the territories in the world that are not now democratic could ever simultaneously become nation-states and consolidated democracies as we have defined these terms.

One of the reasons for this inconvenient fact is that many of the existing states in the world are multinational, multilingual, and multicultural.[30] To make them nation-states by democratic means is extremely difficult. In structurally embedded multicultural settings, almost the only democratic possibilities for the creation of a homogeneous nation-state are voluntary cultural assimilation, voluntary exit, or peaceful creation of new territorial boundaries, financially supported and monitored by the international community, and accepted by all the political leaders. These are truly heroic (and empirically and democratically difficult) assumptions.[31]

The other possibilities for creating a homogeneous nation-state in discongruent settings involve subtle or not so subtle sanctions against those not speaking the language, wearing the national attire, or practicing the religion of the titular nation. Eugene Weber, in his classic study, *Peasants into Frenchmen,* analyzes in extensive detail the wide repertoire of nation-state–mandated policies in the schools, civil service, and military that were systematically designed to repress and eliminate multilingualism and multiculturalism.[32] The French state, inspired by the Jacobin idea of the *nation unie et indivisible,* eventually succeeded in overcoming the cultural and linguistic heterogeneity of France. The purposeful process of nation-building by the French state was an incredible success, which contrasts with the more limited success of the Spanish nineteenth-century liberal centralist state in the same endeavor, although we should not ignore how far Spain and the Spanish state succeeded in its effort to create a Spanish identity

30. In the early 1970s, Walker Connor calculated that only 12 of the world's 132 states that were then in existence were "essentially homogeneous from an ethnic viewpoint." See Connor, "Nation-Building or Nation-Destroying," *World Politics* 24 (1972): 320. For later discussions using somewhat different criteria that also arrived at very low estimates of the number of true nation-states in the world, see Hakan Wiberg, "Self-determination as an International Issue," in Iaonn M. Lewis, ed., *Nationalism and Self-determination in the Horn of Africa* (London: Ithaca Press, 1983), George Thomas Kurian, *The New Book of World Ranking* (New York: Facts on File, 1991), and the various articles brought together in Walker Connor, *Ethnonationalism: The Quest for Understanding* (Princeton: Princeton University Press, 1994). Connor's work is particularly revealing in that he documents that all too often in modern political science the words *nation-state* and *state* are used interchangeably by important authors within the same article. See Connor, "Terminological Chaos ('A Nation Is a Nation, Is a State, Is an Ethnic Group, Is a . . .')," in *Ethnonationalism,* esp. 8.

31. Exceptionally a national community controlling democratically the state—or one of its subunits—might engage in a nation-building process using a wealth of resources, incentives, and limited discrimination and have a partial success. The closest example we can think of is the linguistic "normalization" policies of the government in Catalonia (the Generalitat), which discriminate against Spanish in primary schools. However, we should note that constitutional and political challenges to these normalization policies are emerging.

32. See the outstanding monograph by Eugene Weber, *Peasants into Frenchmen: The Modernization of Rural France, 1870–1914* (Stanford: Stanford University Press, 1976).

over the centuries, particularly in the first seventy-five years of the nineteenth century. From today's perspective those endeavors of modern states appear as far from admirable and represent a cost that many of us would not like to pay. However, it is not just a question of how we evaluate such efforts of state-based nation building but how feasible they are in the contemporary context. Our answer on the basis of a sociological analysis is that, independent of the desirability of such a process (which involves a value judgment), such an effort is today doomed to failure in most societies and certainly in liberal democratic societies. We could go into an analysis of why this is so, but we have to limit ourselves to a few points. In the modern world, even in the less developed peripheral or marginal ethnic, cultural, linguistic minorities, every society produces an intellectual elite which, for emotional reasons and (let us not forget) self-interest, will defend the "primordial" values and characteristics. Such elites did not exist, as Gellner has rightly stressed, in agrarian preindustrial societies. Today they exist even in such agrarian societies. Under modern circumstances, where all significant groups have writers and intellectuals who disseminate national cultures, where communication systems have greatly increased the possibility for migrants to remain continuously connected to their home cultures, and where modern democratic norms accept a degree of multiculturalism, homogenizing policies, even if not formally antidemocratic, would probably not be conducive to democratic crafting. If the titular nation actually wants a truly homogeneous nation-state population, a variant of the "ethnic cleansing" formula is too often a tempting method.

Our inquiry about the impossibility of building nation-states and democracies in some types of polities is also based on how humanity is spatially distributed in the world. One building block for nations is possibly language. But as Ernest Gellner has observed, there are perhaps as many as 8,000 languages (not counting important dialects) in the world.[33] Maybe "national communities" could be the building block; if, however, for the sake of argument we assume that only one out of every ten languages is a base for a "reasonably effective" nationalism, there could be as many as 800 viable national communities.[34] But the most important inconvenient fact is not quantitative, but the existential reality that cultural, linguistic, and religious groups are not neatly segmented into 8,000 or 800 nationalities, each occupying reasonably well-defined territories, but are profoundly inter-mixed and overlapping. The appropriate metaphor is not the demarcated squares of the chess board, but the inextricably blended hues and modulations of tie-dyed cloth.

Let us review some of the spatial patterns of language and ethnicity in some aspirant nation-states. We are not against democratically crafted "velvet divorces."

---

33. See Gellner, *Nations and Nationalism*, 44.
34. This conjecture is developed by Gellner, ibid., 44–45.

However, we should note that relatively clear cultural boundaries facilitate such territorial separations. Latvia would like to be a nation-state. But in none of the seven most populous cities in Latvia is Latvian spoken by a majority of the residents. In the capital of Estonia, Tallinn, quite far from the border with Russia, barely half the people of the aspirant nation-state of Estonia speak Estonian. For these and many other countries no simple territorial division or "velvet divorce" is available.[35]

Some analysts were happy when the separate nationalities of the former USSR became fifteen republics, all based on "titular nationalities," on the assumption that democratic nation-states might emerge. In fact, many of the incumbents in the republics sounded extreme nationalist (rather than democratic) themes in the first elections. One of the possible formulas for diminishing conflict among titular nationalities and "migrants" is what David Laitin calls the "competitive assimilation game." That is, it becomes in the interests of many working class migrants to begin to assimilate competitively to enhance the life chances of their children in the new environment. This can potentially happen to Spanish working-class migrants in culturally and economically vibrant Catalonia. But is it likely among Russians in Central Asia? In 1989 in Alma-Ata, the capital of Kazakhstan, Russians constituted 59 percent of the population and the Kazakhs, the titular nationality, 22.5 percent. Less than 1 percent of the Russians spoke the titular language. In Bishkek, the capital of Kyrgyzstan, the percentages were virtually identical. No voluntary nation-state, through a competitive assimilation process, is plausible in this "settler colonialism" context. In these circumstances, if there ever is to be a nation-state, it will not be achieved by democratic means. In fact, even the effort to achieve a nation-state would only further encourage "colonial settlers" to appeal to Zhirinovsky-type extreme nationalist leaders in Russia for support.[36]

There is another inconvenient fact for nation-state advocates in multinational settings. Many people, if they have been living in multinational states, might, for reasons of identity (or to maintain their portfolio of multiple access points in the economy), enjoy having multiple identities and might resist the movement to-

---

35. See the excellent and sobering book by Anatol Lieven, *The Baltic Revolution: Estonia, Latvia, Lithuania and the Path to Independence* (New Haven: Yale University Press, 1993), 434. Even if there is a relatively clear cultural demarcation, as in the Russian-speaking part of Crimea, which was given to the Ukraine by Khrushchev in 1954, or in dominantly Russian areas of northeast Kazakhstan, it is normally extremely difficult for politicians from the state-bearing nationalities to allow "secession." Prime Minister Klaus's ability to convince his party and most Czechs that they would be economically better off without the Slovaks is quite untypical.

36. For David Laitin's analysis of what he calls a "migrant competitive assimilation game" in Catalonia and his analysis of a possible "colonial settler game" in the Central Asian republics of the former Soviet Union, see Laitin, "The Four Nationality Games and Soviet Politics," *Journal of Soviet Nationalities* (Spring 1991): 1–37. In fact, Kazakhstan could present a particularly complicated case of conflicts between state-bearing nationalists, Russian minorities, and political elites in the Russian "homeland." See Martha Brill Olcott, "Kazakhstan: A Republic of Minorities," in Ian Bremmer and Ray Taras, eds., *Nations and Politics in the Soviet Successor States* (Cambridge: Cambridge University Press, 1993), 313–30.

ward ethnic-state homogenization. Such people are normally the first targets of coercion by ethnic-state entrepreneurs. The empirical and emotional fact is that many human beings in the contemporary world have for a long time identified with more than one culture and history, have intermarried, have friends of different nationalitites, and have moved back and forth within the state. Therefore, it is not surprising that they may have dual identities. Nationalists, representing both the dominant nationality in the state and the oppressed nationality, want people to abandon such dual identities and make either-or choices. Indeed, they often invent or structure dichotomies where none existed before. This is one of the reasons why plebescites can be so divisive and can destroy real social bonds.

MULTINATIONAL STATES AND DEMOCRATIZATION: BEYOND CONFLICTING LOGICS

So how can democracy possibly be achieved in multinational states? We certainly have a strong hypothesis on how not to consolidate democracy in multinational settings. The greater the percentage of people in a given state who were born there or who had not arrived perceiving themselves as foreign citizens, who are denied citizenship in the state and whose life chances are hurt by such denial, the more unlikely it is that this state will consolidate democracy.

Phrased more positively, our hypothesis is that, in a multinational setting, the chances to consolidate democracy are increased by state policies that grant inclusive and equal citizenship and that give all citizens a common "roof" of state-mandated and enforced individual rights.

Such multinational states also have an even greater need than other polities to explore a variety of nonmajoritarian, nonplebiscitarian formulas. For example, if there are relatively strong spatial differences between groups within the state, federalism could be explored. The state and the society might also allow a variety of publicly supported communal institutions, such as media and schools in different languages, symbolic recognition of cultural diversity, a variety of legally accepted marriage codes, legal and political tolerance for parties representing different communities, and a whole array of political procedures and devices that Arend Lijphart has described as "consociational democracy."[37] Typically, proportional representation (rather than large single-member districts, with first-past-the-post elections) can facilitate representation of spatially dispersed minorities. Some strict adherents to the tradition of political liberalism, with its focus on the rights of individuals and universalism, are against any form of collective rights. But we believe that the combination of *collective rights* of nationalities or minorities in a multinational, multicultural society and state, *with the rights of individu-*

37. See his seminal article, "Consociational Democracy," *World Politics* 21 (January 1969): 207–25, and his *Democracy in Plural Societies: A Comparative Exploration* (New Haven: Yale University Press, 1977).

als fully protected by the state, is probably the least conflictual way of articulating such a democratic non–nation-state policy.[38]

In cases where transitions start in a context of a nondemocratic multinational federal system, a strategy of crafting democratic federalism should probably follow an electoral sequence of elections at the statewide level first, so as to generate a legitimate framework for later deliberations as to how to decentralize the polity democratically. If the first competitive elections are regional, the elections will tend to privilege regional nationalists, and ethnocracies, rather than democracies, may well emerge.[39] However, the specific ways of structuring political life in multinational settings needs to be contextualized in each country. Along these lines we believe that it is time to re-evaluate some of the rich experiments with *nonterritorial autonomy* that relate, for example, to the self-government of corporate ethnic or religious communities such as the Jewish Kabal in the Polish-Lithuanian Commonwealth, the millets in the Ottoman Empire, or the "national curias" in the late Hapsburg Empire.[40] These mechanisms will not eliminate conflict in multinational states, but they may moderate conflict and help make both the state and democracy more viable.

We also believe some conceptual, political, and normative attention should be given to the possibility of "state-nations." The states we would like to call state-nations are multicultural, or even multinational states, which nonetheless still manage to engender strong identification and loyalty from their citizens, an identification and loyalty that proponents of homogeneous nation-states perceive that only nation-states can engender. The United States of America is such a multicultural and increasingly multilingual country, as is Switzerland. Neither country is strictly speaking a "nation-state," but we believe both could now be called "state-nations." Under Jawaharlal Nehru, India made significant gains in managing multinational tensions through the skillful and consensual usage of numerous consociational practices. Through this process India became in the 1950s and early 1960s a democratic "state-nation." But if Hindu nationalists win power in the 1990s and attempt to turn India, with its 110 million Muslims, into a Hindu na-

---

38. For interesting arguments that some notion of group rights is in fact necessary to the very definition of some types of individual rights and to the advancement of universal norms in rights, see the work by the Oxford philosopher Joseph Raz, *The Morality of Freedom* (Oxford: Oxford University Press, 1986), esp. 165–216, and Kim Lane Scheppele, "Rethinking Group Rights," paper prepared for a conference on The Meaning of Rights in the Former Soviet Bloc Countries, July 4–5, 1994, Institute for Constitutional and Legislative Policy, Central European University, Budapest. Also see the rigorous book by the philosopher Will Kymlicka, *Multicultural Citizenship: A Liberal Theory of Minority Rights* (Oxford: Oxford University Press, 1995), esp. chap. 3, "Individual Rights and Collective Rights"; chap. 4, "Rethinking the Liberal Tradition"; and chap. 6, "Justice and Minority Rights."

39. We develop this point in greater detail in our "Political Identities and Electoral Sequences: Spain, the Soviet Union and Yugoslavia," *Daedalus* 121 (Spring 1992): 123–39, and in this book in our chapter on Spain and our chapter on stateness in the USSR.

40. For an analytic and bibliographic introduction to these important but neglected experiments, see John Coakley, "Approaches to the Resolution of Ethnic Conflict: The Strategy of Non-territorial Autonomy," *International Political Science Review*, 15, no. 3 (1994): 297–314.

tion-state, almost certainly communal violence would increase and Indian democracy would be threatened gravely.[41]

Let us conclude with a word about *political identities*. Many writings on nationalism have focused on "primordial" identities and the need for people to choose between mutually exclusive identities. However, our research into political identities has shown two things. First, political identities are not fixed or primordial in the *Oxford English Dictionary* sense of "pertaining to, or existing at (or from) the very beginning; first in time, earliest, original, primitive, primeval." Rather, they are highly changeable and socially constructed. Second, if nationalist politicians, by the atmosphere they create (or social scientists and census-takers with crude dichotomous categories) do not force polarization, many people may prefer to self-identify themselves as having *multiple and complementary* identities.[42] In fact, along with a common political "roof" of state-protected rights for inclusive and equal citizenship, the human capacity for multiple and complementary identities is precisely one of the key factors that makes democracy in multinational states possible. Because political identities are not fixed and permanent, the quality of democratic leadership is particularly important. Multiple and complementary political identities can be nurtured by political leadership. So can polar and conflictual political identities.[43] Before the conscious use of ethnic cleansing as a strategy to construct nation-states in Bosnia-Herzegovina, Sarajevo was a multinational urban area, whose citizens had multiple identities and one of the highest rates of interfaith marriages of any city in the world.

The central proposition of this chapter has been that, if successful democratic consolidation is the goal, then would-be democracy crafters in charge of the state apparatus must take into careful consideration the particular mix of nations, cultures, and awakened political identities present in the territory. Holding socioeconomic levels of development equal, some types of democracy are possible with one type of polity, but virtually impossible if elites in charge of the state attempt to build another type of polity. If a territory is culturally multinational, political elites in control of the state could initiate "nationalizing policies" that might not violate human rights or Council of Europe norms for democracy, but that would have the combined effect, in each of the five arenas of the polity, of greatly diminishing the chances of democratic consolidation. An example of such ma-

41. Two pioneering works on this theme are Arend Lijphart, "The Puzzle of Indian Democracy: A Reinterpretation," unpublished manuscript, 1994, and Ashutosh Varshney, "Contested Meanings: India's National Identity, Hindu Nationalism and the Politics of Anxiety," *Daedalus* 122 (Summer 1993): 227–61.

42. For example, in 1982 in Catalonia, when respondents were given the opportunity to classify themselves on a questionnaire offering five possibilities: "Spanish," "more Spanish than Catalan," "equally Spanish and Catalan," "more Catalan than Spanish," or "Catalan," 40 percent (the largest single group) identified themselves as "equally Spanish and Catalan." See Juan J. Linz, "De la crisis de un Estado Unitario al Estado de las Autonomías" in Fernando Fernández Rodríguez, ed., *La España de las Autonomías* (Madrid: Instituto de Estudios de Administración Local, 1985), 527–672 (above data on 560).

43. See Linz and Stepan, "Political Identities and Electoral Sequences: Spain, the Soviet Union and Yugoslavia," 123–39.

Table 2.1. The inter-relationship between State, Nation(s), and Democratization (Assuming No Irredenta)

Degree of Presence of Other "Nations" besides Titular Nation in State Territory	Policies and Actions of State-leaders of "Titular Nation"				
	Drives toward Goal of Nation-State	Extends Some Recognition to Legitimacy of Cultural Diversity	Crafts Some Federal or Quasi-federal Institutions and/or Quasi-consociational Practices	Accepts in Principle Possibility of Peaceful and Democratic Negotiated Secession	No Clear, or Extremely Weak State Leaders
No other nation exists and there is little cultural and/or ethnic differentiation.	Democratic nation-state can easily consolidate and be strong		Mononational democratic state can easily exist		
No other nation exists but extensive cultural diversity	Democratic nation-state possible.	Democratic state-nation can easily exist	Mononational democratic state can easily exist		
Other nation(s) present but not awakened.		Democratic state-nation can easily exist			
Other nation(s) present and awakened.	Generates conflict, making democracy difficult but not impossible.	Democratic state-nation can exist but will be under pressure to move toward →	Multinational state is only democratic possibility. If crafted carefully, democracy can be consolidated.	If a clearly demarcated territorial base exists, peaceful secession is possible with democracy in both new states.	
Other nation(s) present and militant.	Generates so much conflict or repression that democratic consolidation is highly implausible.	Democratic state-nation can exist but to be consolidated should move toward →	Multinational state is only democratic possibility but prospect for consolidation difficult. Pressures toward	If no territorial base exists, "velvet divorce" is impossible and if militancy persists democracy cannot be consolidated.	
No group has sufficient cohesion and identity to be a nation-builder					No State possible so democracy is impossible

Note: The concept of property space as used here was originally formulated by Paul Lazarsfeld. See The Language of Social Research: A Reader in the Methodology of Social Research (Glencoe, Ill: Free Press, 1951) 40–62.

joritarian "nationalizing policies" in each of five arenas would be the following. In the arena of civil society, schooling and mass media could be restricted to the official language. In the arena of political society, nationalizing citizenship laws could lead to a significant over-representation of the dominant nationality in elected political offices. In the arena of the state bureaucracy, a rapid changeover to one official language could *de facto* decrease other nationalities' participation in and access to the services of the state. In the arena of the rule of law, the legal system could subtly privilege a whole range of customs, practices, and institutions of the would-be nation-state. Finally, in the arena of economic society, the state-bearing nationality, as the presumed "owner" of the nation-state, could be given special (or even exclusive) rights to land redistribution or voucher distribution, if there was privatization. In contrast, if the real goal is democratic consolidation, a democratizing strategy would require that less majoritarian and more consensual policies be crafted in each of the above arenas.

A final policy point to stress concerns *timing*. Potentially difficult democratic outcomes may be made manageable only if some type of pre-emptive policies and decisions are argued for, negotiated, and implemented by political leaders. If the opportunity for such ameliorative policies is lost, the range of available space for maneuver will be narrowed and a dynamic of societal conflict will probably intensify until democratic consolidation becomes increasingly difficult and eventually impossible.

To summarize the possibilities and limits of reconciling nation-states and democratization and to call attention to where and when a repertoire of pre-emptive policies are politically possible and democratically indicated, we conclude with Table 2.1.[44]

---

44. Table 2.1 does not include the effect of an irredenta on democracy in both the claimed area and in neighboring states. Depiction of this would call for an even more complicated table.

3

Modern Nondemocratic Regimes

Democratic transition and consolidation involve the movement from a nondemocratic to a democratic regime. However, specific polities may vary immensely in the *paths* available for transition and the unfinished *tasks* the new democracy must face before it is consolidated. Our central endeavor in the next two chapters is to show how and why much—though of course not all—of such variation can be explained by prior regime type.

For over a quarter of a century the dominant conceptual framework among analysts interested in classifying the different political systems in the world has been the tripartite distinction between democratic, authoritarian, and totalitarian regimes. New paradigms emerge because they help analysts see commonalities and implications they had previously overlooked. When Juan Linz wrote his 1964 article "An Authoritarian Regime: Spain," he wanted to call attention to the fact that between what then were seen as the two major stable political poles—the democratic pole and the totalitarian pole—there existed a form of polity that had its own internal logic and was a steady regime type. Though this type was nondemocratic, Linz argued that it was fundamentally different from a totalitarian regime on four key dimensions—pluralism, ideology, leadership, and mobilization. This was of course what he termed an *authoritarian regime*. He defined them as: "political systems with limited, not responsible, political pluralism, without elaborate and guiding ideology, but with distinctive mentalities, without extensive nor intensive political mobilization, except at some points in their development, and in which a leader or occasionally a small group exercises power within formally ill-defined limits but actually quite predictable ones."[1]

In the 1960s, as analysts attempted to construct categories with which to compare and contrast all the systems in the world, the authoritarian category proved useful. As the new paradigm took hold among comparativists, two somewhat surprising conclusions emerged. First, it became increasingly apparent that more regimes were "authoritarian" than were "totalitarian" or "democratic" combined.[2]

---

1. Juan J. Linz, "An Authoritarian Regime: The Case of Spain," in Erik Allardt and Yrjö Littunen, eds., *Cleavages, Ideologies and Party Systems* (Helsinki: Transactions of the Westermarck Society, 1964), 291–342. Reprinted in Erik Allardt and Stein Rokkan, eds., *Mass Politics: Studies in Political Sociology* (New York: Free Press, 1970), 251–83, 374–81. Page citations will refer to the 1970 volume. The definition is found on 255.

2. See, for example, the data contained in footnotes 4 and 5 in this chapter.

Authoritarian regimes were thus the modal category of regime type in the modern world. Second, authoritarian regimes were not necessarily in transition to a different type of regime. As Linz's studies of Spain in the 1950s and early 1960s showed, the four distinctive dimensions of an authoritarian regime—limited pluralism, mentality, somewhat constrained leadership, and weak mobilization—could cohere for a long period as a reinforcing and integrated system that was relatively stable.[3]

Typologies rise or fall according to their analytic usefulness to researchers. In our judgment, the existing tripartite regime classification has not only become less useful to democratic theorists and practitioners than it once was, it has also become an obstacle. Part of the case for typology change proceeds from the implications of the empirical universe we need to analyze. Very roughly, if we were looking at the world of the mid-1980s, how many countries could conceivably be called "democracies" of ten years' duration? And how many countries were very close to the totalitarian pole for that entire period? Answers have, of course, an inherently subjective dimension, particularly as regards the evaluation of the evidence used to classify countries along the different criteria used in the typology. Fortunately, however, two independently organized studies attempt to measure most of the countries in the world as to their political rights and civil liberties.[4] The criteria used in the studies are explicit, and there is a very high degree of agreement in the results. If we use these studies and the traditional tripartite regime type distinction, it turns out that more than 90 percent of modern nondemocratic regimes would have to share the same typological space—"authoritarian."[5] Obviously, with so many heterogeneous countries sharing the same

3. See Juan J. Linz, "From Falange to Movimiento-Organización: The Spanish Single Party and the Franco Regime, 1936–1968," in Samuel P. Huntington and Clement H. Moore, eds., *Authoritarian Politics in Modern Society: The Dynamics of Established One-Party Systems* (New York: Basic Books, 1970), 128–203. Also see Linz, "Opposition in and under an Authoritarian Regime: The Case of Spain," in Robert A. Dahl, ed., *Regimes and Oppositions* (New Haven: Yale University Press, 1973), 171–259.

4. One effort was by Michael Coppedge and Wolfgang Reinicke, who attempted to operationalize the eight "institutional guarantees" that Robert Dahl argued were required for a polyarchy. They assigned values to 137 countries on a polyarchy scale, based on their assessment of political conditions as of mid-1985. The results are available in "A Measure of Polyarchy," paper prepared for the Conference on Measuring Democracy, Hoover Institution, Stanford University, May 27–28, 1988; and their "A Scale of Polyarchy," in Raymond D. Gastil, ed., *Freedom in the World: Political Rights and Civil Liberties, 1987–1988* (New York: Freedom House, 1990), 101–28. Robert A. Dahl's seminal discussion of the "institutional guarantees" needed for polyarchy is found in Dahl, *Polyarchy: Participation and Opposition* (New Haven: Yale University Press, 1971), 1–16.

The other major effort to operationalize a scale of democracy is the annual Freedom House evaluation of virtually all the countries of the world. The advisory panel has included in recent years such scholars as Seymour Martin Lipset, Giovanni Sartori, and Lucian W. Pye. The value they assigned on their scale for each year from 1978–1987 can be found in Gastil, *Freedom in the World*, 54–65.

5. We arrive at this conclusion in the following fashion. The annual survey coordinated by Raymond D. Gastil employs a 7-point scale of the political rights and civil liberties dimensions of democracy. With the help of a panel of scholars, Gastil, from 1978 to 1987, classified annually 167 countries on this scale. For our purposes if we call the universe of democracies those countries that from 1978 to 1987 never received a score of lower than 2 on the Gastil scale for political rights and 3 for civil liberty, we come up with 42 countries. This is very close to the number of countries that Coppedge and Reinicke classify as "full polyarchies" in their independent study of the year 1985. Since our interest is in how countries become democracies we will

typological "starting place," this typology of regime type cannot tell us much about the extremely significant range of variation in possible transition paths and consolidation tasks that we believe in fact exists. Our purpose in the rest of this chapter is to reformulate the tripartite paradigm of regime type so as to make it more helpful in the analysis of *transition paths* and *consolidation tasks*. We propose therefore a revised typology, consisting of "democratic," "authoritarian," "totalitarian," "post-totalitarian," and "sultanistic" regimes.

DEMOCRACY

To start with the democratic type of regime, there are of course significant variations within democracy. However, we believe that such important categories as "consociational democracy" and "majoritarian democracy" are subtypes of democracy and not different regime types.[6] Democracy as a regime type seems to us to be of sufficient value to be retained and not to need further elaboration at this point in the book.

TOTALITARIANISM

We also believe that the concept of a totalitarian regime as an ideal type, with some close historical approximations, has enduring value. If a regime has eliminated almost all pre-existing political, economic, and social pluralism, has a unified, articulated, guiding, utopian ideology, has intensive and extensive mobilization, and has a leadership that rules, often charismatically, with undefined limits and great unpredictability and vulnerability for elites and nonelites alike, then it seems to us that it still makes historical and conceptual sense to call this a regime with strong totalitarian tendencies.

If we accept the continued conceptual utility of the democratic and totalitarian regime types, the area in which further typological revision is needed concerns the regimes that are clearly neither democratic nor totalitarian. By the early

---

exclude those 42 countries from our universe of analysis. This would leave us with 125 countries in the universe we want to explore.

If we then decide to call long-standing "totalitarian" regimes those regimes that received the lowest possible score on political rights and civil liberties on the Gastil scale for each year in the 1978–1987 period, we would have a total of nine countries that fall into the totalitarian classification. Thus, if one used the traditional typology, the Gastil scale would imply that 116 of 125 countries, or 92.8 percent of the universe under analysis, would have to be placed in the same typological space. See Gastil, *Freedom in the World,* 54–65.

6. For discussions of variations within democracy, see Arendt Lijphart, *Democracies: Patterns of Majoritarian and Consensus Government in Twenty-one Countries* (New Haven: Yale University Press, 1984), esp. 1–36; Philippe C. Schmitter and Terry Lynn Karl, "What Democracy Is . . . and Is Not," *Journal of Democracy* 2, no. 2 (Summer 1991): 75–88; and Juan J. Linz, "Change and Continuity in the Nature of Contemporary Democracies," in Gary Marks and Larry Diamond, eds., *Reexamining Democracy* (Newbury Park, N.J.: Sage Publications, 1992), 182–207.

1980s, the number of countries that were clearly totalitarian or were attempting to create such regimes had in fact been declining for some time. As many Soviet-type regimes began to change after Stalin's death in 1953, they no longer conformed to the totalitarian model, as research showed. This change created conceptual confusion. Some scholars argued that the totalitarian category itself was wrong. Others wanted to call post-Stalinist regimes authoritarian. Neither of these approaches seems to us fully satisfactory. Empirically, of course, most of the Soviet-type systems in the 1980s were not totalitarian. However, the "Soviet type" regimes, with the exception of Poland (see chap. 12), could not be understood in their distinctiveness by including them in the category of an authoritarian regime.

The literature on Soviet-type regimes correctly drew attention to regime characteristics that were no longer totalitarian and opened up promising new studies of policy-making. One of these perspectives was "institutional pluralism."[7] However, in our judgment, to call these post-Stalinist polities *pluralistic* missed some extremely important features that could hardly be called pluralistic. Pluralist democratic theory, especially the "group theory" variant explored by such writers as Arthur Bentley and David Truman, starts with *individuals in civil society* who enter into numerous freely formed interest groups that are relatively autonomous and often criss-crossing. The many groups in civil society attempt to aggregate their interests and compete against each other in political society to influence state policies. However, the "institutional pluralism" that some writers discerned in the Soviet Union was radically different, in that almost all the pluralistic conflict occurred in *regime-created organizations within the party-state* itself. Conceptually, therefore, this form of competition and conflict is actually closer to what political theorists call *bureaucratic politics* than it is to *pluralistic politics*.[8]

Rather than forcing these Soviet-type regimes into the existing typology of totalitarian, authoritarian, and democratic regimes, we believe we should expand that typology by explicating a distinctive regime type that we will call *post-totalitarian*.[9] Methodologically, we believe this category is justified because on each of the four dimensions of regime type—pluralism, ideology, leadership, and mobi-

7. The strongest advocate of an institutional pluralist perspective for the analysis of Soviet politics was Jerry F. Hough, especially in his *The Soviet Union and Social Science Theory* (Cambridge, Mass.: Harvard University Press, 1977).

8. The pioneering critique of the institutional pluralist approach to Soviet politics is Archie Brown, "Pluralism, Power and the Soviet Political System: A Comparative Perspective," in Susan Gross Solomon, ed., *Pluralism in the Soviet Union* (London: Macmillan, 1983), 61–107. A useful review of the literature, with attention to authors such as Gordon Skilling, Archie Brown, and Jerry Hough, is found in Gabriel Almond (with Laura Roselle), "Model-Fitting in Communism Studies," in his *A Discipline Divided: Schools and Sects in Political Science* (Newbury Park, Calif.: Sage Publications, 1990), 157–72.

9. Juan Linz, in his "Totalitarian and Authoritarian Regimes," in Fred I. Greenstein and Nelson W. Polsby, eds., *Handbook of Political Science* (Reading, Mass.: Addison-Wesley Publishing Co., 1975), 3:175–411, analyzed what he called "post-totalitarian authoritarian regimes," see 336–50. Here, with our focus on the available paths to democratic transition and the tasks of democratic consolidation, it seems to both of us that it is more useful to treat post-totalitarian regimes not as a subtype of authoritarianism, but as an ideal type in its own right.

lization—there can be a post-totalitarian ideal type that is different from a totalitarian, authoritarian, or democratic ideal type. Later in this chapter we will also rearticulate the argument for considering sultanism as a separate ideal-type regime.[10]

To state our argument in bold terms, we first present a schematic presentation of how the five ideal-type regimes we propose—democratic, totalitarian, post-totalitarian, authoritarian, and sultanistic—differ from each other on each one of the four constituent characteristics of regime type (table 3.1). In the following chapter we make explicit what we believe are the implications of each regime type for democratic transition paths and the tasks of democratic consolidation.

POST-TOTALITARIANISM

Our task here is to explore how, on each of the four dimensions of regime type, post-totalitarianism is different from totalitarianism, as well as different from authoritarianism.[11] Where appropriate we will also call attention to some under-theorized characteristics of both totalitarian and post-totalitarian regimes that produce dynamic pressures for out-of-type change. We do not subscribe to the view that either type is static.

Post-totalitarianism, as table 3.1 implies, can encompass a continuum varying from "early post-totalitarianism," to "frozen post-totalitarianism," to "mature post-totalitarianism." Early post-totalitarianism is very close to the totalitarian ideal type but differs from it on at least one key dimension, normally some constraints on the leader. There can be frozen post-totalitarianism in which, despite the persistent tolerance of some civil society critics of the regime, almost all the other control mechanisms of the party-state stay in place for a long period and do not evolve (e.g., Czechoslovakia, from 1977 to 1989). Or there can be mature post-totalitarianism in which there has been significant change in all the dimensions of the post-totalitarian regime except that politically the leading role of the official party is still sacrosanct (e.g., Hungary from 1982 to 1988, which eventually evolved by late 1988 very close to an out-of-type change).

Concerning *pluralism,* the defining characteristic of totalitarianism is that there is no political, economic, or social pluralism in the polity and that pre-

---

10. For Juan Linz's first discussion of sultanism, see ibid, 259–63. For a more complete discussion of sultanism, see H. E. Chehabi and Juan J. Linz, "Sultanistic Regimes," paper prepared for a conference on sultanistic regimes at Harvard University in November 1990. The results of the conference, which included papers on such countries as Iran, the Philippines, the Dominican Republic, and Romania, will be published in a volume edited by H. E. Chehabi and Juan J. Linz.

11. We believe that readers can readily see for themselves how post-totalitarian regimes are not democratic regimes, so we will not discuss this point separately. We want to make clear that for our analytic purposes in this book that the term *post-totalitarian* refers to a type of nondemocratic regime before the transition to democracy. In this chapter our main concern is with ideal types. However, in chapter 15, "Post-Communism's Prehistories," we provide ample empirical evidence of what a totalitarian or post-totalitarian (in contrast to an authoritarian) legacy means for each of the five arenas necessary for a consolidated democracy that we analyzed in table 1.1 in this book.

existing sources of pluralism have been uprooted or systematically repressed. In an authoritarian regime there is some limited political pluralism and often quite extensive economic and social pluralism. In an authoritarian regime, many of the manifestations of the limited political pluralism and the more extensive social and economic pluralism predate the authoritarian regime. How does pluralism in post-totalitarian regimes contrast with the near absence of pluralism in totalitarian regimes and the limited pluralism of authoritarian regimes?

In mature post-totalitarianism, there is a much more important and complex play of institutional pluralism within the state than in totalitarianism. Also, in contrast to totalitarianism, post-totalitarianism normally has a much more significant degree of social pluralism, and in mature post-totalitarian there is often discussion of a "second culture" or a "parallel culture." Evidence of this is found in such things as a robust underground *samizdat* literature with multi-issue journals of the sort not possible under totalitarianism.[12] This growing pluralism is simultaneously a dynamic source of vulnerability for the post-totalitarian regime and a dynamic source of strength for an emerging democratic opposition. For example, this "second culture" can be sufficiently powerful that, even though leaders of the second culture will frequently be imprisoned, in a mature post-totalitarian regime opposition leaders can generate substantial followings and create enduring oppositional organizations in civil society. At moments of crisis, therefore, a mature post-totalitarian regime can have a cadre of a democratic opposition based in civil society with much greater potential to form a democratic political opposition than would be available in a totalitarian regime. A mature post-totalitarian regime can also feature the coexistence of a state-planned economy with extensive partial market experiments in the state sector that can generate a "red bourgeoisie" of state sector managers and a growing but subordinate private sector, especially in agriculture, commerce and services.

However, in a post-totalitarian regime this social and economic pluralism is different in degree and kind from that found in an authoritarian regime. It is different in degree because there is normally more social and economic pluralism in an authoritarian regime (in particular there is normally a more autonomous private sector, somewhat greater religious freedom, and a greater amount of above-ground cultural production). The difference in kind is typologically even more important. In a post-totalitarian society, the historical reference both for the power holders of the regime and the opposition is the previous totalitarian regime. By definition, the existence of a previous totalitarian regime means that most of the pre-existing sources of responsible and organized pluralism have been eliminated or repressed and a totalitarian order has been established. There is therefore an active effort at "detotalitarianization" on the part of oppositional

---

12. For example, in mature post-totalitarian Hungary the most influential *samizdat* publication, *Beszélö*, from 1982 to 1989, was issued as a quarterly with publication runs of 20,000. Information supplied to Alfred Stepan by the publisher and editorial board member, Miklós Haraszti, Budapest, August 1994.

Table 3.1. Major Modern Regime Ideal Types and Their Defining Characteristics

Characteristic	Democracy	Authoritarianism	Totalitarianism	Post-totalitarianism	Sultanism
Pluralism	Responsible political pluralism reinforced by extensive areas of pluralist autonomy in economy, society, and internal life of organizations. Legally protected pluralism consistent with "societal corporatism" but not "state corporatism."	Political system with limited, not responsible political pluralism. Often quite extensive social and economic pluralism. In authoritarian regimes most of pluralism had roots in society before the establishment of the regime. Often some space for semiopposition.	No significant economic, social, or political pluralism. Official party has *de jure* and *de facto* monopoly of power. Party has eliminated almost all pretotalitarian pluralism. No space for second economy or parallel society.	Limited, but not responsible social, economic, and institutional pluralism. Almost no political pluralism because party still formally has monopoly of power. May have "second economy," but state still the overwhelming presence. Most manifestations of pluralism in "flattened polity" grew out of tolerated state structures or dissident groups consciously formed in opposition to totalitarian regime. In mature post-totalitarianism opposition often creates "second culture" or "parallel society."	Economic and social pluralism does not disappear but is subject to unpredictable and despotic intervention. No group or individual in civil society, political society, or the state is free from sultan's exercise of despotic power. No rule of law. Low institutionalization. High fusion of private and public.
Ideology	Extensive intellectual commitment to citizenship and procedural rules of contestation. Not teleological. Respect for rights of minorities, state of law, and value of individualism.	Political system without elaborate and guiding ideology but with distinctive mentalities.	Elaborate and guiding ideology that articulates a reachable utopia. Leaders, individuals, and groups derive most of their sense of mission, legitimation, and often specific policies from their commitment to some holistic conception of humanity and society.	Guiding ideology still officially exists and is part of the social reality. But weakened commitment to or faith in utopia. Shift of emphasis from ideology to programmatic consensus that presumably is based on rational decision-making and limited debate without too much reference to ideology.	Highly arbitrary manipulation of symbols. Extreme glorification of ruler. No elaborate or guiding ideology or even distinctive mentalities outside of despotic personalism. No attempt to justify major initiatives on the basis of ideology. Pseudo-ideology not believed by staff, subjects, or outside world.

Table 3.1. *(continued)*

Characteristic	Democracy	Authoritarianism	Totalitarianism	Post-totalitarianism	Sultanism
Mobilization	Participation via autonomously generated organization of civil society and competing parties of political society guaranteed by a system of law. Value is on low regime mobilization but high citizen participation. Diffuse effort by regime to induce good citizenship and patriotism. Toleration of peaceful and orderly opposition.	Political system without extensive or intensive political mobilization except at some points in their development.	Extensive mobilization into a vast array of regime-created obligatory organizations. Emphasis on activism of cadres and militants. Effort at mobilization of enthusiasm. Private life is decried.	Progressive loss of interest by leaders and nonleaders involved in organizing mobilization. Routine mobilization of population within state-sponsored organizations to achieve a minimum degree of conformity and compliance. Many "cadres" and "militants" are mere careerists and opportunists. Boredom, withdrawal, and ultimately privatization of population's values become an accepted fact.	Low but occasional manipulative mobilization of a ceremonial type by coercive or clientelistic methods without permanent organization. Periodic mobilization of parastate groups who use violence against groups targeted by sultan.
Leadership	Top leadership produced by free elections and must be exercised within constitutional limits and state of law. Leadership must be periodically subjected to and produced by free elections.	Political system in which a leader or occasionally a small group exercises power within formally ill-defined but actually quite predictable norms. Effort at cooptation of old elite groups. Some autonomy in state careers and in military.	Totalitarian leadership rules with undefined limits and great unpredictability for members and nonmembers. Often charismatic. Recruitment to top leadership highly dependent on success and commitment in party organization.	Growing emphasis by post-totalitarian political elite on personal security. Checks on top leadership via party structures, procedures, and "internal democracy." Top leaders are seldom charismatic. Recruitment to top leadership restricted to official party but less dependent upon building a career within party's organization. Top leaders can come from party technocrats in state apparatus.	Highly personalistic and arbitrary. No rational-legal constraints. Strong dynastic tendency. No autonomy in state careers. Leader unencumbered by ideology. Compliance to leaders based on intense fear and personal rewards. Staff of leader drawn from members of his family, friends, business associates, or men directly involved in use of violence to sustain the regime. Staff's position derives from their purely personal submission to the ruler.

currents in civil society. Much of the emotional and organizational drive of the opposition in civil society is thus consciously crafted to forge alternatives to the political, economic, and social structures created by the totalitarian regime, structures that still play a major role in the post-totalitarian society. Much of the second culture therefore is not traditional in form but is found in new movements that arise out of the totalitarian experience. There can also be a state-led detotalitarianization in which the regime itself begins to eliminate some of the most extreme features of the monist experience. Thus, if there is growing "institutional pluralism," or a growing respect for procedure and law, or a newly tolerated private sector, it should be understood as a kind of pluralism that emerges *out of* the previous totalitarian regime.

However, it is typologically and politically important to stress that there are significant limits to pluralism in post-totalitarian societies. In contrast to an authoritarian regime, there is *no* limited and relatively autonomous pluralism in the explicitly political realm. The official party in all post-totalitarian regimes is still legally accorded the leading role in the polity. The institutional pluralism of a post-totalitarian regime should not be confused with political pluralism; rather, institutional pluralism is exercised within the party-state or within the newly tolerated second economy or parallel culture. The pluralism of the parallel culture or the second culture should be seen as a *social* pluralism that may have political implications. But we must insist that the party and the regime leaders in post-totalitarian regimes, unless they experience out-of-type change, accord *no* legitimacy or responsibility to nonofficial political pluralism.[13] Even the formal pluralism of satellite parties becomes politically relevant only in the final stages of the regime after the transition is in progress.

When we turn to the dimension of *leadership,* we also see central tendencies that distinguish totalitarian from authoritarian leadership. Totalitarian leadership is unconstrained by laws and procedures and is often charismatic. The leadership can come from the revolutionary party or movement, but members of this core are as vulnerable to the sharp policy and ideological changes enunciated by the leader (even more so in terms of the possibility of losing their lives) as the rest of the population.[14] By contrast, in the Linzian scheme, authoritarian leadership is characterized by a political system in which a leader or occasionally a small group exercises power within formally ill-defined but actually quite predictable norms. There are often extensive efforts to co-opt old elite groups into leadership roles, and there is some autonomy in state careers and in the military.

13. Hungary in 1988–89 represents a mature post-totalitarian regime which, by engaging in extensive detotalitarianization and by increasingly recognizing the legitimacy of other parties, had experienced significant out-of-type changes even before the Communist Party lost power. See chapter 17.

14. For example, under Stalin, of the nine members of the Politburo in 1930, five had disappeared or been shot by 1937. See George K. Schueller, *The Politburo* (Stanford: Stanford University Press, 1951), 5–6.

As in a totalitarian regime, post-totalitarian leadership is still exclusively restricted to the revolutionary party or movement. However, in contrast to a totalitarian regime, post-totalitarian leaders tend to be more bureaucratic and state technocratic than charismatic. The central core of a post-totalitarian regime normally strives successfully to enhance its security and lessen its fear by reducing the range of arbitrary discretion allowed to the top leadership.

In contrast to those who say that the totalitarian regime concept is static, we believe that, when an opportunity presents itself (such as the death of the maximum leader), the top elite's desire to reduce the future leader's absolute discretion is predictably a dynamic source of pressure for out-of-type regime change from totalitarianism to post-totalitarianism. The post-totalitarian leadership is thus typologically closer in this respect to authoritarian leadership, in that the leader rules within unspecified but in reality reasonably predictable limits. However, the leadership in these two regime types still differs fundamentally. Post-totalitarian leadership is exclusively recruited from party members who develop their careers in the party organization itself, the bureaucracy, or the technocratic apparatus of the state. They all are thus recruited from the structures created by the regime. In sharp contrast, in most authoritarian regimes, the norm is for the regime to co-opt much of the leadership from groups that have some power, presence, and legitimacy that does not derive directly from the regime itself. Indeed, the authoritarian regime has often been captured by powerful fragments of the pre-existing society. In some authoritarian regimes, even access to top positions can be established not by political loyalties as much as by some degree of professional and technical expertise and some degree of competition through examinations that are open to the society as a whole. In mature post-totalitarian regimes, technical competence becomes increasingly important, but we should remember that the original access to professional training was controlled by political criteria. Also, the competences that are accepted or recognized in post-totalitarian systems are technical or managerial but do not include skills developed in a broader range of fields such as the law, religious organizations, or independent business or labor.

The limited party-bureaucratic-technocratic pluralism under post-totalitarianism does not give the regime the flexibility for change within the regime that co-optation of nonregime elites can give to many authoritarian regimes. The desire to resist the personalized leadership of the First Secretary–ideologue can be a source of change from totalitarian to post-totalitarian, but it can also lead eventually to the oligarchic leadership of aging men supported by the nomenklatura. Attempts at rejuvenation at the top by including or co-opting new men and women from the outside are normally very limited. In extreme cases (i.e., the GDR and post-1968 Czechoslovakia), frozen post-totalitarianism shows geriatric tendencies. Under crisis circumstances, the inability to renovate leadership, not so paradoxically, is a potential source of dynamic change in that a frozen post-totalitarian regime, with its old and narrow leadership base, has a very limited capacity to negotiate. Such a leadership structure, if it is not able to repress opponents in a crisis, is particularly vulnerable to *collapse*. One of the reasons why midlevel cadres in the once all-powerful coercive apparatus might, in time of crisis, let the regime collapse rather than fire upon the democratic opposition has to do with the role of ideology in post-totalitarianism.

The contrast between the role of *ideology* in a totalitarian system and in a post-totalitarian system is sharp, but it is more one of behavior and belief than one of official canon. In the area of ideology, the dynamic potential for change from a totalitarian to a post-totalitarian regime, both on the part of the cadres and on the part of the society, is the growing empirical disjunction between official ideological claims and reality. This disjunction produces lessened ideological commitment on the part of the cadres and growing criticism of the regime by groups in civil society. In fact, many of the new critics in civil society emerge out of the ranks of former true believers, who argue that the regime does not—or, worse, cannot—advance its own goals. The pressures created by this tension between doctrine and reality often contributes to an out-of-type shift from a totalitarian regime effort to mobilize enthusiasm to a post-totalitarian effort to maintain acquiescence. In the post-totalitarian phase, the elaborate and guiding ideology created under the totalitarian regime still exists as the official state canon, but among many leaders there is a weakened commitment to and faith in utopia. Among much of the population, the official canon is seen as an obligatory ritual, and among groups in the "parallel society" or "second culture," there is constant reference to the first culture as a "living lie."[15] This is another source of weakness, of the "hollowing out" of the post-totalitarian regime's apparent strength.

The role of ideology in a post-totalitarian regime is thus diminished from its role under totalitarianism, but it is still quite different from the role of ideology in an authoritarian regime. Most authoritarian regimes have diffuse nondemocratic mentalities, but they do not have highly articulated ideologies concerning the leading role of the party, interest groups, religion, and many other aspects of civil society, political society, the economy, and the state that still exist in a regime we would call post-totalitarian. Therefore, a fundamental contrast between a post-totalitarian and authoritarian regime is that in a post-totalitarian regime there is an important ideological legacy that cannot be ignored and that cannot be questioned officially. The state-sanctioned ideology has a *social presence* in the organizational life of the post-totalitarian polity. Whether it expresses itself in the extensive array of state-sponsored organizations or in the domain of incipient but still officially controlled organizations, ideology is part of the social reality of a post-totalitarian regime to a greater degree than in most authoritarian regimes.

---

15. Extensive discussions and references about "parallel society," "second culture," and the "living lie" are found in our chapter on post-totalitarianism in Hungary and Czechoslovakia (chap. 17).

The relative de-ideologization of post-totalitarian regimes and the weakening of the belief in utopia as a foundation of legitimacy mean that, as in many authoritarian regimes, there is a growing effort in a post-totalitarian polity to legitimate the regime on the basis of performance criteria. The gap between the original utopian elements of the ideology and the increasing legitimation efforts on the basis of efficacy, particularly when the latter fails, is one of the sources of weakness in post-totalitarian regimes. Since democracies base their claim to obedience on the procedural foundations of democratic citizenship, as well as performance, they have a layer of insulation against weak performance not available to most post-totalitarian or authoritarian regimes. The weakening of utopian ideology that is a characteristic of post-totalitarianism thus opens up a new dynamic of regime vulnerabilities—or, from the perspective of democratic transition, new opportunities—that can be exploited by the democratic opposition. For example, the discrepancy between the constant reiteration of the importance of ideology and the ideology's growing irrelevance to policymaking or, worse, its transparent contradiction with social reality contribute to undermining the commitment and faith of the middle and lower cadres in the regime. Such a situation can help contribute to the rapid collapse of the regime if midlevel functionaries of the coercive apparatus have grave doubts about their right to shoot citizens who are protesting against the regime and its ideology, as we shall see when we discuss events in 1989 in East Germany and Czechoslovakia.[16]

The final typological difference we need to explore concerns *mobilization*. Most authoritarian regimes never develop complex, all-inclusive networks of association whose purpose is the mobilization of the population. They may have brief periods of intensive mobilization, but these are normally less intensive than in a totalitarian regime and less extensive than in a post-totalitarian regime. In totalitarian regimes, however, there is extensive and intensive mobilization of society into a vast array of regime-created organizations and activities. Because utopian goals are intrinsic to the regime, there is a great effort to mobilize enthusiasm to activate cadres, and most leaders emerge out of these cadres. In the totalitarian system, "privatized" bourgeois individuals at home with their family and friends and enjoying life in the small circle of their own choosing are decried.

In post-totalitarian regimes, the extensive array of institutions of regime-created mobilization vehicles still dominate associational life. However, they have lost their intensity. Membership is still generalized and obligatory but tends to generate more boredom than enthusiasm. State-technocratic employment is an alternative to cadre activism as a successful career path, as long as there is "correct" participation in official organizations. Instead of the mobilization of enthu-

---

16. Daniel V. Friedheim is conducting major research on the question of collapse in such frozen post-totalitarian regimes. See Friedheim, "Regime Collapse in the Peaceful East German Revolution: The Role of Middle-Level Officials," *German Politics* (April 1993): 97–112, and his forthcoming Yale University doctoral dissertation in which he discusses East Germany.

siasm that can be so functional in a totalitarian regime, the networks of ritualized mobilization in a post-totalitarian regime can produce a "cost" of time away from technocratic tasks for professionals and a cost of boredom and flight into private life by many other people. When there is no structural crisis and especially when there is no perception of an available alternative, such privatization is not necessarily a problem for a post-totalitarian regime. Thus, Kadar's famous saying, "Those who are not against us are for us," is a saying that is conceivable only in a post-totalitarian regime, not in a totalitarian one. However, if the performance of a post-totalitarian as opposed to a totalitarian regime is so poor that the personal rewards of private life are eroded, then privatization and apathy may contribute to a new dynamic—especially if alternatives are seen as possible—of crises of "exit," "voice," and "loyalty."[17]

Let us conclude our discussion of post-totalitarianism with a summary of its political and ideological weaknesses. We do this to help enrich the discussion of why these regimes collapsed so rapidly once they entered into prolonged stagnation and the USSR withdrew its extensive coercive support. Indeed in chapter 17, "Varieties of Post-totalitarian Regimes," we develop a theoretical and empirical argument about why frozen post-totalitarian regimes are more vulnerable to collapse than are authoritarian or totalitarian regimes.

Totalitarianism, democracy, and even many authoritarian regimes begin with "genetic" legitimacy among their core supporters, given the historical circumstances that led to the establishment of these regimes. By contrast, post-totalitarianism regimes do not have such a founding genetic legitimacy because they emerge out of the routinization, decay, or elite fears of the totalitarian regime. Post-totalitarian regimes, because of coercive resources they inherit and the related weaknesses of organized opposition, can give the appearance of as much or more stability than authoritarian regimes; if external support is withdrawn, however, their inner loss of purpose and commitment make them vulnerable to collapse.

Post-totalitarian politics was a result in part of the moving away from Stalinism, but also of social changes in Communist societies. Post-totalitarian regimes did away with the worst aspects of repression but at the same time maintained most mechanisms of control. Although less bloody than under Stalinism, the presence of security services—like the Stasi in the GDR—sometimes became more pervasive. Post-totalitarianism could have led to moderate reforms in the economy, like those discussed at the time of the Prague Spring, but the Brezhnev restoration stopped dynamic adaptation in the USSR and in most other Soviet-type systems, except for Hungary and Poland.

---

17. The reference, of course, is to Albert Hirschman, *Exit, Voice and Loyalty* (Cambridge: Harvard University Press, 1970), 59. For a fascinating discussion of this dynamic in relation to the collapse of the GDR, see Hirschman, "Exit, Voice and the Fate of the German Democratic Republic: An Essay on Conceptual History," *World Politics* 41 (January 1993): 173–202. We discuss the Kadar quote in greater detail in the chapter on varieties of post-totalitarianism (chap. 17).

Post-totalitarianism had probably less legitimacy for the ruling elites and above all the middle-level cadres than had a more totalitarian system. The loss of the utopian component of the ideology and the greater reliance on performance (which after some initial success did not continue) left the regimes vulnerable and ultimately made the use of massive repression less justifiable. Passive compliance and careerism opened the door to withdrawal into private life, weakening the regime so that the opposition could ultimately force it to negotiate or to collapse when it could not rely on coercion.

The weakness of post-totalitarian regimes has not yet been fully analyzed and explained but probably can be understood only by keeping in mind the enormous hopes and energies initially associated with Marxism-Leninism that in the past explained the emergence of totalitarianism and its appeal.[18] Many distinguished and influential Western intellectuals admired or excused Leninism and in the 1930s even Stalinism, but few Western intellectuals on the left could muster enthusiasm for post-totalitarianism in the USSR or even for perestroika and glasnost.

As we shall see in part 4, the emergence and evolution of post-totalitarianism can be the result of three distinct but often interconnected processes: (1) deliberate policies of the rulers to soften or reform the totalitarian system (detotalitarianism by choice), (2) the internal "hollowing out" of the totalitarian regimes' structures and an internal erosion of the cadres' ideological belief in the system (detotalitarianism by decay), and (3) the creation of social, cultural, and even economic spaces that resist or escape totalitarian control (detotalitarianism by societal conquest).

"Sultanism"

A large group of polities, such as Haiti under the Duvaliers, the Dominican Republic under Trujillo, the Central African Republic under Bokassa, the Philippines under Marcos, Iran under the Shah, Romania under Ceauşescu, and North Korea under Kim Il Sung, have had strong tendencies toward an extreme form of patrimonialism that Weber called *sultanism*. For Weber,

patrimonialism and, in the extreme case, *sultanism* tend to arise whenever traditional domination develops an administration and a military force which are purely personal instruments of the master. . . . Where domination . . . operates primarily on the basis of discretion, it will be called *sultanism* . . . The non-traditional element is not, however, rationalized in impersonal terms, but consists only in the extreme development of the ruler's discretion. It is this which distinguishes it from every form of rational authority.[19]

---

18. On the ideological and moral attractiveness of revolutionary Marxist-Leninism as a total system and the "vacuum" left in the wake of its collapse, see Ernest Gellner, "Homeland of the Unrevolution," *Daedalus* (Summer 1993): 141–54.

19. Max Weber, *Economy and Society: An Outline of Interpretive Sociology*, ed. Guenther Roth and Claus Wittich (Berkeley: University of California Press, 1978), 1:231, 232. Italics in the original.

Weber did not intend the word *sultanism* to imply religious claims to obedience. In fact, under Ottoman rule, the ruler held two distinct offices and titles, that of sultan and that of caliph. Initially, the Ottoman ruler was a sultan, and only after the conquest of Damascus did he assume the title of caliph, which entailed religious authority. After the defeat of Turkey in World War I and the proclamation of the republic, the former ruler lost his title of sultan but retained his religious title of caliph until Atatürk eventually forced him to relinquish even that title. Our point is that the secular and religious dimensions of his authority were conceptually and historically distinguished. Furthermore, the term *sultan* should not be analytically bound to the Middle East. Just as there are mandarins in New Delhi and Paris as well as in Peking and there is a macho style of politics in the Pentagon as well as in Buenos Aires, there are sultanistic rulers in Africa and the Caribbean as well as in the Middle East. What we do want the term *sultanism* to connote is a generic style of domination and regime rulership that is, as Weber says, an extreme form of patrimonialism. In sultanism, the private and the public are fused, there is a strong tendency toward familial power and dynastic succession, there is no distinction between a state career and personal service to the ruler, there is a lack of rationalized impersonal ideology, economic success depends on a personal relationship to the ruler, and, most of all, the ruler acts only according to his own unchecked discretion, with no larger, impersonal goals.

Table 3.1 gives substantial details on what a sultanistic type is in relation to pluralism, ideology, mobilization, and leadership. In this section we attempt to highlight differences between sultanism, totalitarianism, and authoritarianism because, while we believe they are distinct ideal types, in any concrete case a specific polity could have a mix of some sultanistic and some authoritarian tendencies (a combination that might open up a variety of transition options) or a mix of sultanistic and totalitarian tendencies (a combination that would tend to eliminate numerous transition options).

In his long essay, "Totalitarian and Authoritarian Regimes," Juan Linz discussed the special features that make sultanism a distinctive type of nondemocratic regime.[20] Since the sultanistic regime type has not been widely accepted in the literature, we believe it will be useful for us to highlight systematically its distinctive qualities so as to make more clear the implications of this type of regime for the patterns of democratic resistance and the problems of democratic consolidation.

In sultanism, there is a high fusion by the ruler of the private and the public. The sultanistic polity becomes the personal domain of the sultan. In this domain there is no rule of law and there is low institutionalization. In sultanism there may be extensive social and economic pluralism, but almost never political pluralism, because political power is so directly related to the ruler's person. However, the essential reality in a sultanistic regime is that all individuals, groups, and institu-

---

20. Linz, "Totalitarian and Authoritarian Regimes," 259–63.

tions are permanently subject to the unpredictable and despotic intervention of the sultan, and thus all pluralism is precarious.

In authoritarianism there may or may not be a rule of law, space for a semi-opposition, or space for regime moderates who might establish links with opposition moderates, and there are normally extensive social and economic activities that function within a secure framework of relative autonomy. Under sultanism, however, there is no rule of law, no space for a semiopposition, no space for regime moderates who might negotiate with democratic moderates, and no sphere of the economy or civil society that is not subject to the despotic exercise of the sultan's will. As we demonstrate in the next chapter, this critical difference between pluralism in authoritarian and sultanistic regimes has immense implications for the types of transition that are *available* in an authoritarian regime but *unavailable* in a sultanistic regime.

There is also a sharp contrast in the function and consequences of ideology between totalitarian and sultanistic regimes. In a totalitarian regime not only is there an elaborate and guiding ideology, but ideology has the function of legitimating the regime, and rulers are often somewhat constrained by their own value system and ideology. They or their followers, or both, believe in that ideology as a point of reference and justification for their actions. In contrast, a sultanistic ruler characteristically has no elaborate and guiding ideology. There may be highly personalistic statements with pretensions of being an ideology, often named after the sultan, but this ideology is elaborated after the ruler has assumed power, is subject to extreme manipulation, and, most importantly, is not believed to be constraining on the ruler and is relevant only as long as he practices it. Thus, there could be questions raised as to whether Stalin's practices and statements were consistent with Marxism-Leninism, but there would be no reason for anyone to debate whether Trujillo's statements were consistent with Trujilloism. The contrast between authoritarian and sultanistic regimes is less stark over ideology; however, the distinctive mentalities that are a part of most authoritarian alliances are normally more constraining on rulers than is the sultan's idiosyncratic and personal ideology.

The extensive and intensive mobilization that is a feature of totalitarianism is seldom found in a sultanistic regime because of its low degree of institutionalization and its low commitment to an overarching ideology. The low degree of organization.means that any mobilization that does occur is uneven and sporadic. Probably the biggest difference between sultanistic mobilization and authoritarian mobilization is the tendency within sultanism (most dramatic in the case of the Duvalier's Tonton Macoutes in Haiti) to use para-state groups linked to the sultan to wield violence and terror against anyone who opposes the ruler's will. These para-state groups are not modern bureaucracies with generalized norms and procedures; rather, they are direct extensions of the sultan's will. They have no significant institutional autonomy. As Weber stressed, they are purely "personal instruments of the master."

Finally, how does leadership differ in sultanism, totalitarianism, and authoritarianism? The essence of sultanism is *unrestrained personal rulership*. This personal rulership is, as we have seen, unconstrained by ideology, rational-legal norms, or any balance of power. "Support is based not on a coincidence of interest between preexisting privileged social groups and the ruler but on interests created by his rule, rewards he offers for loyalty, and the fear of his vengeance."[21]

In one key respect leadership under sultanism and totalitarianism is similar. In both regimes the leader rules with undefined limits on his power and there is great unpredictability for elites and nonelites alike. In this respect, a Stalin and a Somoza are alike. However, there are important differences. The elaborate ideology, with its sense of nonpersonal and public mission, is meant to play an important legitimating function in totalitarian regimes. The ideological pronouncements of a totalitarian leader are taken seriously not only by his followers and cadres, but also by the society and intellectuals, including—in the cases of Leninism, Stalinism, and Marxism (and even fascism)—by intellectuals outside the state in which the leader exercises control. This places a degree of organizational, social, and ideological constraint on totalitarian leadership that is not present in sultanistic leadership. Most importantly, the intense degree to which rulership is personal in sultanism makes the *dynastic* dimension of rulership normatively acceptable and empirically common, whereas the public claims of totalitarianism make dynastic ambition, if not unprecedented, at least aberrant.

The leadership dimension shows an even stronger contrast between authoritarianism and sultanism. As Linz stated in his discussion of authoritarianism, leadership is exercised in an authoritarian regime "with formally ill-defined but actually quite predictable" norms.[22] In most authoritarian regimes some bureaucratic entities play an important part. These bureaucratic entities often retain or generate their own norms, which imply that there are procedural and normative limits on what leaders can ask them to do in their capacity as, for example, military officers, judges, tax officials, or police officers. However, a sultanistic leader simply "demands unconditional administrative compliance, for the official's loyalty to his office is not an impersonal commitment to impersonal tasks that define the extent and content of his office, but rather a servant's loyalty based on a strictly personal relationship to the ruler and an obligation that in principle permits no limitation."[23]

We have now spelled out the central tendencies of five ideal-type regimes in the modern world, four of which are nondemocratic. We are ready for the next step, which is to explore why and how the *type* of prior nondemocratic regime has an important effect on the democratic transition paths available and the tasks to be addressed before democracy can be consolidated.

21. Ibid., 260.
22. Ibid., 255.
23. Ibid., 260.

4

The Implications of Prior
Regime Type for Transition Paths
and Consolidation Tasks

Having analyzed the necessary conditions for a consolidated democracy and then spelled out the key differences among the four ideal-typical nondemocratic regimes, it should be clear that the characteristics of the previous nondemocratic regime have profound implications for the transition *paths* available and the *tasks* different countries face when they begin their struggles to develop consolidated democracies. Within the logic of our ideal types, it is conceivable that a particular authoritarian regime in its late stages might have a robust civil society, a legal culture supportive of constitutionalism and rule of law, a usable state bureaucracy that operates within professional norms, and a reasonably well-institutionalized economic society. For such a polity, the first and only necessary item on the initial democratization agenda would relate to political society—that is, the creation of the autonomy, authority, power, and legitimacy of democratic institutions. We argue in chapter 6 that Spain, in the early 1970s, approximated this position. However, if the starting point were from a totalitarian regime of the communist subtype, democratic consolidation would entail the task of simultaneously crafting not only political society and economic society, but also every single arena of a democracy as well. The full implications of these arguments are spelled out in a more systematic and detailed manner in tables 4.2 and 4.3, but here let us first depict the argument in its most stark form, table 4.1.

The analytic utility of distinguishing between post-totalitarian and totalitarian regimes should now be clear. As table 4.1 demonstrates, it is conceivable that a post-totalitarian regime could begin a transition to democracy with a combination of low-medium or medium scores on each condition necessary for a consolidated democracy except for the autonomy of political society. Hungary in early and mid-1989 came closest to approximating this position. While the tasks facing democrats starting from a mature post-totalitarian regime are challenging, they are substantially less than those facing democrats starting from a totalitarian regime. However, it should also be clear that, precisely because post-totalitarian regimes have a prior totalitarian period, there will be *legacies* to over-

Table 4.1. The Implications of Prior Nondemocratic Regime Type for the Tasks of Democratic Consolidation

Arena Characteristics	Authoritarian	Totalitarian	Post-totalitarian	Sultanistic
Civil society autonomy	Medium to high	Low	Low to medium	Low to medium
Political society autonomy	Low to medium	Low	Low	Low
Constitutionalism and rule of law	Low to high	Low	Medium	Low
Professional norms and autonomy of state bureaucracy	Low to high	Low	Low to medium	Low
Economic society with a degree of market autonomy and plurality of ownership forms	Medium to high	Low (Communist) or medium (Fascist)	Low to low-medium	Low to medium

Note: The character of the arenas in the prior nondemocratic regime in the period relatively close to the start of the transition is of the greatest importance for the tasks democratic leaders will face. The less developed the arena, the greater the tasks democratic leaders will have to accomplish before the new regime can be a consolidated democracy.

come that are simply not found in an authoritarian regime that has never been totalitarian.

Sharp differences between authoritarian and sultanistic regimes in our typology also help direct attention to the fact that the immediate implications of a sultanistic regime for democracy-crafters (as in Haiti) are that they will have to begin the construction of civil society, constitutionalism and a rule of law, professional norms of the bureaucracy, economic society, and political institutions from a very low base.

The delineation of the different regime types also allows us to be more specific about the possibilities and limits of "pacts" as a transition option available or not available in any particular nondemocratic regime type. Before discussing under what conditions pacts are possible, three general analytic points about pacts must be stressed. First, neither theoretically nor historically do democratic transitions necessarily involve pacts. Indeed, of the eight distinctive paths to redemocratization Stepan analyzed elsewhere, only three involved pacts.[1] Second, pacts can range from very democratic to very nondemocratic in their intention and consequences. A pact might be specifically crafted to provide for the rapid dismantling of a nondemocratic regime and the setting of an early and specific date for free elections. Such a pact would be clearly democratic in its intention and, if implemented, its consequences. Or a pact may explicitly entail some nondemocratic constraints for a short period before and after the first foundational election. In contrast, a consociational pact that is not initially undemocratic, if maintained too long, might preclude the entry into politics of new groups and eventually

---

1. See Alfred Stepan, "Paths toward Redemocratization: Theoretical and Comparative Considerations," in Guillermo O'Donnell, Philippe C. Schmitter, and Laurence Whitehead, eds., *Transitions from Authoritarian Rule: Comparative Perspectives* (Baltimore: Johns Hopkins University Press, 1986), 64–84, 170–74.

Table 4.2. The Implications of Prior Nondemocratic Regime Type for Paths to Democratic Transition

Path	Authoritarianism	Totalitarianism	Post-totalitarianism	Sultanism
1. Reforma-pactada, ruptura-pactada	Given that civil society can be reasonably well developed and that some moderate political opposition with a national constituency can exist, *reforma-pactada, ruptura-pactada* between regime moderates and democratic opposition moderates is possible. Either regime leaders or the opposition could win fair elections and complete a transition.	No space for organized democratic opposition or for regime moderates. Thus *reforma-pactada* path is unavailable.	In mature post-totalitarianism, there can be collective leadership and a moderate wing. Likewise, the democratic opposition could have a well-developed "second culture" and incipient political groupings. If leaders of a mature post-totalitarian regime believe that elections are necessary and they have a chance to win, *reforma-pactada* with the leaders of the second culture or incipient opposition leading to free elections is possible.	Given a lack of rule of law and civil liberties on the one hand and personalistic penetration of the entire polity by the sultan on the other, the two prerequisites for a four-player pacted reform, an organized nonviolent democratic opposition and regime moderates with sufficient authority to negotiate a pact, do not exist, leaving the *reforma-pactada* virtually impossible.
2. Defeat in War	Defeat in war or war-related collapse could lead to a democratic transition with weak negotiating power by prior nondemocratic regime if representatives of democratic forces in civil and political society are available and demand an electoral path.	Virtually the only path in which totalitarianism defeated in war could lead rapidly to a democratic regime is by occupation by a democratic regime and externally monitored democratic installation.	In early post-totalitarianism, democratic prospects could resemble totalitarianism. In mature post-totalitarianism, assumption of government by a democratic opposition and the early holding of elections are possible.	Given absence of the rule of law and widespread para-state violence, the democratic path is virtually not available without external monitoring and guarantees.

Table 4.2. (continued)

Path	Authoritarianism	Totalitarianism	Post-Totalitarianism	Sultanism
3. Interim government after regime termination not initiated by regime (coup by nonhierarchical military, armed insurgents, or mass uprising and regime collapse)	In an authoritarian regime, it is possible that an organized democratic opposition in civil society and even political society exists. If they demand early elections, this transition path is quite possible. However, in the absence of effective demand for elections, the interim government will be tempted to exercise revolutionary power in policy areas and to postpone or cancel elections, thus delaying the transition or leading to a new nondemocratic regime.	An interim government is unlikely. However, should a deep crisis lead to a successor government, given flattened civil society and the absence of organized democratic political society, successful pressure for the holding of free elections is unlikely. The successors might search for electoral legitimation, but this does not ensure democratization.	Early elections are only the most likely path in mature post-totalitarianism where opposition activists might form government and proceed to democratization. In early or frozen post-totalitarianism, the most likely regime transition is mass uprising which, if not repressed, could lead to regime collapse and an interim government. The interim government may well be formed by elites connected with the old regime who are able to consolidate their power electorally in the still "flattened society."	High chance that "interim government" will claim to act in the name of the people and will postpone elections in order to carry out reforms. Given previous lack of autonomy of civil or political society, there is a high chance that groups associated with the sultan but claiming legitimacy for having supported the uprising will achieve nondemocratic power. The best chance for democratic transition is if revolutionary upheaval is led by internationally supported, democratically inclined leaders who set a date for elections and allow free contestation of power.

Table 4.2. (continued)

Path	Authoritarianism	Totalitarianism	Post-Totalitarianism	Sultanism
4. Extrication from rule by hierarchically led military	If a regime is led by a hierarchical military, the "military as institution," if it feels under internal or external threat, may play a role in pressuring the "military as government" to withdraw from direct rule and to hold "extrication elections." The length of transition and the extent of the "reserve domains of power" the military can impose as the price of extrication decrease with the severity of the internal or external threat to the military as institution and the strength of democratic forces in civil and political society.	Path not available to this regime type. Primacy of revolutionary party and unconstrained role of leaders make rule by hierarchical military impossible.	Path not available to this type given leading role of the party.	Path not available to this regime type. Sultanism implies a degree of fusion of private and public, and the sultan's interference with bureaucratic norms is incompatible with rule by a hierarchical military.
5. Some regime-specific possible transition paths and likely outcomes	If nondemocratic authoritarian regime is led by nonhierarchical military and this regime collapses or is overthrown, it will be easier to impose civilian democratic control and trials on the military than if the regime had been led by a hierarchical military.	Leadership of totalitarian regime could split, opening the way for popular mobilization, liberalization, and possibly even an interim government that holds elections. Given the level of control prior to the mobilization of protest, a more probable outcome is that the dynamic of mobilization leads to re-imposition by force of totalitarian controls or to shift to post-totalitarianism. See transition paths open to post-totalitarianism.	A post-totalitarian regime, confronted with a serious crisis, could collapse if the option of repression is unavailable. Collapse could lead to non-democratic takeover by alternative elites, democratization, or chaos.	Given dynastic tendencies of sultanism, if sultan dies of natural causes family members will attempt to continue sultanistic regime; thus, normally no regime-led liberalization will take place.

Table 4.2. (continued)

Path	Authoritarianism	Totalitarianism	Post-Totalitarianism	Sultanism
6. Other regime-specific paths	If a civilian-led authoritarian regime initiates a democratic transition, whatever agreements have been made will only tend to have the power the electorate and elected officials give to them. The emerging democracy will therefore normally be less constrained than if the prior nondemocratic regime had been led by a hierarchical military.	If totalitarian regime is supported by an external hegemon, withdrawal of hegemon's support could alter all power relationships. Cost of repression increases. Opposition and mobilization increase, and collapse becomes a possible outcome. If regime falls, chaos or provisional government is most likely. Given the absence of organized democratic opposition, even if provisional government begins a transition, control by people emerging out of the old regime is most likely.	If post-totalitarian regime is supported by external hegemon, it could collapse if hegemon removes coercive guarantee. If it is an early post-totalitarian regime, the successor regime is likely to be authoritarian or controlled by leaders emerging out of the previous regime. If it is a late post-totalitarian regime, civil society leaders of the provisional government could call early and completely free elections.	If the sultan is dependent on a foreign patron, a continuation of a crisis and pressure by the patron might lead to the ruler holding snap elections which he thinks he can control. Defeat in elections is a possibility, especially if an external patron supports the opposition. But democratic governance will be greatly aided by continued engagement of the patron in the democratization process. Foreign patron can sometimes force the sultan to step down.
7. Other regime-specific paths		Totalitarian regime could shift to post-totalitarianism. See transition options for post-totalitarianism.		Most likely domestic cause for the defeat of the sultan is assassination or revolutionary upheaval by armed groups or civil society. Upheaval could be supported even by business groups because of their dislike of the sultan's extreme use of arbitrary power. Provisional government is most likely. See no. 3 above.

become a form of "exclusionary consociational authoritarianism."[2] Finally, a pact that is designed to exclude some groups permanently and vastly to over-represent other groups is clearly undemocratic in its intention and, as long as it is sustained, in its consequences. Third, as Stepan has argued elsewhere, "pact *creation* does not necessarily mean pact *maintenance*—pacts can fall apart. . . . Pacts—with or without consociational elements—cannot be created in all political systems. Party pacts have two requirements: first, leaders with the organizational and ideological capacity to negotiate a grand coalition among themselves; second, the allegiance of their political followers to the terms of the pact."[3]

Much of the transition literature on pacts contains references to "hard-liners" and "moderates." Transitions are frequently seen as involving a pact between the regime moderates and the opposition moderates who are both able to "use" and "contain" their respective hard-liners. This is, in essence, a four-player game theory model.[4] However, two conditions must be satisfied for it to be a true four-player game. The moderate players in the regime must have sufficient autonomy so that they can, over time, conduct strategic as well as tactical negotiations with the players from the moderate opposition. Conversely, the moderates in the opposition need a degree of continued organizational presence, power, and followers in the polity to play their part in the negotiation pacts. For many writers on transitions, the *locus classicus* of such a pact occurred in Spain.[5] In Spain, as we shall see in chapter 6, regime and opposition moderates initially crafted a pacted reform. Eventually, negotiations led to a pacted rupture that allowed the dismantling of the nondemocratic elements of the Franco state and the creation of new democratic structures. This overall process is called *reforma pactada–ruptura pactada*.

While there are often references to the possibility of pacts being a key part of most transitions, full four-player pacts are possible only in two of our four ideal-typical nondemocratic regimes. A regime that approximates the sultanistic ideal type does not have the *reforma pactada-ruptura pactada* available as a transition path because the two moderate players are absent. The essence of the sultanistic ideal type is that the sultan fuses personal and public power. Important figures in the regime are significant not because of any bureaucratic or professional position they hold, but because of their presence on the personal staff of the sultan.

---

2. Jonathan Hartlyn discusses consociational exclusion in *The Politics of Coalition Rule in Colombia* (Cambridge: Cambridge University Press, 1988).

3. Stepan, "Paths toward Redemocratization," 80. Stress in original. For an excellent analysis of the difficulties of pact maintenance, see Eric Nordlinger, *Conflict Regulation and Divided Societies* (Cambridge: Center for International Affairs, Harvard University Press, 1972).

4. See, for example, Adam Przeworski, "The Games of Transition," in Scott Mainwaring, Guillermo O'Donnell, and Samuel Valenzuela, eds., *Issues in Democratic Consolidation* (Notre Dame, Indiana: University of Notre Dame Press, 1992), 105–53.

5. For a rigorous and appropriate application of the game theory approach to the Spanish case, see Josep M. Colomer, *Game Theory and the Transition to Democracy: The Spanish Model* (Aldershot, England: Edward Elgar Publishing, 1995), and "Transitions by Agreement: Modeling the Spanish Way," *American Political Science Review* (December 1991): 1283–1302.

Table 4.3. The Implications of Nondemocratic Regime Type for the Minimal Tasks of Completing Transition to and Consolidation of a Democratic Regime from that Regime Type

Necessary Conditions	Authoritarianism	Totalitarianism	Post-totalitarianism	Sultanism
1. Rule of law and civil society freedom	In some authoritarian regimes there is a tradition of rule of law and civil society that might be quite lively, but civil liberties will need to be extended and protected. Laws giving autonomy to trade unions, media, etc., may need to be enacted and implemented.	Rule of law did not exist. Much of the legal code, to the extent that it existed, was highly politicized and instrumental for the party-state but not for its citizens and therefore was incompatible with democracy. Civil liberties are minimal and need to be legalized, developed, and protected. The "flattened" nature of civil society requires fundamental changes that are difficult to generate in a short time.	An extensive reform of the legal system to assure civil rights and rule of law will be needed.	Given the legacy of the fusion of public and private and the extreme personalization of power, the establishment of a rule of law and guarantees for citizens have a high priority and will be a difficult task.
2. Political society autonomy and trust and legal condition for it	All the normal conditions ensuring the free electoral competition between parties need to be created. In some cases, party competition has only been suspended and can easily be revitalized. In other cases, the formation of parties needs to be legalized and restrictions on specific parties lifted. In some cases the political rights of key political actors need to be re-established. In exceptional cases an authoritarian state party may have to be dismantled.	The party's dominant position in all areas of society and its privileged status and resources must be dismantled, its presence in all institutions removed, and almost all of its property transferred to the state. However, if citizens want to recreate the party they should be allowed to do so, and its support and power should depend on the votes people might want to give to it. Given the flattened social landscape the representation of interests will be particularly difficult.	The dismantling of the privileged status, legal and otherwise, of the dominant party will be needed. Legal reform will also be needed to assure the free formation and competition of political parties. While society may not be as "flattened" as under totalitarianism, the relative lack of economic and political differentiation makes political "representation" of interests difficult and complicates the development of a normal spectrum of democratic parties.	The suppression of semiprivate violence and the creation of a modicum of trust are requirements for the development of political parties, free contestation for power, and sufficient autonomy for the working of democratic procedures and institutions.

Table 4.3. (continued)

Necessary Conditions	Authoritarianism	Totalitarianism	Post-totalitarianism	Sultanism
3. Constitutional rules to allocate power democratically	In some cases, there can be an immediate declaration that a previous democratic constitution has been reinstated; in other cases amendments to a nondemocratic constitution may be viable; in still others a full democratic constituent assembly and constitution-making process are needed.	A paper constitution may exist that, when filled with democratic content, might lead to perverse consequences, since it was not designed for a democratic society. The making of a new democratic constitution will be necessary but difficult due to an inchoate political society, the lack of a constitutional culture, and the legacy created by the verbal commitments of the previous constitution.	Given the fictive character of the constitution, there are serious costs to using these institutions, and the making of a democratic constitution should be a high priority.	A universalistic legal culture will have to be developed. Even while there may be a usable constitution, given the recent abuse of constitutional rules, a spirit of trust and respect for constitutionalism does not exist at the end of a sultanistic period.
4. State bureaucracy acceptable and serviceable to democratic government	To the extent that the bureaucracy has not been politicized and has maintained professional standards, there may be no immediate need for bureaucratic reform. In some cases, a more or less limited purge of bureaucrats, including the judiciary and the military, might be desirable. But if a hierarchical military played a major role in the previous nondemocratic regime, such purges may be quite difficult.	The delegation of major tasks of the state to the party and the penetration of the party into all bureaucratic and social institutions make the creation of a nonpoliticized bureaucracy an imperative and difficult task. The dismantling of the party within the state might seriously reduce the efficiency and coordination of the state apparatus and open the door for a clientelistic take-over by the new democrats or by opportunists. The experience of the party state leaves a legacy of popular distrust of the state.	The fact that many functions of the state, including judiciary functions, were performed by party bureaucrats makes purges and reform of the state bureaucracy a widespread demand but a complex and contentious issue to resolve. The skills of the former bureaucratic elite and the lack of experience of the opposition may well give the former elite a privileged position.	The clientelistic penetration and corruption of bureaucratic institutions limit their efficiency and legitimacy and put extensive reform on the agenda. Even democratically elected leaders may perpetuate clientelistic practices rather than rational administration.

Table 4.3. (continued)

Necessary Conditions	Authoritarianism	Totalitarianism	Post-totalitarianism	Sultanism
5. Sufficient autonomy for economy and economic actors to assure pluralism of civil society, political society, and economic society	If the economy has been a functioning mixed economy, there may be no immediate changes necessary to facilitate the transition and consolidation of democracy. Whatever further reforms are desired or needed will be part of normal political processes that could include more socialization or more privatization of property and more or less social and/or economic regulation of the market.	In communist totalitarianism the almost total public ownership of property and the linkages between the party and the economy make the growth of autonomy of civil and political society particularly difficult. Fundamental reform of the economy is imperative, but the absence of a legal institutional framework for a market economy and the weakness of legal culture make the creation of an "economic society" difficult and facilitate the emergence of illegal or alegal practices.	Ultimate control by the state of all economic activity does not seem conducive to the minimal degree of civil and political society robustness necessary for a democratic polity. Some reforms are necessary to create an institutionalized economic society. A full-blown market economy is not a requirement for democracy.	Dismantling of the patrimonial and clientelistic structures of the ruler and his allies will be necessary to allow the normal development of civil, political, and economic society.

But there is absolutely no room on the "household" staff of the sultan for a moderate player who publicly negotiates the demise of his employer. The other players who never exist in an ideal typical sultanistic regime are moderates from the organized democratic opposition. Neither civil society nor political society has enough autonomy to enable a publicly organized democratic opposition to develop sufficient negotiating capacity for it to be a full player in any pacted transition.[6]

A similar logic would preclude the ideal-typical totalitarian regime from even a full two-player game. There is a big player (the totalitarian hard-line maximum leader and his party-state staff) and a small underground opposition (half a player?) that can struggle to exist and possibly resist but that has absolutely no capacity to negotiate a pacted transition.

Even early post-totalitarian regimes do not have sufficient diversity and autonomy in the ruling party-state leadership or sufficient strength and autonomy within the democratic opposition really to produce all the players needed to conclude successfully a four-player democratic transition game. Indeed, as we argued in chapter 3, if an early or a "frozen" post-totalitarian regime faces a crisis of opposition, it is particularly vulnerable to collapse if it is not able to repress that opposition, given its limited negotiating capability. But a mature post-totalitarian regime (such as Hungary in the mid-1980s) and a wide range of authoritarian regimes (such as Spain and Brazil in the mid-1970s) can produce four-player games. Thus although "pacted transitions" figure prominently in the literature, the classic four-player pacted transitions are in fact available as a transition path only in some authoritarian and mature post-totalitarian regimes.

A transition path that would seem available to most nondemocratic regimes but that, upon closer scrutiny, is in fact available only to the authoritarian regime type concerns the military. If the costs of rule by the "military as government" are considered too great for the "military as institution," a free election may become part of the extrication formula for the hierarchical military in charge of an authoritarian regime.[7] However, the control of the government by a hierarchical military bureaucracy is completely inconsistent with the logics of sultanism or totalitarianism or of the leading role of the party in post-totalitarianism.

We are now ready to present for analysis a resumé of the implications of nondemocratic regime types for *paths* to democratic transition (table 4.2), and of the implications of nondemocratic regime type for the minimal *tasks* of completing the transition to and consolidation of a democratic regime (table 4.3).

6. For example, the only Warsaw Pact country in 1988 not to have one opposition samizdat journal published in the country was Romania, a country that combined under Ceaușescu strong sultanistic and totalitarian tendencies. For the special difficulties of a successful democratic transition from a sultanistic regime, see the introductory chapter by H. E. Chehabi and Juan J. Linz in their edited volume in progress, *Sultanistic Regimes*, and Richard Snyder, "Explaining Transitions from Neopatrimonial Dictatorships," *Comparative Politics* 24 (July 1992): 379–99. Also see Michael Bratton and Nicholas van de Walle, "Neopatrimonial Regimes and Political Transition in Africa," *World Politics* (July 1994): 453–89.

7. An extensive conceptual and political analysis of the distinction between the "military as government" and the "military as institution" is developed in chapter 5.

5

Actors and Contexts

IN ADDITION to our "macrovariables" of prior regime type and stateness, we call attention to some other important variables that affect democratic transition and consolidation and that lend themselves to middle range propositions. Two actor-centered variables concern the leadership base of the prior nondemocratic regime and the question of who initiates and who controls the transition. Three context variables relate to international influences, the political economy of legitimacy and coercion, and constitution-making environments.

THE INSTITUTIONAL COMPOSITION AND LEADERSHIP OF THE PRECEDING NONDEMOCRATIC REGIME

Our central question here concerns the core group that is in day-by-day control of the state apparatus. What is the institutional character of this state elite? Does its character favorably or unfavorably affect democratic transition and consolidation? The organizational base is necessarily analytically distinct from the variable of regime type because, within some regime types (especially authoritarian), there can be dramatically different types of state elites, each with quite different implications for democratic transition and consolidation. Without being exhaustive, four different types of state elites can be distinguished: (1) a hierarchical military, (2) a nonhierarchical military, (3) a civilian elite, and (4) the distinctive category of sultanistic elites.

Hierarchical Military

As shown in chapter 4 on the consequences of prior nondemocratic regime types, only an authoritarian regime has the possibility of being controlled by a hierarchical military organization. Control by such an organization is against the logics of a totalitarian, post-totalitarian, or sultanistic regime.[1] All hierarchical

---

1. In some cases, such as Chile and Uruguay, and especially the "dirty war" in Argentina, the military developed a definition of the enemy in their national security doctrine that gave to the repression a totalitarian dimension. See, for example, Alexandra Barahona de Brito, "Truth or Amnesty—Human Rights and Democratization in Latin America: Uruguay and Chile" (Ph.D. diss., University of Oxford, 1993), 28–61.

military regimes share one characteristic that is potentially favorable to democratic transition. The officer corps, taken as a whole, sees itself as a permanent part of the state apparatus, with enduring interests and permanent functions that transcend the interests of the government of the day. This means that there is always the possibility that the hierarchical leaders of the military-as-institution will come to the decision that the costs of direct involvement in nondemocratic rule are greater than the costs of extrication. Thus, the reassertion of hierarchical authority in the name of the military-as-institution is a permanent danger faced by the military-as-government. Furthermore, as members of a situational elite who derive their power and status from the existence of a functioning state apparatus, the military-as-institution have an interest in a stable state, and this requires a government.[2] This often means that, if a democratic regime is an available ruling formula in the polity, the military may decide to solve their internal organizational problems and their need for a government by devolving the exercise of government to civilians. Paradoxically but predictably, democratic elections are thus often part of the extrication strategy of military institutions that feel threatened by their prominent role in nondemocratic regimes.

We can make parsimonious and much less optimistic statements about hierarchical military regimes in relation to democratic consolidation. Precisely because the military (short of their elimination by foreign powers or by revolution) is a permanent part of the state apparatus and as such has privileged access to coercive resources, members of the military will be an integral part of the machinery that the new democratic government has to manage. Theoretically and practically, therefore, the more the military hierarchy directly manages the state and their own organization on a day-by-day basis before the transition, the more salient the issue of the successful democratic management of the military will be to the task of democratic consolidation. Furthermore, the more hierarchically led the military, the less they are forced to extricate themselves from a nondemocratic regime due to internal contradictions, and the weaker the coalition that is forcing them from office, the more the military will be in a position to negotiate their withdrawal on terms where they retain nondemocratic prerogatives or impose very confining conditions on the political processes that lead to democratic consolidation. More than any of the three other kinds of organizational bases found in nondemocratic regimes, a hierarchical military possesses the greatest ability to impose "reserve domains" on the newly elected government, and this by definition precludes democratic consolidation. This is a particularly acute problem if

---

2. For a more discursive argument about the analytical and historical utility of the distinction between military-as-government and military-as-institution, see Stepan, "Paths toward Redemocratization," 75–78, 172–73. For the concept of the military as a "situational elite" with a special relationship to the state, see Alfred Stepan, "Inclusionary and Exclusionary Military Responses to Radicalism with Special Attention to Peru," in Seweryn Bialer, ed., *Radicalism in the Contemporary Age* (Boulder: Westview Press, 1977), 3: 221–39, 344–50.

the hierarchical military have been involved in widespread human rights violations and condition their loyalty, as a part of the state apparatus, upon not being
punished by the new democratic government. Such a legacy of human rights violations presented severe problems for democratic consolidation in Argentina
and Chile.

This is not meant to imply a static situation. Power is always and everywhere
relational. We simply mean that, if a relatively unified, hierarchically led military
has just left the direct exercise of rule, the complex dialectical tasks of democratic
power creation and the reduction of the domains of nondemocratic prerogatives
of the military must become two of the most important tasks for new democratic
leaders.

Nonhierarchical Military

A nonhierarchical, military-led nondemocratic regime, on the other hand,
has some characteristics that make it less of a potential obstacle to democratic
transition and especially democratic consolidation. Concerning democratic
transition, if a nonhierarchically led military-as-government (e.g., of colonels
and majors) enters into difficulties, the incentive for the military-as-institution
to re-establish hierarchy by supporting an extrication coup is even higher than it
would be if the military-as-government were hierarchically led. The fundamental political and theoretical distinction, however, concerns democratic consolidation. The chances that the military-as-institution will tolerate punishment
and trials of members of the outgoing nondemocratic government are significantly greater if the group being punished is not seen to be the military institution itself, but a group within the military which has violated hierarchical norms.
Likewise, if the colonels have established para-state intelligence operations that
are perceived as threats even to the organizational military, the hierarchical military is much more likely to acquiesce (or even insist) that their reserve domains
of power be eliminated.

Civilian Leadership

In comparative terms, civilian-led regimes (even mature post-totalitarian
civilian-led regimes in which Communist parties are essential components) will
characteristically have greater institutional, symbolic, and absorptive capacities
than either military or sultanistic leaders to initiate, direct, and manage a democratic transition. Civilian leaders are often more motivated to initiate and more
capable of negotiating a complicated reform pact than are the military. They often
have more links to society than do military or para-military sultanistic leaders.
Civilians also can see themselves as potential winners and rulers in a future democratic regime. This option is much less likely for military or sultanistic rulers.

There are, of course, potential problems for full democratic transition and consolidation in such civilian-led political change. Civilian-led liberalization may re-equilibrate the system short of democratic transition or allow groups to win elections by skillful but nondemocratic means because of their privileged access to levers of power. When we consider democratic consolidation, however, it seems to us that the capacity of civilian leaders in a previously nondemocratic regime to create obstacles to democratic consolidation, such as constitutionally sanctioned reserve domains of power, is significantly less than that of a military organization.

An exception to the above assertion might seem to be the case of a civilian-led, nondemocratic regime based on a monopoly party—especially a ruling Communist Party. Should this kind of organizational base be considered an obstacle to democratic consolidation comparable to a hierarchical military organization that has just left power? Some political activists in Eastern Europe feared that a defeated ruling Communist Party and a defeated ruling hierarchical military were functional equivalents in terms of their ability to impede the consolidation of democracy. However, we believe that, in those cases where the Communist Party has been defeated in free and competitive elections (as in Hungary in 1990), this analogy is fundamentally misleading on two grounds: (1) organizational relationships to the state apparatus and (2) incentives. The hierarchical military, unless it has been militarily defeated and dissolved by the new democratic incumbents, will, as an organization, withdraw as a unit into the state apparatus where it still has extensive state missions and state-allocated resources (as in Chile in 1989). A defeated Communist Party, in contrast, while it may well retain control of many resources and loyalties that help it compete in later elections, has no comparable institutional base in the state apparatus, has no continuing claim on new state resources, and has no continuing state mission. Organizationally, it is a defeated party out of office and, though it may win open elections in the future (as in Hungary in 1994), it has less collective resources to impose "reserve domains" than do the military out of office. Our argument here is restricted *only* to those cases where the democratic opposition wins open and contested elections and then assumes control of the government. However, in some societies, normally close to the totalitarian pole, with no legacies of liberal or democratic politics, top nomenklatura figures are able to put on nationalist garb and engage not in democracy building but ethnocracy building. In such contexts civil society is too weak to generate a competitive political society and members of the nomenklatura are able to appropriate power and "legitimate" themselves via elections.

In relation to behavioral incentives, Communists (or ex-Communists) from the former nomenklatura after defeat in free and contested elections will still occupy numerous important positions within the state apparatus, especially in state enterprises. The members of the former nomenklatura through their networks extending over management, administration, and even security services can assure themselves a privileged position in the emerging capitalist economy and with it substantial political influence. However, they normally act for their own individual self-interest. In most post-Communist countries the former nomenklatura do not attempt to overthrow or directly challenge the new regime but to profit by it. In some cases, particularly in the former Soviet Union, this leads to a confusion between the public and the private and with it considerable room for corruption. The more the members of the former nomenklatura act as individuals or democratic state managers, the better their chances of survival as officials. This is particularly so for managers of state production, trading, and banking enterprises, who can use their organizational resources profitably to restructure new forms of recombined public-private property.[3] The incentive system for the former nomenklatura thus has strong individualist or network components, which involve working for advantages by manipulating the new political context more than opposing it per se. The incentive system for the military is fundamentally different. With few exceptions, incentives to the military are collective and derive from the struggles to retain group prerogatives to avoid collective negative actions, such as trials. Therefore, unlike the nomenklatura out of office, for the military out of office there may be significant incentives for acting together in open contestation against the new democratic government.

Sultanistic Leadership

Last, we should briefly consider what the institutional composition of sultanistic rule implies for democratic transitions and consolidation. A sultanistic regime is one in which the ruler personalizes the government and the regime and, in an uninstitutionalized but erratically pervasive way, penetrates the state, political society, and civil society. Fused are not only the private and the public, but also the civilian and the military. Theoretically, it is hard to classify sultanship as either a military- or a civilian-led regime. Sultanistic regimes present an opportunity for democratic transition because, should the ruler (and his or her family) be overthrown or assassinated, the sultanistic regime collapses. However, the very nature of a sultanistic regime means that there is very little space for the organization of a democratic opposition. Therefore, short of death by natural causes, sultanistic dictators are characteristically overthrown by quick, massive movements of civil society, by assassination, or by armed revolt (see table 4.2). This manner of regime termination often leads to the dynamics of a provisional government which, unless there is a decision to hold rapid elections, normally presents dangers for democratic consolidation.[4] Also, the very personalization of power around the dictator may allow close associates of the regime to assume power. Or, even when the group or armed movement leading the revolt eliminates

3. Pioneering work on new network formation and the associated phenomenon of "recombinant property" that is not really private and no longer public is being done by David Stark, "Recombinant Property in East European Capitalism," Working Paper, Collegium Budapest, 1994.

4. We will discuss interim governments in our analysis of the next variable.

those most associated with the sultanistic regime, they may appoint themselves as the "sovereign" representatives of the people and rule in the name of democracy without passing through the free contestation and free election phases that are necessary for full democratic transition and consolidation.

Transition Initiation: Who Starts and Who Controls?

Transitions initiated by an uprising of civil society, by the sudden collapse of the nondemocratic regime, by an armed revolution, or by a nonhierarchically led military coup all tend toward situations in which the instruments of rule will be assumed by an interim or provisional government.[5] Transitions initiated by hierarchical state-led or regime-led forces do not.

Interim governments are highly fluid situations and can lead to diametrically opposite outcomes depending on which groups are most powerful, and especially on whether elections or sweeping decree reforms are considered to be the first priority. If the interim government quickly sets a date for elections and rules as a relatively neutral caretaker for these elections, this can be a very rapid and efficacious route toward a democratic transition. However, if the interim government claims that its actions in overthrowing the government give it a legitimate mandate to make fundamental changes that *it defines* as preconditions to democratic elections, the interim government can set into motion a dangerous dynamic in which the democratic transition is put at peril, even including the postponement of elections *sine die*.

Elections are crucial because without them there is no easy way to evaluate whether the interim government is or is not actually representing the majority. Without elections, actors who did not play a central role in eliminating the old regime will find it very difficult to emerge and assert that they have a democratic mandate. And without elections the full array of institutions that constitute a new democratic political society—such as legislatures, constituent assemblies, and competitive political parties—simply cannot develop sufficient autonomy, legality, and legitimacy.

Elections are most likely to be held quickly in cases of collapse where democratic party leaders (as in Greece in 1974) almost immediately emerge as the core of the interim government or where leaders of civil society who are committed to creating a political democracy as the first order of business (as in Czechoslovakia in 1989) are the core of the interim government. Frequently, however, especially in cases where armed force has brought them into power, interim governments develop a dynamic that moves them away from fully free contestation. Claiming

---

5. For a more detailed discussion of interim governments, see Yossi Shain and Juan J. Linz, eds., *Between States: Interim Governments and Democratic Transitions* (New York: Cambridge University Press, 1995).

revolutionary legitimacy, the provisional government may substitute occasional plebiscites or referenda for multiparty elections. A provisional government that begins with a nonhierarchical coup may open up an explosive situation because it may involve part of the state apparatus attacking another part of the state apparatus, in which outcomes can vary from massive state repression to revolution. The least likely outcome in such a conflict is procedural democracy.

What can we say about state-led or regime-initiated and regime-controlled transitions? For one thing the potential for the emergence of an interim government is virtually absent when the regime controls the transfer of government until elections decide who should govern. This fundamental point made, we need to be aware that regime-controlled transfers can be placed along a continuum ranging from democratically disloyal to loyal. A democratically disloyal transfer is one in which, for whatever reasons, the outgoing regime attempts to put strong constraints on the incoming, democratically elected government by placing supporters of the nondemocratic regime in key state positions and by successfully insisting on the retention of many nondemocratic features in the new political system. A disloyal transfer is most likely to happen when the leaders of the outgoing nondemocratic regime are reluctant to transfer power to democratic institutions and the correlation of forces between the nondemocratic regime and the democratic opposition is one where the nondemocratic leaders retain substantial coercive and political resources. For reasons we have already discussed, this is most likely to happen if the prior nondemocratic government was a hierarchically controlled military regime with strong allies in civil and political society, as we shall see in the case of Chile.

INTERNATIONAL INFLUENCE

The most influential and widely read publication on democratic transitions is the four-volume work edited by Guillermo O'Donnell, Philippe C. Schmitter, and Laurence Whitehead, *Transitions from Authoritarian Rule.* The cases in this study all concerned Southern Europe and Latin America and, with the exception of Italy, the decade of the mid-1970s to the mid-1980s. Generalizing from the experiences within these spatial and temporal confines, O'Donnell and Schmitter in the concluding volume argue that "domestic factors play a predominant role in the transition. More precisely, we assert that there is no transition whose beginning is not the consequence—direct or indirect—of important divisions within the authoritarian regime itself."[6] Laurence Whitehead, in his valuable chapter on

---

6. Guillermo O'Donnell and Philippe C. Schmitter, *Tentative Conclusions about Uncertain Democracies* (Baltimore: Johns Hopkins University Press, 1986), 19.

international influence, offers a more qualified generalization: "In all the peacetime cases considered here internal forces were of primary importance in determining the course and outcome of the transition attempt, and international factors played only a secondary role."[7]

However, if one considers the entire world and all major actual (or potential) cases of democratization in modern times, the analysis of international influences can be pushed much further and a series of nuanced hypotheses can be advanced. To do so, we distinguish between the foreign policy, *zeitgeist*, and diffusion effects.

Foreign Policies

Conceptually, foreign policies can have an influence on domestic contexts in very different ways. To begin with, there *are* in fact three categories of situations in which the use of force in foreign policy actually *determines* outcomes that relate to democracy. First, a nondemocratic country can use force to overthrow a less militarily powerful democracy and either annex or occupy the country or install a nondemocratic puppet regime (e.g., Germany in Czechoslovakia in 1938). Second, a nondemocratic regional hegemon (which can be a single country or a community of countries acting collectively) can in its "outer empire" use military force to reverse a successful democratizing revolutionary effort to overthrow a nondemocratic regime (e.g., Hungary in 1956) or to reverse a liberalizing process (e.g., Czechoslovakia in 1968). Third, a democratic country that is a victor in a war against a nondemocratic regime can occupy the defeated country and initiate a democratic transition by installation (e.g., Germany and Japan in 1945). However, although foreign policies can have determinative force in the democratic transition phase, democratic consolidation in an independent country is ultimately determined by domestic forces.

Another influence of foreign policy on democratic transition and consolidation concerns what we might call *gate opening to democratic efforts*. Formal or informal empires, largely responding to their own internal and geopolitical needs, may open a previously closed gate to democratization efforts in subordinate regimes. Whether there will be a democratic transition or not and whether this will lead to democratic consolidation or not is predominantly domestically determined (e.g., most of the British Empire after World War II, the Soviet bloc in Eastern Europe in 1989).

---

7. Laurence Whitehead, "International Aspects of Democratization," in O'Donnell, Schmitter, and Whitehead, *Transitions from Authoritarian Rule: Comparative Perspectives*, 4. In the body of the article Whitehead gives detailed information about how the European Community played a strongly supportive role in democratic consolidation in southern Europe. In later works, Whitehead, O'Donnell, and Schmitter correctly acknowledged that international influence played a central role in Eastern Europe. Also see the two-volume work edited by Abraham F. Lowenthal, *Exporting Democracy: The United States and Latin America* (Baltimore: Johns Hopkins University Press, 1991); and Geoffrey Pridham, ed., *Securing Democracy: The International Context of Regime Transition in Southern Europe* (London: Routledge, 1990).

Subversion is another kind of policy effect. Regional hegemons (democratic or nondemocratic) can play an important contributing, though seldom determinative, role in helping to subvert a nondemocratic regime (e.g., U.S. foreign policies toward the Philippines in 1987) or in helping to subvert democracy that is opposing the hegemon's policy preferences (e.g., U.S foreign policy toward Chile in 1973). A democratic hegemon may also use its geopolitical and economic power to thwart nondemocratic forces trying to impede a democratic transition process (e.g., President Carter's role in reversing electoral fraud in the Dominican Republic in 1978).

Finally, a regional hegemon may, by a consistent policy package of meaningful incentives and disincentives, play a major supportive (but not determinative) role in helping a fledgling democracy in the region complete a democratic transition and consolidate democracy (e.g., the collective foreign policy of the European Economic Community [EEC] and especially of West Germany toward Portugal in 1974).

Zeitgeist

The concept of *zeitgeist* is taken from the German tradition of intellectual history and refers to the "spirit of the times." We do not believe in any variant of the "end of history" thesis—the thesis, namely, that one ideology, such as the democratic ideology, can or will stop human efforts to respond to problems by creating alternative political visions and ideologies.[8] But we do maintain that, when a country is part of an international ideological community where democracy is only one of many strongly contested ideologies, the chances of transiting to and consolidating democracy are substantially less than if the spirit of the times is one where democratic ideologies have no powerful contenders. The effect of a democratically hostile or a democratically supportive *zeitgeist* can readily be seen when we contrast interwar Europe with the Europe of the mid-1970s and the 1980s. In interwar Europe, in the aftermath of the break-up of the Austro-Hungarian Empire, boundary changes emerging out of the Treaty of Versailles, and various political experiments, eleven states with little or no prior experience of an independent democratic regime made some effort to establish democracies.[9] However, the spirit of the times was one in which the democratic ideal competed with four

---

8. See, for example, Francis Fukuyama, "The End of History," *National Interest* 16 (Summer 1989): 3–18. The return to power in Lithuania, Poland, and Hungary of reform communists as social democrats is but one example of how history can evolve in new and unexpected ways. Another example is the resurgence, in the name of "democratic majoritarianism," of ethnic nationalist dictatorships in parts of the former Soviet Union and Yugoslavia.

9. These states were Spain, Italy, Poland, Hungary, Czechoslovakia, Estonia, Latvia, Lithuania, Bulgaria, Yugoslavia, and Romania. For a discussion of their demise, see Juan J. Linz, "La crisis de las democracias," in Mercedes Cabrera, Santos Juliá, and Pablo Martín Aceña, eds., *Europa en crisis, 1919–1939* (Madrid: Editorial Pablo Iglesias, 1992), 231–80.

other contesting ideologies in Europe, *none* of them democratic. Communism in the Soviet Union was a novel experiment that many felt offered great promise. Fascism in Italy was seen by many others as a powerful contestant to both communism and democracy. Catholicism, after the papal encyclical, *Rerum Novarum,* was the basis of novel forms of corporatist and integralist movements. Finally, in the midst of this intense ideological struggle, many conservatives still remembered positively the political formula of a predemocratic, authoritarian constitutional monarchy, of which Imperial Germany was the esteemed exemplar. All of Europe was influenced in some degree by these nondemocratic ideas. Latin America too was strongly influenced by these European intellectual and ideological currents, as the experience of the Estado Novo under Vargas in Brazil and of Peronism in Argentina shows.

Though democracy is never "overdetermined," even in the context of the most supportive *zeitgeist,* by the late 1970s the *zeitgeist* in southern Europe—indeed in most of the world (with the important exception of a reinvigorated fundamentalism in the Islamic cultural community)—was such that there were no major ideological contestants to democracy as a political system. To be sure, Communism was entrenched in the Soviet Union and by extension in the subordinate regimes of Eastern Europe, but the pronouncement by an eminent Polish philosopher that the 1968 Soviet invasion of Czechoslovakia represented the "clinical death" of Marxist revisionism in Central and Eastern Europe proved prophetic.[10] By 1977, the issue of human rights had acquired such pan-European support that most of the East European regimes became signatories to the Helsinki Accords.[11] Fascism and Nazism were thoroughly discredited after World War II, and no longer represented a pole of attraction. After Vatican II (1961–63) Catholicism developed an ideological and institutional position more amenable to democracy (if not to capitalism) than ever before.[12] In the modern era most of the secure and successful monarchs are now constitutional heads of state in parliamentary democracies. The Egyptian and Peruvian military option so intriguing in the 1960s had few adherents in the world by the mid-1970s. On the other hand, the Latin American left's experience with a new type of modern military-led bureaucratic-authoritarian regime had contributed to a deep revalorization of democracy, not merely as a tactical instrument but as a value in itself.[13] The hopes that some democrats had in Yugoslav worker self-management as a school for democracy have been thor-

10. Leszek Kolakowski, *Main Currents of Marxism* (Oxford: Oxford University Press, 1978), 3: 465.

11. For the effects on the domestic politics of East European countries and the Soviet Union of having signed the Helsinki Accords, see Samuel P. Huntington, *The Third Wave: Democratization in the Twentieth Century* (Norman: Oklahoma University Press, 1991), esp. 85–100.

12. For Vatican II and how it enhanced the status of democracy in Roman Catholic theology, see George Weigel, *The Final Revolution: The Resistance Church and the Collapse of Communism* (New York: Oxford University Press, 1992), esp. 67–74.

13. The revalorization of democracy by the left produced a rich new genre of writings. For one such example see Francisco Weffort, "Why Democracy?" in Alfred Stepan, ed., *Democratizing Brazil: Problems of Transition and Consolidation* (New York: Oxford University Press, 1989), 327–50.

oughly disappointed. In Africa, "one-party" states by the early 1990s had lost almost all their original credibility as "mobilizing regimes" and were increasingly disdained as "rent-seeking" formulas exploited by nondemocratic elites.

Diffusion

Zeitgeist in the world of politics refers to historical eras. But the *diffusion effect* in an international political community, especially in a community tightly coupled by culture, coercive systems, and/or communication, can refer to weeks or even days. Law-like statements about human creations such as democracies are inherently different from law-like statements in the physical sciences because no two moments in history can be exactly alike. Human beings reflect upon previous events and, where the events seem directly relevant to them, often consciously or unconsciously attempt to adjust their behavior so as to achieve or avoid a comparable outcome. Political learning is possible. For example, after the Portuguese revolution had exploded, a Spanish conservative leader, Manuel Fraga, expressed some interest in playing a role in leading democratic change because he "did not want to become the Caetano of Spain."[14] Likewise Prince Juan Carlos in Spain was undoubtedly influenced by the Greek case, where his brother-in-law, King Constantine, lost his throne due to his ambivalence about democracy.

More generally, we posit that the more tightly coupled a group of countries are, the more a successful transition in any country in the group will tend to transform the range of perceived political alternatives for the rest of the group. Indeed, as we shall see when we examine Central and Eastern Europe in 1989, international diffusion effects can change elite political expectations, crowd behavior, and relations of power within the regime almost overnight. For practitioners and theorists alike, diffusion effects have obviously gained in salience in the modern world owing to the revolution in communications. Today, the dramatic collapse of a nondemocratic regime is immediately experienced by virtually the entire population of the neighboring countries through radio and television. This experience in turn instantly becomes a powerful new component of domestic politics.[15]

THE POLITICAL ECONOMY OF LEGITIMACY AND OF COERCION

What is the relationship between citizens' perception of the socioeconomic efficacy of a regime and their perception of the legitimacy of the regime itself?

14. Fraga was referring to the overthrow of the post-Salazar leader of Portugal, Marcello Caetano, who failed to initiate a transition. The diffusion effect here is that Spanish conservatives rapidly began to recalculate the costs and benefits of initiating a democratic transition.

15. All countries discussed in this volume experienced some diffusion effects, but none more dramatically than the countries of Central and Eastern Europe.

How does the economy affect the prospects of a transition away from a nondemocratic regime? If a transition has begun, how does the economy affect the chances of democratic consolidation? Are democratic and nondemocratic regimes equally helped by sustained growth? Are democratic and nondemocratic regimes equally hurt by economic decline?

We accept the well-documented correlation that there are few democracies at very low levels of socioeconomic development and that most polities at a high level of socioeconomic development are democracies.[16] Most of the major modern transition attempts thus take place in countries at medium levels of development. However, this relationship between development and the probability of democracy does not tell us much about *when, how,* and *if* a transition will take place and be successfully completed. Indeed, within this critical context of intermediate levels of development we contend that it is often difficult or impossible to make systematic statements about the effect of economics on democratization processes.[17] However, if one uses an analytical framework that combines politics and economics and focuses on legitimacy, one can make much more meaningful statements. Certainly for transition theory, economic trends in themselves are less important than is the perception of alternatives, system blame, and the legitimacy beliefs of significant segments of the population or major institutional actors. Why?

For theoreticians and practitioners who posit a tightly coupled relationship between the economy and regime stability, robust economic conditions would appear supportive of any type of regime. We would argue, however, that the proposition is theoretically and empirically indefensible. We see good theoretical reasons why sustained economic growth *could* erode a nondemocratic regime. We see *no* theoretical reason why sustained economic growth would erode a democratic regime. Regime type can make a great difference. From the perspective of political economy, we absolutely cannot formulate any valid propositions that take the form, "under conditions of great economic prosperity there will be no incentives for a transition from a nondemocratic to democratic regime." This is so precisely because many nondemocratic regimes, especially those of the statistical

16. The classic initial formulation of this argument was Seymour Martin Lipset, "Some Social Requisites of Democracy: Economic Development and Political Legitimacy," *American Political Science Review* (March 1959): 69–105. Larry Diamond reviewed three decades of literature relevant to the development/democracy debate and concluded that the evidence broadly supports the Lipset theory. See Diamond, "Economic Development and Democracy Reconsidered," in Gary Marks and Larry Diamond, eds., *Reexamining Democracy* (Newbury Park: Sage, 1992), 93–139.

17. The specific relationship between economic growth or economic crisis and the initiation of a transition out of a nondemocratic regime has been the object of considerable debate. José María Maravall, in an outstanding and well-researched work, has analyzed this problem in great detail, with particular reference to southern and Eastern Europe. We find that his analysis converges with our brief analysis, which we had written independently. We are happy to refer the reader to his book for the relevant evidence. See José María Maravall, *Los resultados de la democracia: Un estudio del sur y el este de Europa* (Madrid: Alianza Editorial, 1995).

mode, authoritarian regimes, are originally defended by the state elite and their core socioeconomic allies as necessary given the *exceptional* difficulties (often economic) the polity faces. Thus, prolonged economic prosperity, especially in an authoritarian regime, may erode the basis of the regime's justification based on exceptional circumstances. Prolonged economic success can contribute to the perception that the exceptional coercive measures of the nondemocratic regime are no longer necessary and may possibly erode the soundness of the new economic prosperity.

Prolonged economic growth may also contribute to social changes that raise the cost of repression and thus indirectly facilitate a transition to democracy. Prolonged economic expansion normally contributes to the growth of a middle class; a more important and needed skilled labor force; an expansion of education; greater contacts with other societies via television, radio, and travel; and a more diverse range of possible protests. There is even strong evidence to indicate that, within a territory, increases in regional wealth increase citizens' expectations that they should be well treated by the police.[18]

Empirically, there are a number of cases where sustained prosperity altered relations of power in favor of democratic forces. In fact, three cases in our study, Pinochet's Chile, Brazil in the early 1970s, and Franco's Spain in its last twenty years (as well as South Korea), had some of the world's highest rates of economic growth. Spain's growth contributed to the belief of some of the core constituents of the authoritarian regime and among the industrial elite that they could manage equally well in the future in a more democratic environment. The times had changed and so did the regime.[19] In Brazil, the soft-line military wing announced its liberalization program in September 1973, after five years of unprecedented growth and *before* the oil crisis, soaring interest rates, and its attendant debt crisis. In September 1973 the military felt that the economy was in excellent condition and no significant political threat existed. In the absence of the "exceptional circumstances" that had legitimated their coup in their own eyes, they came to believe that continued authoritarian rule not only was not necessary but might contribute to the autonomy of the security forces and the "Argentinization of Brazil."[20] In Chile many of the key industrialists who had believed that Pinochet

18. For example, seven occupational groups in Franco's Spain, ranging from manual laborers to those in liberal professions, were asked if they expected "equal," "better," or "worse" treatment by the police than other citizens. The data were broken down according to the level of economic development of the respondents' place of residence. In 19 of 21 of the possible comparisons, the greater the regional economic development, the greater the expectation of equal treatment by the police. See Juan J. Linz, "Ecological Analysis and Survey Research," in Mattei Dogan and Stein Rokkan, eds., *Quantitative Ecological Analysis in the Social Sciences* (Cambridge: MIT Press, 1969), 91–131, esp. table 1, p. 113.

19. As Adolfo Suárez said before he became prime minister of Spain, "Our people who at the beginning of his (Franco's) government had asked simply for bread, today ask for quality consumption, and in the same fashion, whereas at the beginning they wanted order, today they ask for freedom—freedom of political association." Speech in the Cortes on June 9, 1976.

20. Stepan, *Rethinking Military Politics*, 32–33.

was indispensable in 1980, by 1988 had come to believe that the risk of fair elections to the economic model was less than the risk of supporting Pinochet in unfair elections.[21] In all three cases, the political economy of prosperity contributed to new perceptions about alternative futures and to lessening resistance to democratic alternatives.

In sharp contrast, when we consider democratizing regimes or consolidated democracies, there are no theoretical reasons or empirical evidence to support an argument that economic growth contributes to regime erosion. Of course, a "revolution of rising expectations" may create new demands on democratic governments, but it cannot attack their *raison d'être*. Indeed, if a regime is based on the double legitimacy of democratic procedures *and* socioeconomic efficacy, the chances of a fundamental regime alternative (given the absence of a "stateness" problem) being raised by a significant group in society is empirically negligible.

Severe economic problems affect democratic and nondemocratic regimes, especially authoritarian ones, very differently. There are good theoretical reasons why sharp economic decline (say five years of continuous negative growth) will adversely affect stability in both democratic and nondemocratic regimes, but it will affect the latter substantially more. Modern nondemocratic (especially authoritarian) regimes are often heavily dependent on their *performance* claims but are not bolstered by procedural claims deriving from their democratic status. Theory leads us to posit therefore that a democratic regime has two valuable sources of insulation from sustained economic downturn not available to a nondemocratic regime: its claim to legitimacy based on its origin and the fact that elections are always on the horizon and hold the prospect of producing an alternative socioeconomic program and an alternative government *without* a regime change. This means that most new democracies have about eight years of breathing space—four years or so for the initial government and four years or so for an alternative government.

This theory-based assumption gains strong empirical support from data compiled by Fernando Limongi and Adam Przeworski. In their study of South America between 1945 and 1988, they found that the probability that a nondemocratic regime would survive three consecutive years of negative growth was 33 percent, whereas the probability that a democratic regime would survive three years of negative growth was 73 percent. More dramatically, their data show that *no* nondemocratic regime survived more than three years of consecutive negative growth, whereas the probability that a democratic regime would survive four or five years of consecutive negative growth was 57 percent and 50 percent respectively.[22]

Let us return to our argument concerning economics and the politics of *alter-*

---

21. See the interview with one of the leaders of a major business interest group in Chile, in Alfred Stepan, "The Last Days of Pinochet?" *New York Review of Books* (June 2, 1988): 33.

22. Fernando Limongi and Adam Przeworski, "Democracy and Development in South America, 1945–1988" (University of Chicago, October 27, 1993, unpublished manuscript).

natives and *system blame* in nondemocracies and in democracies. If the political situation is such that there is no strong perception of a possible alternative, a non-democratic regime can often continue to rule by coercion. However, when the belief grows that other alternatives are possible (as well as preferable), the political economy of legitimacy and coercion changes sharply. If the coercive capacity of the nondemocratic regime decreases (due say to internal dissent or the withdrawal of vital external guarantees), then the political economy of prolonged stagnation can contribute to the erosion of the regime. It is not changes in the economy, but changes in politics, that trigger regime erosion—that is, the *effects* of a poor economy often have to be mediated by political change.

The question of system blame is also crucial for the fate of democracies. As we have discussed elsewhere, the economic crisis of interwar Europe was as intense in countries such as the Netherlands and Norway (which did not break down) as in Germany and Austria (which did break down). Indeed, 30,000 Dutch workers in 1936 went to work in Germany because the Dutch economy was in worse condition than the German economy. What made the crisis of the economy a crisis of the political system in Germany and Austria was that strong groups on the right and the left had regime alternatives in mind and thus attacked the regime. Politically motivated system blame, more than the economic crisis *per se*, caused the German and Austrian breakdowns.[23]

The key question for the democracies is whether their citizens believe that, in the circumstances, the democratic government is a doing a credible job in trying to overcome economic problems. It is important to stress that the political economy of legitimacy will produce severe and perhaps insoluble challenges to democratic consolidation in those cases where the democratic system *itself* is judged to be incapable of producing a program to overcome the economic crisis.

To summarize, what can and cannot we say about transition theory and the political economy of legitimacy? Theory and the Limongi-Przeworski data indicate that consecutive years of negative growth lessen the chance of either a nondemocratic or a democratic regime's surviving. Thus, a country that is experiencing positive growth, other things being equal, has a better chance to consolidate democracy than a country that is experiencing negative growth. This said, the theory and the data also indicate that a democratic regime has more insulation from economic difficulty than does a nondemocratic regime. The ques-

---

23. For a more detailed development of this argument with supporting data, see Juan J. Linz and Alfred Stepan, "Political Crafting of Democratic Consolidation or Destruction: European and South American Comparisons," in Robert A. Pastor, ed., *Democracy in the Americas: Stopping the Pendulum* (New York: Holmes and Meyer, 1989), 41–61. We are indebted to Ekkart Zimmerman for his pioneering studies of interwar Europe. See Zimmerman, "Government Stability in Six European Countries during the World Economic Crisis of the 1930s: Some Preliminary Considerations," *European Journal of Political Research 15*, no. 1 (1987): 23–52 and Zimmerman, "Economic and Political Reactions to the World Economic Crises of the 1930s: Six European Countries," paper presented for the Mid-West Political Science Association Convention, Chicago, April 10–12, 1986.

tion of whether an aspiring democracy can withstand economic difficulties, as the German-Dutch comparison showed, depends to a great extent on the degree of noneconomic system blame and mass-elite perceptions about the desirability of other political alternatives. The question is thus one of relationships. It is theoretically possible, and indeed has occurred, that a newly democratizing regime suffers a decline in citizen perceptions of democracy's socioeconomic efficacy *at the same time* that their belief that "democracy is the best possible political system for a country like ours" increases.[24]

In those cases, however, where the citizens come to believe that the democratic system *itself* is compounding the economic problem or is incapable of defining and implementing a credible strategy of economic reform, system blame will greatly aggravate the political effect of economic hard times. More importantly, economic crises will tend to lead to democratic breakdown in those cases where powerful groups outside or—more fatally—*inside* the government increasingly argue that nondemocratic alternatives of rule are the only solution to the economic crisis.

In a situation where the crisis is permanent, after at least one democratic alternation of government, and where a reasonable argument can be made that the democratic political actors are incapable or unwilling to search for solutions and even compound the problems by such actions as infighting and corruption, key actors will search for alternatives. But alternatives might not be available. Key actors' previous experience with alternatives might have been equally or more unattractive. In such circumstances, many of these actors might resign themselves to a poorly performing democracy. Such resignation may not prevent crises, upheavals, and attempted local coups but is not conducive to regime change. But it certainly makes consolidation difficult and can even deconsolidate a democracy.

CONSTITUTION-MAKING ENVIRONMENTS

A neglected aspect of democratic transition and consolidation concerns the comparative analysis of the contexts in which constitutional formulas are adopted or retained. Without attempting to review all possible variations, let us simply mention six very different possible constitution-making contexts and/or formulas and indicate what problems they present for democratic transition and democratic consolidation. We move from those contexts and formulas that pre-

---

24. In Linz and Stepan, "Political Crafting of Democratic Consolidation or Destruction," 44, we note that, during a period (1978–1981) of rising unemployment, inflation, recession, and terrorism the Spanish citizen's belief in the efficacy of democracy *declined* by 25 percentage points in national polls while the belief that democracy was the best political system for a country like Spain *increased* by 5 percentage points in the same period. The key implication is that the citizenry did not believe, despite the economic problems, that any alternative political system was preferable.

sent the most confining conditions for democratic consolidation in an existing state to those that present the least.[25]

1. The retention of a constitution created by an nondemocratic regime with reserve domains and difficult amendment procedures. These confining conditions may be the price the outgoing nondemocratic regime is able to extract for yielding formal control of the state apparatus. However, if this constitution *de jure* enshrines nondemocratic "reserve domains" insisted upon by the outgoing nondemocratic power-holders, then the transition by our definition cannot be completed until these powers are removed. If the constitution has very difficult amendment procedures this will further complicate the process of democratic transition and consolidation. In this book Chile is the clearest case.

2. The retention of a "paper" constitution which has unexpected destabilizing and paralyzing consequences when used under more electorally competitive conditions. Some nondemocratic constitutions may enshrine a very elaborate set of decision-rules, procedures, and rights that had no effect on the operation of the nondemocratic regime because the constitution was a fiction. However, in more electorally competitive circumstances, this constitution can take on a life of its own that may make it almost impossible to arrive at democratically binding decisions. In such cases, the constitution can help destroy the state and should be changed extremely quickly before its perverse consequences have this paralyzing effect. The most important instances of this type of constitution are found in the Soviet-type, federal constitutions in the former USSR, Yugoslavia, and Czechoslovakia.

3. The creation by a provisional government of a constitution with some *de jure* nondemocratic powers. Even when the old nondemocratic regime is destroyed and many new policies are passed, a democratic transition itself cannot be completed unless the nondemocratic components of the constitution crafted by the provisional government are eliminated, as we shall see in the case of Portugal. Even when these nondemocratic clauses are eliminated, the origin of the constitution in a provisional government may hurt democratic consolidation because of its inappropriateness or weak societal acceptance.

4. The use of constitution created under highly constraining circumstances reflecting the *de facto* power of nondemocratic institutions and forces. Such a constitution may be formally democratic and thus consistent with a transition

25. Some indispensable sources on constitutions and democracy are Jon Elster and Rune Slagstad, eds., *Constitutionalism and Democracy* (Cambridge: Cambridge University Press, 1988); Douglas Greenberg, Stanley N. Katz, Melanie Beth Oliveira, and Steven C. Wheatly, eds., *Constitutionalism and Democracy: Transitions in the Contemporary World* (New York: Oxford University Press, 1993); Bruce Ackerman, The Future of Liberal Revolution (New Haven: Yale University Press, 1992); A. E. Dick Howard, ed., *Constitution Making in Eastern Europe* (Washington: Woodrow Wilson Center Press, 1993); and the *East European Constitutional Review,* published quarterly since 1992 by the Center for the Study of Constitutionalism in Eastern Europe at the University of Chicago Law School in partnership with the Central European University.

being completed, but democratic consolidation may be hampered because a constrained constituent assembly, while believing that other institutional arrangements are more appropriate for the creation and consolidation of democratic politics, may be *de facto* prevented from selecting them. To some extent Brazil is such a example.

5. The restoration of a previous democratic constitution. This formula precludes a potentially divisive debate about constitutional alternatives and is often selected by redemocratizing polities for reasons of speed, conflict avoidance, and the desire to call upon some legacies of historic legitimacy. It should be pointed out, however, that simple restoration presents two potential problems for democratic consolidation. First, when the polity has undergone great changes during the authoritarian interlude, it is possible that a new constitutional arrangement would in fact be more appropriate for democratic consolidation. Second, restoration also assumes that the political procedures and institutions of the old constitution have played no role whatsoever in the democratic breakdown. When the old democratic arrangements have in fact contributed to democratic breakdown, restoration precludes an historic opportunity to construct new and improved arrangements with different procedures and symbols. Uruguay and Argentina are cases worth analyzing from this perspective.

6. Free and consensual constitution-making. This occurs when democratically elected representatives come together to deliberate freely and to forge the new constitutional arrangements they consider most appropriate for the consolidation of democracy in their polity. The constituent assembly ideally should avoid a partisan constitution approved only by a "temporary majority" that leads a large minority to put constitutional revisions on the agenda, thereby making consolidation of democratic institutions more difficult. The optimal formula is one in which decisions about issues of potentially great divisiveness and intensity are arrived at in a consensual rather than a majoritarian manner and in which the work of the constituent assembly gains further legitimacy by being approved in a popular referendum that sets the democratic context in which further changes, such as devolution (if these are to be considered), take place.[26] In this book only Spain fits this pattern.

In the rest of this book we examine how the interplay of our arenas, such as political society, rule of law, and economic society, and our variables, such as regime type, stateness, and those discussed in this chapter, affected the processes of transition to democracy and the consolidation of democracy in three different sociopolitical (and geographic) regions of the world—southern Europe, the Southern Core of Latin America, and post-Communist Europe.

26. For an argument in favor of consensual constitutions produced and ratified by nationwide debates, see Ackerman, *The Future of Liberal Revolution*, 46–68.

Part II

Southern Europe: Completed Consolidations

Although we believe that democratic transition and democratic consolidation are closely interconnected processes, we also believe that social scientists can and should strive to be as explicit as possible as to whether a transition is complete and whether a particular political system is or is not a consolidated democracy. In part 2 we argue that not only have Spain, Portugal, and Greece completed democratic transitions, all three have become consolidated democracies. Since there are many studies of the southern European transitions, but relatively few of consolidation per se, we pay particular attention in our studies of southern European countries to how uncertain and even difficult transitions became consolidated democracies.

6

The Paradigmatic Case of
Reforma Pactada–Ruptura Pactada:
Spain

THERE IS GROWING consensus that the Spanish transition is in many ways the paradigmatic case for the study of pacted democratic transition and rapid democratic consolidation, much as the Weimar Republic became paradigmatic for the study of democratic breakdown.[1] A number of factors contribute to the special (if not actually always paradigmatic) status of Spain in the transition literature. Foremost is the fact that it was one of the first in the cycle of what Samuel Huntington calls the "third wave" of democratic transitions, and it therefore influenced thinking in many countries that would later undertake similar difficult tasks. It was also, in contrast to many transitions, one in which the authoritarian regime had not faced defeat or near-defeat in war, as was the case in Portugal and

1. The bibliography on the Spanish transition is the most extensive of any of the cases we consider in this book. An essential source is José Félix Tezanos, Ramón Cotarelo, and Andrés de Blas, eds., *La transición democrática española* (Madrid: Sistema, 1989). This volume includes outstanding articles by Spanish social scientists, a very complete bibliography, an essay reviewing the different analyses of the transition, and a chronology of the process. Also see the special issue of *Sistema* 68–69 (Nov. 1985), which includes a bibliographic essay, several outstanding articles, and the responses to a questionaire by politicians and intellectuals on their views of the transition process. An indispensible selection of articles is contained in Ramón Cotarelo, ed., *Transición política y consolidación democrática: España (1975–1986)* (Madrid: Centro de Investigaciones Sociológicas, 1992). Other valuable overviews are José María Maravall and Julian Santamaría, "Political Change in Spain and the Prospects for Democracy," in Guillermo O'Donnell, Philippe C. Schmitter, and Laurence Whitehead, eds., *Transitions from Authoritarian Rule: Southern Europe* (Baltimore: Johns Hopkins University Press, 1986), 70–108; José María Maravall, *La política de la transición 1975–80* (Madrid: Taurus, 1981), which is available in English as *The Transition to Democracy in Spain* (London: Croom Helm, 1982); Carlos Huneeus, *La Unión de Centro Democrático y la transición a la democracia en España* (Madrid: Centro de Investigaciones Sociológicas-Siglo XXI de España, 1985); and Donald Share, *The Making of Spanish Democracy* (Westport, Conn.: Praeger, 1986). A well-documented study of the period immediately before and after the transition which pays particular attention to why key activists in the late Franco regime came to accept a democratic transition is Charles T. Powell, "Reform versus 'Ruptura' in Spain's Transition to Democracy" (Ph.D. diss., Faculty of Modern History, Oxford University, 1989). For parties and elections see Richard Gunther, Giacomo Sani, and Goldie Shabad, eds., *Spain after Franco: The Making of a Competitive Party System* (Los Angeles: University of California Press, 1988). For the role of labor, see Robert Fishman, *Working Class Organization and the Return to Democracy in Spain* (Ithaca: Cornell University Press, 1990). A basic source on the political attitudes of Spaniards during the transition and the first election is Juan J. Linz, Francisco Andrés Orizo, Manuel Gómez-Reino, and Darío Vila, *Informe sociológico sobre el cambio político en España 1975–1981* (Madrid: Fundación FOESSA, Euramérica, 1982).

Greece. Likewise, its rulers did not confront a deep economic crisis, as in Latin America and the Communist countries of Eastern Europe and the Soviet Union. Nor was it a case in which an external factor, like the withdrawal of the support by a hegemonic power, influenced the rulers. Rather, it was a case in which those in power thought they could not stay in power without, given the Western European context, excessive repression, while those challenging the regime could not marshal, at least immediately, enough force to overthrow it, particularly in view of the loyalty of the Armed Forces to the regime.[2] In this sense Spain was a "regime-initiated transition," although under the pressure of society.

Another reason for the admiration of many observers of the Spanish transition to democracy has been that Spain appeared to outsiders as a highly conflictual and potentially violent society, owing to the legacy of the civil war. However, the outsider's view did not correspond to the facts of Spanish society in the 1970s. Rather, through the "cultural work" of civil society before the transition and the continued cultural work of civil society and almost all elements of political society during the transition, Spain had transformed the lessons of the civil war into a positive factor that aided the transition. The contrast with the historical meaning of the Croatian-Serbian civil wars of the 1940s could not be more dramatic.[3] To this it should be added that Spain was the first of our examples of an attempted transition to democracy in which problems of a multilingual and multinational state intensified at the same time as the transition process was being initiated.

2. Ten years after the death of Franco, a public opinion poll captured this sense of deadlock. On the one hand only 13 percent of those polled felt that the regime could have continued without change after the death of Franco. On the other hand, only 18 percent of those polled said that "the opposition groups were very strong and could have overthrown the regime." See "Actitudes y opiniones de los españoles ante la constitución y las instituciones democráticas" (Madrid: Centro de Investigaciones Sociológicas, 1985), 105. For the changing calculations of regime forces in the 1969–75 period, see Powell, "Reform versus 'Ruptura,'" 15–54. For an excellent analysis of the role of the military in the same period, see Fernando Rodrigo Rodríguez, "El camino hacia la democracia: Militares y política en la transición española" (Ph.D diss., Facultad de Ciencias Políticas y Sociológicas, Universidad Complutense, 1989), 21–72.

3. As Víctor M. Pérez-Díaz argues so well, Spain's new democratic political culture "is to a certain degree a deliberate institutional and cultural construct. . . . This institutional effort has been considerably helped by a cultural collective attempt, partly conscious and partly unconscious. . . . Looming large in our collective memory of that experience we find a crucial experiment that failed: our II Republic and the Civil War of 1936–1939. . . . The moral implications of that tragic account were: the share of guilt and responsibility was more or less evenly distributed among the contenders, since they were all to blame." See Pérez-Díaz, "The Emergence of Democratic Spain and the 'Invention' of a Democratic Tradition" (Madrid: Instituto Juan March, June 1990, Working Paper #1), quotes from 19, 20, 21, 23. Also see his magisterial *The Return of Civil Society: The Emergence of Democratic Spain* (Cambridge, Mass.: Harvard University Press, 1993). Paloma Aguilar Fernández, in her excellent study of Spanish textbooks, newsreels, theater, and general discourse, documents how, in the twenty years before the death of Franco, the historical memory of the civil war had been culturally reconstructed so that it became a building block for the effort to consolidate democracy. See her *La memoria histórica de la guerra civil española (1936–1939): Un proceso de aprendizaje político* (Madrid: Centro de Estudios Avanzados en Ciencias Sociales, 1995). Despite the passage of more than forty years, the most commonly used descriptions by Croats of their Serbian enemies, and vice versa, are the names of the major contending factions in the civil war, the Croatian *Ustašas* and the predominantly Serbian *Chetniks*. See Ivo Banac, "Post-Communism as Post-Yugoslavism: The Yugoslav Non-revolutions of 1989–1990," in Ivo Banac, ed., *Eastern Europe in Revolution* (New Haven: Yale University Press, 1992), 168–87.

Another circumstance that makes the Spanish case particularly interesting is that the authoritarian regime had lasted thirty-six years and had created a complex institutional structure. It was not possible to use the existing institutions by filling them with democratic content or proceeding to a restoration of the pre-dictatorship democratic institutions, as in some Latin American cases. There was finally a unique factor that appeared to complicate the transition, Franco's installation of a monarchy that had a low historical legitimacy and that could easily be contested by democrats. Today the king is often referred to as *el piloto del cambio* (the pilot of change). However, it is useful to remember that, in Spain, the king by his actions legitimated the monarchy more than the monarchy legitimated the king.[4]

The relatively smooth process of the Spanish transition has, a posteriori, led many people to consider the Spanish model of political engineering as an "overdetermined" success. Indeed, if we reduce the messy historical process, with all its complexities, frustrations, delays and doubts, to a theoretical model, it appears to be an elegant process, even susceptible to a game theoretical analysis.[5] In fact, the comparison between our contemporary theoretical modeling and the inevitably more complex experience of the process should be a warning to those who analyze similar changes while they are still going on. It is well to remember that even the easiest and most successful transition was lived as a precarious process constantly requiring innovative political action.[6] It is doubtful that the Spaniards would have responded in the period 1975–77 with as great a pride about how the transition was made as they did ten years later. Certainly, the so-called *desencanto,* the disappointment or the demystification of the process and its leaders (particularly of Prime Minister Adolfo Suárez in the late 1970s and early 1980s) is by now largely forgotten, but it finds a parallel in most of the transitions in other parts of the world. The potential threat to the transition caused by the attempted military coup on February 23, 1981 tends also to be underestimated in retrospect.[7]

4. For a valuable book-length treatment of the role of the king in the transition, a book that won the Premio Espejo de España, see Charles T. Powell, *El piloto del cambio: El rey, la monarquía y la transición a la democracia* (Barcelona: Editorial Planeta, 1991). For a discussion of the role of the king, see also Juan J. Linz, "Innovative Leadership in the Transition to Democracy and a New Democracy: The Case of Spain," in Gabriel Sheffer, ed., *Innovative Leadership in International Politics* (Albany: State University of New York Press, 1993), 141–86.

5. See, for example, Josep M. Colomer, *El arte de la manipulación política: Votaciones y teoría de juegos en la política española* (Barcelona: Editorial Anagrama, 1990), which is an original and intelligent application of game theory to the transition. An article based on the book is "Transitions by Agreement: Modeling the Spanish Way," *American Political Science Review* (Dec. 1991): 1283–1302.

6. See, for example, Juan J. Linz, "Spain and Portugal: Critical Choices," in David S. Landes, ed., *Critical Choices for Americans: Western Europe* (Lexington, Mass.: Lexington Books, 1977), 237–96. This essay, which was written in 1974 and slightly revised in February 1976, reflects the uncertainties and fears at the start of the reign of Juan Carlos I. A rereading serves to correct the image of transition as a smooth and predetermined process that a theoretical model developed ex post facto might suggest. On the critical role leadership played in transforming the possible into reality, see Linz, "Innovative Leadership in the Transition."

7. There is an extensive literature on the military in the transition and on the failed coup of the 23rd of February 1981. The *Revista de investigaciones sociológicas* 36 (Oct.–Dec. 1986) is devoted to civil-military relations and includes an article by Agustín Rodríguez Sahagun, the first civilian minister of defense under

Finally, the Moncloa Pact has become a standard reference in discussions of the role of pacts in stabilizing transition processes. All too often, however, it is forgotten that the pact constructed in the prime minister's residence called *Moncloa*, was not a *social pact* between trade unions and employers' organizations, but a *political pact*. Adolfo Suárez called the Moncloa meetings, because he wanted to involve political society, and in particular all the parties who after the first free elections had representatives in the Spanish legislature, in negotiations among themselves. Between the Moncloa meetings, the parties consulted with their key constituents in civil society. (Suárez considered this link between political society and civil society particularly crucial in the case of the Communist Party and the trade unions.) Only after these extensive negotiations was the Moncloa political pact formally voted upon in a solemn session of the Cortes.[8] The resolution approving the Moncloa Pact was passed with one vote against by the lower house and with three votes against and two abstentions in the Senate.

We have emphasized these facts before entering into an analysis of our variables because, while we believe our variables to be extremely important, we do not want ourselves or the reader to fall into the trap of believing that the Spanish transition was overdetermined to be successful or that the political engineers at all times followed a rational model. With these important caveats in mind, how does Spain relate to the variables we discussed in Part 1?

From the perspective of the tasks a country must address before it can complete a transition and consolidate democracy, Spain began in a comparatively privileged position. Indeed, from the perspective of Table 4.3, the only task that was immediately urgent in November 1975, when Franco died, was the creation of political institutions with autonomy and support. Given this situation, it is now becoming fashionable to see the Spanish consolidation as being almost inevitable, given its supportive socioeconomic and geopolitical context. We believe that such an unexamined opinion not only leads to a serious misinterpretation of the actual process of democratic transition and consolidation in Spain but also contributes to the dangerous lack of attention to how the transition was actually prepared and how the successful execution of this plan later made it easier to handle

---

Suárez, another by the first socialist defense minister, Narcis Serra, as well as papers by social scientists, public opinion data, and book reviews. The complexity and psychology underlying *desencanto* is beautifully explored in Albert O. Hirschman's chapter, "On Disappointment," in his book *Shifting Involvements: Private Interest and Public Action* (Princeton: Princeton University Press, 1982), 9–24.

8. This account of the political process of the Moncloa Pact is based largely on an interview carried out by Alfred Stepan with Adolfo Suárez on May 24, 1990. Suárez says he initially considered making the stabilization plan an executive decision but rapidly realized it would be more legitimate and more effective if he could arrive at an agreement with the political parties. This complex consensual process within political society, which was a hallmark of the Spanish transition, was, as we shall see, virtually completely absent in the major Argentine and pre-Plan Real Brazilian stabilization plans, which were drawn up in secret by the president and his closest advisors and announced to a shocked nation on television without ever having been discussed in the legislatures. For the relationship between the Communist and Socialist parties, the unions, and the Moncloa Pact, see Fishman, *Working Class Organization and Democracy*, 17, 180, 215–26.

Spain's stateness problem and in fact to consolidate democracy. Let us turn, therefore, to how the transition was actually crafted.

CRAFTING THE SPANISH TRANSITION

The Spanish transition had to deal with a problem recurrent in other later transitions: how to dismantle the nondemocratic regime and its institutions and to gain democratic legitimacy based in elections in order to confront the many problems faced by the society. In contrast to the military regimes in Greece and Latin America (with the partial exception of Chile and Brazil), Franco's civilian and authoritarian regime had built a complete institutional and constitutional structure. The Francoite institutions, with their official single party and their corporatist Cortes (parliament), could by no stretch of the imagination be made serviceable to democracy by filling them with democratically elected personnel, as many believed could be done with the formally ultrademocratic constitutions of the Eastern European Communist regimes. Those Francoite institutions had to go, but the option of a revolutionary overthrow—the rupture demanded by the opposition—was not really feasible (as the Spanish Communist Party leadership acknowledged later), given the overall climate of public opinion and in particular the support the regime had in the armed forces.[9] An unconstitutional declaration by the king to abrogate the Franco constitution, with the support of some radical groups in the armed forces (the small minority inspired by the Portuguese golpe-revolution), was out of the question. So, from the beginning, within the regime, there was thought given to the possibility of using the legality of the Franco Fundamental Laws and the corporatist Cortes to change the regime constitutionally, against the spirit and intent of those laws. A lot of thinking and debate and some unsuccessful starts went into the efforts that finally yielded the Law for Political Reform. The need for legal "backward legitimation," to use Guiseppe di Palma's

---

9. The first thesis of the Spanish Communist Party (PCE) at its IX Party Congress in February 1978 was devoted to explaining why the combination of reformist pressures emanating from the regime and the opposition, as well as international pressures, "obliged the PCE to nuance its ruptural theses." For the full text see *Mundo Obrero*, Madrid (Feb. 2, 1978), 1.

However, as late as 1981, according to the Fishman study, not an insignificant number of the working class leaders at the plant level in Madrid and Barcelona believed that "because of indecision and the errors of many leaders of the opposition, a historic opportunity was lost to create a more advanced democracy on the basis of popular mobilizations and a political ruptura." In Barcelona 68 percent of the leaders identified with Comisiones Obreras (the Communist Union) felt that way compared to 40 percent in Madrid. Among those of the socialist UGT (Unión General de Trabajadores), there were 31 percent and 23 percent in Barcelona and Madrid, respectively, who believed that ruptura would have been possible. Among all the 324 workers' representatives interviewed, 39 percent believed in the possibility of the ruptura, while 57 percent felt that "the balance of forces at the time of the political transition did not permit the step to democracy by ruptura, and the leaders of the left did well in changing strategy to facilitate the reforma which led to democracy." This was the opinion of the majority of UGT representatives in Barcelona (66 percent), Madrid (72 percent), and the Comisiones Obreras in Madrid (55 percent) and only 30 percent in Barcelona. The above data are from Fishman, *Working Class Organization and Democracy*, 144.

phrase, was based on the fact that the king had sworn to defend those laws, that his authority was derived from them, that the government in charge had been appointed according to them, and that the obedience of the armed forces could only be assured if the change took place in that way.[10] The fear of a vacuum of authority, of a sudden transfer of power to the then quite radical opposition forces—foremost the nationalists in the periphery and the Spanish Communist Party and the trade union movements controlled by it—was unthinkable without the risk of involution or political repression. The reformers thus had to act cautiously, and their instrument was legal reform, making possible a democratically elected body that could deal with the many problems on the horizon, including stateness problems and an incipient economic crisis. It also was essential to avoid a separate and open debate about the monarchy, which did not enjoy particularly strong legitimacy.

The way chosen was to convince the Cortes—the legislature created and partly appointed by Franco—to allow the creation of a fundamentally different type of legislative body after open and free elections with the participation of political parties. That is what was achieved by the Law for Political Reform and its subsequent approval by referendum.[11] The equivalent in the USSR would have involved Gorbachev convincing the Communist Party and the legislative organs of the complex constitutional structure of the Soviet Union to allow multiparty, freely contested elections for a parliament of the union which would then have the duty and power to form the government. Failing this, there should at least be a union-wide, direct multiparty competitive election for a president of the Soviet Union. As we shall see, as long as the Soviet Union existed, nothing close to such elections ever happened. How was it actually accomplished in Spain? No one can ignore the structurally favorable conditions in Spain, but there can be no doubt that this particularly successful transition owes much to agency.

A more detailed analysis of leadership during the democratic transition would pay considerable attention to the moderating role of the king, the constructive leadership of Santiago Carrillo (the leader of the Spanish Communist Party), the

10. The concept of *backward legitimation* was first developed by Giuseppe di Palma in his "Founding Coalitions in Southern Europe: Legitimacy and Hegemony," *Government and Opposition* 15 (1980): 162–89.

11. On the "law *for* political reform," see Pablo Lucas Verdú, *La octava ley fundamental*, with a foreword by Enrique Tierno (Madrid: Tecnos, 1976), and Antonio Hernández Gil, *El cambio político español y la constitución* (Barcelona: Planeta, 1981). Some readers might feel that we unfairly privilege in our analysis the role of the main actors in the regime or the opposition. We want to emphasize here the important role of ordinary citizens in generating a crisis of the regime. They often take risks in their opposition and struggle against the regime. They also generate pressures on regime actors to initiate a transition (sometimes thereby avoiding regime collapse). However, in the case of Spain, in support of our approach we have data from a survey shortly after the approval of the Law for Political Reform asking respondents to whom they attributed the positive aspects of the change: 26 percent chose the government, 23 percent the king, 20 percent Prime Minister Suárez, 8 percent the parties of the opposition, 3 percent the Cortes, 21 percent the people and the citizens in general, while 6 percent said there was nothing good and 9 percent did not answer. See Linz et. al., *Informe sociológico sobre el cambio político*, p. 119.

prudence of Cardinal Tarancón (the leader of the Spanish Catholic Church), the support and courage of General Gutiérrez Mellado (the chief of staff to the Spanish Army), the political astuteness of Josep Tarradellas (the exiled leader of the Catalan regional government), the parliamentary negotiating abilities of Torcuato Fernández Miranda, and the cooperation of the conservative leader Manuel Fraga, to mention just a few of the figures involved. In the short space available, we cannot do justice to all these actors and organizations. We would, however, like to call particular attention to the innovative leadership of Adolfo Suárez. We will pay particular attention to how he formulated the key issues of democracy in two of his most politically influential speeches (which, unfortunately, have never been translated into English). As we shall see, for Suárez, the holding of elections was the essence of his task. He was right. Elections are crucial to the democratizing process of dismantling and disempowering the old regime. They are even more crucial to the installation, legitimation, and empowerment of a new democratic regime. While the specificities of this process will vary from polity to polity, we believe that in some of the countries we discuss later—most dramatically the USSR and later Russia—leaders missed opportunities to advance this power erosion/power creation process, with deleterious results for democracy and state capacity.

In the first of two influential speeches, Adolfo Suárez, then speaking as the minister-secretary general of the almost defunct official single party, the *Movimiento,* in the first royal cabinet, made a complex appeal to the corporatist Franco-controlled Cortes that *liberalization* and eventually *democratization* was necessary.[12] It was the beginning of five months of argumentation. Suárez began by referring to "the democratic monarch's" support for reform. He went on to argue that, given the socioeconomic developments under Franco, the government should take the next step in political reform by allowing free political association. "I think that our historic task . . . is very simple: to finish the work [started by Franco]. . . . The government, the legitimate manager of this historic moment, has the responsibility to put into motion the mechanism necessary for the definite consolidation of a modern democracy." He stressed that changes in Spanish society had contributed to a new pluralism, a pluralism which had already assumed, de facto, political forms.

The point of departure [of the proposed political reform of a law legalizing political association] is the recognition of the pluralism of our society. If this society is plural, we cannot allow ourselves the luxury of ignoring it. . . . If we contemplate the national reality with a minimum of sincerity, we have to acknowledge that in addition to this theoretical pluralism, there already exist organized forces. We would entrench ourselves into an absurd blindness if we refuse to see this. These forces, call them parties or not, now exist as a public fact. . . . The aims of parties are

12. Many analysts of the Spanish transition believe that this speech was instrumental in the king's selection of the young Adolfo Suárez to succeed the floundering Arias Navarro as prime minister. Maravall and Santamaría argue that Arias "never accepted the idea of transforming the inherited regime into a pluralist democracy." See Maravall and Santamaría, "Political Change in Spain," 81.

specific and not the least of them is to assume power. So, if the road is not opened by the legality which is being proposed by the state itself, there will only be an apparent peace, below which will germinate the seeds of subversion.

Suárez went on to say that political pacts were being discussed, but he astutely raised the question as to how democratic political representatives could be created to participate in such pacts: "With whom should they [the government] make the pact?" Suárez immediately gave his answer: "Only after elections will there be valid interlocutors and legitimated agents."[13] On July 1, 1976 Prime Minister Arias Navarro was forced to resign and Adolfo Suárez was appointed Prime Minister.

The institutionalization of a democratic process was still very much in doubt at the time of the appointment of Suárez. In many democratic transitions the constitution of the old regime remains in force and inhibits or delays democratic renewal. In Spain the Cortes could have been such a structure. Suárez's seemingly impossible task was to convince the Cortes to vote for a Law for Political Reform that in essence would result in the Cortes' own disappearance. If he could not convince the Cortes, he would have to risk a constitutional confrontation of uncertain consequences for democratic legitimacy (as occurred with Yeltsin's conflict with the Russian parliament in 1993) or accept the Cortes' ability to paralyze the changes needed for democratic transition.

Suárez approached this problem by carefully drafting and negotiating a text of the democratizing Law for Political Reform. Before he submitted the text to the Cortes for the process of legal approval, he went on national television and made his second historic speech. In this speech to the nation, Suárez implicitly warned the Cortes that without new constitutional norms there could be social conflict: "The absence of rules leads to 'ad-hockery' and can lead to anarchy." He also urged the Cortes to avoid conflict by letting the people express their will. He told the nation he was confident that the Cortes would perform this historic task. He then made the crucial step from liberalization to democratization. He advocated free and open elections and set a date. "I have said the word *elections* and in essence this is the key to the proposal. The [proposed] constitutional modification will permit the [new] Cortes to be elected by direct, secret, and universal suffrage as soon as possible and, in all events, before June of 1977. In this manner the people will participate in the construction of their own future since they will express themselves, they will elect their representatives, and these representatives will make the decisions over the questions that affect the national community." For Adolfo Suárez the fundamental task was to manage to make the forces present on

13. All of these quotations are our translations from the speech Adolfo Suárez made to the Cortes on June 9, 1976, in defense of the Law for Political Association. The full text of his speech and the law are found in the pamphlet released by Ediciones del Movimiento in Madrid (1976), entitled "El Derecho de Asociación Política," 9–28.

the street and in civil society participate in the political system without his abdication of his own powers until after the elections. While acknowledging the prestige of opposition groups and leaders, he reiterated his argument that only elections would determine with whom to negotiate. For Suárez it would be via elections that "political groups that today voluntarily present themselves publicly as protagonists (and they are significant and respectable but lack a popular mandate) will come to be representatives of the people."

Suárez made an indirect appeal to the corporatist Cortes that it would be ethically and historically correct to vote themselves out of existence by allowing free elections. He also assured the nation there would be no power vacuum and that the rule of law would prevail. "The government is convinced that the institutions [of the Franco regime] will understand the need for this reform and will support the direct appeal to the people whom these institutions themselves serve. There cannot be and there will not be a constitutional vacuum, and even less a vacuum of legality. Such a vacuum cannot emerge because Spain is a State of Law which is based on the primacy of the law."

Suárez then went on to argue that *only* if the state was restructured and filled with a new democratic power would it be strong enough to address the country's social and economic agenda and its looming stateness problem. For Suárez, the sequence of reform thus had to start with political reform. "When the people have made their voice heard, then there can be resolved other great political problems with the authority which will come from electoral representation. Then issues like institutionalization of the regions, within the permanent unity of Spain, can be approached." For Suárez, political reform was a precondition of economic reform. "As long as political unknowns [*incógnitas*] hang over the country, there cannot be either economic reactivation or stability." He concluded by conveying a sense of hope and implying that the Cortes should allow the people to decide. "The future is not written because only the people can write it."[14]

On the day before the vote, many close observers were not certain that the Law for Political Reform would be passed. However, Suárez and the movement toward democratization had gained such momentum that the Cortes passed the law by a margin of 425 affirmative votes against 59 negative votes.[15] Subsequently, the Law for Political Reform was submitted to a referendum on December 15, 1978. With a strong 77% turnout, it was approved by 94% of those voting.

After the referendum's overwhelming endorsement of the Law for Political Reform, the process of dismantling the authoritarian structure and allowing democratic power gains accelerated. The referendum increased Suárez's power and his

14. See Pablo Lucas Verdú, *La octava ley fundamental*, which contains the full texts of the law (103–8) and of the speech by Suárez to the nation (109–19), from which we have translated excerpts.

15. Juan J. Linz was present in the Cortes for the entire debate and the first vote. This 366-vote margin on November 18, 1976 represented a 121-vote increase over the favorable vote for the much less controversial liberalizing Law for Political Association, held on June 9, 1976.

ability to enter into negotiations to create an inclusive political society. Suárez first met the opposition formally on December 23, 1976, only eight days after the referendum, although in the summer of 1976 he had informally met twice with the Socialist Party leader, Felipe González, and other opposition leaders. Suárez met informally with the leader of the Communist Party, Santiago Carrillo, in January 1977, soon after Carrillo left jail. On April 9, 1977, Suárez successfully took the dangerous step, considering hard-line resistence, of legalizing the Communist Party. The first parliamentary election was held on June 15, 1977. The parliament produced by the election drafted a constitution, which was approved in a referendum on December 6, 1978. The process we have just described illustrates the complex interaction between legality, legitimacy, and power and the importance of *timing* in transitions.[16]

THE LEGALIZATION OF THE COMMUNIST PARTY: AN EXCURSUS ON INCLUSIONARY CHOICES

Once the general principle of a freely elected legislature had been accepted, the most difficult and dangerous decision Suárez faced was whether to legalize the Communist Party of Spain (PCE). Decades of anti-Communist propaganda, suspicions about the Communists' ambitions, and worries about the party's diffuse strength throughout society provided a context in which the right, and especially the military, might well have been mobilized against the transition. Even among the reformers there were those who argued for postponing the legalization of the Communist Party until after the first free elections.

The question of legalization was, however, an issue affecting the inclusiveness of contestation, an essential element of democracy, and therefore the credibility of the Spanish regime's democratizing effort. In addition, the obvious presence of a strong Communist Party, in terms of activists and sympathizers, inevitably created the dilemmas of the cost of repression versus the cost of toleration. In his television address justifying the legalization, Suárez put the issue clearly before the people:

The rejection [of the request of legalization] would not be consistent with the reality that the Communist Party exists and is organized. The struggle against it could only be carried out by repression.

Not only am I not Communist, but I reject strongly its ideology, as it is rejected by the other members of my cabinet. But I am a democrat, and sincerely democratic. Therefore I think that our people are sufficiently mature . . . to assimilate their own pluralism.

16. On the role of timing in regime changes, see Juan J. Linz, "Ill fattore tempo nei mutamenti di regime," *Teoria política* 11, no. 1 (1986): 3–47.

I do not think that our people want to find itself fatally obliged to see our jails full of people for ideological reasons. I think that in a democracy we must all be vigilant of ourselves, we must all be witnesses and judges of our public actions. We have to instore the respect for legal minorities. Among the rights and duties of living together is the acceptance of the opponent (*adversario*). If one has to confront him, one has to do it in civilized competition. Sincerely, is it not preferable to count in the ballot boxes what otherwise we would have to measure on the poor basis of unrest in the streets?[17]

This crucial decision ended any doubts about the sincerity of Suárez's personal commitment to democracy, and Suárez seized the occasion of his television address to announce his candidacy in the elections. The decision to legalize the Communist Party was extremely dangerous, as was shown by the hostile responses of some key military leaders and even of some of the important politicians who had supported the transition. For example, Suárez's announcement provoked the resignation of the minister of the navy, who had to be replaced by a retired admiral because no active duty admiral would assume the post. Suárez's announcement also spurred a unanimous declaration of the Army Supreme Council that "legalization of the Communist Party has produced general repugnance in all the units of the army." However, despite a more intemperate earlier document that had been leaked, they also concluded that, "in consideration of higher national interests, the [council] accepts with discipline the fait accompli [*hecho consumado*]."[18] Suárez's difficult choice proved decisive in assuring the moderate Euro-Communist posture of the Spanish Communist Party and its leader Santiago Carrillo and thus made a vital contribution to the eventual success of the Spanish transition.

We will not enter into a lengthy argument, but obviously for democracy it is a critical choice whether to make an inclusionary decision to allow *all* political forces to participate in the political process or to make an exclusionary decision to exact rules against parties that might, in the view of one or another important sector of the regime or society, be perceived as threatening to them or to democracy. We shall also not enter into the important normative debate as to whether democracy has the right to limit participation in the "democratic game" only to those committed to playing by democratic rules. We would like, however, to be explicit about two empirical implications of an inclusionary choice. Both were adeptly alluded to in the above speech by Suárez. First, the decision to allow participation allows the objective counting in votes of a possible extremist movement's support which would weaken any excess claims to diffuse societal support which could be made if it were prohibited. Second, if extremist parties are out-

17. This and other Suárez speeches in the critical 1976–78 period are found in Adolfo Suárez González, *Un nuevo horizonte para España: Discursos del Presidente del Gobierno 1976–1978* (Madrid: Imprenta del Boletín Oficial del Estado, 1978).

18. For an excellent discussion of the tense situation in the military after the legalization of the Communist Party, see Rodrigo, "El camino hacia la democracia," 185–94, quote from p. 191.

lawed, the democratic regime is involved in jailing, on potential ideological as opposed to actual behavioral grounds, citizens who belong to state-declared illegal organizations.

This does not mean that democrats should be passive against antidemocratic forces. Democrats can oppose and attempt politically to isolate ideological extremists and to jail them if they actually use violence to advance their ideas. Above all, democrats must avoid any semiloyal collaboration with antidemocratic forces.

The Communist Party of Spain loyally contributed to the transition to and consolidation of democracy in Spain. However, the normative and empirical issues raised in 1977 were still salient in Spain in the 1990s. The *Herri Batasuna* (HB), a party that advocates independence and revolutionary change in the Basque Country, does not hide its sympathy and even indirect support for ETA terrorists. However, rightly in our view, given the theoretical and empirical arguments we have advanced, HB has not been outlawed. Indeed, HB has been successful in electing some representatives and officials. But, fundamentally, it has been politically isolated.

Empirically, for the effort to consolidate democracy, the advantage to Spain of having allowed even explicitly antidemocratic extremists to participate in elections becomes apparent when we analyze some key cases. For example, in the 1979 second general elections in Spain, Fuerza Nueva, a neofascist group, campaigned actively throughout the country, claiming to speak for the values of the past and attempting to agglutinate antiregime forces. But, Fuerza Nueva won only 2.1 percent of the total vote, elected only one deputy, and disintegrated as a political force soon after the 1979 election. Even more dramatically, the courts allowed Lieutenant Colonel Antonio Tejero Molina, one of the February 1981 coup organizers, to run the party Solidaridad Española from his jail cell in the 1982 general elections. Once again the claim was that he was representing strong currents of opposition against the direction of the transition. Tejero's party received less than 30,000 (0.13 percent) of the total votes, thereby objectively "counting," to use Suárez's word, the absolute rejection of the putschists by the electorate.

Democracy does not mean that every citizen supports democracy, nor that antidemocrats should not enjoy democratic freedoms for legal and nonviolent acitivities. Violent activities should certainly be punished using legal means (although even some democrats may, in their frustration with terrorism, condone illegal reprisals). The defense of democracy is the duty of democratic parties and leaders and ultimately of the voters, making possible government by democrats.

STATENESS PROBLEMS AND THEIR DEMOCRATIC RESTRUCTURING

If Spain had been a relatively homogeneous nation-state, like Portugal, Greece, and the Latin American cases we will discuss, the Spanish transition to democracy would probably have been completed with the approval of the constitution. However, the strong nationalist feelings in Catalonia and the Basque Country raised problems of stateness. The Catalan and Basque nationalisms were not perceived as central to most of those who wrote about the Spanish transition process. However, the crisis of other multinational states highlights the significance of the steps Spain took to manage its stateness problem, steps which deserve separate attention. It is our contention that Spain was able to manage its stateness problem by successful devolution only because it had first created, by the process we have just analyzed, legitimate state power with the authority and capacity to restructure the polity.

In our judgment, when Spain began its transition, the variable that potentially presented the most dangerous complication for both democratic transition and democratic consolidation was stateness. Because stateness was so critical and because, unlike Yugoslavia and the Soviet Union, it was handled so well in Spain, we will analyze it in particular detail, both for the light it sheds on the Spanish transition and also for the theoretical implications it has for transitions in heterogeneous states with important regional, cultural and national differences, such as Yugoslavia, the Soviet Union, Czechoslovakia, Indonesia, and Nigeria.

When Spain began the process of democratization, the potential for a dangerous stateness problem indeed existed. The most important indicator was that terrorist violence of the nationalist Basque organization ETA (*Euskadi ta Askatasuna*—Euskadi and Freedom) between 1960 and the year of Franco's death, 1975, had caused forty-three deaths. In 1978, the year the constitution was approved, deaths had escalated to sixty-five. There were seventy-eight deaths in 1979 and ninety-six in 1980, the year of the first new regional elections that led to a major devolution of power.[19] This armed violence created the very real potential of military opposition to the democratic transition and consolidation because, while not one army officer was killed during the Basque insurgency in 1968–75 under Franco, or in the 1975–77 transition period, in the postelectoral period of democratic rule between 1978 and 1983, thirty-seven army officers died due to Basque nationalist violence.[20]

Yet, surprisingly, despite the deaths of military officers and the inevitable difficulties of creating Spain's quasi-federal state, *none* of the important statewide interest groups or parties engaged in *system blame*. Adversity was not deliberately used to delegitimate either the fledgling democratic regime or the new constitutional structures that departed from Spain's traditional unitary state organization. In our judgment the main reason for this lack of system blame was Spain's

19. See Fernando Reinares, "Sociogénesis y evolución del terrorismo en España," in Salvador Giner, ed., *España sociedad y política* (Madrid: Espasa Calpe, 1990), 353–96. See especially the table on p. 390, with bibliographic references.

20. Ibid. Also see Francisco J. Llera, *Los vascos y la política. El proceso político vasco: Elecciones, partidos y opinión pública y legitimación en el País Vasco, 1977–1992* (Bilbao: Universidad del País Vasco, 1994).

successful handling of its potentially grave problem of stateness via state wide elections.

Elections, especially founding elections, help create agendas, actors, and organizations, and, most importantly, legitimacy and power. One of our major arguments is that, if a country has a stateness problem, it makes a critical difference whether the first elections are statewide or regional. In Spain the first elections were statewide, and we believe that they helped transcend Spain's stateness problem. The first post-Franco vote, as we have seen, was the referendum to approve a "law *for* political reform." This law committed the government not to any details of political reform, but to a process of clear *democratization,* not just *liberalization.*

The second key vote, on June 15, 1977, was also not merely about liberalization, but about democratization; it was a statewide general election to select deputies who would create a government and draft a new constitution. Because of the statewide stakes involved, four statewide parties conducted a campaign in all of Spain around statewide themes, winning 319 of the 350 seats. Just as importantly, the statewide parties campaigned very hard in areas where the potential for secession was greatest and the history of antisystem sentiment was most deeply rooted—the Catalan and Basque regions. While strong Catalan and Basque nationalist parties did emerge, the four statewide parties and their regional affiliates won 67.7% of the vote in Catalonia, and 51.4% of the vote in the Basque Country.[21]

The deputies and government produced by these statewide elections engaged in prolonged public and private negotiations over the constitution and over how to proceed on the stateness issue. A consensual constitution was finally supported in parliament by the four major parties and the major Catalan nationalist party; 258 of the 274 members voting gave it their approval. Spain's third general appeal to the voters then followed, namely a referendum on the constitution, which was approved by 87.8% of the voters on December 1, 1978. In Catalonia the constitution was approved by 90.4 percent of the voters. In the Basque Country 68.8 percent of those who voted approved the constitution, but voter turnout was only 45.5 percent, which was below the Spanish and Catalan level of 67 percent.[22]

Strengthened and legitimated by these three convocations of its electorate, Spain's government and parliament began negotiations in earnest over the devolution of power to the Catalan and Basque Country provincial representatives, who themselves had been constituted in the aftermath of the general elections. Surrounded by intense controversy the negotiators eventually crafted a system by which Spain would change its historically centralized state structure for a new decentralized one characterized by an unprecedented devolution of power to the

---

21. For the organization of statewide parties and the importance of the general election in transforming the agendas of these parties, see Gunther, Sani, and Shabad, *Spain after Franco,* 37–177. The results of the 1977 election are found on pp. 38 and 311.

22. For details about constitutional votes see Andrea Bonime-Blanc, *Spain's Transition to Democracy: The Politics of Constitution-Making* (Boulder, Colo.: Westview Press, 1987).

peripheral nationalist constituencies. These negotiated agreements over regional autonomy (the Statutes of Autonomy) were submitted to Basque and Catalan voters in October, 1979. The Catalan statute was approved by 87.9 percent and the Basque statute by 90.3 percent of those who voted in the regions.[23] The largest and oldest Basque nationalist party (PNV), which had urged abstention on the earlier referendum on the constitution, adjusted to the new political situation and urged approval of the Statutes of Autonomy.[24]

Had the first elections in Spain been regional rather than statewide, the incentives for the creation of Spain-wide parties and a Spain-wide agenda would have been greatly reduced. Consequently, the statewide parties and their affiliates would have received fewer votes.[25] We also believe that, if the first elections had been on the regional level, issues raised by nationalities would have assumed a much more substantial and divisive role in the electoral campaign than they actually did and the nationalist parties and their affiliates would have been more extreme. Indeed, there is a good chance that peripheral nationalist parties and groups would have been able to shift the discourse of the electoral campaign so that calls for ruptura and mobilization for independence would have become predominant.[26] Strengthened nationalist parties would have gravely complicated the stateness problem in Spain. Relations between the military and the democratizing forces of the central government would almost certainly have been put under greater strain. In a context of heightened stateness conflict, the coup coalition—defeated by the king's personal intervention on February 23, 1981—would probably have emerged earlier and with greater force against a divided and less legitimate government.

The democratic transition in Spain certainly began under favorable conditions, but the clear commitment to democratization and countrywide elections strengthened the legitimacy claims of the central government, helped forge links between

23. See Juan J. Linz, "De la crisis de un Estado unitario al Estado de las autonomías," in Fernando Fernández Rodríguez, ed., *La España de las autonomías* (Madrid: Instituto de Estudios de Administración Local, 1985), 527–672, and Juan J. Linz, *Conflicto en Euskadi* (Madrid: Espasa Calpe, 1986). On the negotiation of the Basque Autonomy Statute, see the account by two journalists, Kepa Bordegarai and Robert Pastor, *Estatuto vasco* (San Sebastian: Ediciones Vascas, 1979).

24. Some extreme separatist groups continued to boycott the vote on autonomy, and the overall voter turnout was 13 percent lower than the Spanish average in the constitutional referendum; nevertheless, the voter turnout of 54 percent was still politically significant.

25. Even when stateness issues are not salient, regional parties in Spain tend to poll 15–25 percent better in regional elections than they do in general elections.

26. One example of such a potential discourse was the fact that the Consejo de Fuerzas Políticas de Cataluña in March 1976 publicly demanded the "establishment of a provisional government of the Generalitat that would assume power in Catalonia from the moment of the 'ruptura democrática' with the commitment to announce and hold in the shortest time possible elections to the Catalan parliament; that government would constitute itself on the basis of the principles that shaped the Estatuto of 1932 and as a first step in the concrete exercise of the right of self determination." As the former exiled leader of the Catalan regional govenment, Josep Tarradellas, comments in his memoirs, "political verbalism was at its height." José Tarradellas, *Ja Sóc Aqui: Recuerdo de un retorno* (Barcelona: Planeta, 1990), diary entry of March 15, 1976, p. 4.

Table 6.1. Multiple Identities in Catalonia: 1982

	Population			
Identity	Both Parents Born in Catalonia	Neither Parent Born in Catalonia	Immigrants	Entire Sample
Catalan	13.7	10.7	2.3	9.0
More Catalan than Spanish	26.5	12.0	4.2	16.9
Equally Catalan and Spanish	48.2	37.5	25.9	40.1
More Spanish than Catalan	5.7	10.5	12.6	8.2
Spanish	5.1	23.7	51.3	23.5
No answer	0.8	5.7	3.8	2.4
	(414)	(69)	(317)	(885)

Source: Juan J. Linz, "De la crisis de un estado unitario al estado de las autonomías," in Fernando Fernández Rodríguez, ed., *La España de las autonomías* (Madrid: Instituto de Estudios de Administración Local, 1985) 560.

Table 6.2. National Identities in Catalonia

	Percentage	
Survey Answer	Catalans	All Spain
"Proud to be Spanish"	73%	85%
"Proud to be Catalan"	82%	N/A[a]
In favor of the unification of Europe via the European Community	83%	76%

Source: The questions on pride are from Francisco Andrés Orizo and Alejandro Sánchez Fernández, *El sistema de valors dels Catalans* (Barcelona: Institut Català d'Estudis Mediterranis, 1991), 207. The question on European unification is from "Los Españoles ante el Segundo aniversario de la firma del Tratado de Adhesión de España a la Comunidad Europa" (Madrid: Centro de Investigaciones Sociológicas, Abril 1988), 53. This table is reproduced with permission from Juan J. Linz and Alfred Stepan, "Political Identities and Electoral Sequences: Spain, the Soviet Union, and Yugoslavia," *Daedalus* 121 (Spring 1992): 128.
[a]N/A, not available.

political society and civil society, and contributed to a new, constitutionally sanctioned relationship between Spain's peripheral nationalisms and the central government. Most importantly, countrywide elections restructured stateness identities in ways that were supportive of multiple identities and democracy in Spain. In the new democratic Spain, *complementary multiple identities* persist. Dual identities in Catalonia are the norm and have never been in question (table 6.1)

Catalans now have political and cultural control over education, television and radio, and indeed over most of the areas where Catalan nationalism had been most repressed in the past. Catalans also participate as a regional group in the European Community (now the European Union), a body that in some important respects is a community of regions as much as a community of states. Finally, in this new context, Catalans, to a greater extent than ever before, accepted their identity as members of the Spanish state. The sequence of elections in Spain helped constitute these mutually supportive legal and affective memberships in national (Catalan), state (Spanish), and suprastate (European Community) polities. The

Table 6.3. National Identities in the Basque Country

	Percentage	
Survey Answer	Basque Country	All Spain
"Proud to be Spanish"	44%	85%
"Proud to be Basque	69%	N/Aª
In favor of the unification of Europe via the European Community	74%	76%

Source: Reprinted, with permission, from Juan J. Linz and Alfred Stepan, "Political Identities and Electoral Sequences: Spain, the Soviet Union, and Yugoslavia," *Daedalus* 121 (spring 1992): 129.
ª N/A, not available.

overwhelming percentage of all Catalans are proud to be Catalan, proud to be Spanish, and very supportive of joining an integrated European political community. Table 6.2 shows these complementary multiple identities very clearly.

The Basque Country presents a more difficult political situation. While the support for membership in a unified Europe is high, the citizenry in the Basque Country are 40 percent less proud to be Spanish than the national average and about 30 percent less proud to be Spanish than the Catalans (table 6.3). There is still routine separatist violence in the Basque Country, but we believe that the overall political situation has been ameliorated by the sequence of elections we have described. Indeed, the Basque Country is a particularly dramatic example of how elections can structure identities and delegitimate certain types of antistate violence.

Let us now focus explicitly on the question of how identities can be constructed by political processes. Between 1977 and 1979 the most heated question in Spanish politics concerned the relationship of peripheral nationalisms to the unitary Spanish state. In this two-year period the percentage of the population in the Basque Country who said they wanted to be independent *doubled,* to represent virtually a third of the entire population. Starting from a smaller base, pro-independence sentiment *tripled* in Catalonia in the same period. Obviously, if these trends had continued for a few more years, there would have been a severe crisis of stateness in Spain. However, once there had been a referendum on the Statutes of Autonomy and governments had been established with Basque and Catalan nationalist parties in office, sentiment for independence declined and later stabilized at lower levels (figure 6.1).

Assassinations, kidnapping and terrorism by pro-independence groups in the Basque Country still continued after the referendum, but their political significance changed dramatically. The terrorism of the ETA was a central factor in the course of the democratic transition, the constitution-making period, the negotiation and approval of the autonomy statutes, the election of the Basque parliament, the formation of a Basque government, and the transfer of functions to the government. At each of those points in time, it was argued that those steps would lead to the end of terrorism; however, more often than not they coincided with an

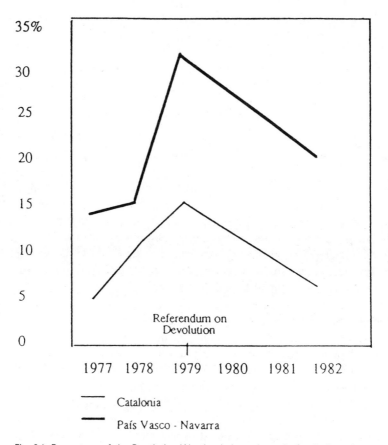

Fig. 6.1. Percentage of the Population Wanting Independence in Catalonia and
País Vasco-Navarra before and after the 1979 Referendum on Devolution of
Power to the Automonías.

Source: Juan J. Linz and Alfred Stepan, "Political Identities and Electoral Sequences: Spain, the Soviet
Union, and Yugoslavia," *Daedalus* 121, no. 2 (Spring 1992): 130. Reprinted with permission from
Daedalus. This table is based on the data originally produced in Juan J. Linz, "De la crisis de un Estado
unitario al Estado de las autonomías," in Fernando Fernández Rodríguez, ed., *La España de las
autonomías* (Madrid: Instituto de Estudios de Administración Local, 1985), 587.

upsurge of terrorist casualties. Terrorism has not disappeared with the consolidation of Spanish democracy and the consolidation of Basque institutions and self-
government.

Does this mean that the steps in the solution of the stateness problem—the existence of peripheral nationalisms—have failed? There is evidence (which we cannot discuss here in full detail) that this is not the case. Terrorism, from having a
central importance, has become a tragic aspect of life, mostly in the Basque country, but that cannot destabilize Spanish democracy. The attempt on the life of the
leader of the opposition Partido Popular, José María Aznar, in 1995 provoked

unanimous condemnation. Terrorism has today its own dynamics, with only minority support in the Basque population.

The public opinion data show basic changes in the attitudes of the Basque population toward ETA, but the comparison of attitudes over time is complicated by some changes in question formulation and the different proportions of "no opinion"and "don't know" (due probably to the practices of the different polling organizations). With this in mind we want to note that in 1979 only 5 percent saw ETA as "criminals"; by 1989, 16 percent did so. In 1979, 17.1 percent saw ETA as patriots; by 1989, only 5 percent saw them as patriots. In the course of a decade of democracy, the proportion saying that ETA were "idealists" dropped from 33 percent to 18 percent; the ambiguous answer "manipulated" dropped from 29 percent to 11 percent; while that of "madmen" increased from 8 percent to 16 percent. Many of those changes were due to larger numbers of don't know and no answers, from 8 percent to 34 percent—reflecting perhaps a tiredness of the whole issue—but that does deflect from the fact that the number of those expressing support by defining ETA as "patriots" and those condemning them as "criminals" have changed.

Another set of data covering several years from 1981 to 1989 shows that, in 1981, 8 percent gave ETA their "full support"; in 1989 the figure was 3 percent. Those agreeing with ETA goals but not the means went from 3 percent in 1981 to 9 percent in 1989. Most importantly, the percentage of respondents expressing "total rejection" went from 23 percent in 1981 to 45 percent in 1989, with 48 percent "don't know, no answer" in 1981 and only 16 percent "don't know, no answer" in 1989.[27]

The comparison of data by party voted between 1979 and 1986 shows that, among those supporting the Socialists (PSOE) the percentage answering "patriots" or "idealists" dropped from 46 percent to 10 percent and the percentage giving negative answers ("madmen" or "criminals") rose from 47 percent to 74 percent. Most significantly, this "identity delegitimization" occurred even among the voters of the main nationalist party, the Partido Nacionalista Vasco (PNV), where the percentage of positive answers dropped from 40 percent to 16 percent. Even among the voters of Herri Batasuna, the positive responses weakened, from 60 percent saying "patriots" to 31 percent, while more said "idealists," 25 percent in 1979 and 40 percent in 1986.[28]

27. For an analysis of the Basque data and a more extensive discussion of democratic politics in the context of political violence, see Goldie Shabad and Francisco J. Llera, "Political Violence in a Democratic State: Basque Terrorism in Spain," in Martha Crenshaw, ed. *Terrorism in Context* (University Park, Penn.: Pennsylvania State University Press,1995), 410–69; Llera, *Los vascos y la política* and Linz, *Conflicto en Euskadi*, 698.

28. Shabad and Llera, "Political Violence." Unfortunately, the comparison of attitudes concerning independence between 1979 and 1989 is not fully possible, since the alternative answer "indifferent" was introduced in 1989. However, those expressing "great desire" or "fairly large desire" for independence constituted 36 percent in 1979 and 31 percent in 1989. Those reporting a desire that was "fairly small," respectively, 15 percent and 8 percent; "very small" were 12 percent and 7 percent; and "none," 29 percent and 19 percent. Offering the alternative "indifferent"allowed 19 percent not to make a choice. In addition, the number of "no answers" increased from 7 percent to 18 percent (probably because of the different practices of the survey organizations).

For Basque nationalists (probably like most nationalists throughout the world), the goal of an independent nation-state will never disappear. But the intensity of that desire and the political means used to advance that desire can and have changed. Accommodation to a democratic multinational state is possible, as the pattern of Spanish-Basque politics of the last two decades shows.

These developments have largely stabilized the multiple levels of identity (the important number of those who feel their Basque identity as well as a Spanish identity) and limited the polarization of the two communities. They also have stabilized the initially strong and growing desire for independence. Not that such a desire has disappeared, although it is increasingly stated as a symbolic long-term goal, while politics, government, and elections take place within the redefined Spanish state. Those developments have also made possible in the Basque country the delegitimation and political isolation of the ETA terrorists. Although Basque political killings continue, they no longer threaten to bring down the democratic government.

The crisis of Spanish stateness has been contained, initially due to the choice of electoral sequence. As we shall see when we discuss the stateness issue in the Soviet Union and Yugoslavia, the electoral sequence in these two countries was profoundly different, and it exacerbated the stateness problem that both countries already had due to their Soviet-style federal constitutions and historical memories. We do not want to overstate the significance of holding first a general election—in which statewide parties competed in the whole country and which also gave a democratic legitimation to the nationalist parties—in the successful resolution of the problem of Spanish stateness in a critical moment. Without all of the subsequent steps taken (the decrees on the pre-autonomias in the fall of 1977, the 1978 constitution, and the approval of the Estatutos in 1979), the problem could have continued being an obstacle to full consolidation of Spanish democracy. We do not say either that the nation-building efforts in the periphery are not problematic, in the sense we have already discussed in chapter 2, in the multilingual Catalan and Basque societies. What we do say is that the postponement of full devolution until after the approval of a Spanish constitution in 1978, the negotiation of the Autonomy Statutes, and their popular legitimation in a referendum allowed a much less conflictual and more institutional recognition of nationalist aspirations and the creation of a new and different state.

Using the definition of democratic transition advanced earlier, we maintain that the Spanish transition began with the death of Franco on November 20, 1975, and was completed at the latest on October 25, 1979, when the Basque and Catalan referendums on regional autonomy were held. A case could, of course, be made that the transition was completed when the principle of government accountability to the parliament was established formally in November 1977 or when the new democratic constitution was approved in the referendum on December 6, 1978. However, we believe that only after the Basque and Catalan regional autonomy formula had been negotiated and voted upon did Spain meet our three requirements for a *completed transition*: a government was in office that was the result of a free and popular vote, the government had sovereign authority to generate policies, and the government did not de jure have to share power with other bodies. Until this point there had been some doubt about whether the military would successfully challenge the government's sovereign right to negotiate and generate new policies in the highly controversial area of regional politics. Furthermore, the legitimacy of a democratically elected government, if it had not solved these problems of regionalization, might have been questioned because the government could have been seen as displaying excessive continuity with the Franquist regime.

EXCURSUS ON VIOLENCE AND DEMOCRATIZATION

It is difficult to assess the importance of political violence in the struggle for democracy. In the cases included in our work, the regimes were not overthrown by armed popular movements, guerrillas, or terrorists, if we ignore the confusing events in Romania. The "liberation by golpe" of the Portuguese Captains is an altogether different case. However, the case of Spain involves the violence of the ETA, which certainly did not lead to the Spanish transition but contributed to the crisis of Franco's regime. The assassination of his premier, Luis Carrero Blanco, in December 1973 was an important event whose political implications for the regime and change after the death of Franco will continue to be debated. It has been argued that, if Luis Carrero Blanco had been prime minister when Franco died, the resistance of the "bunker" [the hard line] would have been greater and the transition probably would have been much different and more difficult. Some facts are clear. ETA violence was a serious problem. Its repression contributed to the international delegitimation of the Franco regime. But the scale of violence reached its height in 1978–80 during the approval of the Constitution, the second free election, the negotiation of Basque autonomy with Basque moderate politicians, and the first election for the Basque regional parliament.

However, the sympathy for or tolerant attitude toward the ETA of much of the opposition during this whole period and the ambiguous attitude of the French government toward ETA members operating in France allowed the ETA to play a disturbing and frustrating role in the new democracy. Although politically increasingly isolated, ETA violence led the Socialist democratic government to condone—we do not know exactly to what extent—illegal actions against the ETA. This is a case in which a democratic government acted in ways that blemished its civil rights record.[29] This has, years later in 1995, contributed to a serious crisis of confidence in the government.

29. As Linz has pointed out, democratic governments are most likely to violate the law and commit human rights abuses in cases where terrorism is combined with nationalistic, linguistic, or religious de-

Table 6.4. "Democracy Is the Best Political System for a Country Like Ours," Spain 1978–1993.

Survey Answer	1978	1980	1981	1982–83	1983	1988	1993
"Yes"	77	69	81	74	85	87	79
"No"	15	20	13	6	10		
"Depends"				12			
"Other, N/A"	8	11	6	7	5		
N	(5,898)	N/A	(1,703)	(5,463)	(3,952)	(4,548)	(1,448)

Source: This table is reproduced, with permission, from Juan J. Linz and Alfred Stepan, "Political Crafting of Democratic Consolidation or Destruction: European and South American Comparisons," in Robert A. Pastor, ed., *Democracy in the Americas: Stopping the Pendulum* (New York: Holmes and Meier, 1989), 44. National surveys by Data S.A., Madrid. For 1978 (July) and 1980 see J. J. Linz, M. Gómez-Reino, D. Vila, and F. A. Orizo, *Informe sociológico sobre el cambio político en España, 1975– 1981* (IV Informe FOESSA, Vol. I, Fundación FOESSA), (Madrid: Euramérica, 1981), 627–29. For 1981, March 4 to 21 (after the February 23 attempted coup), *Cambio 16*, no. 488 (April 6, 1981): 42–45; for 1982–83, November–January, postelection survey with the support of the Volkswagen-Stiftung, unpublished. For the study see Juan J. Linz and J. R. Montero, *Crisis y cambio: Electores y partidos en la España de los años ochenta* (Madrid: Centro de Estudios Constitucionales, 1986). For 1983 (Fall), see J. J. Linz, "La sociedad española: presente, pasado y futuro," in J. J. Linz, ed., *España, un presente para el futuro, I: La sociedad* (Madrid: Instituto de Estudios Económicos, 1984), 57–95, and J. J. Linz, "Legitimacy of Democracy and the Socioeconomic System," in Mattei Dogan, ed., *Comparing Pluralist Democracies: Strains on Legitimacy* (Boulder, Colo.: Westview Press, 1988), 65–113. Data for 1988 and 1993 from the Centro de Documentación de Data, S.A., Madrid. For an important conceptual and empirical analysis, see José Ramon Montero and Richard Gunther, "Democratic Legitimacy in Spain," paper prepared for the International Political Science Association (IPSA), IVI World Congress, Berlin, August 21–25, 1994.

Here we want only to note that the terrorist struggle against a nondemocratic government may leave a difficult legacy for a new democracy, since the terrorists may pursue other goals than democratization and, therefore, not stop their actions when democracy has been achieved. The assassination of one of the intellectual leaders of the right, Senator Jaime Guzmán, in Chile after a democratic government assumed office is another example of how such a legacy complicates the democratic political process.

DEMOCRATIC CONSOLIDATION

There is broad scholarly consensus that Spanish democracy was *consolidated* no later than the peaceful transfer of power to the socialist opposition after the October 1982 general elections. We accept this date. However, a case could be made that democracy was consolidated even earlier, with the completion of the successful trials and imprisonment of the military leaders involved in the February 23, 1981 coup attempt. It is very significant (and a startling contrast to Argentina) that the two major leaders of the coup attempt, Colonel Tejero and General Miláns del Bosch, were sent to jail and that there was never a politically significant movement in the military or in civil society to grant them clemency.

In our theoretical discussion of democratic consolidation, we distinguished the

mands. See his "Types of Political Regimes and Respect for Human Rights: Historical and Cross-National Perspectives," in Asbjørn Eide and Bernt Hagtvet, eds., *Human Rights in Perspective: A Global Assessment* (Oxford: Blackwell, 1992), 177–222, 299–310, esp. 190–93.

Table 6.5. "At This Time, What Do You Think Is Best: Government Only of the UCD (The Unión de Centro Democrático, Then the Ruling Party), a Political Party Coalition, a Civil-Military Government, or a Military Government?" Spain 1981

Survey Answer	Percentage
UCD government	27%
Coalition government	52%
Civil-military government	5%
Military government	2%
Others (no response, don't know, hard to classify)	14%
	100%

(*N* = 1,703)

Note: The question in Spanish was: "En estos momentos, ¿qué cree usted que es el mejor: un gobierno sólo de UCD, un gobierno de coalición entre partidos políticos, un gobierno cívico-militar, o un gobierno militar?"
Source: This table is reproduced, with permission, from Linz and Stepan, "Political Crafting of Democratic Consolidation or Destruction," 45. Data are from a special poll carried out by Data, S.A., Madrid, Spain, between March 4 and 21, 1981, after the putsch attempt of February 23, 1981.

attitudes of the general citizenry from the *behavior* of nationally significant groups and the *constitutional reality* of whether the democratic government was de jure sovereign in the policy sphere. In the Spanish case, the first component to become fully congruent with consolidation was public opinion. By 1978 Spanish public opinion was strongly democratic, and it has remained so ever since (table 6.4).

Not only was Spanish public opinion strongly prodemocratic in the abstract sense, it also overwhelmingly rejected the major possible alternative to democracy, a military government (table 6.5).

Ten years after the death of Franco, 76 percent of the population felt pride in the transition and only 9 percent said that the transition was not a source of pride. This sense of pride was particularly strong on the left, where 82 percent of those who said they would vote Communist and 88 percent of those who said they would vote Socialist expressed pride in the transition.[30]

In terms of the behavior of nationally significant groups, parts of the military spent significant resources attempting to impose conditions, by pressure and if necessary by military force, on democratically elected governments, at least until the failed coup in February 1981. Some scholars, such as Paul Preston, argue that some party activists were in sufficient contact with coup conspirators to be called, in effect, a semiloyal opposition. However, the overwhelmingly negative reaction to the coup expressed by the king, public opinion, and party leaders helped to establish very clearly that the only game in town after February 1981 was a democratic game.[31]

30. "Actitudes y opiniones de los españoles ante la constitución y las instituciones democráticas," 32.
31. Before the coup attempt prominent politicians from a range of parties, including the Socialist Party, engaged in semiloyal discussions with the military about a possible civil-military caretaker coalitional government. All such ambivalent actions on the part of party activists stopped after the coup. For a discussion of the semiloyal behavior of some politicians, see Paul Preston, *The Triumph of Democracy in Spain* (London: Methuen, 1986), 160–88, esp. 181–84.

The final component of democratic consolidation to be put in place was the successful exercise by the democratic government of its right not to have its policy power constrained by non-democratic institutions. The trials and imprisonment of the military were complete by 1982. The trials helped to consolidate democracy because they showed how divided and without an agenda the military "alternative" really was. The most important hard-liners were defeated, disgraced, and jailed. After the trials there was a "steady realization among large numbers of officers that democracy was there to stay and that the military ought to accommodate itself within it."[32] Finally, after they were faced with the solid parliamentary majority achieved by the Socialists in October 1982, "military contestation shifted from politics to more strictly corporate concerns, and from resistance to accommodation."[33] From December 1982 until March 1991 the defense minister of the Socialist government, Narcis Serra, the former mayor of Barcelona, designed and implemented an imaginative and sweeping restructuring of the military, which had begun with UCD goverments and their civilian ministers of defense. When he left office "the once feared *Poder Militar* was now, in many respects, one more branch of the state administration."[34] In terms of civil-military theory, a democratic pattern of civil-military relations is one in which there is low contestation by the military of the policies of the democratically elected government and where the military accepts that they have low "prerogatives" or reserve domains.[35] For more than a decade, Spain has been in this position.

A review of the basic background variables that facilitate or impede a democratic consolidation shows that Spain, with the important exception of the stateness variable we have examined, began its transformation under facilitating conditions on all the other variables. The organizational base of the authoritarian regime was civilian or civilianized pro regime officers. Some may think of the Franco regime as a military regime, but Franco exercised power as head of the party as well as generalísimo of the armed forces and predominantly as chief of state. Numerous studies of decision making in the last twenty-five years of the Franco regime support Felipe Agüero's judgment that "although the military in Spain was highly present in the Franquist structures, it did not delineate or monitor government policy or control its leader," and that "the military in Spain did not participate in the elite nucleus that made the core decisions for the transition."[36] In our judgment it is appropriate, therefore, to call the regime base in the

---

32. Felipe Agüero, "The Assertion of Civilian Supremacy in Post-authoritarian Contexts: Spain in Comparative Perspective" (Ph.D. diss., Duke University, 1991), 300.

33. Ibid., 309.

34. For an excellent discussion of the socialist reform, see ibid., 309–56. This quote is from p. 356.

35. For a more extensive conceptual discussion of "military prerogatives" and "military contestation" and a comparative analysis of Spain, Chile, Uruguay, Argentina, and Brazil, see Stepan, *Rethinking Military Politics*, 93–127, esp. figure 7.3 on p. 122.

36. Both quotes from Felipe Agüero, "The Military in the Processes of Political Democratization in South America and South Europe: Outcomes and Initial Conditions," paper presented at the XV Interna-

years preceding the transition a "civilianized-authoritarian regime." As we have argued, such a base presents fewer potential obstacles to democratic transition and consolidation than does a sultanistic base or a hierarchical military.

In Spain there were, of course, important social and political pressures for change when Franco died. Our emphasis on the formally developed part of civil society in Spain that in part served as a basis, cover, and support for an emerging political society should not lead us to neglect the less organized forms of dissent by people in demonstrations, rallies, and sympathy strikes. Some of those actions were quite spontaneous, and certainly many of those participating did not belong to any of the organizations initiating them.

There is, however, a very important difference between authoritarian Spain and those regimes in Communist Europe with strong totalitarian or frozen post-totalitarian features, such as the GDR, Czechoslovakia, Bulgaria, Romania, and the Baltic republics. There the weakness of civil society and political society before the transition started and during the course of the transition made the more spontaneous actions of citizens congregating in squares, churches, and streets (like those in Leipzig, Dresden, Berlin, Prague, Sofia, and finally in Timisoara and Bucharest) play a much greater role in the crisis of those regimes and their collapse or the initiation of a transformation from above. In some of those cases, there was a serious possibility of a violent Tiananmen Square denouement, an outcome less likely in Spain (except perhaps in the Basque Country) due to the mediating role of civil organizations and the leaders of an incipient political society. The massive demonstration in Spain in February 1977, after the murder of Communist labor lawyers—the Atocha murders—is one example; their lying-in-state at the bar association offices in the Supreme Court building, the authorized character of the mass demonstration, and the control of the militants by the PCE made this an important but orderly event. In this context of heightened societal pressure for and expectations of change, the regime's political leaders, especially Adolfo Suárez, initiated the law for political reform and were in charge when the first elections were held and when the constitution was drafted. Popular pressure kept the transition going forward and contributed to the dialectic captured by the well-known Spanish phrase *reforma pactada-ruptura pactada*. Nonetheless, since the regime played a key role at all stages of the transition, it is appropriate to call Spain a case of negotiated transition, which, consistent with our argument, is a format that avoids most of the problems of a "provisional government."

Concerning the implication of the character of the previous nondemocratic regime, we argued in table 4.3 that it is conceivable that in the later stages of an authoritarian regime a country could arrive at a set of conditions vis-à-vis civil

tional Congress of the Latin American Studies Association, San Juan, Puerto Rico, September 21–23, 1989, 22 and 27. For a similar argument with supporting documentation, see Rodrigo, "El camino hacia la democracia," 21–32, and Stepan, *Rethinking Military Politics*, 118–21.

society, constitutionalism and rule of law, the state bureaucracy, and economic society that would be quite supportive of democratic consolidation, if there was a democratic transition. Spain is the clearest example of the phenomenon. In the words of Víctor Pérez-Díaz, "by the time we get to the mid-70s the economic, social and cultural institutions of Spain were already quite close to those of Western Europe, and the cultural beliefs, normative orientation and attitudes that go with the workings of these institutions were also close to European ones. This is one of the reasons why the political change to democracy worked so swiftly."[37] He further notes that, by the mid-70s (just before the transition), "Spain's economy was a modern economy, ranking tenth among capitalist economies throughout the world, with a large industrial sector, a booming service sector and its agriculture undergoing rapid transformation."[38] Indeed, the Spanish economy had benefited from the overall development of Western Europe, and between 1961 and 1970 it had a growth rate of 7.3 percent, one of the highest in the world.[39] The Spanish transition is particularly relevant to the debates about economic factors in transitions and consolidations of new democracies. The robust economic development in Spain in the 1960s contributed indirectly to the transition by generating a more complex and free society in which there were considerable working class protests and strikes, first on economic issues and later on solidarity demands. In the moment of transition, Spain's close network of organizations limited anomic and violent action, possibly because everybody had something to lose in disorder. However, there was no direct relationship between prolonged economic growth and the onset of the transition nor to the specific political processes leading to democracy. Spain had reached a level of development that should have led to democratization quite a few years before Franco's death in 1975. The business class did not press for change by articulating arguments that the regime had served its function or that further development required democratization. Business did not oppose democratization and might have even privately supported it, but business played no active public role bringing about democracy.

Of the five arenas that were crucial for the consolidation of democracy, as argued in chapter one, Spain began its transition with reasonable supportive con-

---

37. Pérez-Díaz, "Emergence of a Democratic Spain," 14. This is true even in the area of political preferences. For example, although, until shortly before the 1977 elections, the public recognition of leaders and the large number of emerging parties were small, the Spaniards, even before the death of Franco and especially after the transition began, could clearly place themselves on the left-right dimension and express their preference for one or another of the ideological tendencies in the European political spectrum. Most Spaniards from the daily news were quite familiar with European politics and parties. In this respect Spain was very different from most post-totalitarian societies and particularly from the former USSR.

38. Ibid.

39. See J. M. Maravall, "Economic Reforms in New Democracies: The Southern European Experience," *East South System Transformations,* Working Paper #3 (Oct. 1990), Department of Political Science, University of Chicago, 3. For a more detailed evaluation of areas of economic strength and weakness of the Franco regime in 1960–75, see José María Maravall, *Los resultados de la democracia: Un estudio del sur y el este de Europa* (Madrid: Alianza Editorial, 1995), 61–104.

ditions in all of the arenas except political society. Democratic crafters and supporters inherited a civil society already robust and reasonably differentiated, an economic society that needed restructuring but was already institutionalized, a state apparatus tainted with authoritarianism but usable (and certainly so by the first democratically elected government, which came from its ranks), and a reasonably strong recent tradition of rule of law.

Given this situation we do not feel that international influence was critical for Spain's transition and consolidation (as we will argue it was for Portugal), but it certainly was systematically supportive. Democracy in Spain, in fact, was already consolidated before Spain entered the European Economic Community in 1986. However, the fact that the EEC was solidly democratic, and had "set up a stable pattern of rewards and disincentives" for would-be members was helpful to Spain's transition and consolidation.[40] As the former Socialist Minister, José M. Maravall, has noted, "Adolfo Suárez presented Spain's request for membership to the EEC in 1977 and the totality of parliamentary parties supported him. It was widely believed that international isolation and the dictatorship had been closely connected in recent Spanish history. The European Community was seen as a symbol of democracy and development; this symbol had been very important in the struggle against Francoism. Joining the EEC was believed to be a decisive step for the consolidation of democracy."[41] Foreign policies toward Spain and the prevailing *Zeitgeist* in Western Europe were thus very supportive of democratic transition and consolidation. The diffusion effect was also helpful for Spain. The 1974 Portuguese Revolution encouraged some Spanish proregime leaders to push the democratic transition forward rather than wait for a reaction from below, and the loss of the king's throne in Greece probably encouraged King Juan Carlos to support a regime-led democratic transition.

The political economy of legitimacy is extremely interesting because there is absolutely no doubt that the economic situation of Spain deteriorated sharply during the transition and did not improve until three years *after* consolidation in 1982. Spanish unemployment in the early 1970s under Franco was one of the lowest in Europe, hovering around 3 percent. With the transition to democracy, unemployment rose dramatically—in fact, Spain's 20 percent unemployment rate in the mid-1980s was the highest in Western Europe. Economic growth rates, which averaged over 7 percent from 1960 to 1974 and were among the highest in the world, averaged only 1.7 percent between 1975 and 1985.[42] The hypothesis of a tightly coupled relationship between economic efficiency and political legitimacy would lead

40. Whitehead, "International Aspects of Democratization," 22.
41. Maravall, "Economic Reforms in New Democracies," 16.
42. The Spanish unemployment data are from Banco de Bilbao, Economic Research Department, *Situación: Review of the Spanish Economy*, International Edition, no. 10–11, 1986. The Spanish growth rates are derived from *United Nations Statistical Yearbook*, 1976, 1982, and Economic Intelligence Unit, *Quarterly Reports: Spain* (2nd quarter 1986).

us to predict a corresponding decline in the legitimacy of democracy. Although the polls showed a sharp decline in the belief in the socioeconomic efficacy of the regime, there was a significant increase in the number of citizens who answered affirmatively to the question "Is democracy the best political system for a country like ours?"[43] As with the Dutch in the mid-1930s, the Spanish in the 1980s, despite economic decline, struggled all the harder to make the democratic regime work because no alternative seemed more appropriate. Helped by the fact that Spain had started with a reasonably good economy, the sequence of reform actually followed was first political, second social, and only third, economic.[44]

Our final conditioning variable is the constitution-adoption formula. In the absence of a sultanistic background or an armed conflict within the state, a constitution imposed by a provisional government was precluded. The relative absence of the military in the day-to-day governing process of the old authoritarian regime and the fact that the transition was being led by the regime's civilian leaders meant that the military did not attempt to impose authoritarian prerogatives or confining conditions on the constituent assembly.[45] The civil war legacy, the great socioeconomic changes since the 1930s, and the fact that the Franco government had been in power for forty years virtually precluded a restoration. These factors, together with the constant pressure of the democratic opposition, led the regime's leaders to adopt the free constitution-making formula. Within this formula, Spain elected the consensual as opposed to the majoritarian style of constitution making. The issue of consensus underlying the political process of the transition and above all the constitution-making process was emphasized by Suárez in a speech before the Congress of Deputies on April 5, 1978 in these terms:

During a constituent process, the Government must limit the reach of its options, maintaining the level of dissensus at levels which are not substantial, because that is the only way to avoid what would be the most grave danger to the body politic: the nonexistence of a concord located in the country at its roots, concerning the basic elements of national coexistence. This transitory situation, characteristic of all constituent periods, conditions all aspects of political action. . . . the Constitution, as an expression of national concord, must be obtained by consensus, for which it is necessary to take into account the diverse political forces now present."[46]

43. We develop this argument at greater length in Stepan and Linz, "Political Crafting of Democratic Consolidation or Destruction: European and South American Comparisons," in Robert A. Pastor, ed., *Democracy in the Americas: Stopping the Pendulum* (New York: Holmes and Meier, 1989), 42–48; the quote is from p. 43.

44. The seminal work on the sequencing of reform in southern Europe is Maravall, "Economic Reforms in New Democracies." Given the "simultaneity" problem that all post-Communist polities faced, this sequencing was (unfortunately) not considered seriously in that region. Even in the South American countries, the choice, everywhere but Chile, has been to address deep debt-related problems and political problems simultaneously.

45. On this key point see the excellent dissertation by Rodrigo, "El camino hacia la democracia," 273–77.

46. The distinction between the consensual and the majoritarian styles of democratic policy making is developed in Arend Lijphart, *Democracies: Patterns of Majoritarianism and Consensus in Twenty-one Countries* (New Haven: Yale University Press, 1984), 1–36.

The result of the consensual approach to constitution drafting was that the constitution was approved in the lower house by 325, with only 6 votes against and 8 abstentions. To get maximum legitimacy for the new constitution, the Spanish leaders chose to have their collective work submitted to a constitutional referendum where, as we saw, it obtained about 88 percent approval.[47] *None* of the other twelve countries we consider in this volume carried out all of these steps. Probably the most significant consequence of the consensual process is that, ten years after the death of Franco, 65 percent of those polled felt that the constitution "was an accord among almost all political parties," whereas only 10 percent felt it was "imposition by one party on the other." In answer to the question, "Whose ideas prevailed in the constitution—'right,' 'left,' 'center', 'everyone' or 'no one in particular'?" the answer "everyone" was agreed to by 57 percent, whereas the next highest was the "center" with 7 percent.[48] The constitution, therefore, was and is an element of popular consensus in the new democracy.

We do not want to leave the impression that democratic consolidation in Spain was overdetermined by our variables. We have acknowledged the delicacy of the question of stateness, the severity of the military threat to Spanish democracy in February 1981, and the indispensability of the skill and imagination of party leaders and the king for success. Nevertheless, in comparative terms, Spain began the transition with very favorable conditions. This would not have been the case had Spain begun the transition from a totalitarian, post-totalitarian, or sultanistic base. However, as we shall see when we examine Portugal, a transition that begins with a coup by a nonhierarchical military confronts vastly more complicated circumstances, even though it shares the same typological origin as an authoritarian regime.

At the time of making final revisions to our book, the Spanish government is in the midst of a serious crisis unrelated to the transition. This crisis is due to revelations of corruption on the part of the head of the Bank of Spain and the first civilian and socialist head of the Guardia Civil, tolerance or support for the anti-ETA terrorism of the clandestine organization called GAL (Grupos Anti-terroristas de Liberación), the cover-up of the death of an ETA member at the hands of the police, and widespread telephone tapping.

A mixture of complexities derived from the constructive vote of no confidence and the interests of the Catalan party—Convergència i Unió—delayed dissolution and new elections. However, no one questioned the democratic institutions, and the response was the calling of early elections for March, 1996. In this case, the quality of democracy does not jeopardize the consolidation of democracy; in fact, in this and other cases, one could argue that the relative invulnerability of democratic institutions to bad government is proof of consolidation.

---

47. For the votes see Linz, "Innovative Leadership in the Transitions," 185. On the constitution-making process see Bonime-Blanc, *Spain's Transition to Democracy.*

48. "Actitudes y opiniones de los españoles ante la constitución," 50–51.

7

From Interim Government to Simultaneous Transition and Consolidation: Portugal

THE PORTUGUESE transition to democracy presents characteristics that are directly relevant to our theoretical framework. It exemplifies in a particularly dramatic way the problems stemming from a transition initiated by a nonhierarchical military. In Portugal this led to rule by interim governments and a constitution-making process heavily conditioned by nondemocratic pressures. The result was the creation of "reserve domains" of power that precluded, as long they were in place, the completion of democratic transition and therefore democratic consolidation. The Portuguese case also boldly highlights how elections can be an independent factor in transition and consolidation, since elections can sociologically, as well as legally, alter relations of power. Without the formal written commitment of the Armed Forces Movement (MFA) to hold elections within one year (a decision later regretted by some of the revolutionary officers and their allies), the uncertainty and difficulty of the Portuguese transition could well have been much greater than they were.

Why was the Portuguese transition so fundamentally different from the Spanish transition? Regime type does not really help us because the Salazar regime in Portugal was not significantly different from the Franco regime in Spain. To be sure, the regime was at times described as totalitarian, but most scholars now concur that the regime never was totalitarian, even in the worst period of Salazar.[1] The regime did of course have a fascist-style structure of mass organizations, but these structures were actually less important than in Spain, and the official party was not strongly organized. The regime had a nondemocratic constitutional system with strong corporatist features, but more than in Spain it had certain institutions of a liberal origin such as regular elections to a parliament and even a

---

1. For an analysis of the corporatist but not totalitarian nature of the Salazar regime, see Manuel de Lucena, "Interpretações do Salazarismo: Notas de leitura crítica," *Análise social* 20 (1984): 423–51. For an excellent review of the literature, see António Costa Pinto, *Salazar's Dictatorship and European Fascism: Problems of Interpretation* (Boulder: Social Science Monographs, 1995). For a comparison of the regimes of Franco and Salazar, which concludes that neither was totalitarian, see Javier Tusell, *La dictadura de Franco* (Madrid: Alianza Editorial, 1988), 272–305.

short period of tolerated political contestation before the elections.[2] For a while there was even a direct election of the president—in fact, in 1958 the regime's candidate almost lost. The weakness of the single official party and the lesser weight of fascist ideological influences brought the regime even further from the totalitarian model than in Spain. The military were more unruly and politicized than in Spain. Military revolts were routine and both the regime and the opposition attempted to bolster themselves by having military officers as their presidential standard bearers. In fact, all presidents of Portugal from 1926 to 1986 were military men.[3] But the regime was by no means a military regime. Ultimately, like Spain, Portugal's nondemocratic regime can be characterized as a civilianized authoritarian regime with a weak party. Salazar was a university professor who was surrounded by academics, and his successor was a distinguished university professor. Finally, Salazar as the long-time head of government was, like Franco, committed to sustaining the nondemocratic regime he had created.

With such similar regimes in Portugal and Spain, why did Portugal have revolutionary rupture with its past while Spain had a "transition by transaction"? Writing today about the Portuguese upheavals, we all too often tend to see them in the framework set by later transition processes, forgetting that in 1974 Portugal was the first of the transitions in contemporary southern Europe. Thus there was no "Spanish model" available for emulation or reflection, as it was later for government and opposition elites alike in Hungary, Brazil, Uruguay, and South Korea. Portugal as the first transition was also not helped by a diffusion effect. The model of *reforma pactada–ruptura pactada* had not been invented. However, with our interest in assessing the importance of diffusion and political learning, our discussion of Spain opens up the very real possibility that part of the reason why the Spanish transition was so fundamentally different from the Portuguese transition is that the Portuguese upheavals were occurring as Franco died and served for some of the key regime activists in Spain as a point of reference of how *not* to make a transition. This important point aside, one can still speculate counterfactually whether a "transition by transaction" would have been possible in Portugal.

Theorists of these "transitions by transaction," such as Mainwaring and Share, generalizing from Spain and Brazil, have posited that such a transition is most likely if there is (1) a reasonably well-established regime, (2) a low subversive threat, (3) a cooperative opposition, (4) low mobilization, and (5) innovative leadership.[4] With the exception of a small but Stalinist Communist Party, Portu-

2. See Philippe C. Schmitter, "The 'Régime d'Exception' That Became the Rule: Forty-eight Years of Authoritarian Domination in Portugal," in Graham and Makler, *Contemporary Portugal*, 3–46.

3. For the Portuguese military under Salazar and an analysis of twenty-one different cases of insurrection, see Douglas L. Wheeler, "The Military and the Portuguese Dictatorship, 1926–1974: 'The Honor of the Army'," in Graham and Makler, *Contemporary Portugal*, 221–56. Despite these acts of insurrection, Wheeler is clear that the Salazar government was not a military government. "The armed forces leadership after 1933, and especially after World War II, was increasingly controlled by the state" (p. 199).

4. See Scott Mainwaring and Donald Share, "Transition through Transaction: Democratization in

gal at the death of Salazar in 1970 shared great similarities with Spain and Brazil on the first four conditions. What Portugal lacked was an innovative leader who took a major role in initiating a transition.[5] In the end, midlevel professional officers whose status and morale were being destroyed, and many junior officers who were being radicalized by the colonial wars in Angola and most importantly in Mozambique and Guinea, terminated the government that could not or would not terminate the wars. On April 25, 1974, Western Europe's oldest dictatorship was overthrown by junior officers.[6]

Almost immediately, massive crowds filled the streets, supporting the junior officers, crowds that put carnations in their guns, thus helping legitimate and make irreversible the "revolution of the carnations." The success of the liberation by "golpe" rapidly led to the freeing of political prisoners.[7] The liberation opened a period of febrile activity, social protests, more or less spontaneous takeovers of factories and large agricultural units, purges of all kinds of institutions if they were seen as closely related to the previous regime, and constant *assembleas* to decide everything. Parties seen as representing continuity with the old regime were outlawed. The Portuguese Communist Party emerged out of many of the assemblies with key positions of power. Nationalization of the banks put the country on the road to socialism, given the banks' traditional control of much of industry. It was a revolutionary process that attracted worldwide attention, enthusiasm, and fears.

TRANSITION INITIATED BY A REVOLUTIONARY NONHIERARCHICAL MILITARY

Analytically, how did such a revolutionary process begin, and especially how and why did such a process lead to representative parliamentary democracy? Ob-

---

Brazil and Spain," in Wayne Selcher, ed., *Political Liberalization in Brazil* (Boulder, Colo.: Westview Press, 1986), 175–215.

5. For a systematic analysis of how Marcello Caetano, in sharp contrast to the "innovative leadership" of Suárez in Spain, did not take advantage of these favorable conditions for a transacted transition, see Daniel V. Friedheim, "Innovative Leadership: The Failure to Democratize Pre-revolutionary Portugal" (Yale University, July 1990, mimeo). For early comparisons of the Spanish and Portuguese transitions, see Juan J. Linz, "Some Comparative Thoughts on the Transition to Democracy in Portugal and Spain," in Jorge Braga de Macedo and Simon Serfaty, eds., *Portugal since the Revolution: Economic and Political Perspectives* (Boulder, Colo.: Westview Press, 1981), 25–45.

6. The crisis in the military is shown by the fact that, for the 1971 class at the military academy, there were 550 openings, but only 169 candidates applied to take the admissions test; 103 were admitted. See the massively documented book by María Carrilho, *Forças armadas e mudança política em Portugal no séc. XX: Para uma explicação sociológica do papel dos militares* (Lisbon: Estudos Gerais Série Universitária, 1985), 385. The commissioning of drafted university students infuriated the professional officers, many of whom wanted the colonial wars to end. The professionals were worried that, if they lost the wars, they would receive the same humiliating treatment from the government that had been received by the commanders of the Portuguese garrisons who surrendered in Goa.

7. The classic study is by Philippe C. Schmitter, "Liberation by Golpe: Retrospective Thoughts on the Demise of Authoritarian Rule in Portugal," *Armed Forces and Society* 2 (Nov. 1975):5–33.

viously, when we consult the variables discussed in part 1, the revolutionary process had most to do with our variable "who initiates and controls the transition." The character of those who initiated the transition also introduced strong nondemocratic elements into the variable we called "the constitution-making environment."[8]

In Portugal the transition was started to a great extent by captains. Thus, unlike the Greek case we shall explore next, the Portuguese revolution was not initiated by the state. This made for a crisis of normal military structures and also led to a general crisis of the state. Consistent with our analytical framework, this opened up a period of "interim governments" in which the possibilities for full democratic transition, not to speak of democratic consolidation, were very much in doubt. For a while the junior military, pulled along by extensive mass mobilization in Lisbon and in the South, were in essence in alliance with a Stalinist Communist Party and various revolutionary groups in an effort to transform the country.[9] Between 1974 and 1976 the country lived through a turbulent period of provisional governments and a near disintegrating state. Indeed, Kenneth Maxwell alludes to the fact that, on a number of accounts, Portugal was closer in this period to Nicaragua than it was to any southern European or South American transition.[10]

During the period of revolutionary upheavals, the military became deeply involved in all phases of political activity. After April 1974, the Junta of National Salvation, headed by seven officers, assumed sovereign power, elected a new president from its members, and appointed the government. Another revolutionary organ of the new regime, the Council of State, exercised legislative power until the election of the Constituent Assembly; it was composed of twenty-one members, only five of whom were civilians, all appointed by the military. The last five interim governments were all presided over by military men. Forty of the ninety cabinet positions were held by military officers.[11] In addition, in the course of 1974–75, the military jurisdiction was not only not abolished or restricted, but was extended to cover all "counter-revolutionary" crimes, including those exercised by the mass media. The military gave themselves the power to arrest, to carry out police inquiries, and to submit to military jurisdiction any civilians they deemed were involved in offenses concerning the military.[12] The military assumed unilat-

---

8. See chapter 5 for our discussion of these variables.

9. The high degree of autonomous popular mobilization and land seizures is important to stress and is well documented in Nancy Gina Bermeo, *The Revolution within the Revolution: Workers' Control in Rural Portugal* (Princeton: Princeton University Press, 1986).

10. Kenneth Maxwell, "Regime Overthrow and the Prospects for Democratic Transition in Portugal," in O'Donnell, Schmitter, and Whitehead, *Transitions from Authoritarian Rule: Southern Europe*, 113.

11. All of these figures were obtained from the extremely informative article by José Sánchez Cervelló, "El processo democrático portugués (1974–1975)," in Hipólito de la Torre, ed., *Portugal y España en el cambio político (1958–1978)* (Mérida: Universidad Nacional de Educación a Distancia, Centro Regional de Extremadura, 1989), 155–63.

12. Ibid.

eral control of key foreign policy issues. In the words of one of the most radical military leaders of the provisional government, Vasco Gonçalves, "the MFA was the only, and exclusive, group in charge of decolonialization."[13] The military also took over an important role in the mass media. Their *Bulletin of the MFA* had a circulation of 100,000, and the MFA, through the unit called *Dinamização Cultural*, carried out extensive political mobilization efforts in support of the revolutionary process. Even the winner of the competition to participate in the first European Eurovision Music Festival was an officer.[14]

Given the extraordinary political roles played by a nonhierarchical military, the Moscow-line Communist Party, and popular revolutionary actions, *how*, by our criteria, did Portugal on August 12, 1982, *simultaneously* complete its democratic transition *and* its democratic consolidation?

INTERIM GOVERNMENTS AND ELECTIONS

Theoretically and empirically we believe that the strongest democratic countervailing power to the nondemocratic dynamic of an interim government is free elections with a set date. Only such elections can constitute political society. This is so because elections can (1) create new democratic political actors, (2) fill the newly opened political space with institutions associated with democracy, (3) give a claim of democratic legitimacy to forces that have not necessarily played a role in the destruction of the nondemocratic regime, and (4) provide the first opportunity for all the citizens of the country to render a positive or negative judgment on the provisional government.

The Portuguese case supports this general argument. For reasons that still have to be studied, the initial program of the Armed Forces Movements explicitly committed them to holding Constituent Assembly elections within a year.[15] There was the further additional commitment to elections for a parliament and a president, under a framework to be determined by the Constituent Assembly within another year.[16] Let us remember that there are two options in the writing of new constitutions. One is the election of a constituent assembly with no other function and to which the government would not be accountable, and the other is the election of a regular parliament to which a government will be accountable that will engage in law making at the same time that it drafts and approves a constitution. The first alternative may serve, as it did in Portugal, to delay the formation of a parliament-

---

13. Ibid., 162.

14. Ibid., 162–63. The indispensable chronology that reproduces most of the important decrees, manifestos, and speeches of the 1974–75 revolutionary period is the multivolume series, Henrique Barrilaro Ruas, ed., *A revolução das flores; Do 25 de Abril ao Governo Provisório* (Lisbon: Editorial Aster, n.d.).

15. See article 4 of the "Disposições Constitucionais Transitórias" (May 14, 1974). The entire text is reprinted in Barrilaro Ruas, *A revolução das flores,* 308–14.

16. Ibid., 118.

based government until after the approval of a constitution and new elections. It allows the prolongation of a possibly authoritarian interim government. Another consequence might be that the real political leaders might prefer not to be in the constituent assembly, whose product will therefore be more abstract and theoretical than it probably would have been if it had been the result of compromises between the most powerful leaders interested in being in a legislature or the executive while the constituent assembly meets. In comparison, in Nicaragua the broad coalition supporting the Sandinistas did not demand or get such a clear statement concerning the adoption of a constitution by a democratically elected constituent assembly nor a date for the end of the interim government.

The Portuguese Constituent Assembly elections were held on schedule on April 25, 1975. In these statewide elections, a center-left party, a center-right party, and a conservative party, all of which were in favor of procedural democracy, won 72 percent of the vote. In 1976, in the first free parliamentary elections since the 1920s, these same three parties won 75 percent of the vote and 222 of the 263 seats in the assembly.[17]

The crucial analytical point about interim governments is that, after a long authoritarian period, groups who destroy a nondemocratic regime and who form an interim government can always make the claim that they legitimately represent the wishes and needs of the people. It is virtually impossible to verify or dispute their claim without elections. Elections create new democratic claimants. The monopolistic claims of the leaders of an interim government are thus contested, and an important part of the newly created political space is occupied by actors whose origin is in democratic procedures.

The holding of elections does not mean that the struggle over the democratic or nondemocratic direction of the transition is over. In a highly fluid environment, such as existed in Portugal in 1974–75, free elections meant only that a democratic discourse and democratic power resources had been created to contest the discourse and resources held by the forces associated with the interim government. That these two discourses and power bases can be radically different, even following elections, was made strikingly clear in the remarks made by the leader of the Portuguese Communist Party, Alvaro Cunhal, in an interview with the Italian journalist Oriana Fallacci in 1975: "If you think the Socialist Party with its 40 percent and the Popular Democrats with its 27 percent constitute the majority . . . you're the victim of a misunderstanding. . . . I'm telling you the elections have nothing or very little to do with the dynamics of a revolution. . . . I promise you there will be no parliament in Portugal."[18]

17. On elections, see David B. Goldey, "Elections and the Consolidation of Portuguese Democracy: 1974–1983," *Electoral Studies* 2, no. 3 (Dec. 1983): 229–40, and Thomas C. Bruneau and Alex Macleod, *Politics in Contemporary Portugal: Parties and the Consolidation of Democracy* (Boulder, Colo.: Lynne Rienner Publishers, 1986), esp. chap. 2.

18. Maxwell, "Regime Overthrow and Transition in Portugal," 127.

The Reassertion of Military Hierarchy

Why then did a democratic parliament in fact get established in 1976? Here we must go back to the origins of the revolution in the junior officers. In chapter 5 we advanced the argument that a nonhierarchically led military regime perpetually risks being checked by the assertion of control by the officers associated with the military hierarchy. Here we differ somewhat from the important work of Felipe Agüero. He asserts that, if the previous authoritarian regime is civilianized and the transition is begun by a military coup, the relative power position of the military will be "strong."[19] We believe this is correct only when the coup is led by a hierarchical military. When the coup is led by the nonhierarchical military, they are, as we have argued, always vulnerable to a hierarchical countercoup.

In Portugal, politics during the provisional governments increasingly threatened the military chain of command. In some cases, parallel operational command units were set up which refused to comply with orders from their nominal superiors. Mixed groups of officers and enlisted men occasionally met in debating forums. Finally, the solidarity of the self-proclaimed "motor of the revolution" cracked, and this generated sharp intramilitary conflicts about future policy directions and alliance strategies. As Laurence S. Graham has noted, by late 1975 the political involvement of the Portuguese military had reached a point where the "political alignments on the left, the right, and the center all represented different constellations of civilian and military leaders. Seen in organizational terms, by this point the military as an identifiable institution distinct from civilian society had largely ceased to exist. The pre-revolutionary divisions between the services and within them between officers and enlisted men had disintegrated further into warring factions."[20] Indeed, documentation exists to show that at least three strikingly different political tendencies had emerged within the military by August 1975.[21]

Under these circumstances a group of senior officers concerned with institutional matters of unity and discipline began to form around Colonel Ramalho

19. Felipe Agüero, "The Military and Democracy in South America and Southern Europe: Outcomes and Initial Conditions" (paper presented at the XV International Congress of the Latin American Studies Association, Miami, December 4 to 6, 1989). Also see the important book by Felipe Agüero, *Soldiers, Civilians, and Democracy: Post-Franco Spain in Comparative Perspective* (Baltimore: Johns Hopkins University Press, 1995).

20. Laurence S. Graham, "The Military: Modernization and Changing Perspectives," in Kenneth Maxwell, ed., *Portuguese Defense and Foreign Policy Since Democratization* (New York: Camões Center, Research Institute on International Change, Columbia University, Special Report No. 3, 1991), 16.

21. Three completely incompatible political documents were written by competing military factions in July and August of 1975. See in particular the vanguardist prorevolutionary document issued by a group called COPCON and a democratic socialist document signed by officers explicitly condemning the antidemocratic politics of COPCON in Hipólito de la Torre and Josep Sánchez Cervelló, *Portugal en el siglo XX* (Madrid: Ediciones Istmo, 1992), 325–34. Paul Christopher Manuel, *Uncertain Outcome: The Politics of the Portuguese Transition to Democracy* (Lanham, N.Y.: University Press of America, 1995), gives a detailed and documented account of the politics and factions in the MFA from 1974 to 1976.

Eanes. When an officerless group of paratroopers was involved in what appeared to be a leftist putsch on November 25, 1975, it was put down by Colonel Eanes and backed by a strong political coalition of national and international forces. A long process of the reassertion of hierarchical control within the military as organization had begun. Respecting electoral results became a part of the military hierarchy's own depoliticization strategy. As Maxwell says, "The army, which in 1975 talked of itself as a 'revolutionary vanguard' and a 'movement of national liberation' by 1976 praised 'hierarchy' and 'discipline.'"[22]

CONSTITUTION-MAKING ENVIRONMENT: THE NONDEMOCRATIC CONSTITUTION OF 1976

However, the interlude of interim governments and extremely high involvement of the military in politics had left its legacy, especially concerning the variable we call the *constitution-making environment*. In terms of democratic theory and democratic institutions, the price was that, unlike Spain, the Constituent Assembly was not really "sovereign" and able to draft the constitution its members liked. For the 1975 election to the Constituent Assembly to go forward, the parties bowed to revolutionary military power and signed a formal written pact with the MFA (Armed Forces Movement), agreeing to a supervisory role for the MFA even after the election. A second MFA-political parties pact signed on February 26, 1976, while the Constituent Assembly was in process, further constrained the elected officials.[23]

As a result of these pacts, the 1976 constitution contained some clearly nondemocratic features. The predominantly military Council of the Revolution was given the power to pass their own laws and to judge the constitutionality of all laws passed by the assembly. Article 149, paragraph 3, of the 1976 Portuguese Constitution asserted flatly that "decree-laws of the Council of the Revolution shall have the same validity as laws of the Assembly of the Republic."[24] Article 148 stated that the Council of the Revolution would have the competence to "make laws concerning the organizational functioning, and discipline of the Armed Forces." It also stated that "the powers referred to in . . . the foregoing paragraph shall be vested in the Council of the Revolution alone."[25]

22. Maxwell, "Regime Overthrow and Transition in Portugal," 133.
23. The complete text of the first pact is reprinted in "Plataforma Constitucional Partidos—M.F.A.," in Fernando Ribeiro de Mello, ed., *Dossier 2ª República* (Lisbon: Edições Afrodite, 1976), 1:235–41. The complete text of the second pact is reprinted in "Segundo Pacto dos Partidos com o M.F.A.," in Reinaldo Caldeira and Maria da Céu Silva, *Constituição política da República Portuguesa 1976: Projectos, votações e posições dos partidos* (Lisbon: Livraria Bertrand, 1976), 343–52.
24. This power simply reaffirmed the concessions agreed to in article 3, section 2 of the previously cited "Plataforma Constitucional Partidos—M.F.A."
25. This extraordinary "right" of military self-government had also been "pacted" previously in article 3, section 14, of the "Segundo Pacto dos Partidos com o M.F.A."

As long as the Constitution gave these *de jure* prerogatives to an institution whose power did not derive from democratic procedures, Portugal did not meet our criteria of a completed democratic transition. In addition, the Council of the Revolution *de facto* exercised its *de jure* powers. According to Bruneau and Macleod, "the Council adopted an activist stance which upset many civilian politicians, rejecting no fewer than thirty-five of the seventy-four bills that were submitted to it."[26] In the end it took six years of action by the democratic political parties and the acquiescence and at times active support of President Eanes before a Constitutional Revision of 1982 could occur that abolished the Council of the Revolution and established a legal framework for democratic control of the military.[27]

SIMULTANEOUS TRANSITION COMPLETION AND DEMOCRATIC CONSOLIDATION

Democratic transition and democratic consolidation are normally separate processes that follow each other in temporal sequence. However, under some circumstances they can occur simultaneously. We believe such simultaneity occurred in Portugal on August 12, 1982. Why?

Concerning the *attitudinal* dimension of democratic consolidation, we unfortunately do not have much relevant and/or methodologically sound public opinion data on Portuguese attitudes toward democracy until after 1982, but we believe the surprising stability of party preferences in Portugal from 1975 to 1985 indicates that the vast majority of the voting public consistently expressed a preference for prodemocratic, proregime parties. Based on their study of public opinion and their analysis of voting patterns, Bruneau and Macleod assert that "party loyalty was defined early, in 1975, and continued with very little movement of the voters from one party to another between 1976 and 1983."[28] The "founding election" of 1975 is particularly illustrative in this respect. The 1975 election became a contest between a revolutionary military that campaigned openly for abstention or a null vote and the democratic political parties who urged a high turnout. The military's campaign had virtually no effect. Participation was over 90 percent—one of the very highest participation rates of all the founding elections considered in this book—and only 2 percent more of the voters cast null votes than they had in the 1976 elections, when no one campaigned for null votes.[29]

26. Bruneau and Macleod, *Politics in Contemporary Portugal,* 40.
27. For details of the vote abolishing the Council of the Revolution, see *Facts on File,* 41 (1982): 638, 867. By November 1982 the important Law on National Defense, which specified the institutional details of civilian control, was passed. For this gradual process of civilian empowerment and democratic control, see the valuable accounts contained in Bruneau and Macleod, *Politics in Contemporary Portugal,* 12–25, and Graham, "The Military," 14–28.
28. Bruneau and Macleod, *Politics in Contemporary Portugal,* 40.
29. For details of the founding election of 1975, the best source is Jorge Gaspar and Nuno Vitorino, *As eleições de 25 de Abril: Geografia e imagem dos partidos* (Lisbon: Livros Horizonte, 1976).

Even in the absence of conclusive pre-1982 surveys, this voting pattern supports the argument that, attitudinally, Portugal had crossed our threshold for democratic consolidation by 1982. A public opinion study administered in 1985 in Portugal revealed a public opinion profile not unlike that of other consolidated democracies.[30] In a 1988 poll, 90.2 percent of the population were generally favorable to democracy. Actively supporting democracy were 38.9 percent. Passively accepting democracy were 51.3 percent. Significantly, of the 24.6 percent of the population polled who said they were "dissatisfied" with how democracy had functioned in the last ten years, only 5.1 answered that they were *against,* while 19.1 percent said they were *for,* democracy.[31] By 1990 prodemocratic sentiment in Portugal was above the Western European norm. In answer to the standard Eurobarometer question, "How satisfied are you with the way democracy works?" an average of 62 percent of respondents in the European Community answered "very satisfied" or "satisfied." In Portugal the figure was 71 percent.[32]

Behaviorally we believe that after and perhaps even before 1982 no organization or movement of national importance was spending significant resources to attempt to achieve their goals by nondemocratic means. The authors of an important comparative article on the new southern European democracies give Portugal the same "regime support" rating they gave on this dimension to the consolidated democracies of France, Italy, and Finland.[33]

30. For the 1985 poll and Western and southern European comparisons and analyses, see Leonardo Morlino and José R. Montero, "Legitimacy and Democracy in Southern Europe," in Richard Gunther, P. Nikiforos Diamandouros, and Hans-Jürgen Puhle, eds., *The Politics of Democratic Consolidation: Southern Europe in Comparative Perspective* (Baltimore: Johns Hopkins University Press, 1995), 230–60.

31. These results are reported in Franz-Wilhelm Heimer, Jorge Vala-Salvador, and José Manuel Leite Vargas, "Attitudes toward Democracy in Contemporary Portugal" (paper presented to the European Consortium for Political Research, Paris, April 10–15, 1989). Also see Bruneau and Macleod, *Politics in Contemporary Portugal,* for a comparative analysis of polls administered in 1978 and 1984. For a review of Portuguese public opinion data, also see Mário Bacalhau, "Transition of the Political System and Political Attitudes in Portugal," *International Journal of Public Opinion Research* 2, no. 2 (1990): 141–54.

32. Eurobarometer (1991): 18–31. Indeed, in the 1987 *Eurobarometer,* of all the members of the European Community, only Luxembourg was more content with the way democracy functioned than was Portugal. See Philippe C. Schmitter, "Public Opinion and the 'Quality' of Democracy in Portugal," in H. E. Chehabi and Alfred Stepan, eds., *Politics, Society and Democracy: Comparative Essays* (Boulder, Colo.: Westview Press, 1995), 345–59. In Schmitter's article he calls attention to the quite low percentage of those polled who feel that they could influence the government and to the much higher marks given to the nondemocratic government of Caetano than to any of the democratic governments before 1984. However, Schmitter concludes with the judgment, "From the perspective of normative theory, and even more from that of the exhalted aspirations embodied in the *Movimento do 25 do Abril* and its immediate aftermath, the quality of democracy in contemporary Portugal would have to be judged 'disappointing'. However, from the perspective of the actual practice of democracy in Western Europe and North America, it should be judged 'normal'. This may not seem very exciting, but it is a considerable accomplishment when one reflects back on where the country was prior to the overthrow of authoritarian rule" (pp. 358–59). For the most comprehensive collection and analysis of survey data for the first twenty years of the Portuguese transition, see Mário Balcalhau, *Atitudes, opiniões e comportamentos políticos dos Portugueses: 1973–1993* (Lisbon: Edição Mário Balcalhau-Thomas Bruneau, 1994).

33. Arend Lijphart, Thomas C. Bruneau, P. Nikiforos Diamandouros, and Richard Gunther, "A Mediterranean Model of Democracy? The Southern European Democracies in Comparative Perspective," *West European Politics* 11 (Jan. 1988): 19.

Finally, the *constitutional* dimension in the polity of "reserve domains" of nonaccountable power in the Council of the Revolution were still so great in early 1982 that Portugal had not completed its democratic transition. However, when the military accepted the constitutional changes of August 12, 1982, not only was the transition complete, but attitudinally, behaviorally, and constitutionally democracy was consolidated in Portugal.[34]

We believe that the most salient of our seven variables for analyzing the course of the Portuguese transition and consolidation concerns the characteristics of those who initiated the transition. The fact that the transition began with a liberation by a nonhierarchical golpe rapidly opened up the dynamic of interim governments in which revolution was as much an option as parliamentary democracy. The second most influential variable, the constitution-making environment, is closely related to the first. The extraordinarily powerful role played by the nonhierarchical military (backed by the Portuguese Communist Party and by impressive societal mobilization in the capital and its southern environs) led to a highly constricted constitution-making process. None of the other variables were as salient in the transition and consolidation process. However, all, if understood in their dialectic relationship to other forces, can be seen as ultimately supportive of democratic consolidation.

Unlike the Spanish case or, even more, most post-Communist cases, "stateness" was not a problem because Portugal is virtually as close as any country in Europe to being an ideal typical nation-state. Portugal is a monolingual nation-state whose borders have been fixed for hundreds of years. The only possible irredenta is a town of 25,000 bordering Spain. The only potential stateness problem could have been separatism in the Azores islands, perhaps supported by the United States because of their air bases there, should the Portuguese mainland have become Communist, but this in fact never became a salient issue.

Concerning our variable of international influence, foreign policies were ultimately supportive of democratic transition and consolidation in Portugal. Indeed, they were more *critical* than in the Spanish case and require more research. Though certain knowledge will have to await the opening of archives and more complete memoirs, even at this stage there is some evidence to indicate that the United States was so concerned about the revolutionary dynamic in Portugal that they considered a range of covert and even paramilitary operations.[35] Given the

---

34. A conceptualization of the phases of the Portuguese process from April 25, 1974, until democratic consolidation can be found in an article by António Vítorino, a Socialist Party deputy to the European Parliament, a law professor, and a former member of the Constitutional Court, "A democracia representativa," in Adriano Moreira et al., *Portugal hoje* (Lisbon: Instituto Nacional de Administração, 1995), 328–50. Vítorino writes, "The full consolidation of the democratic political system flowed from the first constitutional revision, approved in 1982, which eliminated the Council of the Revolution, thus leading to the redefinition of the political system [so that] popular suffrage became the only source of public power" (p. 329). This essay provides excellent bibliographical references for the literature on the revision of the consitution.

35. Kenneth Maxwell writes that, "as events in Lisbon turned leftward, for a time U.S. policy, dominated

degree of Portuguese mobilization in 1975, if U.S. covert military operations (as in Guatemala in 1954), instead of elections, had been responsible for defeating the revolutionary forces, it is hard to believe that the ensuing atmosphere would have been conducive to democratic consolidation. However, the European Community urged the United States to follow a political and not a military strategy. Furthermore, the European Socialist parties, especially the West German Socialist Party, by funds, organizational links, and moral support, bolstered the most important democratic party in Portugal, the Socialists led by Mário Soares. Once past the founding election of 1975 and especially the 1976 election that produced a government, the European Community became a valuable and steady pole of attraction for Portuguese democratic governments.[36] Foreign policy relationships between Spain and Portugal during the transition also deserve much more attention than they have received to date. In fact, key politicians in Spain and in Portugal worked hard to avoid Spanish-Portuguese conflicts during the 1974–75 revolutionary process. Surprisingly, Spain, ruled by Franco next door, recognized the revolutionary government in Portugal four days after it took power. The Franco government and the succession of revolutionary interim governments in Portugal made meticulous efforts to maintain correct relations between the countries. In September 1975, after the coming to power in Portugal of the more moderate government of Pinheiro de Azevedo following the fall of the pro-Communist government of Colonel Vasco Gonçalves, an obscure but dangerous situation developed. After the execution by the Spanish state of five revolutionaries convicted of committing political murders, the residences of the Spanish ambassador in Lisbon and the Spanish consulate in Porto were burned. False reports of the movement of Spanish tanks to the Portuguese border were widely circulated in Portugal. By omission or commission, radical Portuguese military factions such as COPCON seem to have been involved in the incidents. Only quick and moderate diplomatic activity by the Portuguese and Spanish governments calmed the crisis.[37]

Though it is not one of our generic variables, we would be remiss if we did not discuss the issue of *mobilization*. There was no significant mobilization before the

---

by Henry Kissinger, abandoned hope for a democratic outcome and toyed with various counter-revolutionary options—some paramilitary, some involving separatism in the Azores." See Maxwell, "Portuguese Defense and Foreign Policy: An Overview," in Maxwell, *Portuguese Defense and Foreign Policy*, 6.

36. Rainer Eisfeld, a German scholar, cites documents concerning aid from the German Social Democratic Party to the Socialist Party in Portugal in his "Portugal and Western Europe," in Kenneth Maxwell, ed., *Portugal in the 1980s: Dilemmas of Democratic Consolidation* (New York: Greenwood Press, 1986), 29–62, esp. 55. Also see Thomas C. Bruneau, *Politics and Nationhood* (New York: Praeger, 1984), 52–54.

37. See the well-researched and well-documented book by Josep Sánchez Cervelló, *A revolução Portuguesa e a sua influencia na transição española (1961–1976)* (Lisbon: Assirio e Alvin, 1993), 353–57. What is still not certain is whether or not the burning of the Spanish diplomatic buildings in Portugal was a deliberate effort by COPCON or others to encourage Spanish intervention, as a way to inflame Portuguese nationalist sentiment and therefore radicalize Portuguese politics, analogous to the radicalization that occurred in Iran after the takeover of the U.S. embassy.

"liberation by golpe."[38] But the immediate mass support in the streets that greeted the liberation certainly helped reduce the chances of a successful counterattack by the supporters of the Salazar-Caetano regime. Within a matter of days the members of the dreaded security forces were in disorganized flight, the state was dissolving, and the most extensive purges of all our cases were under way.[39] However, there was another face of mobilization. If we call a phenomenon where millions of people by their own actions play a role in dictating events a form of mobilization, then the fact that millions of Portuguese citizens refused to answer the call for a null vote in the 1975 election was a critical form of mobilization. By their massive revealed preferences the Portuguese citizens played a critical role.

The last variable to evaluate is the political economy of legitimacy and coercion. Between the incapacitation of Salazar in 1968 and the revolution by golpe in 1974, the Portuguese economy averaged 6.5 percent annual economic growth.[40] Thus, economic crisis per se cannot be said to have contributed to the start of the transition. What did contribute to the start of the transition was that a key part of the coercive apparatus, the military, became convinced that the regime could not solve the colonial wars and that this would create a profound crisis for them. They thus became antiregime. Further, many of the regime-associated politicians who had urged liberalization in the 1960s had, by 1974, become convinced that the regime would not lead the transition. They were thus "available" to support the antiregime actions of the military. Politics, not economics, caused the breakdown of the regime and started the transition.

Let us now consider the role of the economy in democratic consolidation. We have argued that democracy was consolidated in Portugal in October 1982. It is

38. As J. M. Maravall shows, "although workers' strikes had increased before the transition, the explosion of demands followed, rather than preceded, the end of dictatorship. It was democracy that liberated demands. There were seventeen strikes in the first week of democracy, thirty-one in the second, eighty-seven in the third and ninety-three in the fourth week." See Maravall, "Economic Reforms in New Democracies," 6, cited in chap. 6, n. 39.

39. António Costa Pinto, in an excellent article, correctly calls attention to the critical role mobilization played in helping dissolve the coercive apparatus of the old regime. He argues that "the State crisis of legitimacy after the coup and the political and social mobilization following it led to great changes in Portugal's society and economy.... On the first days after the military coup there emerged from Portugal's three main cities a powerful atmosphere of liberation followed by demonstrations. Action preceded legislation: the political prisons were surrounded; the headquarters of the previous single party, the censorship offices and the corporative unions were all occupied.... The pressure of left-wing political movements and the effect of 'liberation' prevented any action from the institutions and the national political elite of the dissolved regime." See Costa Pinto, "Dealing with the Legacy of Authoritarianism: Political Purge and Radical Right Movements in Portugal's Transition to Democracy (1974–1976)," in Stein U. Larsen et al., eds., *Modern Europe after Fascism: 1945–1980's* (Bergen: Norwegian University Press, forthcoming).

40. See Maravall, "Economic Reforms in New Democracies," 2–3. Diana Smith, the *Financial Times* correspondent in Portugal for a decade, states that "between 1972 and 1974 economic growth boomed at over eight percent a year." See Smith, "Portugal and the Challenge of 1992" (New York: Camões Center, Research Institute on International Change, Columbia University, 1990), 6. Due to the colonial wars, however, there was a growing financial crisis of the state as the regime devoted between 30 and 50 percent of its budget to its wars in Africa.

important to stress that, due to the oil shocks, the recession in Europe, the return of an overseas population proportionately five times greater than France had to absorb after Algeria, and the economic disarray in the aftermath of the 1974–75 aborted revolution, the Portuguese economy was in severe straits until well after democratic consolidation.[41] The major stabilization plan of 1983–84 further increased economic hardships for most people. However, on the basis of his extensive polling, Thomas Bruneau documented that there was very little *system blame* of the democratic regime due to this economic decline. Ninety-three percent of the people in a 1984 poll said that there was an economic crisis. But, as Bruneau noted, "the survey then asked the causes for the economic crisis and found that the respondents saw little relationship between it and any particular government; rather it was due to the world economic crisis. None of the responses to the question in the survey gave indications of serious alienation from the present regime."[42] Between 1989 and 1991 Portugal had one of the fastest growing economies in Europe.[43] However, since this economic boom occurred after democracy was consolidated, it is more accurate to say that economic growth strengthened democratic consolidation rather than contributed per se to its initial consolidation. What the Portuguese case reveals clearly is that democracy became consolidated during a period of deep economic hardship but not of political despair or of system blame.

41. As Diana Smith indicates, "By December 1982 Portugal had a budget deficit worth 15 percent of the GDP, a 5.6 billion trade deficit, a 3.2 billion balance-of-payments deficit (the worst in its history, equal to 13.5 percent of GDP) and a foreign debt of 14.5 billion—72 percent of the GDP." Ibid., 9.

42. Thomas C. Bruneau, "Portugal's Unexpected Transition," in Kenneth Maxwell and Michael H. Haltzel, ed., *Portugal: Ancient Country, Young Democracy* (Washington, D.C.: Wilson Center Press, 1990), 15.

43. For the boom of 1986–90, see Smith, "Portugal and the Challenge of 1992." By 1989 budget deficits were down to 4.7 percent of GDP, there was an overall trade surplus of two billion dollars, and for 1989–90 Portugal had the highest economic growth rate of the twenty-four OECD countries. For these and other data, see *Portugal Outlook* 1 (1990): 6–9.

8

Crisis of a Nonhierarchical Military Regime: Greece

A STRONG CASE can be made that the Greek transition began on July 21, 1974, and was concluded on December 9, 1974. This 142-day transition is by far the most rapid in our southern European–South American set.[1] What accounts for the rapidity of the Greek transition?

Much is explained by our variable concerning the institutional base of the Greek authoritarian regime. The 1967 military takeover in Greece occurred via a nonhierarchical colonels' coup led by George Papadopoulos. The nonhierarchical nature of the coup is underscored by the fact that the junior officers in the army purged approximately 400 of their senior officers in 1967.[2] They also staged the coup without the active support of the Navy or the Air Force. Of all the non-democratic regimes whose transition we are studying, the Greek junta had the narrowest base within the state. As Diamandouros states so well, the crown's opposition was "latent from the start, open during the ill-planned and ill-executed countercoup of 13 December 1967, and muted but continuous after that." This "clash between crown and colonels resulted in a sharp split within the Greek officer corps, pitting the vast majority of the Navy officers and a large number of the Air Force counterparts against their army colleagues."[3]

In political society, Diamandouros refers to the "quasi-unanimous refusal of the parliamentary right to cooperate with the military."[4] This contrasts markedly with the military regimes in Brazil and Chile, which for many years received the very strong support of the traditional parliamentary right. Finally, the growing mobilization of civil society had been one of the reasons for the 1967 coup. These mobilizations began to pick up again in 1973 and culminated in the student up-

---

1. Brazil is the longest; the transition there began with the March 16, 1974, inauguration speech of Ernesto Geisel and ended sixteen years later with the inauguration of the first freely and directly elected president.

2. Constantine Danopoulos, "Farewell to the Man on Horseback—Intervention and Civilian Rule in Modern Greece" (paper presented for a conference on democratic consolidation organized by the Centro de la Realidad Contemporánea, Santiago, Chile, August 10–11, 1989), 6.

3. P. Nikiforos Diamandouros, "Regime Change and the Prospects for Democracy in Greece: 1974–1983," in O'Donnell, Schmitter, and Whitehead, *Transitions from Authoritarian Rule: Southern Europe*, 146–47.

4. Ibid., 147.

risings at the National Polytechnic in November. The fact that the army colonels had such a narrow base in the state and political society meant that student uprisings received widespread national and international support, which further isolated and divided the military. This contributed to a hard line coup by Brigadier General Ioannides and those of his supporters within the military police and the lower ranks of the army.[5] But this new military coup only led to even deeper divisions and purges in the officer corps and further accentuated the non-hierarchical base of the regime.

This military fragmentation and politically hostile context made the Greek junta operationally incapable vis-à-vis Turkey and unable to respond adequately to the crisis of Cyprus on July 20, 1974. The crisis was precipitated by the junta's clumsy involvement in a Greek-inspired coup against the government of Cyprus, led by Archibishop Makarios, and the junta's inept military response to the Turkish invasion of Cyprus. It was under these conditions, as Diamondouros succinctly says, that "the Joint Chiefs, invoking the threat of war, reasserted the hierarchical lines of command within the armed forces and effectively neutralized the power base sustaining Ioannides and the *hard-liners*. This move signalled the distancing of the armed forces from the disintegrating regime and made easier the search for a transfer-of-power formula under their initial aegis."[6]

We would like to highlight four key institutional dimensions of the Greek transition that directly relate to our conceptual framework. First, the transfer of power was made by groups acting more as a part of the state than of the regime. Within seventy-two hours of the Turkish invasion of Cyprus, the regime-appointed president, General Ghizikis, backed by the heirarchical military, had deposed the non-hierarchical military and, aided by civilian politicians with contacts in the junta, negotiated the return of the conservative political leader, Constantine Karamanlis. The enthusiastic popular response to Karamanlis' return to Athens further strengthened Karamanlis' hand with the military and led to his rapid swearing in as prime minister.[7] Second, because of the military urgency of immediate extrication from government, the "military as institution" was not able to impose any confining conditions on civilians as a precondition for extrication. Indeed, the Greek scholar and civil-military specialist, Thanos Veremis, argues that the military's incapacity in the face of war increased Karamanlis' bargaining power. The hierarchical military wanted him to assume power immediately, but "a condition of Karamanlis' acceptance of office was a pledge that the armed forces should re-

5. Ibid., 156.

6. Ibid., 157.

7. For a discussion of the exact sequence of events in these seventy-four hours, see P. Nikiforos Diamandouros, "Transition to, and Consolidation of, Democratic Politics in Greece, 1974–1983: A Tentative Assessment," in Geoffrey Pridham, ed., *The New Mediterranean Democracies: Regime Transitions in Spain, Greece and Portugal* (London: Frank Cass, 1984), 53–56. We also owe much to the meticulous attention to detail and sequence in Demitras Pappas, "Greece: July 24–November 17, 1974" (Yale University, 1988, unpublished manuscript).

turn to their former military duties, and desist from further interference in government."[8] Third, this transfer of power by a state institution to a caretaker government precluded a revolutionary "interim government," as in Portugal. Fourth, the hierarchical military, who had been purged by the nonhierarchical military, were called back to active duty and assigned to the top positions in the military chain of command of the new civilian government. Constantine Danopoulos estimates that approximately 75 percent of the senior officers purged in 1967–68 were returned to key positions in 1974.[9] The cumulative effect of these four important dimensions of the Greek transition go a long way to explain why in Greece in 1975 many officers were convicted of crimes and the sentences were not resisted by the "military-as-institution."

In comparative terms we can say that in the Spanish case there were strong initiatives within the *regime* that contributed to the democratization process and the regime was able to carry the *state* with it. In complete contrast, in Portugal, the regime showed weak will and capacity to transform itself, and a nonhierarchical military revolution, which rapidly was supported by mobilization in civil society, destroyed the *regime* and much of the *state*. In Greece the outcome was more controlled because part of the *state* (the hierarchical military) overthrew the *regime* and transferred power immediately to a conservative but prodemocratic government.[10]

We believe that the Greek transition was completed on December 9, 1974, when, as a result of free elections and a referendum that abolished the monarchy on December 8, 1974, Parliament opened and Prime Minister Karamanlis became accountable to Parliament. In the 142-day period between the military stepdown and the opening of Parliament, impediments to full democratic transition were removed. Karamanlis, who had been actively complicitous in the restrictive legislation that had marred Greek politics ever since the Civil War, "specifically put an end to Law 509/1948, the last major piece of civil-war discriminatory legislation."[11] He announced that an elected parliament would revise the Constitution; he restored many civil liberties that had been absent since the Civil War and, most significantly, he ended the proscription of the Communist Party. Thus, when Parliament opened the Greek transition was complete.

The question of when (or for some observers even if) Greek democracy be-

8. Thanos Veremis, "Greece: Veto and Impasse, 1967–1974," in Christopher Clapham and George Philip, eds., *The Political Dilemmas of Military Regimes* (London: Croom Helm, 1985), 41. For civil-military relations during the crisis, see Takis Pappas, "The Making of Party Democracy in Greece" (Ph. D. diss., Department of Sociology, Yale University, 1995).

9. Oral exchange between Stepan and Danopoulos during the discussion after Danopoulos presented his previously cited paper in Santiago, Chile, August 10, 1989.

10. For the formulation and significance of the distinction (often overlooked) between *state* and *regime*, see the important review article by Robert M. Fishman, "Rethinking State and Regime: Southern Europe's Transition to Democracy," *World Politics* 42 (April 1990): 422–40.

11. Diamandouros, "Transition to Democratic Politics in Greece," 60.

came consolidated is more difficult to answer. However, we would argue that, at the very latest, democracy was consolidated when the party of the socialist opposition won the 1981 elections and assumed power.

Constitutionally, largely due to the process we have just examined, the hierarchical military neither insisted on "reserve domains" nor contested the newly elected government's decision to go forward with widespread military trials. In Greece in 1975 many officers were convicted of crimes, the sentences were not resisted by the "military-as-institution," and the successful conclusion of the trials within a year of elections made a positive contribution politically and militarily to democratic consolidation. Thanos Veremis makes the following judgment about Greece:

> No doubt the trials and imprisonment of leading members of the dictatorship, and some of their henchmen, left much to be desired in terms of a clean sweep of the armed forces of Junta sympathizers. Yet governments since 1975 felt no threat from the army nor were they in any way obstructed by it. . . . Officers . . . possibly shaken by the disastrous outcome of military rule, choose to abide by the rules of professionalism which had been the hallmark of officer corps in the West.[12]

The aftermath of the military trials enabled a series of constitutional and legislative reforms that restricted areas of military authority within democratic boundaries. Before 1975 ended, a new constitution had been installed (democratically but, as we shall see, over strong opposition) and there were no laws, procedures, or prerogatives that constrained the sovereignty of democratic politics and procedures. In complete contrast to Portugal, constitutional structures in Greece were the first dimension of democracy to be consolidated.

Behaviorally, especially in terms of the acceptance by all major players of each other's right to contest and, if victorious, to exercise power, the institutions and values of Greek democracy had become the "only game in town" with the 1981 election. We do not say 1974, because even after the election of 1974 the major contestants in democratic politics still had important adjustments to make.

The two most important semiloyal or even nondemocratic groups between the Civil War and the 1967 breakdown had been rightist groups, who normally insisted upon "controlled democracy" in which they would deny citizenship rights to those on the left they deemed "non-nationally minded" and the communist parties, which (especially the pro-Moscow KKE) intermittently committed themselves to nondemocratic oppositional tactics.[13] Even the Pan-hellenic Socialist

---

12. Thanos Veremis, "The Military," in Kevin Featherstone and Dimitrios K. Katsoudas, eds., *Political Change in Greece before and after the Colonels* (London: Croom Helm, 1987), 225. Constantine Danopoulou-los, in his "Farewell to the Man on Horseback," makes similar arguments.

13. On the antidemocratic para-constitutional features of Greek political life before the 1967 breakdown, see P. Nikiforos Diamandouros, "The Politics of Constitution-Making in Postauthoritarian Greece: A Macrohistorical Perspective" (paper presented at the 1987 Annual Meeting of the American Political Science Association).

Movement (PASOK), which had been created by Andreas Papandreou in 1968 after he was released from prison, had antisystem overtones. During the 1974 elections the leading group within PASOK were former members of the resistance organizations. This wing of PASOK was more "maximalist" than the Communists. They deeply distrusted the right and were in turn deeply distrusted by the right.[14] Two key aspects of the new political system were not readily accepted by PASOK and the main Communist Party, the KKE. The major parties of the left were sharply critical of the electoral system, which they argued was constructed to over-represent the largest party in the rapidly held election and to under-represent the opposition. In fact the New Democracy Party, created by Karamanlis and supported by most conservatives, won 54.4 percent of the vote but 73.3 percent of the seats. In sharp contrast, PASOK and the Electoral Alliance of the United Left won 23.1 percent of the vote but only 6.7 percent of the seats.[15] This meant that the New Democracy Party had a large majority with which to structure the constitution in 1975 as they wanted. In fact, New Democracy, in telling contrast to the non-majoritarian government in Spain, devoted very little effort to arriving at a constitutional consensus. Karamanlis used his overwhelming majority to get the constitution he wanted. Only limited concessions were negotiated with the opposition. The opposition in particular objected to strong presidential emergency powers. According to Nikos Alivizatos, the "debate led to a major clash, all opposition parties finally withdrawing from the Assembly in May 1975, denouncing the new Constitution as authoritarian. As a consequence, at the final vote on 9 June 1975, the Constitution was approved only by the New Democracy deputies."[16]

Over the next five years, however, all the major players made substantial adjustments in accepting democratic practices and the specific institutions of Greek democracy. For the 1977 election, PASOK, after advancing a less maximalist and more electorally oriented program, emerged as the major opposition party. New Democracy, in turn, did not continue to abuse their majoritarian prerogatives. New Democracy and PASOK each entered the 1981 election accepting the democratic loyalty of the other party and increasingly arriving at a series of tacit understandings on how democratic parliamentary politics should be conducted.[17]

14. On the political evolution of PASOK and their early maximalism, see P. Nikiforos Diamandouros, "PASOK and State-Society Relations in Postauthoritarian Greece (1974–1988)," in Speros Vryonis, Jr., ed., *Greece on the Road to Democracy: From the Junta to PASOK, 1974–1986* (New Rochelle, N.Y.: Caratzas Publishers, 1991), 15–35. An important work on PASOK is George Th. Mavrogordatos, *Rise of the Greek Sun: The Greek Elections of 1981* (London: Kings' College, Center for Contemporary Greek Studies, 1983, occasional paper 1).

15. See Richard Clogg, *Parties and Elections in Greece: The Search for Legitimacy* (London: C. Hurst and Co., 1987), 60.

16. Nikos Alivizatos, "The Difficulties of 'Rationalization' in a Polarized Political System: The Greek Chamber of Deputies," in Ulrike Liebert and Maurizio Cotta, eds., *Parliament and Democratic Consolidation in Southern Europe* (London: Pinter Publishers, 1990), 134.

17. Alivizatos writes that, "over the years, although not openly admitted, a kind of consensus seems to prevail between PASOK and New Democracy on how the parliamentary game should be played, a consensus which is more amazing if one takes into consideration the apparently incompatible socio-economic projects of the two parties." Ibid., 146.

Table 8.1. Evaluation of Authoritarian Regimes of Greece, Spain, and Portugal

Opinion of the Previous Nondemocratic Regime	Percentage		
	Greece (1985)	Spain (1985)	Portugal (1985)
Only bad	59%	28%	30%
In part good, in part bad	31%	44%	42%
It was good	6%	17%	13%
Don't know/no answer	4%	11%	15%
N	1,998	2,488	2,000

Source: Data from Leonardo Morlino and José Ramón Montero, "Legitimacy and Democracy in Southern Europe," in Richard Gunther, P. Nikiforos Diamandouros, and Hans-Jürgen Puhle, eds., The Politics of Democratic Consolidation: Southern Europe in Comparative Perspective (Baltimore: Johns Hopkins University Press, 1995), 236.

PASOK grew to accept most of the specific electoral and constitutional provisions and was able to get Parliament to make revisions to the constitution in 1986. Both communist parties increasingly eschewed antisystem behavior and attempted to achieve their goals within the framework of a democratic regime. Therefore, one could argue that, behaviorally, democracy was consolidated at the latest in 1981. Indeed, some specialists argue that, behaviorally, it was consolidated as early as 1977.

Attitudinally, the colonels' regime never had the kind of support of a significant segment of the population that the long-term dictatorships of Salazar and Franco (and Pinochet) had, nor did it have any comparable achievements in any area to its credit. Therefore, when democratic alternatives were available the colonels encountered the massive rejection of civil society. The legacy of the colonels' junta presented fewer obstacles to democratic consolidation than any of the southern European or South American cases we consider in our study. Unfortunately, we have public opinion data only since the mid-1980s to confirm this, but those data support our conclusion. We believe that the creation by Karamanlis of a new conservative party called, significantly, New Democracy; the legalization and participation of both communist parties, the pro-Moscow KKE and the Eurocommunist KKI (interior); and the evolutionary changes in PASOK helped create attitudes within these critical party groupings and among their mass following that were strongly supportive of democratic consolidation by 1981. Indeed, when public opinion polls for all of southern Europe became available for the first time in 1985, two points emerged clearly. First, the Greeks had a much more negative opinion about the military dictatorship than the Spanish had of the Franco period or the Portuguese had of the Salazar period. In a poll, two times more Greeks than Spaniards or Portuguese answered that the previous authoritarian regime was "only bad" (table 8.1).

Second, possibly because of the above, Greeks, by a greater percentage than the Spanish or Portuguese, expressed a preference for democracy over authoritarianism (table 8.2). These and subsequent polls by other organizations confirm, in our

Table 8.2. Comparison of Attitudinal Support for Democracy in Greece, Spain, and Portugal (1985)

	Percentage		
Opinion about Preferred Polity	Greece	Spain	Portugal
"Democracy is preferable to any other regime."	87%	70%	61%
"In some cases an authoritarian regime, a dictatorship is preferable."	5%	10%	9%
"For people like me it is all the same."	6%	9%	7%
DK/NA	2%	11%	23%

Source: Data from Leonardo Morlino and José Ramón Montero, "Legitimacy and Democracy in Southern Europe" in Richard Gunther, P. Nikiforos Diamandouros, and Hans-Jürgen Puhle, eds., *The Politics of Democratic Consolidation: Southern Europe in Comparative Perspective* (Baltimore: Johns Hopkins University Press, 1995), 236.

judgment, that, with the change of government in 1981, Greece had become a consolidated democracy.

We will not labor our discussion of all the other variables, but on balance they did not present a major problem for democratic consolidation. The "international influence" variable indeed facilitated democratic consolidation in that the EEC applied both sticks (after the colonel's coup Greece's application was shelved) and carrots (the EEC acted very quickly on the Karamanlis government's membership request and Greece was admitted to the EEC in 1981). Concerning the political economy of legitimacy, as in most of Western Europe, 1975–81 were not good years for the economy, but for Greeks this was less important than the very tangible political gains.

Stateness is a more complex issue. Although Greece is a nation-state, Greece since ancient times has had a major diaspora and in recent times irredentist sentiments have colored much of Greek political life. Nationalist feelings interject themselves more into politics than in Portugal or Spain. The memories of a long struggle for independence, the slow incorporation of territories in different wars, the devastating military defeat suffered by the Greek military in the Greek-Turkish war of 1919–22 (known in Greek history as "*the* catastrophe"), which led to the return of over one million destitute Greek-speakers from the Ottoman diaspora in less than a year, and the Greek state's dependency on international power constellations during the cold war led to an exacerbation of nationalist feelings and politics in Greece. The idea of *Enosis* (unification) with Cyprus, the presence of a Greek minority in Albania, and the sense that Macedonia should not assume a "historic Greek name" are issues in Greek and Balkan politics and reflect the disturbing effect of "irredentist" feelings. This feeling did not prevent the consolidation of democracy by 1981 but contributed to the "quality" problem of Greek democracy to which we now turn.[18]

18. An introduction to the extensive literature on "*the* catastrophe" and nationalist and irredentist politics that complicate Greece's stateness problem can be found in Diamandouros, "Regime Change and the Prospects for Democracy in Greece."

The theme of the *quality* of consolidated democracies is one that is really beyond the scope of this book but cries out for a brief discussion. When we circulated earlier drafts of this book in 1991, colleagues frequently expressed reservations about our calling Greek democracy *consolidated*. They correctly pointed out that former Prime Minister Andreas Papandreau and other leaders of his government were under indictment for corruption, that Greece's budget deficit was the highest in the EEC and that no government of any stripe could bring it under control, that the style of political discourse seemed dangerously acrimonious, and that two general elections in a row (June 1989 and November 1989) had produced hung parliaments. However, the fact that these multiple crises did not lead to a major threat to democratic institutions could in our judgment also be interpreted as a sign of democratic consolidation. We believe that it is more accurate to see the above problems as indicative of the poor quality of a consolidated democracy.[19] Within the category of consolidated democracy some democracies deepen and some do not. Some are of relatively high quality and some are of relatively low quality. We consider Greek democracy to be of relatively low quality, and low quality democracies have fewer degrees of freedom than those of high quality and might breakdown more easily. This said, it is probably useful to point out that, despite these problems, Greek democracy has displayed some impressive qualities of flexibility and adaptability.

The "historical memory" of the civil war has now become more like that in Spain (and completely unlike the historical memory of the World War II civil wars between Croatians and Serbians). Significantly, in a public opinion poll, the largest single group (41 percent) blamed *both* the Communists and the government forces for the civil war, and the next largest group (32 percent) did not even offer an opinion.[20] Despite the acrimonious party partisanship of public debate, citizens in private show an increasing propensity to say that they would consider voting for a party of the opposite camp in the future. This indicates that there is less "cultural difference" between the parties and that the realm of democratically acceptable alternatives is broadening.[21]

Finally, we consider the fact of two hung parliaments of less significance than the processes by which political parties responded to their common problem.

19. For the debate in Greece about whether the 1980s was a "lost decade" and a good discussion of the "quality of democracy" problem, see P. Nikiforos Diamandouros, "Politics and Culture, 1974–91: An Interpretation," in Richard Clogg, ed., *Greece, 1981–1989: The Populist Decade* (New York: St. Martin's Press, 1993), 1–25.

20. See the interesting review of Greek public opinion polls by Panayote Elias Dimitras, "Greek Public Attitudes: Continuity and Change," *International Journal of Public Opinion Research* 2 (Summer 1990): 92–115, esp. 103.

21. For example, in the 1985 election in greater Athens the Communist parties won 17 percent of the vote but 30 percent of those polled said they might consider voting for such parties in the future. In 1989 the figures were 15 percent and 44 percent respectively. Both PASOK and New Democracy experienced a similar (but less dramatic) increase in voters who considered themselves willing to consider voting for them in the future. Ibid., 99.

After the indecisive election of June 1989, from June until November 1989, the two "descendents" of the warring sides of the 1946–49 civil war, the pro-Moscow Communist Party and the New Democracy, formed a coalition government. This coalition would have been unthinkable at the start of the transition in 1974. Indeed, if 1949 can be seen as the military end of the Greek civil war and the election of 1974 as the political end, then the 1989 Communist–New Democracy coalition was the cultural end of the civil war. When the November 1989 elections again failed to produce a winner, extensive inter- and intraparty negotiations produced an all-party government that ruled until the April 1990 election that yielded a slender majority for New Democracy.[22]

Despite the very real "quality problems" of Greek democracy, if democracy ever breaks down in Greece, in our judgment it will not be because Greek democracy was never consolidated but because democratic politicians respond to problems in ways that actively exacerbate the crisis. The way to avoid and to analyze any possible crisis of Greek democracy has less to do with the theory and praxis of democratic transition and consolidation than with the theory and praxis of "breakdown."[23]

---

22. Diamandouros, "Politics and Culture." An interesting indicator of the increasing capacity of civil society to attempt to solve problems is that, in the face of the growing fiscal crisis of the state, the two peak organizations, the Greek Federation of Industries and the General Confederation of Greek Workers, signed a broad-ranging two-year collective bargaining agreement in 1990.

23. We are alluding here to patterns that were analyzed in Juan J. Linz and Alfred Stepan, eds., *The Breakdown of Democratic Regimes* (Baltimore: Johns Hopkins University Press, 1978).

9

Southern Europe: Concluding Reflections

WE ARE NOW in a position to summarize our conclusions about southern Europe. Some of them are no doubt obvious, yet it is clear that, taking the entire range of democratic transitions and democratic consolidations in the world, these southern European cases occurred within a relatively limited range of possible initial conditions.

— No southern European transition had a sultanistic origin.

— No southern European transition had a totalitarian or post-totalitarian origin.

— No southern European transition began from an authoritarian regime led by the hierarchical military.

— No southern European transition began from a base of a strong single authoritarian party.

Cumulatively, this means that many of the most salient initial confining conditions present in other parts of the world were absent in southern Europe.

Another major point that we would like to stress concerns *sequence*. The southern European countries were structurally able and consciously chose to concentrate first on politics, second on social welfare policies, and only later on structural economic reforms. We consider this the optimal sequence if it is at all possible. Democracy in any given country entails understandings concerning decision-rules, the creation of institutional arrangements, the removal of barriers to participation, the indispensable element of elections, and the creation of political society. Ideally socioeconomic policies are produced by and flow out of this setting.

In an era when "state-shrinking" is advanced as an imperative for the struggling new democracies of Latin America and post-Communist Europe, we want to record a cautionary historical note. *All* three of the southern European new democracies strengthened their states by increasing tax revenues. *All* used this revenue to increase significantly social welfare expenditures and state employment (table 9.1).

All three southern European countries also became consolidated *before* their economies improved and even before economic restructuring began. Spain did

Table 9.1. Increases of Tax Revenue, Public Expenditures, and Public Employment: Spain, Portugal, and Greece (1976, 1984, 1988)

	Percentage of Gross Domestic Product								
	Spain			Portugal			Greece		
Revenue and Expenditure	1976	1984	1988	1976	1984	1988	1976	1984	1988
Revenue from taxes	25.0	33.2	36.7	31.0	34.6	36.6	29.2	34.2	35.9
Total public expenditure	26.0	38.7	41.7	37.3	41.6	43.7	20.9	44.2	51.3
Public employment expenditure	8.5	12.8	13.8	8.8	13.3	13.8	8.5	9.4	10.1

Source: Data from José María Maravall, "Politics and Policy: Economic Reforms in Southern Europe," in Luiz Carlos Bresser Pereira, José María Maravall, and Adam Przeworski, *Economic Reforms in New Democracies: A Social Democratic Approach* (New York: Cambridge University Press, 1993), table 2.4, p. 103.

not begin major structural economic reform until 1982, Portugal until 1985, and Greece's first unsuccessful effort was in 1985–87.[1] As a corollary of the above, in the critical period between elected governments assuming office and democratic consolidation, in *none* of the southern European countries were issues concerning the design or functioning of the economy as salient as debates about the design and functioning of political power.

Stateness was never a problem for democratic transition and consolidation in Portugal. In Greece stateness was also not a significant problem during the period of its democratic transition and consolidation but has emerged as a problem in the 1990s as Greek nationalism became intertwined with Balkan, especially Macedonian, politics. Stateness could have caused a breakdown of the Spanish transition, but the success of Spanish leaders in handling the transformation of the unitary state into the multilingual and multinational *estado de las autonomías* shows that even new democracies can deal with such problems.

A word about the international environment is also in order. All three countries opted to try to join the European Economic community and to live by the norms of the community. All became full members, but only after their democratic consolidation. The Treaty of Rome's procedures provide for subsidies to the poorest regions within the community. These provisions eventually generated substantial subsidies to Greece, Spain, and Portugal. After thinking about the relationship of these three new democracies to the EEC, we agree with Laurence Whitehead's conclusions that the community itself had set up a stable pattern of rewards and incentives, that the community had a deep and abiding concern with

1. This comes through clearly in José María Maravall, "Politics and Policy: Economic Reforms in Southern Europe," in Luiz Bresser Pereira, José María Maravall, and Adam Przeworski, *Economic Reforms in New Democracies: A Social Democratic Approach* (New York: Cambridge University Press, 1993), 77–131. Also see the important work by José María Maravall, *Los resultados de la democracia. Un estudio del sur y el este de Europa* (Madrid: Alianza Editorial, 1995).

consolidating democracy in its immediate region, and that the prospect of membership in the European Community "produced a substantial long-term pressure for democratization."[2]

Finally, we believe that the specific contribution of political institutions deserves more attention than it has received in the democratic transitions and consolidation literature. Specifically, we believe that the southern European choice of parliamentary or semipresidential (which have turned increasingly parliamentary) constitutional frameworks gave them greater degrees of freedom than if they had chosen U.S.-style presidentialism as their constitutional framework. The fact that no new democracy in southern Europe chose the U.S. style of presidentialism in our judgment increased their degrees of freedom. In Spain, parliamentarianism allowed Suárez, when he had exhausted his support, to step down; it allowed his successor, Calvo Sotelo, to lead the efforts to jail the coup-makers, and it allowed the early calling of elections, which led to the Socialists assuming power. In Greece, the parliamentary framework allowed the formal coalition of New Democracy and the Communists. In Portugal, the semipresidential framework allowed a military president and an increasingly powerful civilian prime minister to coexist, although what are called the three "presidential cabinets" generated considerable tension. None of this would have been possible in a pure presidential system.

The general empirical and theoretical argument in favor of parliamentarianism as a constitutional framework that favors democratic consolidation can be advanced further. Of the forty-one countries in the world that experienced uninterrupted democracies for ten consecutive years between 1981 and 1990, thirty were pure parliamentary systems and only four of them were pure presidential systems. Of the ninety-three countries in the world that became independent between 1945 and 1979, only fifteen were uninterrupted democracies in the 1980–89 period, but *all* began as parliamentary democracies. We do not believe that these numbers occur by chance.[3] We have argued elsewhere that the parliamentary organizational form gives the political system significant advantages over presidentialism in terms of three capacities useful for democratic consolidation: efficacy, the capacity to construct majorities, and the ability to terminate a crisis of gov-

2. Laurence Whitehead, "International Aspects of Democratization," in O'Donnell, Schmitter, and Whitehead, eds., *Transitions from Authoritarian Rule: Comparative Perspectives*, 23. By the mid-1990s some of the European Union's rules generated substantial bitterness and protest, particularly among Spanish fishermen, farmers, and cattle-raisers.

3. The breakdown of the ninety-three countries as to their initial constitutional framework and their later democratic consolidation is as follows. In the universe of ninety-three countries, thirteen began their independence as ruling monarchies, three as semipresidential systems, thirty-six as presidential systems, and forty-one as parliamentary systems. The results of a Pearson's chi-squared test of the complete data by Stepan and Cindy Skach allowed them to reject the null hypothesis that the above distribution is random. The chances of observing this distribution randomly are less than one in a thousand. These and other data are presented and analyzed in Stepan and Skach, "Constitutional Frameworks and Democratic Consolidation: Parliamentarianism versus Presidentialism," *World Politics* 45 (October 1993), 1–22, esp. 5–15.

Table 9.2. Respondents Affirming That "Democracy is Preferable to Any Other Form of Government" in Spain, Portugal, and Greece and Compared with Average of European Union States, 1992 (Legitimacy Indicator)

Respondent's Location	Percentage
Spain	78%
Portugal	83%
Greece	90%
European Union Average	78%

Source: Data from *Eurobarometer,* 37 (1992).

ernment without it becoming a crisis of the regime.[4] Spain and Greece are purely parliamentary systems. Portugal is a semipresidential system but since 1988 has increasingly functioned as a parliamentary system.[5] No new Latin American, Asian, or post-Communist democracy (with the exception of Hungary) initially selected and crafted a pure parliamentary form. Czechoslovakia was close, but neither the prime minister nor the president could dissolve the Parliament and call for new elections. As of 1995 it is perhaps no accident that Hungary, the Czech Republic (where the president is indirectly elected), and Slovenia, (which has a directly elected president with few powers) should be closer to consolidation than any post-communist country with a directly elected president with significant powers. We believe that the arguments in favor of parliamentarianism as an institutional framework that facilitates democratic consolidation deserve more serious consideration by practicioners and theorists alike.

Finally, how do citizens' opinions about the legitimacy and efficacy of the new democracies of southern Europe compare with the rest of the states in the European Union? The answer is quite well (tables 9.2 and 9.3).

In summation, all southern European countries are democratically consolidated, no consolidation took longer than eight years, and the new southern European democracies are becoming increasingly comparable in their political patterns to other West European parliamentary democracies.[6] Although the three

4. See Linz, "Excursus on Presidential and Parliamentary Democracy," in Juan J. Linz and Alfred Stepan, eds., *The Breakdown of Democratic Regimes* (Baltimore: Johns Hopkins University Press, 1978), 71–74, and Linz, "Presidential or Parliamentary Democracy: Does It Make a Difference?" in Juan J. Linz and Arturo Valenzuela, eds., *The Failure of Presidential Democracy: Comparative Perspectives* (Baltimore: Johns Hopkins University Press, 1994), 3–87, and Alfred Stepan, "Parliamentarismo X Presidencialismo no mundo moderno: Revisão de um debate atual," *Estudos Avançados* (São Paulo, Janeiro/Abril 1990): 96–107.

5. Spain, as a constitutional monarchy, never had any semipresidential features. In Greece there was much talk about adopting a Fifth Republic style semipresidentialism but legislation providing for the direct election of the president was never passed and the strong presidential prerogatives provided in the 1975 constitution were weakened significantly by constitutional changes introduced by the Socialists after they came to power in 1981. Portugal in 1995 is still semiparliamentary in form but after 1982 the president's powers were weakened by constitutional changes. Political practice became even more parliamentary once the first civilian, who also happened to be a former prime minister, assumed that office in 1986.

6. This is the central argument of the previously cited article by Lijphart, Bruneau, Diamandouros, and Gunther, "A Mediterranean Model of Democracy?"

Table 9.3. Respondents Who Are "Very Satisfied" or "Fairly Satisfied with the Way Democracy Works" in Spain, Portugal, and Greece Compared with Average of European Union States, 1985–1993 (Efficacy Indicator)

Respondent's Location	Percentage				
	1985	1987	1989	1991	1993
Spain	51	55	60	57	40
Portugal	34	70	60	75	51
Greece	51	49	52	34	39
European Union	49	51	57	50	43

Source: Eurobarometer Trend Variables, 1974–1993 (May 1994).

southern European democratic consolidations seem today to have been accomplished relatively easily, one should not forget that the Spanish and Portuguese transitions began only after extremely long periods of nondemocratic rule and that, in Greece, postwar democracy was questioned by many Greeks, given the legacies of the civil war. Furthermore, all of the southern European transitions started at the beginning of the "third wave" of democratizations and could not benefit from the lessons of other countries.[7]

EXCURSUS ON WHY NEGATIVE EVALUATION OF THE PAST NONDEMOCRATIC REGIME IS NOT A REQUIREMENT FOR DEMOCRATIC CONSOLIDATION

Now that we have finished our analysis of democratic consolidation in what once were Western Europe's two longest standing nondemocratic polities, Portugal and Spain, we would like to address a conceptual point that frequently emerges in the democratization literature. There are students of the transition and consolidation of new democracies who link both processes with the rejection and negative evaluation of the preceding nondemocratic regime. It is even argued that such a rejection is necessary for democratic consolidation, and sometimes rankings of the quality of new democracies include indicators of the evaluation of the previous nondemocratic regime. We reject such arguments on conceptual, historical, and empirical grounds.

Conceptually, we reject such arguments because our definition of consolidation is present and future oriented. Thus, a key indicator for us is whether or not a strong majority of the citizens is in agreement with such phrases as "for a country like ours democracy is better than any other alternative." Analytically, a positive attitude toward democracy as the best alternative for now, and the future does

7. For Samuel P. Huntington, the "third wave" of democratization in the world (1974–) began with Portugal. See Huntington, *The Third Wave: Democratization in the Twentieth Century* (Norman: Oklahoma University Press, 1991), chap. 1.

not require a negative attitude toward the past. People can make an independent evaluation and affirm that the preceding regime had achievements or a least was not all bad and still support democracy as their preferred form of government.

Historically, we reject such arguments because in our judgment the overwhelming majority of consolidated democracies did not actually begin their transition to democracy with a majority of members of the polity or even many of the key agents of the transition being either convinced democrats or citizens who rejected everything about the past regime. Rather, a democratic majority emerges when elites and ordinary citizens alike begin to evaluate, for the societal problems they *then* face and the overall world within which they then live, that democratic procedures of conflict regulation are better or less dangerous than any other form of governance. Thus, for many key elites democratic *behavior* emerges before democratic *attitudes* because elites may make the calculation that breaking the democratic rules of the game—whether they like them or not—will not yield a positive outcome for their interests. Democracy becomes the "only game in town" partly by belief and partly by elite calculation of the cost of compliance versus the cost of mobilization for other governing alternatives.

Empirically, we reject such arguments because for recent transitions we have conclusive documentation showing that it is possible for democracy to become consolidated while only a minority of the public completely rejects the past. Proof of this is that, in 1985 in Portugal and Spain, when according to our criteria democracy had already been consolidated in both countries, less than 30 percent of those polled said that the Franco or Salazar regimes were "only bad," but a strong majority said that "democracy is preferable to any other regime" (table 9.4).

Table 9.4 shows that, if we combine the answers that the Franco regime "was good" and was "in part good, in part bad," of those polled in 1985 61 percent in Spain and 57 percent in Portugal did not completely reject the past and indeed felt that it had some good qualities. In the same poll, however, 70 percent of respondents in Spain and 61 percent in Portugal also answered that "democracy is preferable to any other regime." The first answer was an assessment of the past; the second was a statement of preference for the present and future. The two answers were not incompatible.[8] By 1992 in Portugal, 83 percent of respondents (compared to 61 percent in 1985) preferred democracy to any other regime. The increase in support for democracy was partly due to the fact that people who refused to answer or who said "don't know" had dropped from 23 percent in 1985

8. Indeed, analysis of a 1978 Spanish poll shows that, of the respondents who answered both a question about Franco and a question about democracy, 83.5 percent said that "democracy is the best political system for a country like ours." Of these, only 28.1 percent totally disapproved of "the actions of Franco," and 23.2 percent said there were "many errors that could have been avoided," whereas 32.0 percent approved Franco's action in some form (5.9 percent "totally approved," 15.6 thought the actions were "in general good," and 10.5 felt that they were "mediocre without too many mistakes"). See Juan J. Linz, "El legado de Franco y la democracia," in Juan J. Linz et al., *Informe sociológico sobre el cambio político en España, 1975–1981* (Madrid: Euramérica, 1981), 587–618.

Table 9.4. The Compatibility of a Strong Affirmation of the Desirability of a Democratic Present and Future with a Weak Rejection of the Nondemocratic Past: Spain and Portugal

	Percentage of Respondents			
	Spain		Portugal	
Survey Response	1985	1992	1985	1992
Strong Affirmation of Democracy as Preferred Polity				
"Democracy is preferable to any other regime."	70	78	61	83
"In some cases an authoritarian regime, a dictatorship is preferable."	10	9	9	9
"For people like me it is all the same."	9	7	7	4
"Don't know/no answer"	11	6	23	4
Opinion of the Previous Nondemocratic Regime				
"It was good."	17		13	
"In part good, in part bad"	44		44	
"Only bad"	29		29	
Don't know/no answer"	10		14	
N	(2,488)		(2,000)	

Source: For 1985 data the source is the same as for tables 8.1 and 8.2. The 1992 data are from the *Eurobarometer* 37 (1992).

to only 4 percent in 1992. We do not have data, but we doubt that there was a significant movement in Portugal toward assessing the past as "only bad."

Let us speculate about what sort of psychological and historical processes can combine to allow individuals simultaneously to assess the nondemocratic past as not all bad and still prefer a democratic regime in the present and future. The evaluation of any regime involves a wide range of criteria, dimensions, and experiences of the members of a society, and it would be unrealistic to assume that people who have lived under a nondemocratic regime for decades, who have made their lives in it, and who have seen their success in life linked with participation in the regime's institutions should suddenly reject everything about the regime. In addition, some nondemocratic regimes (Taiwan and South Korea in the 1980s, Spain in the 1960s and early 1970s, Hungary for the middle part of the Kádár period) have to their credit considerable achievements in one or another realm of societal life—achievements that it would be foolish for an objective observer to deny, that reasonable people know were there, and that only ideological rigidity and blindess might deny. That does not mean that the same people will not (correctly) perceive the negative dimensions of the previous regime, which might have affected them or about which they may be knowledgeable. It would be difficult to conceive a society, especially in such regimes as we mentioned above, in which large numbers of people would have only negative or positive experiences, especially if the regime had experienced a prolonged evolution and sometimes a deliberate liberalization process that allowed many people to pursue their own lives within the limits established by the regime. Indeed, more specific questions than are normally asked in surveys show a large number of people saying bad things about certain aspects of the regime, such as the amount of oppression and the limits of freedom, while at the same time many people note positive aspects of the regime, as in the area of economic and social development.[9]

There is a story of a Spanish exile who returned after many years to Franco's Spain, was impressed with the positive changes in Spanish society associated with economic development that made it so different from the one before the civil war, and asked the question, "Was I on the wrong side fighting in the war when all this would be achieved under Franco?" One answer was that much of what he saw as positive would have been achieved under any regime in the European context in the 1950s and 1960s, and it might have been achieved even earlier if the regime had not been there. But why and how it was achieved is not what people think of when they evaluate the performance of the past regime.

Does the simple fact that many people may have some positive assessments of the past constitute an obstacle to their positive commitment to a new democratic regime? The empirical data show that this is not the case. People who do not have a negative opinion of the previous regime, particularly those who have a mixed opinion ("in part good, in part bad"), can be fully supportive of a new democratic regime. Such people's evaluations are based on the added positive dimensions that democracy brings to political life and to the society and, above all, to their basically positive response to the values associated with freedom, participation, control of who shall govern, accountability of those in power, and a certain certitude about political processes. Let us not forget that one of the great worries of people under nondemocratic regimes, particularly when it is personalized, is what will happen when the ruler dies. All maximum leaders disappear from the scene. Thus, all Spaniards lived under Franco with an uneasy feeling that sooner or later the country would have to face the fact that Franco would die and that then new decisions would have to be made for which there were no clear rules and which opened doors to incertitude and possibly even violent conflict. With all the incertitude that Adam Przeworski has correctly emphasized as characterizing democracy, one of democracy's characteristics is also that there are predictable mechanisms by which to change governments and to adapt to a changing society. In democracies there is a constitutional framework, guaranteed by many rules and procedures, that limits the unpredictability of political change and guarantees rights to individuals and groups as no nondemocratic regime can effectively do.

The underlying assumption of linking the consolidation of democracy to the overall negative evaluation of the previous regime often starts from the mistaken idea that such nondemocratic regimes never had much support except from small, privileged, and oppressive minorities. Some people think that, in southern Europe and South America, right-wing authoritarian regimes were supported only by large land owners, the bishops, the generals, the bankers, and a minority

9. Ibid.

of ideological activists, forgetting that there were many nonelites who might have seen their future positively affected by the previous regime.

The same is true for the former Communist societies. "Real existing socialism" created interests and constituencies. Many people were upwardly mobile by conformity with the regime; got fellowships for higher education, medals for their sports achievements, funds for their cultural activities, and careers in the nomenklatura; became successful plant managers, and what not. Those people, whatever their feelings about the ultimate desirability of the regime, their hostility to its Soviet dependence when they were nationalist, and their displeasure about the many small, bureaucratic chicaneries, cannot deny that they had a moderately good life and sometimes even a fairly good life and that the changes that are happening in their societies endanger those achievements. What is most disturbing for many of the old supporters of the nondemocratic regime is that new democrats often deny their personal legitimacy by assuming that, if they had been successful in the past regime, they must have been evil.

Once again we stress our point that most democracies must *craft* a majority of convinced democrats. To insist that only people with impeccable democratic opposition credentials can be loyal democrats may actually weaken democracy.

We are interested in attitudes toward the past regime but only in a nuanced way. For example, in Greece many more people than in Spain or Portugal evaluate the previous nondemocratic regime as "only bad." But we do not believe that this necessarily makes Greeks more convinced democrats than Spaniards or Portuguese. We see the Greek survey results as a correct empirical statement that the short regime of the colonels had no significant achievements to its credit and much to its discredit. What *is* true, however, is that the intense rejection of the Greek dictatorship facilitated punishment of the previous leaders of the military regime for human rights offences. As we shall see, the case of Chile is like those of Spain and Portugal in one respect, that a relatively high degree of people believe that the nondemocratic regime was "in part good and in part bad." The key difference that we will document later is that a disturbing number of Chilean respondents support a continued role in the *present* of some of the nondemocratic institutions created by the Pinochet regime. In this respect Chile is fundamentally different from Spain or Portugal. As will also become apparent later, citizens in most Central European post-Communist countries are able to make complex and independent judgments about the past and the present. Overwhelmingly, respondents in Central Europe (but not in the former Soviet Union) five years after the collapse of Communism simultaneously said that the economy was better under the Communist regime but that the political system was better under the new democratizing regime. Thus, they were able to differentiate between an "economic basket of goods" and a "political basket of goods," between a past that for them as individuals was not all bad and a different political future they aspired to even though they knew they would lose elements of the past they valued.

Part III

South America:
Constrained Transitions

Like the three southern European countries we have considered, none of the four Latin American countries in our set (Brazil, Uruguay, Argentina, and Chile—hereafter referred to as the Southern Cone countries) began from a base of a sultanistic regime, a post-totalitarian regime, or a strong civilianized authoritarian party regime. However, while *none* of the new southern European democracies began from a base of a hierarchical military regime, *all* of the Southern Cone transitions were preceded by a hierarchically controlled military regime. In our opening conceptual discussion we asserted that such a military, unless eliminated by foreign powers or by revolution, would still be a permanent part of the state apparatus during and after the transition and thus an integral part of the machinery that the new democratic government must attempt to manage. We further stated that "the more hierarchically led the military, the less it is being forced to extricate due to internal contradictions, and the weaker the coalition that is forcing them from office, the more the military will be in a position to negotiate their withdrawal on terms where they retain nondemocratic prerogatives or impose very confining conditions on the political processes that should lead to democratic consolidation."

To what extent are these general propositions borne out in the four Southern Cone countries? Further, to what extent did the variable of a hierarchical military, taken by itself, complicate the task of democratic consolidation when we compare the Southern Cone countries to those of southern Europe?

In part 3 we demonstrate that the transitions in all four countries were indeed immensely constrained by hierarchical militaries. However, we will also show that great variation exists within our four countries. In Chile, despite the most favorable economic conditions, to this day military prerogatives are so great that the democratic government will probably not meet our perhaps demanding definition of a completed transition until the end of the 1990s. Uruguay, on the other hand, despite continuing economic problems, has become the only country in our South America set to become consolidated but has such problems of governance (especially efficacy) that we consider it a "risk-prone" consolidated democracy. Until things began to improve in mid-1994, Brazil was further from consolidation in 1992–94 than it was in 1985, at the end of direct military rule. Argentina was in a dangerous state of regime decomposition and military recomposition during the last few years of the first democratically elected government under Alfonsín but reversed both these processes under Menem, yet certain aspects of the role of Menem make us reluctant to consider Argentina a consolidated democracy. Obviously, to explain such variation among these countries we will have to explore other variables besides their common origins in hierarchically controlled military regimes, especially that of the political economy of legitimacy. The arenas of political society and the rule of law also bear extensive analysis due to their very different quality in the four countries.

10

A Risk-Prone Consolidated
Democracy: Uruguay

Our task in this chapter is twofold. First, we will develop the no doubt controversial argument that Uruguay is a consolidated democracy and will assess what conditions enabled it to become the only one of the four former "bureaucratic-authoritarian" regimes of South America to attain this status.[1] Second, we will explain why we judge Uruguay, like Greece, to be risk-prone, and why the question of risk-proneness is better analyzed by the literature and politics on the breakdown of democracies than by the literature and politics of the "transitions to democracy."[2]

Conceptually, Uruguay conforms very closely to our theoretical framework. Uruguay was an authoritarian regime from 1973 to 1985, always dominated de facto by the military and ruled de jure by a hierarchically led military from 1976 until a united military organization handed over power to a democratically elected president in 1985.[3] Consistent with our analysis, the fact that the military remained in office throughout the transition ruled out a provisional government.

In our framework we also argued that hierarchically led military authoritarian regimes normally present a potential advantage for transition (the military-as-institution may come to believe that their interests are best served by an extrication from the military-as-government) but a potential obstacle for democratic consolidation (the military-as-institution, as the price of extrication, may be able

1. For the concept of a "bureaucratic-authoritarian" regime, see Guillermo O'Donnell, *Modernization and Bureaucratic-Authoritarianism: Studies in South American Politics* (Berkeley: Institute of International Studies, University of California, 1973), and David Collier, ed., *The New Authoritarianism in Latin America* (Princeton: Princeton University Press, 1979).

2. That is, it would be better analyzed by using the framework found in Juan J. Linz and Alfred Stepan, eds., *The Breakdown of Democratic Regimes* (Baltimore: Johns Hopkins University Press, 1978) than by classics of the transition literature such as the four-volume study of O'Donnell, Schmitter, and Whitehead, *Transitions from Authoritarian Rule.*

3. We will be quite schematic with our analysis of Uruguay because readers interested in the details of the Uruguayan transition and the problems it presented for consolidation have two excellent recent monographs dedicated precisely to these issues. We refer to Charles Guy Gillespie, *Negotiating Democracy: Politicians and Generals in Uruguay* (Cambridge: Cambridge University Press, 1991), and Luis E. González, *Political Structures and Democracy in Uruguay* (Notre Dame: University of Notre Dame Press, 1991). We were fortunate to work with both of these talented scholars when they wrote these dissertation books at Yale University.

to impose strong constraints on the incoming democratic government). Uruguay illustrates both of these predicted tendencies.

Why did a democratic transition start? What caused the division between the military-as-institution and the military-as-government? Initially, from 1978 to 1980, there were few military officers in Uruguay who favored a return to liberal democracy, but also few who were ready to attempt to institutionalize an authoritarian regime. In terms of systematic repression (but not deaths), Uruguay was the most deeply repressive of the four South American bureaucratic-authoritarian regimes.[4] Civil society and political society were also less powerful loci of resistance than in Brazil or Chile. Nonetheless, in the twentieth century, the Uruguayan military had never directly ruled, the country had lived more years under democratic regimes than any other country in Latin America, and the two traditional catch-all parties (the Colorados and the Blancos) had never received less than 75 percent of the total vote in any presidential election. Uruguayan voters, even by West European standards, had a tradition of high party identification and a clear sense of a left-right index.[5] Most military officers also identified with one of Uruguay's two traditional party "families."

This context helps to explain why, although the military repressed political parties, they did not dare try to displace them. Indeed, in 1976, when they finally overthrew the civilian figurehead president, they were at pains to issue a declaration that they did not "want to share historical responsibility for abolishing the parties" and that "sovereignty resides in the nation . . . as expressed . . . in the popular vote."[6] By 1977 the military announced that they would draw up a new constitution for "strengthening democracy." The new constitution would be submitted to a plebiscite in 1980 and, if ratified, elections with a single presidential candidate, nominated by the two traditional parties and approved by the military, would be held in 1981.

The democratic transition in Uruguay began when, to the surprise of most observers, but especially the military, the democratic opposition won the plebiscite. Legitimacy and power relationships began to change immediately. As we saw in Portugal, elections refute or reinforce legitimacy claims of power contestants. For some prominent military officers, the results of the plebiscite weakened their belief in their right to rule. Indeed, the transcripts of the constitutional working group that met the day after the plebiscite reveal that some of the top military of-

---

4. For example, Amnesty International estimates that Uruguayan citizens were jailed during the early years of the regime at a ratio of 1 per 600 citizens; the corresponding ratios for Argentina were 1 in 1,200 and for Chile 1 in 2,000. See Gillespie, *Negotiating Democracy,* 50–87.

5. González advances extensive evidence to back his argument that Uruguay, before its breakdown, had the strongest democratic tradition in Latin America, in *Political Structures and Democracy in Uruguay,* 1–7. Indeed, Robert A. Dahl goes as far as to say that Uruguay is probably the most striking case "in which a relatively long-standing democratic system has been replaced by an internally imposed authoritarian regime," in *A Preface to Economic Democracy* (Berkeley: University of California Press, 1985), 40.

6. Quoted in Gillespie, *Negotiating Democracy,* 54.

ficials, for the first time ever, began to refer to the military government simply as the "gobierno de facto" (the de facto government).[7] For their part, the traditional political parties emerged from the plebiscite energized, less frightened, and newly self-confident in their legitimacy.[8]

It was the military's defeat in the plebiscite and the fact that the traditional parties presented a newly strengthened alternative that produced the split between the military-as-government (which experimented with a variety of ways to stay in power) and the military-as-institution (which began discussing transitional formulas with part of the democratic opposition). In our conceptual introduction we said that, while the control of the outgoing government by a hierarchical military always presents the threat that they can constrain the transition, the degree to which they are able to do so will depend on the changing dynamics of power relationships. Why were the parties strong enough, vis-à-vis the military, to make the transition and consolidate democracy?

By 1980 the military did not have a defensive project against guerrillas. The guerrillas had in fact been defeated even before the military assumed power in 1973 and had no significant presence in Uruguay by 1980. The military also had no clear economic project, no "foundational" or offensive agenda. Finally, the two major traditional parties presented a nonthreatening alternative. In a revealing public opinion poll taken six months before the plebiscite, by a margin of 2 to 1, upper-class respondents believed that a political opening would *speed* rather than slow economic recuperation. Even more significantly, by a margin of 7 to 1, upper-class respondents believed that a political opening would *improve* rather than worsen tranquility and public order. Significantly, not one single business group took out an advertisement supporting the military in the 1980 plebiscite.[9] In a particularly damaging blow to military pretensions to rule, the president of the normally conservative Rural Association went on television and rather contemptuously dismissed the idea of Uruguay's need for a military drafted constitution. With no internal threat, without significant powerful alliances in civil or political society, and with their loss in the plebiscite, whose results they said they would respect, the military-as-institution's bargaining power with the politicians eroded

7. Diario de sesiones de la Constituente, 1980. This was brought to our attention by Juan Rial and Carina Perelli.

8. For an excellent analysis of the plebiscite and its consequences, see Luis E. González, "Uruguay 1980–81: An Unexpected Opening," *Latin American Research Review* 18, no. 3 (1983): 63–76. González calls this vote a military effort to found a plebiscitary nondemocratic regime. Also see Howard Handelman, "Prelude to Elections: The Military's Legitimacy Crisis and the 1980 Constitutional Plebiscite in Uruguay," in Paul W. Drake and Eduardo Silva, eds., *Elections and Democratization in Latin America, 1980–85* (San Diego: Center for Iberian and Latin American Studies, Center for U.S-Mexican Studies, Institute of the Americas, University of California, San Diego, 1986), 201–14.

9. For these polls and an analysis of the military's absence of either a defensive or an offensive project, see Alfred Stepan, "State Power and Civil Society in the Southern Cone of Latin America," in Peter Evans, Dietrich Rueschemeyer, and Theda Skocpol, eds., *Bringing the State Back In* (New York: Cambridge University Press, 1985), 325–31.

significantly. As in Greece, the civilian politicians refused to continue negotiations about assuming the responsibility of rule until the military softened their demands.[10]

This is not to imply that the military-as-organization was not able to extract a price; they were. The fact that a hierarchically controlled military held power until after the first elections meant that the military was in a position to negotiate the transfer of power in a way that constrained the transition. The most important constraint, negotiated in the party-military Naval Club Pact, was that elections could be held only on the condition that the charismatic leader of one of the two major parties, Wilson Ferreira of the Blanco Party, would not stand as a presidential candidate. Ferreira had won more individual votes than any other candidate in the 1971 election, the last election before the military coup. Due to the peculiarities of the Uruguayan electoral system, he did not win the presidency in 1971. Ferreira would have been a leading contender to win in 1984 if the military had not vetoed him. The first postmilitary election was thus, for some key voters, tarnished. However, the facts that the Blanco Party fielded other candidates and the left-wing coalition (Frente Amplio) agreed to participate in the elections lessened the illegitimacy of the election. The military were also able to extract guarantees concerning the National Security Council and their own autonomy. Nonetheless, the parties' bargaining power was sufficiently strong that the military agreed that these prerogatives would expire at the end of the first year of democratic rule.

The most politically damaging curtailment of the elected government's sovereignty by the military occurred in December 1986. Though no written documentation exists for confirmation, it is widely believed that, by an informal interpretation of the Naval Club Pact, it was tacitly agreed by some key political party and military negotiators that there would be no trials of military officers for human rights abuses committed immediately before and during military rule. In December 1986, some military officers were issued a subpoena to appear in court. On a Friday, the defense minister ordered the officers not to appear in court on the following Monday. For forty-eight hours Uruguayan politicians struggled with a legitimacy-eroding dilemma. If they insisted on the officers appearing in court, they would face a military refusal and therefore a crisis of their own authority. As an alternative, they could hastily pass an amnesty law and avoid the immediate crisis at the cost of the lowered prestige of democratic institutions.[11] After many

10. When confronted with hard-line military demands at the initial negotiations in Parque Hotel, the civilian negotiators walked out and returned only for the more successful Naval Club Pact discussions after the military had softened their terms. For a sophisticated analysis of these negotiations, see chapters 6–8 in Gillespie, *Negotiating Democracy.*

11. This assessment of the dilemma was presented during an interview by Stepan shortly after the event with then President Sanguinetti and Senator Jorge Battle in Montevideo, February 3, 1987. Also see Julio María Sanguinetti, *El temor y la impaciencia: Ensayo sobre la transición democrática en America Latina* (Buenos Aires: Fondo de Cultura Económica, 1991), 63–68.

agonized discussions, they elected the latter course of action, to the widespread dismay of the majority of the population. Eventually, enough signatures (25 percent of the electorate) were gathered to force a referendum on the amnesty. In an April 1989 referendum, 57 percent of those voting agreed to let the amnesty stand. However, public opinion polls indicated that significant sections of the electorate voted to let the amnesty stand, more to avoid a crisis than because they believed it was just.[12] They were almost certainly right to believe there would have been a military crisis. The Uruguayan general who played the most important and constructive role in negotiating the extrication of the military-as-institution, General Hugo Medina, in a 1991 interview, when asked what would have happened if the citizens had voted for military trials, made the following unequivocal assertion: "If I had not assumed the responsibility for a coup, it would have been assumed by the next officer in the hierarchy, if not by him, the next. This is so because this was the thinking of the Armed Forces."[13] Notwithstanding this chilling assessment, once the citizens had voted, this seemed the last major item of contestation concerning the party-military agenda. In December 1989, free elections were held in which all candidates were allowed to participate, and in fact the left coalition, Frente Amplio, won the mayorship of Montevideo, which comprises about half of Uruguay's population.

With the referendum and the election of December 1989, Uruguay fulfilled all our conditions for a completed transition.[14] However, the "transfer price" that the hierarchical military extracted from the new democracy, while low by Brazilian or Chilean standards, was real both in terms of policy sovereignty and political legitimacy.

Despite the constraints the hierarchical military was able to impose on the transition, we believe that Uruguay had become consolidated by 1992, a judgment that may be controversial. Let us first examine the behavioral dimension of consolidation. In the 1968–73 period leading to the coup, Uruguay's Tupamaros were Latin America's best organized urban guerrilla force. The dominant faction of the ruling political party, the Colorados, was led by a president who utilized the guerrilla threat, says González, "to impose . . . a kind of siege which he used to circumvent parliament." González adds that, after 1968, "the already semi-loyal left

12. For example, in a March 1989 Equipos poll, only 27 percent of those polled believed that the military would respect the decision. The most cited reason for people voting to uphold the amnesty was their desire to consolidate democracy. The official title of the law that was supported was "Ley de Caducidad de la Pretensión Punitiva del Estado" (Law Abrogating the Punitive Claim of the State).

13. The first major published interview with General Hugo Medina appeared in *Búsqueda* (March 7, 1991): 32–37. This quote is from p. 37. For an account of the debates concerning the referendum over what was called the "law of impunity," see Lawrence Weschler, *A Miracle, a Universe: Settling Accounts with Torturers* (New York: Random House, 1990), 173–236.

14. For this election see Carina Perelli and Juan Rial, "El fin de la restauración: La elección del 26 de noviembre de 1989," *Cuadernos de orientación electoral,* no. 10, (Montevideo: Peitho, April 1990). Also see the excellent work by Alexandra Barahona de Brito, "Truth or Amnesty: Human Rights and Democratization in Latin America: Uruguay and Chile (Ph.D. diss., St. Antony's College, University of Oxford, 1993).

was openly pushed to plain disloyalty by the government and most of the leadership of the major parties—with the significant exception of the Blanco majority. Besides, by 1971 the very idea of loyalty was unclear: the government itself did not abide by the existing rules."[15] And of course, well before the July 1973 coup, the military had unilaterally assumed control of the dirty war against the guerrillas and, as Gillespie correctly wrote, "tragically, the most important catalyst to the military intervention was the secretive courting of Generals by politicians on all sides."[16] In essence, Uruguay in 1968–73 was a system in which most nationally important political actors were "disloyal" or at best "semiloyal" to the democratic regime.[17]

Political learning can help consolidate democracy. For one thing, citizens can learn from previous breakdowns and change the composition of parliament by their voting behavior. In Uruguay all the major rightist and leftist political factions most associated with the 1968–73 breakdown have been "punished" by the electorate. Both the traditional parties had extreme rightist factions that were clearly disloyal or semiloyal in 1968–73. The right-wing Colorado faction that acted disloyally before the breakdown received 56 percent of the vote in 1971, 31 percent in the internal party election in 1982, and 24 percent in 1984. An even more dramatic trend occurred in the Blanco Party, where the faction that supported authoritarian behavior received 34 percent in 1971, 26 percent in 1982, and only 3 percent in 1984. Finally, in the coalition of left-wing parties, the Frente Amplio, the winners in the 1984 elections were the centripetal forces in each party (the opposite of Sartori's model of dangerous "centrifugal polarization"). As González summed up, the "process of displacement toward the center . . . weakened all the antisystem forces of the political spectrum."[18]

For the consolidation of democracy the loyal democratic behavior of parties is important, but it is as important that all the major political parties *perceive* that the other major parties are loyal to the process. If all the major parties perceive each other as loyal this decreases the cost for losers (because they will have another chance to contest elections and the rights of the minority will be respected) and it increases the cost of "intertemporal" disengagement from the democratic process (because of the perception that democracy is the most important political game being played).[19] Gillespie constructed a survey question to identify po-

15. The citations are from González, *Political Structures and Democracy in Uruguay*, 42, 41.

16. Gillespie, *Negotiating Democracy*, 44.

17. For the importance of the categories of "semiloyalty" and "disloyalty" for the analysis of democratic breakdown, see Juan J. Linz, *The Breakdown of Democratic Regimes: Crisis, Breakdown and Reequilibration* (Baltimore: Johns Hopkins University Press, 1978), 28–45.

18. All the electoral percentages and the citation are from González, *Political Structures and Democracy in Uruguay*, 70–71. Also see Juan Rial, "The Uruguayan Election of 1984: A Triumph of the Center," in Drake and Silva, eds., *Elections and Democratization*, 245–72.

19. Adam Przeworski makes a related point when he talks of the importance for consolidation of increasing the "intertemporal" benefits of playing the democratic game. Given that this game generates both winners and losers, Przeworski asks, "Why would those who suffer as the result of the democratic interplay

litical factions' perceptions of the loyalty, semiloyalty and disloyalty of their party opponents. On a ten-point scale in which four to six is semiloyal and above seven is disloyal, in 1985 not *one* of the twelve major factions of the three leading parties was judged by its rivals as disloyal. In contrast, using the same procedure, four of the nine major factions for the 1968–73 period were judged retrospectively as disloyal by at least one opposition party.[20]

Another critical piece of evidence concerning political behavior and consolidation is whether parties that were once treated as unacceptable power-holders come to be treated as "acceptable." In 1971, important groups of the Colorados and Blancos considered the left-wing coalition (Frente Amplio) unacceptable. But ever since the Frente Amplio's important participation in the Naval Club Pact of 1985, its members have been increasingly seen as normal and accepted participants in the democratic system. In 1989 a socialist, Tabaré Vásquez, from the Frente Amplio coalition, was elected mayor of Montevideo. There were no significant arguments about his right to run or to assume office. His behavior as mayor of Montevideo was seen as even-handed. Indeed, in 1990, whereas only 22 percent of polled Montevideo residents believed President Lacalle of the traditional Blanco Party paid attention to the needs and demands of *all* the voters, 63 percent of polled Montevideo residents believed Vásquez did. More significantly, voters for President Lacalle judged Vázquez, by 17 percentage points, to be more attentive to all the voters' demands and issues than was Lacalle himself.[21] By mid-1992 most analysts began to see Tabaré Vásquez as a major challenger whom former president Jorge Sanguinetti and his Blancos rivals would have to face in the 1994 presidential elections. In an interview with one of the authors, Vásquez stated, "I have absolute confidence that whoever wins the election in 1994 will assume the government. Our military are not antidemocratic."[22] The mere fact that Vásquez was considered a possible president of Uruguay increased his power to moderate

---

not seek to subvert the system that generates such results?" He goes on to argue that the losers "comply with present defeats because they believe that the institutional framework that organizes the democratic competition will permit them to advance their interests in the future." See Przeworkski, *Democracy and the Market: Political and Economic Reforms in Eastern Europe and Latin America* (New York: Cambridge University Press, 1991), esp. 18–19.

20. This is computed from tables 3.6 and 10.5 in Gillespie, *Negotiating Democracy.*

21. Surveys done by Equipos Consultores Asociados in June 1990.

22. Interview with Alfred Stepan, Montevideo, March 25, 1992. Vásquez went on to add that, after assuming the office of mayor, he made courtesy calls to all the commanders of the Armed Forces garrisons in Montevideo. Since then he has given out awards at the graduation of the Naval Academy and the Police Academy and attended an Air Force graduation. He said he would like to attend an army graduation but to date had not been invited. When Stepan asked one of Uruguay's top generals what the army would do if Vásquez won the election, he said the army would be "correct but nothing more." For a pioneering analysis of political space and how the discourse of Tabaré Vásquez allowed him to emerge as a new democratic leader in Uruguay, see Carina Perelli, "Un líder transgresor: Tabaré Vásquez o la intendencia como espacio político," in Carina Perelli, Fernando Filgueira, and Silvana Rubino, *Gobierno y política en Montevideo: La intendencia municipal de Montevideo y la formación de un nuevo liderazgo a comienzos de los años '90* (Montevideo: Peitho, 1991), 109–51.

the behavior of his coalitional allies. In 1992 the Frente Amplio had been integrated into the Uruguayan democratic political system by all significant parties. Indeed, Tabaré Vásquez was almost elected president in the November 1994 election when he polled more than any other single candidate. He did not win the presidency because, in the Uruguayan election system, total party votes accumulate. In the near three-way tie, his coalition, the *Encuentro Progresista* (EP), came in third place, 36,005 votes behind the Colorados and 13,206 behind the Blancos. However, in all the pre-election and post-election talks about the need for cooperation to make Uruguay governable, the Frente Amplio were considered legitimate participants in the political system. Senator Danilo Astori, leader of the group that won the most votes in the EP, played a particularly active role in governability discussions after the 1994 elections.[23]

What about the military? After the 1989 referendum on the decision by the Congress not to prosecute the military, the military made no explicit or implicit threats or demands on the democratic political system. In terms of prerogatives, they almost reverted back to the pre-authoritarian regime pattern of civil-military relations. In 1990, they certainly had fewer prerogatives than the military had in Chile, Argentina, or Brazil.[24] One of the reasons that the military was not very powerful in Uruguayan politics after free elections was that they had virtually no allies. In poll after poll, business elites, politicians, and mass publics alike rejected military involvement in politics. For example, in answer to the question, "If similar circumstances to 1973 occurred in Uruguay would you think it good if the military assumed power?" 92 percent of executives and technical specialists said "no." Also, the inevitable "desencanto" (disenchantment) with democracy has not contributed to any nostalgia for the nondemocratic past. Uruguay in essence had been ruled by five authoritarian presidents from 1968 to 1985 and then by the democratically elected Sanguinetti. In a December 1988 poll respondents were asked to evaluate under which president the country was better off in each of seven different categories. In every single category the democratic president Jorge Sanguinetti was given the highest marks.[25] In August 1985, of nine institutions evaluated in terms of trust, political parties ranked highest, with a net score of plus 57, and the armed forces ranked lowest, with a net score of minus 73. Only 5 percent of the population viewed the armed forces "sympathetically" and 7 percent "neutrally," in contrast to those 78 percent who viewed the military with "antipathy."[26] In no coun-

23. For the final results of the 1994 election, see "Uruguay; Sanguinetti Seeks All-round Accords," *Latin American Regional Reports: Southern Cone Report* (Feb. 9, 1995): 7. In the Senate the Colorados received eleven seats, the Blancos ten, the Frente Amplio nine, and Nuevo Espacio one. In the Chamber of Deputies the Colorados won thirty-two seats, the Blancos thirty-one, the Frente Amplio thirty-one, and Nuevo Espacio five.

24. For documentation and analysis of military perogatives in Uruguay, Chile, Argentina, and Brazil, see Stepan, *Rethinking Military Politics*, 93–125, esp. 116–18.

25. Equipos, December 1988 poll.

26. Equipos, August 1985 poll.

try in our thirteen-country sample, with the possible exception of Greece, did democracy start with such a complete rejection of the political role of the military.

In a context with no violent enemies (there was only one significant act of violence associated with the left in the first seven years of democratic rule), a virtual elimination of disloyal opposition among political parties, and the popular rejection of the military as a political ally, it would have been extremely risky for the military as an institution to attempt to assume power or to block the inauguration of a possible victorious Frente Amplio presidential candidate in 1994. In 1992, Stepan asked a top ranking active-duty general what would happen to Uruguay politically if Tabaré Vásquez were elected president in 1994. The general's answer implied that he, too, accepted that the system was already a consolidated democracy. In the event of a 1994 victory of Tabaré Vásquez, the general saw the task of ensuring political order not as something that would emerge out of military action, but rather out of the normal functioning of politics. He quoted approvingly a remark by a senior Uruguayan politician to the effect that "the Frente Amplio, like all other parties, will need to make accords with parties to rule effectively. In Uruguay the office of the presidency in itself is not power. For power, accords are necessary and accords depend on acceptable behavior."[27]

In March 1992, after one of our many research visits to Uruguay, we arrived at the conclusion that Uruguay was consolidated. Shortly thereafter, an office occasionally used by ex-President Sanguinetti was bombed by a group claiming to be composed of retired midlevel officers with the help of some active-duty officers. Naturally, we thought about whether our judgment was still valid. We decided that the best way to evaluate the meaning of the bombing was to examine political reactions. After all, Spain routinely experiences terrorist bombing, but Spain is consolidated because after 1981 there has been no significant semiloyal or disloyal behavior by parties and institutions of statewide significance. In Uruguay, all major political groups explicitly condemned the bombing. The hierarchical military also condemned the bombing in forceful terms. Despite this worrisome terrorist act, our judgment concerning the behavioral dimension of Uruguay's consolidation was ratified. By 1992, there was no semiloyal or disloyal behavior by any major party or organization in Uruguay.[28]

Uruguay is also consolidated *institutionally;* with the agreed-upon lapse of the Naval Club Pact, one year to the day after the inauguration of a democratic parliament, there were no de jure constraints on the policy freedom of the democratic government. The de facto limit on the democratic government from 1985 to 1989 stemming from military refusal to be tried for human rights abuses was of course a serious constraint. But, for better or worse, the results of the 1989 refer-

27. Interview, March 25, 1992, in Montevideo. Not for direct attribution.

28. However, the military said there was no evidence to show that the military was actively involved. Of course our final judgment will have to wait until we are able to determine whether the military cooperates fully with the investigation and supports the court's decision if the perpetrators are tried and found guilty.

Table 10.1. Comparison of Attitudinal Support for Democracy in Uruguay and Three Consolidated Democracies in Southern Europe: Spain, Portugal, and Greece

	Percentage of Respondents:			
Opinion about Preferred Policy	Uruguay (1991)	Spain (1985)	Portugal (1985)	Greece (1985)
"Democracy is preferable to any other form of government."	73	70	61	87
"In some cases, a nondemocratic government could be preferable to a democracy."	10	10	9	5
"For people like me, a democratic and a nondemocratic regime are the same."	8	9	7	6
DK/NA[a]	9	11	23	2

Source: For Uruguay, data supplied by Equipos, Consultores Asociados, Montevideo. For Spain, Portugal, and Greece, data from Leonardo Morlino and José Ramón Montero, "Legitimacy and Democracy in Southern Europe," in Richard Gunther, P. Nikiforos Diamandouros, and Hans-Jürgen Puhle, eds., *The Politics of Democratic Consolidation: Southern Europe in Comparative Perspective* (Baltimore: Johns Hopkins University Press, 1995), 236.
[a]DK/NA, don't know or no answer

endum on the amnesty have removed this item from the agenda. Parliament reviews military budgets, there is a civilian (but relatively weak) minister of defense, and the president has a free hand in selecting the commander-in-chief of the three services. To be sure, there are certainly civil-military problems in Uruguay. There is still no serious analysis by the president, Parliament, or the minister of defense as to what type of armed forces Uruguay really wants. The interview with Medina also revealed a still disturbing difference between civilian and military opinion about human rights. Other incidents, like the confusion and conflict in 1993 surrounding the harboring of a Chilean military intelligence agent in Uruguay without the government's approval, lead us to the opinion that the quality of civil-military relations in Uruguay in 1993–94 was still not really high.

Nevertheless, given the overall balance of power in Uruguay, the military is no longer a threat to the consolidation of democracy. In this respect it is useful to remember that the quality of civil-military relations in Spain was still poor in 1982 when Felipe González assumed the prime ministership. Spain, like Uruguay, became a consolidated democracy with relatively poor civil-military relations. Improving the quality of these relations was the work of another decade under the inspired leadership and strategy of Narcís Serra. Whether Uruguay will have comparable leadership and strategies and the necessary fiscal strength to implement new programs is still very much in doubt. But Uruguay in 1992, like Spain in 1982, had crossed a threshold.

Finally, is the *attitudinal* support for democracy consistent with calling Uruguay consolidated? If we compare citizens' attitudes toward democracy in Uruguay with those in the three consolidated democracies of southern Europe, we see that the attitudinal dimension of consolidation is similar in all four countries (table 10.1).

Table 10.2. Attitudes in Uruguay toward Democracy According to Geographic Region and Respondents' Ideological Self-identification (December 1991)

Opinion about Preferred Polity	Montevideo (1988)	Percentage of Respondents by Region			Percentage of Respondents by Ideological Self-identification					
		Montevideo	Interurban	Nation	Left	Center Left	Center	Center Right	Right	Not Defined
"Democracy is preferable to any other form of government."	79	78	69	73	74	81	80	75	69	57
"In some cases, a nondemocratic government could be preferable to a democracy."	9	10	10	10	11	11	11	10	11	6
"For people like me, a democratic and non-democratic regime are the same."	6	6	9	8	8	4	6	11	9	10
DK/NA[a]	6	6	12	9	7	4	3	4	11	27

Source: Data from Equipos, Consultores Asociados, Montevideo.
[a]DK/NA, don't know or no answer.

These data suggest a high level of overall general attitudinal support for democracy in Uruguay. However, since our analysis is concerned with democratic *consolidation*, we must disaggregate and examine these attitudes more closely. If any substantial group, on either the left or the right or within specific geographic regions, were to remain attitudinally unsupportive of democracy, this would constitute an obstacle to consolidation. Yet in Uruguay, as table 10.2 demonstrates, support for the democratic system is fairly strong across the entire country and the political spectrum.

Let us turn to the final conceptual and political issue that the Uruguayan case raises—the question of the quality of a consolidated democracy. Obviously, within the world of consolidated democracies there are three very different logical possibilities: (1) some can deepen and improve their degrees of equity, participation, and support; (2) others may have serious problems (such as high degrees of social conflict or the persistence of an underclass) that hurt the quality of, but may not contribute to a breakdown of, a democracy; and (3) a consolidated democracy may live with a series of problems that it does not solve—or a new set of problems may emerge—which finally contribute to a qualitatively and quantitatively new level of semiloyal and disloyal behavior that leads to the progressive deconsolidation of the regime and eventually to its breakdown. In Linz's 1978 discussion of the breakdown of democratic regimes, he remarked that, "In the last analysis, breakdown is a result of processes initiated by the government's incapacity to solve problems for which disloyal oppositions offer themselves as a solution."[29]

Although we consider Uruguay to be a consolidated democracy, in our judgment democracy in Uruguay has a more "risk-prone configuration" than it does in Spain or Portugal.[30] If the democratic political system cannot address critical problems, then there is a risk that significant political actors—the chief executive, political parties, opinion makers or social movements—might begin to pose antisystem alternatives. The quality and quantity of semiloyal and disloyal behavior could begin to increase. At this critical juncture, in our judgment, the intellectual and political categories of most relevance to examine have more to do with "the breakdown of democracy" literature than they have to do with "transitions" literature.[31]

Writing in 1995, the three key elements of the risk-prone configuration of Uruguay's political system are the perceived crisis of efficacy, the growing perception that this crisis of efficacy is directly related to the specific institutional arrangements that are long-standing features of democratic competition in Uruguay, and a military that, while not opposing democracy, has not, as in Spain, been organizationally and ideologically reconfigured and incorporated into the political system on a more secure basis. The third component could gain increased relevance precisely because of its potential to interact with the other two elements in Uruguay's risk-prone configuration in ways prejudicial to democracy.

While Uruguay in 1980 had a gross national product (GNP) per capita income of $2,820 (higher than that in Argentina, Brazil, or Chile), the highest literacy rate (94 percent) of the four countries, and probably Latin America's best income distribution, the country has been in a relative decline since the mid-1950s.[32] A well-documented empirical pattern is that democratic political systems are normally seen as more legitimate than their economic systems, be they market oriented or not.[33] Also, citizens' belief in the "appropriateness" (or legitimacy) of democracy can for a time *increase* even though their belief in the capacity (efficacy) of democracy to resolve their economic problems is *decreasing*. Spain in 1976–82 exemplifies such a case. We will call this distinction legitimacy versus efficacy. In Spain, for a brief period in the dangerous year of the failed coup (1981), 81 percent of the population believed that democracy was the best political system for a country like

---

29. Linz and Stepan, *The Breakdown of Democratic Regimes*, 50.

30. González applies this phrase to Uruguay in *Political Structures and Democracy in Uruguay*, 161. We find his argument convincing and the concept worthy of incorporation into the general scholarly analysis of consolidation. As we have seen, the way in which Greek democratic politics embroiled itself in Balkan politics made it more risk-prone in the mid-1990s than it had been in the mid-1980s.

31. Of course, some types of transitions may directly contribute to the creation of a democracy that, although consolidated, has features that make it risk-prone.

32. For a discussion of these comparative data, see González, *Political Structures and Democracy in Uruguay*, 2–4.

33. This literature is analyzed in Juan J. Linz, "Legitimacy of Democracy and the Socioeconomic System," in Mattei Dogan, ed., *Comparing Pluralist Democracies: Strains on Legitimacy* (Boulder, Colo.: Westview Press, 1988), 65–113.

theirs, but only 43 percent felt that democracy allowed the resolution of problems that they as Spaniards faced. By 1983 this 38 percent gap between Spain's legitimacy and efficacy indicators had been reduced to 24 percent.[34] In Montevideo, the capital of Uruguay, however, the gap between legitimacy and efficacy in 1988 was 41 percent. In 1990 the gap had grown to 43 percent. Furthermore, in December 1988 only 13 percent of those polled in Montevideo said the country was progressing, while 31 percent said the country was declining. Three years later these figures had deteriorated further to 9 percent and 39 percent, respectively.[35]

Uruguay's prolonged efficacy-legitimacy gap alone would make democracy "risk-prone." However, the configuration would become even more risk-prone if Uruguay's institutions of democracy themselves were perceived as contributing to policy inefficacy. As we argued in chapter 5, economic problems become particularly acute for a democracy when nondemocratic alternatives are proposed as the solution *and* when the existing democratic institutions are perceived as contributing to the economic problems. In Uruguay there is at the moment no nondemocratic alternative being proposed as a solution. Up until recently there was also relatively little system blame because politicians blamed themselves or the international system for their country's stagnation. This could change.

During Uruguay's golden age (1918–1956) the norm was a two-party system with a dominant party that produced presidents with a double majority—a personal majority and a legislative majority. There was a party system that was analogous to another presidential system where democracy worked (i.e., the United States), in that there was low fragmentation and low polarization. Uruguay's long-standing and unusual electoral system (known as the double simultaneous vote) allows all parties to run multiple candidates for the presidency and for all the votes for a party's label (whether for the extreme left candidate or the extreme right candidate) to accrue to the party.[36] Until the late 1950s, this electoral system did not present significant problems. But the number of parties, intraparty factions, and presidential candidates per party have grown considerably since 1960.[37] Presidents are now routinely elected with less than 25 percent of the popular vote because winning parties have had 2 to 4 factions. From this fragmented base presidents can count on legislative support of less than a quarter of the legislature. This party-institutional context makes the creation of a coherent policy majority to address Uruguay's stagna-

34. See the discussion about this in chapter 6.

35. Equipos, *Informe de Coyuntura*, June 1990, and Equipos, December 1991.

36. See Oscar A. Bottinelli, "El sistema electoral uruguayo: descripción y análisis," *Peitho*, Documentos de Trabajo, no. 83, 1991.

37. A classic study of these issues is Giacomo Sani and Giovanni Sartori, "Polarization, Fragmentation and Competition in Western Democracies," in Hans Daalder and Peter Mair, eds., *Western European Party Systems: Continuity and Change* (London: Sage, 1983), 307–40. González replicates much of their analysis to show that from 1954 to 1984 Uruguay has changed, in comparative terms, from near the bottom of their fragmentation scale to near the top of their scale. González, *Political Structures and Democracy in Uruguay*, pp. 85–112.

tion extremely difficult. Many of Uruguay's most distinguished analysts and politicians are now making the case that it is precisely Uruguay's combination of party fragmentation, the electoral system, *and* presidentialism that has created legislative impasse and short-lived policy coalitions.[38] From a game theory perspective, the only groups that can change this system are the Parliament and the party leaders, yet it is precisely these groups that have been the "winners" with the system. It will thus be difficult to get a majority to change the system until there is a clear perception of crisis. However, if the institutions of Uruguay's political system are increasingly seen as contributing directly to Uruguay's stagnation, there could be growing system blame of the democratic regime itself. The fact that Uruguay chose to restore both the constitution and electoral system that were in effect before military rule, notwithstanding their contribution to the breakdown, means that an opportunity for constitutional and institutional innovation after the dictatorship was missed.

This brings us to the third component of Uruguay's risk-prone configuration—the military. As we have argued, the Uruguayan military has yielded their nondemocratic prerogatives and is not currently a plausible coalition partner for any nondemocratic group. However, Uruguay's prolonged economic stagnation has contributed to a fiscal crisis of the state that exacerbates civil-military relations. The Uruguayan military since 1985 have been in a double crisis—an "existential crisis" concerning their mission and a resource crisis brought about by extensive budgetary cuts.[39] Democratic governments have cut military budgets, but unlike in Spain they have not yet played a role in rethinking military organization, mission, and force-structure or in rethinking how to reincorporate the military socially and ideologically back into the democratic polity. Such a situation, if it is not altered, could make Uruguay's democracy even more risk-prone should disloyal and semiloyal behavior among politicians begin to emerge and the military suddenly find the allies that they have not had during the period 1980–1995.

We want to stress that such semiloyal and disloyal behavior does not now exist and that we see no credible "coup" coalition on the horizon.[40] Such antidemo-

38. In various political fora in Uruguay, Juan Rial and Luiz Eduardo González have increasingly argued this point. For their writing on this subject, see González, *Political Structures and Democracy in Uruguay,* 161–64, and Juan Rial, "Reforma constitucional: Invitación a una discusión necesária," text of a speech given to young Uruguayan politicians, November 1991. A major Colorado political party leader, Jorge Batlle, in a self-criticism of what he calls "Uruguayan nomenklatura," argues that "a government that is born without majorities, as a consequence of our electoral system, not only creates problems for government, but worse the system consecrates the irresponsibility of everyone," public speech, July 15, 1990.

39. For an excellent analysis, especially of the existential crisis, see Carina Perelli, "El nuevo ethos militar en America Latina: Las crisis existenciales de las fuerzas armadas de la región en los 90," *Peitho,* Documentos de Trabajo, no. 80, 1991.

40. In fact, we see the opposite. As the economies of Argentina, and even Brazil, grew robustly in 1994 and as the government was able to negotiate what was seen as better terms for Uruguay's role in the MERCOSUR (the new common market of Brazil, Argentina, Uruguay, and Paraguay), confidence in the future experienced a significant upturn for the first time since 1988. According to a poll conducted by Equipos in August 1990, 66 percent of those polled in a national survey said that they believed the economy was "bad" or "very bad." In October 1994 those who felt the economy was "bad" or "very bad" had declined to below 40 percent. Furthermore, the presidential approval rating, which had hit a new historic low of 11 per-

cratic behavior and such a correlation of forces supportive of breakdown would be the result of a future unresolved crisis of democracy.[41] We also want to stress that Uruguay's configuration of democratic institutions, practices, and values discourages the syndrome that Guillermo O'Donnell calls "delegative democracy" that plagues so many presidential systems and that we will discuss in the Argentinian and Brazilian cases.[42] However, if democratic politicians cannot or will not realign Uruguay's risk-prone configuration, they could—as in most historical cases of breakdown—be direct contributors to such an outcome.

---

cent in August 1992, had risen to 29 percent by October 1994. Indeed, in contrast to all 1992–93 political predictions, the Blanco ruling party, as we have seen, almost won the November 1994 presidential elections. These and other Equipos polls were published in *El Observador* on October 24, 1994.

41. Many party leaders expressed concern after the November 1994 election that Uruguay's traditional two-party system could become an even weaker base of government support as Uruguay became a three-party system. In an effort to overcome problems of governability, all parties with representatives in the legislature agreed to open negotiations on important electoral and socioeconomic reforms. See "Uruguay: Congress Seeks to Update its Image," *Latin American Regional Report: Southern Cone Report* (April 20, 1995): 7.

42. For a discussion of these positive aspects of Uruguayan democracy, see Juan J. Linz, "Presidential or Parliamentary Democracy: Does It Make a Difference?" in Juan J. Linz and Arturo Valenzuela, eds., *The Failure of Presidential Democracy* (Baltimore: Johns Hopkins University Press, 1994), 36-37, and Guillermo O'Donnell, "Delegative Democracy," *Journal of Democracy* 5, no. 1 (January 1994): 55–69, esp 64.

11

Crises of Efficacy, Legitimacy, and Democratic State "Presence": Brazil

Oᴏ ᴛʜᴇ sᴇᴠᴇɴ southern European and South American countries we analyze in this book, Brazil has experienced the most difficulty in consolidating democracy. Brazil shares with the other six countries the same previous regime type—authoritarian—so this cannot explain the variation. Unlike Spain and many of the East European countries, it had no significant stateness problem, so this variable also is of no explanatory use for the crisis of consolidation.[1] It shared with Uruguay, Chile, and Argentina the extremely unfortunate consequences of the international debt crisis, but although it had the largest total debt of all countries in the world outside of the United States, its per capita debt throughout the 1980s was substantially less than that of Chile or Argentina, both of which by the early 1990s had managed their debt crises better.[2] The Brazilian transition's origins in a hierarchically controlled military regime did, of course, have numerous deleterious consequences for the democratization process, which we will evaluate. However, Brazil is not as constrained by the military as is Chile, and, as we shall see, Chile is not experiencing such multiple crises of the polity.

The major distinctive problem in Brazil concerns our variable of the political economy of legitimacy. Brazil has by far the most unequal distribution of income and the worst social welfare and educational standards of any of the southern European or South American or, for that matter, Central European countries in our set, and this certainly has not helped the effort to consolidate democracy.[3]

1. However, it is true that, in the midst of a prolonged fiscal (and political) crisis of the state, Brazil in 1992–93 saw numerous movements in the North and West demanding that some states be subdivided to form new ones, and a secessionist movement with strong racist overtones emerged in the relatively homogenously developed and predominantly white states of Rio Grande do Sul, Santa Catarina, and Paraná. A forthcoming book by Aspásia Alcântara de Camargo will review the growing problems of Brazilian federalism.

2. See, for example, the frequent publications of the World Bank in the 1980s called the *World Bank Debt Table*.

3. For example, the World Bank has data on income distribution for forty-one countries. In this group Brazil has the *highest* percentage of gross domestic product (GDP) per capita going to the top decile of the population and the *lowest* percentage going to the poorest two deciles of the population. See *World Devel-*

Furthermore, Brazil has historically had the least structured system of political parties of the four South American countries we analyze in this book. In this context, between 1985 and 1993, seven different reform packages were launched, failed, and were abandoned by a political society unable to craft together a sustainable policy coalition.[4] Like some post-Communist countries we will examine later, such as Russia, this political inefficacy had an erosive effect on each of the basic dimensions of a democratic polity. Constitutionalism and rule of law—never strong in Brazil's highly unequal society—weakened further. The prolonged economic crisis diminished the state's fiscal and moral capacity to play an integrating role in society and to provide basic services to citizens. The autonomy and value attached to the institutions of political society became more and more tenuous. As the state withdrew and political society was not able to craft sustained support around any policy alternatives, society became more anomic and the value of citizenship declined.

Our analysis of Brazil is divided into six parts. First, we briefly place Brazil's initial transition in comparative context. Second, we document how the hierarchical Brazilian military imposed severe constraints on the first democratic government. Third, we explore the nature of the crisis of the political economy of legitimacy. Fourth, we document how this crisis of the political economy of legitimacy has contributed to a degree of ambivalence about democracy that was not found in any other of our southern European or South American cases. Fifth, we explore some of the darker and more difficult problems this prolonged crisis had on citizenship, the state, and the polity and analyze some necessary and plausible reforms. Sixth, we briefly assess how Brazilians, facing the abyss in 1993, began in 1994 to piece together and support more promising plans to address Brazil's multiple crises.

A LONG, CONSTRAINED TRANSITION

The Brazilian transition from authoritarianism began with the inauguration of General Ernesto Geisel as president on March 15, 1974. From their base in government, Geisel and his closest political adviser, General Golbery do Couto e Silva,

---

opment Report 1990: Poverty (World Bank, 1990), 236–37. Also see Bolívar Lamounier, "Brazil: Inequality against Democracy," in Larry Diamond, Juan J. Linz, and Seymour Martin Lipset, eds., *Democracy in Developing Areas: Latin America* (Boulder, Colo.: Lynne Rienner, 1989), 111–58.

4. Luis Carlos Bresser Pereira, a well-known Brazilian economist and former finance minister, reviews why each one of these failed in "The Failure to Stabilize," his keynote speech to the conference "Brazil's Economic, Political and Social Reform," Institute of Latin American Studies of the University of London, February 16–17, 1993. Although he argued that some plans were weak technically because they did not address the specificities of Brazil's "inertia inflation," all plans, even those that were in his judgment technically correct, were aborted because of the inability to sustain political support once they encountered difficulties. Also see Albert Fishlow, "The State of Economics in Brazil and Latin America: Is the Past Prologue to the Future?" in Alfred Stepan, ed., *Americas: New Interpretive Essays* (New York: Oxford University Press, 1992), 58–79. An eighth and more successful plan, the Plan Real, was launched on July 1, 1994, with broader negotiated political support than the other plans. We will discuss the Plan Real at the end of this chapter.

began a complex process of seeking out allies in civil society in order to check the growing autonomy of the security community, which they considered dangerous for the military-as-institution and unnecessary because all guerrilla movements from the left had been destroyed. They initiated a controlled liberalization but soon there began a long process of what Stepan has analyzed as a dynamic of "regime concession and societal conquest."[5] The democratic transition in Brazil was not completed until the directly elected president, Fernando Collor de Mello, assumed office on March 15, 1990. This sixteen-year transition is almost twice as long as the Portuguese transition (which is the longest in our southern Europe set). The length of the Brazilian transition appears even more dramatic when we consider that the Brazilian authoritarian regime only began on March 31, 1964.

Both the extraordinary length of the Brazilian transition and the fact that the military "opening" (*abertura*) was six years longer than the military "closure" seem to us directly related to the fact that the authoritarian regime, although *it* never fully institutionalized, was hierarchically led by a military organization that had sufficient power to control the pace of the transition and extract a high price for extrication.[6]

From February to June 1984, Brazil experienced the most sustained and massive political movement in its history—the campaign for *Diretas Já*, or Direct Elections Now. The most significant forces in political and civil society wanted direct elections. In fact, no major group in civil society, including business, spoke out against direct elections.[7] However, the military insisted on indirect elections and the first civilian government since 1964 thus came into being in 1985 via indirect elections. To make matters worse, the popular but indirectly elected Tancredo Neves died before assuming office, and the compromise vice-presidential choice, José Sarney, who had been president of the proregime party, served for the next five years as president, even though by 1988 three out of four Brazilians wanted his term to be cut short.[8] The constraining conditions imposed by the outgoing

5. For interviews with Golbery and Geisel about why they began this process, see Stepan, *Rethinking Military Politics: Brazil and the Southern Cone* (Princeton University Press, 1988), 30–44. For the conquest dynamic within civil society that eventually pushed the military liberalization plans toward democratization, see Alfred Stepan, "State Power and the Strength of Civil Society in the Southern Cone of Latin America," in Peter B. Evans, Dietrich Rueschemeyer, and Theda Skocpol, eds., *Bringing the State Back In* (Cambridge: Cambridge University Press, 1985), 331–43.

6. For articles by two key social theorists and party leaders (Fernando Henrique Cardoso and Francisco Weffort) about the Brazilian transition; on civil society resistance by Ralph della Cava, Margaret E. Crahan, and Scott Mainwaring; and on the evolution of the political system by Bolivar Lamounier and Maria do Carmo Campello de Souza, see Alfred Stepan, ed., *Democratizing Brazil: Problems of Transition and Consolidation* (New York: Oxford University Press, 1989).

7. See the special issue of *Veja* (January 16, 1985). Also see Alfred Stepan, "State Power and the Strength of Civil Society in the Southern Cone of Latin America," in Evans, Rueschemeyer, and Skocpol, eds., *Bringing the State Back In*, 331–343.

8. For documentation of Sarney's lack of support, see Bolívar Lamounier and Alexandre H. Marques, "A democracia brasileira no final da 'década perdida,'" in Bolívar Lamounier, ed., *Ouvindo o Brasil: Uma Análise da Opinião Pública Brasileira Hoje* (São Paulo: Editora Sumaré, 1992), 143.

hierarchically controlled military regime affected not only the origins of the new civilian government but its performance. On a whole range of key policy issues, the civilian government, at best, shared sovereignty with the military. Throughout the entire government of the first civilian president, José Sarney (1985–90), there were six military ministers in the cabinet. On numerous occasions the military unilaterally decided whether or not to send military units to quell strikes. Active duty army officers continued in control of the National Intelligence Service. None of Brazil's controversial nuclear projects were discussed in Congress. The military played a major role in setting the boundaries to agrarian reform.[9]

Military influence on the Constituent Assembly was significantly strong to warrant placing Brazil's constitution in our category of a "constitution created under highly constraining circumstances reflecting the de facto power of nondemocratic institutions and forces." The military, via a skillful combination of threats and lobbying, succeeded in eliminating, softening, or subverting most of the proposed constitutional clauses that would have curtailed military autonomy.[10] The most dramatic instance of military involvement in constitution-making concerned their maneuvering with the president to forestall Latin America's first experiment in parliamentarianism or, more likely, "semi-presidentialism," along the lines of the French Fifth Republic. Support among the members of the Constituent Assembly for a more parliamentary form of government was such that the first seventy-seven articles were drawn up and approved in final form in a language that supposed that the basic form of the government would be parliamentary and not presidential. However, just before the crucial vote on article 78 that would have explicitly established a parliamentary form of government in Brazil, the military helped alter the balance of power. The indirectly elected president, José Sarney, who did not want his term or his powers to be curtailed, and the army, which did not want to be subject to parliamentary votes of no confidence and which wanted to retain their direct relationship to the president, joined forces. President Sarney and the military launched a powerful counterattack of pork-barrel payoffs and threats, and presidentialism triumphed in a last-minute vote change in the Constituent Assembly.[11]

COMBINED CONSTITUTIONAL, POLITICAL, AND ECONOMIC FRAGILITY

This sudden use of military-backed presidential power contributed to Brazil's constitutional, political, and economic fragility as it attempted to consolidate

9. For extensive documentation see Stepan, *Rethinking Military Politics,* 103–14.

10. See Eliézer Rizzo de Oliveira, "O papel das forças armadas na nova constituição e no futuro da democracia no Brasil," *Vozes* 82, no. 2 (July–Dec. 1988): 21–27.

11. The above discussion is based on extensive interviews by Alfred Stepan conducted in Brasília in December 1989.

democracy in the 1990s. In fact, the members of the Constituent Assembly never altered the first seventy-seven "parliamentary" articles. The 1988 constitution thus featured greatly enhanced legislative powers consistent with a parliamentary constitution so that the president, especially in budgetary areas, cannot—except by decree—rule with any efficacy without strong legislative support.[12] However, President Collor, a classic example of the antipolitics and antiparty politician that presidentialism and television can produce, began his presidency backed by a party that controlled less than 5 percent of the seats in congress.

The first major policy initiative of the Collor presidency, the stabilization or "Collor plan," quickly revealed the threats such a weak congressional base present for democratic consolidation. In dramatic contrast to Spain, where the stabilization agreement, the Moncloa Pact, was the result of complex party negotiations and was formally ratified in Parliament, in Brazil President Collor's plan was announced on television to a shocked nation with absolutely no prior consultation with political parties or congress. A dangerous game of policy deadlock or presidential intimidation had begun.[13] Two key "provisional decrees" were quickly challenged as unconstitutional by the courts and withdrawn. But the president threatened Congress that he would mobilize the masses to support his plan. "There is no doubt that I have an intimate deep relation with the poor masses," he announced. He warned Congress that it "must respect me because I am the center of power."[14] Even one of President Collor's strongest supporters, the influential conservative former minister of finance, Senator Roberto Campos, lamented, "This is juridical butchery, which dashes confidence in the Collor plan."[15]

Unlike President Fujimori in Peru, President Collor did not attempt an "auto-coup," but less than halfway through his presidency his isolation from civil and political society contributed to the fact that he had tried and failed with two different drastic stabilization plans.[16] He was also personally mired in corruption scandals.[17] In any democratic regime there is always the risk of a "crisis of gov-

12. For an analysis by an important economist who became Minister of Planning in 1995, see José Serra, "A constituição e o gasto público," *Planejamento e Políticas Públicas* no. 1 (June 1989): 93–106.

13. For a pioneering comparative account of the politics of policy planning in Spain and Brazil, see Luis Carlos Bresser Pereira, José María Maravall, and Adam Przeworski, *Economic Reforms in New Democracies: A Social Democratic Approach* (New York: Cambridge University Press, 1993).

14. Latin American Regional Reports: *Brazil*, May 3, 1990, 6. This is, of course, the type of discourse that Guillermo O'Donnell so deftly analyzes in his "Delegative Democracy," *Journal of Democracy* 5, no. 1 (Jan. 1994): 55–69.

15. See "Mounting Criticism of 'Authoritarian Governments' Novo Brasil Plan," *Latin American Regional Reports: Brazil*, June 7, 1990, 1–3; Campos quote on p. 2.

16. See Luiz Carlos Bresser Pereira, *Os tempos heróicos de Collor: Adventuras da modernidade e desventuras da ortodoxia* (São Paulo: Nobel, 1991).

17. The best source on the breadth and depth of the corruption that surrounded Collor's presidency is the 371-page congressional report, Brazil, Congresso Nacional, "Relatório Final da Comissão Mista de Inquérito" (August 1992). For an analysis of this report, see Luiz Felipe de Alencantro, "O Relatório da CPI: Um Retrato do Brasil," *Novos Estudos CEBRAP* no. 34 (Nov. 1992): 3–7. Also see the cover page article by James Brooke, "Looting Brazil," *New York Times Magazine*, November 8, 1992, 30–33, 42–45, 70–71.

ernment." By June 1992, Brazil faced an acute crisis of government. The key issue for democracy is that a crisis of government be resolved reasonably quickly before it becomes a "crisis of regime" so that a new political coalition can be reconstituted to attempt anew to combine policy efficacy with democratic legitimacy. In a parliamentary system without direct elections for the chief executive, Collor would not normally have been selected prime minister since his party controlled less than 5 percent of the votes in Congress. Even if a majority had passively supported him in the beginning, faced with the crisis of government by mid-1992 he would almost certainly have been peacefully and quietly replaced by someone who could command at least a temporary majority. In Brazil's presidential system, however, the only way to get a new government was to impeach President Collor, a process which all key political players initially felt would be extremely difficult and dangerous.[18] The constitutional crisis created a setting where key politicians toyed with the dangerous precedent of hastily moving up the scheduled date for a referendum on parliamentarianism, influential commentators and a near majority of public opinion wanted the president to resign, but the president insisted on filling out his "mandate."[19] While the military was not directly to blame for this turn of events, without their key supportive role in vetoing the parliamentary plans of the Constituent Assembly, Brazil's democratic consolidation would not have been threatened by such an intense legislative-executive conflict in the 1990–94 presidential term. Fortunately, when faced with the crisis, both Brazilian civil society and political society rallied forces and were successfully able to carry out South America's first impeachment in the twentieth century. But the weak vice-president, Itamar Franco, who became acting president and eventually president, was initially just as incapable as President Collor of implementing a coherent economic policy.

AMBIVALENT ATTITUDES TOWARD DEMOCRACY

Given this context it would be surprising if the Brazilian public had attitudes that were as strongly supportive of democracy as in the consolidated democracies of Spain, Portugal, Greece, or Uruguay. Indeed, on the eve of President Collor's second aniversary in power, and thus two months before the corruption and im-

18. Constitução Republica Federativa do Brasil, 1988 (article 86) stipulates that the removal of a president requires a two-thirds vote in the House of Representatives and then a trial by the Senate (for a political crime) or by the Supreme Court (for ordinary penal crimes). Impeachment was further complicated by the fact that the implementing legislation, spelling out procedures, had not yet been passed (article 85).

19. Much of President Collor's support in the 1989 presidential election had come from his pledge that he would fight corruption. By June 1992, only 19 percent of those polled felt he was innocent of the criminal charges of corruption, but 71 percent felt he would not be convicted. Nonetheless, 47 percent wanted him to resign or take a temporary leave of absence from the presidency as legal processes advanced. See *Folha de São Paulo,* June 25, 1992, 1. For military and political calls for Collor's resignation, see James Brooke, "Brazil's President Damaged by Corruption Inquiry," *New York Times,* June 28, 1992, A-9.

Table 11.1. Comparison of Attitudinal Support for Democracy in Brazil versus the Four Consolidated Democracies of Uruguay, Spain, Portugal, and Greece

	Percentage of Respondents				
Opinion about Preferred Polity	Brazil (1992)	Uruguay (1991)	Spain (1985)	Portugal (1985)	Greece (1985)
"Democracy is preferable to any other form of government."	42	73	70	61	87
"In some cases, a nondemocratic government could be preferable to a democracy."	22	10	10	9	5
"For people like me, a democratic and a nondemocratic regime are the same."	24	8	9	7	6
DK/NA[a]	12	9	11	23	2

Source: For Uruguay, same as table 10.1. For Spain, Portugal, and Greece, same as table 8.2. For Brazil, data from "Avaliação do Governo Collor apos dois años de mandato," *Datafolha* (São Paulo: Feb. 1992), national sample of 2,500.
[a]DK/NA, don't know or no answer.

peachment crisis we have just been discussing, a national opinion poll revealed that Brazilian citizens had attitudes that were strikingly more ambivalent about democracy than in the four consolidated democracies we have discussed (Spain, Portugal, Greece, and Uruguay) (Table 11.1).

These 1992 results were so stark that we inventoried all the polls given in Brazil on these questions to see if the March 1992 results were anomalous or part of a more persistent pattern. Fortunately for our research these identical questions had been asked six times in Brazil between 1988 and 1992, by four different organizations using somewhat different samples and polling techniques. Unfortunately for Brazilian politics, in *every* single poll, Brazil scored lower than Spain, Uruguay, Portugal, or Greece on *each* of the three core questions (table 11.2).

In the 1986–92 period, the high point of support for democracy was in December 1989, immediately after Brazil's first direct presidential election in twenty-nine years.[20] By 1991 and 1992, however, this support had declined to new lows. The results of Tables 11.1 and 11.2 are so clear that, taken by themselves, one would have to render the judgment that Brazilian democracy is far from consolidated. We have argued that support for democracy must always be assessed in comparison to other alternatives. In the case of Uruguay we saw that there was a severe efficacy-legitimacy gap. However, this gap was rendered less dangerous for democracy in Uruguay because the political parties filled most of the political space and the military was not accepted as an alternative. Indeed, we saw that the democratic government of President Sanguinetti, despite its difficulties, was judged to be more effective than the military on all seven policy areas where their perfor-

20. For an analysis of how increased participation during the election increased support for democracy, see the forthcoming book by José Alvaro Moises, *Cultura Política*, as well as his "Democratization and Mass Political Culture in Brazil" (St. Antony's College, Oxford University, March 1992, unpublished manuscript).

Table 11.2. Evolving Attitudes toward Democracy in Brazil, 1988–1992

Opinion about Preferred Polity	Percentage of Respondents					
	December 1988	September 1989	December 1989	March 1990	April 1991	April 1992
"Democracy is preferable to any other form of government."	43	43	55	56	39	42
"In some cases, a nondemocratic government could be preferable to a democracy."	21	18	15	17	17	22
"For people like me, a democratic and nondemocratic regime are the same."	26	22	16	17	28	24
DK/NA/other	10	17	14	10	14	12
Sample size	800	2,083	2,510	2,480	3,650	2,500
	(São Paulo)	(National)	(National)	(National)	(National)	(National)
Organizer of poll	IDESP	CEDEC	CEDEC	CEDEC	IBOPE	Datafolha

Source: The December 1988 poll was organized by two researchers from IDESP and reported in Judith Muszynski and Antonio Manuel Teixera Mendes, "Democratização e opinão pública no Brasil," in Bolívar Lamounier, ed., De Geisel a Collor: O balanço da transição (São Paulo: Editora Sumaré, 1990), 61–80, esp. 70. The September 1989, December 1989, and March 1990 studies came from a multiyear research project on political culture organized by José Alvaro Moises from CEDEC and will be reported in a forthcoming book. The April 1991 results are by IBOPE, Brazil's largest commercial polling organization which uses telephone interviewing. The IBOPE results are reported in Bolívar Lamounier, ed., Ouvindo o Brasil: Uma análise da opinião pública brasileira hoje (São Paulo: Editora Sumaré, 1992), 137–58, esp. 150–51. The April 1992 survey was conducted by Datafolha, the public opinion polling organization of the newspaper Folha da São Paulo.

mances were compared. The situation in Brazil was substantially more dangerous. Both efficacy and legitimacy were quite low and a significant proportion of the population judged the military government to have been more efficacious than civilian government. In 1989, on five out of seven items, citizens believed that the situation was better under the military regime of 1964–85 than under the first four years of civilian democratic rule (table 11.3).

Even more dangerous than a high valuation of the *past performance* of the military is the question of future preference. In dramatic contrast to Uruguay or even Argentina, a significant percentage of Brazil's citizens have persistently seen the return of the military as a *desired future alternative*. For example, in a December 1988 comparative study of new democracies in Brazil, Argentina, and Uruguay, only 6 percent of the Montevideo residents polled felt a return of the military would make things better, only 15 percent in Argentina felt so, but 40 percent of the inhabitants polled in São Paulo felt so.[21] In a national poll a year later, in response to the statement, "The country would be better off if the military returned to power," 38 percent concurred and only 45 percent disagreed.[22]

21. See Judith Muszynski and Antonio Manuel Teixeira Mendes, "Democratização e opinião pública no Brasil," in Bolívar Lamounier, ed., De Geisel a Collor: O balanço da transição (São Paulo: Editora Sumaré, 1990), 71.
22. This poll is discussed in Cultura Política, no. 1 (Sept. 1989).

Table 11.3. Citizen Satisfaction with Brazil's Performance in the Military Regime of 1964–1985 and the First Four Years of Civilian-led Democracy (New Republic)

	Percentage of Respondents			
Item Evaluated	Better in the Military Regime	Better in the New Republic	Equal in Both Periods	Don't Know or No Answer
Overall situation	46	17	28	9
Economic situation	52	13	26	9
Inflation	56	14	21	9
Foreign debt	37	18	30	15
Corruption	35	18	32	15
Political liberties	19	48	18	15
Freedom of expression	16	50	17	17

Source: Data from Ibope (April 1989), *N*=2,750, national poll. Cited in Bolívar Lamounier and Alexandre H. Marques, "A democracia brasileira no final da 'década perdida,'" in Bolívar Lamounier, ed., *Ouvindo o Brasil: Uma análise da opinão pública brasileira hoje* (São Paulo: Editora Sumaré, 1992), 149.

Why do so many Brazilians feel ambivalent about democracy? One possible hypothesis is that, in a country with possibly the worst income distribution in the world, the poorest citizens feel that the combination of inefficacious government and prolonged politics of austerity has meant that democracy has made no positive impact on the economic quality of their life. In fact, when we run the three classic questions about support for democracy against citizens' statements concerning their economic situation, we see a mixed picture. On two of the three questions, the poorest citizens were indeed the least supportive of democracy. However, on one key question, "in some circumstances a dictatorship is better than a democracy," they were the *most* supportive of democracy. The general picture that emerges is that in inequality-ridden Brazil, support for democracy is relatively low in *all* groups (table 11.4).

When we explore further citizens' ambivalence about democracy in Brazil, we find ourselves confronting disturbing information concerning three of the arenas of consolidated democracies—rule of law, a usable state, and a strong political society—we discussed in chapter 1. In Spain, Portugal, Greece, and Uruguay, these three arenas were not problematical for the consolidation of democracy, so we did not devote much attention to them. Brazil, however, forces us to explore these arenas of democracy in greater detail.

Democracy is less a normative utopia than an agreement about arrangements for regulating conflict. The state itself must respect the law and be a resource for citizens in the regulation of conflict. For the state (under the direction of a democratic government and shaped by democratic institutions) to carry out its conflict regulation and social integration tasks, two things are necessary. First, the state must be normatively and institutionally present throughout the territory.

Table 11.4. Correlation between Respondents' Attitudes toward the Adequacy of Their Income and Their Attitude toward Democracy: Brazil

	Percentage of Respondents				
Opinion about Preferred Polity	Entire Sample	"My income is more than sufficient."	"My income is precisely what I need."	"My income is not sufficient."	"My income is very small and this creates difficulties."
"Democracy is preferable to any other form of government."	42	52	49	49	35
"In some cases, a dictatorship could be preferable to a democracy."	22	26	24	23	21
"For people like me, a democratic and a nondemocratic regime are the same."	24	16	23	21	27
DK/NA[a]	12	7	5	7	16
N	2,500	55	11	864	1,247

Source: Data from Datafolha, Brazilian National Survey, February 1992.
[a]DK/NA, don't know or no answer.

Second, the state must be seen as a relatively usable and fair vehicle for settling conflicts in the polity. We are living in a period when there are cries for shrinking the role of the state in all areas. But one of the normative promises of democracy is that citizens will have their rights respected. If one group in civil society, because of its superior economic or coercive resources, denies the rights of other groups in civil society, then, if democracy is indeed to be a vehicle for regulating conflict and providing rights to its citizens, the state must be effectively present. It is in this basic sense that citizenship and democracy assume the normative and institutional presence of the state. Modern citizenship and modern democracy require a state. Even before the auto-coup by President Fujimori, the Peruvian state had shrunk so much that citizenship and democracy had already lost most of their meaning. Brazil too is a country with great problems concerning the normative and institutional presence of the state. Study after study reveals that the over-riding majority of Brazil's citizens do not believe that the state attempts to enforce laws on all its citizens impartially. In particular, citizens believe that the justice system fundamentally exists to protect the powerful and that the police are not to be trusted (table 11.5).

The police and the legal system are virtually not present concerning detection and prosecution of rural violence against the poor. Between 1964 and 1989, 1,566 citizens (rural workers, indigenous people, and some lawyers and religious people) were killed in conflicts involving land disputes. Only 17 people were ever tried for these killings. Only 8 were convicted. The absence of access of ordinary citi-

Table 11.5. Degree of Agreement or Disagreement with Statements about the Fairness of the Justice System and the Police in Brazil, 1989

	Percentage of Respondents			
Assertion	Completely Agree	Partially Agree	Partially Disagree	Completely Disagree
"In Brazil the justice system only functions to help the powerful."	58	26	7	6
"The police arrest and kill innocent people."	39	39	9	9

Source: Data from CEPAC-IBOPE national poll of eighty questions administered in April 1991 to a national sample of 3,600 respondents. The results are partially reported by the director of CEPAC; Rubens Figuiredo, "Verdades e mitos sobre a cultura brasileira," in Lamounier, *Ouvindo o Brasil*, 95–115. In May 1989 the São Paulo Commission on Peace and Justice did focus group analysis on citizen perceptions of the justice system, the police, and the fairness of the state. The qualitative results strongly support the quantitative findings of CEPAC-IBOPE. See *Pesquisa direitos humanos: Primeira fase relatorio final* (São Paulo: Comisão Justiça e Paz, Maio, 1989).

zens to the law is demonstrated graphically by the fact that, of the eight convictions, three cases involved priests, three involved lawyers, and two involved international organizations coming to the defense of indigenous peoples.[23]

In urban areas the state is present in the form of police but the use of deadly force is extremely high by world standards for a democracy. For example, one measure of estimating whether deadly force is excessive is the ratio of police killed to citizens killed in gun fire exchanges in the line of duty. In 1990 in New York City, 7.8 citizens were killed in such exchanges for every policeman. In 1990 in the city of São Paulo, the ratio was 28 to 1. In greater São Paulo, where much of the poorer population lives, the ratio was closer to 40 to 1. Another key indicator to explore is wounded to killed ratios, that is, the number of citizens wounded in encounters with police in relation to the number of citizens killed in such encounters. In Chicago from 1971 to 1974, the ratio was three people wounded by the police to every one killed by the police (393 citizens were wounded and 131 citizens were killed). In São Paulo in 1990 however, 251 citizens were wounded and 588 citizens were killed by the police. That is, the killed to wounded ratio was 7 times that of Chicago. Such a killed to wounded ratio indicates that many citizens were probably not so much killed in gun fights with the police as executed by the police.[24]

These indicators help explain why many reports in Brazil show that people are

23. See Paulo Sérgio Pinheiro, "Democracia, derechos humanos y desarrollo económico y social: Obstáculos y resistancias. El caso de Brasil," *Nucleo de estudios da violência*, (Dec. 1991): 11.

24. For a pioneering study of these and other indicators, see Paul G. Chevigny, "Police Deadly Force as Social Control: Jamaica, Brazil and Argentina," *Nucleo de estudos da violência*, (1991). These questions are brilliantly reviewed and documented in Wanderley Guilherme dos Santos, "Fronteiras do Estado Mínimo: Indicações sobre o híbrido institucional brasileiro," in *Razões da desordem* (Rio de Janeiro: Rocco, 1993), 77–116. For an excellent and disturbing analysis of a cycle of public sector nonperformance in the areas of justice, which helps generate civil society vigilantism and hostility toward defenders of human rights, which in turn feeds indiscriminate police violence, see the chapter, "Police Violence and the Failure of the Rule of Law," in Teresa Pires do Rio Caldeira, "City of Walls: Crime, Segregation and Citizenship in São Paulo" (Ph.D. diss. Department of Anthropology, University of California at Berkeley, 1992), 159–223.

so afraid of the police that they seldom will ask for their help in regulating conflict. As we shall see, this contrasts sharply with Chile, where 76 percent of the total population, and even 72 percent of those who identify themselves as being on the left, believe they would receive favorable treatment if they went to the police with a problem.[25]

The fiscal crises of the state in Brazil exacerbates many of these problems. For example, the National Police Academy, which could possibly have become the source of new research, socialization, and training by the new democratic government, has been closed since 1985 due to fiscal constraints.[26]

Guillermo O'Donnell has made a fundamental observation about the theme we have just been discussing. He argues that if one could color a map green where the state and the democratic government are effectively present, grey where they are only intermittently present, and blank where their services, laws, and norms are not felt, a consolidating democracy should be getting greener. Unfortunately, the combination of low efficacy, high corruption, indiscriminate neoliberal state bashing, and fiscal crisis has meant that from 1985 to 1993 the grey and blank areas of Brazil expanded more than the green areas.[27]

In late April 1993, six months after President Collor's impeachment and the assumption of office by President Itamar Franco, Brazil continued with inflation at near 30 percent a month. Many analysts expressed their doubts that any serious constructive change could happen until a new president was inaugurated in January 1995. Numerous politicians and citizens alike voiced their fear that the presidential election would polarize the country and produce another minority government. Commentators even worried at the time that, if hyperinflation hit Brazil, President Itamar Franco might resign and this could produce a political and constitutional crisis.[28]

25. The Chilean data are contained in "Estudio social y de opinión pública," Centro de Estudios Públicos, Documento de Trabajo, no. 173 (Santiago, Chile, Feb. 1992), 65. The wariness of the Brazilian population about the police is captured by the song by Chico Buarque de Holanda, "Help! Call the Thief!" (instead of "Help! Call the Police!")

26. Interview of Stepan with Celio Borja, Minister of Justice, Brasilia, April 7, 1992. In the same interview, when asked to comment on why Brazilians had doubts about the justice and police systems, he answered "they are right to have such doubts." But he went on to lament that he had virtually no financial resources to allocate to improve the situation.

27. Guillermo O'Donnell, "Notes on State, Regime and Crisis—or how I am finding it useful to think about countries that are not moving at all toward a consolidated democratic regime" (paper prepared for a conference of the East-South System Transformation Project, Toledo, Jan. 1991). We have, for stylistic reasons, taken the liberty of changing some of O'Donnell's colors, but his fundamental observation remains. A somewhat revised version of O'Donnell's seminal work was published as "On the State, Democratization and Some Conceptual Problems (a Latin American View with Glances at some Post-Communist Countries)," *World Development* 21 (1993): 1355–69.

Also see dos Santos, "Fronteiras do Estado Mínimo," in the book *Razões da desordem*. In the same book also see "Primeiro, terceiro e outros mundos possíveis, ou como se tornar um país mais pobre e predar o planeta," 117–48.

28. One of Brazil's leading newsletters, "Carta Política," in its April 5–11, 1993, issue, actually ran an elite poll on who should succeed President Franco if he resigned. In conversations with Stepan in April 1993, some deputies said that, before President Itamar Franco could be encouraged to resign, the next official in

In this context, one of Brazil's most influential journalists wrote the following editorial in Brazil's largest newsweekly:

"The March Towards a Coup"

Below follows a small list of assumptions about which it is reasonable to suppose that there exists a form of consensus in Brazil.

1. The country is without a currency.

2. The Brazilian economy is passing through the worst crisis of this century and there is no hope of recuperation in the next two years. Much less recuperation within the current rules of the game.

3. The crisis of the public security services of the great cities has made the citizens frightened to go out into the street.

4. The executive power entered into a collapse ten years ago.

5. The legislative power is without prestige.

It is possible to live with some of these plagues for a long time, or even with all five for a short time, but it is impossible to endure all indefinitely.

Brazil is on the road to a coup d'etat. This situation cannot last two more years. How the coup will come is difficult to say. Depending on the results of the presidential elections next year, and the conduct of the winner, it could be more similar to 1937 (a coup with the president) than to 1964 (against the president).

... To say that there is no danger of a coup because the armed forces are out of politics is nonsense. The people who make coups in Brazil are the fat cats of civilian life. ... There is not a coup in march. What there is, is a situation that will bring the middle class and the empresarios to march in the direction of a coup.[29]

Even without the above editorial we believe that we have given more than enough evidence to demonstrate that Brazil in 1993 was far from a consolidated democracy. Indeed, the central questions to conclude with are what could be done to avoid a further erosion of Brazil's fragile democracy or, more positively, to improve the quality of Brazil's democracy. These questions of course merit many full-length economic, social, and political studies. We will limit ourselves to a few observations that flow directly out of our initial theoretical framework concerning the five arenas of a consolidated democracy we discussed in table 1.1: a lively civil society, a relatively autonomous and valued political society, a rule of law, a usable state, and an institutionalized economic society. Is democracy in Brazil an overdetermined failure or, in the Hirschmanian sense, are there some possibilistic opportunities?

DEMOCRATIC ARENAS IN BRAZIL: POSSIBILISTIC RESTRUCTURING?

Let us first address the question of a rule of law. The concept of "accountability" is central to the modern theory and practice of democratic control of the state.

---

the constitutional line of succession, the president of the Chamber of Deputies, who also was involved in corruption charges, should be forced out of office.

29. Elio Gaspari, *Veja* (April 28, 1993): 23.

Unfortunately, there is no word for accountability in Portuguese. The closest word is *responsabilidade*, which conveys the idea that, if something goes exceptionally wrong, the person in charge will assume responsibility. In modern democratic practice, however, accountability carries broader connotations. It implies that all financial records will be *routinely* subject to inspection and that it is the obligation of the officials who use public funds to follow transparent procedures. Increasingly, the concept is used to help draw boundaries between acceptable use of public funds for public purposes and the unacceptable use of public funds for private purposes. Bureaucrats and officials who treat state resources as their "patrimony" are held accountable and can be put in jail.[30]

As we have seen, a major reason why the rule of law is so weak in Brazil is that state officials are perceived by citizens not to be even-handed in the administration of justice. Worse, state officials often violate the law with impunity. In this respect the impeachment of President Collor was a victory for democratic procedures and the first major victory against "impunity." From a theoretical point of view, what was impressive about the impeachment proceedings is that, in the midst of the multiple crises of democracy, every major component of the Brazilian polity carried out its fundamental democratic tasks. The charges of corruption in the Collor administration were first fully aired by civil society in a series of excellent magazine and newspaper stories. Then, instead of downplaying the charges or seeking extraconstitutional help from the military, the relevant part of political society—the Brazilian Congress—correctly assumed the responsibility to carry out a full investigation. The state also played its appropriate role. The newly redefined office of the attorney general conducted an independent inquiry, and the Justice Ministry allowed the federal police to carry out certain indispensable investigations. As the results of the multiple investigations became public, civil society, this time through numerous mass public demonstrations, urged political society to vote for impeachment and against impunity. At no time did any significant force outside or inside the military attempt to involve the military in decelerating or accelerating the working of democratic procedures.[31] It is too

30. For a succinct comparison of Max Weber's classic distinction between a modern bureaucracy and the system of administration under patrimonial rule, see Reinhard Bendix, *Max Weber: An Intellectual Portrait* (New York: Anchor Books, 1960), 423–25. The six key principles of bureaucratic rule, all of which contrast with patrimonial practice and all of which the democratizing champions are still attempting to achieve in Brazil, are the following: (1) "Official business is conducted on a continuous basis." (2) "It is conducted in accordance with stipulated rules." (3) "Each official's responsibilities and authority are part of a hierarchy of authority." (4) "Officials and other administrative employees do not own the resources necessary for the performance of their assigned functions but they are *accountable* for their use of these resources. Official business and private affairs, official revenue and private income are strictly separated." (emphasis added) (5) "Offices cannot be appropriated by their incumbents." (6) "Official business is conducted on the basis of written documents." Ibid., 424.

31. No full-blown academic studies of the impeachment have yet been published. However, an important start is Maria D'Alva Gil Kinzo, "The Political Process of Collor's Impeachment" (paper prepared for the conference, "Brazil: The Struggle for Modernization," Institute of Latin American Studies, University of London, Feb. 18–19, 1993, to be published in the conference proceedings by the institute). For the political

early to make any judgments, but it is possible that the impeachment of Collor has helped the rule of law more generally in Brazil by at least putting the issue of impunity of state officials and legislators on the democratic agenda.[32]

Let us turn to the question of Brazil's "political society" and its relationship to the economy. One of the principal tasks that a democratic political society must perform is the aggregation of interests in such a way that elected governments can develop sufficient democratic power to address effectively many of the major problems society faces. As we have documented, the failure of seven different stabilization plans between 1985 and 1992 was one of the many signs of the lack of efficacy and democratic power in Brazil.

Brazil was not an economy in complete ruins in this period. For example, in 1992, while Mexico had a trade deficit of 22.8 billion dollars, Brazil had a trade surplus of more than 15 billion dollars and reserves of more than 20 billion dollars. But, largely due to its political crisis, the first three civilian presidents were unable to gain support for any stabilization policy, the real income of workers deteriorated, and eventually the state faced such a fiscal crisis (defined as virtually no credit so that the state can only borrow at very short term and at very high interest rates) that real interest rates in 1992 approximated 30 percent. This high real interest rate made new private sector investment prohibitively costly for those who needed to go to capital markets and made the Brazilian government's internal debt service so burdensome that the state could deliver fewer and fewer collective goods to its citizens. Weak governments in Brazil from 1985 to 1993 would not or could not address the fiscal crisis and stabilize the economy. The price of legislative support was almost always an agreement not to put fiscal reform on the agenda or to give special subsidies to constituents of congressmen and governors.

Many things contributed to this situation, but certainly a major role has been played by Brazil's combination of a fragmented party system and populist, voluntarist presidents. Fragmented multiparty systems and presidentialism make an extremely unsupportive combination for an enduring democracy.[33] This is one of

---

process of impeachment, also see Marcos Nobre, "Pensando o Impeachment," *Novos Estudos CEBRAP,* no. 34 (Nov. 1992): 15–20.

32. For example, *Veja* (March 24, 1993), 16–25, ran two articles contrasting *impunity* for corruption in Brazil with *imprisonment* in Italy. Among other things, *Veja* pointed out that a 1988 census of the 8,700 prisoners in the state of Rio de Janeiro did not unearth one person who was in jail for abuse of political funds or influence peddling. The Ministry of Justice in April 1993 was replicating the study for the 126,000 prisoners in Brazil's jails and had tentatively found virtually no white-collar criminals or former high state officials in prison for any of Brazil's well publicized corruption scandals. Another sign of the new climate were the serious investigations and unprecedented number of indictments that resulted from the massacre of 111 prisoners by the state police following a prison riot in São Paulo. The riot occurred shortly after the impeachment of Collor.

On a more cautionary note, almost no one went to jail for any of the Collorgate scandals or the São Paulo massacre. The reforming attorney general of the republic, Aristides Junqueira, has argued that, unless the penal system and the judicial system are reformed so as to help yield convictions in cases of proven wrong-doing, the new public consensus against impunity could turn to deepened cynicism.

33. See the powerfully argued article by Scott Mainwaring, "Presidentialism, Multipartism, and De-

the many reasons we believed that the adoption of parliamentarianism in the Brazilian plebiscite of April 21, 1993, would have given valuable degrees of freedom to the country's fragile democratic system. Let us elaborate why we believe the defeat of parliamentarianism in April 1993 was unfortunate.

Governments in a parliamentary system cannot form and cannot endure without at least the compliance of a majority. Therefore, parliamentarianism over time develops many incentives to produce coalitional majorities. Presidentialism has far fewer coalition-inducing incentives.[34] Because of parliamentarianism's greater facility in creating enduring majorities out of multiparty coalitions, it has a greater capacity to endure with a large number of parties in the legislature than does presidentialism. In fact, between 1979 and 1989 as many as eleven consolidated parliamentary democracies had—using the Laakso/Taagepera index to count "effective" parties—between three and seven "effective" political parties in their legislatures.[35] In sharp contrast, *none* of the long-standing presidential democracies had more than 2.7 "effective" political parties in their legislatures. Using the same index, Brazil in 1992 had 8.5 parties in the lower house, making it *three times* more fragmented (or less aggregated) than any long-standing, consolidated presidential democracy in the world (table 11.6). Parliamentarism, with its

mocracy: The Difficult Combination," *Comparative Political Studies* 26, no. 2 (July 1993): 198–228. He will develop this argument in greater detail for the case of Brazil in "Dilemmas of Multiparty Presidential Democracy: The Case of Brazil," in Scott Mainwaring and Matthew Shugart, eds., *Presidentialism and Democracy in Latin America* (forthcoming).

34. The general argument for parliamentarism first appeared in print in Juan Linz's brief "Excursus on Presidential and Parliamentary Democracy," in Linz and Stepan, *The Breakdown of Democratic Regimes*, 71–74. There is a growing literature regarding the comparative advantages of presidentialism and parliamentarism, much of which is brought together in Juan J. Linz and Arturo Valenzuela, eds., *The Failure of Presidential Democracy* (Baltimore: Johns Hopkins University Press, 1994). For an article that gives empirical, cross-national evidence that supports the parliamentary thesis, see Alfred Stepan and Cindy Skach, "Constitutional Frameworks and Democratic Consolidation: Parliamentarism versus Presidentialism," *World Politics* (Oct. 1993): 1–22. For a sophisticated quantitative analysis that demonstrates that paliamentary regimes are more conducive to economic growth and survive economic hard times better than do presidential regimes, see Adam Przeworski and Mike Alvarez, "Parliamentarianism and Presidentialism: Which Works? Which Lasts?" (paper prepared for presentation at the triennial congress of the Polish Sociological Association, Lublin, June 27–30, 1994).

Another of the many reasons we favor parliamentarianism is because it is a form of mutual dependence between the legislature and the executive. The legislature can dismiss the government, and the government can call for new elections. This mutual dependence helps produce coalitional majorities or, failing that, provides routine impasse-breaking devices. In contrast, presidentialism is a system of mutual independence. The president has a fixed and independent mandate, and the legislature has a fixed and independent mandate. Governments can and do form without majorities and, in systems with many parties like Brazil, such minority governments routinely face a situation of long-term legislative impasse with no routine constitutionally available impasse-breaking device. Under these conditions legislatures can vote for budgets without assuming the responsibility of government.

35. The "effective" number of parties is calculated using the Laakso/Taagepera index, which takes into account the relative strength of parties according to the number of seats they hold in the lower house of the national legislature. See Markku Laakso and Rein Taagepera, "'Effective' Number of Political Parties: A Measure with Application to West Europe," *Comparative Political Studies* 12, no. 1 (April 1979): 3–27. See Stepan and Skach, "Constitutional Frameworks and Democratic Consolidation," 8–9.

Table 11.6. A Laakso/Taagepera Index of "Effective" Political Parties in the Legislatures of the Parliamentary, Semipresidential, and Presidential Continuous Democracies, 1979–1989

Parliamentary		Semipresidential		Presidential	
3.0 or More Parties	Fewer than 3.0 Parties	3.0 or More Parties	Fewer than 3.0 Parties	3.0 or More Parties	Fewer than 3.0 Parties
	Kiribati[a]				
	Nauru[a]				
	Tuvalu[a]				
	Botswana 1.3				
	St. Vincent 1.4				
	Dominica 1.5				
	Jamaica 1.5				
	Bahamas 1.6				
	Trin&Tob 1.6				
	Barbados 1.7				
	St. Lucia 1.7				
	NewZeal. 2.0				USA 1.9
	Canada 2.0				
	UK 2.1				Colombia 2.1
	India 2.1				
	Greece 2.2				Dom.Rep. 2.3
	Austria 2.4				Cost.Ric. 2.3
	Australia 2.5				
	Solomons 2.5				
	Mauritius 2.5				Venez. 2.6
	Ireland 2.7				
	Spain 2.7				
	Japan 2.9				
W.Germ.3. 2		France 3.2			
Norway 3.2					
Sweden 3.4					
Luxemb. 3.4					
Israel 3.6		Portugal 3.6			
Nether. 3.8					
Italy 3.9					
PapNeGu. 4.0					
Iceland 4.3					
Denmark 5.2					
Belgium 7.0					

Note: Switzerland and Finland are "mixed" systems with 5.4 and 5.1 effective parties, respectively.
Source: This table is reproduced from Alfred Stepan and Cindy Skach, "Constitutional Frameworks and Democratic Consolidation: Parliamentarism versus Presidentialism," *World Politics* (Oct. 1993): 8–9. See also Markku Laakso and Rein Taagepera, "'Effective' Number of Parties: A Measure with Application to West Europe," *Comparative Political Studies* 12, no. 1 (1979): 3–27.
[a] Given the absence of formal parties, there are fewer than two "political groupings."

strong incentives for party discipline and coalition-building, would, in our opinion, encourage Brazil's political society to aggregate interests.

Having missed what we believe was an historic opportunity to change from a
presidential to a parliamentary system, what, if anything, could be done to improve the aggregative and government-producing capacity of Brazilian political
society?[36]

In contrast to Chile and Uruguay, or even Argentina, Brazil has a political culture of weak party identities. But, while political culture is very important, so are
specific *incentives* that inhibit or reward party proliferation. In this respect, a good
case could be made that Brazil has one of the most permissive sets of electoral,
party, and congressional decision-rules of any country in the world. These decision-rules give extensive and very tangible incentives for "rent-seeking" behavior
by political entrepreneurs who create parties to use as tradeable assets or as a way
of avoiding party discipline.[37]

There are numerous important branching points in any "decision-tree" of
legislation that can encourage or discourage party proliferation. One major decision involves the type of electoral system a nation chooses for determining its legislature's composition. Here, the decision is usually between a majority system, on
the one hand, and some form of proportional representation (PR), on the other
hand. Although PR systems are considered more "representative" in that they tend
to reproduce in parliament the relative weight of political forces in the country,
these systems also tend to produce a more fragmented legislature. Majority systems and single-member districts, contrariwise, are designed to produce a parliament that represents only those main political forces in the country which are,
electorally, the strongest. Therefore, the majority system tends to produce fewer
parties in the legislature.[38] While this system may not appear to be as "representative" of the various political forces in a society (as compared to PR), it nevertheless encourages the formation of a legislature with majority parties and discourages party proliferation.

At each branching point, Brazil has chosen the decision-rule that *most* en-

36. Bolivar Lamounier has written two excellent articles that explore these questions in detail. See his
"Brazil: Toward Parliamentarianism?" in Linz and Valenzuela, eds., *The Failure of Presidential Democracy*,
179–219. He analyzes the defeat of the parliamentary option on pp. 215–16. The depressing mood in Brazil
in early 1994 is captured starkly in Lamounier, "Latin America's Critical Elections: Brazil at an Impasse,"
Journal of Democracy 5, no. 3 (1994): 72–87.

37. The oldest political parties with a significant history in Brazil are the PMDB (Partido do Movimento
Democratico Brasileiro) and the PT (Partido dos Trabalhadores), both of which were founded in the 1970s.
The three other South American cases in our analysis (Uruguay, Chile, and Argentina) all have some major
political parties that can trace their lineage to nineteenth century party roots. For a pioneering set of quantitative and qualitative comparisons, see Scott Mainwaring and Timothy R. Scully, "Introduction: Party Systems in Latin America," in Scott Mainwaring and Timothy R. Scully, eds, *Building Democratic Institutions:
Party Systems in Latin America* (Stanford: Stanford University Press, 1995), 1–34.

38. See the classic study by Maurice Duverger, *Political Parties* (New York: Wiley, 1954). Also see Duverger's more recent work, "'Duverger's Law': Thirty Years Later," in Bernard Grofman and Arend Lijphart,
eds., *Electoral Laws and Their Political Consequences* (New York: Agathon Press, 1986), 69–84.

courages party proliferation. Brazil chose proportional representation, but within PR a country can have a high threshold (5 percent) for a party to be represented in parliament or no threshold. Brazil has a threshold of close to zero. A party can get representation in the National Congress with as little as 0.04 percent of the national vote.[39] Concerning party discipline, the branching point is between a closed-list system, where the party ranks the top candidates and hence creates strong incentives for party discipline, or an open list, in which any candidate is free to run and those candidates who get the most votes believe they have received a "personal vote" rather than a party vote. Brazil has an open list. Legislative procedure can punish or not punish members who change parties. Brazil has no sanctions whatsoever.[40] A country can choose *not* to give any free media time to parties during elections, to give free media time only to major parties, or to give time to all registered parties no matter how small. Brazil's current legislation gives two hours of free time a year on national television and radio networks and one hour of free time on statewide television and radio stations to all of the *seventeen* registered parties.[41]

Could this extraordinary system of institutional incentives for party proliferation and undiscipline be altered? According to the constitution of 1988, anytime between October 1993 and elections in 1994 a constitutional revisory assembly could have come into being; in this assembly the two chambers would have met jointly and laws concerning constitutional statutes could have been passed by a simple majority. Unfortunately, they missed this opportunity. If a simple majority of the Constituent Assembly had so decided, they could have changed the Brazilian incentive system in numerous ways so as to discourage party fragmentation. For example, if they had chosen a German-style mixed electoral system (half PR with a 5 percent threshold and half single-member districts), Brazil would most likely have cut its party index in half. Unfortunately, as table 11.6 shows, while this is a perfectly normal number for a parliamentary system, it would still be substantially higher than that of any long-standing, democratic presidential system in the world. But our point is that despite Brazil's antiparty political cul-

39. This point is developed by Scott Mainwaring, "Parties, Politicians and Electoral Systems: Brazil in Comparative Perspective," *Comparative Politics* (Oct. 1991): esp. 43 n. 7.

40. Survey reported in *Folha de São Paulo*, October 27, 1990, A-4. For an extensive documentation of pary indiscipline, see the excellent article by Scott Mainwaring, "Brazil: Weak Parties, Feckless Democracy," in Mainwaring and Scully, eds., *Building Democratic Institutions,* 354–98. In this context electoral volatility in Brazil is extremely high. In fact, according to the Pedersen index of electoral volatility, which measures the percentage of seats (or votes) that change party hands from one election to another, the average volatility over a century in eighteen advanced industrial democracies was below 9 percent (in votes). Uruguay's volatility on the Pedersen index from 1971 to 1989 was 9.1 percent, Argentina's from 1983 to 1993 was 12.7 percent, Chile's from 1973 to 1991 was 15.8 percent, Brazil's from 1982 to 1990 was 40.9 percent, one of the highest ever recorded. Much of Brazil's volatility came from the choices of the politicians, not the electorate. For example, more than one-third of all federal deputies elected in 1986 had changed their party by 1990. See p. 374 for data on the Pedersen index.

41. Announcement of Tribunal Superior Eleitoral reprinted in "Horario eleitoral gratuito recomeça dia 6," *O Estado de São Paulo,* April 24, 1993, 6.

ture, the current democratic representatives, if they ever want to reduce the number of parties to a more manageable size or to improve party discipline in the legislature, have a vast range of incentive systems they could use. If they do use them, they will, in our judgment, increase the capacity of Brazil's political society to aggregate interests and to generate democratic power. If they refuse to do so, they may weaken rather than strengthen political society. This is not overdetermined.

In chapter 1 we argued that democratic consolidation required a "usable state." We also argued that, despite the occasional state-bashing rhetoric of some who argue for "state shrinking," serious and effective privatization paradoxically requires a reasonably strong state regulatory apparatus.[42] The goal of such a state coordinated privatization strategy is to *restructure* the state so that the fiscal crisis is overcome, state revenues are enhanced, and the overall market economy is stronger. This strategy entails a simultaneous effort to narrow the scope of the state, to sell off industries, and to downsize unnecessary personnel so that the private sector is not unduly constrained and the state's capacity to carry out its core responsibilities in health, education, law, and justice are enhanced. In different ways both old and new democracies try to grapple with more or less success with this difficult dual task.

Many international observers criticized President Collor's corruption but praised his privatization. However, we believe that when privatization under Collor is studied systematically the record will reveal that the combination of a fragmented political society and a voluntaristic president produced a radically suboptimal style of privatization that had dangerous consequences. For example, in a country where the most serious estimates are that the dollar value of tax evasion is greater than the dollar value of tax collection, President Collor in his hasty rush to reduce state personnel continued the shrinking of tax collectors that had begun with the 1979 oil shock. In Brazil in 1979 there were 12,000 federal tax agents. In 1992 there were only 5,700.[43] Worse, the combination of presidential corruption and an erratic series of economic reforms with no sustained political base led to a taxpayer revolt. The index of nonpayment of income tax by juridical persons who had acknowledged the amount of tax they owed (and thus were not the normal "evaders" but actual "defiant declarers") grew from 1.6 percent in 1988 (the year before President Collor assumed office) to 50.7 percent in 1991 (his last full year in office).[44]

---

42. As Miles Kahler argues, "orthodoxy has not dealt successfully with the paradox of using the state—its only instrument—to change policy in a less statist direction." Kahler, "Orthodoxy and Its Alternatives: Explaining Approaches to Stabilization and Adjustment," in Joan M. Nelson, ed., *Economic Crisis and Policy Choice: The Politics of Adjustment in the Third World* (Princeton: Princeton University Press, 1990), 33–61, quote from p. 55.

43. See the informative article on the erosion of the state's capacity to tax by Lourdes Sola, "State, Structural Reform and Democratization in Brazil: Economic Liberalization by Default," in C. Acuña, E. Gamarra, and W. Smith, eds., *Democracy, Market and Structural Reform in Contemporary Latin America* (New Brunswick, NJ: Transaction Publishers, 1994).

44. Data supplied to Alfred Stepan by the chief economist of the Brazilian congressional commission

Many of the state-shrinking reforms were so poorly drafted by the presidential office that they were counterproductive. Critical parts of the "brain" of the state were endangered by ill-thought-out privatization. For example, in the Ministry of Industry and Commerce, support for computerized data banks concerning all of Brazil's industries was canceled and much of the data lost. This eliminated an important potential resource for an effective tax collection effort. Analogously, in the Ministry of Agriculture, a key animal inspection facility was drastically cut, which weakened the state's quality control capacity vital to both health administration and export promotion. Finally, many of the best civil servants in Brasilia left government service after President Collor exercised a line-item veto that would have cut their retirement pay packages substantially. Some top civil servants were almost immediately rehired by other parts of the state and now receive two state paychecks monthly. Many others were lost to public service or remained in a demoralized condition.[45] Greater selectivity by state privatizers could have saved more money and brainpower and could have more efficiently reduced redundant or incompetent personnel.

Neoliberal reform can be done in such a way as to shrink unnecessary state expenditures, eliminate the fiscal crisis, and increase the net sum of state social expenditures and investments in infrastructure. Between 1986 and 1990 two reform governors in the state of Ceará, Tasso Jereissati and Ciro Gomes, cut total paychecks from 152,000 to 112,000 (paychecks, not necessarily personnel, since some individuals had received as many as seven paychecks) and went from spending 69 percent of the state budget on personnel and debt to 39 percent. With the extra money the state of Ceará increased infrastructure investments and vital social services. In the process, Ceará created an award-winning grassroots preventive medicine health program, reduced infant mortality by 32 percent in four years, developed a highly participatory self-help housing program, and built roads at one quarter the cost per mile of roads built in other states. The two governors of Ceará also generated the highest approval ratings of any governors in Brazil.[46]

President Collor's brand of neoliberalism and state-shrinking exacerbated the fiscal crisis, paralyzed private sector investment, disorganized the state, and weakened democratic support. Governor Tasso Jereissati's and Ciro Gomes' brand of neoliberalism ended the fiscal crisis, increased public sector social and infra-

---

on fiscal reform from a table on "Índices de Inadimplência—Brasil" to be published in the forthcoming "Relatório Final da Comissão Parlamentar Mista de Inquérito" on fiscal reform. Also see Sola, "State, Reform and Democratization in Brazil."

45. Stepan's interviews with staff members and a senator from the Brazilian Congressional Commission for Economic Reform, April 22, 1993. The civil service decree was Decree 8112, December 12, 1990.

46. For the program to reduce infant mortality that won Ceará UNICEF's Maurice Pate Prize, see UNICEF, "Ceará: Como Reduzir a Mortalidade Infantil" (June 1991). For a report on the reversal of the fiscal crisis, see Ceará, Secretaria de Planejamento de Ceará, "A caminho do Ceará melhor: A rota das mudanças" (Fortaleza: 1993), and "Hope from the North-East," *Economist* (Dec. 7, 1991): 18–20.

structure investment, led to a boom in private sector industry, restructured and strengthened the state, and deepened democratic support.

Let us conclude with a comment about "civil society." Brazil has historically had one of the worst income distribution patterns in the world. From 1980 to 1992 income distribution deteriorated further.[47] Thus, in some fundamental sense, the Brazilian economic crisis is clearly not due to an *excess* of effective demand for redistribution by the poor. In fact, there is ample evidence to indicate that for Brazilian democracy to improve, not only must political society be able to *aggregate* demand more effectively, but the poorest of the poor should be able to *articulate* their demands more effectively, so that they have greater access to the rights of citizenship and their potentially substantial weight is more routinely incorporated in the decision calculations of political society. Two recent studies of participation and democracy in Brazil show that the clearest way for this to happen is by increased education. One study of social organization shows that, if one divided Brazil into five regions and each region had three levels of education, in fourteen of the fifteen observations the more education a person had, the more likely they were to join an organization.[48] A multiyear public opinion study of political culture also shows that the less educated people were, the less critical they were of government and the more distant they were from politics (a supportive mix for the persistence of nonresponsive or antidemocratic governments). But, among manual laborers, the more educated a person was, the more critical they were of government services, but the more supportive they were of participatory politics and engagement with the system (an attitude that, given Brazil's current social deficit and political crisis, is supportive of democratic reform).[49]

Brazil is a case of an unconsolidated democracy. Part of its problem is due to the constraints posed on the transition by the military and the debt crisis. But if democracy erodes further in Brazil, it will mainly be because Brazilian democracy has been unable to solve problems that emerged after the transition. Our brief review of five critical components for a consolidated democracy, namely a system of law and justice that is a recourse for citizens, a civil society that can articulate demands, a political society that can aggregate demands, a state that performs vital collective good functions, and an economic society that produces both taxes and wealth, indicate that in every arena there are choice points where policies could improve the situation. Neither breakdown nor consolidation is overdetermined. However, unless there are important changes in most of the five key dem-

47. See Lamounier, "Brazil: Inequality against Democracy."

48. See dos Santos, "Fronteiras do Estado Minimo," table 15, p. 97.

49. This is a major finding of the multiyear public opinion research project by José Álvaro Moisés, "Cultura Política e Consolidação Democratica no Brasil," to be published in book form. For a brief review of the results of this project in English, see José Álvaro Moisés, "Democratization, Mass Political Culture and Political Legitimacy in Brazil" (Center for the Advanced Study in the Social Sciences, Juan March Institute, Madrid, estudio/working paper 1993/94, Feb. 1993).

ocratic arenas we have just discussed, the margin of error for democratic politics will be decreased and the chances of a breakdown will be increased.

Brazil 1994–1995: A Turn Away from Democratic Deconsolidation

In 1993, as we have seen, some influential analysts were discussing the possibility of the breakdown of democracy in Brazil. However, in the context where the military were not accepted as a legitimate and viable ruling alternative and where the regional *zeitgeist* was still supportive of democracy, *no* important groups in Brazil devoted significant resources to mobilizing support for a coup. With no nondemocratic alternative that was attractive or credible, but with fears of a hyperinflation and political unrest growing, a consensually oriented finance minister, the famed sociologist and senator from São Paulo, Fernando Henrique Cardoso, publicly crafted a parliamentary coalition to support a new approach to stabilization. His Plan Real started on July 1, 1994. By July 1, 1995, according to the *Economist*, "inflation had plunged, from several thousand per cent a year to less than 30%."[50]

Many political analysts had feared that the 1994 presidential election would be a polarizing conflict between the right and the left in the second round. As it was, the confrontation was between two basically social-democratic candidates, with albeit different projects, constituencies, and styles, who had been leaders of the civil society opposition to authoritarianism, Fernando Henrique Cardoso and the equally famed union leader, Luís Ignácio "Lula" de Silva. Cardoso, a leading advocate of parlimentarianism, was elected president of Brazil in the first round. In contrast to Fernando Collor, President Cardoso brought great legislative prestige and experience to the chief executive office. On July 1, 1995, on the first year anniversary of the Plan Real, public opinion polls showed that Cardoso had a 72 percent approval rating. At the elite level, conversations about democracy had changed radically by mid-1995 from those in 1993. There were few, if any, conversations about democracy breaking down.[51] Nonetheless, all serious analysts, which very much includes President Cardoso and his minister of planning, José Serra, are painfully aware that all of the problems documented in this chapter concerning extreme social inequality, a fragmented party system, problems of

50. See "Brazil: Happy Birthday," *Economist*, July 8, 1995, 46.
51. Public opinion poll conducted by *Jornal do Brasil/Vox Populi* between July 21 and July 24, 1995, supplied to us. Our observation about 1995 versus 1993 elite conversations is based upon a speech given by Bolivar Lamounier in Brasília on the first anniversary of Plan Real. In that speech Lamounier nonetheless stressed the critical need for major changes in Brazil's political institutions.

rule of law, and a porous fiscal system remain on the agenda.[52] Change in the fiscal system will be particularly hard, given the politics of Brazil's federal system. Support for the new president may be high, but changing ambivalent Brazilian attitudes toward democracy is no doubt the work of a decade. Nonetheless, the Southern Cone's most troubled transition entered 1995 with a surprising lack of *desencanto*.

52. Awareness of the need to develop a political strategy to overcome these problems was repeatedly stressed in public and private conversations by Cardoso and Serra at a meeting attended by us in Brasília, December 2–3, 1994. We must note that the four-year maximum time horizon for the Cardoso administration is a more confining context for democratic reform than would be the case if Brazil had a parliamentary system.

12

From an Impossible to a Possible Democratic Game: Argentina

Argentina from 1976 to 1983 was a hierarchically led military regime. Within this broad context the Argentine military regime had some distinctive specificities that left an impact on the transition and on efforts to consolidate democracy. Uruguay's military regime imprisoned more people per capita than Argentina and applied very systematic repression. However, in Argentina military specialists and entrepeneurs in violence contributed to at times an anarchic reign of terror between 1975 and 1977. Thirty-two times more people per capita "disappeared" in Argentina than in Uruguay, and more than three hundred times more people per capita disappeared in Argentina than in Brazil. While the overall regime lacked the coherence of ideology and organization of a totalitarian regime, many of the military's statements about the need to exterminate their enemies had a totalitarian edge.[1] The military government was in fact much more of an authoritarian "situation" than a institutionalized "regime."[2] The military never created parties or held elections as in Brazil. They never formulated a "guided democracy" constitution and submitted it to a plebiscite as in Uruguay or Chile. Moreover, throughout the period of military rule there were numerous conflicts between the services and within the army which led to abrupt changes in tentative political alliances and actual economic policies. There was no sign of a long-range plan to yield power via competitive elections. If anything, General Galteri's invasion of Malvinas was a bid to create a new base for military rule and

1. A few quotes will suffice. General Iberico St. Jean asserted "first we'll kill the subversives, then their collaborators, then . . . their sympathizers, then . . . those who remain indifferent." The fact that ideology and not actions was a sufficient cause for execution is captured in the statement by General Luciano Menéndez, "We are going to have to kill 50,000 people; 25,000 subversives, 20,000 sympathizers, and we will make 5,000 mistakes." Both quotes are from the valuable study by James W. McGuire, "Interim Government and Democratic Consolidation: Argentina in Comparative Perspective," in Juan J. Linz and Yossi Shain, eds., *Between States* (New York: Cambridge University Press, 1995), pp. 179–210; quotes from p. 183. The most detailed record of the style and pattern of military terror is found in *Nunca Más: The Report of the Argentine National Commission on the Disappeared* (New York: Farrar, Straus and Giroux, 1986). For a table showing the comparative rate of "disappearances" in the southern cone, see Stepan, *Rethinking Military Politics,* 70.

2. The distinction between an "authoritarian situation" and an "authoritarian regime" is developed in Juan J. Linz, "The Future of an Authoritarian Situation or the Institutionalization of an Authoritarian Regime: The Case of Brazil," in Alfred Stepan, ed., *Authoritarian Brazil: Origins, Policies and Future* (New Haven: Yale University Press, 1973), 233–54.

his personal leadership. Given this overall context, when the Argentine military surrendered to the British in Malvinas on June 14, 1982, the military were not seen as a reliable or competent ally by any major section of Argentine civil or political society and internal military dissension, recriminations, and lack of discipline reached such unprecedented levels that some officers worried about intramilitary armed conflict and the dissolution of the military as an organization.[3]

In his extremely informative comparative study, Felipe Agüero constructs a typology of the post-transition power of the military, in which the key variables are whether the previous regime was militarized or civilianized and whether the transition path is via a pacted reform, a military coup, or a military defeat and regime collapse. In his typology, if the authoritarian regime is militarized and the transition path is military defeat and regime collapse, the relative position of the military will consequently be "weak." His two examples are Argentina and Greece.[4]

We feel this typology is quite useful for the analysis of transition. However, if we want to analyze the political consequences of military defeat for democratic consolidation, we must be very careful to distinguish between those cases where the authoritarian military regime is hierarchically led and those cases where it is not and between cases where the regime actually "collapses" and cases where it does not. The defeat and disgrace of the Argentine military in the Malvinas war contributed, as did the Greek military fiasco in Cyprus, to the end of the military government. As in Greece, the departing military tried to impose some conditions as the price of their extrication. But the combined weight of their internal disunity, their low prestige, and the institutional urgency of rapid extrication from rule meant that neither the Greek nor the Argentine military establishment was in a position to impose constraining conditions on successor governments as the price of allowing a transition.

But there are important differences between Greece and Argentina that all too often are overlooked. The fact that the Argentine military organization had been hierarchically led, while the Greek military was not, meant that the Argentine military did not in fact "collapse" and thus were in a position to gravely complicate

3. For example, in an interview on July 24, 1982, in Buenos Aires with Stepan, an Argentine general argued that internal military conflict could lead to the de facto dissolution of the military and that the Russian Revolution had occurred only because the Czarist army had disintegrated. The most graphic account and systematic analysis of internal military conflicts in this period is Andrés Fontana, "De la crisis de Malvinas a la subordinación condicionada: Conflictos intramilitares y transición política en Argentina" (Helen Kellog Institute for International Studies, University of Notre Dame, August 1986, working paper no. 74).

For the professional incompetence of the Argentine military during the Malvinas conflict and its relationship to the politics of repression, see the well-documented and scholarly work on the Argentine military, from the junta to the Menem presidency, by a Spanish colonel, Prudencio García, *El drama de la autonomía militar: Argentina bajo las juntas militares* (Madrid: Alianza Editorial, 1995). For the origins of the dirty war and its development and an exhaustive study of political violence, see María José Moyano, *Argentina's Lost Patrol: Armed Struggle, 1969–1979* (New Haven: Yale University Press, 1995).

4. See Felipe Agüero, "The Military in the Processes of Political Democratization in South America and South Europe: Outcomes and Initial Conditions" (paper presented at the XV International Congress of the Latin American Studies Association, San Juan, Puerto Rico, September 21–23, 1989).

the task of consolidating democracy. A brief resume of the basic narrative sequence of events should suffice to lead us away from the "collapse" metaphor. The Argentine surrender in Malvinas was on June 14, 1982. The same day General Galtieri resigned under pressure as commander-in-chief of the army. He was succeeded by General Cristiano Nicolaides. General Nicolaides, without permission of his junta allies in the air force or the navy, designated a retired army general, Reynaldo Bignone, as a caretaker president. Bignone became president July 1, 1982. Shortly thereafter the military announced that elections would be held no later than the end of 1983. Elections were indeed held in October 1983, and in December 1983 Raúl Alfonsín was inaugurated as Argentina's new president. Eighteen months do not a "collapse" make.[5] Thus, though Portugal, Greece, and Argentina are often lumped together in the transition literature as regime collapses due to external defeat, the metaphor of collapse obscures some critically different power relationships in the countries.

In Portugal nonhierarchical officers who were angry and afraid at being involved in a losing war overthrew the regime, junior officers helped form a provisional revolutionary government, and in the midst of an enormous popular mobilization the *state* collapsed. In Greece, a nonhierarchical military regime, in a Malvinas-like adventure, almost led Greece into a war with Turkey. The nonhierarchical military regime was overthrown by the hierarchical military, who within twenty-four hours gave power to a caretaker civilian government pledged to elections. The state did not collapse. A weak, nonhierarchical military regime was overthrown, and the military as organization gave their weight after the elections to the purge and prosecution of the nonhierarchical military who had committed human rights violations.[6]

The particularly violent nature of the Argentine military government, their internal dissension, their loss of an external war, and the ability of the hierarchical military to hold on to the reigns of government for eighteen months after the defeat in war had five somewhat contradictory consequences. First, the fact that the military was able to retain control of the government for eighteen months after their defeat and to give over the presidency to the victor in elections meant that an interim government with the possibility of revolutionary policies, as in Portugal, was precluded.

Second, although the military held on to government, they were in fact weakened in power terms because, much more than in Uruguay, the military as institution was so gravely divided that they feared internal armed conflict. Their perceived need of extrication was much more intense that that of the Uruguayan military. In these circumstances the political parties were able to refuse military

5. The previously cited article by McGuire, "Interim Government and Democratic Consolidation," is particularly convincing on this point.

6. For the importance of the state versus regime distinction, see Robert M. Fishman, "Rethinking State and Regime: Southern Europe's Transition to Democracy," *World Politics* (April 1990): 422–40.

overtures to enter into a pact. Three times the military made pact overtures, and three times the parties refused. This power relationship explains why the Argentine transition began with fewer agreed-upon restrictions by the political parties than in Brazil, Uruguay, or Chile. The parties did not accept an indirect presidential election as Brazilian parties did in 1985. The parties did not accept the exclusion of a major presidential candidate as they did in Uruguay. And the parties did not have to agree to begin government with key parts of the authoritarian regime's constitution still in effect as they did in Chile. Argentina had the only unpacted and the most classically free transition of our four South American cases.

Third, this set of power relationships also explains why, alone among the South American cases, the incoming democratic government, as in Greece, prosecuted, convicted, and imprisoned numerous military officers for human rights violations.

Fourth, the indiscriminate violence of the military and their ill-thought-out foreign military adventure seriously weakened their currency as a political ally in Argentine politics. In relational terms this increased the currency value of electoral politics.

Fifth, in Greece the trials of the military helped consolidate democracy. In Argentina, trials almost led to the breakdown of democracy. The key explanatory variable here is the difference between a nonhierarchically led and a hierarchically led military government. In Greece, the military as an institution saw the trials and imprisonment of the nonhierarchical leaders of the military government as a way to reconsolidate military hierarchy. In Argentina, the military as organization saw efforts to imprison the hierarchical leaders of the former military government as a mortal attack on their institution. Between April 1987 and January 1990 there were four military uprisings by midlevel officers that weakened the authority of President Alfonsín, shifted his attention away from other critical policy tasks, and forced him to make damaging concessions.[7]

We do not want to overstress the issue of civil-military relations. President Alfonsín had many other problems in his presidency. He announced upon taking office that he would move forward quickly to redress the accumulated social plight of the Argentine population. But he never had a majority in both houses. Worse, he was never able either to arrive at an understanding with or to control the Peronist trade unions, which led thirteen general strikes against his economic plans. In 1986 Raul Alfonsín's major stabilization plan, the Plan Austral, was abandoned. In the October 1987 election he lost control of both houses. In a parliamentary system Alfonsín almost certainly would, and should, have left office at this time. Condemned to office by the presidential calendar, with growing military pressures, and without a winning coalition in civil and political society, Al-

7. For a very careful comparative analysis of the four uprisings and their effect on the Alfonsín government, see Carlos H. Acuña and Catalina Smulovitz, "¿Ni olvido, ni perdón? Derechos humanos y tensiones cívicos-militares en la transición Argentina," Buenos Aires, CEDES, *Documento CEDES*, no. 69, July 1991, esp. 19–31.

fonsín saw a dangerous decline in his government's support, the administration's ability to implement economic policy, and indeed the prospects for democratic continuity.[8] By June 1988 inflation was growing sharply, the government had an approval rating of only 12 percent, and 49 percent of the population felt there could be a military coup.[9] By June 1989, in the midst of Argentina's first-ever "hyperinflation," his government in ruins, a humiliated Raúl Alfonsín left office six months early. But, in an extraordinary turnabout, by June 1992 many politicians and analysts in Argentina began to argue that Argentina had stopped its 60-year decline, and some even suggested that democracy was consolidated.

Later in this section we examine the emergence of a new set of historical relationships, but here we briefly call attention to two major changes that occurred under President Menem. The first concerns the military. When the junior officer uprisings began in 1987, the painted-face rebels (the *carapintadas*) received the tacit support of the military-as-institution because the carapintadas' major announced objective was to defend the military's hierarchical institutions against "unjust" trials. However, the carapintada phenomenon took on a dynamic of its own that made the military-as-institution increasingly wary of them. The revolts became more explicitly political. More and more they were motivated by the personal goals of their junior officer leaders. Eventually, they came to represent less a defense of the military-as-institution than a nonhierarchical attack against not only President Alfonsín but the army high command. Furthermore, in October 1989, President Menem gave a massive pardon to the military for human rights offenses under the juntas, and armed insubordination under the democratic government of Raul Alfonsín, leading some of the released junta leaders to proclaim that they had been vindicated. In this new context, when junior officers and numerous noncommissioned officers started an uprising in December 1989, the carapintada cycle ended as the president and the commander-in-chief joined forces to smash the uprising in the name of military discipline and political democracy. Whereas President Alfonsín lost authority by military uprisings, an antihierarchical military revolt gave President Menem an opportunity to enhance his authority.[10]

8. Three manuscripts that reflect this eroding quality of Argentine democracy in 1987–89 are David Rock, "The Decline and Fall of a Democratic Regime: The Alfonsín Government, 1986–1989," Andrés Fontana, "La política militar en un contexto de transición: Argentina 1983–1989 (both papers prepared for a conference at the Schell Institute, Yale University, March 1990); and Marcello Cavarozzi and María Grossi, "De la reinvención democrática al reflujo político y la hiperinflación (la Argentina de Alfonsín)" (paper prepared for a conference at CERC, Santiago, Chile, Aug. 1990).

9. These data are from polls designed by Edgardo Catterberg and reported in his very informative *Argentina Confronts Politics: Political Culture and Public Opinion in the Argentine Transition to Democracy* (Boulder, Colo.: Lynne Rienner, 1991). The data are from pp. 91 and 110.

10. The previously cited publication by Acuña and Smulovitz, "¿Ni olvido ni perdón?" 39–45, is excellent on how and why the carapintada cycle came to an end. For a strong documented critique of Menem buying peace with the military at the expense of reversing hard-won court decisions, see the previously cited work by the Spanish colonel, García, *El drama de la autonomía militar,* 269–76.

The other major improvement concerned citizens' perception of the economy. Part of this was due to some generic aspects of democracy as a system and part was due to a specifically Argentine phenomenon in the Menem presidency. The generic dimension concerns the political economy of legitimacy. We argued in chapter 5 that most authoritarian regimes have difficulty sustaining a government after three consecutive bad economic years because their claims to rule are based on efficacy, not legitimacy. In contrast, we argued that democratic regimes have two sources of insulation from economic bad times; some legitimacy for the system qua democratic system and the prospect that, with upcoming elections, there can be a vote for an alternative. In Argentina, in November 1988, 70 percent of the people polled felt that conditions in the country had worsened in the last five years. However, 74 percent nonetheless still affirmed that "democracy is always preferable to a dictatorship." Only 15 percent of those polled—in contrast to Brazil's 40 percent—felt that things would be better if the military returned. The economy deteriorated further in the next six months. There was no objective sign that things had improved. However, there had been elections. Even though the winner, Carlos Menem, received 49 percent of the vote, the percentage of citizens who expressed belief that the economy would improve had gone up from 32 percent to 72 percent.[11]

Let us turn to some specifically Argentine dimensions of the economic problem. Whereas President Alfonsín was weakened by thirteen general strikes, President Menem in his first three years of rule did not face one general strike, even though his neoliberal policies shocked the Peronist rank and file. Menem undoubtedly profited by the diffuse support he received in Peronist circles, notwithstanding the turn in his policies. He also benefitted from the widespread support he received from local and international capital. Unlike Alfonsín, who came into office at the height of the debt crisis, Menem was helped by the fact that he came into office just as the world debt crisis was ending and international capital was seeking new outlets. But, finally, President Menem reached back into the classic corporatist repertoire for controlling labor. Much of the funds and power of labor leaders and unions is due to their official recognition. President Menem, like Getúlio Vargas of Brazil and Lázaro Cárdenas of Mexico before him, used the weapon of official recognition to strengthen allies that created new leadership groups and to deny legal recognition to his challengers (such as the CTA). Wildcat strikes were declared illegal and unions that persisted in strikes risked losing their official status or some of the state support for their specific activities. Most importantly, like Vargas and Cárdenas in the 1930s, Menem gained something even Perón never had, extensive government control over the unions' vast social welfare funds.[12]

11. For these polls see Catterberg, *Argentina Confronts Politics*, 110 and idem, "The Balance of Transition: Perceptions of Government Efficacy in the Southern Cone" (paper prepared for the XVth World Congress of the International Political Science Association, Buenos Aires, July 21–25, 1991.)

12. For a brief but revealing review of Menem's strategy to control labor, see Rosendo Fraga, "1991, fin

Despite the absence of strong labor resistance, President Menem's first economic plan was no more successful than President Alfonsín's plan. Forced by the fear of a second hyperinflation, President Menem in February 1991 selected a new minister of finance, Domingo Cavallo, who appealed to the Congress where Peronists and their allies had a majority and to all sectors of society for support, so as to avert a spiral of hyperinflation and economic decline. With inflation low and the economy growing, the approval rating of the government's economic policy rose in Buenos Aires from 16 percent in March 1991 to 68 percent in December 1991.[13] By mid-1992 many in Argentina argued that, after a long period of government with low efficacy and low legitimacy, Argentina was beginning to develop a polity with moderate efficacy and some legitimacy.

Beyond the Impossible Game?

In a justly famous work Guillermo O'Donnell used an elaborate game-theoretical model of Argentine electoral politics to show that party democracy as it was played in Argentina during 1955–66 was an "impossible game."[14] While we will not use the exact categories O'Donnell used, let us schematically review the three core assumptions and rules that in fact made democratic politics an impossible game in this period.

The first core assumption was that, while the Peronistas were the largest single party, they should not be allowed to compete in elections because they would almost certainly win and, if they won, they would not rule democratically and could not be removed from office by elections. Juan Peron's ambivalence toward democratic practices and doctrines when he was in power from 1943–55 allowed groups who may have been undemocratic themselves to disguise their undemocratic behavior in the democratic discourse of protecting democracy.

A second core assumption of O'Donnell's impossible game was that the largest anti-Peronist party, the Radicals of the People, would never be strong enough to win in an election unless there were some restrictions against the Peronists. However, even if they came into office via semifree elections, the Radicals could not be an effective government given the strength of Peronism in the unions.

The third fundamental assumption was that the bourgeoisie accepted the military as the umpire of the electoral game. The umpire had two key functions. First,

de un poder sindical," *Ambito Financiero* Dec. 30 1991: 18. On the origins of the Peronist labor model of incorporation and corporatist control, see Ruth Berins Collier and David Collier, *Shaping the Political Arena: Critical Junctures, the Labor Movement and Regime Dynamics in Latin America* (Princeton: Princeton University Press, 1991), 331–50.

13. Greater Buenos Aires polls done by Estudio Mora y Araujo, Noguera y Asociados.

14. Guillermo O'Donnell, "An Impossible 'Game': Party Competition in Argentina, 1955–66," in *Modernization and Bureaucratic-Authoritarianism: Studies in South American Politics* (Berkeley: Institute of International Studies, University of California, 1973), 166–200.

if the bourgeoisie felt there was what they considered a crisis of legitimacy (such as a victory of Peronists or small parties allied to the Peronists), the umpire was allowed to terminate that round of the electoral game. Second, if the bourgeoisie felt there was a crisis of efficacy (such as the inability of weak anti-Peronist parties to rule effectively), the umpire could terminate that round of the electoral game. The military umpire was delegated these powers by the bourgeoisie because they considered the military a reliable ally or a temporary ruler who would not try to create a permanent nonelectoral game. Rather, the assumption of the game was that after an interval, in which the rules were changed somewhat, another round of the electoral game would begin.

O'Donnell does not explicitly argue the point, but we believe that the rules of the game led to a long-term, double crisis of the Argentine polity, a crisis of democratic legitimacy because of the degree of exclusion and a crisis of efficacy because of the narrow support base of elected governments. This double crisis, plus the fact that the umpire normally did not try to create a Mexican-style authoritarian hegemony and if they attempted to do so they failed, contributed to Argentina's prolonged developmental crisis. No combination of actors could create either a sustained democratic or a sustained nondemocratic base of support for a policy program. In such a context "rational actors" strove to accumulate and use nondemocratic resources, and almost no one wanted to continue with any given round in the electoral game. O'Donnell summarized the situation thus:

> Once one round of this game has been played and knowledge of the rules is perfect, it is evident that it is a futile game which no one can win. Consequently, a rational player becomes "non-allegiant" (he rejects the game, or at least has no interest in its continuation) and "irresponsible" (since everyone will lose eventually, whatever short-term gains are possible should be pursued). Not only is the game futile, but its dynamic has increased polarization. With no players to seek its continuation, it can easily be terminated.[15]

Although O'Donnell's classic analysis was published in 1973, we believe the Argentine military regime of 1976–83 can be seen as a horrifying and ultimately completely unsuccessful effort to use force to change Argentina's economy and polity and to create a new game. The game the military and their allies tried to construct failed dramatically in both efficacy and legitimacy. No one wanted to play round three of the "bureaucratic-authoritarian" game, round one being 1966–73 and round two being 1976–83.

In terms of the categories we have used in this book, the O'Donnell game of Argentine electoral politics in 1955–83 had the following characteristics. Democracy was never the only game in town. Democracy was always marked by semiloyal and frequently disloyal behavior by most groups. There were few intertem-

15. Ibid., 180.

poral incentives for the major actors to continue any given democratic game. System blame of electoral politics was endemic.

One important way to examine cases of attempted redemocratization is to see whether many of the elements that led to the previous breakdown are still present or whether, due to new circumstances, the passage of time, or political learning, a fundamentally new context exists for the renewed effort to institutionalize and consolidate democracy. It is clear that the characteristics of Argentine electoral politics we have described were sufficient by themselves to make a consolidated democratic game impossible. Is there any evidence to indicate that Argentine politics was becoming a possible democratic game after 1992? Very schematically let us re-examine the three core assumptions of the impossible game. Do they still exist, or have they been transformed?

Let us begin with the relationship in the impossible democratic game between the bourgeoisie, the military, and the Peronist party. For the bourgeoisie the electoral game was never the only game in town because the dominant electoral force—Peronism—was not only an unacceptable ally but an unacceptable winner. They could risk their at best semiloyal participation in electoral politics because for them the military was an acceptable umpire of the electoral game or, between rounds, an acceptable ally. However, the military's effort to create their own game in 1976–83 changed the bourgeoisie-military-political party relationships fundamentally. The indiscriminate killing and torture by the military meant that many members of the hitherto "untorturable classes" had their sons and daughters tortured and/or "disappeared." Also, the military's adventure in Malvinas, if it had been prolonged another few months, might well have led to widespread expropriations of English property in Argentina. A victory in Malvinas would have opened up possible Third World policy alignments that would have seriously harmed the social identities and economic alliances of the Argentine bourgeoisie. The military also revealed themselves as dangerously divided and weak. Given this post-Malvinas set of social, economic, and military circumstances, the military by 1983 was no longer seen as a reliable ally or a credible umpire by the bourgeoisie. Finally, when Menem adopted and, more importantly, implemented most of the neoliberal policies long championed by a weighty faction of the bourgeoisie, the Peronist party was transformed in their eyes from being an unacceptable to a potentially acceptable—indeed in the early 1990s an *actual*—ally. The old impossible democratic relationship between the bourgeoisie, the military, and the Peronist party no longer existed.[16]

16. The fundamental change in conservative-business-military relationships is explored in much greater detail in two excellent doctoral dissertations by Carlos H. Acuña of the University of Chicago and Edward L. Gibson of Columbia University. Acuña argues that democracy has become the only game in town and the military an unacceptable ally in "Intereses empresarios, dictadura y democracia en la Argentina actual (o, porqué la burguesía abandona estrategias autoritarias y opta por la estabilidad democrática)" (Buenos Aires: CEDES, Feb. 1992). Edward L. Gibson focuses on the political party ramifications of the military becoming an unacceptable ally and on the new neoliberal alliance between Menem

The second key component of the impossible democratic game was that for many players in the electoral game, competitive, free, and inclusive elections could not be risked because, so the argument went, the Peronists would always win and would never play by fully democratic rules and, if somehow the Radicals did win, they could not govern effectively given Peronist power. Indeed, O'Donnell commented that as early as the Frondizi presidency (1958–62) the largest anti-Peronist party, the Radicales del Pueblo, had become convinced that, "given the situation then prevailing, they would never be able to win an election."[17] The overwhelming victory of the Peronists in 1973 and their tolerance and even encouragement of the para-military violence of the Montoneros further contributed to what many called the "iron law of Argentine politics"—that in free elections Peronists always won and did not respect minority rights. When Raúl Alfonsín and his Radicals triumphed in the free elections of 1983, he broke this iron law of Argentine politics. Menem was re-elected as president in 1995. However, the Radicals (and FREPASO, a new party that outpolled the Peronists in the capital in 1995) have hopes that by 1999 the Argentine polity will be ready for an alternation in party rule. If the democratic game continues, activists in the three major parties believe they can win. The prospect of winning increases the intertemporal incentives for party leaders in all parties to keep the democratic game going.

However, there are some elements of the old game that worry some Radical Party activists. The fact that Peronist unions led thirteen general strikes against the Radical Party administration of Alfonsín and that the Radicals in office were not able to sustain an effective economic policy is a carryover from the impossible game. Nonetheless, in 1992–94 some Radical Party leaders began to argue privately that, if Menem were able to sustain a viable economic model and curb the autonomy of the trade unions, a future Radical government—not faced by a disloyal military and economic crisis—might well be more efficacious than they had been in the past.

The third characteristic of the impossible game was the dangerous discourse about Argentina having a permanent majority party that at best was ambivalent about democracy. Part of this discourse was, as we have seen, weakened by the Peronist defeat in the 1983 elections. Time, both biological and historical, has also reduced the power of this discourse. Some feuds in politics die only when the key protagonists die. Part of the impossible game in Argentina was that Perón, as long as he lived, represented an extraordinary pole of attraction and repulsion in Argentine politics. As a leader who rose to prominence when Mussolini still ruled, Perón was able to create and sustain a semifascist, populist-nationalist rhetoric. With Perón alive Peronism was more movement than party. Perón's policy and

---

and conservative parties in "Conservative Parties and Democratic Politics: Argentina in Comparative Perspective," (Ph.D. diss., Department of Political Science, Columbia University, 1992).

17. O'Donnell, "An Impossible 'Game,'" 188.

doctrinal ambivalence helped perpetuate his dominance of both movement and party. Given, after 1955, the almost permanent hostility of the military as an institution and of important sectors of the bourgeoisie to Perón, elections were never the only game in town for Perón. He thus harbored and generated a wide variety of extraparty and extrademocratic resources.

Menem, however, has come to power in a different world historical time. Like the successors of Franco, he could not sustain the rhetoric of an historical *Zeitgeist* that no longer existed. Also, after his attack on the Peronist unions, Menem and even more so his most probable successors in the party will increasingly have to base their power strategies on democratic electoral power rather than on the movement. If this dynamic does indeed develop, then the last component of the impossible game will have been transformed.

We cannot say that a change in these three interconnected components of the former impossible game is sufficient for democratic consolidation. However, we can say that these changes were a precondition for developing a possible democratic game. Indeed, the changes in these three components have increased the type of behavior that makes democratic politics a possible game. The three major parties and the leading business groups are displaying no outright democratically disloyal behavior. There is less system blame of democratic institutions because efficacy rose rather than declined in 1990–94. With all three major parties believing they have a chance to win and to govern effectively in the future—and not to be subject to extreme harm if they lose—intertemporal incentives to play the democratic game have increased. Finally, given the widespread perception that the military is no longer a reliable nondemocratic coalition partner, democracy is more and more becoming the most important—and increasingly the only— game in town. However, while we believe that democracy has become a possible game in Argentina, we will close by examining some disturbing questions concerning the quality of the democracy that is emerging.

THE QUALITY PROBLEMS OF ARGENTINE DEMOCRACY

In chapter 1 we discussed the five arenas of a consolidated democracy and how ideally, within each arena, activities are carried out and norms are developed that strengthen democratic practices and values in the other arenas (see table 1.1). Let us review briefly President Menem's influence on the quality of democracy in the five arenas we discussed.

If the government of a new democracy consistently operates at—or over—the margin of the constitution, it obviously weakens the rule of law and its primary organizing principle, constitutionalism. With President Menem's style of governance very much in mind, Carlos Nino, the late distinguished legal theorist of Argentina, observed that "the fear of a coup or a breakdown of democracy is increasingly receding but those risks have been replaced by fears about the degradation and emptying of democracy." The Argentinian political sociologist, Juan Carlos Torres, also primarily worried about the quality of democracy, remarked that Menem's style of rule, unless checked, would produce a "low intensity democracy with low intensity citizenship."[18] Judging from the evidence, President Menem's ambivalent attitude toward the rule of law has weakened not only constitutionalism, but also the quality of democratic practices and norms in the state apparatus and in civil, political, and economic society.

In his first four years in office President Menem took advantage of a clause in the constitution that allowed the president to issue decrees if he affirms that they are "necessary and urgent." Between 1853 and 1989 his predecessors had issued fewer than 30 such decrees. Between 1989 and 1993 President Menem issued 244. Furthermore, the constitution required ex post facto consideration of the decrees by the legislature. Only 74 percent of President Menem's 244 decrees were ever submitted to Congress, and only 4 percent went through the full ratification process. However, almost all of the decrees stayed in effect because the legislature, where President Menem had a majority, did not challenge them.[19]

When President Menem was faced with possible resistance by the Supreme Court, he used his legislative majority to increase the number of Supreme Court judges from five to nine. Only forty-one seconds of congressional debate were devoted to this unannounced change. Worse, Menem's closest advisers had been at the center of major corruption charges, some of which implied a connection to President Menem himself.[20] Criminal investigations were on the horizon. In this context Menem created an upper criminal tribunal that was second only to the Supreme Court and was endowed with the judicial faculty to review and reverse any criminal court in the country. Menem staffed the court almost entirely with his supporters. All the new appointees were given life appointments. If Menem were ever to be convicted for corruption, during or after his presidency, he would have to be convicted by this court.[21]

While there has been little direct censorship of the press, a diffuse "culture of fear," almost eliminated under President Alfonsín, re-emerged under President

18. Alfred Stepan, discussions with Carlos Nino and Juan Carlos Torres, Buenos Aires, Argentina, July 26–29, 1993.

19. Study by Mateo Goretti and Della Ferreira Rubio, cited in *Latin American Regional Reports: Southern Cone Report* (Sept. 9, 1993), 8.

20. Argentina's leading investigative journalist, Horacio Verbitsky, reviews the charges of corruption, justice tampering, and constitution flaunting in a long interview, "Menem es el jefe de la corrupción," *La Maga* (March 11, 1992), 1–3. Also see his best-selling book, *Robo para la corona: Los frutos prohibidos del árbol de la corrupción* (Buenos Aires: Planeta, 1991).

21. Alfred Stepan, discussion with Carlos Nino, Buenos Aires, July 25, 1993.

Menem. For example, the leader of the Argentine Journalists' Union claimed that, in the first forty-two months of Menem's government, 139 journalists received anonymous threats and that there were fifty cases of physical assault. He asserted that most of the anonymous threats had "been traced to people with government connections." In the first five-month period leading up to the 1993 congressional elections, the main conservative newspaper, *La Nación,* charged that twenty-two of their journalists received death threats, specifically warning that they should stop criticizing President Menem.[22]

The 1853 constitution, which was reinstated after the inauguration of President Alfonsín, explicitly prohibited the immediate re-election of the president. During 1992–94 President Menem devoted most of his energies to changing this constitutional clause. The political atmosphere became so charged that his minister of the interior resigned with a warning that he believed that some of Menem's political operatives were determined to ensure the continuity of Menem "whatever the cost."[23] The leading opposition party issued a statement in which they said that the Menem government was on the verge of "breaking the legitimacy" of any possible process of revising the constitution.[24] But, after the Peronists had done well in the October 1993 congressional elections, former President Alfonsín, in a move that caught other major leaders of his party by surprise, entered into a personal pact with President Menem to allow a constituent assembly that eliminated the clause prohibiting a sitting president from running for immediate re-election, in return for any number of reforms.[25] Eventually, Alfonsín's party, in a rancorous and sharply divided party convention, approved the Menem-Alfonsín pact. In the May 1995 election, despite a UNICEF report that mortality rates in the northwest of Argentina had soared, continuing revelations about corruption, and Menem's condemnation by human rights groups for his equivocal comments to the mili-

22. See "Politics and Press: Menem's Attitude 'Authoritarian,'" *Latin American Regional Report: The Southern Cone Report* (Sept. 9, 1993), 6–7.

23. See the excellent account of the constitutional crisis by Mario Daniel Serrafero, *Las formas de la reforma: Entre Maquiavelo y Montesquieu* (Buenos Aires: Centro Editor de América Latina, 1994). For the resignation of the minister, see vol. 2, pp. 173–75.

24. Ibid.

25. There is no consensus as to why Alfonsín entered into the pact. Some say he did so because he believed that it was the best way to avoid a breakdown of constitutionality a la Perón in 1949. Others say it was to reinsert himself as a leading power broker in Argentinian politics. Alfonsín stressed the importance of the proposed constitutional revisions that would "attenuate hyperpresidentialism." However, Serrafero's close analysis of the Menem-Alfonsín agreement (sometimes called the Olivos Pact) reveals that most of the proposed constitutional revisions would not actually attenuate the more extreme presidential prerogatives. The proposed office of the chief of the cabinet, billed as quasi-prime ministerial, has in reality few real powers; there is no significant diminution of presidential state-of-siege powers, and new provincial intervention procedures, while giving the legislature a larger role, would still be quite large for a democratic federal system. Finally, the proposed constitutional revisions would in fact accord a degree of de jure constitutional legitimacy to "delegated legislation" by the president. For the full text of the Olivos Pact and an astute commentary on its clauses, see Serrafero, *Las formas de la reforma,* 2:195–224.

tary that "we triumphed in that dirty war" (as well as for the beatings received by the mothers of the Plaza de Mayo), Menem, in a personal triumph, polled more than twice as many votes as his party and won re-election. Menem thus won control of the presidency until the turn of the century.[26] However, given the relative absence of an independent legislature or judiciary and a constitutional revision process marred by personalism, the consolidation of a high-quality democracy in Argentina is far from assured.

President Menem's opponents, especially in the Radical Party, have at times discussed his impeachment on grounds of constitutional violation.[27] His allies insist Menem is on, but not quite over, the margin of constitutionality. In fact, public opinion gives President Menem quite low marks for his respect of the legal system and the legislative system.[28] The president's performance at the margin of the constitution and the public's approval of his style of politics are not the optimal mix for democratic consolidation. Guillermo O'Donnell would say it bears all the worrying characteristics of "delegated democracy." For O'Donnell, some of the major characteristics of delegative democracy are that (1) winning presidential candidates present themselves as above parties, (2) institutions such as Congress and the judiciary are a nuisance and accountability to them is an unnecessary impediment, (3) the president and his personal staff are the alpha and omega of politics, and (4) whereas in consolidated democracies elected executives are embedded in a network of institutionalized power relations, in delegative democracies the president insulates himself from most existing political institutions and organized interests and becomes the sole person responsible for the success of "his" policies. For O'Donnell, delegative democracies may or may not become authoritarian, but they cannot become consolidated democracies.[29]

The ideal combination for a consolidated democracy would be high efficacy

26. In the election the radicals received their worst vote in a free election in a hundred years, but a new, broad, center-to-left opposition coalition emerged—Frepaso, which actually received more votes in congressional elections than did the Peronist party. In the campaign, Frepaso stressed such issues as social welfare and corruption. For the final election results, see "Politics: Menem Exceeds All Expectation," *Latin American Regional Reports: Southern Cone Report* (July 1, 1995): 2–3, and "Dead Return to Haunt Menem: Government Would Prefer the Past to Remain Buried," *Latin American Regional Reports: Southern Cone Report* (April 20, 1995): 3.

27. For example, Deputy Jorge Vanossi filed a long detailed case for impeachment on grounds of multiple violations of the constitution in February 1992. However, because of Menem's control of Congress and the judiciary, Vanossi argued that it was never seriously considered.

28. For example, in a Catterberg poll of Greater Buenos Aires ($N = 500$) in December 1991, 61 percent of those polled felt that the country was going in a good direction but 84 percent felt that there was "much" or "quite a lot" of corruption in the national government, 60 percent felt the judiciary had little or no independence, and only 14 percent felt that the government respected the Congress.

29. Guillermo O'Donnell, "Delegative Democracy?" (East South System Transformations Project, Department of Political Science, University of Chicago, 1991, working paper no. 21.) Politicians with strong delegative tendencies have been Fujimori in Peru, Menem in Argentina, Perot in the United States, and Collor in Brazil. For an abbreviated version of O'Donnell's article, see *Journal of Democracy* (Spring 1994): 55–69.

and high legitimacy. But, even in periods of relatively low governmental efficacy, high legitimacy can help a consolidated democracy weather inevitable economic downturns. Was the price of Argentine high efficacy in the 1990s a legacy of delegated democracy and only moderate legitimacy? If so, what happens to such a political system if efficacy decreases?[30]

30. One thinks, for example, of the harmful implications for Venezuelan democracy of Carlos Andrés Pérez's style of governance. He was popular when he was efficacious (due to high oil prices) but corrupt in the 1970s. When he returned for a second term in the early 1990s and was inefficacious (partly due to low oil prices) and corrupt, Venezuelan democracy almost broke down. Some good economists who are close observers of the Argentine economy argue that the low inflation/high growth economy of 1992–94 had three sources of potential weakness that could eventually decrease efficacy: (1) an overvalued peso tied to the dollar, which could lead to balance of payment problems; (2) a structural budgetary deficit obscured by one-time sale of state assets via privatization; and (3) a relatively low investment level in core industry. The fact that Argentina's economy, unlike Chile's, or even Brazil's, was significantly weakened by the Mexican "tequila effect" in 1995 reinforces these concerns. The 1995 downturn aggravated the continuing "social deficit" of Argentina's neo-liberal policies.

13

Incomplete Transition/Near Consolidation? Chile

THE CHILEAN military, especially the army, entered the struggle over the terms of transition in a far stronger position (institutionally and with their civilian allies) than did their Brazilian, Uruguayan, or Argentine counterparts. In Brazil, the military, for their own reasons, initiated the liberalization in 1974 which led to a long process of "concession and conquest" in a context of growing economic disarray that saw key industrialists join the democratic opposition. In Uruguay, by 1980 all of the major parties had joined forces against the military and their proposed constitution. The bourgeoisie, who by that time did not believe that the military had a necessary "defensive" project or a credible "foundational" project, carried out no actions to maintain the regime in power. In Argentina the military left power humiliated, defeated, and divided. In sharp contrast the Chilean bourgeoisie, through the 1980s, was willing to abandon any pretense of day-to-day political leadership in return for the military's "defensive" project against the left and in return for the credible foundational project the military, with their help, was conducting in the economy. In 1988, after fifteen years in power, the army was united, the authoritarian regime still had a solid core of supporters in civil society, and Pinochet had a plan to rule via the constitution for at least another decade.[1]

1. For a more extensive analysis of the very different mixes of "offensive" and "defensive" projects in Brazil, Argentina, Uruguay, and Chile and the degree to which the military was resisted or supported by civil society, see Alfred Stepan, "State Power and the Strength of Civil Society in the Southern Cone of Latin America," in Peter B. Evans, Dietrich Rueschemeyer, and Theda Skocpol, eds., *Bringing the State Back In* (New York: Cambridge University Press, 1985), 317–43. For an analysis of Chilean democracy and the reason for its breakdown in 1973, see Arturo Valenzuela, "The Breakdown of Chilean Democracy," in Juan J. Linz and Alfred Stepan, eds., *The Breakdown of Democratic Regimes* (Baltimore: Johns Hopkins University Press, 1978) (also available as a separate paperback book). The Chilean political scientist who develops special attention to the foundational project of the military regime is Manuel Antonio Garretón, *El Proceso Político Chileno* (Santiago: FLACSO, 1983), esp. 163–71. For the problems this presented for transition, see Garretón, "The Political Evolution of the Chilean Military," in O'Donnell, Schmitter, and Whitehead, eds., *Transitions from Authoritarian Rule: Latin America* (Baltimore: Johns Hopkins University Press, 1986), 95–112, esp. 98–103. For the first analysis to show how General Pinochet had transformed the Chilean military into a base for a new type of regime, see Genaro Arriagada, *El pensamiento político de los militares* (Santiago: CISEC, 1986). For an assessment of why the Chilean neoliberal economic restructuring actually went further than similar efforts that rapidly failed in Uruguay and Argentina, see Alejandro Foxley, *Latin American*

Pinochet yielded power only because the opposition united and mobilized to take advantage of the one possible vulnerability in Pinochet's own constitution. In 1980, General Pinochet and his followers constructed an authoritarian constitution and submitted it to a plebiscite. Most of the traditional right and business groups in Chile, unlike in Uruguay, campaigned actively for ratification of the constitution. Though the voting procedures were quite flawed, this constitution was indeed "ratified" in a further plebiscite. The constitution called for a plebiscite in 1988 in which, if the nominee unanimously selected by the four-person military junta won a majority of votes, he would rule as an "elected" president for eight more years.[2] However, as the world knows, Pinochet was the nominee and, though he received 44 percent of the votes, he did not receive the 50.1 percent he needed for eight more years of rule.[3]

This set the framework for the 1989 presidential election and the March 1990 transfer of power.[4] This also set the framework for an extremely constrained transition and the most democratically "disloyal" transfer of power of our southern European and Southern Cone cases.

In our conceptual introduction we argued that the most constraining constitutional formula for a new democratic government is one where the incoming government has to agree to rule with an authoritarian constitution crafted by an outgoing authoritarian regime. Given General Pinochet's strong bargaining position, he was able to extract this price. The newly elected government in Chile agreed to begin their rule with the 1980 constitution (partially amended in 1989) and to try to eliminate its authoritarian features by the difficult constitutional amendment procedures stipulated in the constitution itself.

Despite these continuing constraints on democratic policy-making, on August 7, 1991, President Aylwin announced that the Chilean transition had been com-

---

Experiments in Neoconservative Economics (Berkeley: University of California Press, 1983). For a valuable collection of essays by leading specialists inside and outside of Chile on what effect the foundational project did and did not have on labor, political parties, and social movements, see Paul W. Drake and Iván Jaksic, eds., *The Struggle for Democracy in Chile, 1982–1990* (Lincoln: University of Nebraska Press, 1991).

2. For a discussion of how the 1980 constitution opened up this possibility and how the democratic opposition was beginning to mobilize to maximize their opportunity, see Alfred Stepan, "The Last Days of Pinochet?" *New York Review of Books* 35 (June 2, 1988): 32–35.

3. Although the victory was highly satisfying for the democratic opposition, it was still disturbing to them to see that Chile's nondemocratic ruler received what was one of the highest votes of a nondemocratic incumbent in any transition that had occurred to date. For an analysis of the plebiscite and of public opinion polls that shed light on why voters, when organized by a united democratic front, voted against Pinochet, see Manuel Antonio Garretón, "El plebiscito de 1988 y la transición a la democracia en Chile" (Santiago: FLACSO Cuadernos de Difusión, 1988), and Roberto Méndez, Oscar Godoy, Enrique Barros, and Arturo Fontaine Talavera, "¿Por qué ganó el 'No'?" *Estudios Públicos* no. 33 (Summer 1989): 83–134. An extensive collection of surveys about the plebiscite was published by CERC (Centro de Estudios de la Realidad Contemporanea), coordinated by Marta Lagos and Carlos Huneeus.

4. For the 1989 electoral campaign and its results, see Alan Angell and Benny Pollack, "The Chilean Elections of 1989 and the Politics of the Transition to Democracy," *Bulletin of Latin American Research* 9, no. 1 (1990): 1–23, and Arturo Fontaine Talavera, Harald Beyer, and Luis Hernán Paúl, "Mapa de las corrientes políticas en las elecciones generales de 1989," *Estudios Públicos*, no. 38 (Autumn 1990): 99–128.

pleted and that his major task before his term ended in March 1994 would be to consolidate democracy.[5]

We argued in chapter 1 that it is politically as well as intellectually important to be explicit about whether a transition has actually been completed. It is politically important because, if people accept that a transition has been completed when it actually has not, this may indicate that key members of the aspiring democracy have begun to accept nondemocratic constraints as bearable, or, in the worst hypothesis, in some way even useful for the tasks of governing.

This said, it might be useful to return to our definition of a completed transition. The definition we offered in chapter 1 had three components: first, that a government has to be in power as a result of a free and popular vote; second, that this government has authority to generate new policies; and, third, that the executive, legislative, and judicial powers generated by the new democracy do not have to share power with other bodies de jure. By this definition, by the time the Aylwin government left power in March 1994, only the first of these criteria had been completely met. The presidential election of December 1989 was free and popular, as were the parliamentary elections, even though they were conducted with highly controversial electoral laws that cost the parties of the democratic coalition—"Concertación"—possibly as many as seventeen seats.[6] Pinochet's 1980 constitution—even after the democratic opposition negotiated important changes that were ratified in a 1989 plebiscite—clearly contained features that meant that the incoming democratic government had to share power de jure with individuals and institutions whose bases were not democratic in origin.

A key de jure limitation on democratic sovereignty, which in turn limited the democratic government's authority to generate new policies, is the fact that the outgoing nondemocratic government gave itself the constitutional right to appoint nine of the Senate's forty-seven members.[7] In the Chilean context this was critical because almost all of the controversial features of the 1980 constitution and the numerous last minute complementary "organic laws" that Pinochet issued which set the rules of the game for the electoral system, the composition of

5. For an extensive defense of this affirmation by the director of communication and culture of the Aylwin government, see Eugenio Tironi, "Sobre el fin de la transición" *APSI* (Oct. 21–Nov. 3, 1991): 19–21. In 1993 President Aylwin correctly reversed himself and noted that the transition still had important aspects to achieve before it could be considered completed.

6. For the electoral law—and especially a simulation to show how it could have very unexpected consequences—see the pioneering article by Arturo Valenzuela and Peter Siavelis, "Ley electoral y estabilidad democrática: Un ejercício de simulación para el caso de Chile," *Estudios Públicos* no. 43 (Winter 1991): 27–87.

7. See *Constitución Política de la República de Chile: 1980*, article 45. For an astute analysis of how some critical authoritarian features of the 1980 constitution were removed by negotiations followed by a plebiscite in 1989, see Carlos Huneeus, "En defensa de la transción: El primer gobierno de la democracia en Chile," Universität Heidelberg, Institut für Politische Wissenschaft, (February 1995), 9–13. For a review of what was changed and not changed in 1989 and in 1991 via amendments, see Mark Ensalaco, "In with the New, Out with the Old? The Democratizing Impact of Constitutional Reforms in Chile," *Journal of Latin American Studies* 26, no. 2 (May 1994): 409–29.

courts, the regulatory bodies, and the semiautonomous agencies that were an integral part of the authoritarian state required a 60 percent vote in both houses.[8] The Concertación in fact won twenty-two of the thirty-eight Senate seats open to vote and would thus have normally been only one vote short of 60 percent. But with nine "designated senators" in a senate of forty-seven members, this meant that the Concertación was in fact two votes short of even a simple majority and six votes short of the twenty-eight votes needed for major constitutional changes of the nondemocratic features of the constitution.[9]

Another de jure limit on the authority of the new democratic government concerns the *continuity* of military leadership. The constitution gave General Pinochet the prerogative of unremovability *(inamovilidad)* as chief of the army until March 1998 and the same prerogative to the other three junta members from the navy, air force, and police.[10] All four also had the right to voice and vote in the eight-person National Security Council.[11]

The capacity of the military and their allies in civil and political society to constrain the democratic government's ability to set policies and norms was enhanced further by the strong material, ideological, and leadership bases for autonomy the military constructed for themselves. Twelve days before President Aylwin was sworn in, an Organic Constitutional Law of the Armed Forces was signed by Pinochet and approved by the Constitutional Tribunal Pinochet had created and appointed in 1980.[12] This law greatly increased the institutional autonomy of the armed forces. In the critical area of personnel policy, the law removed the president's right to order officers into retirement (a key legal instrument that President Aylwin might have used to remove from active duty some of the more notorious torturers and violators of human rights) and made the gatekeeping nominations to major general (from which all future commanders-in-chief would be drawn) the exclusive prerogative of the commander-in-chief, thus reinforcing ambitious officers' dependence on Pinochet.[13] The task of democratic

---

8. Ibid., articles 116–19.

9. For an excellent analysis of the problems presented by the constitution and the 1989 election results, see Manuel Antonio Garretón, "La redemocratización política en Chile: Transición, inauguración y evolución," *Estudios Publicos* no. 42 (Autumn 1991): 101–35.

10. *Constitución Política,* Disposiciones Transitorias, Octava.

11. For the composition and powers of the National Security Council, see ibid., articles 95 and 96. Two civilian members of the National Security Council were the president of the Supreme Court and the controller-general of public administration, both of whom were appointed by Pinochet and had long terms. Thus, of the eight members of the National Security Council, only two were strongly associated with the new democratic government: the president of Chile, Patrício Aylwin, and the president of the Senate, Gabriel Valdés.

12. See Ministerio de Defensa Nacional, "Ley Orgánica Constitucional de las Fuerzas Armadas," *Diario Oficial de la República de Chile,* no. 18.948 (Feb. 27, 1990): 1678–83. In the same issue the Constitutional Court formally approved the law, thus requiring a constitutional change to reverse it.

13. Ibid., articles 24–32 and esp. article 53. The president of the republic does not have the right to nominate but can refuse to sign, and thus allow, a promotion. On a few occasions President Aylwin exercised this prerogative. See Huneeus, "En defensa de la transición," 23–24. Normally, however, all recommendations for promotion by General Pinochet are accepted. See, for example, "Chile: Army Promotions Ac-

resocialization of the officer corps was made extremely difficult by the fact that all military curriculum choices and all military doctrinal publications were explicitly placed under the exclusive control of the commander-in-chief.[14] Finally, the democratic power of the purse strings over the armed forces was weakened significantly. The law precluded the military budget from ever getting below the quite high 1989 budgetary level. More importantly, the military was given 10 percent of the foreign exchange from the sale by the state enterprise of Chile's main export, copper, and the right to retain the income from any sales of military property, which included extensive land and buildings.[15]

Power relations are never static. The relative power of the democratic government vis-à-vis the military began to grow after Aylwin's inauguration because of its elected origin, the excellent performance of the economy under the astute political and technical direction of the minister of finance, Alejandro Foxley, and a series of military scandals, but the struggle to eliminate these de jure nondemocratic prerogatives of the military may well continue until the late 1990s.

The 1980 constitution, with its designated senators and special guarantees, was crafted to have numerous other defenses. Any law to change the constitution or any of the many "organic constitutional laws" that were an integral part of the state crafted by the military regime had to be approved by the Constitutional Court *before* promulgation. But the composition and function of this court had been structured by the 1980 constitution with an aim to insulate it from direct democratic pressures. When the democratic regime came to power in 1990, it confronted a Constitutional Court with seven members, all appointed by Pinochet, not one of whom was removable until he reached retirement age of seventy-five. Further, the constitution mandated that the incoming democratic president could in the future nominate only one of the court's seven members even when they were eventually renewed. Two would be nominated by the National Security Council, three by the Supreme Court (most of whom in 1990 were Pinochet appointees), and one by an absolute majority of the Senate (where, due to designated senators, the democratic government did not have a majority).[16]

---

cepted," *Latin American Regional Reports: Southern Cone Report* (Nov. 24, 1994): 5. Pinochet's control over promotion went much further in this respect than that of Franco's vis-à-vis the Spanish army.

14. Ibid., article 47. Article 1 explicitly states that one of the constitutional missions of the armed forces is to "guarantee the institutional order of the Republic."

15. Ibid., article 47, clause L, and articles 93–97. For a good discussion of these provisions, see Guillermo Pattillo, "El gasto militar de Chile en la década de los ochenta: Un analíse introductorio," in Guillermo Pattillo, Fernando Bustamante, and Miguel Navarro, ¿*Cuál debe ser el gasto militar en el Chile de los 90?* (Santiago: CED—Editorial Atena, 1991), 13–51. For a review of the parliamentary and extraparliamentary debates on military budgetary prerogatives, see Claudio Fuentes, "Debate en torno al gasto militar: Nuevas perspectivas," *Fuerzas Armadas y Sociedad* 6, no. 4 (1991): 24–49.

16. For this recruitment system see article 81 of the *Constitución Política*. In 1991 one of the seven judges died and President Aylwin exercised the right to appoint Eugenio Velasco, a leading figure of the Concertación, to the judgeship. Our understanding of the Constitutional Court was aided greatly by a meeting of Stepan with Judge Velasco on March 7, 1992, in Santiago.

In addition, when it became increasingly clear that the democratic opposition would win the election and form the next government, General Pinochet devoted most of his energies to putting in place laws and institutional entities to further constrain the policy freedom of the incoming democratic government. Illustrative of the brazenness of this disloyal transition is that, in the waning months of the Pinochet government, highly attractive financial inducements were given to Supreme Court judges to retire early so that Pinochet could appoint young loyalists to these posts. A major state-owned television channel was sold off, and an "independent" TV and Radio Council was appointed before the new government was in power. Pinochet issued laws that gave security of tenure to most of the public sector. For example, in the Ministry of the Interior, of the 556 authorized positions, only 12 were theoretically open for new appointments by the newly elected government.[17]

Gramsci used the metaphor of a series of moats that surround a fortress to describe a strong authoritarian state.[18] The Chilean social scientist, Manuel Antonio Garretón, labels such protective devices "authoritarian enclaves," and elsewhere Alfred Stepan has discussed the concept of military prerogatives that must be reduced by new democratic governments.[19] Whatever term is used it is clear that, until the interlocking system of nondemocratic prerogatives is removed or greatly diminished, the Chilean transition cannot be completed and, by definition, Chilean democracy cannot be consolidated.

Key participants have obliquely indicated in articles or in private conversations with us that, before the democratic government assumed power, one of their highest priorities had originally been to obtain a broad settlement to eliminate the most serious of the obstacles to a democratic transition. The strategy was to combine a direct appeal to the public by the new president and agreements with

---

17. These and numerous other laws and decrees are pejoratively known as "binding laws" (*leyes de amarre*). For discussion and extensive documentation, see Angell and Pollack, "The Chilean Elections of 1989," 1–23. For a knowledgeable discussion of how the incoming Aylwin government was able to get control of the Central Bank and to loosen the bindingness of some of the laws, such as that concerning the television, see Huneeus, "En defensa de la transción," 9–16.

18. See Antonio Gramsci, *Selections from the Prison Notebooks* (New York: International Publishers, 1971), 238.

19. For his excellent discussion of the "authoritarian enclaves," see Manuel Antonio Garretón, *La posibilidad democrática en Chile* (Santiago: FLASCO Cuadernos de Difusión, 1989), 51–62. For Stepan's discussion of prerogatives, see his *Rethinking Military Politics*, 93–127. For detailed follow-up evaluations of Stepan's 1988 analysis of prerogatives that document that most were still in place in Chile in 1995, see Mark Ensalaco, "Military Prerogatives and the Stalemate of Chilean Civil-Military Relations," *Armed Forces and Society* 21, no. 2 (1995): 255–70, and Wendy Hunter, "Two Steps Forward, One Step Back: Civil Military Relations in Post-authoritarian Argentina and Chile" (paper prepared for a conference on Fault Lines of Democratic Governance in the Americas, North-South Center, University of Miami, May 4–6, 1995). President Frei made elimination of nondemocratic prerogatives part of his 1993 campaign platform. However, by November 1994 it appeared that the most important military prerogatives would be contested by the democratic government only in the fourth phase of the Frei administration's phased reform, possibly in 1997, as the terms of the commanders-in-chief of the army, navy, air force, and police and the designated senators approached their end. See "Chile: Phased Reform of the Constitution," *Latin American Research Report: Southern Cone Report* (Nov. 24, 1994), 3 and Hunter, "Two Steps Forward, One Step Back."

some of the democratic right in the Parliament. The highest priorities in this overall settlement were to have been to eliminate the designated senators, to ensure the presidental right to put officers into retirement, to change the "immobility" status of Pinochet and his other commanders-in-chief, to restructure the composition and mission of the Constitutional Court, to alter Chile's executive form of presidentialism toward a semiparliamentary model, and to have direct elections for municipal offices. However, at the end of President Aylwin's administration, the only one of these political priority items to have been accomplished was that of municipal elections, which were held in June 1992.

When asked why they did not attempt a broad settlement to eliminate the interlocking system of nondemocratic prerogatives, key government officials replied that they simply did not have the votes in the Senate, in the National Security Council, or in the courts. Furthermore, they stressed that they had a broad economic and social agenda which, while not requiring constitutional change, required that they structure their overall policy package so that they could win the support of part of the right-wing opposition in the Senate. Given these perceptions of the danger and difficulty of removing the authoritarian enclaves, the first democratic government decided to live with them as the price of stability and a modicum of policy support on other issues from the democratic right.

In terms of our theoretical framework, Chile is thus a clear confirmation of the hypothesis we advanced in chapter 5. We argued that the type of prior government that can impose most constraints on a transition is one in which the nondemocratic regime's base is a hierarchical military that is united and has strong civilian allies. In these conditions we argued that the outgoing military regime would have great resources to impose confining conditions on any transition and that they would simply withdraw into the state, where they could hold state-sanctioned missions and resources. This has happened in Chile. We also said that, of the six types of constitution-making processes, the least democratic would be one where the incoming democratic government has to agree to try to increase its power via the rules of the game that are spelled out in the constitution written by the old authoritarian regime. This too occurred in Chile. Politically, Chilean democracy began under more constrained constitutional circumstances than were the case in any of the Latin American or southern European countries we consider in this book.[20]

In conceptual terms, where did the Concertación government start in March 11, 1990, and where were they able to go in four years? The democratic government

---

20. In Poland, the particular circumstances in which the roundtable negotiated the institutions for the transition had similar confining conditions that were eventually overcome, but, as we shall see, they left a complex legacy. The difference between Chile and Poland was that in Poland the nondemocratic regime was backed by the Communist apparatus, but not by the full force of the hierarchical military. Another interesting case is Nicaragua, where the democratically elected president Violeta Chamorro has de facto and partially de jure had to "co-habit" with the leader of the Sandinista military, Commander Daniel Ortega.

faced a difficult task. Much of the state, due to the mechanisms just described and the tactical withdrawal of a relatively autonomous military back into the state apparatus, was not really in their control. Further, these authoritarian enclaves had significant ideological and coalitional resources because civil society, in two separate highly contested votes, gave 43 percent of their support to the authoritarian regime or their allies. In this respect, Chile contrasts sharply with the 7 to 12 percent range the old regime's allies received in Hungary, Poland, Czechoslovakia, and East Germany in the first contested elections.

The new democratic government's greatest strength was in political society where, despite all the constitutionally imposed limits, they at least controlled the government, having a majority in the lower house and a plurality in the Senate. Four years later the government had altered power relations in its favor in the state, in civil society, and in political society.

In the rest of this section we will explore two scenarios about Chile. In one scenario, which will probably take until at least 1998, Chilean democracy will arrive at a "simultaneity" outcome like that of Portugal. That is, when the last authoritarian enclave is finally displaced, Chile will on that same day complete its transition and consolidate democracy.

The second scenario seems almost churlish to consider. That is one where the consequences of the long-deferred consolidation might set into motion a series of reactions that would reduce the legitimacy and capacity of democratic governance. Or, worse, might even contribute to part of the initial democratic coalition coming to prefer the "governance advantages" of the protected democratic constitution.

Let us consider first the "Portuguese" or "simultaneity" formula, which we consider the most plausible scenario. During the plebiscite of 1988, Pinochet repeatedly warned that a victory by the opposition would bring back party chaos, social conflict, and economic disarray. Precisely because many voters still believed in Pinochet's offensive and defensive projects he won 43 percent of the vote—as much as Margaret Thatcher ever received in England. However, as in Spain and Uruguay, both civil society and political society had in fact reflected on the previous breakdown and applied much of their learning to making democracy work. As in Uruguay political parties have played a key role. Despite Pinochet's predictions the coalition of twelve parties, led by the Christian Democrats, in the Concertación developed an admirable capacity to work together and to pursue policies consistently. Political violence continued but became less intense and more marginalized and, most importantly, was systematically rejected by all political parties. Inflation, far from increasing, reached lower levels than in the last two years of Pinochet's presidency. Furthermore, given the solid political base of the government's economic policies, international financial investment in Chile reached new highs.[21]

21. Typical of the international financial community's positive reaction to the performance of the first year of the democratic government was a report by John F. H. Powell, Joyce Change, and Dirk W. Damrau,

The legacy of human rights abuse was more difficult to handle given the continuing presence of Pinochet's judicial, military, and political power resources. Given this correlation of forces, the Aylwin government decided that the Argentine model of extensive trials was not possible. Indeed, they diagnosed the Argentine civil-military crisis of 1984–87 as having been due to a process by which one component of the state (the military-as-organization) was in strident conflict against another component of the state (the executive of the democratic government). To avoid an Argentine-style conflict and what they saw as an excessive policy of "forgetting" in the Uruguayan government, the Aylwin government decided on a middle course, which was to pursue a "regime of truth" concerning the abuses of civil rights under the previous military regime.

The government commissioned a full scale inquiry into human rights abuses and crimes of political violence in the 1973–85 period and published the results.[22] However, the compromise decision was made that prosecutions would be undertaken only by individuals against individuals so as to avoid the Argentine intrastate conflict. Their formula did not fully satisfy the claims of justice (it is very hard for individuals to prosecute individuals) or the hopes of human rights activists. Despite significant reservations, both on the left and on the right, many Chileans accepted the formula reluctantly as the best outcome that was politically feasible in the circumstances.

Backed by a coherent coalitional majority in the lower house and working hard to arrive at an almost consociational formula with part of the democratic right in the Senate, the Aylwin government—unlike the decree-ridden "delegative democracy" style of Brazilian and Argentine governments or the dead-locked Uruguayan government—proved very efficacious. They were able to formulate and implement a coherent set of programs in all areas that were not vetoed de facto by the 1980 constitution and the decreasing, but still powerful, Pinochet-backed conservative coalition.

"Chile: An Investment-Grade Credit" (New York: Solomon Brothers, May 1991), in which they argued "in our opinion Chile should be viewed as Latin America's first investment grade sovereign credit for the following reasons: There is a strong consensus on economic policy goals. . . . Chilean political stability is sustainable. . . . Prudent macroeconomic arrangements have produced healthy results. . . . Chile has significantly reduced its vulnerability to external shocks" (p. 1). Chile's solid economic performance in 1995, despite the Mexican "tequila effect" which rocked Argentina, confirmed that these judgments were sound.

22. President Aylwin released the two-volume report of the Comisión Nacional de Verdad y Reconciliacion in a moving, nationally televised ceremony. The report is commonly referred to as the Rettig Commission. José Zalaquett, one of the eight members of the commission and a former president of the International Executive Committee of Amnesty International, compared the Uruguayan, Argentine, and Chilean responses to human rights abuses in "Derechos humanos y limitaciones políticas en las transiciones democráticas del Cono Sur," Colección Estudios CIEPLAN no. 33 (Dec. 1991): 147–186. Our understanding of what was and was not done by the Rettig Commission was deepened by an interview of Stepan with Zalaquett on March 5, 1992. For a valuable full-scale evaluation, see "Human Rights and the 'Politics' of Agreements: Chile during President Aylwin's First Year" (New York: Americas Watch, July 1991). See the excellent comparative analysis of Chile and Uruguay by Alexandra Barahona da Brito, "Truth or Amnesty. Human Rights and Democratization in Latin America: Uruguay and Chile" (Ph.D. diss., University of Oxford, 1993).

Table 13.1. Legitimacy and Efficacy in Chile and Spain

Indicator	Chile		Spain		
	1 yr after redemocratization (March 1991)	2 yr after redemocratization (March 1992)	1 yr after redemocratization (1978)	3 yr after redemocratization (1980)	11 yr after First election (1988)
Legitimacy "Democracy is the best political system for a country like ours."	86.6	79.1	77	69	87
Efficacy "Democracy allows the resolution of the problems that we ["as Spaniards/as Chileans"] face."	78.7	67.0	68	45	56
N			(5898)	(3132)	(4548)

Source: For Chile, data from "Evaluación del segundo año de gobierno democrático" (Santiago: Centro de Estudios de la Realidad Contemporanea, May 1992), table 33. For Spain, data from José Ramón Montero and Richard Gunther "Democratic Legitimacy in Spain," paper presented at the International Political Science Association XVI World Congress, Berlin, Aug. 21–25, 1994.

Given this context Chile had already won by mid-1992 attitudinal support for democracy that compared quite favorably to the consolidated democracies of Spain, Portugal, Greece, and Uruguay. Chile in 1992 was the only one of our four Latin American cases whose citizens attested their belief in both the legitimacy and the efficacy of democracy. In fact, by these measures Chile and Spain were remarkably similar (table 13.1). A comparison of the citizens' perception of high efficacy in Chile with that of Brazil is particularly striking (table 13.2).

Chile, even more than Spain, also underscores the fact that citizens can believe that a previous authoritarian regime was "in part good, in part bad" while having an overwhelming opinion in favor of democracy once a democracy is functioning well. In Spain, table 9.4 showed that 44 percent of Spaniards felt that the Franco regime was "in part good, in part bad." In Chile, 55 percent of the population had such an opinion about Pinochet in October 1989.[23] However, the fact that Pinochet was seen as presenting obstacles to democracy contributed to the fact that, a year and a half after the inauguration of a democratic government, his prestige was vastly lower than that of the leading democratic figures. In December 1991 a poll was carried out on the positive and negative images of thirty-one public figures. The leading figures of the democratic government—President Aylwin, Finance Minister Alejandro Foxley, and the Minister of Education Ricardo

23. "Informe Encuesta Nacional," CERC, Santiago, October 1989, table 8.

Table 13.2. Citizens' Perceptions of Governmental Efficacy on the Second Anniversary of Democratic Rule under Freely Elected Presidents (Aylwin in Chile, Collor in Brazil)

Indicator	Chile (March 1992)	Brazil (Feb. 20–22, 1992)
"This government is resolving the economic problems of the country."	23.1	3
"This government is not resolving the economic problems of the country but needs time."	54.1	32
"This government cannot resolve the economic problems of the country."	12.8	29
"No government can resolve the economic problems of the country."	8.3	30
Don't know/not answered	1.8	6

Source: Chile: data from same source as for table 13.1, table 58, N =1,500, national sample. Brazil: data from Datafolha, national sample, N =2,500.

Lagos (a socialist who was the founding president of the social-democratic Party for Democracy)—were overwhelmingly popular. The young president of the democratic right party, Andres Allamand, also received a very favorable rating. The two figures with the largest net unpopularity were General Pinochet and the leftist leader Volodia Teitelboin, who, as late as 1988, had been talking about the need for a mass uprising.[24]

Finally, as we argued in part 1, a consolidated democracy needs to have a state apparatus that is considered usable and reasonably even-handed by its citizens. We saw in the case of Brazil that citizens have great fears of the police. In Chile, despite the fact that they were close to the Pinochet regime, the National Police Force (the Carabineros) managed to survive with some of its professional image intact. In Chile, two years after the democratic opposition won the election, 76 percent of a national sample and 71 percent of those who identified themselves as on the left said that they believed that the Carabineros would be helpful to them or to people like them.[25]

Given these early favorable attitudes in 1992 toward the regime's legitimacy, efficacy, and fairness, the attitudinal dimension of Chilean democracy seemed to indicate that Chile was on the road to consolidation. Also, given the decline in disloyal and semiloyal behavior of many political actors—with the far from negligible exception of the military—the behavioral dimension of consolidation also looked favorable. This situation gave credence to the likelihood of our Portuguese scenario. That is, when all of the de jure limitations on the ability of democratically sanctioned institutions to make policy are finally overcome, on that day the Chilean transition to democracy and the Chilean consolidation of democracy would probably occur simultaneously.

24. A CERC poll given to the authors.

25. See "Estudio social y de opinión pública," Centro de Estudios Publicos, Documento de Trabajo, no. 173 (Feb. 1992): 65. La Policía Civil de Investigaciones (PCI) was also quite effacious and nonviolent. Between 1991 and June 1994, fifty-three members of the top leadership of one of Chile's most active terrorist groups, Movimento Juvenil Lautaro, were captured in "bloodless operations" and put in jail. See "Entire Lautaro Leadership in Gaol," Latin American Research Report: Southern Cone Report (Aug. 1994), 7.

This leads us to our final question. What, if any, costs could there be to Chilean democracy if it has to wait until the end of the 1990s to eliminate nondemocratic prerogatives and to create a democratic constitution? Before the vote that led up to the defeat of Pinochet had taken place, many of the leading political figures of the Chilean democratic opposition, from the left to the right, reviewed the causes of the breakdown of democracy in Chile in 1973 and discussed how to consolidate democracy in the future. There was a very widespread recognition of the fact that Chile was naturally a multiparty system with strong party ideologies. In the past the democratic opposition leaders had argued that this combination tended to produce minority governments, legislative impasses, and attempts by popularly elected presidents to rule by decrees or use extraparliamentary measures. Many of the Chilean exiles had lived in Italy, Germany, and Spain, and modern parliamentarianism seemed to them an appropriate response for Chile.[26] At this time a near consensus had emerged that presidentialism had problems that needed to be addressed. Some even argued that, in the first democratic government, while the coalition was still holding together and before future presidential campaigns completely divided them, the democratic opposition should move toward a parliamentary system of the semipresidential variety. Once in power, however, and faced with resistance to constitutional reform by the Pinochet coalition and by their own desire to press forward with socioeconomic policy measures, the government decided to let political reform wait.

By early 1992, however, the two leading components of the Concertación coalition, the Christian Democrats and the Socialists, had undeclared but powerful presidential candidates organizing their campaigns and inevitably creating some tension in the Concertación.[27] Our theoretical and comparative analysis leads us to think that the arguments advanced by many Chilean politicians and theoreticians in 1985–88 were right then and are still right. However, we believe that in politics timing is crucial. The logic of electoral competition and the lure of holding the office of the presidency will make it much more difficult for Chile to put together a winning coalition for parliamentarianism in the late-1990s than it would have been in the early 1990s. This, in turn, will make the task of putting together coalitions for governance more difficult. Why?

26. Both of the authors attended a three-day conference in Chile in August 1989 on this theme. At the concluding public session, Ricardo Lagos, the president of Partido por la Democracia (or Party for Democracy—PPD); Andres Zaldivar, the president of Partido Demócrata Cristiano (or Christian Democratic Party—PDC); and Andres Allamand, the president of the major democratic right party, Renovación Nacional all advanced arguments on the need to re-examine Chile's presidential system. A later secretary general of the Chilean Christian Democratic Party, Genaro Arriagada, wrote a pioneering article on the theme of how Chile's multiparty presidential system produced "double-minority" governments and thus needed parliamentarianism.

27. The two leading "precandidates" came from the two major parties of the Concertación, Eduardo Frei of the Christian Democrats and Ricardo Lagos of the social democratic Party for Democracy. By mid-1992 Eduardo Frei had a commanding lead in the polls for the December 1993 election. In the end Lagos withdrew as a candidate, and Frei won easily.

Some have argued that, given the existence of the Concertación and the powerful consensual majority it had developed in the lower house, Chile had achieved the coalitional virtues of parliamentarianism even without shifting to a parliamentary system. This is possible. But the Concertación's capacity in 1990–94 owed much to the high incentives for coalitional compromise that were created by the constraints imposed by the 1980 constitution. There was, of course, internal political learning within the coalition, but the constitution and Pinochet's control of part of the state apppartatus acted as powerful factors of agglutination. If this reasoning is correct, then, as the Pinochet presence wanes and multiparty competition in the context of presidentialism grows, Chile's coalitional calculus could once again become quite difficult.[28]

But the cost of Pinochet's continued opposition to trials for human rights violations, and his penchant and ability to block the democratically elected government's efforts to reform the constitution and to eliminate the interconnected system of military prerogatives, might be that democracy begins to lose some of its attractiveness, and even legitimacy, in the eyes of its citizens. By 1993 there were worrying signs that this was beginning to happen. Despite continued excellent economic performance and the exceptionally high personal popularity of President Alywin, respondents expressing themselves as "very satisfied" or "satisfied" with democracy declined from 75 percent in August 1990 to 37 percent in August 1993.[29] In the aftermath of a military show of force by Pinochet in June 1993 and the president's inability to carry out his announced policy changes vis-à-vis military prerogatives, the percentage of respondents who said "democracy is fully installed," which was 25 percent in October 1991 and 20 percent in March 1992,

---

28. This assertion is based on the theoretical premise that, in a multiparty parliamentary system, there will be more incentives for forming enduring coalitions than in a multiparty presidential system. The quantitative evidence of the world's long-standing democracies gives strong empirical support to the theoretical argument. In 1980–89 there were fourteen parliamentary or semipresidential systems with three to seven "effective" political parties on the Laakso-Taagepera scale. The "highest effective party index" for a presidential democracy with ten years duration in that period is Venezuela with 2.6 parties, but Chile before Pinochet often had a party index near 6—perfectly normal for a parliamentary democracy but highly exceptional for a presidential democracy. See Alfred Stepan and Cindy Skach, "Constitutional Frameworks and Democratic Consolidation: Parliamentarianism vs. Presidentialism," *World Politics* 46 (Oct. 1993): 8–9. For the general argument in favor of parliamentarianism and an analysis of the Chilean problems with presidentialism, see the articles by Juan J. Linz and Arturo Valenzuela, respectively, in the volume they edited, *The Failure of Presidential Democracy* (Baltimore: Johns Hopkins University Press, 1994).

The Aylwin government of 1989–93 had significant consociational and quasi-parliamentary features. President Frei's government is more presidential in style. For example, President Frei removed the most important Socialist member of his cabinet without any prior consultation with his Socialist Party coalition members. Such behavior would be highly improbable in a parliamentary coalition. The general secretary of the Socialist Party warned that "the lack of consultation undermines the very foundations that have made possible the governing coalition." See "Chile: Socialists Angered by Loss of Top Post," *Latin America Research Review: Southern Cone Report* (Oct. 20, 1994), 6.

29. This decline appeared in various CERC polls shown to the authors by Marta Lagos, who designed the polls and who believes, by the analysis of related questions, that the most likely explanation for the decline in the legitimacy indicator is citizens' negative reaction to the military's continued ability to control key parts of the policy agenda. See "Informe de Prensa Encuesta Nacional," CERC, Oct. 1993.

dropped near the end of the Aylwin administration (October 1993) to a new low of 16 percent.[30] Indeed, 40.6 percent of those polled in October 1993 actually believed that the military wanted to return to power.[31]

In June 1995, retired General Manuel Contreras, the former head of the much feared secret police, DINA, was given a jail sentence for his involvement in the 1976 Washington assassination of a major Chilean opposition leader, Orlando Letelier. But, before he could be jailed, military helicopters spirited the convicted Contreras from his ranch to a naval hospital. After a four-month standoff, Contreras was eventually put in a special jail with military guards. Military acts of intimidation and defiance of the democratic government such as these were, in 1993–95, significantly greater in Chile than they were in Brazil, Uruguay, or Argentina. Such acts continued to underscore to the Chilean citizens that there continued to be, seven years after the transition began, important policy areas outside the effective control of the democratic regime.

Let us conclude with a final reflection. The 1980 constitution greatly strengthened the prerogatives of the government of the day—Congress must adhere to a strict timetable specified by the executive, they cannot initiate important money bills, and the office of the presidency is insulated within the structures that Pinochet designed for himself. Mitterand, when he was in the opposition, used to call de Gaulle's Fifth Republic Constitution a "permanent coup d'état."[32] The irony is that, upon being elected president, it was Mitterand who gave the Gaullist constitution its final legitimation. It would be a sad irony if the quality of Chilean democracy eventually turned out to be lower than it might have been if the democratic government found some of the 1980 Constitution's prerogatives so convenient for governance that they routinized and legitimized them.

---

30. Ibid., table 5.
31. Ibid., 23–24.
32. Francois Mitterand, *Le coup d'état permanent* (Paris: Plan, 1965).

14

South America: Concluding Reflections

Tне ғаст тнат the Southern Cone cases of democratic transitions and consolidation began from bases of hierarchically controlled military regimes contributed to powerful constraining conditions in all four countries under consideration. We argue that this variable, taken by itself, explains an important degree of the variance concerning democratic consolidation in the Southern Cone compared to the southern European cases.

However, we also believe that other factors, not all directly related to this variable, help explain the difficult task of democratic consolidation in the Southern Cone. We concluded our southern European section with a rapid review of factors that were positive. In the Latin American cases, the same factors are present but in a more problematic way.

Schematically, the major differences are the following:

1. The European community represented a positive political and economic network to which Spain, Greece, and Portugal could aspire. Membership in the community offered some financial incentives. In southern Europe, integration into the EEC held out the positive transfer of close to 5 percent of GNP. No comparable positive economic or political network existed for the Southern Cone. The market-democratic countries led by the United States were seen primarily as sources of foreign indebtedness. In the 1980s continued market integration for the Southern Cone countries meant debt payment of close to 5 percent of GNP for Brazil, Argentina, and Uruguay. However, by the mid-1990s the common market of Brazil, Argentina, Uruguay, and Paraguay (MERCOSUR) was beginning to help trade and growth among these four countries.

2. Greece and Portugal had been members of the North Atlantic Treaty Organization (NATO) in nondemocratic periods. However, on balance, membership in NATO in the 1980s for Greece, Portugal, and Spain (especially for the air force and navy) helped ease the militaries' transition to democracy because it gave support to missions and identities based on enhanced military professionalism. Adhesion to NATO, especially in the case of Spain, produced considerable controversy among politicians and within public opinion at large. But membership has also meant that the tension-fraught question "Why do we need a military in democracy?" was not a major source of civil-military conflict. The Southern Cone

countries have no NATO-like roles. The major international role that the Reagan and Bush administrations encouraged the Latin American militaries to perform concerned the politically explosive area of joint antidrug trafficking operations.

3. We argued that, for southern Europe, in no country were "issues concerning the direction or functioning of the economy as salient as the debates about political power." We believe this helped focus attention on the political aspects of democratic consolidation. In Latin America, partly due to the debt crisis, economic issues rapidly became as important as and eventually more important than political issues, and we believe that this hurt democratic consolidation. The only exception to this was Chile, where the economy was in good condition but the political constraints were severe.

4. In contrast to Europe, no Latin American country carried out an unconstrained constituent assembly. Brazil tried and was constrained by the military and the president. Democratic politicians in Chile are still slowly attempting to unshackle themselves from an authoritarian constitution. Uruguay and Argentina opted for restoration formulas. Although in Argentina there was a discussion of fundamental reforms, ultimately, as we have seen, there was an ad hoc reform to make possible the reelection of Menem.

5. All Southern Cone countries began their transitions with presidents with fixed terms and continue with presidential systems. In Brazil, Argentina, and Uruguay, this contributed to some institutionally specific problems. In Brazil, executive-legislative deadlock has been the norm, and the "accidental" president, José Sarney, served five years and helped block the Constituent Assembly's choice for parliamentarianism. President Sarney often relied upon military power. In Argentina, the difference in electoral timetables blocked any possibility for a popular President Alfonsín to win a majority in 1984–85 and forced an unpopular President Alfonsín to continue ruling in 1987–89, after he had been roundly defeated in congressional elections. In Uruguay, the first three civilian presidents have been minority presidents. The weak incentives in presidentialism for coalitions make effective coalition government difficult in all three countries. Whether Chile's new-found spirit of coalitional cooperation can survive the waning of Pinochet's presence remains to be seen.

6. Given the civil-military conflicts that have often constrained sovereignty and weakened legitimacy, the prolonged economic crises, and the weak coalitional capacity of presidentialist governments, it is understandable that public perceptions about whether the country was faring well under democracy were dangerously low even before the first civilian presidents finished their terms.[1]

1. For example, in November 1988 as the terms of presidents Alfonsín, Sanguinetti, and Sarney were ending, the percentage of people who classified the situation of their respective countries as "bad" or "very bad" was 84 percent in Brazil, 60 percent in Argentina, and 57 percent in Uruguay. Only 1 percent of respondents in Brazil and 4 percent of respondents in Argentina and Uruguay felt that their country's situa-

Philippe C. Schmitter coined a chilling phrase when he remarked that some countries may be "condemned to democracy" because the alternatives are even weaker. Fortunately, the authoritarian alternative was still very unattractive toward the end of the mandates of the first civilian presidents in Brazil, Argentina, and Uruguay. In all three countries presidential elections in 1989 brought a resurgence of confidence in the new presidents. However, from the perspective of democratic theory and stability, the plebiscitary style of President Menem in Argentina and of the eventually impeached President Collor in Brazil related more to "delegated democracy" (with all its hopes and dangers) than to democratic consolidation.

7. In summation, in contrast to Spain, Portugal, and Greece, all of which are consolidated, of our four South American cases only crisis-prone Uruguay, with its mix of high legitimacy and difficult political economy, is democratically consolidated. Given military prerogatives the Chilean transition itself is still far from complete. Brazil was further from consolidation in 1993 than in 1986. Argentina has tamed inflation, but the president flouts legality. On the plus side, in all four countries civil societies' demands for "transparency" and accountability in state and government have reached unprecedented levels, and all four countries are still strongly committed to electoral politics.

Addendum: How Citizens View Democracy

In August 1995, as we were correcting the edited copy of this book, we received advance results of the first ever Latino Barometer. This survey used a common questionnaire and a common method. Table 14.1 summarizes the results that relate to democratic legitimacy, democratic efficacy, and expectations about the future. All implications of this important survey must await rigorous full-scale analysis by the projects' coordinators. However, even at this stage we can draw attention to some of the results most relevant to our book.

The reader of the preceding chapters can see that the answers to the question about the legitimacy of democracy and corresponding attitudes toward an authoritarian alternative under certain circumstances clearly confirm our conclusions about the attitudinal support for the consolidation in Uruguay and our concern about the case of Brazil. Additional data referred to later in this addendum provide the reader with even more supporting information about these basic patterns in both countries.

The Argentine and Chilean responses on the legitimacy question pose more

---

tion was "very good" or "good." The percentage of respondents who felt that the situation was "neither good nor bad" was 15 percent in Brazil, 36 percent in Argentina, and 38 percent in Uruguay. Figures are taken from *Proyecto Cono Sur,* as reported in Edgardo Catterberg and María Braun, "Notas para un balance de la transición" (paper prepared for a conference on democratic consolidation organized by the Centro de la Realidad Contemporánea [CERC], Santiago, Chile, Aug. 10–11, 1989), 19.

Table 14.1. Attitudes toward the Legitimacy and Efficacy of Democracy and Expectations about the Future: Uruguay, Argentina, Chile, and Brazil, 1995

Survey Response	Percentage of Respondents			
	Uruguay	Argentina	Chile	Brazil
"With which of the following phrases are you most in agreement?" (Legitimacy Indicator)				
"Democracy is preferable to any other form of government."	80	76.6	52.2	41.0
"In some circumstances an authoritarian government can be preferable to a democratic government."	8	10.9	18.5	21.1
"For someone like me, a democratic or a nondemocratic regime makes no difference."	6	6.1	25.3	23.3
"Don't know"	4	6.4	2.4	13.8
No answer	2	—	1.5	0.8
"Some people say that democracy allows the solution of problems that we have in our country. Other people say that democracy does not solve the problems. Which of the following phrases is the closest to your way of thinking?" (Efficacy Indicator)				
"Democracy allows the solution of the problems."	54	52.9	47.6	45.6
"Democracy does not solve the problems."	34	36.6	46.4	44.6
"Don't know"	9	10.5	4.3	9.2
No answer	3	0.1	1.7	0.7
"Would you say that the country is . . . ?" (Expectation Indicator)				
"Progressing"	29	30.6	52.6	43.7
"Stagnant"	45	43.2	39.1	37.7
"Moving backward"	22	22.8	5.8	15.8
"Don't know"/N.A.	4	3.4	2.4	2.9
N	(1,213)	(1,200)	(1,240)	(1,200)

Source: Latino Barometer, project directed by Marta Lagos. Full results to be published by the end of 1995. We are extremely grateful to Marta Lagos for making these data available to us. The interpretation, however, is our responsibility.

complex problems. In our chapter on Chile, we documented the downward trend in citizen satisfaction with democracy. However, for a variety of reasons we develop later, the difference between the 52.2 percent support for democracy in Chile in 1995 (down from 63.8 percent in 1991) and the 76.6 percent support for democracy in Agentina is perplexing.

The responses to the question about whether an authoritarian government might be preferable show the small potential constituency for authoritarianism in Uruguay and Argentina. The data show a larger potential constituency for authoritarianism in Brazil but also in Chile. In fact, the percentage of people answering that "for someone like me a democratic or a nondemocratic regime makes no difference" is about four times higher in Brazil and Chile than in Uruguay or Argentina. The reader will note that the lower overall commitment to democracy in Brazil is not due to a larger number of authoritarian or "indifferent" responses but to the larger number of "don't knows," which is 13.8 percent in Brazil compared to 2.4 percent in Chile.

The answers to the efficacy question about "democracy [allowing] the solution of the [country's] problems" should, in the opinion of many scholars, provide an explanation of the above differences. However, the first thing that strikes us is that the maximum difference between the countries on efficacy (8.4 percent) is not nearly as great as the maximum difference on the legitimacy question (39.0 percent). Once again this demonstrates that it is a conceptual and political mistake to presume that legitimacy and efficacy are always tightly linked.

Although the difference between efficacy in Uruguay and Brazil is congruent with the legitimacy of democracy, it is by no means an explanation of the full difference.[2] What is most surprising in the data is that the efficacy response in Chile is both less positive (and more negative) than that in Argentina. Readers might think that this explains the difference concerning the legitimacy indicator in Chile and Argentina but might also feel that this is counterintuitive because they know that the economic performance of Chile has been superior to that of Argentina and that some aspects of democracy are of a higher quality in Chile than in Argentina. The readers are not wrong when they perceive Chile in a positive light because 52.6 percent of the Chileans believe that the country is making progress whereas only 30.6 percent of the Argentines believe their country is progressing. Also, only 5.8 percent of the Chileans said Chile was "moving backward," in sharp contrast to Argentina's 22.8 percent for the same question. Nonetheless, the strong objective economic indicators in Chile and the hopeful subjective expectations of the Chileans are not transferred to their commitment to the legitimacy of democracy. This is a great paradox that is not easy to explain. However, we believe that the survey results are in line with our analysis of the *incompleteness* of the Chilean transition, the correspondingly different place of the military in Chilean and Argentine society in the mid-1990s, and the constraints under which Chilean democracy has been operating.

On a whole series of indicators, Chileans are somewhat more satisfied with the quality of democracy than are the Argentines. In Chile, in contrast to Argentina, fewer people think corruption has increased significantly in the last five years (14 percentage points fewer), more think that access to television is equitable (7 percentage points more), and more think that elections are cleaner (6 percentage points more). In the area of the economy, more Chileans than Argentines per-

2. In fact, whereas 43.7 percent of the Brazilians see the country as "progressing," only 29 percent of the Uruguayans see their country as progressing. This indicates that the response that "democracy is preferable to any other form of government" (39 percentage points higher in Uruguay than in Brazil) is a complex judgment that involves much more than a sense of economic or other forms of nonpolitical progress. Questions such as perceptions of justice and equality no doubt enter into judgments concerning legitimacy.

Table 14.2. Attitudes toward the Power of and Confidence in the Military in Argentina, Uruguay, Brazil, and Chile, 1995

Survey Response	Percentage of Respondents			
	Argentina	Uruguay	Brazil	Chile
"Who do you believe has the most power in (your country)? Name up to three groups."				
"The Military"	18	22	30.9	46.8
"And who would you like to have more power in (your country)?" Name up to three groups."				
"The Military"	5.4	8	32.9	10.6
"How much confidence do you have in . . . ?" (Percentage answering "much" or "some")				
"The Military"	37.5	44	58.7	54.3

Source: Latino Barometer (see table 14.1).

ceive that their standard of living is higher than their parents' (19 percentage points more) and fewer Chileans than Argentines believe that poverty has "increased a lot" in the last five years (39 percentage points fewer).

However, as table 14.2 makes clear, in relation to the military there are major differences in the opposite direction between Chile and Argentina, but also Uruguay and Brazil. The Argentine data are the easiest to interpret. Fewer citizens in Argentina than in any other country in the Southern Cone believe that the military is powerful. Also, the lowest percentage of respondents in the Southern Cone who want the military to have more power is in Argentina and the least trusted military is in Argentina. These data reinforce our previous argument that the military's role as an autonomous and trusted political actor has been reduced greatly in Argentina. In Brazil, the percentage of people who would like the military to have more power is the highest and is congruent with Brazil's low legitimacy indicator. Once again, the Chilean data are the most complex. More Chileans by far perceive the military as the most powerful group in the country, but only in Brazil do more people have trust in the military. In sharp contrast to Argentina, Chilean military supporters and military opponents alike state that the military is still obviously a major actor in the political system.

The breakdown of democracy and the repressive rule of the military probably left a different legacy in Chile than in Argentina; we can only hint at this legacy, and it deserves much more research and analysis. In Chile an important segment of the society felt deeply threatened by the Unidad Popular government and the parties linked with it. These groups supported Pinochet and continued doing so in the plebiscite, and many of them continue to support the parties of the right and the continuance of military prerogatives. In Argentina, citizens felt threatened not so much by a government or by a party or parties, but by the breakdown of government and the political violence of the guerrilla-terrorists and the state-terrorists. However, there is no salient and weighty presence in Argentina in 1995 of the actors of the drama that led to the tragic years of military rule. In addition, that rule has nothing to its credit. In contrast, in Chile, part of the right still believes that some leftist parties are a potential threat and should be banned. For their part, much of the left see the coup by Pinochet as an attack on democracy, see the coup victims as innocent citizens who were identified with legitimate options, and dislike the continuation of military prerogatives. The human rights issue therefore retains a different saliency and meaning in Chile than in Argentina and remains on the political agenda in Chile in a way that it is not in Argentina. In Chile, the persistence of military prerogatives and the limits imposed on human rights–related trials are unfinished parts of the process of democratization. This is so because the effective answer given to requests by human rights activists for trials in Chile was not given as in Uruguay (however reluctantly) by citizens in a referendum, as in Argentina (however controversially) by a pardon granted by a twice democratically elected president, but by the auto-amnesty the military gave themselves.[3]

After six years of democratic rule, the transition is still not complete and the military retain extensive prerogatives and often act with impunity. This might help to explain why, even though the economy continues to improve, there is a declining number of confident democrats in Chile.

Table 14.1 suggests that, in the area of public opinion, Argentina seems to be transcending parts of its nondemocratic past, although the leadership style of Menem and the voters' tolerance of his questionable attitude toward law and corruption remind us of some of the legacies of Argentina's recent social and economic turmoil. In Chile, however, there seems to be a degree of uneasiness about the present, the past, and the political future that contributes not only to the relatively low legitimacy indicator in table 14.1, but also to a cluster of attitudes not found in consolidated democracies (table 14.3).

Among those who believe that "democracy allows the solution of the problems of the country," we would not expect significant differences in legitimacy belief among the four countries. However, the differences in the commitment to democracy we found continue independently of the positive view of the potential efficacy of democracy (table 14.4).

Indeed, as table 14.4 makes clear, among those who consider democracy efficacious there is significant variation as to whether respondents consider democracy legitimate or not. Among those who consider democracy efficacious, the percentage who consider democracy preferable in Uruguay is 89.8 percent, in Argentina is 89.3 percent, in Chile is 72.9 percent, and in Brazil is 55.2 percent.

If the link between efficacy and legitimacy were tightly coupled, one would expect that, among those who shared a belief in the inefficacy of democracy, differ-

3. This was graphically demonstrated in June 1995 when, after the conviction of General Contreras (for his involvement in a political assasination), a poll asked whether "reconciliation had taken place in Chile." Of those polled 68.9 percent said that Chileans were not reconciled. Among the left, 63.7 percent wanted more trials, whereas only 22.2 percent on the right did. See Encuesta Nacional CERC (Santiago, July 1995).

Table 14.3. Attitudes toward Political Liberties and Trust in Chile, Brazil, Argentina and Uruguay, 1995

Survey Response	Percentage of Respondents			
	Chile	Brazil	Argentina	Uruguay
"All parties should be permitted."	38.6	62.8	59.0	67
"Extremist parties should be prohibited."	53.6	25.6	29.0	24
"Democracy can function without parties."	33.6	42.2	18.1	15
"A little bit of a governmental strong hand (*mano dura*) is not bad for the country."	62.9	51.8	46.8	45
"People normally say what they think about politics."	28.5	31.3	46.4	NA

Source: Latino Barometer (see table 14.1).
NA, not available.

ences in legitimacy beliefs would be narrowed. The fact is that they are more marked. This would suggest that, with lower legitimacy in the society, the lack of perceived efficacy has a greater effect on the responses of the citizens. Incidentally, this would be congruent with our analysis of the influence of the loss of efficacy during the world depression in interwar Europe.[4] The difference in the preference for democracy between those who believe in the efficacy of democracy and those who do not in Uruguay (respectively, 89.8 percent and 71.5 percent) is 18.3 percentage points, in Argentina is 24.2 percentage points, in Brazil is 26.2 percentage points, and in Chile is 39.8 percentage points.

Preference for the authoritarian alternative is always higher among those not believing in the efficacy of democracy. The group who lack belief in the efficacy of democracy and prefer authoritarianism is small in Uruguay (14.5 percent) and in Argentina (18.3 percent) but larger in Chile (25.7 percent) and in Brazil (27.7 percent). Lack of efficacy also leads to a larger percentage of respondents who feel that "for people like themselves democracy makes no difference." But again, the effect is modest in Uruguay (8.3 percent) and Argentina (11.7 percent) but great in Chile (37.9 percent) and Brazil (30.7 percent). The high proportion in Chile accounts for much of the "democratic" deficit, which in Brazil is also explained by a larger number of politically uninterested or uninformed.

Let us conclude this addendum with an attempt to construct an empirically based typology of legitimacy and efficacy and to locate the populations of the four Southern Cone countries in our typology. The first dimension of our typology concerns legitimacy. For simplicity let us assign a label to our three answers on our legitimacy indicator. We will call respondents *democrats* if they answered positively to the statement "democracy is preferable to any form of government." We will call respondents *authoritarian* if they gave a positive answer to the statement "in some circumstances an authoritarian government can be preferable to a

4. See our "Political Crafting of Democratic Consolidation or Destruction: European and South American Comparisons," in Robert A. Pastor, ed., *Democracy in the Americas* (New York: Holmes and Meier, 1989), 46–47, 58.

Table 14.4. Perception of Capacity of Democracy to Solve the Problems of the Country and Attitude toward Democracy in Uruguay, Argentina, Chile, and Brazil (Percentages of Respondents)

	Efficacy							
	"Democracy is able to solve the problems."				"Democracy is not able to solve the problems."			
Survey Response	Uruguay	Argentina	Chile	Brazil	Uruguay	Argentina	Chile	Brazil
Legitimacy "With which of the following phrases are you most in agreement?"								
"Democracy is preferable to any other form of government."	89.8	89.3	72.9	55.2	71.5	65.1	33.1	29.0
"In some circumstances an authoritarian government can be preferable to a democratic government."	3.9	5.3	11.7	16.8	14.5	18.3	25.7	27.7
"For someone like me, a democratic or a nondemocratic regime makes no difference."	3.8	1.9	13.4	17.2	8.3	11.7	37.9	30.7
No answer or "don't know"	2.5	3.5	2.0	10.8	5.7	4.9	3.3	12.7
N	(660)	(617)	(590)	(547)	(411)	(427)	(575)	(535)

Source: Latino Barometer (see table 14.1).

democratic government." We will call respondents *alienated* if they answered positively to the statement, "for someone like me, a democratic or nondemocratic regime makes no difference."

The second dimension of our typology concerns efficacy. We will simply make a dichotomy between those who believe that "democracy allows the solution of the problems that we have in our country" and those who do not believe this to be so. These two dimensions create a legitimacy/efficacy typology of six types. In this typology we shall call people who support democracy and believe it to be efficacious *confident democrats*. Those who support democracy but do not believe it capable of solving the country's problems we call *worried democrats* (table 14.5).

We can now turn to the distribution of the population among those interviewed who expressed an opinion about the legitimacy and the efficacy of democracy. Using these variables and the *Latino Barometer* results, we can empirically locate the percentage of respondents from each Southern Cone country within our typology (table 14.6). Respondents who consider democracy the most preferable form of government and capable of solving the problems of the country (*satisfied democrats* they were called in some Spanish and southern European studies) are 57.4 percent in Uruguay, 54.9 percent in Argentina, 37.9 percent in Chile, and 31.6 percent in Brazil.[5] Those who think that democracy is the most

5. See the important article by Leonardo Morlino and José R. Montero, "Legitimacy and Democracy in Southern Europe," in Richard Gunther, P. Nikiforos Diamandouros, and Hans-Jürgen Puhle, eds., *The Politics of Democratic Consolidation: Southern Europe in Comparative Perspective* (Baltimore: Johns Hopkins University Press, 1995), 231–60.

Table 14.5. Typology of Democratic "Legitimacy" and "Efficacy"

	Efficacy Indicator	
Legitimacy Indicator	Democracy solves problems.	Democracy cannot solve problems.
Democracy is preferable.	Confident democrats	Worried democrats
Under certain circumstances an authoritarian government is preferable.	Authoritarians (potential democrats)	Authoritarians (with no positive expectations about democracy)
For someone like me there is no difference.	Alienated (even if democracy works)	Alienated (do not expect democracy to work)

Table 14.6. Empirical Placement of Uruguay (U), Argentina (A), Chile (C), and Brazil (B) on a Typology of Legitimacy and Efficacy: 1995 (in Percent)

		Efficacy Indicator		
Legitimacy Indicator	Country	Democracy solves problems	Democracy does not solve problems	Total
		Confident democrats	Worried democrats	Total democrats
Democracy is	U	57.4	28.5	85.9
preferable.	A	54.9	27.7	82.6
	C	37.9	16.8	54.7
	B	31.6	16.2	47.8
		Authoritarian/potential democrats	Authoritarian (with no positive expectations about democracy)	Total authoritarian
Under certain	U	2.5	5.8	8.3
circumstances	A	3.3	7.7	11.0
authoritarian	C	6.1	13.0	19.1
government is	B	9.6	15.5	25.1
preferable.				
		Alienated (even though democracy could work)	Alienated (do not expect democracy to work)	Total alienated
For someone like	U	2.4	3.3	5.7
me there is no	A	1.2	5.0	6.2
difference.	C	7.0	19.2	26.2
	B	9.8	17.2	27.0

Source: Latino Barometer (see table 14.1). Respondents who did not answer both questions are not included. The percentages are therefore based on the total of those answering both questions. The number of cases included in the typology is 1,031 in Uruguay, 1,002 in Argentina, 1,135 in Chile, and 955 in Brazil. The percentages of total respondents not included because they did not answer one or the other of the questions are respectively 14.3, 6.6, 8.4, and 20.4. Of those in Brazil who are not included, almost one-half answered the democracy question, and half of them were favorable to democracy.

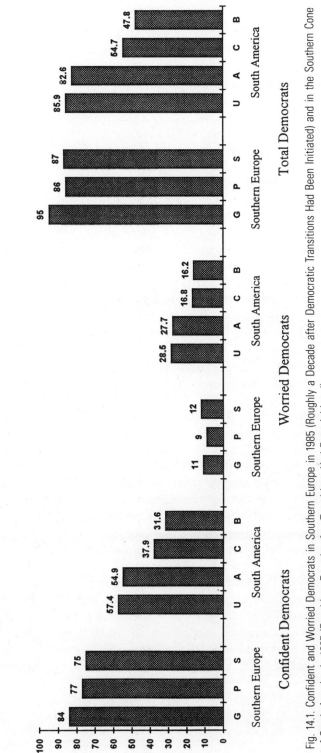

Fig. 14.1: Confident and Worried Democrats in Southern Europe in 1985 (Roughly a Decade after Democratic Transitions Had Been Initiated) and in the Southern Cone of South America in 1995 (Roughly a Decade after Transitions Had Been Initiated).

Code: For southern Europe, G = Greece, P = Portugal, and S = Spain. For the Southern Cone of South America, U = Uruguay, A = Argentina, C = Chile, and B = Brazil.
Source: For southern Europe, Leonardo Morlino and José R. Montero, "Legitimacy and Democracy in Southern Europe," in Richard Gunther, P. Nikiforos Diamondouros, and Hans-Jürgen Puhle, eds., *The Politics of Democratic Consolidation: Southern Europe in Comparative Perspective* (Baltimore: Johns Hopkins University Press, 1995), 231–60. For South America, *Latino Barometer* (see table 14.1). As in table 14.6, only respondents who answered both the legitimacy and efficacy questions are included.

preferable form of government but do not consider it able to solve problems (often identified as *critical democrats* in the southern European studies) are 28.5 percent in Uruguay, 27.7 percent in Argentina, 16.8 percent in Chile, and 16.2 percent in Brazil. These two groups added together are those who considered democracy preferable; they add up to 85.9 percent in Uruguay, 82.6 percent in Argentina, 54.7 percent in Chile, and 47.8 percent in Brazil.

Those who think that "under certain circumstances an authoritarian government is preferable" generally express no confidence in the ability of democracy to solve problems, but there are a few who, despite their acceptance of authoritarian rule, believe in the potential efficacy of democracy. They are few in Uruguay (2.5 percent) and Argentina (3.3 percent) but more numerous in Chile (6.1 percent) and in Brazil (9.6 percent).

Finally, there are those indifferent about democracy and authoritarian rule, most of them with little confidence in the capacity of democracy to solve problems. Again, we find in Chile and Brazil a larger number who, despite the fact that they believe democracy is capable of solving the problems, do not believe that it makes a difference for people like themselves (7.0 percent in Chile and 9.8 percent in Brazil). This contrasts with only 2.4 percent in Uruguay and 1.2 percent in Argentina.

Unfortunately, the questions asked in southern Europe do not allow us to construct exactly the same typology, since only the legitimacy dimension is measured by the same question. Those answering that "democracy is preferable" were 87 percent in Greece, 70 percent in Spain, and 61 percent in Portugal (which, if we ignore the "don't know"-no answer group, become, respectively, 88.8 percent, 78.6 percent, and 79.2 percent). The democrats can be divided concerning their efficacy beliefs on the basis of the question: With which of the following statements do you agree? (1) our democracy works well, (2) our democracy has many defects but it works, (3) our democracy is getting worse and soon will not work at all. Taking the first two answers as positive, the percentage of respondents who were positive on legitimacy and positive on efficacy (77 percent in Portugal, 75 percent in Spain, and 84 percent in Greece) would seem to be substantially higher in the new democracies in southern Europe than in the Southern Cone of South America. If we take the third answer as negative on efficacy, we have 9 percent "worried democrats" in Portugal, 12 percent "worried democrats" in Spain, and 11 percent in Greece. With these caveats about the absence of strict comparability in mind, the reader can consult figure 14.1 to see the comparative percentages of confident democrats and worried democrats roughly a decade after democratic transition processes had been initiated in southern Europe and in South America.

Part IV

Post-Communist Europe: The Most Complex Paths and Tasks

The year 1989 was a historic date when all of the Communist regimes in Europe (counting the USSR) started a momentous process of political, economic, and social change. Where there were nine states in 1989, there are now twenty-seven, fifteen of them successor states of the USSR. Obviously, an accurate depiction of the specificities of this massive transformative process will take decades and will be the work of scholars on the region who command the requisite linguistic and historical skills. Our task in part 4 is necessarily more spatially and empirically delimited and must be primarily conceptual in nature.

In each chapter our fundamental intention will be to build upon and to help elucidate the major theoretical issues we discussed in part 1. Our hope is that, by incorporating post-Communist Europe systematically into the theory building endeavor, we can sharpen and where necessary reformulate or reject aspects of current democratization theory. In the end, by a process of what Albert O. Hirschman would call "trespassing," our aim is not only to expand the scope and utility of democratic theory, but also to make a small contribution to the monumental task of analyzing the world historical transformation in post-Communist Europe.

The theoretical problems we will explore in the seven chapters of part 4 have the following structure. In chapter 15 we address the question of the "prehistories" of post-Communist Europe, attempting to do justice to the elements of commonality and the elements of difference in the region.[1] Since most of the commonalities in the outer empire of the USSR were a result of policies imposed by the USSR, we examine the influence of these policies and why, how, and with what consequences these policies changed. We also develop further the analysis we began in part 1 concerning the special legacies the totalitarian and post-totalitarian regimes present in each of the five arenas whose effective functioning is helpful to the task of consolidating democracy.

The first country to break out of the USSR's outer empire was Poland. In chapter 16 we explore why Poland, alone of all the Communist countries of Europe, never completely conformed to the Soviet totalitarian regime type, and how this gave Poland, by the late 1970s, some unique resources with which to challenge the Communist system. However, as the first country in the region to make a round table pact on transition, Poland paid a price that has been underestimated from the perspective of the problems this has created for democratic consolidation. One of the most acute of these problems is the style of opposition that became dominant in Poland; it engendered values and patterns of action in the arena of

---

1. The prehistory we focus on most is the Communist period. Older prehistories are, of course, also extremely important. The classic works that analyze the specific pre-Communist sociopolitical history of each of the countries of East Central Europe that we analyze in this part of the book are Joseph Rothschild, *East Central Europe between the Two World Wars* (Seattle: University of Washington Press, 1977), and his *Return to Diversity: A Political History of East Central Europe since World War II* (New York: Oxford University Press, 1989); the latter is especially good for the account it gives of the specific way each country became Communist after World War II. See also Hugh Seton-Watson, *Eastern Europe between the Wars: 1918–1941* (Boulder, Colo.: Westview Press, 1986).

civil society that impeded the construction of a democratically effective political society. The parallels with Brazil are instructive here.

In our analysis of nondemocratic regimes in part 1, we argued that post-totalitarianism had significant within-type variation, from early, to frozen, to mature. In chapter 17 we expand the argument by examining the most developed example in the world of mature post-totalitarianism (Hungary in the late 1980s), a graphic example of frozen post-totalitarianism (Czechoslovakia in 1968–89), and a case of very early post-totalitarianism (Bulgaria in 1988–89). Our interest lies in the textures of politics and the different but analytically predictable democratic transition paths available from different starting points in the post-totalitarian continuum.

Another regime type analyzed in part 1 of this book is the sultanistic regime. There we argued that, if a specific regime approximated a fusion of the totalitarian and sultanistic ideal-types, the *reforma pactada–ruptura pactada* transition path that we find in Spain and Hungary would not be available. We further argued that, if a regime change occurred in such a context (probably through a revolution or due to a change in international forces), democratic consolidation would entail the especially difficult tasks of crafting democratic values and patterns of action in *each* of the five arenas of a democratic polity. In chapter 18 our analysis of Romania will allow us to explore this theoretical argument empirically, since the Ceauşescu regime had elements of sultanism in addition to totalitarianism.

The handling of the triangular relationship among stateness, nationalism, and democracy has been seen to be essential to the success of the democratic transition in Spain. The failure to negotiate this triadic relationship has been crucial in the failure of democratic transition in many post-Soviet countries. No chapter can do justice to the importance and difficulties of the failure of democratic transition in the USSR. We can, however, within the context of our previous theoretical discussion of stateness, put into a sharp comparative perspective some aspects of that failure (chap. 19). We can also indicate why the particular form of state disintegration became a difficult legacy in Russia for would-be democracy crafters.

In many of the new states of the former Soviet Union, the failure of democratic consolidation is almost overdetermined for the foreseeable future. Ethnic civil wars and the economic chaos partly caused by the nearly stateless quality of some of the strife-torn polities make the creation of the rule of law, as well as democratic civil, political, and economic societies, extremely difficult.[2] However, of the new states of the former Soviet Union that are beginning their transformations, Estonia, with its impressive democratic experience of 1918–33 and its relatively strong economy, began its transition—in contrast to most of the other successor states of the former Soviet Union—with many relatively favorable conditions

<hr />

2. These new polities are some of the most telling examples of what Ken Jowitt brilliantly predicted could be a "new world disorder" of weak societies and weak states. See Jowitt, *New World Disorder: The Leninist Extinction* (Berkeley: University of California Press, 1992).

(chap. 20). Thus, the inability to satisfy our definition of democracy was not overdetermined in Estonia. The major problem Estonia (and even more, as we shall see, Latvia) had on its transition agenda was how to handle its large Russian-speaking population. The Baltic Republics thus present us with a particularly interesting area in which to explore, in demoi that are actually multinational, the possibilities of transcending (and the costs of not transcending) the sometimes conflicting logics of nation-state–building and democracy-building.

We conclude the book with a broad-ranging and necessarily tentative analysis of the democratic prospects of post-Communist Europe from the perspective of modern democratic theory and practice. In chapter 21 we include in the analysis all of the states of post-Communist Europe, both to document and to begin to explain their variations in terms of democratic efficacy and legitimacy.

15

Post-Communism's Prehistories

ANY SERIOUS comparative political analysis of the inter-regional differences between democratization in southern Europe, South America, and post-Communist Europe and the great intraregional differences within post-Communist Europe must pay special attention to the stateness issues we discussed in chapter 2. In addition, comparativists must consider carefully how three of the variables that we discussed in part 1 inter-relate. These variables are international influences, the political economy of coercion and legitimacy, and the special legacies of totalitarian and post-totalitarian regimes.

INTERNATIONAL INFLUENCES AND TRANSITION

When we place in comparative perspective the transitions in the Soviet Union and the ex-Warsaw Pact countries of East Central Europe (Poland, Hungary, Czechoslovakia, the German Democratic Republic, Romania, and Bulgaria), one of their most distinctive qualities concerns the variable we call *international influence*. One of the editors of the classic four-volume study of the transitions in southern Europe and South America, Laurence Whitehead, argued that "in all the peacetime cases considered here internal forces were of primary importance in determining the course and outcome of the transition attempt, and international factors played only a secondary role."[1] Clearly, such a judgment would obviously be unwarranted for East Central Europe, given the speed with which Communism collapsed in 1989 and the fact that Czechoslovakia, Romania, and Bulgaria began their transitions almost *before* any significant domestic changes had occurred.[2] Many scholars have documented the prolonged economic stagnation and legitimacy problems of most of the region. However, economic stagnation and weak legitimacy alone (which had existed for a long time before 1989) cannot explain the rapidity of the domino-like collapse of the countries. For this we need

1. Laurence Whitehead, "International Aspects of Democratization," in O'Donnell, Schmitter, and Whitehead, *Transitions from Authoritarian Rule: Comparative Perspectives,* 4.

2. Adam Przeworski captures how these regimes were swept away as if by a dam breaking in *Democracy and the Market: Political and Economic Reforms in Eastern Europe and Latin America* (Cambridge: Cambridge University Press, 1991), 4–6. See also Samuel P. Huntington's discussion of "snow-balling" in *The Third Wave: Democratization in the Late Twentieth Century* (Norman: University of Oklahoma Press, 1991), 33.

to explore the special linkage in the region between international and domestic politics.

Indeed, in Eastern Europe between 1948 and 1989, the very use of the words independent, sovereign, and domestic to describe politics is strained, given the ideological, political, military, and economic linkages between the Soviet hegemon and its East Central European "outer empire."[3] The nature of these linkages in turn reduced the normal international influence of major democratic and market polities of the sort that were significant, though not determinative, in southern Europe and South America. Here we must pause, therefore, to discuss how comparativists should and should not approach the question of the international influence of the Soviet Union.

Much of the pre-1989 literature of the countries of the region suffered from two analytic problems. Initially, a major strand of the literature began with such an exclusive focus on the region's shared status as "satellites" that the significant heterogeneity of the pre-Communist and Communist state-society relations of each country was played down. Later, many scholars, in a reaction against Cold War excesses, began to emphasize the uniqueness of the countries on which they specialized. In the process important commonalities in the economies, politics, and societies of the entire region were understressed. However, as comparativists interested in problems of democratic transition and the tasks that must be faced before democracy can be consolidated, our conceptual endeavor must be to show how, why, and with what consequences elements of commonality and elements of difference can be simultaneously present.

The Soviet Union was not just a system or the center of an empire, but the emanating source of a major utopian vision. During the post–World War II phase of Soviet expansion in Eastern Europe, there were important military and economic gains for the Soviet Union. However, power relations within the bloc were reinforced, during the period of "high Stalinism," by the claims of ideology. Indeed, the 1968 Brezhnev Doctrine of limited sovereignty, which was used to justify the repression of the Prague Spring experiment, was explicitly based on such claims: "The sovereignty of independent socialist countries can not be set against the interests of world socialism and the world revolutionary movement."[4]

Limited sovereignty was reinforced by a regionwide trading, planning, and investment network (the Council for Mutual Economic Assistance, CMEA) centered around Moscow and a regionwide military alliance (the Soviet-led Warsaw Pact). In addition, the Soviet Politburo's strong involvement in leadership

---

3. See, for example, the use made of the concept *outer empire* in Alex Pravda, ed., *The End of the Outer Empire: Soviet–East European Relations in Transition, 1985–90* (London: Royal Institute of International Affairs and Sage Publications, 1992). The term *inner empire* is now increasingly used to describe relations between the USSR and the fifteen former soviet republics.

4. For this quotation and a discussion, see Mark Kramer, "Beyond the Brezhnev Doctrine: A New Era in Soviet–East European Relations?" *International Security* (Winter 1989–90): 25.

changes in Eastern Europe and their external monitoring of ideological frameworks and party-state administrative structures gave the Eastern European Warsaw Pact countries an unusually high degree of regional commonality and dependence on a common hegemon.[5]

Furthermore, Soviet military presence was a clear and determinative factor in
beating back the impressive range of heterogeneous resistance these "satellites"
still managed to generate. Soviet troops were garrisoned in four of the seven Warsaw Pact countries, namely Poland, Czechoslovakia, Hungary, and the German
Democratic Republic. In three of the four, during the GDR riots in 1953, during
Hungary's Revolution in 1956, and after the Prague Spring of Czechoslovakia in
1968, Soviet troops were used to alter the course of domestic politics. In Poland in
1981 the perceived threat of the use of Soviet troops played a critical role in the
regime's ability to impose martial law and to repress Solidarity forces, which in a
Gramscian sense had become hegemonic within Polish civil society. If we consider these countries independent, then the "irreversibility of Communism"
much proclaimed by thinkers such as Jeanne Kirkpatrick was obviously wrong.
Hungary in 1956 was, as Joseph Rothschild correctly says, a "victorious revolution
[that] was defeated only by overwhelming foreign force."[6] If Hungary had been
located in a geopolitical space analogous to Spain or Brazil, Communism would
have almost certainly stayed reversed and a democratic transition might have
begun in 1956. Likewise, if the Prague Spring of 1968 had occurred in such a space,
Czechoslovakia might have evolved from a post-totalitarian to an authoritarian
regime with the wider range of transition options such a regime type represents.[7]

5. On the embeddedness of Eastern Europe in such structures, see Robert L. Hutchings, *Soviet–East European Relations: Consolidation and Conflict* (Madison: University of Wisconsin Press, 1983), and Christopher
D. Jones, *Soviet Influence in Eastern Europe: Political Autonomy and the Warsaw Pact* (New York: Praeger Publishers, 1981). Western democracies, especially the United States, certainly played a covert or even overt role
in the subversion or overthrow of democracies in such countries as Brazil (1964) or Chile (1973). However,
Western support for Pinochet in Chile and for the military in Brazil was never unequivocal because the
coups were rationalized in the name of democracy even by coup defendants and were opposed in the name
of democracy and human rights by sectors of opinion and some powerful political leaders. Even more importantly, the democratic opposition to rulers such as Pinochet normally could mobilize extensive political
alliances in Italy, Germany, and even the United States that had a major influence inside countries such as
Chile. The domestic democratic opposition had no such comparable networks inside the Soviet empire.

6. Joseph Rothschild, *Return to Diversity: A Political History of East Central Europe since World War II.*
(Oxford: Oxford University Press, 1989), 160.

7. For speculation on how Czechoslovakia might have evolved, see H. Gordon Skilling, *Czechoslovakia's
Interrupted Revolution* (Princeton: Princeton University Press, 1976). Skilling argues that "there was a powerful dynamic at work, within the party and in society at large, which suggested that, barring outside intervention, the process of change would have been accelerated rather than slowed down or blocked, and
would eventually have produced a thoroughly revised socialism, democratic in form, and national in content. . . . The Prague experiment seemed doomed to failure for external reasons rather than inherent domestic ones" (pp. 842–43). However, as comparativists we believe that there is no evidence to suggest that
Alexander Dubček wanted a Western-style democracy. Dubček never proposed multiparty politics. He did,
however, clearly favor liberalization. Given Prague's history and setting, we believe that this liberalization
might well have created a context in which other forces could have been energized and could have pushed
for a democratic transition.

Instead, as Timothy Garton Ash, writing in 1986 observed, "one spring was followed by fifteen winters."[8]

The outcomes in the GDR in 1953, in Poland in 1956 and 1981, in Czechoslovakia in 1968, and even more emphatically in Hungary in 1956 did not illustrate the irreversibility of Communist-style regimes. The outcomes did reveal, however, that the presence of foreign combat troops, controlled by a Communist hegemon that was ideologically confident and geopolitically willing to use force, could thwart potential transitions to democracy.

Why was the Soviet hegemon willing, again and again, to use force? Partly because, from the Soviet perspective, the use of force had so few costs. Given the balance of nuclear terror in existence, the West allowed the Soviets to use force to repress Hungary in 1956 and to build the Berlin Wall in 1961. Until Gorbachev, the Soviet Union did not want Western direct investment, so negative Western reaction to the Soviet use of force did not raise any significant perceived opportunity costs for the Soviet Union. The Soviet leaders also still believed (or at least articulated the belief) in the inevitable global victory of their socioeconomic and doctrinal system. In this East-West calculus of interests, the costs of Soviet repression of Eastern Europe did not exceed the costs of toleration.

The international embeddedness of the Warsaw Pact countries of Central and Eastern Europe and their dependence on a hegemon were thus unlike anything center-periphery theorists encountered in the politics of the peripheral states of Spain, Portugal, or Greece or what dependency theorists could document for Argentina, Chile, Uruguay, or Brazil.[9] In this context, without a domestic change in the hegemon—and here domestic factors in the USSR were crucial—it was extremely difficult for either Central and East European elites (dependent on Soviet political control) or Central and East European masses (coercible by domestic elites credibly supported by the hegemon) to initiate new political processes that might have led to democratic transitions.

Yugoslavia was not in the Soviet bloc, but Tito's "straddling" between East and West weakened international pressures toward democracy as we have defined it. United States foreign policy-makers, largely for "divide and rule" reasons, accorded Yugoslavia a de facto "most favored Communist" status. Likewise, democratic theorists put Yugoslavia in a different category from all other Communist systems because they believed that worker self-management was a form of democracy and could evolve positively. A widely used external "exit" option, particularly to Germany, also released some pressures for democratization. The significant degree of liberalization—especially concerning travel and many university freedoms—lessened Western criticism of Yugoslavia's still considerable "democratic deficit."

---

8. Timothy Garton Ash, "Czechoslovakia under the Ice" in *The Uses of Adversity: Essays on the Fate of Central Europe* (New York: Random House, 1989), 62.

9. However, U.S. use of force in the Caribbean and in Central America under the ideological guise of first the Monroe Doctrine and later counterinsurgency and low-intensity warfare is another matter.

When 1989 arrived, many of those holding power in the different republics could resist full democratization and liberal values on the basis of their nationalist stand vis-à-vis their neighbors and internal minorities. Thus, the independence of majoritarian ethnocratic "nation-states" increasingly became privileged over liberal democratic values and democratization as we have defined them.[10]

The Altered Political Economy of Coercion and Legitimacy in the Soviet Union and Its International Consequences

What led to domestic changes in the hegemon, and what effect did these changes have vis-à-vis the West and vis-à-vis the cost of maintenance of the outer empire in Central and Eastern Europe? Hundreds of articles and books, by scholars better qualified than we, have been and are being written on this question. However, as comparativists interested in shifting power relationships, we maintain that some changes seem to be fundamental.

The initial change occurred within the ideology and power structure of the hegemon. In 1985 the new leader of the Communist Party, Mikhail Gorbachev, and his core supporters were convinced that the Soviet Union was in a state of dangerous stagnation requiring far-reaching restructuring.[11] Gorbachev's vehicle for change was perestroika and later glasnost. But both strategies fundamentally altered the place of Eastern Europe, the West, and the political economy of coercion in his calculations. To be successful, perestroika needed to enhance flows of investment and technology and indeed to build a much closer network of relations with the public and private sectors of the United States and the European Community. This network of relations and resource flows could be accomplished much better in a post–cold war environment than in a cold war environment.

Furthermore, the greatest single source of potential savings to be used for new investment in the Soviet Union was decreased military expenditures. Indeed, early in the Gorbachev period his advisers came to the conclusion that the size of the Soviet GNP was smaller than previously estimated and that military expenditures were greater.[12] In a spirited defense of Gorbachev's reforms against party hardliners, Foreign Minister Shevardnadze at the 1990 Party Congress defiantly

10. For the emergent ethnic nationalist dictatorships in parts of the former Yugoslavia, see George Soros, "Nationalist Dictatorships versus Open Society" (New York: Soros Foundation, January 1993, pamphlet).

11. Three basic sources for their widespread perception of stagnation and their strategies to overcome this predicament are Mikhail Gorbachev, *Perestroika: New Thinking for Our Country and the World* (New York: Harper and Row, 1987); Edward Wilkes Walker, "Structural Pressures, Political Choice and Institutional Change: Bureaucratic Totalitarianism and the Origins of Perestroika" (Ph. D. diss., Department of Political Science, Columbia University, 1992); and the magisterial book by Archie Brown, *The Gorbachev Factor* (Oxford: Oxford University Press, 1996).

12. This point was stressed in an interview with Stepan by one of Gorbachev's key advisors, Aleksandr Yakovlev, in Moscow, October 24, 1989.

asked the congress whether the members really thought it was possible or indeed in the Soviet Union's interest to continue its extremely heavy defense expenditures, which in his judgment had led to the "economic and social ruin" of the Soviet Union.

Having come to the Ministry of Foreign Affairs and having obtained access to the appropriate information, I learned that in the past two decades alone ideological confrontation with the West added R700 trillion rubles as the cost of military confrontation. . . .

The prospects have opened up the possibilities to enter a new era, and to build completely new relations between the two superpowers. . . . But it is obvious that if we continue as we did before, comrades—I state this with all responsibility—to spend a quarter, I stress a quarter, of our budget on military spending—we have ruined the country—then we simply won't need defense, just as we won't need an army for a ruined country and poor people.

There is no sense in protecting a system that has led to economic and social ruin. There is just one way out: policy should take upon itself the task of creating a reserve of security with accompanying reductions in defense spending. . . .

Our calculations show that in the current five-year plan period, the total peace dividend resulting from the foreign policy line based on new thinking could amount to R240 to R250 billion. Our country does not have a future outside integration into the worldwide system of economic and financial institutions and ties. We need to get out of the self-isolation from the world, and from progress, into which we have driven ourselves.[13]

The Soviet Union's defense expenditures were even higher than Shevardnadze implied. From a comparative perspective the Soviet Union's security-related expenditures were more than three times as great as that of the United States, six times as great as the EEC average, and twenty times as great as that of Japan. Furthermore, in all these open, high-information market economies, there were greater spillovers between military technology and globally competitive export industries than in the USSR. In comparative economic terms, therefore, the country that stood to benefit most from the "end of the cold war" was the Soviet Union. See figure 15.1, which also shows that Soviet defense expenditures were also at least three times higher than any South European or South American case we have considered in this book.

When it came to Eastern Europe, influential Soviet analysts believed that the entire Council of Mutual Economic Assistance would benefit economically and politically from shifting in the direction of perestroika and glasnost.[14] In an important mid-1988 document, significantly written for a conference on "The Place and Role of Eastern Europe in the Relaxation of Tension between the U.S.A. and the U.S.S.R.," authoritative Soviet specialists advanced the argument that eco-

13. See Shevardnadze's speech on July 3, 1990, at the 28th Communist Party of the Soviet Union (CPSU) Party Congress, reprinted in *Foreign Broadcast Information Service*, Daily Report, Soviet Union, July 5, 1990, pp. 7–10. Note that he speaks not so much of military confrontation but ideological confrontation.

14. Well before Gorbachev, some important analysts in the Soviet Union and the United States had also argued that the "outer empire" in Eastern Europe had changed from an asset to a liability for the Soviet

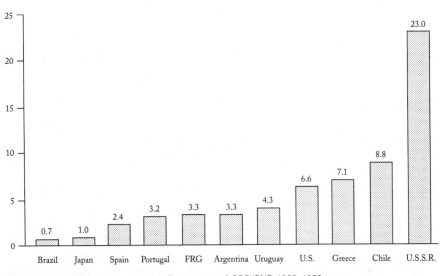

Fig. 15.1. Defense Expenditures as a Percentage of GDP/GNP, 1983–1989.

Sources: The 1989 data for the Soviet Union are from Dimitri Steinber, "The Soviet Defense Burden: Estimating Hidden Costs," *Soviet Studies* 44, no. 2 (1992): 258. All other data are for 1984 (except Uruguay, which is for 1983) and are drawn from Stockholm International Peace Research Institute, *World Armaments and Disarmament: SIPRI Yearbook, 1984* (Stockholm: SIPRI), 129–31, and *1986*, pp. 243–47.

nomic and political liberalization would be a good thing for Eastern Europe and the Soviet Union. The document was clearly critical of the intense level of previous Soviet military and political intervention in Eastern Europe. We quote from this document at length because it was written *before* the momentous changes in Eastern Europe in 1989.

The administrative-state model of socialism, established in the majority of Eastern European countries during the 1950's under the influence of the Soviet Union, has not withstood the test of time, thereby showing its socio-political and economic inefficiency. . . . It was inadmissible to extend the postulate of the primary role of the Communist party of the Soviet Union to relationships among socialist states. . . . The model for the existing system was created in the Soviet Union during the 1930's and 1940's. . . . The process of *perestroika* is already shaping a new multifaceted political reality, one full of contradictions and conflicts. In terms of the scale and depth of integration processes and the intensity of the interweaving of economic, scientific and technological interests and relations, the CMEA countries turned out to be far behind the countries of the European Community. . . . Interest in preserving peace, a prerequisite for which is the positive development of relations between the two systems, necessitates that new politi-

---

Union. See, for example, the extremely high estimates of Soviet subsidies by M. Marrese and J. Vanous, *Soviet Subsidizing of Trade with Eastern Europe: A Soviet Perspective* (Berkeley: Institute of International Studies, University of California, Berkeley, 1983). For a review of the evidence and much lower estimates, see Charles Wolf, Jr., "The Costs and Benefits of the Soviet Empire," in Henry S. Rowen and Charles Wolf, Jr., eds., *The Future of the Soviet Empire* (New York: Institute for Contemporary Studies and St. Martin's Press, 1987), 121–142.

cal thinking guide the policies of the great powers with respect to crisis situations in the whole world, including those in the socialist countries of Eastern Europe. . . . It is inadmissible that *either side* interfere in the internal problems of a country finding itself in a difficult position. . . . Should crisis situations develop, they should under no circumstances be allowed to deter progress in East-West relations.[15]

Six months after that document was written, Gorbachev made his momentous announcement in December 1988 to the United Nations that, by the end of 1990, independent of Western action on arms reductions, the Soviet Union would withdraw some 240,000 men, 10,000 tanks, and 820 combat aircraft from Eastern Europe and from the Western military district of the Soviet Union closest to Eastern Europe. According to Charles Gati, "more than any other single event, that announcement set the stage for the dramatic developments of 1989. By suggesting that Moscow was prepared to remove Soviet forces from its East European dominion, Gorbachev put the region's Communist leaders on notice that Soviet tanks would no longer protect their rule. It did not take long for the people of Eastern Europe to understand that their leaders were therefore vulnerable—that some of them were, in effect, on the run."[16] When Gorbachev made this statement the Gang of Four, the Brezhnevite repressive leaders of Czechoslovakia, East Germany, Romania, and Bulgaria, were all resisting and often censuring his statements about glasnost, and only in Bulgaria had perestroika been approved even in theory.

We show, in following chapters, that in every single instance the regional hegemon (the Soviet Union) took some specific action to weaken each one of the Gang of Four. Unfortunately, we do not have data for East Germany, but we do have data from a public opinion poll administered in 1986–87 in Bulgaria, Romania, and Czechoslovakia that indicates that numerous citizens in these countries felt that glasnost and perestroika would be good for these countries (table 15.1).

Though Gorbachev's preference was for Central and Eastern Europe to embrace "within-system" Soviet-like changes, he gravely underestimated how illegitimate and unpopular many of the regimes were and how destabilizing the combination of his statements in *favor* of glasnost and perestroika and *against* Soviet military intervention would be.[17] Given the hegemonic relations that the Soviet Union had previously had in Eastern Europe, Gorbachev's endorsement of change altered power relationships everywhere in the Warsaw Pact countries. It weakened

15. "The Place and Role of Eastern Europe in the Relaxation of Tensions between the USA and the USSR" was written by the staff of the Institute of Economics of the World Socialist System (Moscow) for a conference in Alexandria, Virginia, and widely circulated because the Soviet authors allowed it to be published in its entirety in *Problems of Communism* 37, nos. 3–4 (May–August 1988): 55–70.

16. Charles Gati, *The Bloc That Failed: Soviet–East European Politics in Transformation* (Bloomington: Indiana University Press, 1990), 166–67. Alex Pravda offers some evidence that East European leaders were told, as early as November 1986, that the Soviet Union would not use force to uphold their rule. See "Soviet Policy towards Eastern Europe in Transition," in Pravda, *The End of Outer Empire*, esp. 17–18.

17. For evidence and arguments on this theme, see Pravda, *The End of Outer Empire*, 1–34, and Gati, *The Bloc That Failed*, 102–3.

Table 15.1. "Do you believe that Gorbachev's leadership is good or bad for [respondent's own country]?"

Reply	Percentage of Respondents		
	Bulgaria	Czechoslovakia	Romania
Good	64	53	40
Bad	8	8	10
Neither	24	34	38
Other/no answer	4	5	12
Number of cases	556	436	541

Source: East European Perceptions of Gorbachev and Soviet Reforms (Munich: Radio Free Europe, Audience and Public Opinion Research Department, July 1988). Reprinted in Gati, *The Bloc That Failed,* 68.

antiglasnost Communist Party leadership in Bulgaria, Romania, East Germany, and Czechoslovakia, it strengthened reform wings of the Communist Party in Hungary and Poland who wanted to establish a new relationship with the democratic opposition, and it emboldened the democratic opposition in all countries of Eastern Europe.

Two fields of force were felt by actors in mid-1989. First, the ideological self-confidence defined by the Brezhnev Doctrine, in the Soviet Union's right of intervention, had been steadily waning. This waning force was felt by the Soviet leadership, by East European heads of government, and by the opposition. But there remained a second countervailing force. Key democratic activists, especially in Poland and Hungary, insisted that they could not count on nonintervention by the USSR. They awaited, in effect, the proof of an actual case of Soviet nonintervention at the moment of regime change away from Communism. Among the reasons they cite for their caution and their reluctance to mobilize force was that there was always the possibility that Gorbachev would fall and that hard-liners and/or nationalists would assume power. As the coup attempt in the Soviet Union in August 1991 and the December 1993 election results in Russia showed, their apprehension was not unfounded.[18]

Whatever Gorbachev's initial calculations were, by the fall of 1989 Soviet policy had already profoundly changed relations of power in the bloc. Existing Communist governments were weaker and the democratic oppositions were stronger.[19] In

18. For informative studies of the Brezhnev Doctrine of "limited sovereignty" and how and why it was changed by Gorbachev, see Robert A. Jones, *The Soviet Concept of "Limited Sovereignty" from Lenin to Gorbachev* (New York: St. Martin's Press, 1990), and Mark Kramer, "Beyond the Brezhnev Doctrine: New Era in Soviet-East European Relations?" *International Security* (Winter 1989–90), 25–67.

19. However, some of the elites still believed in the ideology of socialism and in the possibility of economic and social reforms allowing them to stay in power and incorporate moderate oppositions as long as they did not need to use massive violence. This meant that, with the exception of Hungary, and in a unique way in Poland, Communist rulers in the Warsaw Pact did not initiate a reform type of transition to democracy, as in Spain or Brazil. The transition to democracy was forced on them: in Germany, not by the round

this context, Soviet use of armed force to crush change would have dramatically altered the course of perestroika in the Soviet Union. Economic and financial relations with the West would have experienced a grave setback. Gorbachev's hopes for reductions in military expenditure would have been cancelled. In the fall of 1989, to paraphrase Robert Dahl, the cost of intervention was greater than the costs of toleration.[20]

LEGACIES OF (COMMUNIST-STYLE) TOTALITARIAN AND POST-TOTALITARIAN REGIME TYPES FOR DEMOCRATIC CONSOLIDATION

Many analysts have correctly noted that a major difference between East European and post-Soviet transitions on the one hand and those in southern Europe and South America on the other is the "simultaneity problem." In Eastern Europe and in the Soviet Union, in addition to making a political transition to democracy, the countries have simultaneously had to make a transition to market economies.[21] We obviously agree that both of these profound changes are necessary. However, the analysis must go much further.

All of the regimes in the region, with the partial exception of Poland, which we will argue (controversially) was never a completely installed totalitarian regime, were at one time "totalitarian." Some later became "post-totalitarian." As we specified in table 1.1, there are five reinforcing arenas of a modern consolidated democratic polity concerning civil society, political society, rule of law, the state apparatus, and economic society. We further specified, in table 4.3, that, when a specific transition starts from a prior base that approximated our totalitarian or post-totalitarian ideal type, this *necessarily* implies a very distinctive and difficult set of tasks in *each* of the five arenas, tasks that must be accomplished before that polity can become a consolidated democracy.

Since none of the nondemocratic regimes we have considered thus far in southern Europe or South America was totalitarian or post-totalitarian, the challenges

---

table but by exit to West Germany and by voice in the streets of East Germany. In Czechoslovakia the events leading to regime collapse were even less expected. The fact that these regime leaders did not plan for a transition to democracy has contributed to the use of the word *revolution* (as in "velvet revolution"). The word *revolution* is not used to describe any of the southern European or South American transitions we have discussed except that of Portugal, which was a revolution unleashed after a nonhierarchical military coup.

20. Robert Dahl's famous axiom about the costs of toleration is found in his *Polyarchy: Participation and Opposition* (New Haven: Yale University Press, 1971), 15. In China, which is also in some ways an empire, the cost of repression in its periphery (such as Tibet and Sinkian) is not, as of this writing, higher than the cost of repression. This is partly due to Tibet's and Sinkian's great geographic and cultural distance from the West. Also, given the size and growth of the Chinese market, the cost of resistance by the West is perceived as too high by many powerful actors. In addition, there is latent ethnocentric feeling in much of the West that nondemocratic rule is "intolerable" in the West but "tolerable" in other parts of the world.

21. Claus Offe goes further and speaks of the triple (political, economic, and socioterritorial) transformations that are necessary. See "Capitalism by Democratic Design? Democratic Theory Facing the Triple Transition in East Central Europe," translated by Pierre Adler, *Social Research* 58 (Winter 1991): 865–92.

for all the countries we consider here in part 4 (including Poland) are thus different in kind than those considered heretofore. While our argument has been laid out also in tables 1.1 and 4.3 (and we urge the reader to consult those tables again) and will be explored empirically in the chapters to follow, it might be useful to pause at this point to illustrate some of the generic problems that are particularly salient in each of the five polity arenas, given a totalitarian or post-totalitarian legacy.

Civil Society

The classic approach is to include in this term organizations and groups that are relatively independent of the state. If we use this definition, the key observation to make is that, with Poland being a partial exception, the overwhelming majority of unions, agrarian collectives, cultural societies, communications systems, and other organizations in Eastern Europe and the USSR existing at the time of transition were originally created in the totalitarian period and were maintained by the party state even in the post-totalitarian period. The hidden, but known and in some cases parallel, presence of intelligence agents further weakened these organizations and often compromised their leaders' capacity to play a role in the transition. This phenomenon was most important in the GDR, Czechoslovakia, Romania, Bulgaria, and the USSR. In contrast, in the authoritarian regimes of southern Europe and South America, though many of the trade union, entrepreneurial, and newspaper organizations were brutally repressed, they were not totally penetrated by an official party or even by police and intelligence agents.

Religion needs special discussion. In all societies religion is the social reality most difficult to control by those in power. Communism, with its commitment to atheism, was particularly committed to limit as much as possible the role of religion in civil society. There were, however, important differences between religions. Orthodox christianity, with its legacy of caesaropapism and therefore its tendency toward dependence on the state and toward being a national church, did not serve as a basis for oppositional activity. At best it was a small source of limited cultural dissidence. As a consequence, it has not, except for nationalism in the post-Communist countries, been a source for major new leadership or issue articulation. The presence of the internationally organized Roman Catholic Church (especially in Poland and Lithuania) and Protestant dissidents (especially in East Germany in the late 1980s) contributed to a different civil society.

In democratic societies, religion, the churches, and the voluntary groups linked with them play an important role in bringing people together, articulating moral positions (that often have political implications) and helping in organizing a variety of interests. In this respect massive secularization may weaken an active society. Communism made a deliberate effort to secularize societies, persecute religious organizations, control and infiltrate them, and bar from elite postions and education those loyal to the churches. The data collected by Richard Rose show the effect of those policies, which failed only in some Catholic countries, like Poland. The percentage of respondents saying that they never or rarely went to church was 71.1 percent in Belorussia, 60 percent in Ukraine, 68 percent in the Czech Republic (where secularization was already advanced before Communism) 66 percent in Bulgaria, and 66 percent in Hungary, contrasting with 41 percent in Slovakia, 46 percent in Romania, 44 percent in Slovenia, and 16 percent in Poland.[22]

Not only were most organizations, normally considered in other settings part of civil society, integrated into the party-state in Communist Europe, but they had a material presence that was, and often still is, the beneficiary of a series of state subsidies. It is not necessarily therefore in the perceived interest of such potential actors in an autonomous civil society to *want* to become autonomous. In post-Communist Europe, many workers in Bulgarian collectives, Polish mines, and Russian factories; intellectuals in the massive Academy of Science systems in all the countries; or people in hundreds of other state-subsidized organizations worry that they will be voting against their material self-interest if they support the proposed utopian alternatives offered by most market-oriented democrats. It is important to stress that this legacy extends well beyond the nomenklatura. Many citizens in Eastern Europe live every day in some tension between their goals for the future and their present material interests.

One of the leading analysts of this legacy, the Polish sociologist Edmund Mokrzycki, argues that it is a mistake not to understand that "so-called real socialism—that is, the system that took shape in the Soviet Union and in European socialist countries—is a social system in the strong sense of the term; it has its own equilibrium mechanisms, its own dynamics, and the ability to reproduce its constitutive characteristics."[23] The continued strong showing in two consecutive elections of groups associated with the old regime in Bulgaria and Romania and the return to power in 1992–94 of parties associated with the Communists in Lithuania, Poland, and Hungary, show how sociologically grounded in real interests are groups associated with "real socialism." Elsewhere, Mokrzycki and a coauthor take much of the "democratic transition" literatures to task for failing to incorporate this issue into their analyses:

In the process of rejecting "really existing socialism," democracy was proclaimed the promised land. . . . A critical paradox, however, has emerged since 1989. Whereas in the West European and American experience, democracy was proclaimed and institutionalized by the same social groups, in Eastern Europe—most vividly demonstrated by the case of Poland—the social groups that articulated democracy are the very groups threatened by the institutionalization of

22. For church attendance data see Richard Rose and Christian Haerpfer, "Adapting to Transformation in Eastern Europe: New Democracies Barometer-11," *Studies in Public Policy* no. 212 (1993): table 35.

23. See his thought-provoking "The Legacy of Real Socialism, Group Interests, and the Search for a New Utopia," in Walter D. Connor and Piotr Ploszajski, eds., *Escape from Socialism: The Polish Route* (Warsaw: IFiS Publishers, 1992), 269.

democracy in its liberal capitalist form. . . . None of the existing approaches to transition has paid adequate attention to the socio-economic structures that evolved under Leninism and the impact they have on the processes of political democratization.[24]

Political Society

When we turn to political society, the tension between future utopian desires and present material interests, in the context of the relatively flattened landscape left by post-totalitarianism, creates problems for political representation. Politicians frequently claimed in the founding elections to represent independent entrepreneurs and independent trade unions, groups that in most countries in Eastern Europe did not yet exist. Democratic political society, moreover, is not only about political representation; it is also about political parties. But forty-five years of party-state rule in Eastern Europe and more than seventy in the Soviet Union have given the very word *party* a negative connotation throughout the region. Indeed, almost none of the major political movements in Eastern Europe called themselves parties (viz. Solidarity in Poland, Civic Forum in Czechoslovakia, Hungarian Democratic Forum in Hungary, popular fronts in the Baltic countries, and Union of Democratic Forces in Bulgaria). Furthermore, the charismatic leaders in the region, Walesa in Poland, Havel in Czechoslovakia, and Yeltsin in Russia, refused to join and lead political parties.

Here a comparison between Communist Europe and other areas is useful. In sharp contrast to Eastern Europe and the Soviet Union, the opposition parties in Spain, Uruguay, and Chile struggled to create a more solid and autonomous civil society, but most of their energies were devoted to the articulation of an alternative political future, a future in which parties would play the leading role.[25] These parties, *before* the transition to democracy began, had developed competitive alternative political programs, spelling out what they intended to do when they came to power via democratic elections. In some countries the entire spectrum of political parties continued in existence underground, and thus an "a-legal" or "illegal" but real and visible political society existed even under the nondemocratic regime.[26]

---

24. Edmund Mokrzycki and Arista Maria Cirtantas, "The Articulation and Institutionalization of Democracy in Poland," *Social Research*, 60, no. 4 (1993): 787–819.

25. As we have seen, the major exception to this was Brazil, where civil society was the celebrity of the transition and parties, while they existed and played a significant role, were constantly changing their identity.

26. See Juan J. Linz's discussion of *tolerated, illegal,* but especially *a-legal* opposition in Spain in the late Franco period, "Opposition to and under an Authoritarian Regime: The Case of Spain," in Robert A. Dahl, ed., *Regimes and Oppositions* (New Haven: Yale University Press, 1973), 171–260, esp. 216–30. In Chile and Uruguay a foreign political analyst in the course of a two-week visit could, and normally would in the decade before the transition, meet with representatives of virtually every political party that later emerged as politically meaningful (either by themselves or as a member of a multiparty coalition) in the founding elections. As we shall see, in all of Eastern Europe only Hungary (after December 1988) approximated anything like this degree of development of political society in the period that preceded the transition.

The Rule of Law

We next turn to the arena of rule of law and its primary organizing principle, constitutionalism. There is, of course, no consolidated democracy without a relatively autonomous rule of law. Some of the legal traditions and norms that help create and sustain the relative autonomy of law are that legal codes are developed to a significant degree on the basis of precedent or their own internal logic. Furthermore, an independent judiciary plays a crucial role in interpreting old laws, the constitutionality of new laws, and the state's implementation of law.

Under high Stalinism, the conception of law was totally different. Indeed, the first president of the USSR Supreme Court wrote in 1927 that "Communism means not the victory of socialist laws, but a victory of socialism over any law."[27] Under Stalin, the leading legal theorist of the regime, E. B. Pashukanis, advanced principles that were totally dependent on the revolutionary mission of Communism.[28] One of Pashukanis's central tenets in effect was that "under developed socialism, policy and plan would replace law."[29] For our analytic purposes, since the leader and party-state create both policy and plan, there is no space for a legal system to constrain or bind the leader or the party-state. This, of course, is consistent with the ideal type of totalitarianism, in which one of the four defining characteristics is that a leader "rules with undefined limits."

A system in which the leader rules with "undefined limits" is the conceptual opposite of modern democratic constitutionalism, which entails that elected political leaders, the state, and even the sovereign citizenry have agreed to a complex series of "self-binding" mechanisms.[30] Part of this self-binding quality of a law-bound democratic polity is that there is a clear hierarchy of laws, with pre-established and relatively rigid norms and procedures for their change.[31]

To be sure, in those countries in which politics evolved in a post-totalitarian

27. For an analysis of law in the totalitarian period, see Harold J. Berman, *Justice in the USSR* (New York: Vintage, 1963); quotation is from p. 26. Berman's book was originally published by Harvard University Press in 1950.

28. In this respect Hitler's and Stalin's legal codes were similar in their disdain for precedent or the internal principles of legal logic. Article 1 of the Nazi-drafted *Volksgesetzbuch* (*People's Code*), which was to replace the nineteenth-century civil code *Bürgerliches Gesetzbuch*, stated the following: "The highest law is the welfare of the German People." (article 1) "German blood, German honor and hereditary health are to be kept pure and to be defended. These are the basic forces of the German People's Law." (article 2) "The Judge in his decision is not subject to any instruction. He dictates law out of free conviction derived from the total factual situation and according to an interpretation of law supported by the National Socialist world view." (article 20) *Volksgesetzbuch: Grundregeln und Buch I. Entwurf und Erläuterungen,* presented by Justus Wilhelm Hedemann, Dr. Heinrich Lehrmann, and Dr. Wolfgang Siebert (Munich: C. H. Beck, 1942).

29. See the entry under law in Tom Bottomore, ed., *A Dictionary of Marxist Thought* (Cambridge: Harvard University Press, 1983), 276.

30. For a rich discussion of the "self-binding" dimension of democratic constitutionalism, see Jon Elster and Rune Slagstad, eds., *Constitutionalism and Democracy* (Cambridge: Cambridge University Press, 1988), esp. the introduction by Jon Elster, pp. 1–18.

31. For example, all long-standing continental European democracies have virtually the same fourfold hierarchy of laws which is supported by the judiciary and, if it exists, by the constitutional court. In de-

direction, socialist legality became somewhat constraining on the state apparatus. However, the "leading role" of the party in the party-state still rendered most laws instrumental and heavily dependent on the party's initiative and interpretation. The distinguished Australian scholar, T. H. Rigby, writing in 1980, underscored the weakness of "self-binding" in post-totalitarian socialist legality: "The Soviet Constitution, even in its latest variant, is a notoriously misleading and incomplete guide to the distribution of power in the system. . . . [The] core aspect of the Soviet system, the party-state relationship, is regulated, as it always has been, by discretion and not by law. . . . The Soviet regime . . . has never been prepared to limit itself within the rules which it itself prescribes."[32]

Some of the most important new norms to emerge in the post-Stalinist period were aimed less at creating a generic rule of law for all the citizenry than at creating specific procedures to limit the leaders' freedom to control other party elites. Important generic binding procedures occurred only in mature post-totalitarian regimes concerning specific issue areas where the party had made a prior decision in favor of extending legal rights (e.g., private property rights in Hungary after 1983). The central point is that legal culture, especially a "self-binding" democratic constitutional culture embedded in a hierarchy of laws, must be the creation of the new democracies.

Once again, in comparison to post-Communist Europe, some of the long-standing authoritarian dictatorships we have considered in Franco's Spain, Salazar's Portugal, and Pinochet's Chile left more to build on in the way of a constitutional culture. In all these countries the law schools maintained their traditional approaches and students were exposed to the legal scholarship of other countries—including the democracies. In all three cases most of the principles of Western democratic law, while abused or put in abeyance in practice, were not fundamentally challenged normatively or theoretically by a completely new system of law and legal thinking.[33]

Usable State

The next task relates to a usable state bureaucracy. What does a totalitarian or a post-totalitarian legacy imply about the availability of a usable state bureau-

scending hierarchical order they are (1) the constitution, which can be changed only by pre-established, relatively rigid rules that call for special majorities; (2) laws passed by the parliament but that cannot violate the constitution; (3) decree laws issued by the cabinet which normally have a limited duration and, to remain valid, have to be ratified actively or passively by the parliament; and (4) administrative orders, which can be issued by ministries but which cannot violate any of the above.

32. T. H. Rigby, "A Conceptual Approach to Authority, Power and Policy in the Soviet Union," in T.H. Rigby, Archie Brown, and Peter Reddaway, eds., *Authority, Power and Policy in the USSR* (New York: St. Martin's Press, 1980), 12.

33. In Spain the Franco regime paid at least formal respect to article 3 of the 1889 Spanish Civil Code, which established the legal hierarchy of norms complemented by the general principles of law. In addition, particularly in the late years of the regime, the subjection of the administration to legal controls and administrative courts was expanded in comparison to the pre-Franco past. The last dictator of Portugal was

cracy at the beginning of a possible democratic transition? We believe, with Joseph A. Schumpeter, that modern democracies are best served when elected politicians (often amateurs) are supported by a strata of professional bureaucrats. Per se, bureaucrats are not democratic, but they have a function in making democracies efficacious.[34] However, to the extent that the bureaucracy of the previous nondemocratic regime has been recruited by political criteria defined by the old regime and to the extent that the political leadership of the old regime has deeply colonized the bureaucracy, the bureaucracy presents problems of serviceability to a new regime. Among the potential problems that will be present at the beginning of the transition from a totalitarian or post-totalitarian ideal type of regime are the following: (1) The lack of a clear distinction between the party and the state (indeed, the party generally dominates the state)[35] means that the collapse, disintegration, or massive rejection of the party can also disrupt much of the normal functioning of the state bureaucracy.[36] (2) Efficacy is damaged when many

---

the law professor Marcello Caetano. In the standard legal text he wrote, he paid extensive homage to western principles of jurisprudence.

34. While we do not necessarily subscribe to everything he says, the classic observations by Joseph A. Schumpeter are worth quoting at length: "Democratic government in modern industrial society must be able to command . . . the services of a well-trained bureaucracy of good standing and tradition, endowed with a strong sense of duty and a no less strong *esprit de corps*. Such a bureaucracy is the main answer to the argument about government by amateurs. Potentially it is the only answer to the question so often heard in this country: democratic politics has proved itself unable to produce decent city government. . . .

It is not enough that the bureaucracy should be efficient in current administration and competent to give advice. It must also be strong enough to guide and, if need be, to instruct the politicians who head the ministries. In order to be able to do this it must be in a position to evolve principles of its own and sufficiently independent to assert them. It must be a power in its own right." From Joseph A. Schumpeter, *Capitalism, Socialism and Democracy* (New York: Harper and Row, 1975), 293.

35. The most copiously documented case is East Germany. Especially telling and authoritative self-descriptions may be found in the two-volume handbook of the GDR published by the regime itself in 1985 as the *DDR Handbuch*. Particularly revealing are the entries under S.E.D. (the official party, the Socialist Unity Party of Germany) and the "Staatsapparat" (state apparatus). Top state officials sat in the Partieleitung (party-leadership), and top party officials attended Sitzungen (meetings) of state bodies. Politburo and Central Committee decisions were completely binding on the state. The handbook of the GDR regime explicitly stated that "leading functions in the state are exercised by members of the S.E.D. which de facto perform state functions as commissioners of the party" (2: 1274). Indeed, the state apparatus is accorded no professional bureaucratic autonomy at all and is depicted explicitly in the handbook as an instrument of the party. "The party apparatus [of the S.E.D.] shall lead the state as the most important instrument of the party" (2: 1275). Party structures inside the state and the secret police completed the control mechanisms (2:1188–89). In the state apparatus, 2,125,054 East Germans worked directly for their government, [Klaus König, "Bureaucratic Integration by Elite Transfer," *Governance* 6, no. 3 (1933): 386–96], of whom approximately 500,000 were vetted by the party as nomenklatura appointments, [Gerd Meyer, *Die DDR Machtelite in der Ära Honecker* (Tübingen: Francke, 1991), 89]. Research on the GDR before the 1989 regime change concluded that the nomenklatura covered all middle- and top-level jobs, a small number of which were reserved for members of the non-SED parties in the National Front [Gero Neugebauer, "Die führende Rolle der SED," in Ilse Spittmann, ed., *Die SED in Geschichte und Gegenwart* (Deutschland Archiv, 1987), 70]. More than 99 percent of army officers belonged to the SED (ibid., 69). The *Kleines Politisches Wörterbuch* (Berlin: Dietz, 1973) defines *Kaderpolitik* (cadre policy), therefore, quite broadly as the "selection, education, qualification, as well as deployment of capable cadres devoted to the task of the working class and its Marxist-Leninist party in all realms of societal life" (p. 390).

36. The most extreme examples of the implosion of the party occurred in the former Soviet Union and Yugoslavia. We discuss the fragmentation of the party-state in the USSR in chapter 19.

potentially loyal and effective civil servants are fired due to guilt by association or when administrative positions are immediately "colonized" by antiregime (but possibly incompetent) forces. Both massive purging (as in East Germany) or the absence of any significant change (as in Romania) will create problems for democracy. (3) The informer legacy causes problems. Regimes that approximate totalitarianism or even early post-totalitarianism have all-encompassing ideologies and organizational schemes. There is thus the tendency in such regimes to induce ordinary citizens (and not only intelligence specialists) to inform and spy on other citizens.[37] This legacy of the informer presents inevitable problems for the new regime, most prominent of which is the demand on the part of many citizens for "lustration" [purification] of the state apparatus, even if this violates due process and civil rights and creates legitimacy problems.[38] If new democracies engage in large-scale lustration policies, another consequence might be that those threatened by lustration and their families might turn to vote for the successor, reformed Communist parties as a pressure group for their interests.

These totalitarian or early post-totalitarian legacies contrast sharply with the legacies of the authoritarian regimes of the sort we considered in parts 2 and 3.[39] The informer legacy (and thus the lustration demand) was less severe because most of the spying on citizens was done by members of the state intelligence or coercive apparatus and not by ordinary citizens. To be sure, many authoritarian regimes leave a difficult legacy of human rights abuses by the military, police, and intelligence agencies. And, as we have documented, the new democratic governments in Argentina, Uruguay, and Chile have had little success in imprison-

37. For example, in East Germany, out of a population of not more than eighteen million people, Stasi intelligence files were maintained on six million subjects, of whom four million were GDR residents. Stasi full-time employees (*Hauptamtliche Mitarbeiter*) were capped at 85,000; the precise figure for 1982 was 81,487, according to the Gauck Behörde, which occasionally cites the higher figure of 99,000. David Gill and Ulrich Schröter, *Das Ministerium für Staatssicherheit: Anatomie des Mielke -Imperiums* (Berlin: Rohwolt, 1991), 34, 37. Total informants (*Informelle Mitarbeiter*) numbered at least 109,000, most of whom signed written statements of collaboration, but there could have been more, since many documents were destroyed during the regime change. Gauck cited 150,000 in a television appearance. He also cites 100,000 *Gehaltsempfänger* (salaried persons) in his own book, Joachim Gauck, *Die Stasi-Akten* (Hamburg: Rohwolt Taschenbuch, 1991), 27.

38. These problems were most severe in Czechoslovakia, Bulgaria, and East Germany (all three of which in 1989 approximated our description of "early" or "frozen" post-totalitarianism). In Czechoslovakia, the parliament passed a lustration law that violated many basic tenets of democratic law and civil liberties (see chapter 17). In Bulgaria the lustration issue split the Union of Democratic Forces between "revolutionary democrats" and "procedural democrats." Germany's ready-made "inheritor state" of West Germany has addressed this legacy by purging of a sort that would be extremely difficult (and democratically dangerous) in most new democracies. For example, 27 percent of all administrative-level employees in the ministries of the new Bundesländer were imported from the West, and 51 percent of the highest level appointments were filled by such imports. In the Justice Department of Brandenburg, West German imports topped 70 percent. The GDR data were supplied to us by Daniel V. Friedheim from his forthcoming Yale University doctoral dissertation on the GDR regime change. Also see König, "Bureaucratic Integration by Elite Transfer."

39. However, regimes that approximate the sultanistic ideal type predictably will present grave problems of the serviceability of the old bureaucracy because by definition the sultan did not respect any bureaucratic norms. As we (and Weber) argued, there are no "state careers" in a sultanistic regime, only members of the "household staff" of the sultan.

ing human rights offenders. However, because the scope of these hierarchically led military regimes was less extensive than in the totalitarian or even early post-totalitarian regimes and because there were no official state parties in Argentina, Uruguay, or Chile (and only a relatively weak official party in Brazil), many members of the state apparatus were left in place, or positions were not completely politicized in the authoritarian period, or both. In this respect, much more of the state apparatus was "available" and usable by the new democratic forces during and after the transition.[40] In this regard, the contrast between the degree to which the state apparatus was politicized in the period before the transition in East Germany and Spain is particularly dramatic. In East Germany there were 500,000 nomenklatura jobs; in Spain there were almost none. In the decade before Franco's death, entrance to the civil service was by a competitive exam in which candidates were identified only by number. Indeed, by the 1960s the only position in the Spanish government that required membership in the official party, the Movimiento Nacional, was the post of provincial governor because the incumbent of this post was also the head of the provincial Movimiento organization.[41]

Economic Society

We conclude with a brief discussion here of the last of our five tasks of consolidation, which concerns economic society. We will not say much about what a totalitarian regime of the Communist type implies about markets because this subject has been written about extensively. However, we note here that, in our judgment, most commentaries fail to highlight the crucial social, political, and state requisites of modern market economies. Advanced market economics are neither mechanistic nor spontaneous. The economic societies of the advanced democracies, in their great diversity, have all been socially constructed by economic incentives *and* a complex interplay of societal norms, governmental policies, and state-sanctioned rules that regulate (among other things) contracts, the rights and privileges of private (and public) property, and banking and credit systems.

In a totalitarian regime of the Communist type, *none* of the above-listed (minimal) components of an effective, socially constructed, economic society exist.

---

40. For example, though the military in Uruguay banned elections when they assumed power in 1973, they did nothing to alter the traditional system of electoral registers or districts. They also left in place Uruguay's highly proficient and neutral electoral court. Therefore, when the military decided to hold a constitutional referendum in 1980, the professional bureaucrats implemented Uruguay's traditional and virtually tamper-proof democratic voting procedures. In these circumstances, the democratic opposition were able to profit by this "usable state" and defeat the military's proposal for a semiauthoritarian constitution.

41. Significantly, even in this one nomenklatura position, most appointees became party members only *after* being nominated to the post of governor. Indeed, in one celebrated case in the early 1960s, the nominee to Sevilla refused to join the party but was allowed to assume his position anyway. For the increasing professionalization and independence of the Spanish civil service, see Miguel Beltrán Villalva, "Política y administración bajo el Franquismo: La reforma administrativa y los planes de desarrollo" in Raymond Carr, ed., *La época de Franco* (Madrid: Espasa Calpe, forthcoming).

The easiest component to create and the one that normally appears first is a degree of market incentives. However, there are innumerable other problems that must be addressed before an effective economic society is consolidated. There is first and foremost the problem of an effective state.[42] A revolutionary upheaval can do away with a command economy, but if the party-state also implodes and there is no effective political power, how will the new regulatory framework of economic society be constructed? Witness Russia. There is also the problem of property. If the right of private property is introduced, inevitably there are questions of how the new rights of private ownership should be established. By restitution? From what date? Before the Communists? Before the Nazis? How should public companies be sold? By auction? Who has enough capital? Are there enough effective buyers? Should foreign capital be assigned a fixed quota? Should there be manager buy-outs? Will these be seen as nomenklatura buy-outs? Should spontaneous privatization be permitted? Is this actually theft of public property? These and a hundred other questions are predictably on the agenda in the aftermath of a Communist totalitarian or post-totalitarian regime, and similar problems will be the legacy in different ways of most sultanistic regimes. However, in an authoritarian regime of the Chilean or Spanish sort, very few of these questions will be found.

Post-Communism's Diverse Paths

In this chapter, we have sought to evaluate important Russian and especially Central and East European commonalities because of their coexistence within the coercive system of Soviet dominance and the fact that the Soviet Union attempted to impose a similar social, political, ideological, and economic regime type on them all. However, our primary task in the chapters that follow is to take this common heritage as an important background factor and to explore the under-analyzed variation within the region in democratic (or nondemocratic) transition *paths*. We also want to explore the substantial variation in the *tasks* that polities must accomplish if they are ever to become democratically consolidated. A significant part of this within-region variation comes from their pre-Communist histories and their geopolitical location. But an important part of this variation is also explicable in terms of their distinctive regime types (or subtypes) and/or the severity of their stateness problem.

The erosion of the Soviet Union's ideological confidence and geopolitical will to use coercion to manage its outer and inner empires changed power relations

---

42. The role of the state in the transformation of post-Communist economies is a major research vacuum. Indeed, when we asked a leading North American economist researching post-Communist Europe for academic references on the subject, he commented that "neglect of the role of the state in the transformation by economists borders on the criminal."

throughout the region. However, the consequences of this new international environment varied greatly and comparative *path-dependent* analysis is called for. For example, since the late 1970s Poland, by our criteria, approximated an authoritarian (not a totalitarian or post-totalitarian) regime. Given the changed Soviet political economy of coercion, a democratic opposition in Poland that had been *blocked* became unblocked. In mature post-totalitarian Hungary, a four-player game of democratic opposition that would not have even started in the past was allowed to play out to the end. In "frozen" post-totalitarian polities (e.g., the G.D.R. and Czechoslovakia), old guard Brezhnev era leaders who needed external support to make their coercive threats credible *collapsed* when their middle-level cadres either no longer believed in the regime's utopian ideological claims or at least were unwilling to use large-scale violence against protesting crowds. Regimes that had experienced virtually no domestic changes, such as sultanistic-totalitarian Romania and barely post-totalitarian Bulgaria, were *reconstituted* by nondemocratic elites after they divested themselves of their long-standing leaders.

In most of the southern part of the Soviet Union's near totalitarian inner empire, the stateness crisis of the Soviet Union allowed nondemocratic elites, who were close to the levers of power in the republics, to shift from a party-state to an ethnic state discourse without tolerating pluralism, respecting minority rights, or building a democratic civil society. Such changes certainly relate to the literature on post-Communist politics, but ethnoauthoritarianism, ethnic conflict, and state erosion are more dominant features of many of these polities than is democratization or even full liberalization. In fact, as we document in chapter 19, the discourse of "national liberation" was privileged over democratization and the discourse of collective rights of "titular nationalitites" was privileged over individual rights. As our contribution to the new comparative politics of post-Communist regimes, we will explore the sources and consequences of such major variations.

16

Authoritarian Communism, Ethical Civil Society, and Ambivalent Political Society: Poland

Our purpose in this chapter is to locate transformations in Poland within the overall context of the literature and politics of democratic transitions. We do this by developing four inter-related arguments. First, we will advance the thesis that Poland is the only country in Eastern Europe that was always closer to an authoritarian than to a totalitarian regime, even in the 1949–53 period when totalitarian tendencies were strongest. Second, we show how from 1976 to 1988 the dominant ethos, structure, and language of conflict in Poland were between the nation's "ethical civil society" and the regime's internationalized authoritarian party-state. Third, we argue that, precisely because Poland in 1988–89 was an authoritarian regime led by party-soldiers—and was the *first* of East Europe's transitions—the regime initiated and the opposition accepted a "pacted transition" comparable in its confining conditions to those we have seen in Chile and Brazil. Fourth, we explore how the new democracy's origins in an ethical civil society, a pacted transition, and, very rapidly, a semipresidential system with a directly elected charismatic leader created a legacy of ambivalence toward political society which must be transcended before Poland can consolidate democracy.

THE INABILITY TO INSTALL TOTALITARIANISM

Let us first evaluate the question of regime type. More than any other country we will consider in this section, Polish society resists classification as having ever been a fully installed totalitarian regime. We certainly do not deny that there were some efforts (as in Spain after the Civil War) to install a totalitarian regime in Poland and that much of the totalitarian state apparatus and official party ideology found elsewhere in Eastern Europe was found in Poland. However, some fundamental elements of Polish politics do not really fit the totalitarian regime type as we analyzed it in chapter 3. In particular, we believe that Poland always had a significant de facto degree of societal pluralism. We further believe that this de facto societal pluralism increased the ability of parts of civil society to resist the regime's ideology and somewhat checked the will of the aspirant totalitarian regime to impose intense mobilization, especially in the ideological area. These limits on totalitarian penetration had in turn an effect on the regime's leadership style. Our argument, therefore, is that in each of the four key typological dimensions of totalitarianism—most clearly in pluralism but also in mobilization, ideology, and leadership—Poland contained some totalitarian but even stronger authoritarian tendencies.[1]

At all times the Polish Catholic Church maintained a sphere of relative autonomy which gave it organizational and ideological capacities to resist its and the Polish nation's full incorporation into totalitarian structures. This de facto social pluralism of the Catholic Church generated a complex pattern of reciprocal power recognition and even negotiation between the Catholic Church and the state not found in any Communist regime we would call totalitarian. For example, in April 1950 the government agreed to allow religious education in public schools and not to interfere with the church press. In return the church agreed to refrain from overt political activities and to restrain priests from active opposition.[2] In one of the most committed Catholic nations in the world, the fact that the atheistic party-state even temporarily granted this concession was a limit on its goal of total ideological hegemony.[3] There was a renewed effort to control the church in 1953–56, during which the primate of Poland, Cardinal Stefan Wyszyński, was kept under house arrest.[4] A measure of how fearful the Soviet-backed

---

1. Milovan Djilas reviewed the history of totalitarianism in all the countries in Eastern Europe, and he also argued that only in Poland was totalitarianism never installed. "It would not be incorrect to conclude that Poland was never a totalitarian state, if only because some form of spiritual life—in the first place the Catholic Church—preserved a measure of autonomy. Also, peasant holdings remained largely private property. On top of that, thanks to the Warsaw uprising in 1944 and the armed and other resistance immediately after the war, the vast majority of Poles received both the new regime and Soviet control without any illusions about Soviet 'liberators.' Poland has been, in fact, largely a police state. The 1956 revolt in Poznan had a crucial significance for Poland's internal autonomy. [Gomulka] . . . retarded but did not stop the anti-totalitarian movement in Poland; it is there that the totalitarian idea has been most decisively rejected." Milovan Djilas, "The Disintegration of Leninist Totalitarianism," in Irving Howe, ed., *1984 Revisited: Totalitarianism in Our Century* (New York: Harper and Row, 1983), 145–46.

2. For discussions of the dynamic power struggles of concession and conquest between the Communists and the Catholic Church, see Ronald C. Monticone, *The Catholic Church in Communist Poland, 1945–1985: Forty Years of Church-State Relations* (New York: Columbia University Press, 1986), esp. 26–130. Another analysis of "conflicts and co-existence" between the Polish church and state and of the political role of the church in Poland since 1945 is Bogdan Szajkowski, *Next to God . . . Poland: Politics and Religion in Contemporary Poland* (New York: St. Martin's Press, 1983). For a comparative perspective of the Polish Catholic Church in an authoritarian-government/opposition dynamic, see the essay by Hank Johnston, "Toward an Explanation of Church Opposition to Authoritarian Regimes: Religio-oppositional Subcultures in Poland and Catalonia," *Journal for the Scientific Study of Religion* 28, no. 4 (1989): 493–508.

3. Communist Poland had substantially more priests per capita than did Catholic Latin America. For example, in 1968 Poland had 52 priests per 100,000 population. The highest ratio of priests per capita of the twenty Latin American countires that year was in Chile, with 27. Brazil had only 13 priests per 100,000 population, and Cuba had 3. See Luigi Einaudi, Richard Maullin, Alfred Stepan, and Michael Fleet, *Latin American Institutional Development: The Changing Catholic Church* (Santa Monica: Rand Corp., 1969), 18.

4. See *A Freedom Within: The Prison Notes of Stefan Cardinal Wyszyński* (San Diego: Harcourt Brace Jo-

party authorities were of the Catholic Church is that, in contrast to Hungary or Croatia, the Polish authorities did not put the cardinal on trial. The assault on the church generated even more resistance on the part of Polish society and exacerbated the distance between the "us" of the Polish nation and the "them" of the Soviet-supported party-state. As Joseph Rothchild summarizes, "the Polish Catholic Church more than recouped its post-war material losses through its flock's renewed fervor . . . social groups that had been indifferent or even anti-clerical gave it their allegiance as a mark of political and spiritual protest against Stalinist trends."[5] By 1956 the moderately nationalist reform Communist, Gomulka, to make his government more palatable, allowed the reintroduction of religious instruction in state schools.[6] In fact, on a number of occasions between 1956 and 1989 the government implicitly or even explicitly had to ask the church to contain crisis situations that might have led to Soviet intervention by playing a moderating role in Polish politics. Symbolically, in 1986 a statue of Cardinal Wyszyński was erected in Warsaw's most prominent boulevard outside of a church.

Another telling indicator of limited pluralism as opposed to monism was agriculture. Nationalization of agriculture by means of collectivization or cooperatives was soft-pedaled even by the Polish Stalinists in the late 1940s. Gomulka's consistent rejection of forced collectivization was an essential component of his "Polish road to socialism," which was branded heretical and then visionary by Moscow. The tradition of peasant cooperatives predominated over collectivized state farms. Indeed, independent, privately owned farms remained in the over-

---

vanovich, 1982), in which the Cardinal documents the fluctuations in state policies toward the church at the time of, during, and after his internment. Also see Andrzej Micewski, *Cardinal Wyszyński* (San Diego: Harcourt Brace Jovanovich, 1984). In addition to this symbolic gesture of Communist control over the church hierarchy in 1953, "Patriotic priests acceptable to the state were pushed into key church positions, and the PAX movement of progressive Catholics was supported by the authorities." However, this policy failed when it was opposed by the church. See Dieter Bingen, "The Catholic Church as a Political Actor," in Jack Bielasiak and Maurice D. Simon, eds., *Polish Politics: Edge of the Abyss* (New York: Praeger Press, 1984), 213. Also see M. K. Dziewanowski, *The Communist Party of Poland: An Outline of History* (Cambridge: Harvard University Press, 1976), esp. 241–51.

5. Joseph Rothchild, *Return to Diversity* (New York: Oxford University Press, 1989), 87.

6. For the specifics of allowing religious education in Polish public schools, see Monticone, *The Catholic Church in Communist Poland,* esp. 26–28. Monticone discusses the Joint Commission of Representatives of the Government and the Episcopate, which was established in 1956 to address the "many unresolved problems in mutual relations." The discourse of the joint commission's communiqué, issued on December 8, suggested that both the government and the church hierarchy would assume a policy of full, mutual understanding. Monticone contends that "the most important part of the agreement pertained to the teaching of religion after school hours in all schools where the majority of parents favored it. . . . As a result . . . religious instruction was given in the vast majority of schools throughout Poland" (pp. 27–28). Gomulka's liberalization policy toward the church, including the release of Cardinal Wyszyński from house arrest, was part of his "Spring in October," a period of Polish liberalization accompanying the de-Stalinization process occurring in the Soviet Union. As Nicholas Bethell argues, "In 1956 he [Gomulka] and the Cardinal were on good terms . . . to secure the Cardinal's release from detention was one of Gomulka's first political acts. In return the Cardinal helped Gomulka to consolidate his rule and to restrain irresponsible elements." Nicholas Bethell, *Gomulka, His Poland and His Communism* (London: Longmans Press, 1969), 248–49. See also Lawrence Weschler, *The Passion of Poland* (New York: Pantheon Books, 1982), esp. 211–18 for a chronology of Polish events during de-Stalinization.

whelming majority, never dipping below 70 percent of Poland's agricultural hold-ings.[7] Once again, this is a mark of incomplete state penetration and a sign of so-cial power and autonomy outside the grip of the totalitarian state.

Finally, the overall reversals of policy and ideology that marked the shifts of leadership from the mini-Stalinism of Boleslaw Bierut, to the relative tolerance and Polish nationalism of Gomulka (1956–70), to the experiment with massive foreign borrowing of Gierek (1971–80), to the repression of the military-led regime of Jaruzelski (1981–89) is a pattern of policy alternation and changing leadership styles more consistent with an authoritarian regime than a totalitarian regime. In fact, during the period of the greatest effort to impose totalitarianism in Poland (1949–53), President and First Secretary Boleslaw Bierut was *primus inter pares* in a triumvirate including the ideologist, Jakub Berman, and the economist, Hilary Minc. This collegial power-sharing exemplifies another of Poland's differ-entiations from extreme totalitarianism, the dictator and the cult of personality.

Why did this peculiar pattern of authoritarian Communism emerge in Po-land? Specifically, how did the unique Polish quality of resistance by civil society contribute to this pattern and to the fact that Poland became the first country in the world to force a ruling Communist Party to enter into a power dyarchy with a democratic opposition?

The stateness variable has particular importance in Poland, but in a pro-foundly different way than in the Soviet Union. The extermination of Poland's Jews, the expulsion of the ethnic Germans, and the incorporation of Byelorussian and Ukrainian populations into the Soviet Union in the aftermath of World War II left the overwhelming majority of Poland's citizens ethnically Polish and Roman Catholic. This was the first true nation-state in Polish history.[8]

Moreover, the Polish people's support for the nation was one of the most emo-tionally and historically intense in Europe. Poland had gone from being one of the major European powers to being "stateless" from 1795 to 1918 owing to conquest and partition at the hands of Russia, Prussia, and Austria. In this period of state-lessness the Catholic Church became a particularly strong and beloved cultural

7. See Andrzej Korbonski, *Politics of Socialist Agriculture in Poland: 1945–1960* (New York: Columbia University Press, 1965), 212–312, and "Peasant Agriculture in Socialist Poland since 1956: An Alternative to Collectivization," in Jerzy F. Karcz, ed., *Soviet and East European Agriculture* (Berkeley: University of California Press, 1967), 411–31. See also Janine Wedel, *The Private Poland* (New York: Facts on File Publications, 1986), 54, for data on the relatively substantial, informal, nonagricultural private sector in Poland in the late 1970s and early 1980s.

8. As late as 1939, Poles (92 percent of whom were Roman Catholic) only "constituted about 90 percent of the population in the western vojevodships . . . about 80 percent in the central . . . and 60 percent in the southern." See Jan Tomasz Gross, *Polish Society under German Occupation, The Generalgouvernement, 1939–1944* (Princeton: Princeton University Press, 1979), 12. K. A. Jelenski argues that, "paradoxically, the communist Poland that emerged from the Yalta agreements corresponded to an old dream of the most ex-treme kind. . . . It is—for the first time in its history—a country of one ethnic group and one religion, with all faiths other than Catholicism accounting for only a tiny percentage of the population." See his essay, "Paradoxes of Polish Nationalism," in Leopold Labedz, ed., *Poland under Jaruzelski: A Comprehensive Sourcebook on Poland during and after Martial Law* (New York: Scribner's Sons, 1983), 391.

and institutional expression of Polish nationality. The Polish state again formally disappeared when Germany and the Soviet Union partitioned the country after the German-Soviet Pact of August 23, 1939. The new division of Poland led to repressive rule of Poles, deportation into the Soviet Union of the Polish Army, deliberate destruction of much of the Polish intelligentsia, and mass murder in Kathyn, which was blamed on the Germans but was later recognized as a Soviet act. [9] However, along with Yugoslavia, Polish society developed the strongest resistance movement in Europe. Unlike Yugoslavia, however, in Poland the resistance movement and the government in exile were unified and in close contact. The Red Army stood by and did nothing while Polish resistance fighters struggled against the Nazis in the Warsaw uprising. Complete Soviet military domination in Poland was established only after the defeat of Polish resistance forces in the civil war of 1945–47.[10] Because Poland had been part of the victorious Allied coalition in World War II, the Soviet Union (unlike in East Germany, Hungary, or Slovakia) could not attempt to legitimate their occupation by the claim that they represented Allied occupation over Nazi collaborators.[11] Thus, from the beginning, Polish stateness was a source of nationalist antagonism against the Soviet hegemon and provided a deep reservoir of sources of resistance.

This leads us to the question of totalitarianism and its control of the coercive apparatus. A completely totalitarian regime, since it relies so much on societal penetration and control by the state, must have total organizational and ideological control of the security apparatus, especially the military. More than any other country in Eastern Europe, Poland conducted a civil war in 1945–47 against Soviet and Communist forces. This left a paradoxical legacy in civil-military relations. Polish military unreliability was recognized by the fact that it was the only country in Eastern Europe where a Russian citizen, indeed a Soviet marshal and a deputy minister of defense, Konstantin Rokossovsky (admittedly of Polish extraction), was made commander-in-chief. This only made more transparent the "foreign," illegitimate status of the Communist government.[12] The Soviet Union

9. See the two outstanding studies by Jan T. Gross, *Revolution from Abroad: The Soviet Conquest of Poland's Western Ukraine and Western Belorussia* (Princeton: Princeton University Press, 1988), and Gross, *Polish Society under German Occupation.*

10. For example, it was only "between 1948 and 1955, [that] the Polish armed forces underwent a major transformation conforming them to the then current Soviet model." Paul C. Latawski, "The Polish Military and Politics," in Jack Bielasiak and Maurice D. Simon, eds., *Polish Politics: Edge of the Abyss* (New York: Praeger Press, 1984), 271.

11. This point was stressed repeatedly to Stepan in October 1989 and July 1990 by a variety of Polish officials and analysts coming from the Communist Party or the military.

12. For the Soviet background of most of the Polish high command from 1949 to 1956, see George Sanford, *Military Rule in Poland: The Rebuilding of Communist Power, 1981–1983* (London: Crown Helm, 1986), 57. Latawski, a student of Polish foreign policy and history, asserts that, after 1949, "the most significant change for the army was the importation of Soviet Officers, who eventually made up half the entire officer corps." Latawski, "The Polish Military and Politics," 271, 288 n. 12. See also Dale Herspring, "The Polish Military and the Policy Process," in Maurice D. Simon and Roger E. Kanet, eds., *Background to Crisis: Policy and Politics in Poland* (Boulder, Colo.: Westview Press, 1980), esp. 222–24.

made some effort to make a link with Polish national tradition by allowing Poland to be the only country in Eastern Europe in which officers retained much of their prewar uniform. But, at critical moments, the army, by their ambivalence and slowness to act, de facto checked the possibility of totalitarian state power. An important early example of this is that the army did not fire upon the Poznan strikers in June 1956.[13] At other times the army played a key role in party struggles. Wiatr argues that "in October 1956 when the USSR tried to blackmail the Polish leaders to slow down the process of de-Stalinization, the Polish military threw its support to the new Party leadership headed by Wladyslaw Gomulka, showing also its determination to resist Soviet intervention."[14]

Before we conclude these comments on totalitarianism, we would like to make a general observation about political pluralism and the Roman Catholic Church. There have, of course, been numerous periods throughout history of the Roman Catholic Church's collaboration with conservative and corporatist authoritarian regimes, most notably in Spain and to a lesser extent in Portugal.[15] However, it is our contention that, sociologically and politically, the existence of a strong Roman Catholic Church in a totalitarian country is *always* a latent source of pluralism, precisely because it is a formal organization with a transnational base. The papacy can be a source of spiritual and material support for groups that want to resist monist absorption or extinction. The papacy can also impose sanctions and withdraw recognition from local bishops who might under pressure agree to cooperate with totalitarian governments. In the Polish case, for example, once or twice some Polish priests came close to accepting agreements with Communist governments, but the authority of these agreements was explicitly disowned and rejected by the pope.

This source of higher international power is of course not available in a political system (such as Bulgaria, Romania, or most of the former Soviet Union) which has Orthodox churches that are national but not transnational in scope and that historically have accepted a form of "caesaropapism" in which the emperor or head of state was the supreme temporal and spiritual authority.[16] It is also not available in a predominantly Islamic society because Islam as a religion is

---

13. For Poznan events, see A. Ross Johnson, Robert W. Dean, and Alexander Alexiev, *East European Military Establishments: The Warsaw Pact Northern Tier* (Santa Monica: RAND, 1982), 60. For a discussion by Khrushchev of how the "Poles had vilified us in 1956" and the movement of Soviet troops toward Warsaw, as well as the editor's comment about the possibility of armed resistance by the Polish troops, see Jerrold L. Schecter with Vyacheslav V. Luchkov, eds., *Khrushchev Remembers: The Glasnost Tapes* (Boston: Little, Brown and Co., 1990), 113–20.

14. Jerzy J. Wiatr, *Four Essays on East European Democratic Transformation* (Warsaw: Scholar Agency, 1992), 62. For a similar judgment, also see Andrzej Korbonski "The Dilemmas of Civil-Military Relations in Contemporary Poland: 1945–1981," *Armed Forces and Society* 8, no. 1 (1981): 3–20, esp. 10.

15. But even in Spain the church eventually contributed to the delegitimation of the authoritarian model. Juan J. Linz, "Church and State in Spain from the Civil War to the Return of Democracy," *Daedalus* 120, no. 3 (1991): 159–78.

16. For *caesaropapism* and orthodox churches, see Max Weber, *Economy and Society*, ed. Guenther Roth and Claus Wittich (Berkeley: University of California Press, 1978), 2:1159–63.

a community of believers in which all believers can be preachers and where there is no formal transnational hierarchy. This excursus on Catholicism as a transnational actor is of course especially appropriate for our analysis of Poland because on October 16, 1978, Cardinal Karol Wojtyla, the archbishop of Poland's second most important city, Kraków, became Pope John Paul II, and even greater anti-regime resources were mobilized with consequences we explain later.

We do not want to overstress our point. The effort to impose a totalitarian regime in Poland definitely left some legacies in post-Communist Poland not found in a typical postauthoritarian regime. The most important legacy was that, despite the important degree of private agricultural holdings, the state played the commanding role in the economy, whose industrial and service sectors were overwhelmingly socialized. Even if Poland was never fully totalitarian, Poland's "really existing socialism" of 1945–89 left numerous structures of group interests in post-Communist Poland.[17] The reality of Communist authoritarianism also meant that resistance, if it was to be effective, had to be based in civil society because oppositional parties as an expression of political society were never either formally permitted or informally tolerated.

THE EMERGENCE OF OPPOSITIONAL HEGEMONY AND THE EROSION OF THE COMMUNIST PARTY

With Gomulka's agreement in 1956 to allow the church to teach religion in public schools, the church was never again mortally threatened.[18] After 1956 Polish universities and researchers developed, along with Yugoslavia, by far the greatest degree of autonomy and creativity in Eastern Europe in such politically relevant areas as political sociology, philosophy, history, and economics.[19] Polish intellectuals and citizens, despite a degree of regime constraints and surveillance, had a significant degree of freedom for international travel.

17. See Edmund Mokrzycki, "The Legacy of Real Socialism, Group Interests, and the Search for a New Utopia," in W. C. Connor and P. Ploszajski, eds., *Escape from Socialism: The Polish Route* (Warsaw: IFiS Publishers, 1992), 269–81.

18. The German scholar of the Polish church and Solidarity, Dieter Bingen, notes that, "in May 1957, Gomulka explained that he saw a need for coexistence between believers and nonbelievers and between the church and socialism." Although tensions between church and state—inherent in many regime concession/societal conquest dynamics—did continue after this period, the church was never again threatened seriously. It remained, in Bingen's terms, "the stable anchor of Poland's political system." Dieter Bingen, "The Catholic Church as a Political Actor," 213, 236.

19. In the 1970s, a group of intellectuals from Warsaw started a series of independent lectures devoted to the social sciences and history. The effort, attended mainly by university students, "known colloquially as 'The Flying University,' proved to be popular.... In January, 1978, some sixty prominent intellectuals and academics signed a declaration calling into being the Society for Academic Courses.... In its first year, 120 lectures were offered by the Flying University to at least 5,000 people in major towns countrywide." See Janusz Bugajski and Maxine Pollack, *East European Fault Lines: Dissent, Opposition and Social Activism* (Boulder, Colo.: Westview Press, 1989), 226. See also Karol H. Borowski, "Secular and Religious Education in Poland," *Religious Education* 70, no 1 (1975): 70–76.

From a comparative and theoretical perspective, the moral and organizational style of Polish opposition put Poland in the vanguard of Eastern Europe. A crucial difference between Poland and all the other East European Communist states was the extraordinary "horizontal relationship of civil society with itself."[20] This degree of "self-organization" of Polish civil society was possible in an authoritarian regime, but impossible in a totalitarian regime and beyond the bounds of anything we would want to call post-totalitarian. This relationship was crafted over time. In 1968 students and intellectuals protested but received little support from workers. Indeed, workers were recruited by the government into special gangs to break up demonstrations in an attempt to polarize workers and the intelligentsia. In late 1970 and early 1971, workers had mass demonstrations but intellectuals did not join them. In 1976, however, intellectuals formed an organization called KOR (Committee for the Defense of Workers) to help workers punished for strike activities. When the massive protests led by Lech Walesa and the workers broke out in 1980 at the Lenin Shipyard in Gdansk, other civil society groups, from intellectuals to the church, helped interweave the weft and warp of the tightly textured Polish resistance. At Solidarity's height, 10 million workers, representing the majority of employed workers in the country, were members. Solidarity's power position in the economy and the polity was so strong that in August 1980 any claim of the party-state to be the sole representative of the people was smashed when Solidarity became the first independent trade union in any Communist country to win legal recognition. Solidarity also was able to get the government to soften the nomenklatura system. The Polish government agreed that future appointments in factories would be "made on the basis of qualification and not on party membership."[21]

Poland has the largest and best tradition of public opinion survey research in Eastern Europe. These surveys repeatedly reveal a deep societal rejection of a totalitarian vision of state and society. A poll taken in November 1981 showed that "between 60–80 percent of the respondents declared themselves in favor of a polycentric power model—that is the principle of full autonomy of institutions, limited central planning, increased participation of the Church in social life, and

20. The concept of the "horizontal relationship of civil society with itself" is developed by Alfred Stepan, "State Power and Strength of Civil Society in the Southern Cone of Latin America," in Peter Evans, Dietrich Rueschemeyer, and Theda Skocpol, eds., *Bringing the State Back In* (Cambridge: Cambridge University Press, 1988), 317–43. The complex and extremely important process of the interweaving of civil society in Poland to form the fabric of opposition is similar to that of Brazil, where a fabric composed of "new unionism," base community groups, the "people's church," and intellectuals was crucial in democratizing, not just liberalizing, the regime. See the essays in Alfred Stepan's edited volume, *Democratizing Brazil: Problems of Transition and Consolidation* (Oxford: Oxford University Press, 1989), esp. 143–296.

21. Wlodzimierz Pankow, "The Solidarity Movement, Management and the Political System in Poland," in Jadwiga Koralewicz, Ireneusz Bialecki, and Margaret Watson, eds., *Crisis and Transition: Polish Society in the 1980s* (Oxford: Berg Publishers, 1987), 112–15. The political culture in which KOR and Solidarity emerged is studied in great depth in Andrzej W. Tymowski, *The Unwanted Revolution: From Moral Economy to Liberal Society in Poland (The Social Origins of Reform and Counter-Reform)* (Ph.D. diss. Department of Political Science, Yale University, 1995), esp. 126–241.

curtailment of Party life . . . some 70% of the respondents said they were in favor of the activities of the independent self-governing trade-union Solidarity."[22]

Polish forms of self-organization of society against the state were in fact an inspiration to organizers of civil society in other parts of the world, particularly Latin America. In Poland's self-organized society, people dared to organize, act, think, and live, in the famous phrase of Adam Michnik, "as if they were free." Indeed, the power and legitimacy of Solidarity after one year of existence was such that Stefan Kania, first Secretary after Gierek and before Jaruzelski, took pains to deny that a situation of dual power existed in Poland (i.e., between the collapsing party and Solidarity).

In Gramscian terms, Solidarity in the fall of 1981 possessed hegemony in civil society, and the party maintained its power only to the extent that it controlled the coercive forces of the army and the security services and the shadow of the Soviet Union limited a challenge to the regime. It was against this increasingly self-organized society that a further sign of the weakness of the Polish Communist Party appeared. On December 13, 1981, General Jaruzelski, who did not mention the Communist Party or use the word *comrade,* and who defined himself simply as a "soldier and the head of the government of Poland," declared, "I hereby announce that today a Military Council for National Salvation has been constituted" and that Poland was under martial law.[23] The de facto loss of the leading role of the party was implicitly recognized by the fact that the leader of the government and almost all key ministers were not party officials as such, but Polish party-soldiers under the direction of General Jaruzelski. Unlike any Communist regime in history, the Polish Communist regime from 1981 until the assumption of office by Solidarity's first prime minister in August 1989 was directed by the military, who, while members of the Communist Party, were primarily military officers.

General Jaruzelski, simultaneously holding the positions of prime minister and minister of defense, appointed high-ranking military officers to several key ministries, state enterprises, and numerous local government offices. He created and ruled through the Military Council for National Salvation (*Wojskowa Rada Ocalenia Narodowego,* or WRON). All twenty-one members of this council held high military posts, and they emerged as the leading authority in the country. The Polish scholar Jadwiga Staniszkis describes the martial law regime as Jaruzelski's

22. Ireneusz Bialecki, "What the Poles Thought in 1981," in Koralewicz, Bialecki, and Watson, eds., *Crisis and Transition,* 30.

23. As a document, the declaration of martial law is strikingly similar to many documents issued by leaders of hierarchical military organizations in Latin America as justifications for their seizure of power. The document also lacks any of the ideological claims that one would find in totalitarian or even post-totalitarian discourse. Jaruzelski alludes to "interminable conflict" and "chaos" that have brought the country to the "edge of an abyss," which explains the "burden of responsibility which falls upon me." The complete document is reproduced in Robert Maxwell, ed., *Jaruzelski: Prime Minister of Poland* (Oxford: Pergamon Press, 1985), 28–30.

effort to redefine the institutional regime and to move from a party state toward an "authoritarian-bureaucratic, non-ideological army state."[24] The primary position of the military, a set of party-soldiers who at the same time formed an institution distinct from the Communist Party, made a difference to the regime's decisions to initiate liberalization and to recognize Solidarity as a legitimate, acceptable, and even necessary "player" with which the regime would negotiate. As Korbonski correctly states, the Polish military had been historically a "moderating" power in politics, occasionally exercising a veto over the domestic agenda and particularly over Communist policies. In 1981, however, this moderating power role broke down, the military became the government, and a unique five-way power relationship between the security services (headed by Minister of Interior General Czeslaw Kiszczak, who retained his post until the summer of 1990), the army, the Soviet-related party (led by a solid Warsaw Pact officer, General Jaruzelski), the Catholic Church, and Solidarity developed.[25] It is crucial to recognize that all five institutions then interacted to shape the timing and tempo of the eventual transition.

PACTED TRANSITION

When martial law was declared on December 13, 1981, the set of major power actors in Poland included on one side the Solidarity movement (much of organized labor and the intellectutal and social movements associated with it) and the Catholic Church, and on the other side the hierarchically controlled military, the security services, and the remnants of the official party under their control. The message of the Solidarity movement was amplified by what Bronislaw Geremek called the "indestructible empire" of more than a thousand informal and formal publications. The Catholic Church, despite its identification with the opposition, was occasionally used by the regime as an unofficial mediator and moderator.

---

24. Jadwiga Staniszkis, *Poland: Self-limiting Revolution* (Princeton: Princeton University Press, 1986), 320.

25. See Cindy Skach, "Military Regimes and Negotiated Democratic Transitions: Poland and Brazil in Comparative Perspective" (1991, unpublished manuscript). There are several good analyses concerning the military dimension of authoritarianism in Poland. George C. Malcher, *Poland's Politicized Army: Communists in Uniform* (New York: Praeger, 1984), is one of the few authors to recognize and document the militarization of the Polish administration after 1981. Polish sociologist Jerzy Wiatr discusses the evolution of the party-soldier in *The Soldier and the Nation: The Role of the Military in Polish Politics, 1948–1985* (Boulder, Colo.: Westview Press, 1988). Andrew Michta's book, *Red Eagle: The Army in Polish Politics, 1944–1988* (Stanford, Calif.: Hoover Institution Press, 1990), contains less substantive analysis of military-authoritarianism but provides a good and recent historical account of the military institution.

Some of the best discussion and analysis of historical civil-military relations in Poland are found in Andrzej Korbonski's works. See in particular his article with Sarah M. Terry, "The Military as a Political Actor in Poland," in Andrzej Kolkowicz, ed., *Soldiers, Peasants and Bureaucrats: Civil-Military Relations in Communist and Modernizing Societies* (London: George Allen and Unwin Press, 1982), 159–80, and "The Dilemmas of Civil-Military Relations in Contemporary Poland: 1945–1981," in *Armed Forces and Society* 8, no. 1 (1981): 3–20.

This is a set of actors (even if we accept the transnational Soviet presence) closer to those found in authoritarian Brazil and Chile than to those in totalitarian or even post-totalitarian countries.

This analysis of power actors leads us directly to our argument that Poland, more than any other country in Eastern Europe, is an example of a pacted transition, where the opposition paid a price for the transition analogous to those we have analyzed in Brazil and even more in Chile. In both Chile and Poland, the pacted transitions meant that democracy started with the old regime's constitution and with the old regime still retaining strong positions in the legislature and in the state apparatus. Let us see how this paradoxical but very real pacted transition occurred.

In 1987–88 Poland was an authoritarian regime facing growing problems and growing opposition. In June 1987 Pope John Paul II made his third visit to Poland and called for the re-legalization of Solidarity. The regime realized the seriousness of its economic problems, but in November 1987 General Jaruzelski's proposal for a package of economic changes to be backed by society was defeated in a national referendum because it failed to obtain the required majority of those eligible to vote. The losing of a referendum (impossible in a totalitarian regime and unprecedented in pre–round table post-totalitarian regimes) is a unique event in Communist Europe and contributed to the further erosion of the regime.

In May 1988 a new round of Solidarity strikes, initiated by a new generation of younger and more militant trade unionists, began. To some extent both Jaruzelski as a regime moderate and Walesa as an opposition moderate were facing potential challenges from their radicals. Eventually, the classic four-player game of transition (regime radicals, regime moderates, opposition moderates, opposition radicals) had appeared.

In the early summer of 1988, General Kiszczak, the minister of the interior, through an interview asked Lech Walesa if he would like to begin exploratory talks. Walesa agreed in a letter of July 21, 1988. On August 26, during a second wave of Solidarity strikes General Jaruzelski, at a politburo meeting, proposed negotiation with Solidarity.[26] As the critical prenegotiation process advanced, it became clear that the government wanted some support for its economic policies from Solidarity. The government did not want to risk a total Solidarity boycott of the upcoming 1989 parliamentary elections. Solidarity in turn wanted legal recognition, which only the government could give.[27] We stress these points because we want to emphasize that the government wanted the negotiations but still acted as if it pos-

26. Our discussion of the Round Table owes much to the Polish legal constitutional theorist Wiktor Osiatynski, who observed the round-table talks and later carried out extensive archival and interview research. He reports his findings in "The Round Table Negotiations in Poland" (Center for the Study of Constitutionalism in Eastern Europe at the University of Chicago Law School in partnership with the Central European University, 1993, working paper no. 1). To be included in Jon Elster, ed., *The Roundtable Talks and the End of Communism* (Chicago: University of Chicago Press, forthcoming).

27. For the importance of the August–December 1988 prenegotiation talks (and an illustration of the four-player game dynamics), see Jadwiga Staniszkis, *The Dynamics of the Breakthrough in Eastern Europe:*

sessed significant coercive strength. As it turned out, both the government and the opposition overestimated the government's strength.[28] Indeed, even as Round Table talks evolved, they were always surrounded by a "Rawlsian veil of ignorance," in that both sides, not knowing what would happen in the future, made concessions they would not have made if they could have known what the results would be.[29]

Of course, the Polish Round Table talks set into motion the chain of extraordinary events of 1989 in Europe. As a result of the talks the first completely free election of one house, the Senate, occurred in Eastern Europe in forty years. Because of the unexpectedly overwhelming triumph of Solidarity in the elections in June 1989, in August the first non-Communist prime minister in Eastern Europe in forty years came to office after the Communists were unable to form a government when some of their former satellite Peasant Party allies defected. The installation of the first non-Communist prime minister was strongly conditioned by international power relationships. A Soviet intervention in Poland would have meant the death of Gorbachev's detente with the West, with deleterious consequences for his perestroika project. Gorbachev thus faced a stark choice he had not expected or desired: intervene in Poland or let a non-Communist government come to power. New power relationships in authoritarian Communist

---

The Polish Experience (Berkeley: University of California Press, 1991), 195–202, and Osiatynski, "Round Table Negotiations in Poland," 7–12. For a defense of why Solidarity entered the Round Table that emphasizes the costs of going first and the achievements attained, see Bronislaw Geremek, "Post-Communism and Democracy in Poland," *Washington Quarterly* 13, no. 3 (1990): 125–31.

28. A chief negotiator for the government (and later chairman of the successor to the Communist Party, the Union of Social Democracy), Aleksander Kwaśniewski, later told Osiatynski, "This illusion [of our strength] saved us from the Romanian experience. If the Party leadership realized how weak it was, there would never have been the Round Table and peaceful change" (p. 7). A chief negotiator for Solidarity, Zbigniew Bujak (who later became a co-founder of the ROAD Party) stressed to Osiantynski that Solidarity worked to "come close to the borderline between merely improving the existing system and real reforms that would set off an avalanche" (p. 47). Osiantynski goes on to say that "on April 5, 1989 almost no one believed that this line would be crossed almost immediately after the Round Table." Six years after the Round Table Pact, some of its agreements, such as the office of the presidency, still stand.

29. Indeed, as Adam Przeworski indicates in *Democracy and the Market: Political and Economic Reforms in Eastern Europe and Latin America* (Cambridge: Cambridge University Press, 1991), 87, "If everyone is behind the Rawlsian veil, that is, if they know little about their political strength under the eventual democratic institutions, all opt for a maximum solution: institutions that introduce checks and balances and maximize the political influence of minorities. . . . Hence constitutions that are written when the relation of forces are still unclear are likely to counteract increasing returns to power, provide insurance to the eventual losers, and reduce the stakes of competition." Consequently, "institutions adopted when the relation of forces is unknown or unclear are most likely to last across a variety of conditions." See also John Rawls, *A Theory of Justice* (Cambridge: Harvard University Press, 1971), 136–37, where he first elaborated theoretically his concept of the original position behind the veil of ignorance. "The idea of the original position is to set up a fair procedure so that any principles agreed to will be just. . . . Somehow we must nullify the effects of special contingencies which put men at odds and tempt them to exploit social and natural circumstances to their own advantage. Now, in order to do this I assume that the parties are situated behind a veil of ignorance. They do not know how the various alternatives will affect their own particular case and they are obliged to evaluate principles solely on the basis of general considerations."

In Algeria, the regime in 1991, without reaching any prior agreement with the opposition on institutions, allowed the FIS (Islamic Salvation Front) to win the first round of the elections; the regime then cancelled the second round and proclaimed martial law. Once the veil of ignorance was lifted by the election results, a negotiation on the conditions for the transition had become much more difficult.

Poland structured Gorbachev's decision.[30] But, once the decision was made, the Polish example in turn had an international demonstration effect that altered power relationships in all the other post-totalitarian, near-totalitarian, and even sultanistic regimes in Eastern Europe as well.

Poland's historic contribution to the fall of Communism in Eastern Europe is now widely and correctly understood. Less well understood, however, is the price Poland paid for being first. Poland's pacted transition delayed its own full transition, and, most importantly, the legacy of its path to transition had an unforeseen harmful effect on Poland's efforts to create the political institutions necessary for democratic consolidation. We concur with Jan T. Gross's assessment that "critical situations engineered within the logic of an epoch's closing days not only marked the end of the old order but, largely unbeknownst at the time, are also a legacy that the new epoch will have to control. . . . The source of today's political crisis in Poland is institutional."[31]

The Round Table Pact entailed three critical compromises. The party-soldiers around Jaruzelski were very intent on stopping Solidarity from boycotting the upcoming 1989 election. Solidarity mainly wanted legal recognition. To entice Solidarity to participate in the elections of 1989, the party-soldiers, against very strong nomenklatura opposition, agreed that 35 percent of the seats in what was then Poland's only chamber, the Sejm, would be open to free, competitive elections. Solidarity did not believe that a full transition to democracy was then possible, but they did believe that they could use elections to get Solidarity relegalized and to start the process of free political campaigning. Solidarity thus accepted an even more partial victory than the Brazilian, Uruguayan, or Chilean opposition had accepted in their own negotiations with regimes still directly managed by hierarchical militaries. The Polish compromise turned out to mean, however, that, from August 1989 until December 1991, the Communist Party and their allies had a majority in the lower house, although the satellite peasant party, as in the GDR and in Bulgaria, soon asserted some independence.[32]

---

30. Alex Pravda captures nicely this complex dialectic between Polish advances and Soviet reactive permissiveness: "As Poland pioneered the transition from 'defensive liberalization' to power sharing, so it prompted a shift in Soviet policy from liberalization to reactive permissiveness. Three critical junctures stand out in the transition of Polish politics and the evolution of Soviet policy: the legalization of Solidarity, its electoral victory, and the formation of the Mazowiecki government. In each case Poles determined the timing and nature of change, though with an eye to Moscow which in each instance placed its weight on the side of permissiveness rather than obstructionism in the hope of minimizing instability." Alex Pravda, "Soviet Policy towards Eastern Europe in Transition: The Means Justify the Ends," in Alex Pravda, ed., *The End of the Outer Empire: Soviet-East European Relations in Transition, 1985–1990* (London: Royal Institute of International Affairs and Sage Publications, 1993), 24.

31. See Jan T. Gross, "Poland: From Civil Society to Political Nation," in Ivo Banac, ed., *Eastern Europe in Revolution* (Ithaca: Cornell University Press, 1992), 57, 65.

32. This greatly complicated constitution making. It raised questions: Did Solidarity have the votes to get the constitution it wanted? Did the Communist majority in the Sejm have the legitimacy to co-author a new constitution?

The second and third major compromises involved the creation of the Senate and Presidency. These emerged as a complex trade-off. The party-soldiers and the nomenklatura both wanted to create a strong presidency that would ensure that "general interests" (e.g., the party) were guaranteed. The government first proposed that the Sejm and other bodies indirectly elect the president. Solidarity refused to accept this. To break the impasse, the government offered to create a Senate and to allow free elections for the Senate with the understanding that the Sejm and the Senate, by a simple majority which the government expected to win, would elect the president. After much discussion about the powers of the president, Solidarity agreed to the creation of the presidency and the creation of the Senate.[33]

The Round Table agreed to the following powers of the president, which were entered as amendments to Poland's constitution by the Polish Sejm within a week of the signing of the Round Table Pact. The first president was to be indirectly elected by the legislature for a six-year term. The president was ex officio made chairman of the Committee of National Defense and commander-in-chief. He was empowered to represent Poland in international affairs, to make nominations for the prime ministership to the Sejm, and to dismiss the prime minister under special circumstances. Important presidential acts required the countersignature of the prime minister except when they "concern matters reserved for the executive—i.e. foreign policy, defense, and national security. . . . The president is also empowered to declare a state of 'emergency' for a period of up to three months."[34]

From the perspective of transition theory, these agreements introduced two complicating legacies for Poland's efforts to complete its transition and to consolidate democracy. The fact that 65 percent of the Sejm would be elected in noncompetitive elections but given co-equal authority with the Senate meant that a body with nondemocratic origins was given an important role in the drafting of a democratic constitution. Also, an ambiguous office of the presidency (whose first incumbent was assumed to be and was General Jaruzelski), with special powers in the areas of internal security, defense, and foreign relations and some emergency powers, was written into the existing constitution. This concession took on added importance over time. Because it was so difficult to draft a constitution in the conditions created by the pacted transition, the constitutional "rights" of the president acquired a life of their own.

Solidarity began Poland's transitional government with great societal support because of its role in the opposition and its overwhelming triumph in those seats in the Parliament that were open to free contestation. This societal legitimacy also accounts for the great support initially given to Finance Minister Balcerowicz's

33. Because of difficulty of approving a constitution, these amendments had, by mid-1992, acquired additional authority as the "constitutional rights" of the president. For details on the Senate-presidency trade-off in the Round Table, see Osiatynski, "Round Table Negotiations in Poland," 40–43.

34. Osiatynski, "Round Table Negotiations in Poland," 45–46.

stabilization plan, which was the most audacious in Eastern Europe and laid part of the groundwork for Poland having the fastest growing economy in all of Europe in 1993–94.[35] However, our basic point remains. Solidarity, like the democratic opponents in Brazil, Uruguay, and Chile, agreed to a pacted transition. In fact, no South American transition began with 65 percent of the lower house and a parallel executive in the hands of the previous nondemocratic regime.

POLITICAL SOCIETY AND THE PROBLEMS OF DEMOCRATIC CONSOLIDATION

Let us now conclude this chapter with a tentative analysis of the legacies left by a democratic opposition anchored in civil society and a pacted transition with the party-soldiers. In chapter 1 we argued that a consolidated democracy requires, among other things, the crafting of agreements about the institutions for generating public policies. Such crafting requires a certain autonomy for political society, as well as the attitudinal belief by public opinion and key actors that these democratic institutions are more appropriate for their society than any other alternative arrangements. How has Poland progressed toward these necessary goals?

Taking political society first, a central characteristic of a democratic polity is that it represents a form of *conflict* that is carried out within agreed-upon procedures. A consolidated democracy is a polity that legitimizes and accepts as normal conflict within the democratic framework. A modern democratic polity also requires that parties aggregate and represent the organized interests of society. All post-Communist societies, even postauthoritarian Poland, will have special problems with the task of *representation*. In the "flattened" post-Communist landscape, independent capital and even labor and many other important social groups are still in the rudimentary process of self-definition. For capital, the dilemma of how to represent interests that are not yet organized or even in existence was captured succinctly in the confirmation hearings of the Polish Sejm, when a nominee to be minister of industry said, "I represent subjects that do not yet exist."[36] The function of representation is further complicated by the fact that, although the goal of most of the post-Communist regimes in Eastern Europe is to create market economies and societies, few people at the start of the transformation process have *actual material interests* (as opposed to potential theoretical interests) in such reforms. It is difficult, therefore, to represent material interests

35. As Adam Przeworski argues, "If people trust the government, voters may opt for the 'horse therapy,' to use the Polish description of the Balcerowicz plan. . . . In Poland, an overwhelming proportion of the population (±90 percent) supported the Mazowiecki government in spite of the drastic deterioration in living conditions during the first months of the new economic program." See Przeworski, *Democracy and the Market*, 165.

36. Staniszkis, *The Dynamics of Breakthrough*, 184.

that do not yet exist.[37] Even in those cases where material interests did exist—industrial labor, for example—it was hard in 1989–90 to create a social-democratic party to represent the social-democratic *space* because of society's deeply ambivalent attitude toward the Communist Party that claimed to represent labor.[38] However, as privatization proceeded and management and capitalism were held responsible for problems, political parties, even post-Communist parties that claimed to represent the social-democratic space, did increasingly well by 1993–94.

This general problem of post-Communist representation and the authentication and legitimization of political society were compounded and given a distinctive specificity in Poland because of the length and ethos of the opposition campaign. *Civil society*, like many other key political words such as *democracy*, can be used by different theoreticians and different social movements in different ways.[39] In Poland and in a slightly different way in Brazil, the idea of civil society developed some very distinctive and politically powerful overtones. In Poland *civil society* referred to the sphere of uncoerced activity not created by the state and virtually independent of the state. We also believe that Poland was a particularly strong case of a "civil society against the state" dichotomy, which had strong cultural roots in the struggle of the nation against foreign-controlled state authority.[40] This was a politically useful concept in the opposition period because it allowed a sharp differentiation between "them" (the Moscow-dependent party-state) and "us" (Polish civil society).[41] The language associated with civil society further strengthened the opposition's position against the party-state because it

37. Ibid. 216. As Przeworski notes, even "in several capitalist countries in which private entrepreneurship was feeble—Brazil, France, Mexico, South Korea—the state not only led the accumulation of capital but in time created a local bourgeoisie. Eastern European countries have no local bourgeoisie, and the prevailing mood is so radically antistatist that the state cannot play the same role in the near future. . . . In Poland, private savings amounted to about one-third of GNP, or about 8 percent of the capital stock, by the end of 1989." Przeworksi, *Democracy and the Market*, 159, 156.

38. This is a major theme in the writing of Iván Szelényi. See his "Socialist Opposition in Eastern Europe: Dilemmas and Prospects," in Rudolf L. Tökés, ed., *Opposition in Eastern Europe* (Baltimore: Johns Hopkins University Press, 1979), 187–208, and "Social and Political Landscape, Central Europe, Fall 1990," in Banac, *Eastern Europe in Revolution*, where he says "most unsurprisingly the newly formed social democratic parties were humiliated by devastating defeats" (p. 227).

39. For a discussion of the different meanings of *civil society* in various philosophical approaches and how it began to be used in Eastern Europe, see Jean L. Cohen and Andrew Arato, *Civil Society and Political Theory* (Cambridge: MIT Press, 1992). For a selection of different approaches and for a good essay on how *civil society* became central to the theory, practice, and life of East European opposition movements, see John Keane, ed., *Civil Society and the State* (London: Verso, 1988). A revisionist critique of *civil society* is now emerging. See, for example, the chapter arguing that civil society was the "last ideology of the old intelligentsia," in Klaus von Beyme, *Systemwechsel in Osteuropa* (Frankfurt an Main: Suhrkamp, 1994), 100–123.

40. For an argument that the sharp "civil society versus the state" dichotomy is empirically a rare exception in Communist systems and that the norm is infiltration and manipulation of the party-state by counterforces or reformists within the state, see X. L. Deng, "Institutional Amphibiousness and the Transition from Communism: The Case of China," *British Journal of Political Science* 24 (July 1994): 293–318. We believe that Deng's critique is particularly useful to bear in mind when a country such as Hungary in the 1980s is evaluated.

41. By now there is an extensive literature on many aspects of Polish civil society. Some of the best works include Timothy Garton Ash, *The Polish Revolution: Solidarity* (New York: Charles Scribner's Sons, 1983);

was encoded in a moral discourse of "truth" and the existential claim of "living in truth." This discourse was particularly functional for what was in effect the national liberation movement, which was waged in Poland from 1976 to 1989. In any movement of liberation, an extremely high value is attached to "unity" within the struggle, and the ideas of *compromise* or *internal conflict* are spoken of pejoratively. Given the difficulties of the opposition's struggle against a highly organized state, there was an understandable tactical and strategic need for immediacy, spontaneity, and antiformal modes of operation. Imperceptibly, the instrumental aspects of immediacy, spontaneity, and antiformalism became ethical standards of personal and collective behavior. Taken as a whole, this language and behavior is what some Polish analysts call "ethical civil society," which no doubt was one of the most powerful and innovative features of the Polish opposition and, ultimately, of the Polish path to democratic transition.[42]

While the idea of "ethical civil society" contributed to a very powerful politics of opposition, many theorists and practitioners went even further. They were so eager to avoid becoming captured in the routines and lies of the party-state that they elevated the situational ethics of oppositional behavior into a general principle of the "politics of anti-politics."[43] This "politics of antipolitics" entailed the aspiration of creating a sphere of freedom independent of the state.

Jadwiga Staniszkis, *Poland's Self-limiting Revolution*, ed. Jan T. Gross (Princeton: Princeton University Press, 1984); and Andrzej M. Tymowski, "The Unwanted Social Revolution: From Moral Economy to Liberal Society in Poland (The Social Origin of the Transformation of 1989) (Ph. D. diss., Yale University, 1995).

Rudolf L. Tokés' edited volume, *Opposition in Eastern Europe* (Baltimore: Johns Hopkins University Press, 1979), contains excellent essays on Poland, including that by Jacques Rupnik, "Dissent in Poland, 1968–78: The End of Revisionism and the Rebirth of Civil Society." Two essays in this volume, Iván Szelènyi's "Socialist Opposition in Eastern Europe: Dilemmas and Prospects" and Alex Pravda's "Industrial Workers: Patterns of Dissent, Opposition and Accommodation," discuss Poland's civil society in comparative Central European perspective. For discussion of the self-organization of civil society, see Z. A. Pelczynski, "Solidarity and the 'Rebirth of Civil Society' in Poland, 1976–81," in John Keane, ed., *Civil Society and the State* (London: Verso, 1988), 361–80.

There are also numerous autobiographies by past and current leaders of Polish civil society. Memoirs of the historian Adam Michnik, one of the founders of the Committee for the Defense of Workers (KOR), are published in *Letters from Prison and Other Essays* (Berkeley: University of California Press, 1985).

In addition, the spring 1981 edition of *Telos*, volume 47, was dedicated to examining "Poland and the Future of Socialism." This volume contains numerous essays on civil society by Polish and East European intellectuals. That of the Hungarian scholar, Andrew Arato, "Civil Society against the State: Poland 1980–81," Adam Michnik's perspective in "What We Want to Do and What We Can Do," and the essay "Solidarity's Tasks" by Tadeusz Mazowiecki (the Solidarity expert invited to serve as president of the Committee of Experts for the All-Plants Strike Committee of Gdansk) not only exemplify the diversity of Poland's intellectual community, but also document the thoughts of civil society's leaders during the crucial and difficult 1980–81 period. An earlier essay on civil society by Michnik, "The New Evolutionism," is found in *Survey* 22 (1976): 267–77. See also *Survey* 17 (1971): 37–52, for Leszek Kolakowski's thoughtful essay, "Hope and Hopelessness."

42. The theme of "ethical civil society" is developed in Piotr Ogrodzinski, "The Four Faces of Civil Society" (Warsaw, 1991, unpublished manuscript).

43. David Ost argues that a significant part of the Polish opposition "rejected the state not just because it could not win there, but also because it did not want to win there. . . . This opposition did not want to possess power so much as to abolish it. . . . So 'anti-politics' is not just the necessary rejection of the state, but also the deliberate rejection of the state, the belief that what is essential to a just order is not a benign

Table 16.1. The Contrasting Language of "Ethical Civil Society in Opposition" and "Political Society in a Consolidated Democracy"

Value or Attitude	Ethical Civil Society in Opposition	Political Society in a Consolidated Democracy
Basis of action	Ethics of truth	Interests
Actors	The ethical nation	Groups
Attitude toward "internal differences"	Viewed pejoratively	Accepted as normal
Attitude toward "internal conflict" within democratic community	Effort to repress	Effort to organize, aggregate, and represent
Attitude toward "compromise"	Negative	Positive
Attitude toward routinized institutions	Negative	Positive
Attitude toward "antipolitics"	Positive	Negative
Attitude toward "state"	Operate outside it	Strive to direct it

Unfortunately, Poland's pioneering and heroic path to democratic transition via ethical civil society inevitably created discourses and practices that, until they can be transformed, will generate systemic problems for the creation of a democratic political society. Ethical civil society represents "truth," but political society in a consolidated democracy normally represents "interests." In political society the actor is only seldom the "nation," but more routinely "groups." "Internal differences" and "conflict" are no longer to be collectively suppressed, but organizationally represented in political society. Compromise and institutionalization are no longer negative but positive values. Antipolitics is dangerous for democratic politics. In new democracies, the effort should no longer be to live parallel to state power but to conquer and direct state power. In fact, most of the values and language of ethical civil society that were so functional to the tasks of opposition are dysfunctional for a political society in a consolidated democracy (table 16.1).

Under the best of circumstances it would have required excellent political leadership and sustained craftsmanship for Poland's new democracy to undergo the normative, discursive, and behavioral changes required in the shift from the ethical civil society of opposition to a political society of democratic consolidation. However, the legacy of Poland's pacted transition made such a transformation substantially more difficult. With 65 percent of the Sejm still in the hands of the Communist Party and their former minor party allies and with the office of

government and good people in power, but rather a vital, active, aware, self-governing and creative society." David Ost, *Solidarity and the Politics of Anti-Politics: Opposition and Reform in Poland since 1988* (Philadelphia: Temple University Press, 1990), 2.

Some of the more influential statements with a strong antipolitics overtone are the Hungarian, George Konrad's, *Anti-Politics* (San Diego: Harcourt Brace Jovanovich, 1984), and Václav Havel's *The Power of the Powerless* (London: Hutchinson, 1985). Havel claims, "It is of great importance that the main thing—the everyday, thankless and never-ending struggle of human beings to live more freely . . . never imposes any limits on itself, never be half-hearted, inconsistent, never trap itself in political tactics, speculating on the outcome of its actions or entertaining fantasies about the future" (p. 88). Also see the essay by the Czech journalist and former dissident, Jiří Ruml, "Who Really Is Isolated?" in Havel, *The Power of the Powerless*, 178–97.

the presidency and, by extension, key parts of the state's coercive apparatus in the hands of the creator of martial law, General Jaruzelski, and the minister of the interior who had been in office continuously since the start of martial law, General Kiszczak, the Solidarity leaders continued to place a great stress on the "us" versus "them" dichotomy. They spent an inordinate amount of energy and emotion trying to maintain the unity of Solidarity as a national movement. They also wanted to use this unity as a key resource with which to advance their audacious plan for radical economic reforms. This meant that within the "us" there was a continued pejorative connotation attached to internal dissent, group conflict, and any organizational efforts outside the Solidarity umbrella aimed at creating normal interest-based political parties. Solidarity's "nonparty bloc" in Parliament, in cooperation with the government, attempted, according to the Polish social scientist Jadwiga Staniszkis, to implement a virtual blockade against the articulation and representation of different interests.[44]

Even when Solidarity did break into two major party groups (Ruch Alternatywny Akcja Demokratyczna [ROAD] and Center Alliance) in mid-1990, one commentator remarked that both groups still sought "to maintain their ties to the ethos and values of Solidarity.... What is distinctive about ROAD and Center Alliance, at least until now, is their refusal to define themselves as political parties and provide a clear programmatic self-definition. Both movements prefer to appeal to society as a reflection of Solidarity's legacy, its consensus norm and collective stance."[45]

The problems of Polish political society were further compounded by the choices made by Lech Walesa. In retrospect the apolitical style of Solidarity seems to have directly contributed to its fragmentation into many small parties, its waning power as a political force in 1990–92, to the surprisingly strong victory of the former communists and their Peasant Party allies in the September 1993 parliamentary election, and to the election of a former Communist, Aleksander Kwaśniewski, as President in 1995.

The first apolitical choice that had deleterious implications for political society was made by the leader of the ethical civil society, Lech Walesa, the most charismatic leader in Eastern Europe. He chose not to direct his great influence and energy to running for a political office, creating a political party in the Sejm, or insisting upon becoming the first prime minister. Instead, he chose to stay outside of Poland's incipient political society and to remain a moral tribune of civil society. When he eventually did decide to run for an office, he ran as a nonparty candidate for the office of president.

The Solidarity government rapidly compounded this initial problem by choosing to use the moral capital of the Solidarity movement to rule in a techni-

---

44. Staniszkis is particularly strong in her criticism of the antipolitics of the first Solidarity government in *The Dynamics of Breakthrough*, 203–6.

45. Jack Bielasiak, "The Dilemma of Political Interests in the Postcommunist Transition," in Connor and Ploszajski, *Escape from Socialism*, 209.

cal, apolitical way. This technical, antipolitical focus led, among other things, to the failure of the prime minister, Tadeusz Mazowiecki, even to consult Lech Walesa in the formation of his cabinet.[46] This oversight or slight set into motion the distancing of Solidarity as a movement, led by Walesa, from Solidarity as government, led by Mazowiecki.

The next fatal antipolitical choice made by Solidarity leaders in Parliament and government was not to press for new and completely free parliamentary elections in early 1990. Solidarity's Round Table partner, the official Communist Party (PZPR), dissolved itself in January 1990. Lech Walesa in April 1990 informally announced his presidential ambition.[47] Given Solidarity's overwhelming moral triumph in the 1989 elections, the inability of the Communists to form a government after the elections, the dissolution of the Communist Party and the expressed desire of Lech Walesa to wage a battle for early elections, simultaneous parliamentary and presidential elections in the fall of 1990 seem to us to have been a historical possibility. However, Solidarity leaders in Parliament and the government wanted to postpone parliamentary elections. This led to the famous split in Solidarity in which the Solidarity leader of political society, Mazowiecki, and the Solidarity leader of civil society, Lech Walesa, competed against each other in a direct presidential campaign.[48] The Solidarity prime minister was not only defeated by Lech Walesa but by a populist, apolitical expatriate unknown, Stan Tyminski. In his campaign for the presidency, Walesa deepened divisions within Solidarity and continued his antipolitical stance. He ran as a nonparty candidate for the office of president. As a candidate he articulated the need to maintain the value of spontaneity and antiformal politics, not of institutionalization. Where democratic consolidation in Poland would have required the authentication of parties and the routinized empowerment of Parliament and the prime minister, Lech Walesa campaigned as an interventionist president who would be "running around with an ax."[49]

Let us turn now to the question of political parties and their role in political society. A consolidated democracy requires that a range of political parties not only *represent* interests but seek by coherent programs and organizational activity to *aggregate* interests. Poland held its first completely competitive elections to both houses of Parliament in October 1991, twenty-six months after the formation of the first Solidarity government. One of the instruments of modern political society to help a few parliamentary parties aggregate interests is to set a minimum threshold of over 3 to 5 percent of the total national vote before parties can

---

46. This point was initially brought to our attention in private communication by Timothy Garton Ash and was later confirmed by a leading intellectual of Solidarity.

47. Timothy Garton Ash reviews some important Polish-language books by major participants in this period in his excellent "Poland after Solidarity," *New York Review of Books* (June 13, 1991): 46–58.

48. On the missed opportunity for earlier parliamentary elections, see ibid., 54.

49. Quoted in Gross, "Poland: From Civil Society to Nation," 63.

be represented in Parliament. In Poland it was decided, after a bitter struggle, that no minimum threshold should be established.[50] A further factor that hindered aggregation was that, while Lech Walesa maintained his no-party stance, he gave ambivalent signs to numerous political groupings that he looked upon them with some favor. For their part, the fragmenting ex-Solidarity groups, by maintaining their claim to be the heirs of the consensual mystique of Solidarity's era, did not articulate programmatic alternatives or seek to become interest-based parties. Ethical discussions of non-negotiable values persisted as the dominant discourse. Nonparties with an organizational style of antipolitics proliferated. As one commentator stated,

during the early phase of the transition . . . interest groups certainly have been quite weak. Sectorial interests are virtually non-existent in the political scene. . . . Besides their mini-party status, the significant element about the vast majority of the new organizations is the reliance on normative, often exclusionary values, as the basis of their political activism. The mini-parties operate, in general, along a dimension of values, traditions and norms.[51]

Twenty-nine parties ended up being represented in the Sejm. No party received even 14 percent of the vote. The four largest parties were strongly polarized and controlled less than 50 percent of the seats (table 16.2).[52]

When we apply the standard Laakso/Taagepera weighted formula for constructing an index of "effective" political parties in Parliament, Poland emerges with an index of 10.8 political parties. As table 16.3 makes clear, this is substantially more parties than any existing democracy in the world with ten years' duration.

In this context the first freely elected parliament of Poland's new democracy found it extremely difficult to form a government. When the government was finally formed after a crisis of almost two months, it still had great difficulty creating a coalition for a program.[53] In the first seven months there were three different prime ministers, none of whom commanded a stable coalitional majority. Relations between the prime minister and the directly elected president became dangerously conflictual, with charges and countercharges of nondemocratic intentions and even actions.

50. Lech Walesa promoted either a higher threshold or a first-past-the-post electoral system to encourage larger parties. The former Communists wanted proportional representation because they were worried that they would be eliminated with a first-past-the-post electoral system. Many of Walesa's former Solidarity allies voted against him to limit his power. See David McQuaid, "The 'War' over the Election Law," *Report on Eastern Europe* 2, no. 3 (1991): 11–28.

51. Bielasiak, "Dilemma of Political Interests in Postcommunist Transition," 211, 210.

52. David McQuaid, "The Parliamentary Elections: A Postmortem," *Report on Eastern Europe* (Nov. 8, 1991): 15–21.

53. For details, see Louisa Vinton, "Impasse Reached on Talks on New Government," *Report on Eastern Europe* (Nov. 29, 1991): 19–25; idem, "Poland: Government Crisis Ends, Budget Crisis Begins," *RFE/RE Research Report* (Jan. 17, 1992): 15–21; and idem, "The Polish Government in Search of a Program," *Report on Eastern Europe* (March 27, 1992): 5–12.

Table 16.2. Effective Number of Political Parties in Poland's Sejm after the October 1991 Elections

Party	Number of Seats
Democratic Union	62
Democratic Left Alliance	60
Catholic Electoral Action	49
Polish Peasant Party—Programmatic Alliance	48
Confederation for an Independent Poland	46
Centre Citizens' Alliance	44
Liberal Democratic Congress	37
Peasant Accord	28
Solidarity	27
Beer Lovers' Party	16
German Minority	7
Christian Democracy	5
Party of Christian Democrats	4
Polish Western Union (labor minority)	4
Janusz Korwin-Mikke (Union of Realpolitik) Solidarity	4
Party X	3
Union of Real Politics	3
Silesian Autonomy Movement	2
Democratic Party	1
Orthodox Believers	1
Union of Wielkopolska and Lubuski Region Inhabitants	1
Peasant Electoral Alliance Piast	1
Union of Podhale Region Inhabitants	1
Bydgoszcz List of Peasant Unity	1
Party for Wielkopolska and Poland	1
Cracow Coalition "In Solidarity with the President"	1
Women's Alliance against Adversity	1
Democratic Social Movement	1
Solidarity 80	1
Total Seats Held	460
'Effective' Number of Parties	10.8

Source: Polish election results from "New Digest for October, 1991," *Kessings Record of World Events.* The formula for calculating the "effective" number of parties is found in Markku Laakso and Rein Taagepera, "'Effective' Number of Parties: A Measure with Application to West Europe," *Comparative Political Studies* 12, no. 1 (1979): 3–27.

Semipresidentialism without a Constitution

The subject of directly elected presidents and prime ministers responsible to parliament is so important that it requires a brief excursus. As both of us have independently argued elsewhere, there are strong theoretical grounds for worry about potential problems within a democratic government that has a dual executive with two independent sources of legitimacy.[54] Maurice Duverger, in his pioneering

54. See Juan J. Linz, "Presidential or Parliamentary Democracy: Does It Make a Difference?" in Juan J. Linz and Arturo Valenzuela, eds., *The Failure of Presidential Democracy: Comparative Perspectives* (Baltimore:

Table 16.3. A Laakso/Taagepera Index of "Effective" Political Parties in the Polish Legislature (1991) Contrasted with the Legislatures of Parliamentary, Semipresidential, and Presidential Continuous Democracies in the World (1979–1989)

Parliamentary		Semipresidential		Presidential	
3.0 or More Parties	Fewer than 3.0 Parties	3.0 or More Parties	Fewer than 3.0 Parties	3.0 or More Parties	Fewer than 3.0 Parties
	Kiribati[a]				
	Nauru[a]				
	Tuvalu[a]				
	Botswana 1.3				
	St.Vincent 1.4				
	Dominica 1.5				
	Jamaica 1.5				
	Bahamas 1.6				
	Trin&Tob 1.6				
	Barbados 1.7				
	St.Lucia 1.7				
	NewZeal.2.0				USA 1.9
	Canada 2.0				
	UK 2.1				
	India 2.1				
	Greece 2.2				
	Austria 2.4				Dom. Rep. 2.3
	Australia 2.5				Cost.Ric. 2.3
	Solomons 2.5				
	Mauritius 2.5				
	Ireland 2.7				Venez. 2.6
	Spain 2.7				
	Japan 2.9				
W.Germ.3.2		France 3.2			
Norway 3.2					
Sweden 3.4					
Luxemb. 3.4					
Israel 3.6		Portugal 3.6			
Nether. 3.8					
Italy 3.9					
PapNeGu 4.0					
Iceland 4.3					
Denmark 5.2					
Belgium 7.0					
		Poland 10.8			

[a] Given the absence of formal parties, there are fewer than two "political groupings."
Note: Switzerland and Finland are "mixed" systems with 5.4 and 5.1 effective parties, respectively.
Source: This table is reproduced from Alfred Stepan and Cindy Skach, "Constitutional Frameworks and Democratic Consolidation: Parliamentarism versus Presidentialism," World Politics 46, no. 1 (1993): 8–9. See also Markku Laakso and Rein Taagepera, "'Effective' Number of Parties: A Measure with Application to West Europe," Comparative Political Studies 12, no. 1 (1979): 3–27.

analysis, labels governments "semipresidential" if they meet three conditions: the president is directly elected, the office of the president has significant de jure and de facto powers, and the prime minister enjoys the confidence of the directly elected parliament.[55] Only two of the thirty-seven countries that were continuous democracies during the 1980–89 decade met Duverger's definition, namely France and Portugal.[56] Austria, Iceland, and Ireland have directly elected presidents and prime ministers responsible to a directly elected Parliament, but, Duverger argues and we concur, that they are not semipresidential because the president does not have significant de facto powers.[57] Finland is often called semipresidential because the president has significant de jure and de facto powers, but the president until 1988 was not directly elected but was indirectly chosen by party blocks.[58] One of the surprising results of the Central European transformations was that the only countries to select for all their free elections a classic parliamentary system, where the prime minister is the chief executive and the president is indirectly elected, were Hungary and Czechoslovakia. Most of the post-communist countries have chosen semipresidential systems, presumably inspired by the French Fifth Republic.

Often, given the turmoil of the post-Communist transitions and the relatively weak legal and historical traditions of constitutionalism, the de jure definition and the de facto expectation is that the most important executive office is the presidency.[59] However, these presidents often encountered opposition in the legislature leading to deadlocks, conflicts, and occasionally even armed struggle, as in Russia and Georgia.

When we say that there are strong theoretical grounds to be wary about a "dual

Johns Hopkins University Press, 1994), 3–87, esp. 58–69. See also Alfred Stepan and Ezra Suleiman, "The French Fifth Republic: A Model for Import? Reflections on Poland and Brazil," in H. E. Chehabi and Alfred Stepan, eds., *Politics, Society and Democracy: Comparative Studies* (Boulder, Colo.: Westview Press, 1995), 393–407.

55. See the classic article by Maurice Duverger, "A New Political System Model: Semi-presidential Government," in *European Journal of Political Research* 8 (1980): 165–87. Such a political system is called *premier-presidentialism* in Matthew Soberg Shugart and John M. Carey, *Presidents and Assemblies: Constitutional Design and Electoral Dynamics* (Cambridge: Cambridge University Press, 1992), 53–57.

56. See Alfred Stepan and Cindy Skach, "Constitutional Frameworks and Democratic Consolidation: Parliamentarianism versus Presidentialism," *World Politics* 46, no. 1 (1993): 1–22.

57. "The constitutions of Austria, Ireland and Iceland are semi-presidential. Political practice is parliamentary." See Duverger, "A New Political System Model," 167.

58. Until 1988 in Finland, citizens elected an electoral college by proportional representation and this body in turn chose, by a three-tiered vote, the president. Ibid. 166. Under the current system, the president is directly elected by the population unless any candidate fails to secure a majority of the popular votes, in which case the president is chosen by an electoral college. For a discussion of presidential elections in Finland, see Shugart and Carey, *Presidents and Assemblies,* esp. 266–69. On the semipresidential nature of Finland's constitution and the power relationships between the dual executive offices until 1988, see Jaakko Nousiainen, "Bureaucratic Tradition, Semi-presidential Rule and Parliamentary Government: The Case of Finland," *European Journal of Political Research* 16, no. 2 (1988): 229–49.

59. See, for example, Russia, Georgia, Croatia, Romania, and Serbia. For the evolving role of the presidency in post-Communist Europe, see the special double issue of *East European Constitutional Review* 2, no. 4, 3, no. 1 (1993–94). Also see Ray Taras, ed. *Presidential Systems in Post-Communist States: A Comparative Analysis,* a book-length volume in progress. The title is tentative.

executive," we mean that, if the president is directly elected and the prime minister is responsible to a directly elected parliament, there is a possibility for deadlock and constitutional conflict. A deadlock can become particularly dangerous if the president has special authority over the security forces and some emergency powers. Theoretically we can posit only two positions wherein this potential for dual executive deadlock and conflict is minimized. If the president is the leader of a party or a party coalition and this coalition wins a clear majority in Parliament, there should be no deadlock or crisis because the power relationship can become one of clear constitutional presidential superiority. The only other possible steady state we can posit is one where the prime minister is a party leader and has a single or multiparty majority and the system can operate in a parliamentary fashion notwithstanding the president's special prerogatives in the area of defense, internal security, and foreign affairs.

Since the French Fifth Republic is often held up as the example to be emulated, not only in Poland but in Eastern Europe and the new states of the former Soviet Union, it might be useful to point out some underanalyzed conditions that have helped French semipresidentialism avoid the potential theoretical problems we believe are intrinsic to the semipresidential formula. The Fifth Republic began in 1958, but only a 1962 referendum introduced a direct election for the president, which was held for the first time in 1965. For the first twenty-six years of French semipresidentialism, the president was a party leader and he was able to lead a party or party coalition that commanded a clear majority in Parliament. This yielded the constitutionally sanctioned primacy of the president. There were thus no deadlocks or constitutional conflicts between the prime minister and the president. For twenty-seven months during 1988–90, the president did not control a majority. However, in this period the prime minister did control a majority. The system thus functioned as one where the prime minister was de facto the chief executive. During these twenty-seven months, called *co-habitation*, there was no deadlock or constitutional conflict. After the 1990 parliamentary election the president's party coalition won a majority and the system shifted back to one where the president was dominant. The key point is that at no time in the first thirty years of French semipresidentialism did either the president or the prime minister fail to control a majority.[60]

This excursus made, it should be clear that the initial model of Polish semipresidentialism did not have any of the supportive conditions found in France. Lech Walesa was not a party leader. He did not direct a coalitional majority in the Sejm. Likewise, due to Poland's extreme party fragmentation, none of Poland's

---

60. Other important changes in France that were made to help generate these majorities were an electoral law with a high de facto threshold, a first-past-the-post runoff, and party regulations (unlike Poland's) that encouraged party institutionalization. See Stepan and Suleiman, "The Fifth Republic: A Model for Import?" in Chehabi and Stepan, eds., *Politics, Society and Democracy*, 396–98.

prime ministers in the first freely elected lower house ever commanded a clear majority.

The Polish case was further complicated by the fact that the respective powers of the office of the president and the Parliament were not clearly defined by a constitution before the political actors confronted each other.[61] As we have seen, the office of the president derived from the demands of the Communist government during the Round Table Pact. This office has poorly defined but potentially major powers. Furthermore, many political actors in the democratic Sejm perceive the powers of the president as de facto in origin, rather than democratically chosen.

Walesa, in the first round of the 1990 presidential election, running mainly against the Solidarity prime minister, Tadeusz Mazowiecki, and a previously unknown Polish businessman from Canada, Stan Tymiński, won only 39.9 percent of the vote. Tymiński received 21.1 percent, Mazowiecki 18.0 percent, and the next three candidates combined received 18.8 percent. These percentages were certainly not the results expected for Solidarity's historic and charismatic leader. On the second runoff ballot against Tymiński, Walesa received 74.3 percent of the vote, but voter participation was a disappointingly low 53.4 percent. [62]

Despite these less than overwhelming electoral results, Walesa continued to see himself as a charismatic leader, as tribune of the people, and with more legitimacy than the parties and Parliament. This belief was not shattered by fluctuating but low and tendentially lower support in public opinion polls during the following five years. This contrast between popular support and self-image within an already risk-prone governing formula of semipresidentialism explains much of the institutional conflict that plagued Poland, to which we now turn.

In chapter 5 we said that the most unencumbered constitution-making process would be one in which the constituent assembly, without a directly elected sitting president, is free to discuss and chose what form of constitutional government is most appropriate for their country. Lech Walesa was directly elected as president *before* the first democratically elected Parliament began its discussions. This fact complicated the constitution-making process in general and exacerbated the conflicts between minority prime ministers and the no-party president in particular.

61. If such a system is to work it is particularly important that the powers of the president and the legislature are clearly defined in a legitimate constitution.

62. Krzysztof Jasiewicz in his study of the 1990 election remarked that Walesa's vote "was for many of his supporters, as well as for himself, a most unpleasant surprise." See his "Polish Elections of 1990: Beyond the 'Pospolite Ruszenie,'" in Conner and Ploszajski, *Escape from Socialism*, 194. Frances Millard agrees: "The results of the first round on 25 November came as a shock. Walesa had failed to achieve the first round victory he had sought," and Tyminski, whom she describes as an "unknown Polish expatriate businessman," not Mazowiecki, had come in second. Frances Millard, *The Anatomy of the New Poland: Postcommunist Politics in Its First Phase* (Aldershot, U.K.: Edward Elgar Publishing Co., 1994), 115–32, quotations from pp. 129 and 128. One of the arguments for presidential or semipresidential systems was that a charismatic president can help to overcome the apoliticism seemingly endemic to post-Communist societies. The low participation rate in the Polish presidential election and the low support for the charismatic Walesa both in his election and particularly in recent public opinion polls do not seem to support that expectation.

A few examples will illustrate the complexity and dangerousness of Poland's constitutional conflict. Soon after the first freely elected Parliament met, its members received an eight-page document from President Lech Walesa, which proposed a "little constitution" that Walesa hoped would be ratified quickly and eventually incorporated into the new constitution. Walesa proposed, in essence, to increase the power of the president over that of the prime minister by giving the president the right to name the prime minister and the right to dismiss the prime minister and the cabinet at his own initiative. The Parliament's countervailing right to dismiss a prime minister by a majority vote, on the other hand, would be subject to a presidential veto that could be over-ridden only by a two-thirds majority.[63]

The Parliament was critical of the proposal and Walesa eventually withdrew it. However, in numerous forums he indicated that he would use the presidential mandate to fight for his policy views. For example, shortly after he withdrew his "little constitution," he went to his original base at Gdansk and proclaimed, "I will make demands in the name of the masses who elected me. I am returning to the masses. I will not accept responsibility for what the government does, but I will be with you."[64] In April, after a series of conflicts with the prime minister over who had the right to appoint key officials in the defense ministry, Walesa went on national television to say that he would petition the Sejm "for greater rights for the president, whereby the Prime Minister would be subordinate to the president, just like in the French system. . . . After the experience we have been through, we probably all agree that the only situation for Poland is an above-party government, a government we will form out of specialists."[65]

Two of his previously close supporters voiced worries about a breakdown of democracy initiated by actions from Belvedere, the presidential palace. Jadwiga Staniszkis, who had worked for Walesa's election as president, wrote about the problem of combining presidential bonapartism and executive dualism: "Poland does not yet see the breakdown of democracy, but it may be on the brink of it. . . . There is mounting evidence of a coming executive coup (against the politicians)."[66] Jaroslaw Kaczyński, chairman of the Center Alliance, had been Walesa's presidential chief of staff. However, in answer to a reporter's question, "Does the

---

63. Walesa's five-page proposal is contained in a December 3, 1991, letter to the president of the Sejm, Wieslaw Chrzanowski. A copy of the letter and the proposal is now available in the library of the Sejm. For some details of the letter, see Louisa Vinton, "Five-Party Coalition Gains Strength, Walesa Proposes 'Little Constitution,'" *Report on Eastern Europe* (Dec. 6, 1991): 7–8.

64. Cited in *Radio Free Europe* (Jan. 17, 1992): 15. For an extremely interesting interview with Lech Walesa that yields important insights into Walesa's conception of his role as president, see Wiktor Osiatynski, "A Profile of President Lech Walesa," *East European Constitutional Review* 2, no. 4, 3, no. 1 (1993–94): 47–50. In the same issue on pp. 47–50 Osiatynski also has an interview with Walesa's predecessor, General Wojciech Jaruzelski.

65. Quoted in *FBIS-EEU* (April 30, 1992): 14.

66. See Jadwiga Staniszkis, "Continuity and Change in Post-Communist Europe" (The Hague: Netherlands Institute of International Relations, June 1992), 27.

Belvedere really constitute the worst threat to democracy?" he answered, "It is the political arrangement by which one of the power centers remains practically outside any control but itself controls all the others which constitutes a threat. After all, by sending his draft constitution to the Sejm, the president showed his hand. He wanted all power for himself."[67]

In fact, President Walesa did not control all the other power centers, and he did not attempt an executive coup. But, at the very least, we argue that Polish semi-presidentialism contributed to great constitutional and intragovernmental conflicts that impeded rather than helped democratic consolidation.

For his part the first prime minister appointed by the newly elected Parliament, Jan Olszewski, waged a series of campaigns against the president. To defend his government and to embarrass the president, who advocated a cautious policy toward Communist collaborators and agents, the prime minister, in violation of a prior resolution of the Sejm, released a list of sixty-four supposed collaborators of the past Communist regime. The minister of the interior at the same time allegedly mobilized a special police unit to intimidate (and possibly arrest) the president and his key staff. For these acts the minister of the interior was voted out of office and a Senate committee recommended criminal investigation.[68]

By August 1992, a still-divided Sejm selected Poland's third prime minister in four months. The new prime minister, Hanna Suchocka, argued that it was impossible to govern if the president and prime minister were at odds, so the coalition she formed accelerated work on a new version of the "short constitution." She said that the president's "constitutional rights" should be respected. She thus gave her support to the normalization of the special powers of the president that had their origins in the Round Table Pact. The Sejm accepted her recommendation, without any of the special conditions that allowed semipresidentialism to work well in France, and Poland went a step further toward making "executive-dualism" a permanent part of Poland's fragile democracy.[69] Because of party fragmentation and its dualistic deadlock, Poland's effort to advance toward a balanced budget and a mixed economy stalled. As *The Economist Intelligence Unit* reported, "though the real economy proved surprisingly resilient to the lack of political steer, key developments were seriously delayed. Perhaps most important here was the sheer immobility of the mass privatisation programme where

67. Interview in *East European Reporter* (March–April 1992): 51.

68. See "Reversal of Fortunes," *Warsaw Voice: Polish and Central European Review* (July 26, 1992): 5.

69. This paragraph is based on discussions of Stepan with members of the Sejm's Constitutional Commission (July 22–26, 1992) in Warsaw.

70. *The Economist Intelligence Unit* (EIU) confirmed that the political stalemate constituted a major obstacle to economic policy formulation and implementation in 1992. To the extent that the economy remained modestly robust and inflation was controlled, it did so "despite the politics" in the country, managing to "withstand the policy vacuum of the past six months." EIU's prediction for the second half of 1992 suggested that "after six wasted months the quality of economic policy making may improve." See *The Economist Intelligence Unit Country Report: Poland* (3d quarter, 1992): 6, 4, 8, respectively.

Table 16.4. Party Identification in Five Eastern European Countries: 1990–1991
Question: "Among the political parties and political movements in our country, is there any that you feel closer to?"

Country	Percentage		
	Yes	No	Don't Know
Poland	17%	72%	11%
Bulgaria	67%	28%	5%
Czechoslovakia	53%	46%	1%
Hungary	51%	47%	3%
Romania	64%	30%	5%

Source: László Bruszt and János Simon, *Political Culture, Political and Economic Orientations in Central and Eastern Europe during the Transition to Democracy: The Codebook of the International Survey of 10 Countries* (Budapest: Institute of Political Science of the Hungarian Academy of Sciences, 1992).

nothing happened for a good six months, so further eroding Poland's credibility in the West."[70]

Public Opinion, Elections, and Polish Democracy

Three years after the assumption of power of the first post-Communist government, was Polish public opinion strongly supportive of a democratic political society? Or, as some analysts feared, was Polish public opinion actually dangerously ambivalent about some of the principles and practices of democracy?

Let us look at a series of indictors that would help us explore this question. Let us start with the least worrisome indicator, Poland's extremely low party identification, not surprising given the high index of party fragmentation. Between November 1990 and August 1991, two well-trained Hungarian political sociologists, László Bruszt and János Simon, coordinated a comparative public opinion survey in seven East European countries and three republics of what is now the former Soviet Union. A finding from that study reinforces our historical-structural analysis about Poland's low political definition. Of the five Eastern European countries in the poll, Poland had by far the lowest percentage of respondents expressing closeness to any political party or even political movement (table 16.4).

In the same survey Poland also had, by a less strong margin, the lowest percentage of respondents who expressed a clear preference for a multiparty system. Even more troublesome, at the height of the conflict between the president, the prime minister, and the Sejm in May 1992, Polish public opinion had a more disfavorable opinion toward these three key components of political society than they did toward any other major organization in Poland. Indeed, there was a popular Polish saying to the effect that anyone who got caught in the "Bermuda Triangle" between the warring president, prime minister, and Sejm would be in-

Table 16.5. Disapproval Rate of Major Political Institutions: February 1990, October 1991, May 1992

| | Disapproval Rate | | |
Institution	Februrary 1990	October 1991	May 1992
Lower chamber of legislature	14%	54%	60%
Government and ministries	14%	48%	53%
President	N/A	43%	52%
Catholic Church	12%	25%	44%
Local authorities	N/A	33%	33%
Police	N/A	21%	21%
Armed forces	15%	10%	12%
Ombudsman	N/A	9%	10%

Source: Centrum Badania Opinii Spolecznej (Public Opinion Research Center, CBOS, Warsaw). Data and translation provided by the director, Lena Kolarska-Bobińska.

Table 16.6. Support for a Range of Emergency Measures in Poland, May 1–3, 1992

| | Percentage | | | | |
Measure	Strongly Approving	Rather Approving	Rather Disapproving	Strongly Disapproving	Difficult to Say
"Law of strong hand and ban on democracy"	11%	19%	19%	37%	14%
"Government can rule by decree."	10%	35%	16%	15%	24%
"President can rule by decree."	9%	24%	17%	30%	20%
"Significant limitations on right to strike"	14%	29%	21%	21%	15%
"Creation of new government with president as prime minister"	14%	18%	14%	29%	25%
"Call for general strike"	7%	20%	21%	41%	11%

Source: Same as for Table 16.5.

jured. In contrast, the three most popular institutions were the relatively neutral powers: the armed forces, police, and ombudsman, which were seen as giving service to the citizens and were not involved in the Bermuda Triangle conflict. Interestingly, the church, which had emerged as a strongly partisan antiabortion advocate, was viewed with growing disapproval (table 16.5).

The Public Opinion Research Center in Warsaw, directed by the distinguished Polish sociologist Lena Kolarska-Bobińska, did not design any questions to explore explicitly antidemocratic sentiment in 1989–91. However, in the midst of the political crisis of May 1992, the Center conducted a poll to determine whether emergency measures, ranging from the right of the government (or the president) to rule by decree to a ban on democracy, were acceptable (table 16.6).

The results are open to various interpretations. However, if we call antidemocratic those who would approve of a "law of strong hand and ban on democracy," then 30 percent of those polled were antidemocratic. If we call those who answered "difficult to say" ambivalent democrats, 44 percent of the Polish popu-

Table 16.7. Percentage of Respondents Approving Authoritarian Antipolitical Options in Poland, the Czech Republic, Slovakia, Hungary, and Austria: 1991–1993

	Percentage of Respondents		
Country	"Approve dissolution of parties and Parliament" (1992)	"Prefer a one-party system" (1992)	"Approve rule by a strong man" (1993)
Poland	40%	31%	39%
Hungary	24%	22%	26%
Slovakia	20%	14%	19%
Czech Republic	19%	8%	22%
Austria	8%	N.D.	22%

Source: Fritz Plasser and Peter A. Ulram, "Zum Stand der Demokatisierung in Ost-Mitteleuropa," in Fritz Plasser and Peter A. Ulram, eds., Transformation oder Stagnation? Aktuelle Politische Trends in Osteuropa (Vienna: Schriftenreihe des Zentrums für angewandte Politikforschung, 1993), 2:46–47.

lation polled in May 1992 expressed antidemocratic or ambivalent democratic opinions. In late July 1992, however, when a more consensual prime minister was appointed and there were signs that the conflict within the Bermuda Triangle had diminished, antidemocrats dropped from 30 percent to 25 percent.

We ask the readers to look again at table 16.1. In our judgment the core attitudes of ethical civil society are not authoritarian, but they are fundamentally different from a Lockean concept of a liberal democracy. More importantly, the set of core attitudes depicted in table 16.1 is close to apolitical communitarianism in that they seem to be opposed to the institutionalization of conflict in democratic politics. In fact, on three of the classic indicators of authoritarian antipolitics (the willingness to approve the dissolution of parties and Parliament, the preference for a one-party system, and the approval of rule by a strong man), Poland in different public opinion polls between 1991 and 1993 was much more antipolitical than was the Czech Republic, Slovakia, Hungary, or Austria (table 16.7). A final piece of evidence that Poland had at best ambivalent attitudes toward democratic political society is obtained when we compare the political attitudes in Poland (and Brazil) with the political attitudes in the four consolidated democracies we have studied (Spain, Portugal, Greece, and Uruguay) (table 16.8).

We are not exactly sure to what we would attribute this ambivalent attitude toward democratic institutions, although we certainly think that the apolitical legacy of ethical civil society has played a role. Many analysts will argue that the primary explanation has to do with economic decline and disruption with the transition to the market. However, from a comparative perspective, we should point out that objectively Poland had by far the strongest positive growth in GNP in the 1992–94 period in post-Communist Europe.[71] Subjectively, in a poll administered between 1993 and October 1994 in the Czech Republic, Slovakia, Hun-

71. See Table 21.1 in this book.

Table 16.8. Comparison of Attitudinal Support for Democracy in Poland and Brazil versus the Four Consolidated Democracies of Uruguay, Spain, Portugal, and Greece

	Percentage of Respondents					
Opinion about Preferred Polity	Poland	Brazil	Uruguay	Spain	Portugal	Greece
"Democracy is preferable to any other form of government."	31	42	73	70	61	87
"For people like me, a democratic and a nondemocratic regime are the same."	40	24	8	9	7	6
"In some cases, a nondemocratic government could be preferable to a democracy."	13	22	10	10	9	5
DK/NA[a]	16	12	9	11	23	2

Source: For Poland, same as table 16.5, survey taken November 1992. For Uruguay, same as table 10.1. For Spain, Portugal, and Greece, same as table 8.2. For Brazil,"Avaliação do Governo Collor apos dois años de mandato," *Datafolha* (São Paulo: Feb. 1992): national sample of 2,500.
[a] DK/NA, don't know or no answer.

Table 16.9. Respondents' Approval Rating of the Economic System and Their Level of Trust in the Government and the President: Six Countries of East Central Europe, November 1993 to March 1994

	Percentage of Respondents			
		Trust in Executive of Political System		
Country	Approval of Economic System	Government	President	Total Combined Trust
Poland	50%	25%	20%	(45%)
Bulgaria	14%	13%	40%	(53%)
Hungary	27%	21%	65%	(86%)
Romania	35%	27%	48%	(75%)
Slovakia	31%	32%	62%	(94%)
Czech Republic	67%	57%	67%	(124%)

Source: Richard Rose and Christian Haerpfer, "New Democracies Barometer III: Learning from What Is Happening," *Studies in Public Policy,* no. 230 (1994): tables 23, 52, 58.

gary, Poland, Romania, and Bulgaria, Poland had the second highest evaluation of the economy but by far the lowest overall trust in the two sources of executive power, the government and the president (table 16.9).

For some insights into table 16.9 let us return to our discussion of the possible perils of semipresidentialism with a dual executive. In general theoretical terms, a conflict between the president and the legislature, and the government emerging from them, is not necessarily detrimental to democracy when both sides respect each other and do not intend to eliminate the other. However, when supporters of one or the other component of semipresidentialism feel that the country would be better off if one branch of the democratically legitimated structure of rule would disappear or be closed, the democratic system is endangered and suffers an overall loss of legitimacy, since those questioning one or the other will tend to consider the political system undesirable as long as the side they favor does not prevail. In a pure parliamentary system there is not a dual executive so this source of delegitimation of the democratic institutional framework does not exist. There is of course conflict in a democratic parliament, but it tends to be between parties over policies. However, in a semipresidential system, policy conflicts often express themselves as a conflict between two branches of democracy.

Table 16.9 shows the mutual delegitimation of the government and the president that occurred in Poland despite comparative economic robustness. A particularly dangerous round of this conflict occurred in January and February 1995. The president wanted the existing government to step down and, in private conversation with key actors and occasionally publicly in complex language, implied that, if the government did not step down, he would unilaterally dissolve Parliament and call for new elections even though he had no clear consitutional right to do so. President Walesa addressed Congress with a clear sense of his moral legitimacy to act (despite the fact that he had the lowest presidential approval rating of the six countries polled in table 16.9) because he believed in his charismatic mission, shored up by the fact that he was directly elected. Guillermo O'Donnell would of course classify Walesa's speech as the archetypal discourse of "delegated democracy."[72] Walesa spent some time decrying the slowness of Parliament and the government:

The decisions that are most important for the country are postponed. The only quick decisions are those that serve personal and party interests. . . . Poland does not have the time to sit at a yellow light. For that reason, if there is nothing more that the government and the parliament can do, if there is nothing that can be done for the good of Poland, then I ask you to step down because history will not forgive you or us all. And if you do not have any other ideas or other people [to offer], and only have this simple will to survive, then I will make the decision, in the full conviction that it is in Poland's interests. . . . In democratic elections, the nation entrusted me with responsibility for the state. . . . I am trying to change things using democratic and peaceful methods. But to achieve these results, I will do as I see fit.[73]

The ruling coalition changed the prime minister. But the spectacle of the president ridiculing and threatening Parliament did little to increase the democratic legitimacy of the two democratically legitimated sources of authority.

Poland's political society took an unexpected turn in 1993. Parliamentarians who were aware that the legislature's extreme party fragmentation made the question of creating enduring coalitional majorities difficult passed a new electoral law on May 28, 1993. This electoral law, supported by all seven parties in the then ruling pro-Solidarity coalition and eventually by some opposition parties, mandated that a party could not be represented in the lower house in the Sejm unless it received more than 5 percent of the valid national vote. For a coalition of parties to get into the Sejm, an even higher threshold of 8 percent was established. To further reward the largest parties, only those who received at least 7 percent of the vote would be eligible for redistribution of the national remainder for proportional representation votes that went to parties above the threshold.

The electoral law contained two other provisions that the literature on electoral systems shows have a strong tendency to strengthen the one or two largest parties in the system. First, the Polish electoral law opted for the d'Hondt formula for calculating the distribution of seats within the overall proportional representation system. Arend Lijphart in his magisterial empirical and theoretical review of electoral systems is categorical on the effect of the d'Hondt formula. "Among the highest averages formulas, the d'Hondt method . . . is the least proportional and systematically favors the larger parties."[74] Finally, some electoral districts were split, thus reducing their "district magnitude," defining that phrase as meaning the number of representatives elected in a district. The recurrent finding of electoral studies is that the smaller the overall district magnitudes, the fewer the parties in the legislature, and the more disproportionate a proportional representative system will become.[75]

Shortly before this electoral law—which included four vectors all in the direction of rewarding the first and second largest parties—was formally passed in the Sejm, the majority of parliamentarians in the Solidarity splinter party helped bring down the pro-Solidarity government of Prime Minister Hanna Suchocka. To the surprise of many parliamentarians, the historical leader of Solidarity, Lech Walesa, called for early general elections to be held by September 1993.

"Rational choices" do not always lead to the preferred "rational outcomes." The new incentives of the electoral law would have produced the desired outcome sought by its principal framers only if they had calibrated their behavior so as to win within the new rules they had created. They did not.

Four Catholic parties considered a coalition but in the end only two entered the coalition, just before the deadline, and they polled only 6.4 percent of the vote. In Catholic Poland none of the principal four Catholic parties crossed the threshold.[76] The Liberal Democratic Congress, which despite differences had been major advocates of the post-1989 reform economic plan, could not arrive at a coalition with the other major former Solidarity party which also supported the

---

74. Arend Lijphart, *Electoral Systems and Party Systems: A Study of Twenty-Seven Democracies, 1945–1990* (Oxford: Oxford University Press, 1994), 23.

75. This was a major argument in Douglas W. Rae's classic, *The Political Consequences of Electoral Laws* (New Haven: Yale University Press, 1967), 114–25, and was supported by comparative studies of Rein Taagepera and Matthew S. Shugart, *Seats and Votes: The Effects and Determinants of Electoral Systems* (New Haven: Yale University Press, 1989), 112, and Lijphart, *Electoral Systems and Party Systems*, 10–14. For other details of the election law, see Louisa Viron, "Poland's New Election Law: Fewer Parties, Same Impasse," *RFE/RL Research Report* 28 (July 12, 1993): 7–17. The threshold principles did not apply to ethnic minorities.

76. See Anna Sabbot-Swidlicka, "The Political Elections: The Church, the Right and the Left," *RFE/RL Research Report* 40 (October 8, 1993): 24–31, esp. 25.

Table 16.10. Votes versus Seats: Parties That Crossed and Did Not Cross Poland's Electoral Threshold in the September 1993 Parliamentary Elections to the Sejm (Lower House)

Electoral Threshold	Party	Percentage of Popular Vote	Percentage of Seats
Above the threshold	SLD (Democratic Left Alliance)	20.41%	37.10%
	PSL (Polish Peasant Party)	15.40%	28.60%
	UD (Democratic Union)	10.59%	16.08%
	UP (Union of Labor)	7.28%	8.90%
	KPN (Confederation of Independent Poland)	5.77%	4.70%
	BBWR (Non-Party Bloc for Support of the Reforms)	5.41%	3.40%
	German Minority (not subject to threshold rules)	0.70%	0.80%
Subtotal		65.56%	100%
Below the threshold	Fatherland Catholic Election Committee	6.37%	0
	Solidarity Trade Union	4.90%	0
	Center Alliance	4.42%	0
	Liberal Democratic Caucus	3.99%	0
	Union of Real Politics	3.18%	0
	Self-defense	2.78%	0
	Party X	2.74%	0
	Coalition for Republic	2.70%	0
	Peoples' Alliance	2.37%	0
	Political Party of Beer Lovers	0.10%	0
	Others	0.89%	0
Subtotal		34.44%	0

Source: Compiled from data in Edmund Wnuk-Lipinski, "Left Turn in Poland: A Sociological and Political Analysis," Institute of Political Studies, Polish Academy of Sciences, Warsaw (Nov. 1993), and "Bulletin of Electoral Statistics and Public Opinion Research Data," *East European Politics and Societies* 8, no. 2 (1994): 371.

reform, the Democratic Union (UD), because of a dispute over the share of seats they would be allocated in the coalition. The Liberal Democratic Party did not cross the threshold. In fact, six of the seven parties in the Suchocka coalition that helped formulate the electoral law did not cross the thresholds they devised.

President Walesa refused to support any party, but he did create a Non-Party Bloc of Support of the Reform (BBWR), which crossed the threshold with 5.4 percent of the vote but was not eligible for the distribution of the remainder because of the requirements of the 7 percent clause. In the end, an extremely high 34.4 percent of the total votes went to parties that did not cross the thresholds (table 16.10).[77]

77. For an analysis of the 1993 election, see Edmund Wnuk-Lipinski, "Left Turn in Poland: A Sociological and Political Analysis" (Institute of Political Studies, Polish Academy of Sciences, Warsaw, Nov. 1993); "Bulletin of Electoral Statistics and Public Opinion Research Data," *East European Politics and Societies* 8, no. 2 (1994): 369–73; Louisa Virton, "Poland Goes Left," *RFE/RL Research Report* 40 (October 8, 1993): 21–23; and Voytek Zubek, "The Reassertion of the Left in Post-Communist Poland," *Europe-Asia Studies* 46, no. 2 (1994): 801–37.

Table 16.11. Lijphart Index of Disproportionality for Polish Election to the Sejm (Lower House) in September 1993 and the Average for the Twenty-one Continuous Democracies in the World, Classified by Electoral System, 1945–1980

Electoral System	Country	Index of Disproportionality
Proportional representation	Poland	35.1
	Luxembourg	3.2
	Norway	3.1
	Iceland	3.0
	France IV	2.8
	Ireland	2.4
	Italy	2.2
	Germany	2.1
	Austria	2.0
	Finland	1.6
	Switzerland	1.5
	Sweden	1.2
	Israel	1.1
	Netherlands	1.1
	Denmark	0.9
Single nontransferable vote	Japan	4.2
Plurality and majority	France V	12.3
	Canada	8.1
	New Zealand	6.3
	United Kingdom	6.2
	Australia	5.6
	United States	5.6

Source: For Poland, same as table 16.8. For all other countries, Arend Lijphart, *Democracies: Patterns of Majoritarian and Consensus Government in Twenty-One Countries* (New Haven: Yale University Press, 1984), 160.

Specialists on electoral laws have compiled a variety of formulas to measure what Douglas Rae calls "manufactured majorities" or what Arend Lijphart calls "vote/seat disproportionality." Lijphart has analyzed elections via a simple index of disproportionality that measures the deviation between the total votes received by the two largest parties versus the total seats they received.[78] He has calculated the average "index of disproportionality" for all twenty-one continuous democracies in the world between 1945 and 1980. The highest average index of disproportionality in a democracy that used a plurality and majority electoral system is the French Fifth Republic with 12.3 percent. The highest average index of dispro-

78. For a review of the strengths and weaknesses of various formulas that measure vote/seat disproportionality such as the Rae index, the Loosemore-Hanby index, the Lijphart index, and Michael Gallagher's least-squares index, see the excellent chapter, "Disproportionality, Multipartism, and Majority Victories," in Lijphart, *Electoral Systems and Party Systems*, 57–77. Lijphart discusses his index on pp. 61–62. Douglas Rae has constructed a different formula to measure "manufactured majorities," a phrase he uses to indicate a party or a coalition that did not receive a majority of votes in the election but nonetheless was allocated a majority of seats in the legislature.

portionality for any of the fifteen continuous democracies that used a proportional representation electoral system is Luxembourg with 3.2 percent. The 1993 Polish elections to the Sejm used proportional representation. The two largest parties received 35.8 percent of the vote and 65.9 percent of the seats, thus producing according to Lijphart's formula, an index of disproportionality of 35.1 percent (table 16.11).

The point of this excursus has been that key players in Poland's political society did not "rationally" adjust their behavior to operate within the incentives created by new election rules they themselves created.[79] Their behavior gave the reform Communist Party and their pre-1988 ally, the Peasant Party, not only an absolute majority in the Parliament, but the theoretical capacity to unilaterally draft and pass the constitution in the Parliament. As we shall see in the concluding chapter of this book, most of the dire predictions concerning the "return of communism" or the "end of democracy" did not actually develop, partly because both the former ruling parties in the Communist era and most social groups and parties outside of the Parliament after the 1993 elections seem to have accepted democracy as "the only game in town." Nonetheless, Poland's recent electoral history of an unprecedented score on the Laakso-Taagepera index that measures party fragmentation in 1991 and an unprecedented score, in the opposite direction, on the Lijphart index of disproportionality in 1993 shows how far Poland still had to go before it produced party attitudes and behaviors that would allow political society to make its necessary contribution to democratic consolidation in Poland.

Having made these critical analytic points about political society, we do not want to end this chapter without calling attention to some of Poland's extraordinary achievements. More than any other country in post-Communist Europe, Poland contributed to making the possibility of the 1989 regime changes a reality. The constant pressure of Polish civil society and Solidarity helped to broaden the parameters of the game which Gorbachev and the Soviet Union were playing vis-à-vis the rest of Eastern Europe. This concrete fact is an important historical achievement that helps ratchet Poland forward toward democratic consolidation.

Another important achievement is that Poland had a higher GNP growth rate than any country in Western Europe in 1993 and 1994. This achievement helped bolster domestic and international confidence in Poland. Although the rate of privatization of the state sector did not proceed anywhere near as quickly as in the Czech Republic, the dynamism of the new small and middle-sized private enterprises meant that possibly more than half the economically active population were working in the private sector by the start of 1995.

79. As one Polish analyst observed, the "KLD could have joined the Democratic Union, PL could have joined with KKW, and had KdR not split from PC, all these groups would now have representation in the Lower House. Especially since there is no significant difference between KLD and Democratic Union, PC and KdR, and also between KKW and PL. Political leaders . . . ignored the implications of the new electoral law and had to pay the price." Wnuck-Lipinski, "Left Turn in Poland," 16.

Just as Poland's economy exhibits a healthy robustness, so too do parts of Poland's society. While we have been concerned with the ability of Poland's civil society to work productively with political society, we do not want to seem pessimistic about Polish civil society in general. With a tradition starting much before the historic changes of 1989, Poland's civil society in some areas continues to produce some strong achievements. For example, two former Solidarity leaders, Adam Michnik and Helena Luczywo, have created one of Europe's most dynamic newspapers, *Gazeta Wyborcza,* which circulates seventeen different metropolitan editions daily.

Because of these and many other achievements, as well as its critical geopolitical position, many observers inside and outside of Poland believe that Poland's chances of entering the European Union by the end of the 1990s are good. The very fact that this is an option for Poland creates incentives for Polish political actors to act in a responsible, democratic manner.[80] This usable future as well as elements of its usable past will contribute significantly to hindering democratic breakdown and assisting democratic consolidation.

80. As we discuss in chapter 21, for many countries with severe stateness problems and intense ethnic strife, entry into the European Union is not even a distant possibility. Thus, the set of European Union-related incentives and disincentives that we showed playing a positive role in Southern Europe and a comparable role in Poland are simply not present. In November 1995, Aleksander Kwaśniewski, the former leader of the reform Communist Party, was elected President of Poland. During and after the campaign, Kwaśniewski (unlike Communist Party leaders in Russia) argued that joining the European Union and NATO were two of Poland's highest priorities. As long as these priorities are maintained, Poland will continue to be subject to European Union pressures to conform to liberal and democratic standards.

17

Varieties of Post-Totalitarian Regimes:
Hungary, Czechoslovakia, Bulgaria

Twenty-six of the twenty-seven post-Communist states in Europe (the only exception, as we have argued, being Poland) had at one time approximated the totalitarian ideal type during the period of high Stalinism or before the Yugoslavian "heresy." Most of them later came to approximate the post-totalitarian ideal type. The term *post-totalitarian* itself indicates that this type of regime had not been conceived initially by its founders as a distinctive type of polity but was the result of changes in a system that had once approached the totalitarian model. Thus, *post-totalitarianism* (unlike democracy, totalitarianism, authoritarianism, or sultanism) is not a genetic type but an evolutionary type. That is, no one would or could create a post-totalitarian regime unless there had already been a prior totalitarian regime.

Conceptually the two dominant paths, from within the regime, to post-totalitarianism can be called "post-totalitarianism by choice" and "post-totalitarianism by decay." In the former path, regime elites (often for their own sense of personal safety) may collectively decide to constrain the completely arbitrary powers of the maximum leader, to reduce the role of terror (if that had been prominent), and to begin to tolerate some non-official organizations to emerge in what had been virtually a completely flattened civil society. In "post-totalitarianism by decay" (or post-totalitarianism by reluctant acquiesence), commitment to ideology may simply become hollow, mobilization may degenerate into bureaucratic ritual, and pockets of resistance or relative autonomy may emerge, more due to regime incapacity or reluctant acquiesence to foreign pressure than to any choice. Forces outside the regime can also generate a situation of "post-totalitarianism by societal conquest," in which civil society groups struggle for, and win, areas of relative autonomy.[1] Whatever the path, all post-totalitarian regimes, by definition, emerge out of totalitarian regimes.[2]

1. There are, of course, other paths out of totalitarianism. Totalitarianism can be ended by conquest and occupation by democratic polities, as happened to Germany and Japan after World War II. In these cases there never was a post-totalitarian regime, but rather a sequence of totalitarianism followed by occupation and liberalization followed by democratization. See table 4.2, The Implications of Prior Nondemocratic Regime Type for Paths to Democratic Transition.

2. Specific concrete cases of a shift from a totalitarian to a post-totalitarian regime often may empirically contain some elements of post-totalitarianism by choice, post-totalitarianism by decay, and post-totalitarianism by societal conquest.

The empirical fact that change from totalitarianism is normally not to a typical authoritarian regime but to a distinct type of post-totalitarian regime confirms the argument of Linz that there is no continuum from totalitarianism to authoritarianism.[3] However, the fact that post-totalitarianism cannot be understood without reference to totalitarianism also explains that it can be conceived of as a continuum from an almost totalitarian system to one in which the former totalitarianism elements are almost survivals (in the anthropological sense). This also accounts for the difficulty of determining at what point the transition from a totalitarian to a post-totalitarian regime has taken place.

Because post-totalitarianism is a continuum, we will dedicate extensive space to presenting some of the textures of life within different kinds of post-totalitarian regimes. We will also attempt to conceptualize and discuss the major possible variations within the post-totalitarian type, which can range from an early post-totalitarianism close to the border with totalitarianism, to a frozen post-totalitarianism that shows no significant tendency to evolve toward greater pluralism, to even a mature post-totalitarianism, which may be close to an out-of-type change toward a democratic or authoritarian regime. Only after we have an understanding of such variation within the post-totalitarian type are we analytically prepared to study, evaluate, and even predict the extensive range of transition paths that actually could and do occur within post-totalitarianism. Most of the post-Communist states in Europe began their transition away from Communism from a post-totalitarian starting point. All of the post-totalitarian regimes were affected by the "domino-like" events of 1989, but the style and consequences of the actual transition depended greatly, as we shall see, on the specific post-totalitarian subtype found in each individual country.

Empirically, what do we mean by variations within post-totalitarianism? The variation was most stark in the cases of Hungary and Bulgaria. As we will document, Hungary by February 1989 (i.e., the same month in which the Polish Round Table began) was in fact already close to an out-of-type change from post-totalitarianism to a still undetermined democratic or authoritarian regime. In contrast, we believe we will provide convincing documentation for the argument that Bulgaria, as late as 1988, was close to the totalitarian pole concerning autonomous groups in civil society. Czechoslovakia, in contrast to Bulgaria, had had for more than a decade some important post-totalitarian characteristics in the area of civil society, since the human rights group Charter 77, linked to the Helsinki process, had emerged in 1977. However, detotalitarianization in Czechoslovakia in the 1980s—which was a case essentially of "detotalitarianization by decay"—was nowhere as deep or extensive as it was in Hungary, which had much stronger elements of "detotalitarianization by choice."

3. See Juan J. Linz, "An Authoritarian Regime: Spain," in Erik Allardt and Stein Rokkan, eds., *Mass Politics: Studies in Political Sociology* (New York: Free Press, 1970), 251–83, esp. 253.

If we call Hungary an example of mature post-totalitarianism, and Bulgaria an example of early post-totalitarianism, Czechoslovakia can be considered an example of frozen post-totalitarianism. In essence, Hungary, Czechoslovakia, and Bulgaria in the late 1980s had different state, rule of law, economic, civil, and political society mixes. These different mixes structured much of the negotiating capacity of regime and opposition alike, opened and/or blocked certain transition paths, and helped generate distinct constellations of consolidation tasks.

Our purpose in this chapter is to explain how and why—and with what consequences—Hungary, Czechoslovakia, and Bulgaria had sharply different transition paths. In Hungary, the Communist Party increasingly led by reformists on the one side and an organized democratic party opposition on the other side, *negotiated* an agreement that the next government would be produced by free elections. In these elections, the largest of the Opposition Round Table parties won the most seats and formed a coalition government with a strong parliamentary majority. In Czechoslovakia, after the Berlin Wall was torn down, students and artists led a protest against police brutality. The hard line regime *collapsed* and handed over power to a provisional government headed by the most famous leader of the civil society opposition, Václav Havel.[4] In Bulgaria, a still unreformist Communist Party experienced some societal protests but was able to *control* the transition. The Communist Party, via an internal coup, rid itself of its old leader, Todor Zhivkov, gained some legitimacy by participating in a round table, and eventually won the first competitive election against the still weak democratic forces.

All of these cases were, of course, strongly affected by our variables concerning diffusion effects and the political economy of legitimacy. However, our central thesis is that the most powerful way to explain these three strikingly different transitions (negotiation, collapse, and control) is by exploring the causes and consequences of their variation within the post-totalitarian regime type.

Before examining these three cases, let us briefly mention a cruel paradox. Hungary (and authoritarian Poland) increasingly experimented with a variety of economic reforms and in the process opened themselves up to Western international credit, which eventually made them two of the most indebted countries of the world. This indebtedness contributed to pressures for regime transition; however, it left a difficult economic legacy for democratic consolidation, especially for Hungary, which did not reschedule before or after the transition. In contrast, the frozen post-totalitarian regime in Czechoslovakia engaged in no economic experiments or reforms and received almost no Western foreign credits and thus

---

4. If we had not excluded the GDR on account of its disappearance as a result of unification with the Federal Republic, it would have been a case of early post-totalitarianism leading to regime collapse. Like Czechoslovakia, the GDR only began any efforts to negotiate a transition when collapse was already imminent. Credible negotiators within the regime were weak in both Czechoslovakia and the GDR. However, in the case of the GDR the successive changes of leadership of the regime and perhaps the international dimension of the Germany case gave a bit more breathing space for the incumbents.

faced fewer economic pressures pushing for a transition. However, Czechoslovakia's lack of foreign debt, of course, not so paradoxically became an asset in the democratic consolidation phase.

HUNGARY: A NEGOTIATED TRANSITION FROM MATURE POST-TOTALITARIANISM

For readers familiar with the standard works on negotiated transitions and pacts in southern Europe and Latin America, the East European country that is by far the most familiar in terms of the dynamics of the transition is Hungary.[5] Indeed, most of the basic vocabulary used to describe the Spanish and Uruguayan transitions can be used to describe the Hungarian transition.[6] Regime *blandos* (soft-liners) sought out alliances with some of the leaders of the moderate opposition; regime *blandos* endeavored to use their roles as sponsors of liberalization to strengthen their positions against their own hard-liners; both *blandos* and opposition leaders increasingly focused on the political mechanics of transition, and elite negotiations figured prominently. Why did such a similar political process of regime transition occur in such dissimilar political systems?

Of all the regimes in East Central Europe we will analyze, the Hungarian one underwent the sharpest set of changes. Hungary had free elections in 1945, a very totalitarian period from 1948 to 1953, a reform period that led to a successful popular revolution in 1956, a Communist counter-revolution from 1956 to 1962, and detotalitarianization starting in 1962. By the mid-1980s Hungary was the world's leading example of mature post-totalitarianism.[7]

Between 1945 and 1947 Poland saw a civil war between Polish partisans and Soviet-backed forces. In Hungary, however, possibly because of its less strategic position for the Soviet Union, the Soviet military administration allowed an election in November 1945 that has often been called the freest ever held in Hungary

5. See, for example, Guillermo O'Donnell, Philippe C. Schmitter, and Laurence Whitehead, eds., *Transitions from Authoritarian Rule* (Baltimore: Johns Hopkins University Press, 1986); John Higley and Richard Gunther, eds., *Elites and Democratic Consolidation in Latin American and Southern Europe* (Cambridge: Cambridge University Press, 1992); and Giuseppe di Palma, *To Craft Democracies: An Essay on Democratic Transitions* (Berkeley: University of California Press, 1990).

6. Indeed, a Spanish social scientist draws extensive parallels between Hungary and Spain; see Carmen González Enríquez, *Crisis y cambio en Europa del Este: La transición húngara a la democracia* (Madrid: Centro de Investigaciones Sociológicas / Siglo XXI de España, 1993), esp. 50–80 on pacts and 340–68 for an overall comparison of the Hungarian and Spanish transitions.

One of Hungary's leading public opinion specialists, János Simon, learned Spanish to be able to study the Spanish transition and occasionally publishes his work, often with László Bruszt, in Spain. See their "La mayoría más silenciosa" (Madrid and Budapest, 1990, unpublished manuscript).

7. References to all these changes will be found in this chapter. For a classic book on pre-Communist Hungary that is particularly strong on the country's dualistic electoral principles after 1922 (secret and free in the cities but unsecret and manipulated in the countryside) and an interwar authoritarian period with a reasonably robust press and areas of rule of law, see Andrew C. János, *Politics of Backwardness in Hungary: 1825–1945* (Princeton: Princeton University Press, 1982).

to that date. The Smallholders won the election with 57 percent of the vote, the Social Democrats received 17.4 percent, and the Communists 17 percent.[8] However, in the less-free 1947 parliamentary elections, the Communists received the largest single vote with 22.3 percent and then used a variety of tactics to get the Parliament to prorogue itself for a year. From 1948 to 1953 Hungary underwent one of the most intense periods of Stalinization in Eastern Europe, ranging from a show trial of Cardinal Jozsef Mindszenty to coercive collectivization of agriculture to the summary execution of two thousand "local undergrounders" of the Communist Party. This period is called by many Hungarian commentators "totalitarian."[9]

After Stalin's death in 1953, Khrushchev, as part of his anti-Stalin campaign, replaced the Hungarian mini-Stalin, Mátyás Rákosi, with the more moderate Imre Nagy, who inaugurated the "sharpest and earliest reversal of mature Stalinism to be initiated in any people's democracy."[10] The detotalitarianization of Hungary had begun, but it was to prove a stop-and-go process. From April 1955 until his removal by the Soviets again in July 1956, Rákosi returned to power, to be succeeded by Ernö Gerö and, in the face of widespread student and intellectual demands, by Nagy. Under Nagy, the Hungarian protests rapidly became revolutionary. In Rothschild's judgment, the events in Hungary from October 23 to November 4, 1956, were "a genuine and domestically victorious revolution with national-political as well as socioeconomic aims. This revolution was defeated only by overwhelming foreign force," Soviet tanks.[11]

The evolution of the Hungarian regime from counter-revolutionary repression in 1956 to near out-of-type change by February 1989 deserves a book-length analysis. Our contribution is necessarily more restricted and driven by democratic theory. We believe that the dynamic process of detotalitarianization should and can be analyzed. We also believe that post-totalitarianism is not and should not be a static concept. In addition, we believe that the specific forces and processes by which some post-totalitarian regimes have evolved is an important area of inquiry for scholars interested in democratization. Therefore, we will now attempt to show how detotalitarianization started. We will also attempt to

8. Charles Gati argues that the openness of the elections was largely due to Stalin's fears, until 1946, that he might have to trade away Hungary to the West for his demands on Poland and Germany. See his *Hungary and the Soviet Bloc* (Durham: Duke University Press, 1986), 118.

9. For example, Rudolf Andorka's paper to the XII World Congress of Sociology in Madrid, July 1990, "Transitions from a Totalitarian to a Democratic Political System: The Case of Hungary," argues that "after 1947 Hungary clearly became a Totalitarian state under the rule of the Communist Party the power of which was based on the presence of the Soviet army.... The first relaxation of totalitarianism came after the death of Stalin" (p. 1).

10. Joseph Rothschild, *Return to Diversity: A Political History of East Central Europe since World War II* (New York: Oxford University Press, 1989), 154.

11. Ibid., 160. For a revealing analysis of the process of regime division and social protest that led to this too-often-forgotten case of the internal reversibility of totalitarianism, see Paul Kecskemeti, *The Unexpected Revolution: Social Forces in the Hungarian Uprising* (Stanford: Stanford University Press, 1961).

demonstrate how, in each of the five *arenas* of a consolidated democracy we discussed in chapter 1, some important changes occurred in Hungary before the regime change in 1989. We will likewise show how changes in each arena increasingly reinforced each other. Our task, therefore, is to analyze and illustrate the dynamic process of interacting changes. We will proceed by exploring changes in the rough sequence in which they occurred: ideology, the economy, the state, the rule of law, civil society, and finally political society.

The first area in which Hungary became post-totalitarian was the area of ideology. The revolution of 1956 was followed by repression and the execution of Nagy, but it also left a preoccupation in Khrushchev's Soviet Union and among the team led by Nagy's successor, János Kádár, with how to avoid policies that might precipitate a revolutionary reoccurrence. The search for passive compliance, rather than a totalitarian attempt to mobilize enthusiasm, became a hallmark of Kádár's political style. The first explicit argumentation that reflected the post-totalitarian turn was articulated by Kádár when he advocated a "politics of alliance" at the Plenum of the Central Committee in March 1962. At the plenum, Kádár explicitly distanced himself from the totalitarian aspirations of the Stalinist dictator Mátyás Rákosi when he announced that, "whereas the Rákosites said that someone who is not on our side is against us, we say, those who are not against us, are with us."[12]

The next major step toward detotalitarianization was the introduction in 1968 of the New Economic Mechanism, which despite a partial reversal from 1972 to 1979 represented the most pervasive experimentation of any Warsaw Pact country with markets and quasi-private property.[13] This experiment could not have started without a prior ideological change toward post-totalitarianism, but the New Economic Mechanism itself further eroded the classic Communist utopian ideology and represents the beginning of the process of detotalitarianization by choice. Much has been written about the Hungarian reform from an economic perspective but relatively little about how attendant social and legal changes altered both the state and society. Numerous state-society interactions growing out of the New Economic Mechanism pushed Hungarian society and the regime further away from the totalitarian pole. Evidence abounds. State control over individual job mobility de jure was lessened when in 1968 workers were allowed to

12. In 1962 Kádár was still to complete the last phase of recollectivization that finished his 1956–62 reconsolidation, but no leader committed to maintaining a system that approximated totalitarianism could have issued such a classic post-totalitarian dictum. For the context of Kádár's speech, see González Enríquez, *Crisis y cambio en Europa del Este,* 9.

13. As Charles Gati explains, "the New Economic Mechanism (NEM), begun in 1968, had introduced a measure of rationality into the economy. By focusing on agriculture, small-scale industry, and the service sector, the reforms succeeded in creating an economy in which plan and market could somehow co-exist and living standards rise as well. Kádár's 'goulash Communism'—perhaps an early version of perestroika—was also assisted by his regime's relative political tolerance and openness—perhaps an early version of glasnost." See his *The Bloc That Failed: Soviet East European Relations in Transition* (Bloomington: Indiana University Press, 1990), 95.

change their jobs, to relocate, and legally to work part-time in private, small-scale industry.[14] The state's near-monopoly over worker income sources was demonopolized to the extent that the proportion of total income "derived from the second economy by about three-quarters of the population amounted to at least two-thirds of wages paid in the first economy."[15] The state monopoly over housing was also broken. By 1984, 55 percent of all new housing in Hungary was constructed by the second economy and was open to private purchase and ownership.[16]

Hungary also made important changes toward increased rule of law, especially toward a regulated framework not of a command economy but of what we have called an *economic society*. In 1982 a new set of regulations passed which legalized property rights in much of the second economy.[17] The political import of this was twofold. On the one hand, for society it reduced the party-state discretionary authority and increased the sphere of legally protected rights and thus the rule of law. On the other hand, for party-state officials, it made it legal for nomenklatura families to diversify their "portfolios" and to participate in the second economy.[18]

This new regulatory framework thus began to alter the career and network opportunities for members of the second economy and the state apparatus alike. The groundwork was laid for a "hollowing out" of the state sector and, indirectly, for "nomenklatura buyouts" seven years before the end of Communism. For the nonagricultural state-controlled cooperative sector, reorganization and restructuring of public property began almost immediately as groups of up to one hundred people could legally "break off from a non-agricultural state-cooperative, taking equipment and capital with them."[19] As Anna Seleny has argued, the second economy in Hungary became high-trust networks of everyday people *and* highly placed and well-connected individuals which, without an explicitly political purpose, began to have political implications. Possibly more than anywhere else, we will analyze in this book how the spread and institutionalization of the

14. See Anna Seleny, "Hidden Enterprise and Property Rights Reform in Socialist Hungary," *Law and Policy* 13 (April 1991):156–58. This article and her 1993 MIT doctoral dissertation in the Political Science Department, "The Long Transformation: Hungarian Socialism 1949–1989," are pioneering works on how the New Economic Mechanism had many unintended consequences in the legal, social, and political arenas and how it began to create an "economic society" in Hungary. For a discussion of "contested language and meanings" within the Hungarian Socialist Workers' Party, see her "Constructing the Discourse of Transformation: Hungary, 1979–82," *East European Politics and Societies* 8, no. 3 (1994): 439–66.

15. Seleny, "Hidden Enterprise and Property Rights," 162.

16. See table 19.5 in János Kornai, *The Socialist System: The Political Economy of Communism* (Princeton: Princeton University Press, 1992), 441. Upon publication this book by a Hungarian economist who was a long-time consulant of Hungarian economic reforms and is now a chairholder in economics at Harvard became an instant classic on the problems of command economies and the limits to efforts to partially reform them.

17. This is discussed at length in Seleny's "The Long Transformation."

18. For the consequences of the new structure of rational-choice opportunities for state managers, see László Urban, "Hungarian Transition from a Public Choice Perspective" in András Bozóki, András Körösényi, and George Schöpflin, eds., *Post-Communist Transition: Emerging Pluralism in Hungary* (London: Pinter Publishers, 1992), 88–95.

19. Seleny, "Hidden Enterprise and Property Rights," 163.

Hungarian second economy makes it difficult empirically or analytically to distinguish between economic society and political society. Some Communist systems *collapsed*, as in Czecholsovakia; others, as in Hungary, *adapted*. In Hungary the complex networks of the second economy were a key part of the nomenklatura's capacity and propensity for adaptation. Political out-of-type change did not begin until early 1989. But economic out-of-type change began in 1982.

Despite these important changes in the arenas of economic society, law, and the state, it is important to stress that Kádár never allowed changes in the leading role of the party. Also, until 1987 there was virtually no significant organized political opposition, and associational life in civil society was quite weak. In these arenas Hungary was still early post-totalitarian.

However, by the mid-1980s the political economy of the Kádár regime—and the Communist party-state—came under increasing pressure. Despite the resumption of economic experiments in 1979, the economy experienced growing problems. Foreign debt soared throughout the 1980s. Indeed, by 1989, public external debt soared to over 16 billion. The country's debt per capita of $1,561 was the largest in the world, dwarfing Brazil's $622 per capita debt.[20] A reform wing in the party became increasingly critical of Kádár and sought out alliances in the party and in society. By 1987 independent groups in society, tacitly supported by party reformers, had also become critical of Kádár. The *samizdat* publication, *Beszélö*, in the first half of 1987 issued a special publication, "Social Contract," that began with the assertion that "Kádár Must Go." A normal *Beszélö* publication had a circulation of 4,000. "Social Contract" was reissued and sold 12,000 copies and was widely read by party reformers, whose leaders, Rezsö Nyers and Imre Pozsgay, met privately with the authors in sympathetic discussions.[21] We believe that these events could not have occurred without a power struggle within the regime already going on and without some legitimacy for both regime moderates and opposition moderates. In fact, by October 1987 Hungary's first opposition protoparty, the Hungarian Democratic Forum, had its organizational meeting, which was attended by Pozsgay.[22]

It is true that before 1989 Hungary had no social movements remotely comparable to Solidarity in Poland or multitudes in the streets as in East Germany or even in Czechoslovakia, but it would be a mistake to see the Hungarian transition as being initiated and controlled solely by reformers in the regime. In 1988 a

20. Per capita debt figures calculated from public and publicly guaranteed long-term debt data in the *World Debt Tables, 1991–1992* (Washington: World Bank), as reported in the *Statistical Yearbook 1993* (New York: United Nations), 1051–53. Population figures from *Statistical Yearbook 1993*, 59–67.

21. The above is based on a conversation of Alfred Stepan in Prague (December 16, 1992) with the principal author of the "Social Contract," the political philosopher János Kis, who later became president of the Alliance of Free Democrats after free elections.

22. Pozsgay's supportive relationship with the Hungarian Democratic Forum is discussed in detail in Robert M. Jenkins, "Movements into Parties: The Historical Transformation of the Hungarian Opposition" (Program on Central and Eastern Europe, Working Papers Series, no. 25, Harvard University, 1993).

plethora of largely self-organized associational groups emerged as new actors. One of the most important of the new social movements was an ecology group who effectively organized demonstrations against a dam on the Danube. The focus of two other important groups that emerged in 1988 was explicitly to advocate an institutional framework that would help engender a stronger and more autonomous civil society. In the area of communications, the Publicity Club was organized by journalists and other professionals to advance freedom of speech. In the legal area 135 lawyers created an Independent Forum of Jurists to help empower civil (and later political) society with sufficient expertise to actively review and revise the growing number of legal and constitutional proposals being raised both by the regime and by the new social groups.[23]

One of the great political problems for the newly elected regimes in Eastern Europe is the question of political representation due to the "flattened" post-totalitarian economic and social landscape. In Hungary, however, the economic reforms begun in 1968—with earlier precedents back to 1953—and given legal recognition in 1982 created a more variegated and pluralist environment in which to articulate interests. Anna Seleny captures this relationship nicely.

In sum, private business expanded more rapidly than many officials expected, and its legal and political institutional consequences have proved surprising. The seemingly endless round of amendments, modifications and subsequent reforms which the Ministry of Finance was forced to undertake between 1982 and 1989 indicates that once property rights are granted to groups thereby newly legally enfranchised, the pressure to broaden those rights grows from its own logic. . . . The net effect of such decrees was the broadening of second-economy entrepreneurs' property rights and space for action. . . . Once endowed with legal status, individual entrepreneurs and various organized groups pressed for further changes. Transmission-belt organizations, responsible for "representing" the interests of the small traditional legal private sector of manufacturers and retailers, were internally disrupted because the government changed the economic landscape overnight without specifying their new mandates. In 1987 entrepreneurs formed their own independent interest representation organization which helped extract concessions vis-à-vis the private sector (e.g., on tax policy); and a year later, entrepreneurs formed a political party. The 1982 reform of private property rights was a turning point . . . it was insufficient to stabilize the economy, further destabilized Party ideology, social attitudes and behavior, and proved incompatible with state-socialism as an institutional-political system. The legalization of private entrepreneurship on a wide scale challenged the state's claims on rights to control not only production but economic organization and association.[24]

Shortly after the entrepreneurs organized, a Union of Scientific Workers was created to be followed by other independent unions. While relatively small and largely confined to intellectual workers, these unions pushed the boundaries of post-totalitarianism in a more pluralist direction. As Andrew Arato states, "all these

23. An excellent analysis of these new social movements is contained in Andrew Arato, "Civil Society in the Emerging Democracies: Poland and Hungary," in Margaret Latua Nugent, ed., *From Leninism to Freedom: The Challenges of Democratization* (Boulder, Colo.: Westview Press, 1992), 127–52.

24. Seleny, "Hidden Enterprise and Property Rights," 165–66.

organizations of the defense of worker interests, influenced by different aspects of the model of Polish Solidarity, understood themselves as promoting a fabric of thick social self organization from below, as building and fighting for a civil society with important elements of participation in economic and political life."[25]

The final arena in which Hungarian opposition forces began to organize was political society. The more politically inclined members of social movements developed protopolitical parties. Populist and somewhat rural and traditional nationalist intellectuals met at Lakitelek in 1987 and formed the Hungarian Democratic Forum (MDF). In March 1988 a protoparty, the Federation of Young Democrats, was formed. In the spring of 1988 a loose alliance of new social movements, greens, journalists, reform economists, and independent student and worker organizations formed a more urban and socially liberal grouping called the Network of Free Initiatives. By autumn 1988 this group formed the basis of the Alliance of Free Democrats. One of the distinctive facts about Hungarian politics is that none of the above-mentioned parties was a historic pre–World War II party; they had instead emerged in mature post-totalitarian Hungary. This combination of new social and political movements contributed, by late 1988, to the passage of a new law of association which in turn helped pave the way for a multiparty system. Once this new law of association was passed, three historic parties—the Independent Smallholders Party, the Social Democratic Party, and the Christian Democratic Party—announced their reactivation.[26]

One of the most frequently asked questions about the Hungarian transition is why the Hungarian Communist Party began to accept competitive politics, even before the Polish Round Table was completed and the first non-Communist government was formed in Poland. To begin to answer this question, we have to step back and look at the changing context of Kádár's and the Communist Party's legitimacy. In chapter 5 we argued that a traditional measure of a regime's legitimacy is whether a particular regime is perceived by its citizens to be "the most appropriate one given the circumstances." For much of the 1970s, the Kádár regime's economic and political policies were widely seen as being relatively successful within the parameters of the "Brezhnev Doctrine." Given the geopolitical constraints of the "Brezhnev Doctrine," the most relevant reference group for Hungarians was the Soviet Union and Eastern Europe.

However, by the late 1980s, even before the so-called "Sinatra Doctrine" was

25. Arato, "Civil Society in the Emerging Democracies," 139.

26. On the emergence and increasing formalization of these opposition parties, see László Lengyel, "The Character of Political Parties in Hungary (Autumn 1989)," in András Bozóki, András Körösényi, and George Schöpflin, eds, *Post-Communist Transition: Emerging Pluralism in Hungary* (London: Pinter Publishers, 1992), 30–44, and Jenkins, "Movements into Parties." For the effective mobilization of pressure that led to a law of association much more democratizing in final form than the regime had originally intended, see Gábor Halmas, "Representation and Civil Society in Hungary: The Recodification of the Right of Assembly and Association," *Law and Policy* 13 (April 1991): 135–47. This is a clear example of the dynamic of "detotalitarianization by societal conquest."

Table 17.1. Hungarian Assessment of Their Declining Quality of Life, Equality, and Personal Political Efficacy: A Five-Country Comparison, 1985 and 1989

	Percentage of Respondents	
Country	1985	1989
"In which country do the people live better?"		
Austria	49.9	80.3
Hungary	28.7	12.7
Soviet Union	4.3	0.9
Czechoslovakia	0.3	0.6
Yugoslavia	0.3	0.3
Romania	0.0	0.1
"In which country is there greater equality among the people?"		
Austria	9.8	48.9
Hungary	17.8	19.6
Soviet Union	38.2	9.5
Czechoslovakia	1.1	3.9
Yugoslavia	0.8	1.3
Romania	0.4	0.9
"In which country do the people have the greatest possibility to participate in political matters?"		
Austria	14.1	52.3
Hungary	23.0	24.0
Soviet Union	25.0	4.7
Czechoslovakia	0.6	0.8
Yugoslavia	1.1	2.6
Romania	0.1	0.0

Source: László Bruszt and János Simon, La mayoría más silenciosa (Budapest: Institute of Social Sciences, 1990). Based upon a poll they administered for the Gallup Poll of Hungary.
Even if we would suspect a certain caution in the 1985 responses, or what is called by polling specialists a spiral of silence, the fact that people expressed their attitudes so freely in 1989 would reflect a significant change in itself. The table does not include other answers, and DK/NA, therefore, does not add up to 100.

formally articulated, the relevant reference group increasingly became Western Europe, especially Hungary's neighbor up the Danube, Austria.[27] Table 17.1 shows how in 1989, after four years of Gorbachev, Hungarians increasingly viewed their situation negatively in areas involving the quality of life, equality, and personal political efficacy.

What is clear from table 17.1 is that Gorbachev's reforms were seen as a relative failure by 1989 and that Austria was seen as overwhelmingly the best on all three measures surveyed, even including the issue area most Communist systems felt was their greatest comparative strength—equality. In this overall context, by 1987 the elements of a complex transition game were coming into place in Hungary.

As Stepan has argued elsewhere, a split in the state apparatus (or in Hungary

27. Vladimir Tismaneanu explains that the "Sinatra Doctrine" was "the Soviet decision to allow each East European country to pursue its own variety of reform." In effect, it allowed them to go "their own way." See his Reinventing Politics: Eastern Europe from Stalin to Havel (New York: Free Press, 1993), 216.

in the "party-state") may set into motion a "downward reach" by part of the state to mobilize part of civil society so as to increase its own power position within the state.[28] This sets the framework for concession. However, if civil society is not strong enough, what is given by one part of the state can, when it has served that state group's purpose, be taken away. But, if opposition forces in society are strong enough, a complex dialectic of "regime concession and societal conquest" may ensue that will help push the overall system toward a boundary change, first in the direction of liberalization and finally crossing the line of a democratic transition.[29] Awareness of the potential for such a political process to occur alerts us to look at some transitions as cases of competitive bidding by parts of the state vis-à-vis civil society. Thus, while the optic of civil society *versus* the state is often correct, part of the growth and empowerment of civil society may be due to a momentary *alliance* of parts of the state with parts of civil society, both parts betting, of course, that in the end they will become the ultimate winner. No faction of the Hungarian Communist Party, even the faction of the most advanced reformer, such as Pozsgay, started regime concessions accepting the fact that it might lead to the loss of power. Why then, did the dialectic of regime concession and societal conquest result in Hungary passing beyond the boundary from mature post-totalitarianism to free competitive democracy?

By 1987 the party-state, in a situation of a growing economic crisis and a new geopolitical context, had at least four distinct factions: (1) a hard line hoping that Gorbachev would fall and interested in imposing a post-1968 Czechoslovak-like "normalization strategy" in Hungary, (2) a status quo group around the aging leader Kádár, (3) a moderate reform group led by Károly Grósz interested in economic decentralization but little political change, except for an increasingly lawbound state, and (4) a reform group led by Pozsgay interested in economic, legal, and political change. Starting in mid-1987 the two party reform factions supported each other and both used the party mechanisms they controlled to help build pressure against Kádár.[30] Kádár's major challenger was Károly Grósz, who became prime minister in July 1987. Grósz used this normally weak position as a

---

28. For Stepan's argument about intrastate conflict and the courtship of civil society, see "State Power and the Strength of Civil Society in the Southern Cone of Latin America," in Peter Evans, Dietrich Rueschemeyer, and Theda Skocpol, eds., *Bringing the State Back In* (Cambridge: Cambridge University Press, 1985), 317–46, and *Rethinking Military Politics: Brazil and the Southern Cone* (Princeton: Princeton University Press, 1988), chaps. 1 and 3.

29. For Stepan's analysis of a "regime concession and societal conquest" dialectic in Brazil, see his *Rethinking Military Politics,* esp. 39, 45–46.

30. It is important to stress that the two reform factions in the party and their numerous technocratic allies had little to do with a Polish style dichotomous "civil society versus the state" dynamic. In fact, the increased space for civil society groups in Hungary was partly due to numerous networks created by reformers *inside the state* with civil society. See the important work by X. L. Deng, which recasts traditional thinking about "civil society versus the state" in his "Institutional Amphibiousness and the Transition from Communism: The Case of China," *British Journal of Political Science* 24 (July 1994): 293–318. Deng correctly cites the work of the Hungarian social scientist Elemér Hankiss as documenting important instances of "institutional amphibiousness" in Hungary (p. 301).

platform from which to criticize Kádár in his campaign to be his successor. An excellent study of the intraparty leadership competition notes that "the Grósz strategy pursued a controlled mobilization and radicalization of the elites to pressure the Kádárist leadership. . . . Grósz went beyond ideology to seek the advice and support of party and non-party alike and, in so doing, fatally undermined Kádár's authority as a national leader."[31]

One of Grósz's tactical allies in this campaign was his reform rival Pozsgay, who had great influence over the media. Pozsgay both helped nonparty social movements gain some access to the media and was in turn helped by them. Pozsgay attended the important organizational meeting of the Hungarian Democratic Forum in September 1987 and ensured the publication of their statement in a party-controlled newspaper. In fact, Pozsgay actually spoke at the meeting and urged the attendees to present an alternative program for reform. One scholar who has studied the transformation of the Hungarian Democratic Forum (MDF) from a social movement to a political party offers the following judgment: "The resources provided by Pozsgay through the People's Patriotic Front—organizational support and access to the media—did play a role in helping the MDF. . . . This group might not have undertaken the formation of an organization without the decisive protection provided by the coalition of party reformers. . . . This alliance benefited both camps. It gave Pozsgay and his reform colleagues popular support in the internal [Communist Party] struggle."[32]

The dynamic between regime concession and societal conquest was dramatically clear in the acceleration of events in early 1989. The Hungarian political scientist, András Körösényi, graphically captures how an increasingly empowered civil society and numerous protoparties pushed Hungary's post-totalitarian regime to the brink of an out-of-type political change by recognizing the legitimacy of multiparty elections.

What pushed events forward was Pozsgay's action at the end of January 1989. Pozsgay recognized that there could be no consensus without the revaluation of the events of 1956. While Károly Grósz enjoyed the mountains of the Alps in Switzerland, Pozsgay declared in a radio interview that what happened in Hungary in 1956 was not a counter-revolution, as the official Communist historiography considered the event, but a "national uprising." The effect was dramatic. Grósz called together an extraordinary session of the Central Committee of the HSWP [the Communist Party] in two weeks time. During these two weeks hundreds of social and political organizations expressed their agreement with Pozsgay, or at least their appreciation of his statement. Backed by public opinion and the press, Pozsgay and the reformers won the battle. The Central Committee session of February accepted not only the revaluation of the events of 1956, but the multiparty system as well.[33]

31. George Schöpflin, Rudolf Tökés, and Ivan Völgyes, "Leadership Change and Crisis in Hungary," *Problems of Communism* (Sept.–Oct. 1988): 34, 36.

32. Jenkins, "Movements into Parties," 67, 60.

33. András Körösényi, "The Decay of Communist Rule in Hungary," in Bozóki, Körösényi, and Schöpflin, eds., *Post-Communist Transition*, 6–7.

With the Hungarian Communist Party's acceptance of multiparty elections, especially with Pozsgay's explicit statement that multiparty competition "entails the possibility of losing power," a new regime-society relationship had emerged and a democratic transition was close to being born.[34] By our regime criteria of pluralism, ideology, mobilization, and leadership, Hungary by February 1989 had already arrived—before the dramatic events of the Polish election—at the brink of a boundary change away from post-totalitarianism. The rest is history, well told by others.[35] However, as comparativists we would like to review how Hungary's mature post-totalitarianism opened up a transition *path* not available to Czechoslovakia and Bulgaria—or to any other post-totalitarian regime in Eastern Europe. In table 4.2 we referred to this path as *reforma pactada–ruptura pactada.*

Most of the elements for understanding why Hungary had this option in the first place have been presented. However, not all options that are *available* are *realized.* Let us be more explicit about what the *reforma pactada–ruptura pactada* requires and why this possible path was actually taken in Hungary.

Four of the most important facilitating conditions for a *reforma pactada–ruptura pactada* path are that (1) both moderates in the regime and moderates in the democratic opposition have some power capacity, (2) both of the above "players" come to believe that, considering all the alternatives, negotiations are the preferred alternative, (3) both moderate players have and/or develop strategic and tactical negotiating capacity, and (4) the moderate players become the dominant players on their side.

We believe that we have clearly demonstrated that both regime moderates and democratic opposition moderates had some power capacity. Negotiation became the preferred possibility for both moderate players because both sides were aware that they could not triumph by their own efforts alone, both recognized the depth of the social and economic crisis, and both feared what a repeat of 1956 would do to their futures. The memory of the Hungarian revolution in fact helped both moderate sets of players come to the negotiating table and helped make them the dominant players of their side. László Bruszt and David Stark nicely depict how the legacy of 1956 affected regime and opposition alike. "For the Communist elite,

34. The Pozsgay quote was in an interview in *Magyar Hirlap,* an official Communist Party daily, and was cited in Charles Gati, *The Bloc That Failed: Soviet–East European Relations in Transition* (Bloomington: Indiana University Press, 1990), 171. For the symbolic significance of the Pozsgay statement, see András Sajo, "Round Tables in Hungary" (Center for the Study of Constitutionalism in Eastern Europe, University of Chicago Law School, working paper, no. 2, August 1991), 5.

35. Three excellent studies are László Bruszt and David Stark, "Remaking the Political Field in Hungary: From the Politics of Confrontation to the Politics of Competition," in Ivo Banac, ed., *Eastern Europe in Revolution* (Ithaca, N.Y.: Cornell University Press, 1992), 13–55; Timothy Garton Ash, *We the People: The Revolution of '89 Witnessed in Warsaw, Budapest, Berlin and Prague* (London: Granta Books, 1990), 47–60, which gives a particularly graphic account of how the symbolic and power relations were changed further in the direction of democrats by Nagy's reburial; and the previously cited book by the Spanish social scientist who makes interesting comparisons of the Spanish and Hungarian transitions, González Enríquez, *Crisis y cambio en Europa del Este,* esp. 362–68.

the ghosts of 1956 were the memories of the fury that can be unleashed when society has been pushed beyond its limits. It was above all the *fear of society* that so deeply inscribed in the Communist leadership an instinct to do everything to avoid another 1956. As the economic and political crisis deepened throughout 1988, so increased the references to 1956 in party leaders' speeches."[36] Likewise, for much of the democratic opposition, Bruszt and Stark argue,

it was the lesson of the Russian intervention in 1956 that made the leaders of the newly emerging social and political groups hesitant to question the legitimacy of the regime and to seek, instead, a compromise with its leaders. Mikhail Gorbachev did not automatically alter those calculations, for the limits of his toleration were neither clearly articulated nor yet tested in this period. . . . The first clear test of the end of the Brezhnev Doctrine was the Soviets' acceptance of the non-Communist Mazowiecki government in Poland [August 1989].[37]

The opposition in early 1989 was made up of numerous parties and social movements. The regime made an attempt to enter into negotiations with each fragment of the opposition singly. However, a major step forward in developing the democratic opposition's negotiating capacity was their refusal to negotiate singly. They first created their own "Opposition Round Table" on March 23, 1989. The eight groups who participated in the Opposition Round Table represented conflicting interests and opinions. But, they greatly enhanced their strategic and tactical bargaining capacity by forging an internal agreement that the central purpose of any round table with the regime should not be about social policies or sharing power but *fundamentally* about the details for arriving at a free election by which future power in Hungary would be determined.[38] Unlike any other Eastern European round table, negotiations were between the regime and an already constituted political society, not civil society. The political groups had to reach an agreement among themselves before they could or would negotiate. In fact, in critical events like the reburial of Nagy, political society convoked and organized civil society.

When the National Trilateral Negotiations (the Round Table) began, parts of the regime had not fully accepted the principle of free and competitive elections. However, in a context where political space was constantly being reconfigured by the extraordinary outpouring of national sentiment around Nagy's reburial and the Polish elections, Pozsgay and the Communist Party reformers became dominant within the party and moved toward accepting the uncertainty of democratic elections.[39]

36. Bruszt and Stark, "Remaking the Political Field in Hungary," 24, emphasis in original.
37. Ibid., 25.
38. See László Bruszt, "1989: The Negotiated Revolution of Hungary," *Social Research* (Summer 1990): 365–88, esp. 375; András Bozóki, "Hungary's Road to Systemic Change: The Opposition Round Table," *Eastern European Politics and Societies* 7, no. 2 (1993): 276–308, esp. 285; and Sajo, "Round Tables in Hungary," 20–25.
39. László Bruszt, as national secretary of the Democratic League of Trade Unions, was an official participant in the Opposition Round Table and the Government-Opposition Round Table. Because he both

At this point we need to pause and explore why the reformers in the Communist Party could accept the uncertainty of elections as the best alternative and get many other weighty elements of the party, state managers, and the army to acquiesce in their decision. From the reform Communist viewpoint, a successful crackdown of the regime, such as that attempted by the coup coalition in the USSR in August 1991, could well have led to their purge, as in Czechoslovakia in 1968. However, the reform Communists considered that they had a reasonably good chance to do well in competitive elections. In fact, a June 1989 survey indicated that they would win the first plurality, 26 percent, and that if presidential elections were held soon no opposition candidate had the name recognition and support of Pozsgay.[40] Even if they did not win the first plurality, there was the prospect that they could be legitimate contestants in a democratic multiparty system. As Bruszt and Stark said of the reform Communists' calculations, "their perceptions of the weakness of the opposition and their assessment of their own electoral prospects gave them confidence. . . . With this they made the decisive step of accepting the principle of 'certain institutions of uncertain outcomes' that is at the core of liberal democracy."[41]

Certainly, parts of the party hardline and secret police were not prepared to accept this uncertainty principle, but a weighty part of the party-state, especially the state-enterprise managers, who were normally "pragmatic conservatives," had to make their calculation as to whether it was more in their interest to support a crackdown or possibly to side with the reform Communists. While we will not go so far as to argue that the golden parachute possibility of "nomenklatura buyouts" made state-enterprise managers *active coalitional* partners with Pozsgay, we do believe that the state-enterprise managers' good prospects of "converting" their locational assets as public sector managers into personal economic assets may help explain their *passive acquiescence* in the rise of reform Communists within

---

was a trade union officer and knew some Polish, Bruszt was sent as an observer to the Polish Round Table. His "1989: The Negotiated Revolution of Hungary" is particularly acute in demonstrating the interactive comparative dynamics of events in Poland and Hungary and how this dynamic helped the reform Communists become dominant in the Hungarian Socialist Workers (Communist) Party.

40. In the same June 1989 Gallup poll in Hungary, the largest opposition party, the Hungarian Democratic Forum, received only 9 percent. Most important, as late as the fall of 1989, Pozsgay was convinced that, because of the lack of name recognition of opposition leaders, he could win a direct presidential election. For the poll, see Elemér Hankiss, "In Search of a Paradigm," *Daedalus* (Winter 1990): 206. For a review of a variety of polls, many of which in 1989 offered some encouragement to Communist reformers, see László Bruszt and János Simon, "The Change in Citizens' Political Orientations during the Transition to Democracy in Hungary (Reflected by Public Opinion Survey and Electoral Studies, 1990–1991)," (Budapest: Institute of Political Science, Hungarian Academy of Sciences, 1991). As late as July 6, 1989, Sajo characterized the general opinion of the pro-Prozsgay participants in the round tables as follows: "It was taken for granted that the winner of the popular presidential elections would be Pozsgay." Sajo, "Round Tables in Hungary," 25.

41. Bruszt and Stark, "Remaking the Political Field in Hungary," 45. Their reference to the "principle of uncertain outcomes" in their internal quote refers to Adam Przeworksi's "Democracy as a Contingent Outcome of Conflicts," in Jon Elster and Rune Slagstad, eds., *Constitutionalism and Democracy* (New York: Cambridge University Press, 1988), 59–80.

the Communist Party.[42] As László Urban argues, the opportunity structure opened up by the second economy altered their rational choice calculations.

Why did the reformers gain control gradually within the Communist Party and within the government, and why were they not blocked and replaced by conservatives who resisted the transformation? The short answer is that the reformers took over the lead easily because the pragmatic conservatives let them do that. Why? Because the political supporters of the pragmatic conservatives, the rent-seekers of the old regime, had their own business to take care of, which offered high positive returns for them as opposed to organizing political resistance against the transformation of the system.[43]

A pioneering survey of new elites shows that for some state managers this calculation turned out to be correct. Eighty-one percent of the new private sector economic elite in Hungary in 1993 had been employed by the party-state in areas concerning the economy in 1988 (50 percent in managerial jobs in the state sector of the economy and 30 percent in economic command posts).[44]

What about the army? A crackdown, especially one that could not count on the Soviet army, would probably have had to use the Hungarian army as well as the Hungarian secret police. But, unlike the Yugoslav Army, with its predominantly Serbian officer corps, who perceived it to be in their interest actively to support the war with Croatia and ethnic cleansing in Bosnia-Herzegovina, or the Polish Army, which was a leading part of the party-state from 1981 to 1989, or the Romanian army, which helped capture the Romanian uprising for the nomenklatura, the Hungarian army stayed absolutely neutral during the Hungarian transition. Once again, given Hungary's recent political history, the army calculated that a passive acceptance of peaceful negotiated change would not hurt its interests. János Simon, in one of the first evaluations of the role of the army in the Hungarian transition in 1989, argues that "in 1956 the [Hungarian] military either supported the revolution or deserted from the army, but there was no organized force which supported the Russian invasion. . . . From the very beginning of the regime change the demand of the withdrawal of Soviet troops was on the agenda." The army's gamble paid off in terms of trust. In an annual study of citizens' trust

---

42. The "passive acquiescent" behavior of Hungarian state managers was not qualitatively different from the passive acquiescent behavior of capitalist business elites in transitional cases we have discussed such as Spain, Uruguay, or Chile. In fact, the only transition case in our set, where some entrepreneurs were, for a while, "active coalitional partners" with the democratic opposition, was in Brazil. See Fernando H. Cardoso, "Entrepreneurs and the Transition Process: The Brazilian Case," in O'Donnell, Schmitter, and Whitehead, *Transition from Authoritarian Rule: Comparative Perspectives*, 137–53.

43. See the previously cited Urban, "Hungarian Transition from a Public Choice Perspective," in Bozóki, Körösényi and Schöpflin, *Post-Communist Transition*, 91–92.

44. However, if one takes the entire group of the old economic elite in 1988, 23.4 percent had experienced downward mobility by 1993 and 47.6 percent were forced into early retirement. See Szonja Szelényi, Iván Szelényi, and Imre Kovách, "The Fragmented Hungarian Elites: Circulation in Politics, Reproduction in Economy," in Iván Szelényi, Edmund Wnuk-Lipínski, and Donald Treiman, eds., *Circulation of Elites? Old and New Elites in Post-Communist Society*, tentative title of a book-length manuscript in process.

in institutions, in every year between 1989 and 1992, the army ranked the highest of the six institutions polled.[45]

Given the overall position within the party, the state apparatus, and the army on the one hand and the politically organized opposition on the other hand, it should be clear why a *reforma pactada–ruptura pactada* was not only a possible path but the actual path.

Let us now briefly look at what the specificities of Hungary's mature post-totalitarianism implied for the tasks the incoming democratic government and Parliament had to address before democracy could be consolidated. In table 1.1 we spelled out how one could conceptualize a consolidated democracy as being composed of five major inter-relating arenas. It might be too early to address the question as to whether or not Hungary is democratically consolidated. However, it is not too early to say that, if one reviews all five polity arenas, Hungary, despite important stateness problems and civil society representation problems that we will discuss, had significant advantages vis-à-vis the tasks of consolidation over the other East European countries that began transitions in 1989.

The first arena we will consider is political society. Unlike any other post-totalitarian country in Eastern Europe, Hungary's political society had assumed much of its organizational structure *before* the transition. In fact, though the founding election was not held until March 1990, by December 1988, fifteen months before the election, *every* one of the six parties that eventually won representation in the Hungarian Parliament as a result of the 1990 elections had already been formed.[46] Furthermore, unlike Poland, organized political parties that were already beginning to make the necessary shift from the unitary *we* of civil society to being competitive components of political society were the weightiest parts of the opposition in the round table.

From our theoretical and comparative perspective, political society made a further step toward the capacity to function well in that, unlike the Philippines, Korea, or any country in Latin America, Hungary selected a pure parliamentary model of government. Pozsgay wanted a direct election for the presidency before free elections for the Parliament. In fact, he won support during the round table from the Hungarian Democratic Forum for a direct election of the president in November 1989.[47] In our judgment, if such an election had occurred, Hungary

45. János Simon, *Fieldmarshal's Baton and Peace (Judgements on the Role of the Military in Hungary during the Regime-Change between 1988–1992)* (Budapest: Erasmus Foundation for Democracy, 1993), quote from 7–8, poll data found in table 3.

46. For tables on votes and seats, see András Körösényi, "The Hungarian Parliamentary Election, 1990," in Bozóki, Körösényi and Schöpflin, *Post-Communist Transition*, 72–81. In fact, these *same* six parties were the only parties returned to Parliament after the 1994 elections. No new parties entered Parliament. No old parties were eliminated. See Attila Ágh and Sándor Kurtán, "The 1990 and 1994 Parliamentary Elections in Hungary: Continuity and Change in the Political System," in Attila Ágh and Sándor Kurtán, eds., *Democratization and Europeanization in Hungary: The First Parliament, 1990–1994* (Budapest: Hungarian Centre for Democracy Studies, 1995), 13–26.

47. See Bruszt and Stark, "Remaking the Political Field in Hungary," 48–50.

would have had a semipresidential form of government with some of the attendant problems of this form of governance. Likewise, the constitutional revision process, the first free parliamentary elections, and the government formation process all might have been complicated somewhat by a sitting president legitimated by direct election. In the event, two democratic opposition parties (the Alliance for Free Democrats and the Young Democrats) were sufficiently well organized and sufficiently capable of strategic and tactical behavior that they were able to gather the constitutionally mandated number of signatures for a referendum, one of whose five items was whether parliamentary elections should be held before or after the president was elected. After a spirited campaign, the "parliamentary elections first" option won by a narrow margin. The newly elected Parliament, after deliberations, then decided to elect the president indirectly.[48]

The contrast between Hungary and Poland concerning the arena of political society is extremely sharp. The Hungarian Round Table agreement did not lead to a power-sharing formula but to direct popular elections of the Parliament. The early structuring of political parties and the relatively unconstrained negotiations led to free and competitive elections in March and April 1990, whereas in Poland the first fully competitive parliamentary elections were not held until October 1991. This meant that in Poland the democratic parties suffered the consequences of assuming the responsibilities of government twenty-one months before free parliamentary elections.[49]

Hungary did not have the constitution-making formula that we argued in chapter 5 was optimal, in that a new constitution was not made by a freely elected legislature or constituent assembly and then submitted to a referendum. Rather, all of the major parties during the round table and the two major democratic parties in a pact after the parliamentary elections heavily amended the existing constitution to make it workable.[50] However, in a context where political parties al-

48. The above discussion was informed by an interview of Alfred Stepan with János Kis, Budapest, July 5, 1991, and the previously cited articles by Bozóki and by Bruszt and Stark.

49. This may help account for the fact that, whereas in Poland voter turnout was reported as 42 percent for the first free parliamentary election, in Hungary the first round of the parliamentary elections in March 1990 had a reported voter turnout of 63 percent. Also, in Poland "commentators blamed the low turnout on disaffection with the Solidarity led government's draconian economic austerity measures . . . and on confusion about the programmes of the more than 80 competing political parties and dozens of associations." See *Kessings Record of World Events: 1990*, 37464–65, 37325, respectively, quotation from p. 37465. However, we would like to note that the number of parties appearing on the ballot in almost all "founding elections" is normally extremely large. In most cases the voters quickly whittle them down, as they did in Hungary. In fact, in Hungary fifty-four parties were registered in 1989, of which only twelve managed to satisfy the requirements, intelligently established, to appear on the national list. Indeed, only nineteen parties even presented provincial lists. The earlier structuring of political society in Hungary allowed, in contrast to Poland, a reasonably well-structured party system to emerge. See González Enríquez, *Crisis y cambio en Europa del Este*, 149–50, and Körösényi, "The Hungarian Parliamentary Election, 1990," 74–81.

50. For the constitution-amending process and its results, see Andrew Arato, "Legitimation and Constitution Making in Hungary" (paper prepared for the American Sociological Society Annual Meeting, Miami Beach, August 16, 1993), and András Bozóki, "Political Transition and Consolidated Change in Hungary," in Bozóki, Körösényi and Schöpflin, *Post-Communist Transition*, 60–71.

ready existed and where there was no sitting elected president to pre-empt decisions, the debate about possible governing formulas was broadly informed by
modern European democratic constitutional thinking and practice.[51] While suboptimal, Hungary's approach rapidly produced the rules of the game for political
society, a rule of law, and procedures for adjudicating a hierarchy of governmental and state authority. Hungary never had constitutional impasse of the sort we
analyzed for Poland and will analyze for Czechoslovakia, the USSR, and Russia.
Likewise, while Hungary's constitution-making process lacks the full "origin
legitimacy" of a voted constituent assembly or the "ratification legitimacy" of a
referendum on the constitution, the relatively consensual process of amending
the constitution avoided a sense of "majoritarian imposition," which, as we will
see, led significant minorities in Bulgaria and Romania to question the legitimacy
of the constitution. Hungary also did not face the decisional paralysis produced
by the fictive soviet-type federal system that contributed to the disintegration of
the former USSR, Czechoslovakia, and Yugoslavia. Finally, Hungary's hierarchy of
legal authority precluded a war of laws like the one that plagued Gorbachev's
USSR and Yeltsin's Russia. Nonetheless, the fact that Hungary had amended a
Communist-made constitution, rather than creating a new one, was still a source
of political conflicts in 1995.

In the arena of economic society, property laws, contract laws, capital market,
and banking structures, all had an earlier pretransition start in Hungary than in
any other country in Eastern Europe. Much of the regulatory framework for what
we call an *institutionalized economic society* was in place before the first democratically elected government of Prime Minister Antall assumed office. As one
analyst has summed up,

The actions of the old regime made matters much easier for the Antall government: the legalization of the second economy wherein resided the entrepreneurial skills which would put
Hungary at a comparative advantage vis-à-vis the other East European countries after the political transition; the launching of a capital market and a commercial banking system capable
of providing the intermediary services vital to the privatization effort; the establishment of the
legal mechanisms necessary for the launching of new private firms and the transformation of

51. In the constitution-amending process, Hungary adopted the famous German (and later Spanish)
"constructive vote of confidence" formula, which helps avoid excessive government instability in that a vote
of no confidence can pass only if there exists a positive majority for an alternative government. Hungary
also created a strong constitutional court, which on a number of occasions has checked the government's
tendency to abuse its majority. On the constitutional court see Ethan Klingsberg, "Hungary: Safeguarding
the Transition," *East European Constitutional Review* 2, no. 2 (1993): 44–48. The electoral law they designed
also helps avoid excessive party fragmentation because some districts are single member and other districts
have proportional representation based on a high 4 percent threshold. However, unlike the German law,
which ensures the election of individual candidates in the districts and a reasonable level of proportional-
ity at the national level, the Hungarian law makes possible a significant over-representation of the most successful party or parties. This element of over-representation contributed to what Douglas Rae would call a
"manufactured majority" in the 1994 election.

existing state enterprises into private ownership forms; the enactment of the most forgiving foreign investment laws in existence in Eastern Europe.[52]

In the above quotation it is not just the size of the second economy that is critical, but that this new market is part of an institutionalized and thus more predictable framework. Our statement about Hungary's relatively developed economic society is not merely our academic judgment. Self-interested financial leaders will buy bonds at low premiums only if they believe that the risk is acceptable. An institutionalized economic society helps produce this lower risk environment. Two of the most influential assessors of comparative "sovereign risk" are Moody's Investors Service and Standard and Poor's. Amazingly, within just three years of Hungary's 1990 elections, in all of Latin America (countries with a long background of capitalist economies and erratic economic societies), only Chile was accorded a higher credit rating than Hungary.[53] Foreign investors also made a very positive assessment of Hungary's comparative attractiveness. In 1991, for example, they invested as much money in Hungary as they did in the rest of Eastern Europe combined.[54]

Concerning the question of a usable state apparatus, as in every East European country there were some demands to purge former members of the nomenklatura and the security apparatus. Given Hungary's relatively open educational system, which permitted many policy specialists to visit or teach routinely in Western Europe or the United States, the high level of informal contacts between party reformers and many parts of the democratic opposition, and the fact that the Hungarian state had become increasingly subject to economic processes, institutions, and a regulatory framework, the societal demand for revolutionary purges and ex post facto justice was substantially lower in Hungary, as we shall see, than in a frozen post-totalitarian country such as Czechoslovakia. In these circumstances most technical experts and even judges were considered usable by much of the new

52. See David Bartlett, "The Political Economy of Privatization: Property Reform and Democracy in Hungary," *East European Politics and Societies* (winter 1992): 73–118, citation from 104–5.

53. On Standard and Poor's finely tuned twenty-one-grade scale ranging from the most creditworthy ranking of AAA to D (for default), Chile had a BBB and Hungary was one rung lower at BB+. Mexico tied Hungary with BB+. Oil-rich but politically troubled Venezuela was given a lower rating of BB. Brazil, Argentina, and Russia were unranked. Moody's uses a somewhat different formula but ranked Hungary three grades above Argentina and four grades above Brazil. Hungary's ratings are all the more impressive when one remembers that in 1988 Hungary had a per capita foreign debt more than twice as high as Brazil's; see John F. H. Purcell et al., "Rating of Sovereign, Sovereign-supported, Local Government, and Supranational Issuers" (New York: Solomon Brothers, January 8, 1993). The ratings in our text are taken from a June 16, 1993, update of the above document.

54. Hungary has only 10 percent of Eastern Europe's population, but was the recipient of more foreign private capital in 1991—over $1.4 billion worth—than all the other countries in the region combined. Dirk W. Damrau, "The Role of Foreign Investment in East European Privatization: Hungary, Poland and Czechoslovakia," in John R. Lampe, ed., *Creating Capital Markets in Eastern Europe* (Baltimore: Johns Hopkins University Press, 1992), 33–46, quote from p. 44.

democratic government. A qualified purge law was passed by the Parliament but overturned by the Constitutional Court.[55] In 1993 there were further efforts in Parliament to pass ex post facto "lustration" laws, but their focus was largely restricted to those who had played major coercive roles in the 1956 revolution.[56]

Three factors that helped Hungary handle the potential crisis of the state due to excessive lustration laws deserve special mention. First, all political actors, including the former Communists, who participated in the negotiated transition to democracy via the round tables acquired at least some political capital, a source of political capital not generated for the former Communists in frozen posttotalitarian Czechoslovakia, where the regime, as we shall see, simply collapsed. Second, the indirectly elected president Arpád Gönz, whose office and power had its ultimate legitimization in the freely elected Parliament, skillfully and authoritatively used his constitutionally granted moderating powers to refer doubtful legislation to the Constitutional Court. Third, the Constitutional Court acted within its charter and maintained its legitimacy and authority even though it reversed more parliamentary laws than is the norm in Western European consolidated democracies.

The last of our five arenas is civil society. Here we have a bit of a paradox. Some Hungarian analysts called 1988 the year of civil society and 1989 the year of political society.[57] This should have prepared the ground for a mutually supportive relationship of the type we discussed in chapter 1. However, political society after 1989 effectively demobilized civil society. The parliamentary majority of the government was sufficiently strong in 1990–93 that they tended to neglect inputs from civil society. The government also blocked legislation that would have allowed wider civil control of and access to the media. We agree with those analysts such as Arato who believe that Hungarian democracy would be improved by the creation of more effective and more diverse ways for civil society to exercise a mediating effect on political society. Many potentially important interests, such as social democratic constituencies, were not really represented in the opposition parties that emerged during the transition.[58]

55. See the special forum on the Hungarian Constitutional Court decision that overturned the retroactivity law in *East European Constitutional Review* (summer 1992): 17–22.

56. See Edith Oltay, "Hungary Attempts to Deal with Its Past," *RFE/RL Research Report* 2, no. 18 (1993): 6–10.

57. This phrase was intended to call attention to the rapid growth of civil society in 1988 and to its subsequent immediate conversion into political society in 1989. As Bruszt and Stark explain, "the transition from social movements to political parties could be measured in months rather than years." They go on to explain that the leaders' mobilization of civil society against the state "was brief; and the week that this mobilization crescendoed on June 16, 1989, was the same week that it began rapidly to subside. The summer of 1989 was not a season of organizing society but of negotiating with other political parties." Bruszt and Stark, "Remaking the Political Field in Hungary," 52–53.

58. See, for example, the discussion of why the social democratic constituency was under-represented in Tamás Kolosi, Iván Szelényi, Szonja Szelényi, and Bruce Western, "The Making of Political Fields in Post-Communist Transition (Dynamics of Class and Party in Hungarian Politics, 1989–1990)," in Bozóki, Körösényi, and Schöpflin, eds., *Post-Communist Transition*, 132–62.

There is a debate in Hungary as to whether this civil society–political society imbalance is reversible. János Simon reviewed some public opinion questions that were asked in 1985, 1989, and 1991. Two findings struck us as particularly important. First, on all twelve issue areas polled citizens wanted *more* from the government in 1991 than in 1985. Second, in an impressive continuing upward trend, citizens increasingly said that, if their interests were violated, they "could do something about it" at the local and the national level.[59] If the media are free, if people have the right to organize, and if elections are fair, future elections may provide an opportunity for an improved representation of civil society within political society.

Let us close our discussion of Hungary with a word about stateness. At the Treaty of Trianon in 1920, Hungary was severely truncated. Hungary lost *two-thirds* of its former territory, *three-fifths* of the total prewar population, and *one-third* of the Hungarian-speaking population.[60] Hungarians living under nationalist governments in Romania, Slovakia, and Serbian-controlled Vojvodina are a constant issue in Hungarian politics. For democrats, the issue is the advocacy of the human rights of Hungarians living abroad. For some of the rightist nationalists, it is a question of irredenta, as it was for German and Austrian rightists during the interwar years. The potential for delegitimating a democratic government if it does not "protect" all Hungarians and for system blame politics based on irredenta was real. Some of the greatest struggles within the ruling coalition of 1990–94 revolved around this issue. A vice-president, István Csurka, of the major party in the coalition, the Hungarian Democratic Forum, issued a racist manifesto.[61] In a less politically developed environment, the government probably would have turned to an increasingly nationalist and nondemocratic course.[62] Indeed, the Hungarian Democratic Forum equivocated and was slow to respond to Csurka's provocation. Eventually, with the standing of the Hungarian Democratic Forum in the opinion polls at an all-time low, elections looming in 1994, and a desire to be "coalitionable," the ruling party expelled the racist-nationalist faction's leader, Csurka.

With a war on their border, refugees in their cities, anxiety about maintaining their standard of living, and pressure from the European Union for minority

59. János Simon, "Post-paternalist Political Culture in Hungary: Relationships between Citizens and Politics during and after the 'Melancholic Revolution' (1989–1991)," *Communist and Post-Communist Studies* (June 1993): 226–38.

60. Joseph Rothschild, *East Central Europe between the Two World Wars* (Seattle: University of Washington Press, 1974), 155.

61. See Edith Oltay, "Hungarian Democratic Forum Rent by Dispute over Extremists," *RFE/RL Research Report* 1, no. 47 (1992). George Soros effectively challenged Csurka's declaration both inside Hungary and on the op-ed page of the *New York Times*.

62. Only Romania, which has manipulated Hungarian threats, scored higher on the sense of threat from neighboring countries in the survey of the countries reported in Richard Rose and Christian Haerpfer, "Adapting to Transformation in Eastern Europe: New Democracies Barometer—II," *Studies in Public Policy*, no. 212 (1993): table 19.

treaties with their neighbors, irredentist nationalism that could lead to internal and external conflict did not look like a winning electoral formula in Hungary. In fact, in the 1994 parliamentary elections, the two extreme nationalist parties, Csurka's Hungarian Truth and Life Party and the Green Party, received 1.6 percent and 0.7 percent of the vote, respectively, and did not get into Parliament. This vote was less than a fifth of the number of votes extreme right-nationalist parties had received in France in 1993 or in Italy in 1994.[63]

Despite the 1994 election results, it would be a mistake to believe that nationalist and stateness issues will disappear from the political agenda in Hungary. These issues will no doubt reappear in a more modern form and may affect the quality of democracy in Hungary, but in our judgment they will probably not stop democracy from being consolidated. Mature post-totalitarian and now democratic Hungary has managed its stateness problem reasonably well.

CZECHOSLOVAKIA: TRANSITION BY THE COLLAPSE OF "FROZEN" POST-TOTALITARIANISM

The Czech lands of modern Czechoslovakia, as a component of the Austrian part of the Habsburg Empire, had one of the strongest traditions of law in Eastern Europe. Czechoslovakia, until its partition and occupation by Germany in the aftermath of the Munich Agreement, was also the only country in Eastern Europe to experience uninterrupted democracy from its independence in 1918 until 1938. Finally, Czechoslovakia also had the most developed industry and the most fully literate population in Eastern Europe.[64] This pre-Communist legacy and the fact that Prague is west of Vienna and is the Central European capital closest to Berlin, the de facto political center of Europe, means that the homogeneous Czech Republic, its stateness problem behind it, has reasonably good prospects to become a developed, democratic member of Western Europe.

However, Czechoslovakia, in sharp contrast to Hungary, was not able to have a negotiated transition. After ten days of public demonstrations, the regime simply collapsed. The provisional government that emerged from the Velvet Revolution had strong antipolitics tendencies and rejected an opportunity to develop statewide political parties. Likewise, the provisional government was sufficiently uninterested in the formal structures of decision making that it did not focus on

---

63. In France, Le Pen's National Front received 12.4 percent of the votes in the first round parliamentary elections in 1993. In Italy, the neofascist National Alliance, formerly known as the Italian Social Movement, received 13.5 percent of the direct PR votes in Italy's 1994 parliamentary elections, as reported in *Kessings Record of World Events: 1993*, 39381–82, and *1994*, 39918–20, respectively.

64. For an appreciative comparative assessment of law and democracy in interwar Czechoslovkia, see Jacques Rupnik, *The Other Europe* (London: Weidenfeld and Nicolson, 1988), 3–23, esp. 13–18. In terms of an overall industrial complex, the Bohemian—or Czech-lands—part of the Austro-Hungarian empire was more advanced than the Austrian part.

changing the fictive Soviet-style federal constitution until it was too late to rene-
gotiate and save the federation. Finally, the elected Parliament of Czechoslovakia
passed one of the most morally and democratically dubious pieces of ex post
facto state purging legislation in all of East Europe.[65] To understand why and how
the above events occurred, it is important to analyze certain central characteristics of the rulers and the democratic opposition in Czechoslovakia's frozen post-
totalitarian regime.

Let us first look at the rulers. Alone in Eastern Europe, the Communist Party in
the interwar years enjoyed the legal right to participate in the political system. Indeed, in Czechoslovakia, Skilling says the party was regarded as a "legitimate heir of
Austrian social democracy."[66] After 1941 the Czechoslovak Communists supported
the Soviet efforts to fight the Nazi occupation. Both the Soviet Union and the local
Communist Party emerged from World War II in a vastly more favorable light in
Czechoslovakia than they did in Poland. In fact, in the first free parliamentary elections in the postwar period the Communists emerged with a plurality of 38 percent.[67] The Communist Party thus had a strong base to build on in Czechoslovakia.

After the 1948 Communist coup, Czechoslovaks became subject to extensive
repression which "left the country as, arguably, the most Stalinist of all the peoples democracies." This dogmatic Czechoslovakian Stalinism endured intact after
Stalin's death. As late as 1957 the party chief denounced the word *destalinization*
as being synonymous with "weakness and yielding to the forces of reaction."[68]
The historically somewhat weak (especially in the Czech lands) Catholic Church
was subject to more systematic and effective repression than in any other country
in Eastern Europe.[69]

65. The comparison with Hungary is captured on the cover title page of *East European Constitutional Review* (Spring 1992): "Backward-looking Justice in Czechoslovakia" and "Forward-looking Justice in Hungary." The campaign in Czechoslovakia is called *lustration;* its Latin roots lie in the concept of "purifying" sacrifice. The law was denounced by most international legal and human rights groups. A major source for the compilation of the lists of collaborators came from the Ministry of Interior files of people they approached to collaborate. If a person's name appeared in the files, there was a near presumption of guilt. Only those accused of the lower level of collaboration had a right of appeal. Higher level Communist officials had few appeal rights. See Vojtech Cepl, "Ritual Sacrifices," *East European Constitutional Review* (Spring 1992): 24–26. For a strong critique from a human rights perspective, see the article by the executive director of the Helsinki Watch Committee, Jeri Laber, *New York Review of Books,* April 23, 1992. For a comparative analysis of Czechoslovakia's particularly dubious lustration procedures, see Herman Schwartz, "Lustration in Eastern Europe," *Parker School Journal of East European Law* 1, no. 2 (1994): 141–71.

66. See H. Gordon Skilling, *Czechoslovakia's Interrupted Revolution* (Princeton: Princeton University Press, 1976), 3–10, quote on p. 6.

67. For the comparative strength of the Czechoslovak Communists after World War II, see Rothschild, *Return to Diversity,* 89–97, and Jan Urban, "The Politics of Power and Humiliation," in Tim D. Whipple, ed., *After the Velvet Revolution: Václav Havel and the New Leaders of Czechoslovakia Speak Out* (New York: Freedom House, 1991), esp. 269–70.

68. Both of the above quotes are from Rothschild, *Return to Diversity,* 166.

69. For the regime's comprehensive five-part strategy to control the Catholic Church and the church's slight recovery after 1986, see Sabrina Petra Ramet, "The Catholic Church in Czechoslovakia, 1948–1991," *Studies in Comparative Communism* (Dec. 1991): 377–93. In a ten-country survey in 1993, the Czech-lands had the second highest percentage of respondents who "never" or "rarely" go to church (68 percent). This

With Moscow's initial approval, a Slovak leader, Alexander Dubček, in 1968 began a cautious party-led effort at reform that rapidly emerged as the peaceful and still party-led Prague Spring. But Soviet tanks, leading troops from some of the Warsaw Pact countries, crushed the Prague Spring and began the era of the Brezhnev Doctrine.[70] From 1969 to 1989 the major leader, first as secretary-general of the party and later as president, was Gustáv Husák. He was a much less flexible and compromising leader than Kádár in Hungary. Indeed, the aftermath of the Prague Spring led to probably the largest purge of Communist Party membership in the history of Eastern Europe. Approximately one-third of the party quit or were purged. Reform-minded Communists, if they remained in the party at all, were, in sharp contrast to Hungary, quiet and marginalized.[71]

Again in sharp contrast to Hungary, the party-state adhered to economic orthodoxy. Pretransition Czechoslovakia never tried any market or reform experiments. It therefore borrowed little from the West and thus was not subject to the debt-based pressure for economic and political reforms that Poland and Hungary experienced.[72] After 1968, university life in Czechoslovakia, especially in the social sciences, experienced almost none of the pockets of vitality, excellence, and activity one could normally find in Poland, Hungary, or Slovenia. Lacking the citizenship in a developed democracy available to all East Germans in West Germany, the mass exit option as a trigger to regime decomposition was also not present.[73] Total identification of Husák with the Brezhnev Doctrine and the lack of reforms within the party made the Czechoslovakian party resistant to Gorbachev's thinking.

The area where the regime was furthest from the totalitarian ideal type was in the degree of pluralism—especially for some expression of dissent by civil society. The Soviet Union and thus even Czechoslovakia signed the Helsinki Final Act in 1975 as one of the thirty-five member states of the Conference on Security and Cooperation. All signatories to the Helsinki accord agreed to international monitoring of human rights. Czechoslovakia's adhesion to the Helsinki accords opened up an organizational opportunity for the human rights activists in

contrasts dramatically with Poland, where the comparable figure was 16 percent. See Rose and Haerpfer, "Adapting to Transformation in Eastern Europe," table 35. In the same survey, by almost a factor of two, the Czech Republic had the highest percentage of nonbelievers (47 percent). Poland and Romania had the lowest percentage of nonbelievers (2 percent). Ibid., table 34.

70. The classic book on the Prague Spring is Skilling, *Czechoslovakia's Interrupted Revolution*.

71. One of the leaders of Civic Forum in the Velvet Revolution was Jan Urban. His father had once been a high-ranking member of the Central Committee of the Communist Party. Urban writes that after the Soviet invasion "about a half a million Party members were purged and about 800,000 lost their jobs. From that moment on, the CPCz (Communist Party of Czechslovakia) established itself in opposition to the nationalist and humanist forces within society. . . . This party could no longer reform. Henceforth, it could only control the people through corruption and fear. The word 'reform' became a curse." See Urban, "Politics of Power and Humiliation," 276.

72. Kornai, *The Socialist System*, 427.

73. Albert O. Hirschman, "Exit, Voice, and the Fate of the German Democratic Republic: An Essay in Conceptual History," *World Politics* 45, no. 2 (1993): 173–202.

Czechoslovakia.[74] Groups like Charter 77 and the Committee for the Defense of the Unjustly Persecuted continued to function, despite regular jailings, more or less continuously from 1977–78 until the Velvet Revolution.[75] Unlike Hungary, post-totalitarianism did not evolve toward any out-of-type change but, in return for acquiescence, the regime made few attempts to mobilize enthusiasm.

Thus far, because we dealt first with authoritarian Poland and mature post-totalitarian Hungary, we have not really described the texture and atmosphere of post-totalitarian cultural life, although in chapter 3 we discussed the characteristic post-totalitarian retreat from politics and hollowing of ideology. In the following pages we will therefore quote at length from two eloquent writers, Václav Havel and Timothy Garton Ash, who discuss what "living a lie" under frozen post-totalitarian meant both for the limits of the regime and for the organizational limits of a political opposition.[76] We say *frozen* to capture the notion that the regime was neither in the early months of post-totalitarianism (as Bulgaria was in 1989 concerning pluralism) or evolving toward a possible out-of-type change from mature post-totalitarianism (as in Hungary in the late 1980s). Czechoslovakia was a frozen, post-totalitarian-by-decay regime from 1968 to 1989 and in some small areas was post-totalitarian by societal conquest.

The most significant dissident group in post-totalitarian Czechoslovakia was the Charter 77, whose members, though completely peaceful, were often jailed.[77] One of the founding Chartist leaders, the playwright Václav Havel, wrote of the "parallel culture" of independent thinkers who tried to "live in truth." In 1981 ten million Poles had inscribed in the legally recognized independent trade union. Havel, writing in 1984, the year before Gorbachev came to power, spoke of the "hundreds, possibly thousands of people of all sorts and conditions—young, old, gifted, untalented, believers, nonbelievers—gathered under the umbrella of 'parallel culture,' [who] were led to it exclusively by the incredible narrow-mindedness of a regime which tolerated practically nothing."[78]

Timothy Garton Ash, the Oxford historian, also writing in 1984, nicely captures the frozen post-totalitarian dimension of Czechoslovakia. Whereas a totalitarian regime makes an intense effort at a "mobilization of enthusiasms," Garton Ash,

---

74. For the importance of the Helsinki Rights Accords for democratization in Eastern Europe, see Samuel P. Huntington, *The Third Wave: Democratization in the Late Twentieth Century* (Norman: University of Oklahoma Press, 1991), 89–94.

75. For a useful inventory of these independent groups, see the Helsinki Watch report, *Toward Civil Society: Independent Initiatives in Czechoslovakia* (New York: Helsinki Watch, 1989).

76. Nothing can convey better what frozen totalitarianism means than the writings of Václav Havel and Timothy Garton Ash which we shall refer to. We now realize that our term "frozen" is an echo of one of the essays of Garton Ash called "Czechoslovakia under the Ice."

77. For an excellent discussion of the early history of Charter 77, see H. Gordon Skilling, *Charter 77 and Human Rights in Czechoslovkia* (London: George Allen and Unwin, 1981).

78. Václav Havel, "Six Asides about Culture" (1984), in Jan Vladislav, ed., *Václav Havel: Living in Truth* (London: Faber and Faber, 1986), 128.

following the great Czech writer Milan Kundera, called Husák "the President of Forgetting." "*Forgetting* is the key to the so called normalization of Czechoslovakia. In effect, the regime has said to the people: Forget 1968. Forget your democratic traditions. Forget you were once citizens with rights and duties. Forget politics. In return we give you a comfortable life. . . . We don't ask you to believe in us or our fatuous ideology. All we ask is that you will outwardly and publicly conform."[79]

The leadership, far from having a charismatic leader and change-oriented party militants of the totalitarian ideal type, was pure careerist post-totalitarian. Garton Ash writes, "the Party is little more than a union for self-advancement. . . . The country's politics are frozen into immobility—a fifteen-year Winter after one Prague Spring. . . . No impulses of reform come from the purged, cowed, and corrupt apparat. Younger party leaders are devastatingly critical—but cynically and in private, while most Czechs do not look to the Party for anything at all. . . . I have never been in a country where politics, and indeed the whole of public life, is a matter of such supreme indifference."[80]

Havel captures the lack of real political pluralism and the inauthenticity and boredom of membership in what had once been a party organization of mobilization. "In societies under the post-totalitarian system, all political life in the traditional sense has been eliminated. . . . The gap that results is filled by ideological ritual. In such a situation, people's interest in political matters naturally dwindles. . . . Individuals need not believe all their mystification, but they must behave as though they did. . . . they must live within a lie."[81]

In his famous letter to Dr. Gustáv Husák, Havel raises almost all the themes of post-totalitarianism we discussed in chapter 3; he talks of "self-alienation," of the "principle of dissimulation," of "political apartheid," of the "escape from the sphere of public activity which the authorities welcome."[82] The hope Havel holds out is that the parallel culture may grow because it inevitably must be in permanent tension with the "first culture" of the post-totalitarian party state. He also holds out the prospect that "power shifts at the center of the bloc can influence conditions."[83]

Writing in 1984, Timothy Garton Ash knew that a Polish "self-organizing" society could not develop in Czechoslovakia but, like Havel, he held out hope for an externally initiated change.

Of course the Chartists see that a Czech Solidarity is as likely as fire under ice. But they also see that the development of the *samizdat* counterculture, and the growing alienation of private

79. Timothy Garton Ash, "Czechoslovakia under the Ice," in *The Uses of Adversity: Essays on the Fate of Central Europe* (New York: Random House, 1989), 62. Emphasis in original.

80. Ibid., 63.

81. Václav Havel et al., *The Power of the Powerless: Citizens against the State in Central-Eastern Europe* (Armark, N.Y.: M.E. Sharpe, 1985), quotes from pp. 49 and 31.

82. Havel, "Letter to Dr Gustáv Husák," in Vladislav, *Václav Havel: Living in Truth*, 3–35.

83. Václav Havel, "The Power of the Powerless," in Vladislav, *Václav Havel: Living in Truth*, 105.

opinion, combined with economic and political stagnation, have begun at least to make the ice mushy on the underside. If ever a real thaw comes—from above? After change in Moscow? . . . They know from their own experience in 1968 . . . how suddenly a society that seems atomized, apathetic, and broken can be transformed into an articulate, united civil society. How private opinion can become public opinion. How a nation can stand on its feet again. And for this they are working and waiting, under the ice.[84]

Let us now turn back to the dissidents. How were they living under the ice? A number of groups besides Charter 77 emerged in 1988 and 1989, but none of them could be considered an organized political opposition. They were protest groups in civil society. In comparison to Poland they were only, of course, a minute fraction of the population. In comparison to the social movements in Hungary, which turned into political parties by late 1988, they were small, unorganized, and anti-political. Jan Urban, a leading dissident in Charter 77, in a self-critical article written on the eve of the secession of Slovakia, observed that,

in the summer of 1989 we received a copy of a secret paper for party propagandists, based on an analysis the StB (the Czechoslovak secret police) had prepared for the Politburo. In it, the StB estimated the hard core of "anti-socialist opposition groups" to consist of about sixty people with some five hundred supporters and collaborators. Their estimate was right. And it remained right. . . . We believed in the regime's invincibility until it *collapsed* on its own. We did not know how to organize ourselves to form a political opposition. . . . We did not know the non-society we lived with. All we knew was our enemy and he—spiteful bastard—all of a sudden ran away. Without him we were left alone with an unknown atomized non-society—and with power over it. Had the Communists been able to bargain longer, or had they tried to resist, the new power elite would have learned at least something about how to organize political support and how important it is to institutionalize it. . . . Blinded by the easiness of taking power, we did not think about its nature and institutions. . . . Because of our own anti-political way of existing as political creatures before the change, we were bound to lose—unless we ourselves changed into politicians. By now we know we have failed.[85]

These quotations give some insight into why, as we argued in chapter 3, a frozen post-totalitarian regime is one in which *collapse*, rather than negotiation, is a more likely transition path and why the opposition, surprised by its unexpected success, normally has not developed an articulated political approach.

We have now said enough to allow us to analyze why Czechoslovakia, unlike Hungary, did not have a *reforma pactada–ruptura pactada*. Mature post-totalitarian Hungary met the two necessary (and the four facilitating) conditions for such a pact. Frozen post-totalitarian Czechoslovakia met none. In particular, the Czechoslovak hard-line regime gave no space for reformist moderates in the party-state. Likewise the opposition, while a great moral presence, had no nego-

---

84. Ash, "Czechoslovakia under the Ice," 70.
85. Jan Urban, "The Powerlessness of the Powerful" (Prague, Nov. 1992, unpublished manuscript), 22, emphasis added.

tiating capacity with the regime and indeed was not institutionally organized to conduct strategic and tactical negotiations.

A second dimension of our intra-post-totalitarian comparison relates to differences between Czechoslovakia and Bulgaria. Why did the Czechoslovakian regime *collapse* (as the above quote from Urban indicates), whereas, as we will demonstrate, the Bulgarian regime, via a complex process of adjustment, repression, and negotiation, was able to *control* the transition? For us, the operative word in the above sentence is *collapse.*

Regime collapse is a phenomenon that we believe needs much more conceptual and empirical work. Collapse can be counterposed both to being overthrown and to transition through negotiation. Collapse is different from a regime overthrow in that there is no storming of the seats of power and no occupation of the television station, the governmental buildings, the army bases, or the communication network, either by the military in a coup or by revolutionary activists and masses. There is no arrest, shooting, or immediate flight of the regime leaders trying to save themselves from their opponents, who take over power proclaiming a provisional government, a national salvation junta, or a military junta. Consequently there is no violence.

Regime collapse is also different from our model of negotiated reform and transition in that the incumbents cannot negotiate the conditions under which they will leave power. They cannot impose rules governing the transition, delay the process significantly, or exercise some control of the future. They cannot do so because they believe that, if they should attempt to hold power until an election, they will provoke an immediate outburst of popular anger or a coup. Incumbents no longer believe they can count on the coercive apparatus to support them. In addition, on the side of the democratic opposition, there is no reason to negotiate conditions for the transition because they are convinced of their overwhelming relational power. Collapse is the result of rigidity, ossification, and loss of responsiveness of elites that does not allow them to make timely decisions anticipating crises and change.[86] Rather than being a step ahead of the demands of opposition, the regime is forced to respond on the march, like the GDR leadership, or on the spot, as in Czechoslovakia. In both cases incumbents lost so much control that the best descriptive phrase of the transition is "regime collapse."

Our hypothesis, therefore, is that regimes collapse, not so much due to external forces, but in those circumstances where, when the regime is challenged, multiple and almost simultaneous defections occur within the interior of the state, particularly within the middle levels of the coercive apparatus.[87] To explain such

---

86. For the critical role of timing in regime change, see Juan J. Linz, "Il fattore tempo nei mutamenti di regime," *Teoria Politica* 2, no. 1 (1986): 3–47.

87. We believe that two of the most prominent examples of this are Czechoslovakia and East Germany. Fortunately, David V. Friedman of Yale University is writing a dissertation on the collapse in East Germany, which promises to be an important contribution. His preliminary findings were reported in "Regime Col-

a phenomenon of collapse, the concept of legitimacy is indispensable. Legitimacy in the polity can be a question of what millions of people believe. However, legitimacy within the staff of a coercive apparatus in the early stages of a challenge often depends on what tens, hundreds, or at the most thousands of members of the state apparatus, who will have to *give* and/or *implement* orders, believe.

In crisis situations the question in Weberian terms is whether the coercive staff of the ruler believe in the legitimacy of the orders to use force. For Weber "normally the rule over a considerable number of persons requires a staff, that is, a *special* group which can normally be trusted to execute the general policy as well as the specific commands. . . . Custom, personal advantage, purely affectual or ideal motives of solidarity, do not form a sufficiently reliable basis for a given domination. In addition, there is normally a further element, the belief in *legitimacy*."[88]

We do not have data for Czechoslovakia. However, an outstanding survey designed to probe precisely this Weberian question was administered by Daniel V. Friedheim in the GDR to 119 leading cadre in the *Einsatzleitungen*.

Friedheim writes that his "sample was defined by membership in secret crisis management teams (Einsatzleitungen) in the greater Berlin, Dresden (South) and Rostock (North) areas. At the central, district, and local levels, these teams brought together the top party secretaries, government representatives, and regular police, army and secret police commanders who decided whether or not to deploy force against demonstrators in the fall of 1989."[89] Using Weberian criteria this is an excellent example of a ruler's "coercive staff." What did this coercive staff think in the fall of 1989?

In the course of writing this book, again and again people have asked us, Why did the Communists in Eastern Europe not shoot, as in Tiananmen Square, to maintain themselves in power? Friedheim's survey provides powerful answers. He asked a battery of questions. The first set of questions showed that, when they joined the Communist Party (SED), 97.4 percent of the coercive staff polled believed that "no other political system could better realize the social goals of the G.D.R." In the period before the demise of the GDR 65 percent of them personally still believed that. However, there had been a sharp erosion in their belief in the legitimacy to use force against what the state declared were illegal protests (table 17.2).

If massive Tiananmen Square–type coercion had been imposed early against

---

lapse in the Peaceful East German Revolution: The Role of Middle Level Officials" (paper prepared for the Eighth International Conference of Europeanists, Chicago, March 27–29, 1992). Claus Offe also analyzes the process of collapse in East Germany in his *Der Tunnel am Ende des Lichts.Erkundungen der politischen Transformation im Neuen Osten* (Frankfurt am Main: Campus Verlag, 1994), chap. 2.

88. See Max Weber, *Economy and Society: An Outline of Interpretive Sociology*, ed. Guenther Roth and Claus Wittich (Berkeley: University of California Press, 1978), 1:212–13. Emphasis in original. Also see in the same volume Weber's discussion of the threat of the use of force by the state (pp. 53–55 and 314–15).

89. From a draft of his Ph.D. dissertation, Department of Political Science, Yale University. Cited with permission from the author.

Table 17.2. Erosion of the GDR Coercive Staff's Belief in the Right to Use Force against State-declared Illegal Protests. Question: (1) Just like any government in the world, the GDR always tried to implement the law despite the disagreement of some citizens. When you began your career with the Party did you believe that the state was entitled to use the police to resist illegal protests? (2) In the Fall of 1989, as more and more citizens left your country or demonstrated in the streets, did you still believe the state was entitled to do that?

Answer	Percentage of Respondents	
	In the Past	Fall 1989
Yes	78.4	8.8
Mostly	18.9	21.2
Subtotal	(97.3)	(30.0)
Had Doubts	0.9	31.0
No	1.8	38.8
Subtotal	(2.7)	(69.9)
Total	100.0	100.0

Source: Daniel V. Friedheim, Ph.D. dissertation in process, Department of Political Science, Yale University. Data reproduced with permission.

the protesters in the GDR, some analysts believe that the Communist regime might well have prevented its subsequent collapse. However, Friedheim asked the GDR coercive staff what they thought about the possibility of using Tiananmen Square–type force. The answers reveal that in the European context they overwhelmingly believed that such use of force would be illegitimate and impossible even in defense of socialism (table 17.3).

With this empirical excursus on the GDR taken into account, let us state our argument about how regimes collapse more formally. In critical stages of a regime crisis, vital parts of the state coercive staff equivocate, rebel, or melt away. Seeing this sudden absence of effective force, demonstrators swell in numbers and are emboldened in spirit. At a certain moment there can be so many antiregime demonstrators and so few regime defenders that the leaders of the regime lose all capacity to negotiate. At this moment, the regime is not so much overthrown as it collapses.[90]

Let us explore this process in Czechoslovakia. The wall started coming down in Berlin on November 9, 1989. Eight days later on Friday, November 17, students

90. A valuable formalized model of people's lessening fear in the streets as more people join the protests and the regime's coercive presence becoming less salient is contained in Gary Marks, "Rational Sources of Chaos in Democratic Transition," in Larry Diamond and Gary Marks, ed., *Re-examining Democracy* (Newbury Park: Sage Publications, 1992), 47–69, esp. 53–55. Also see Timur Kuran, "Now Out of Never: The Element of Surprise in the East European Revolution of 1989," *World Politics* 44, no. 1 (1991): 7–48. In the People's Republic of China, should a situation like Tiananmen Square emerge again, the combination of the loss of ideological legitimacy of socialism and the evident self-promotion of the nomenklatura in the new business ventures might lead to a situation where neither the regime nor the opposition has moderates empowered to negotiate. In such a situation, if, as in Czechoslovakia and East Germany, the soliders do not use force, the regime could *collapse*. During Tiananmen Square neither the regime nor the opposition had the capacity to negotiate. However, unlike Czechoslovakia and East Germany, the regime did have the capacity to coerce.

Table 17.3. Response of the GDR Coercive Staff Members to the Question: "What Was Your Opinion at the Time about the Most Important Lessons to be Derived from the Events on Tiananmen Square in June 1989?"

Answer	Percentage
"It could have been possible in the GDR."	1.2
"A bloodbath like that is only possible in the People's Republic of China or Asia."	42.5
"Socialism is not worth that bloodbath."	26.4
"I never saw it as a bloodbath."	29.9

Source: Daniel V. Friedheim, Ph.D. dissertation in process, Department of Political Science, Yale University. Data reproduced with permission.

at a regime-approved march to commemorate the first student killed in the Nazi invasion turned the march into an antiregime demonstration and were brutally beaten. Saturday morning, with Havel and most of the leading dissidents in the country on vacation, the students decided to go on a protest strike. A strike proclamation was read at a popular theater that afternoon, where many theater directors, as well as a normal audience, were assembled. Discussion of a peaceful general strike began.

Before going further with the sequence of events, let us establish some parameters so that the readers can appreciate how *early* the internal collapse began. On Tuesday, November 21, Havel in Prague addressed an outdoor rally for the first time. The major mass demonstration at Letná occurred on Sunday, November 26. The two-hour general strike (so peaceful that many workers agreed to work overtime to make up the lost time) was held on Monday, November 27. The regime, however, was experiencing mass defections from within its core institutions even before Havel spoke.[91]

On Sunday evening, November 19, the Youth Union of the Communist Party, whose chairman Vasil Mohorita had a seat on the Central Committee of the Communist Party and which controlled their own newspaper *Mladá Fronta (Young Front)*, issued a call for an inquiry into the beatings of the students and condemning the use of force by the state. "A majority of young people are calling for and supporting fundamental and essential political reform in our society.... We regard a political solution to the current situation as essential ... We consider violence in this case to be undemocratic ... It is not possible in our society for certain subjects to be forever forbidden."[92] On Monday morning this Communist youth union "turned over its office accommodation on each faculty, complete

91. Two day-by-day, book-length accounts of the Velvet Revolution that reproduce invaluable documents are Bernard Wheaton and Zdenek Kavan, *The Velvet Revolution: Czechoslovakia, 1988–1991* (Boulder, Colo.: Westview Press, 1992), and John F. N. Bradley, *Czechoslovakia's Velvet Revolution: A Political Analysis* (Boulder, Colo.: East European Monographs, distributed by Columbia University Press, New York, 1992).

92. The entire text is reproduced in appendix B of Wheaton and Kavan, *The Velvet Revolution*, 209–10.

with telephone and copying facilities, to the strike committees, giving them significant help in the struggle to communicate directly with the people."[93] On that same day "a police patrol told the students guarding a technical college building to remove the strike posters from the windows. The request was ignored and no further police action was reported at this or any other college or faculty."[94]

Early Tuesday, November 21, after a Central Committee meeting, the government issued various statements that they would resist further antisocialist actions by "all possible means."[95] But that afternoon Havel spoke to his first large public demonstration. The ambivalence of the police was evident to the demonstrators. "Policemen sighted during the demonstration were sporting the national colors on their lapels, a sign of solidarity with the demonstrators, and were also seen cheering Havel."[96]

On Wednesday, November 22, the police began to put in writing what they had been practicing. "We, Communists of the basic organization of the party in the police force in the North District of Prague, turn to you in the Presidium of the Central Committee.... The events of the recent days oblige us to take up a position with the aim of achieving a political solution.... It is no longer possible to use us, the officers of the law, to cover up unsolved political and other problems."[97]

That same day, before and while Havel spoke, other parts of the state apparatus were experiencing defection and resistance. The general director of state television was called to a mass meeting where 700 of his 1,500 employees had signed a petition demanding, among many other things, that video films of police brutality be shown. He capitulated.[98] At the state radio station, "300 staff members of the basic organization of the CPC [Communist Party of Czechoslovakia] met and condemned the Central Committee stance and expressed support for the C.F. [Civic Forum]." They also demanded two hours of air time per day to be open for public discussion "as a reflection of the pluralist tendency of different sectors of the population."[99]

In 1948 factory workers outside of Prague had played a major role in the Communist Party's coup. Factory militias were a crucial part of the regime's reserve coercive apparatus. On Tuesday, November 21, the hard-line leader of the Prague City Council, Miroslav Štepán, made an appeal to "the workers of Prague, members of the People's Militia, and other armed units to deal with the anti-socialist circles."[100] Militia after militia met in angry mass meetings and voted themselves out of existence.[101] In this context the commander of the army, General Vaclavík,

---

93. Ibid., 60.
94. Bradley, *Czechoslovakia's Velvet Revolution*, 78.
95. Ibid., 79.
96. Ibid., 85.
97. The full document is produced in Wheaton and Kavan, *The Velvet Revolution*, 204–5.
98. Ibid., 67.
99. Ibid., 68.
100. Wheaton and Kavan, *The Velvet Revolution*, 70.
101. Ibid., see documents 13 and 17 in appendix B and pp. 70–71 of the text.

who was later appointed minister of defense by Havel, gave a rambling speech on television where, according to Bradley, he said "the army would not fight the people." Bradley adds, "the reason was obvious: soldiers would not obey their officers' orders. This was a deathblow to the Communist leadership."[102]

On Friday November 24, the internal defections within the state (three days before the scheduled general strike was actually held), had already led to a crisis at the elite level of the regime. After an all-day meeting of the Central Committee, at which a variety of proposals including repression were considered, Secretary-General Jakeš submitted his resignation as well as that of his secretariat and his politburo.[103] By December 4 Husák announced his resignation as president. On December 29 the Communist Parliament voted the only candidate, Václav Havel, president of Czechoslovakia.[104]

Why did this collapse occur? Let us refer to a brilliant, prophetic observation by Václav Havel. For Havel, in his famous 1975 "Letter to Dr. Gustáv Husák," the hope for frozen post-totalitarian Czechoslovakia was for "a moment to arrive" in which the "entropic regime" could not respond. "In trying to paralyze life, the authorities paralyze themselves and, in the long run, incapacitate themselves for paralyzing life." For Havel, when that moment comes "the dead weight of inertia crumbles and history steps out again into the arena."[105] Havel's hope was fulfilled. The regime *had* incapacitated itself for paralyzing life and *collapsed*.

As social scientists our hypothesis is that the type of internal collapse that occurred in Czechoslovakia owes much to its frozen post-totalitarianism, especially to the atmosphere of growing inauthenticity of ideology, the pro forma support for the regime, and the modest space for dissent in civil society that can be the base for an alternative. These are good reasons to believe that this type of situation is more likely to happen in a frozen post-totalitarian regime than in any other type of polity. In a full totalitarian regime or a very early post-totalitarian regime, as in Bulgaria in 1989, ideological commitment will tend to be more real, at least, for the cadre, who are the key staff needed to implement coercive policies. In an evolving, mature post-totalitarian regime, reform communists have greater negotiating capacity. In most authoritarian regimes the governments will tend to react via a new coup or extrication from rule by using elections.

In the chapters on Spain and Brazil, we could have described events very similar and even on a larger scale, comparable to the actions of students, professionals, crowds, and strikers in Prague. We did not because they had little direct effect on the transition and the final demise of the regime. Those in power could count on the loyalty and obedience of the police and, if necessary, of the armed forces

102. Bradley, *Czechoslovakia's Velvet Revolution*, 93.

103. Ibid., 98.

104. As in Hungary, a compelling eyewitness account of many of the crucial events is contained in Garton Ash, *We The People*, 78–130.

105. Václav Havel, "Letter to Dr. Gustáv Husák" (1975), Vladislav, *Václav Havel: Living in Truth*, 3–35, quote from p. 27.

and never considered giving up power as a response to such pressures. There was no collapse and no prospect for collapse.

Stateness and the Velvet Divorce: A Neo-Institutionalist Analysis

Our final question concerns stateness. At midnight on December 31, 1992, barely three years after the Velvet Revolution, Czechoslovakia divided into two separate states, the Czech Republic and Slovakia.[106] There have been a number of excellent studies that correctly call attention to some important social, cultural, and historical differences between the two component parts of the former federation of Czechoslovakia. The Czech-lands were a part of the Austrian half and Slovakia was a part of the Hungarian half of the Austro-Hungarian Empire. During the empire, the Czech-lands became one of the most industrial parts of the Empire and Slovakia remained one of the most agrarian. The two components of Czechoslovakia spoke different but mutually intelligible languages. Slovakia has historically been more Catholic than the Czech-lands. Slovakia from 1939 to 1945 was a quasi-independent Nazi puppet state. Slovakia underwent rapid heavy industrialization under Communist rule, a form of subsidized industrialization oriented toward the USSR that resulted in greater structural vulnerabilities in the post-1989 movement toward a market economy. As a result, before 1992, Slovakia had an 11.3 percent unemployment rate compared to 2.7 percent in the Czech-lands.[107]

Having acknowledged these sociocultural and historical differences between the Czech-lands and Slovakia, we believe that it would be a mistake for analysts to overstress the determinate role of mass nationalist sentiment in the breakup of Czechoslovakia. There are many allusions in the press to stateness problems being driven by "irrational" and primordial mass feelings. However, in our judgment the available evidence suggests strongly that intense *mass* separatist and national demands were never dominant in either the Czech Republic or Slovakia until long after the political elites had already begun crafting the divorce after the June 1992 elections (table 17.4).[108]

106. An overall treatment of this subject is found in Jirí Musil, ed., *The End of Czechoslovakia* (Budapest: Central European Press, 1995). Jon Elster explores critically six possible explanations for the breakup in his "Explaining the Breakup of the Czechoslovak Federation: Consenting Adults or the Sorcerer's Apprentice?" *East European Constitutional Review*, 4, no. 1 (1995), 36–41. In essence, we provide a seventh explanation. Four articles on the breakup, two by major political actors (Petr Pithart and Jan Carnogursky), are contained in *Scottish Affairs*, no. 8 (Summer 1994).

107. Two excellent reviews of the literature, which discuss and document these and other differences, are Jirí Musil, "Czech and Slovak Society: Outline of a Comparative Study," in *Czech Sociological Review* 1, no. 1 (1993), 5–21, and Sharon Wolchik, "The Politics of Ethnicity in Post-Communist Czechoslovakia," *East European Politics and Societies* 8, no. 1 (1994), 153–88.

108. "Many citizens in Czechoslovakia share the view that political leaders were primarily responsible for the growth of ethnic tensions and the difficulties that arose over the form of the state. . . . Seventy-one percent of respondents in the Czech-lands and 65 percent in Slovakia surveyed in late 1991 for Radio Free Europe agreed or strongly agreed that politicians were using nationalism for their own purposes." Wolchik, "Politics of Ethnicity in Czechoslovakia," 176.

Table 17.4. Preferred State Arrangements (November 1991–July 1992) in Czech-lands (CR) and Slovakia (SR) (in percentages)

Type of State Arrangement	November 1991		May 1992		July 1992	
	CR	SR	CR	SR	CR	SR
Unitary state	39	20	34	12	38	14
Federation	30	26	28	33	19	27
"Lands-based republic"	20	6	22	6	18	8
Confederation	4	27	6	31	3	30
Two independent states	5	14	6	11	16	16
Don't know	2	7	4	7	6	5

Source: Reproduced with permission from Sharon L. Wolchik, "The Politics of Ethnicity in Post-Communist Czechoslovakia," 180. Based on polls taken by the Institute for Opinion Research.
Note: In addition to the results displayed in this table, the Director of the Association of Independent Social Analysis (AISA) in Prague gave us the results of a national sample conducted in October-November 1992, according to which only 22 percent of respondents in the Czech-lands and 19 percent in Slovakia wanted two completely independent states, even though the political leaders had already agreed on the separation date of December 31, 1992. The "lands-based republic" option was not fully defined but normally was understood to entail a system based on three units: Bohemia, Moravia, and Slovakia.

In fact, an overwhelming majority of citizens wanted a referendum to decide the future of the country. In July 1992, "eighty-two percent of respondents in the Czech-lands and 84 percent in Slovakia agreed that the further existence of the state should be determined not by politicians but *only by citizens in a referendum.*"[109]

In July 1992, another public opinion poll was structured to ascertain the "least preferred" and the "most preferred" of the three most plausible options: federation (the existing model), confederation, or separation. The least preferred option in Slovakia (47 percent) and in the Czech-lands (46 percent) was separation.[110]

Part of the reason for fears about separation was economic. Only 21 percent of those polled in the Czech-lands and only 34 percent in Slovakia felt that their standard of living would be improved by a separation.[111] The major difference of opinion was about the constitutional arrangements of a federation or a confederation. The model most preferred (62 percent) in the Czech-lands was the existing model, federation. By a slight plurality (38 percent) this was also the most preferred model in Slovakia, but 35 percent of those polled most preferred confederation and 20 percent most preferred separation.[112]

If the mass publics of the Czech-lands and Slovakia did not demand separate states, why and how did Czechoslovakia break up? Much research should be carried out on the subject before definitive monographs can be written. However, we suggest that such works cannot be written if they do not give full attention to the interaction of the Soviet-style federal constitutional system with the antipolitical

109. Ibid., 178, our emphasis.
110. For the methodology of this poll by the Institute for Public Opinion Research, see ibid., 180–81.
111. Ibid. However, both component parts of the federation felt that the other region benefited most from the distribution mechanisms used by the federal government.
112. Ibid.

style of the democratic leadership who unexpectedly inherited state power after the sudden collapse of the frozen post-totalitarian regime. Our working hypothesis is strongly neo-institutionalist. Specifically, *without* the impasse-creating mechanisms of Czechoslovakia's Soviet-style federal system, we doubt that the historical, cultural, and economic differences between the Czech-lands and Slovakia would have resulted in the division of Czechoslovakia.[113] Let us consider some basic arguments and data about institutions, attitudes, missed opportunities, and strategic elite choices.

After the regime collapsed in November 1992, the new democrats inherited a parliament (National Assembly) that was bicameral but with a de jure and de facto potential actually to be tricameral. The lower house, the Chamber of the People, had 150 members and was based on population. The Upper House, the Chamber of Nations, also had 150 members, composed of a 75-member Czech section and a 75-member Slovak section. Legally, both the Czech and Slovak sections could deliberate and vote separately. More importantly, on a whole range of issues, especially those that had any relevance to the working of the federation, the constitutional power to block was extremely high. A measure could be approved only if it received the positive vote of 60 percent of *all* members in each chamber, whether they were present or not and whether they voted or not. David Olson captures the blocking power of small groups quite well when he argues that the post-totalitarian constitution that Havel inherited "provided a small number of members (30), if they were so determined or merely absent, with a veto power within the Assembly. . . . As federalism increased in importance . . . the Federal Assembly could not adopt proposed legislation on the most important question before it—stateness."[114] This potential for impasse had long been noted by H. Gordon Skilling, who in his classic work on Czechoslovakia had commented that the post-1968 constitution meant that a very small minority could block "the ratification of the government's program and a vote of confidence in the government."[115] Skilling went on to note that the constitution did not really affect the party-state, which remained unitary. Since the party-state was in charge, the constitution was fictive. Once the transition occurred the constitutional potential for impasse became more real because, unlike a standard West European parliamentary democracy, in Soviet-style constitutions neither the prime minister nor the head of state could dissolve the Parliament and call for new elections in the case of impasse.[116]

---

113. In fact, given the distribution of opinion in the Czech-lands and in Slovakia, probably a *necessary* condition of separation was the existence of institutions that eventually seemed (because of missed opportunities) unworkable and unchangeable.

114. David M. Olson, "The Sundered State: Federalism and Parliament in Czechoslovakia" (paper presented at the Conference on Comparative Parliamentary Development in Eastern Europe and the Former USSR at the Center for Soviet, Post-Soviet and East European Studies, Emory University, Atlanta, April 9–10, 1993), 7.

115. Skilling, *Czechoslovakia's Interrupted Revolution*, appendix B.

116. Personal conversation of the authors with Professor Leon Lipson, a law professor at Yale University and a specialist on Soviet-style constitutions. Also see Paul Wilson, "Czechoslovakia: The Pain of Divorce," *New York Review of Books*, 39 (Dec. 17, 1992): 69–75.

A constitution of the sort we have just analyzed may be fictive for the party-state, but it can take on a new and dangerous life the longer it is not changed in the new democratic context.

As comparativists, we believe that in the crucial period after the collapse of the frozen post-totalitarian regime the new democrats could have rapidly put on the agenda a number of fundamental issues concerning the future of democratic institutions and decision-making arrangements. One possible early agenda item could have been a decision on whether or not to elect a constituent assembly to approve a new and more viable constitution for the federation. Another option could have been for Havel, backed by the authority of the Velvet Revolution, to have asked the existing Federal Assembly to modify the constitution shortly after he was elected president. This was the option Adolfo Suárez followed successfully in Spain with the "Law for Political Reform," as we have documented.

The decision, or better nondecision, to hold elections in June 1990 *within* the confines of the ultra federal and blocking characteristics of the Soviet-style federal constitution constrained severely the manner in which the stateness problem of Czechoslovakia could be handled. The disintegrative potential of the constitution was increased when Havel, unlike Adolfo Suárez of Spain, decided not to try to form a statewide party.

What happened and what did not happen, concerning the soviet-style federal constitution? Unfortunately, the atmosphere of dissident life in frozen post-totalitarian Czechoslovakia did not generate much attention to formal institutional matters. Indeed, the style of Havel and of many of his closest advisors, in sharp contrast to the opposition leadership in Hungary or Spain, was actively antipolitical and anti-institutional.

On the eve of the dissolution of Czechoslovakia, leaders of the Velvet Revolution increasingly commented on the costs of their initial antipolitics and anti-institutionalism. A close confidant of Havel, Petr Pithart, who initially headed the Coordinating Center of Civic Forum and was later prime minister of the Czech Republic from 1990 to 1992, later said that Havel "underestimated the impediments of the inherited constitution. He felt the élan of the Velvet Revolution would carry them by the problem." As we argued in our discussion of Spain, a unified statewide party could have helped. However, Pithart went on to argue that, a few days after the Velvet Revolution was over, leaders from the Slovak capital of Bratislava came to talk to Havel about the Civic Forum party apparatus in Slovakia. Havel urged them to create their own separate party in Slovakia. They left and eventually set up People against Violence.[117] Pithart says that this reflected the "widespread negative attitude toward anything that resembled a party. Havel was a symbol of this. He completely dissociated himself from the party."[118] Pithart's successor as Civic Forum coordinator, Jan Urban, is even more critical of

117. Interview in Prague with Stepan, December 16, 1993.
118. Ibid.

Havel's antipolitics. "He became President as a leader and representative of the Civic Forum, but very soon declared himself a non-partisan President above any political parties . . . Already in February 1990, after several weeks of mutual isolation, the joint delegation of Civic Forum (Czech lands) and Public against Violence (Slovakia) had to force Havel to meet them officially. He received them in one anteroom, not even inviting them to the meeting room."[119]

This inattention to politics and political parties no doubt contributed to the fact that the electoral campaigns of 1989 were largely run by Czech-based and Slovak-based groups. Indeed, of the eleven parties that gained seats in the federal parliament, only one, the former Czechoslovak Communist Party, had representatives from both republics. The Czechoslovak "founding election" paid almost no ideological or organizational attention to the formation of federation-wide parties. Like Spain (and unlike the Soviet Union and Yugoslavia), Czechoslovakia *did* have a founding election sequence that began with statewide elections. However, unlike Spain, the central government leadership made no effort—and in fact discouraged—the formation of a statewide party.[120]

In separate interviews a year after the Velvet Divorce, Stepan asked Pithart and Urban if they believed that Havel and the Civic Forum leaders could have successfully asked the sitting parliament to change the fictive constitution. One can never be certain with complex historical counterfactuals. However, it is worth noting that in the retrospective judgment of both Pithart and Urban, the Civic Forum in late 1989 or early 1990 *could* have achieved some key changes, such as going to a simple majority system for both houses or a constituent assembly. A variety of other formulas could have avoided constitutional impasse. But the central point was that serious constitution-building was not then on the agenda. As it turned out, Havel, despite great efforts in 1991 and 1992, was never able to change the constitution. No referendum on dissolution was ever held. The June 1992 elections did not produce overwhelming mass fervor in either the Czech-lands or the Slovak Republic for separation. However, it did produce a prime minister of the Czech Republic, Václav Klaus, and a prime minister of Slovakia, Vladimír Mečiar, with electoral pluralities, with different economic and political agendas, and with veto power over each other.

In the "terminating" election of June 1992, Vladimír Mečiar's party (HZDS) won only 12 percent of the vote for the lower house of the Federal Republic of Czechoslovakia and a first plurality of only 33.8 percent of the vote to the Slovak Chamber of Nations. However, this was more than sufficient in the Soviet-style trichamber federal system of power to give his party an absolute veto over any significant reform in the federal system they opposed. The Válcav Klaus–led coali-

---

119. Urban, "Powerlessness of the Powerful."

120. On the importance of electoral sequence *and* the formation of statewide parties, see chap. 6 on Spain in this book and Juan J. Linz and Alfred Stepan, "Political Identities and Electoral Sequences: Spain, the Soviet Union, and Yugoslavia," *Daedalus* (Spring 1992): 123–39.

tion won 27 percent of the valid federal votes, and this also gave Klaus's coalition an absolute veto (table 17.5).

Two of the major issues in the June 1992 election in Czechoslovakia concerned the future of federal relations and alternative development models. After the elections Václav Klaus, who favored a Thatcher-like rapid move to the market and a stronger role for the central government, emerged with the first plurality (not a majority) in the Czech lands. Mečiar, who favored a slower, more statist Austrian move toward a market and substantially more autonomy for Slovakia emerged with the first plurality (not a majority) in Slovakia. However, in essence the Soviet-style federal system gave each republic's prime minister de facto veto power over the other. Mečiar possibly would have settled for a confederal state with socioeconomic autonomy, but Klaus could deny him his confederal state. Klaus possibly would have settled for a federal state as long as he could advance his economic reform agenda, but Mečiar could deny him the capacity to implement his market plan. Given their separate goals and their mutual veto power, the rational solution for each leader was to sunder the state. The divorce was peaceful, if not velvet, because the nations were reasonably demarcated territorially and each leader was able to get, because of his control over his respective legislature, a vote for the division they eventually both wanted.[121]

BULGARIA: A REGIME-CONTROLLED TRANSITION FROM EARLY POST-TOTALITARIANISM

The secondary and monographic literature on the Bulgarian transition is still much less rich than it is for Hungary or Czechoslovakia, so our analysis is necessarily more tentative. However, this literature, supplemented by our visits and interviews, allows us to assert with some confidence that, unlike the transitions in Hungary or Czechoslovakia, the early post-totalitarian regime in Bulgaria *initiated* and *never lost control* of the transition and that the leaders of that regime emerged from the first free elections not only with a plurality of the vote but with

---

121. For reasons we cannot discuss here, the Czech Republic emerged from the divorce with better chances to consolidate democracy. In the sociopolitical sphere, the separation may help the Czech Republic move toward democratic consolidation because the new state, with few Germans or Jews (because of World War II) and few Slovaks (because of the Velvet divorce), was, with the possible exception of Moravian sentiment, close to being a nation-state, so it should have no major stateness problems. Also, the Czech Republic's constitutional choice, made at the time of the separation, for a pure parliamentary model also helps avoid the political type of problems that may result from an independently elected president with significant powers and an independently selected prime minister with broad powers. Furthermore, following our prior argument about parliamentarism, the parliamentary system should help create an environment in which parties can develop and where there are incentives for enduring party coalitions. It should be noted that Klaus is a skillful politician committed to building a party.

The division left Slovakia in a somewhat more difficult situation in that Mečiar wanted to build a majoritarian nation-state, but he had significant Hungarian, Gypsy, and Ukrainian minorities. Even after the 1994 election, he only held a bare plurality. In Slovakia, nation-state and democracy could be conflicting logics.

Table 17.5. The "Terminating" Election of Czechoslovakia in 1992: Party Vote and Seats for the Federal Chamber of People and Chamber of Nations, Compared with Votes Needed in Chamber of Nations to Veto any Significant Federal-related Legislation Passed by the Chamber of People

Party	% of Total Votes Received for Federal Chamber of the People	% of Seats Won to Federal Chamber of People after 5% Threshold	% of Votes Won in Slovakia for Chamber of Nations	% of Seats Won in Slovakia for Chamber of Nations after Threshold Effect	% of Votes Won in Czech Lands Chamber of Nations	% of Seats Won in Czech Lands Chamber of Nations after Threshold Effect	Number of Seats Obtained in Chamber of Nations	Number of Seats Needed in Chamber of Nations to Veto Any Major Federal Legislation Passed by Chamber of People
Mečiar-led party (Slovak Democratic Movement)	12	16	33.85	44	—	—	33/75	30/75
Václav Klaus-led coalition (ODS-KDS)	26	32	3.66	—	33.43	49.33	37/75	30/75

Source: Keesing's Record of World Events, News Digest for June 1992, 38944–45, and David M. Olson, "The Sundered State: Federalism and Parliament in Czechoslovakia," paper presented at the Conference on Comparative Parliamentary Development in Eastern Europe and the Former USSR, at the Center for Soviet, Post-Soviet and East European Studies, Emory University, Atlanta, Ga., April 9–10, 1993.

a newly reconstituted claim to power. What accounts for such a different path out of post-totalitarianism in Bulgaria, in contrast to Hungary and Czechoslovakia? Much of the explanation seems to be found in the nature of the previous early post-totalitarian regime and the limited role the democratic opposition was able to play in that regime, given its intermittent and illegal nature.

Among the four dimensions of a totalitarian regime (pluralism, mobilization, ideology, and leadership), Bulgaria in terms of pluralism—unlike Hungary or even Czechoslovakia—still approximated the totalitarian ideal type until 1988.

To document this assertion and to illustrate the texture of the regime, let us quote at length from a valuable study of the birth of the democratic opposition in Bulgaria by Deyan Kiuranov, one of the leaders of Bulgaria's most influential opposition group, Ecoglasnost, founded in February 1989.[122] Kiuranov argues that before 1988 there were some individual acts of resistance but "unfortunately these truly heroic acts did not have any social effect at the time . . . we knew literally nothing about them when they were committed."[123] For Kiuranov, the first truly nongovernmental protest organization to appear in Bulgaria was the Hungarian Rights Association founded in a small provincial town in January 1988 by a former political prisoner, Edward Genov. Genov and the other activists were rapidly "banished from the country."[124] However, small support groups grew up in the country. These groups "were constantly arrested and harassed; they were effectively prevented from meeting organizationally, not to speak of doing something together. In fact, the police forced them to revert to the tactics of the pre-group period: individual action. However, unlike previous "martyrs," they were heard [due to Radio Free Europe and B.B.C.]. This made all the difference."[125]

At about the same time as the Human Rights Association was formed and broken up, an antipollution group in Ruse created a support group that had 300 founding members. But, Kiuranov notes, "after its founding meeting, this group never met again."[126] In Sofia a group saw a film about the Ruse protest and, in March 1988, 30 notable figures, some of them members of the Central Committee of the Bulgarian Communist Party, founded the Ruse Support Committee. On the day after the committee's formation, the 30 signatories were summoned by the

---

122. Deyan Kiuranov, "Political Establishment of the Bulgarian Opposition (January 1988–April 1990)" (unpublished paper prepared for the Center for the Study of Constitutionalism in Eastern Europe at the University of Chicago Law School in partnership with the Central European University, April 25, 1991). Other valuable accounts of the very late and thin emergence of a democratic opposition are by Roumen Daskalov and Boris Nikolov, "Bulgaria, 1989: The Birth of the Opposition" (Center for Cultural Studies, Sofia University, no date, unpublished paper), and Richard Crampton, "The Intelligentsia, the Ecology and the Opposition in Bulgaria," *World Today* (Feb. 1990): 23–26. Also see the article by Roumen Dimitrov, "March across the Institutions: Formation of the Bulgarian Opposition, 1989–1991," *Bulgarian Quarterly* 1, no. 2 (1991): 43–52.

123. Kiuranov, "Political Establishment of the Bulgarian Opposition," 7.

124. Ibid., 8.

125. Ibid.

126. Ibid., 9.

politburo and accused of *"creating structures parallel to already existing ones."*[127] For us, this charge is virtually a definitional statement demonstrating that, in the arena of pluralism, Bulgaria in 1988 still approximated a totalitarian regime. In any case, the regime's action "forestalled any other activity of the Committee. Two months after its founding it had disappeared from the scene."[128] Other groups formed and were dispersed, and, as Richard Crampton notes, "the backlash intensified at the end of 1988 and with the early months of 1989. The most troublesome leaders of the independent groups were expelled, while many of those who remained at home were harassed and subjected to a vilification which was more reminiscent of the Stalinist purges than of Gorbachev's era of glasnost."[129]

From February 1989 until November 1989, other important independent groups emerged, the most important of which was Ecoglasnost. Under the protective cover of a Conference on Security and Cooperation in Europe (CSCE) held in Sofia in October and November 1989, Ecoglasnost became the first group to carry out explicitly political coordinated public protests. However, even Ecoglasnost felt that its existence was in jeopardy right up to the internal party coup that overthrew Todor Zhivkov on November 10, 1989. Zhivkov had ruled the Bulgarian Communist Party from 1954 until the Bulgarian Politburo removed him in 1989. One of the key leaders of Ecoglasnost, Deyan Kiuranov, in an interview said that, despite the Ecoglasnost protests, the regime was still in complete control in early November 1989. In fact, Ecoglasnost leaders feared that they would be massively repressed by the regime as soon as the CSCE delegation left town.[130] "I did not believe in Zhivkov's downfall until it happened—and indeed for some time after. Ecoglasnost was preparing a deep defense for the post-CSCE period. We assumed our major visible leaders would be deported. We were planning for a leaderless organization. A few people were being saved by not going public so they could be in a position to try to coordinate some activities."[131] In his written work Kiuranov is just as clear that the regime, not the opposition, led to the overthrow of Zhivkov. "Despite speculations to the contrary, my opinion is that the activities of the opposition of the green umbrella were not the direct cause of the anti-Zhivkov coup . . . it was essentially an internal party affair. Much as I would have liked it, I cannot give Ecoglasnost or the opposition credit for the sophisticated palace coup."[132]

---

127. Ibid., 9, emphasis added.

128. Ibid., 10.

129. Crampton, "Intelligentsia, Ecology and Opposition in Bulgaria," 24.

130. This perception is also part of the reason that, unlike Hungary, where the organized opposition also sprang up relatively late in the game, in Bulgaria prodemocratic groups had little echo in society and "the prevailing feeling among Bulgarians was that the Zhivkov regime still had enough strength to disarm the opposition and to curb any genuine reformist efforts." See Vladimir Tismaneanu, *Reinventing Politics: Eastern Europe from Stalin to Havel* (New York: Free Press, 1992), 221.

131. Interview by Alfred Stepan with Deyan Kiuranov, Sofia, September 4, 1992.

132. Kiuranov, "Political Establishment of the Bulgarian Opposition," 15.

One of the leaders of the first independent trade union, Podkrepa, concurred that "10 November 1989 was a coup d'état within the party. In November and most of December 1989, the party still had control of the country. We only made our first public appeal for a strike more than a month after the internal party coup."[133] Compare this fact with the strike rate in the late years of the Franco regime, the strikes in Poland, and those in the industrial belt of São Paulo.

Our conclusion is that independently organized democratic opposition activity emerged as an effective force in Bulgaria only by mid-1989. Until that time the Bulgarian regime in the area of pluralism approximated a totalitarian model.[134] Even frozen post-totalitarian Czechoslovakia had had a continuous political opposition from 1977 to 1989, and the Charter 77 groups had visible protest leaders such as Havel and produced numerous policy papers on a wide range of issues. In fact, as the regime collapsed in Czechoslovakia, Havel and his supporters emerged as a clear moral alternative that had substantial hegemony in civil society. In sharp contrast, in early post-totalitarian Bulgaria, the opposition was thin, had few nationally known leaders, and, as subsequent events were to prove, had been deeply infiltrated by the regime so that again and again leaders were exposed as "informers" and lost credibility. Quantitatively, compared to authoritarian Poland, frozen post-totalitarian Czechoslovakia, or mature post-totalitarian Hungary, Bulgaria had significantly fewer independent movements in 1989. Since power is always relational, this weakness of the democratic opposition enhanced the capacity of the nondemocratic regime. Let us now turn to how the regime started and controlled the transition.

One of the two key leaders of the internal party coup against Zhivkov was Petar Mladenov, who eventually was selected by the Communist Party of Bulgaria to be the Secretary General of the party and who, with the Communist Party's support, was elected president of Bulgaria by the People's Assembly. That he was a pro-regime but anti-Zhivkov actor is clear from his extraordinary letter of resignation of October 24, 1989, addressed to Zhivkov, the Politburo, and the Central Committee. Initially, Zhivkov did not circulate the letter, but the following are extracts from the letter that Mladenov later circulated and never denied. It clearly demonstrates that at most he was a staunch properestroika Communist. He began by saying that both his father and mother were members of the Bulgarian Communist Party (BCP) and that he had attended the Moscow Institute of International Relations for six years. He went on to stress that

133. Interview by Alfred Stepan with Boyko Proytchev, political advisor to Podkrepa, in Sofia, September 2, 1992.

134. Even private initiatives in the economy were severely curtailed, contributing to the rather flat configuration with respect to pluralism. There was very little private economic activity and "virtually no experience with marketlike incentives." See Jacek Kochanowicz, Kalman Mizxei, and Joan M. Nelson, "The Transition in Bulgaria, Hungary and Poland: An Overview," in Joan M. Nelson, ed., *A Precarious Balance: Democracy and Economic Reforms in Eastern Europe* (San Francisco: ICS Press, 1994), quotation from p. 10. In the same volume also see Ekaterina Nikova, "The Bulgarian Transition: A Difficult Beginning," 125–162.

I was appointed chief of the Propaganda and Agitation Department of the CC of the BCP . . . In 1977 I was elected member of the Politburo of the CC of the BCP (i.e., for more than 18 years now I have been participating in the supreme governing body of our Party) . . . I think that the true reason for Comrade Zhivkov's irritation and crudeness [toward Mladenov] is his understanding that he has led the country to a profound economic, financial and political crisis . . . [Zhivkov] "succeeded" to isolate Bulgaria from the world, to isolate it even from the USSR, and now we (and we alone) are in a boat with the rotten regime of family dictatorship of Ceauşescu. In a word, Todor Zhivkov's policy has thrown Bulgaria outside the stream of time . . . I think that we are all aware that the world is undergoing a major change, and that if Bulgaria wants to be in tune with the world, our policy must be updated. Even if we don't believe anyone else, we have to believe the USSR and the Communist Party of the Soviet Union.[135]

In the first month after the overthrow of Zhivkov, it was not clear whether Mladenov wanted either perestroika or regime liberalization. But, after major effective public protests against the regime began one month after Zhivkov was overthrown, Mladenov from December 1989 to February 1990 initiated a series of liberalizing steps. One of the more important of these steps was removing article 1 from the constitution, which declared the Communist Party to be the sole leading force in society.[136]

Another major document of the Bulgarian transition that shows that the regime controlled the pace of change is a detailed study of the Bulgarian Round Table.[137] Unlike the Hungarian Round Table, where the democratic opposition first held an Opposition Round Table and set out firm principles of negotiation even before they agreed to enter negotiations, in Bulgaria the preparatory meetings for the Round Table were coordinated by Andrei Lukanov, one of the Bulgarian Communist Party leaders of the coup, who "chaired all meetings, set up the agenda and led the discussions."[138]

The opposition was further weakened in that some of the leaders of the democratic opposition, such as G. Tanbuev, S. Prodev, S. Russev, and Ch. Kiuranov, who were in 1989 among the co-founders of the oppositional organization, all had rejoined the Bulgarian Communist Party, many before the round-table talks actually began.[139]

135. Letter reprinted in *The Insider: Bulgarian Digest Monthly*, no. 1 (1990): 41–42. In the same issue Kostadin Chakurov, a close political advisor to Zhivkov in 1988–89 confirmed the receipt of the letter by Zhivkov, p. 39.

136. At the Fourteenth (extraordinary) Congress of the Bulgarian Communist Party (BCP), Mladenov laid out the foundations for liberalization in his report, "On Restructuring the Party and Building a Democratic Socialist Society." The report called for a "socially oriented market economy" and stated that the BCP was to be "de-Stalinized." According to *Keesing's* the report was "followed by a heated debate which illustrated the division between reformers and conservatives." See *Keesing's Record of World Events*, News Digest for February 1990, p. 37253.

137. Rumyana Kolarova and Dimitr Dimitrov, "Bulgaria," in Jon Elster, ed., *The Roundtable Talks and the Breakdown of Communism* (Chicago: University of Chicago Press, forthcoming). Future references will be to the 1991 unpublished manuscript, "Round Table Talks in Bulgaria."

138. Kolarova and Dimitrov, "Round Table Talks in Bulgaria," 12.

139. Ibid., 8. Prodev returned to become the editor of the party newspaper, "making it as diverse and interesting as the opposition press" and contributing to the party's new, liberalized image. See John D. Bell, "'Post-Communist' Bulgaria," *Current History* (Dec. 1990): 417–20, 427–29, quote from p. 420.

After the round-table talks began in January 1990, Aleksandar Lilov was elected the Communist Party leader and, in the judgment of Kolarova and Dimitrov, the reality that Lilov was in a position "to have total control over power and make concessions was considered by the general public as proof of transformation and democratization and was a powerful legitimizing factor. The fact that all major concessions were announced by the party leader A. Lilov and intensely propagated has to be emphasized."[140] The Bulgarian Communist Party, due to its control of the Parliament, was also able to set a date for elections in June 1990, earlier than the fledging opposition would have liked. Another victory for the Bulgarian Communist Party was that they were able to convince many potential voters that Zhivkov, rather than the Communist Party (after March 1990 known as the Bulgarian Socialist Party [BSP]), was the major cause of Bulgaria's troubles.[141]

In an early post-totalitarian context, where the ruling party was able to personalize the dictatorship, to take credit for its overthrow, and to present itself as the initiator of liberalization and where the opposition was still divided, where the Soviet Union was never seen as the major enemy of nationalism, and where the opposition barely had an organizational presence in the countryside, the ruling party, unlike in Hungary or Czechoslovakia, won the first free and fair elections.

We concur with most election observers that the Bulgarian Socialist Party had numerous structural advantages in the 1990 elections but that the elections were basically fair. Most pre-election polls in fact gave the Bulgarian Socialist Party a slight lead. This makes us believe that fraud on election day was not great. The Union of Democratic Forces (UDF) won in most of the major cities but did poorly in the countryside, where their modernizing message, if heard, was distrusted by a significant part of Bulgaria's relatively old rural population.[142]

Some analysts are harsher in their judgments and argue that local BSP activists manipulated rural voters' fears. "The people there were simply told they would be deprived of essential supplies if they voted for the opposition. After June 1990, a number of Muslim villages in southern Bulgaria were in fact deprived of supplies when it was discovered that they had supported the Movement for Rights and Freedoms or the Union of Democratic Forces."[143] The victory by the Bulgarian

140. Kolarova and Dimitrov, "Round Table Talks in Bulgaria," 33–34.

141. For example, in a pre-election poll 60 percent of the sympathizers for the Bulgarian Socialist Party blamed "Zhivkov and his Mafia" for Bulgaria's crisis, but only 7 percent of them blamed the previous Communist Party. See an analysis of these pre-election polls in "The Political Change in Bulgaria: Pre-Election Attitudes," in *Stability and Transition to Democracy in Bulgaria* (Center for the Study of Democracy, Sofia, 1990, occasional paper 1), 15.

142. See "The Political Change in Bulgaria: Post-electoral Attitudes," in *Stability and Transition to Democracy in Bulgaria*, 19–38.

143. See Plamen S. Tzetkov, "The Politics of Transition in Bulgaria: Back to the Future?" *Problems of Communism* (May–June 1992): 34–42, quote from p. 34, n.1. Analysts interested in comparative analysis might well compare Bulgaria with Paraguay, where close allies of General Stroessner overthrew his dictatorship, gained much credit for initiating liberalization, and were able to use the Colorado Parties' resources against a divided and weak opposition to win the first free election with a particularly strong showing in the rural areas.

Socialist Party in the June 1990 elections meant that the party controlled the parliament and the government and had succeeded in reconstituting its rule on the basis of participation in the round-table discussions and a popular mandate.

After the elections the Bulgarian Socialist Party's impetus for continued symbolic or substantial reform slowed somewhat. The newly named Bulgarian Socialist Party continued to occupy the former headquarters of the Bulgarian Communist Party. At a Party Congress of the Bulgarian Socialist Party in September 1990, the party chose to emphasize a degree of continuity with the past by calling the meeting the Thirty-ninth Party Congress (instead of the First Party Congress) of the Bulgarian Socialist Party. Of the 151 representatives to the Party Congress elected to the Supreme Council, few strongly identified with a reform faction. Aleksandar Lilov, who was one of the leaders of the internal party coup against Zhivkov but who was also Zhivkov's chief ideologist from 1974 to 1983, was reelected party president.[144]

On the opposition side the victory of the former Communist Party created some difficulties for the consolidation of sound democratic practices in political society. The most intense explosion of opposition in civil society occurred *after*, not before, the election, and for a while the streets seemed to displace the parliament as the center of politics. 'Tent cities' of young protesters sprang up in some of the major cities during the summer of 1990. In a still unexplained but dangerous incident, on August 26, 1990, the Bulgarian Socialist Party headquarters was "burned in a pogrom," as the General National Assembly officially called this fire.[145] The Bulgarian social scientist Ekaterina Nikova describes this period thusly: "During the whole period of 1989–1992, Bulgarian politics remained in a phase of prepolitics or antipolitics. Revolutionary rhetoric was kept alive, together with an anachronistic paranoic preoccupation with the past, the KGB, Moscow, and various conspiracies."[146] In conditions rather analogous to East

---

A June 1991 survey may provide us with a clue for the success of the Bulgarian Socialist Party (BSP) in the rural areas. In the survey there was no large difference between cities and rural areas in their response to the question "Do you prefer the system of governing that we have now or the system we had before the Revolution?" Positive answers were given by, respectively, 80 percent and 70 percent. However, when we turn to a battery of eight questions concerning that system of governing, the percentage of rural "don't knows" ranges between 42 and 64, compared to only 17 to 26 percent in the cities. Significantly, to the statement that "everybody is free to say what he or she thinks," 45 percent of rural respondents versus 17 percent of city respondents answered "don't know." We suspect that these high rates of rural "don't knows" reflected a climate of social control that leads to caution. On the other hand, it should be acknowledged that the rural population is particularly favorable to a controlled economy (78 percent). See NAPOC survey, "Divisions within Bulgaria: Results of a Survey of Economic and Political Behavior," *Studies in Public Policy*, no. 199 (1992): questions 57, 58, 63.

144. See the detailed article by Duncan M. Perry, "The Bulgarian Socialist Party Congress: Conservatism Preserved," *Report on Eastern Europe* (Oct. 26, 1990): 4–8.

145. For an analysis of the fire, of the charges by the BSP that it was opposition-inspired violence, and of countercharges by the Union of Democratic Forces (UDF) that it was done by the BSP to burn incriminating documents, see Mark Baskin, "The Politics of the Attack on BSP Headquarters," *Report on Eastern Europe* (Sept. 28, 1990): 8–12.

146. Nikova, "The Bulgarian Transition," 137.

German politics after the fall of the early post-totalitarian regime, a number of key leaders of the former democratic opposition lost legitimacy when it was revealed that they had been "police informers" under the previous regime.[147]

Possibly the most dangerous attitudes for the legitimacy of democratic institutions involved the reluctance of some members of the UDF to accept the legitimacy of a "formal democracy" led by the BSP. A faction of the UDF (called the "Dark Blues") in opposition to what was originally the mainstream of the UDF party, the "Light Blues," protested the moral legitimacy of the formal majority of the BSP to write the constitution for the new democracy. Their protest tactics included walking out of the constitutional debates in the National Assembly.[148] They were particularly enraged that the constitution made it difficult to prosecute former regime officials for acts that were not illegal when they were committed. In numerous interviews in the press and with Stepan, this group questioned whether formal democratic constitutional procedures should have precedence over the moral imperatives of justice. In terms of our categories, at times the Dark Blues were only semiloyal democrats in opposition in 1990–91. Even in the 1991–92 period, after the UDF had won the general election in October 1991 and a Dark Blue militant, Filip Dimitrov, had been prime minister for a year, they engaged in some semiloyal activity.[149]

Despite these problems, by 1995 Bulgaria was still a functioning democratic system. In 1991 the BSP began to renovate itself internally in a more democratic fashion after they were voted out of power. At the December 1991 Fortieth Party Congress of the BSP, the leadership began to be renewed with many young people assuming positions of importance. The UDF, in contrast, faced greater difficulties. In 1994, in protest against continued Dark Blue control of the UDF, the Democratic Party and major groups from Ecoglasnost left the UDF. In fact, Ecoglasnost, the most prominent civil society opposition group in the October–November 1989 antiregime demonstrations, *joined* in an electoral coalition with

147. The most damaging case involved the leader of the UDF, Petar Beron, who was forced to resign in December 1990 when accusations were made that for many years he had been an informer for the State Security. See Rada Nikolaev, "Between Hope and Anger," *Report on Eastern Europe* (Jan. 4, 1991): 5–10.

148. In May 1991, fifty UDF delegates walked out of the National Assembly demonstrating their unwillingness to work with the BSP, but "two-thirds of the opposition deputies remained in the parliament, arguing that a more conciliatory attitude toward the communists might win the latter over to democracy." See Plamen S. Tzvetkov, "The Politics of Transition in Bulgaria: Back to the Future?" *Problems of Communism* (May–June 1992): 35.

149. Interviews by Alfred Stepan in Bulgaria, August 31 to September 4, 1992. While some members of the opposition "advocated an eventual reconciliation and opposed the idea of reprisals against BSP officials," another faction (the Dark Blues) "adopted a far more strident tone, frequently referring to the BSP as 'murderers' and a 'Mafia,' giving the impression that the UDF would conduct a wholesale purge of the government if it won. Both the BSP and some members of the UDF referred to this as a policy of 'McCarthyism.'" See Bell, "Post-Communist" Bulgaria, 427. J. F. Brown goes further in his critique of the Dark Blues. He argues that they contributed to dangerous confrontational politics in 1992–93. "The former communists (now socialists) were not the ones most to blame; instead 'totalitarian' anti-communists had threatened to run riot." J. F. Brown, *Hopes and Shadows: Eastern Europe after Communism* (Durham: Duke University Press, 1994), 105–14, quote from p. 113.

the BSP. In December 1994, for the second straight general election, the UDF experienced a decline in its total vote share. The BSP coalition, with 43.5 percent of the votes, won 52 percent of the seats. In January 1995, this led to the second peaceful alternation of party power since 1991, as Zhan Videnov of the BSP was sworn in as prime minister.[150]

In early 1995 the UDF was thus in opposition again and still was divided about whether it should be a party or a movement. For example, the UDF continued to give an equal vote to each of the seventeen disparate groups in its organization. In other words, the UDF had yet to tranform itself from its prepolitical origins as an umbrella movement that had emerged out of an early post-totalitarian context into a modern democratic party.

From the perspective of prior regime type, Bulgaria from 1989 to 1995 probably "overperformed" democratically. The Bulgarian case needs much more study by observers more qualified than we are. However, we offer two hypotheses to explain this democratic "overperformance": one to do with institutional choice and another to do with an overlooked aspect of Bulgaria's pretransition civil society. The institutional choice question concerns Bulgaria's initial use of a parliamentary framework and its continued use of proportional representation which facilitated minority representation. The parliamentary form of government gave some flexibility to the fragile Bulgarian democracy that a presidential or semipresidential system would not have. For example, when president Mladenov became involved in a scandal about his possibly urging the use of tanks against protestors, the parliament was able to select the leader of the UDF opposition, Zhelyu Zhelev, the dissident philosopher of great prestige, as the president in August 1990. (The July 1991 Constitution subsequently introduced a semi-parliamentary system with direct election of the president.)

The elections in October 1991 were won by the Dark Blues, helping to bring them a bit more into normal politics. The choice of a parliament elected by proportional representation has also meant that politically motivated attacks on Bulgaria's Turkish minority have been softened somewhat, since both major parties intermittently wanted to follow policies that made them a plausible "coalition partner" with the Muslim-based Movement for Rights and Freedom (MRF), which in the first few elections provided the swing vote. In fact, the MRF was a crucial partner in a BSP minority government and in a UDF minority government.[151]

---

150. We owe our information on the 1994 election to an unpublished paper by Dessislava Zagorcheva, "The Transition to Democracy in Bulgaria and Hungary" (Department of Political Science, Central European University, Budapest, January 1995), and to Stefan Krause, "Bulgaria: Socialists at the Helm," *Transition* 1, no. 4 (1995): 33–38.

151. Indeed, Nikova asserts that "the Dimitrov government was in fact a minority government whose fate depended on cooperation with the MRF. The UDF-MRF coalition was disciplined, voting as a bloc on major issues. . . . In a situation unique in Eastern Europe, a small, ethnically based movement has assumed the role of a real national party, thereby thwarting the combined efforts of UDF and BSP extremists." See Ekaterina Nikova, "Bulgaria's Transition and the New 'Government of Privatization,'" Woodrow Wilson Center East European Studies Meeting Report, no. 82, p. 1. MRF's swing role in 1990–94 probably enhanced Bulgaria's capacity to deal with its potential stateness problems.

Our second hypothesis to explain Bulgaria's overperformance concerns an unexpected finding about civil society. Concerning oppositional organization, we are convinced that Bulgaria was close to the totalitarian ideal type until as late as 1988. However, the life of the university and researchers was not as closed as this implies. As long as academics did not organize protests or write critical reports, they were able to read a surprisingly wide variety of material in the national library—much more than their counterparts in Czechslovakia or the USSR. This has meant that Bulgaria had more intellectual capital than our category *early post-totalitarian* would suggest. We are happy to call attention to the specificity of this anomaly of Bulgarian early post-totalitarianism.[152] Notwithstanding this optimistic hypothesis, we are nevertheless concerned about the degree to which some of the legacies of early post-totalitarianism (i.e., nearly flat civil, political, and economic societies and a strong antipolitics strain in the parties and much of the public) mutually reinforce each other *negatively.* Thus, the challenge to rebuild each of these arenas is a difficult but necessary task for democratic consolidation.[153] In this respect we should record some sobering evidence. In a survey conducted in Bulgaria, the Czech Republic, Slovakia, Hungary, Poland, and Romania, in answer to the question as to whether it was "best to get rid of Parliament and elections and have a strong leader who can quickly decide things," 45 percent of Bulgarians polled strongly agreed or somewhat agreed. Hungary and the Czech Republic were much closer to meeting our criteria of "attitudinal" support for democratic consolidation in that, respectively, only 18 percent and 16 percent of the population strongly agreed or somewhat agreed with this antidemocratic statement.[154]

We have concluded that there is great variety and that there are some possibilities of evolution from the post-totalitarian regime type. We are now ready to explore an even more difficult type of regime configuration for democratic transition and consolidation. We consider it the most difficult and least understood regime configuration—one that combines sultanistic and totalitarian tendencies.

---

152. This observation is based on Alfred Stepan's review of the holdings as of 1989 in various libraries in Prague, Moscow, and Sofia and was confirmed by Bulgarian academics such as the economist Maria Todorova and the social scientist Deyan Kiuranov, who have conducted research in both Moscow and Bulgaria in the pre-1989 period.

153. With respect to the importance of pluralism in economic society and its expression in political society, Herbert Kitschelt notes that "Bulgaria's transition to democracy was shaped by the preemptive strike of segments in the communist party who then acquired a position to shape much of the economic transformation because the opposition forces do not have a competent counter-elite that could effectively organize the political-economic transformation. . . . What is missing in the Bulgarian political landscape is a genuinely libertarian pro-market political force equivalent to those found in Poland or Hungary." Herbert Kitschelt, "Emerging Structures of Political Representation in Eastern Europe" (paper prepared for the conference on the Social and Political Bases of Economic Liberalization, Warsaw, September 23–26, 1994), quotes from pp. 14 and 32.

154. Richard Rose and Christian Haepfer, "New Democracies Barometer III: Learning from What Is Happening," *Studies in Public Policy*, no. 230 (1994): table 45.

18

The Effects of Totalitarianism-cum-Sultanism on Democratic Transition: Romania

Oᴏ ᴛʜᴇ ꜰᴏʀᴍᴇʀ Warsaw pact countries in Eastern Europe (Bulgaria, Czechoslovakia, East Germany, Hungary, Poland, and Romania), Romania has numerous distinctions.[1] It had the last transition. It had the most violent regime termination. It was the only country that had nothing remotely close to a national round table. It is the country where the successor regime committed the most egregious violations of human rights. It is the only country where the democratic opposition has yet to win a national election. It is the only country where a former high Communist official was not only elected to the presidency in the first free election, but re-elected.[2]

Dᴇᴄᴏɴsᴛʀᴜᴄᴛɪɴɢ Rᴏᴍᴀɴɪᴀɴ Exᴄᴇᴘᴛɪᴏɴᴀʟɪsᴍ

What explains such exceptionalism? We should first acknowledge that there is more debate about some of the most basic "facts" concerning the transition in Romania than about any other transition we consider in this book. For example, the uprising that sparked Ceauşescu's downfall began in the town of Timisoara. There has been an intense dispute about how many citizens were killed in

1. This chapter draws upon some material previously presented in Alfred Stepan, "Romania: In a Sultanistic State," *Times Literary Supplement* (Oct. 1992), 26–27. Permission to reprint is acknowledged gratefully.

2. Part of this "exceptionalism," of course, has historical roots that precede the Communist period. Romania had one of the weakest experiences of interwar democracy and one of the strongest indigenous fascist movements (the Legion of the Archangel Michael or Iron Guard) in Eastern Europe. For this period see the important studies by Eugene Weber, "Romania," in Hans Rogger and Eugene Weber, eds., *The European Right: A Historical Profile* (Berkeley: University of California Press, 1966), 501–74, and Henry L. Roberts, *Rumania: Political Problems of an Agrarian State* (New York: Yale University Press, 1951). For the purposes of this chapter, the best biography of Ceauşescu is by the Oxford historian Mark Almond, *The Rise and Fall of Nicolae and Elena Ceauşescu* (London: Chapmans, 1992). Anneli Ute Gabanyi, *Die unvollendete Revolution: Rumänien zwischen Diktatur und Demokratie* (Munich: Piper, 1990), is particularly useful for the complex politics of the overthrow of Ceauşescu. A useful modern history of Romania that contains seven short chapters on the post-Ceauşescu period is Martyn Rady, *Romania in Turmoil: A Contemporary History* (London: I. B. Tauris, 1992). See also Daniel Nelson, ed., *Romania after Tyranny* (Boulder, Colo.: Westview Press, 1992).

Timisoara, who killed them, and whether the uprisings in Timisoara and later in Bucharest were spontaneous, manipulated, or even planned by Communists for their own ends.[3] In Romania a major explanation for the country's exceptionalism involves variations of the theme of captured revolution and a well-planned conspiracy.[4] For an immersion in the atmosphere of elation, fear, rumor, confusion, disinformation, and disillusionment that surrounded the fall of Ceauşescu in the winter of 1989 and that contributes to the conspiracy theory, one can do no better than read the account by the award-winning poet Andrei Codrescu of his return to Romania after a twenty-five-year exile in the United States.[5] One of his best chapters, subtitled "Seize the Means of Projection," describes the young students, poets, peasants and former officials in front of the cameras, urgently presenting their views of what was happening to an electrified country and the world. Securitate terrorists were still believed to be a counter-revolutionary threat. Rumors of deliberately poisoned water supplies, of 10,000, 60,000, even 100,000 dead, filled the news channels and the streets. Codrescu had his reservations about many of the new converts to revolution from the old regime, but he, like everyone else, was amazed by the ability of the revolutionaries to use television for their purposes and was swept up in the revolutionary spontaneity of events.

Six months later, on a return visit, Codrescu's euphoria had turned to despair. The old Communists, now the neo-Communists organized in the National Salvation Front, had not only "captured the revolution" (the government itself, led by Ion Iliescu and his former Communist allies), but also captured the words and the meanings of the revolution. President Iliescu had called out vigilante miners to smash the students (who represented to Codrescu the most authentic part of the revolution in Bucharest). Codrescu was distressed to find that many of his friends hailed Iliescu for thanking the miners publicly for their patriotic and disciplined rampage. Then, too, the body count in Timisoara had apparently been inflated by digging up bodies from nearby paupers' graves. Codrescu was thoroughly disillusioned and disoriented. It seemed to him that the whole revolution had been a fake, a film scripted by the Romanian Communists, with a "beautifully orchestrated piece of Kremlin music conducted by Maestro Gorbachev."[6]

3. Comparativists interested in Romania are fortunate that two anthropologists with many years of field work in Romania have dedicated an excellent article to a careful rereading of myths concerning the fall of Ceauşescu. See Katherine Verdery and Gail Kligman, "Romania after Ceauşescu: Post-Communist Communism?" in Ivo Banac, ed., *Eastern Europe in Revolution* (Ithaca: Cornell University Press, 1992), 117–47. For a much-needed analysis of the myths concerning Timisoara, see 118–22. See Michel Castex, *Un mensonge gros comme le siècle: Roumanie, histoire d'une manipulation* (Paris: Albin Michel, 1990), for one such myth, the revolution as a KGB plot.

4. Verdery and Kligman go so far as to call "'the plot mentality' characteristic of virtually every Romanian's description of events prior to, during, and after December 1989." Verdery and Kligman, "Romania after Ceauşescu," 119. Nestor Ratesh devotes a forty-page chapter to a review of conspiracy theories in his *Romania: The Entangled Revolution* (New York: Praeger, 1991), 80–119.

5. Andrei Codrescu, *The Hole in the Flag: A Romanian Exile's Story of Return and Revolution* (New York: William Morrow, 1992).

6. *Ibid.*, 206.

Codrescu's difficulty in knowing what happened is ours too. We do know that the number of people killed in the collapse of Ceauşescu's regime is closer to two thousand than sixty thousand. We also know that Codrescu is probably right in thinking there was an element of a staged counter-revolution, even to the extent of simulated gunfire, and that disinformation played an important role in the events. If, during the uprising, the forces of Iliescu in the Central Committee building in Bucharest's main square were under siege by Securitate loyalists, why are the surrounding buildings destroyed and the Central Committee building unscarred by bullets?

We dwell on Codrescu's book because the idea of a "scripted" revolution, implying a sinister plot written in advance whose enactment allowed its authors to "capture" the revolution, is still probably the reigning framework for analyzing the events in the country. But, as we have indicated, of all of the transitions from Communism that occurred in Eastern Europe, Romania's is the one where we are least able to know what really happened, and, of all the narratives, that of the scripted revolution allows the fewest ambiguities and contradictions. The value of Codrescu's book, then, lies not in its account of connected events as they occurred, but in its documentation of how myths are replaced by countermyths. Indeed, what we are arguing is that, for Romania more than for any other transition in Eastern Europe, any primarily narrative account is necessarily unsatisfying; what we need, rather are studies of the dynamics of myth creation and the function of disinformation—a deconstruction of the revolution itself. The best effort along these lines is the superb piece by two anthropologists, Katherine Verdery and Gail Kligman. They too have sifted through the supposed facts and evidence, and they know all the literature, but their concern is with the very terms by which the events in Romania were experienced, described, and understood: *the miners, the demonstrators, the front, the revolution, neo-communism.* This makes for a lot of italics, but is illuminating.[7]

Most importantly, to analyze the Romanian transition we need to think more deeply about the nature of the Ceauşescu regime and to place Romanian politics in comparative perspective. Of the Warsaw Pact countries in Eastern Europe, Romania had the weakest organized opposition. Indeed, civil society is still so weak that many members of the two innovative organizations, the Civic Alliance and the Group for Social Dialogue, want the monarchy back in order, they say, to give civil society a chance to develop.

The exceptionalism of Romania is most apparent when we consider it in relation to Poland, Hungary, and Czechoslovakia. However we classify the latter regimes in political terms, in all of them, but not in Romania, some space for organized opposition already existed before the transitions began. Ceauşescu's Romania was a fundamentally different place. In Romania, there were no autonomous or even semi-

7. Verdery and Kligman, "Romania after Ceauşescu."

autonomous career paths in the state apparatus. Even the top nomenklatura were hired, treated, mistreated, transferred, and fired as members of the household staff. There was growing personalism, beginning with the appointment of Elena Ceauşescu to the Politburo in 1972 and ending with the well-known "socialism in one family" of the 1980s.

In essence, Ceauşescu treated Romania as his personal domain. Max Weber called this kind of extreme patrimonialism "sultanistic." The Middle Eastern associations of the term are unfortunate because regimes as geographically diverse as Kim Il Sung's in North Korea, Bokassa's in the Central African Empire, and Somoza's in Nicaragua all exhibited strong sultanistic tendencies. In our judgment, understanding the combination of sultanistic and totalitarian tendencies in Ceauşescu's Romania clarifies much more that is distinctive in Romania's past, present, and foreseeable future than the framework of a Communist plot or a "captured revolution."[8]

Totalitarianism: Anti-Soviet Stalinism and the Missed Post-Totalitarianism Turn

Before we explore the sultanistic component of Ceauşescu's rule, let us first examine the totalitarian component. Specifically, did Romania ever come close to being post-totalitarian, by which we mean did Romania ever loosen any of the controls of a fully totalitarian system? And, if it did, how and why—unlike in most East European countries—did totalitarianism re-emerge? Personalism and the manipulation of nationalism are a key part of this and the subsequent sultanistic story.

Whereas most of the East European countries underwent destalinization periods under Khrushchev's influence, Romania under Gheorghiu-Dej and his close associate, Nicolae Ceauşescu, actually resisted destalinization. However, in the last two years of Dej's rule (1963–65), a combination of anti-Soviet nationalism and domestic liberalization gave the regime a somewhat greater degree of internal support.

When Dej died in March 1965, Ceauşescu, by no means the clearly pre-eminent surviving member of the Politburo, was selected within three days as the First Secretary. Ironically, Ceauşescu successfully used appeals to "collective leadership" and respect for colleagues in his effort to consolidate power. Indeed, as Ken Jowitt

---

8. The totalitarian-sultanistic combination is not such an unlikely combination as is often thought. In a trenchant and pioneering manner, Kenneth Jowitt has long insisted on the patrimonial dimension of many Leninist regimes. In his opinion both the Soviet and Romanian regimes had strong patrimonial tendencies before Stalin's death in 1953. He goes even further. He develops an argument, using the same quotes from Max Weber that we cited in chapter 3, that "patrimonialism in its sultanistic form was dominant in the Romanian Party at least from 1957 until 1965." See Kenneth Jowitt, *Revolutionary Breakthroughs and National Development: The Case of Romania 1944–1965* (Berkeley: University of California Press, 1971), 190–197, quote from 193. For Dej's fusion of Leninism and patrimonialism and how this was in some ways congruent with traditional Romanian ascriptive structures of personal patronage, see pp. 147–149.

and Mary Ellen Fisher make clear in their perceptive studies, Ceauşescu's rise to power was aided precisely by the fact that he appealed to those party leaders who wanted a more institutional approach to party rule. The 1965–68 period is a crucial period in Romanian development because mutual fear among the party elite might have contributed, as it had earlier in the Soviet Union, to the regime becoming post-totalitarian.[9]

However, Ceauşescu skillfully used nationalism to go from *primus inter pares* to undisputed leader. Alone among the Warsaw Pact leaders, Ceauşescu condemned the 1968 Soviet invasion of Czechoslovakia. This act greatly increased his national and international support. Both sources of support augmented his relative independence from the collective leadership and from criticism. A leading Romanian intellectual captures how nationalism helped Ceauşescu: "At the end of 1968 Romania was the only country in Eastern Europe where the communist leader was strongly supported by intellectuals. To criticize Ceauşescu we had to undergo a process of rejection that was not easy for us because each gesture against Ceauşescu was seen as a gesture for the Soviet Union."[10] An analogous process, which yielded important material and moral resources and helped demoralize the domestic opposition, occurred among Western leaders. Leaders from De Gaulle to Nixon came to Romania and praised Ceauşescu for his independence. Such international acclaim distracted attention from the fact that Ceauşescu was not like Czechoslovakia's Dubček, who combined anti-Soviet and anti-Stalinist practices, but was actually creating a new form of "anti-Soviet Stalinism."[11]

By the Tenth Party Congress in 1969, collective leadership was interred. Ceauşescu managed to change the party statutes so as to increase his freedom

9. Jowitt cites a key 1965 Ceauşescu speech to the Party Congress as an example of his appeal to a more collegial style of leadership. He also notes that "another element is the very real fear which most members of the elite coalition probably had of Draghici, the head of the security police, to obtain leadership of the Party." Ibid., 226; see also 192–97, 224–28. Jowitt's argument is similar to the reasons he gives for the emergence of a more collegial post-totalitarian leadership style in the Soviet Union after Stalin's death. "The party leadership favored Khrushchev's Party Magna Carta—that is, strictures against a Party sultan like Stalin and his possible use of a patrimonial secret police against the leadership itself." Kenneth Jowitt, *New World Disorder: The Leninist Extinction* (Berkeley: University of California Press, 1992), 251. The most extensive analysis of the rise and demise of collective leadership in Romania under Ceauşescu is Mary Ellen Fischer, *Nicolae Ceauşescu: A Study in Political Leadership* (Boulder, Colo.: Lynne Rienner Publishers, 1989), 66–140.

10. Interview by Alfred Stepan with Pavel Campeanu, Bucharest, June 23, 1991. A comparable remark was made by another prominent intellectual who otherwise has a quite different political outlook than Campeanu. Ovidiu Trasnea, who was a vice president of the International Political Science Association in 1984, argues that "Ceauşescu from 1968–1971 succeeded in gaining the sympathy of the people. This was his most brilliant period." Interview with Stepan, Bucharest, June 25, 1991. Martyn Rady also comments on the importance of Ceauşescu's condemnation of the 1968 Soviet invasion of Czechoslovakia for the consolidation of his power: "Ceauşescu's defiance of Moscow made him a national hero. He and the survival of the Romanian nation became for a time inextricably bound together in the public imagination and opposition to him became temporarily confused with betrayal of the country." Rady, *Romania in Turmoil*, 42.

11. As Mark Almond notes, "It is difficult today to recall that Dubček and Ceauşescu were often mentioned in one breath as the great hopes for reform." Almond, *Rise and Fall of Ceauşescu*, 65. He goes on to say that, in fact, Ceauşescu never repudiated Stalin; indeed, four months before his death he affirmed that "Stalin did everything a man in his position should have done." 67.

from collective leadership. The instrument that was most potentially useful for collective leadership was the fact that the Politburo and the Central Committee had the prerogatives of appointing and removing the General Secretary. Ceauşescu was able to shift these prerogatives to the much larger Party Congress, over which he had greater personal control. His arguments were that this should be done for reasons of national autonomy because the Congress would be harder for Moscow to manipulate, and for democracy, because the Congress should be the sovereign body of the party.[12]

In 1971 Ceauşescu visited China at the height of the cultural revolution and made the first of his many trips to North Korea. As Mark Almond comments, "He was even more impressed by the cult of Kim Il Sung in Pyongyang than by the adoration of Mao on display in Peking."[13] Upon his return to Romania, Ceauşescu almost immediately eliminated the last vestiges of a more relaxed post-totalitarian cultural life.[14] In 1974, he was inaugurated president in a ceremony mimicking a coronation, which completed the fusion of all key party and state roles.[15]

SULTANISTIC ACCRETIONS

After 1974 the Romanian regime never became less totalitarian, but it did become increasingly sultanistic. This combination made the Romanian regime very resistant to any form of nonviolent transformation.

In chapter 3 we spelled out what a regime with strong sultanistic tendencies would be like vis-à-vis the four key dimensions of regime type: leadership, pluralism, ideology, and mobilization. We start with the regime feature that is most distinctive of sultanism—leadership. Ceauşescu's policies and personal style made it clear that he was unbounded by rational-legal constraints like collective leadership and party statutes, and his rule was highly personalistic and arbitrary.

We argued that sultanistic regimes, because of their personalism and the fact that all power derives from the sultan, tend to exhibit strong dynastic tendencies. The extreme tendency of the "sultan" to place his family in most key positions differentiates it from the strong personalism of totalitarianism. Under Ceauşescu, his wife Elena was formally and informally the second most powerful person in the country. Among the titles she held were First Deputy Prime Minister, Chairman of the Commission on Cadres of the Romanian Communist Party, and

---

12. Previously cited interview with Ovidiu Trasnea; also Fischer, *Nicolae Ceauşescu*, 152–59.

13. Almond, *Rise and Fall of Ceauşescu*, 70.

14. From 1970 to 1972 the minister of culture in Romania was Mircea Malitza. Almost immediately after Ceauşescu's visit to China and North Korea, Ceauşescu criticized Malitza for being too tolerant, ordered the cancellation of an experimental course in Western management techniques, greatly curtailed the study of foreign languages, and made all ideological courses revolve around his personal thought. Interview with Mircea Malitza by Stepan, June 22, 1991, Bucharest.

15. For details see Fischer, *Nicolae Ceauşescu*, 160–70, and Almond, *Rise and Fall of Ceauşescu*, 70–71.

Chairman of the National Council on Science and Technology. President Ceau-şescu's four brothers all held key levers of power, while other ministerial positions rotated in and out at the pleasure of Ceauşescu (often called the *Conducator*). In the Ministry of Defense, his brother, Ilie, was Chief of the Main Political Direc-torate. In the all-powerful and hated security police (Securitate), his brother, Nicolae, was in charge of the personnel department. His brother, Ioan, was Vice-Chairman of the State Planning Commission, and his brother, Florea, was a mem-ber of the staff of *Scinteia*, the party daily. The list of other family members in high positions goes on and on. And, of course, his son, Nicu, was widely seen as being groomed as his successor.[16]

The leadership style also became increasingly personalistic. Ceauşescu's 160 "books" were translated into thirty languages and the Romanian philosophical dictionary gave more space to President Ceauşescu's doctrine of Marxism than to the entries for Marx, Engels, and Lenin combined.[17] By the mid-1970s, Mary Ellen Fisher writes, "no Romanian official could deliver a report or write an article without referring to President Ceauşescu's personal insight and leadership as the major source of inspiration and guidance."[18]

Ceauşescu's sultanistic leadership style was again and again manifested in poli-cies. He personally designed, with virtually no technocratic or party help, many huge industrial projects. He destroyed much of historic Bucharest as he capri-ciously designed and endlessly redesigned all of the approach routes and the cen-tral edifice of the most brutal architectural project in Eastern Europe, The Palace of the People.[19] The construction of huge steel mills was a product of this style.[20] One of the most devastating of Ceauşescu's personal decisions was his pronatal-ist and antiabortion campaign, which led to compulsory humiliating gynecolog-ical examinations of women in factories, unwanted pregnancies, abandoned chil-dren and, given the weakness of Romania's hospital system, an AIDS epidemic among children in orphanages.[21]

16. On the dynastic dimensions of Ceauşescu's rule, see R. de Fleurs, "Socialism in One Family," *Survey* 28, no. 4 (1984): 165–74, and Ronald H. Linden, "Socialist Patrimonialism and the Global Economy: The Case of Romania," *International Organization* 40, no. 2 (1986): 347–79. For an extensive list of family mem-bers in key public positions, see Vladimir Tismaneanu, "Personal Power and Political Crisis in Romania," *Government and Opposition* 24, no. 2 (1989): 177–98, esp. 192–93.

17. See Vlad Georgescu, "Romania in the 1980s: The Legacy of Dynastic Socialism," *East European Poli-tics and Society* 2, no. 1 (1988), 82, and Vladimir Tismaneanu, "Ceauşescu's Socialism," *Problems of Commu-nism* 34 (Jan.–Feb. 1985): 63.

18. Mary Ellen Fisher, "Idol or Leader? The Origins and Future of the Ceauşescu Cult," in Daniel N. Nel-son, ed., *Romania in the 1980s* (Boulder, Colo.: Westview, 1981), 118.

19. Almond devotes an entire chapter, "The Architect of Socialism," to this revealing sultanistic episode. Almond, *Rise and Fall of Ceauşescu*, 153–71.

20. For the arbitrariness of these and other policies, see Daniel N. Nelson, *Romania: Politics in the Ceauşescu* Era (New York: Gordon and Breach Science Publishers, 1988), esp. xiii–xvii, and Vlad Georgescu, "Romania in the 1980s: The Legacy of Dynastic Socialism," *East European Politics and Societies* 2, no. 1 (1988), 66–93.

21. See Gail Klingman, "The Politics of Reproduction in Ceauşescu's Romania: A Case Study of Politi-cal Culture," *East European Politics and Societies* 6, no. 3 (1993): 364–418; Daniel J. Rothman and Sheila M.

These totalitarian and sultanistic tendencies combined to make all individuals, groups, and institutions permanently subject to the sultan's arbitrary intervention. The essence of pluralism in sultanism is that no one is free from the exercise of despotic power by the sultan, from top party officials to pregnant women. Tismaneanu captures the personal despotic power of Ceauşescu deftly: "He behaves like an absolutist monarch humiliating party bureaucrats (his vassals) and treating citizens like his property."[22] This extreme personalization of power inevitably meant that there was no degree of institutional autonomy or pluralism in Romania. Career lines in the party and in important state organs such as the military were constantly disrupted. According to Tismaneanu, "the leading role of the party has been superseded by the absolute power of the General Secretary and his family. The level of independent initiatives by party apparatchiks has been reduced to a minimum. In order to stay in office, these people must excel in servility and conformity. . . . Under Ceauşescu the communist elite has virtually disintegrated and the Political Executive Committee is nothing but a rubber-stamp body dominated by the President and his wife."[23]

The Romanian Orthodox Church had no autonomy. In the late 1980s a few priests began to protest against the regime, but according to Romania's Sakharov, Mihail Botez, "all priests who took some very tough stands against state-church cooperation were expelled or voluntarily left the country. For Romanians, they are no longer important."[24]

In 1977 the most significant unrest before 1989 broke out during the miners strike in the Jiu Valley. The two most important leaders of the strike were Constantine Dobre and Engineer Jurca. After the strike was settled via a combination of Securitate intervention and Ceauşescu populism, Dobre disappeared and Jurca was murdered.[25] In 1979 there was an attempt by fifteen people in Bucharest to try to form an independent trade union. According to Nelson, "Ceauşescu's reaction was swift; Vasile Paraschiv, a principal organizer, was arrested and his fate remains unknown."[26]

There was absolutely no space in Ceauşescu's Romania for the development, as in post-totalitarian Czechoslovakia, of a second culture. Typewriters had to be registered with the police (decree 98 of March 1983), and failure to report a conversation with a foreigner was a criminal offense (decree 408 of December 1985).[27]

Rothman, "How AIDS Came to Romania," *New York Review of Books*, November 8, 1990, 5–8; and Rady's chapter on the environment and AIDS in *Romania in Turmoil*, 78–82.

22. Comments during a round-table discussion, *Romania: A Case of Dynastic Socialism* (*Perspectives on Freedom* no. 11, general ed., James Finn) (New York: Freedom House, 1989), 30. This fascinating book reproduces on pp. 5–93 a late 1988 round-table discussion among ten Romanian dissidents.

23. Tismaneanu, "Personal Power and Political Crises," 192–93.

24. In round-table discussion mentioned in note 20, *Romania: A Case of Dynastic Socialism*, 76.

25. Ibid., 80–81.

26. Nelson, *Romania: Politics in the Ceauşescu Era*, xiv.

27. See Georgescu, "Romania in the 1980s," 84. In interviews with Stepan, a number of writers made a point of insisting on the draconian effectiveness of these control mechanisms.

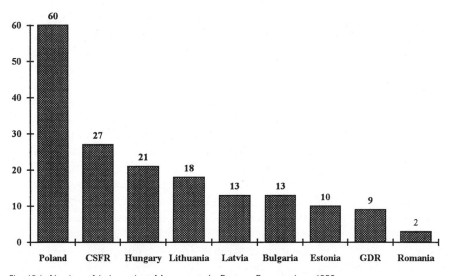

Fig. 18.1. Number of Independent Movements in Eastern Europe, June 1989.

Source: Jiri Pehe, "An Annotated Survey of Independent Movements in Eastern Europe," Radio Free Europe Research, RAD Background Report/100 (Eastern Europe), June 13, 1989, pp. 1–29.

In the last chapter we showed that Bulgaria had substantially fewer independent organizations in civil society than had Hungary or Czechoslovakia. However, in comparative terms, sultanistic and totalitarian Romania was even much more repressive of independent groups than was the country closest to the totalitarian/post-totalitarian boundary, Bulgaria. According to a comparative study by Radio Free Europe, in June 1989 Bulgaria had thirteen independent organizations, all of which had leaders whose names were publicly known. In sharp contrast, in June 1989, Romania only had two independent organizations with bases inside the country, *neither* of which had publicly known leaders (figure 18.1).

Stepan interviewed a number of the dissidents who in 1991 and 1992 were often cited as having made the most courageous attempts to print and distribute material critical of the regime. They all told varieties of the same tale. They worked alone or almost alone. They virtually had to hand-make their printing equipment, and they were all arrested either before or immediately after they attempted to disseminate their critique or calls to action.[28] Of all the countries we consider

28. Radu Filipescu, who in 1992 was president of Apador, a human rights and election watch organization, had three times personally made and distributed (with one other person) a one-page flyer for a symbolic protest. Two of the three times Filipescu was caught and arrested. Gabriel Andreescu, a key figure in two of the major vehicles of post-Ceauşescu civil society, the Group for Social Dialogue and the weekly 22, spent three years trying to get a dissident text smuggled out of the country. When Stepan asked him how many people in Romania had ever seen his dissident statements, Andreescu said "five or six." When Stepan asked, "Why so few people?" Andreescu replied, "I fear that was too many." Andreescu was once arrested for treason and once sent into internal exile. Probably the largest effort to create a dissident publication was by

in this book, Romania is the *only* country where not one genuinely full-blown *samizdat* publication appeared.[29] In no country was the penetration by, and fear of, the ruler and his security services so intense.

This is not to say there were not forms of private dissent among people who spoke a coded language. There was. One of the most famous involved a literary critic. A poetry group called "Cenaclul de Luni" (Monday Circle) met at the University of Bucharest from 1977 until 1983 under the supervision of the renowned literary critic, Nicolae Manolescu, as part of a compulsory cultural activity. One of the members of the Monday Circle, the poet Bogdan Lefter, notes that, while the group never had a journal or the opportunity to publicly express itself politically, it did evolve its own standards. "The best literary critics refused to praise bad writers who praised the regime. They did not invert the scale of values. The poets developed a way to describe society via 'small realism'. We depicted a small symbolic scene in a way that made a comment, without doing what we were not allowed to do, such as direct criticism. We were able to transform an official institution into a free, critical and creative institution." Precisely because the regime feared the élan of the Monday Circle, the university's ideological officer closed the circle in 1983.[30]

Another event that gave spirit to intellectuals who opposed the regime was the publication of two widely read books of dialogues by a disciple of the almost monastically reclusive philosopher, Constantin Noica. The books acquired great significance precisely because the very idea of a socratic dialogue introduced the idea of disagreement and pluralism of thought.[31] But the fact that the Monday Circle and the socratic dialogue were two of the most widely discussed expressions of independent thought and life indicates how far away from organized public dissent "living in truth" remained in Romania.

---

the journalist Petre Mihai Bacanu (who in 1992 was editor of the most important independent daily, *Romania Libera*). For eight months, Bacanu worked with six colleagues and used scrap material to build, "like Gutenberg," a small movable-type printing device so they could publish a newspaper. They made 2,000 copies of one sheet printed on both sides. All seven dissidents were arrested before the paper was distributed, probably because they tried to extend their group to thirty people to create a distribution network. Bacanu was released from prison on the day that Ceauşescu fled Bucharest. This note is based on interviews with Stepan in Bucharest, June 21–25, 1991, and August 25–31, 1992.

29. Future research will no doubt unearth some examples of a *samizdat* publication, but the key point is that most political activists insist they never saw one. Let us quote from some of our interviews with important political activists: "No *samizdat* existed in Romania. Occasionally a single person would put out a flyer, but no journal even had a single issue" (Pavel Campeanu). "We did not exactly have any *samizdat* here. But we had jokes of extremely high quality" (Senator Sorin Botez of the National Liberal Party and a former political prisoner). "No real *samizdat* of any sort, just an occasional flyer but even this was difficult because all the typewriters had to be registered with the police and their typeface analyzed once a year. There is not much study of the opposition under Ceauşescu because there was nothing that significant" (Calin Anastasiu, social scientist who won election as an opposition deputy in September 1992). Ibid.

30. Interview by Stepan with Ion Bogdan Lefter, poet and an editor of the important cultural journal *Contrapuncte* in Bucharest, August 27, 1991.

31. The "school" of the philosopher Constantin Noica is the subject of a chapter in the important book on cultural politics by Katherine Verdery, *National Ideology under Socialism: Identity and Cultural Politics in Ceauşescu's Romania* (Berkeley: University of California Press, 1991), 256–301.

In authoritarian Poland the parallel society was led by a trade union with ten million members eight years before the transition. In the highly repressive post-totalitarian Czechoslovakia, the leader of the parallel society was a playwright who helped lead an organization that in the twelve years before the transition issued 570 reports. In sultanistic/totalitarian Romania, the leaders were poets, literary critics, and philosophers, all of whom spoke a deeply encoded language of dissent, but none of whom were nationally known organizers of any form of public resistance. When the sultan fell there was no nationally known democratic movement or individual who could contest effectively for control of state power.

We now turn to the question of ideology. Under Ceauşescu there was indeed an elaborate ideology of the sort that is a key characteristic of totalitarianism and that is not normally associated with sultanism. This ideology had many of the standard features of Marxism-Leninism: a focus on collective property, the vanguard role of the party, and the articulation of utopian goals. The massive industrialization policy and the schematization plan to eliminate the rural-urban distinction by razing seven thousand traditional villages and forcibly putting peasants in three- or four-story buildings represent the subjection of the society's specificity in the name of totalizing, abstract ideology. However, under Ceauşescu, especially in the 1980s, there were also increasingly strong sultanistic tendencies that weakened the guiding function of ideology because Ceauşescu's ideological messages became increasingly contradictory, erratic, and personalistically opportunistic. In chapter 3 we argued that in sultanism there is "no elaborate and guiding ideology" but a "highly arbitrary manipulation of symbols" and an "extreme glorification of the leader." Countless analysts of Ceauşescu underscore the extraordinary manipulation of ideology. A few citations will suffice.

One of us asked a Romanian social scientist what ideology meant to Ceauşescu. The answer was revealing:

> He gave much importance to ideological problems but he was very mobile, very attentive to changes in the national and international environment, so one of his preferred slogans was 'enrichment of socialist theory.' In his mind it was a serious effort, but there was a constant tendency to interpret ideology in his favor, and for the last three or four years his resolve to search for such ideological enrichment became weaker and weaker. Slogans were repeated without argumentation. . . . He convinced few people with his ideology. There was a declining curve of commitment and identification with Ceauşescu.[32]

A European scholar, writing while Ceauşescu still ruled, also captured the degree to which ideology increasingly became neither a constraining framework for Ceauşescu nor a guiding parameter of action for followers. "Ceauşescuism," he wrote,

> contains a core of basic tenets constantly violated in practice, thus introducing a sense of unreality, fiction, and a Kafkaesque atmosphere of insecurity, anxiety and erratic behavior. As a style

32. From the previously cited interview by Alfred Stepan with Ovidiu Trasnea.

of operation it is characterized by extreme centralization of power, irrationality, and bombastic symbolism. . . . As a set of parameters for subelite behavior, Ceauşescuism is unpredictable . . . thus rendering predictable parameters and standards of performance invalid and dependent upon the attitudes of the movement in the inner circles of the Ceauşescu-Petrescu clan.[33]

Gheorghe Sencovici, son of a former Romanian Central Committee member and a computer scientist who left Romania in 1982, asked in 1986: "Who is Ceauşescu today? Is he a Communist? Is he a Stalinist? Is he obsessed by lack of legitimacy? Is he representing a doctrine? I am afraid he does not represent anything at all. . . . He is closer to Idi Amin, Hitler, Reza Pahlavi and Bokassa than to some other Communist leaders who are still driven by the doctrine."[34] Significantly, of the four figures whom Sencovici compares with Ceauşescu, only Hitler was not in our judgment close to the sultanistic type.

In this context Marxism as a living ideology virtually died in Romania. As Katherine Verdery concludes in her systematic and impressive study of ideology and cultural politics under Ceauşescu, "Marxist philosophy in Romania did not reproduce itself into a second generation: in the 1980s scarcely anyone was carrying on serious philosophical inquiries of a materialist sort."[35] In fact, her central thesis is that the extreme nationalism of the sort that Ceauşescu espoused and endorsed undermined the universalism of Marxism-Leninism. "This national ideology disrupted the Marxist discourse and thus—despite the Communist Party's apparent appropriation of it—was a major element in destroying the Party's legitimacy."[36]

The final regime characteristic we discuss is mobilization. This is the hardest for us to classify clearly. Certainly Romania under Ceauşescu approximated the totalitarian ideal type, in that there was "extensive and intensive mobilization into a vast army of regime-created organizations." As one Romanian social scientist commented, "in no other East European country were so many organizations politicized. Even small organizations with no intrinsic political character, such as an 'organization of people concerned with bees,' were organized by the party-state. The system interfered more deeply in aspects of your life than in any other East European country."[37] Certainly there was a degree of "voluntary" work on Saturdays, and a constant round of state-sponsored mobilization not normally characteristic of either a post-totalitarian or a sultanistic regime.

33. Trond Gilberg, *Nationalism and Communism in Romania: The Rise and Fall of Ceauşescu's Personal Dictatorship* (Boulder, Colo.: Westview Press, 1990), 56.

34. See the previously cited Freedom House round-table discussions, *Romania: A Case of Dynastic Socialism*, 19.

35. Verdery, *National Ideology under Socialism*, 269. Juan Linz in a private conversation with a top candidate for public office in Catalonia supported by the PSUC, the Partido Socialista Unificado de Cataluña (the Catalonian wing of the Communist Party), who had been a guest of Ceauşescu in Bucharest, heard the candidate comment that the regime that he considered most similar to Ceauşescu's was Somoza's Nicaragua.

36. Ibid., 4.

37. From the previously cited interview by Alfred Stepan with Ovidiu Trasnea.

If there was a deviation from totalitarianism concerning mobilization, it was that it was designed not so much to "mobilize enthusiasm" as to ensure the sultan's control of the population by reducing private space and the scope for any form of unauthorized activity. Certainly, the mass ritualized adulation of Ceauşescu had as much a sultanistic as a totalitarian quality. By the 1980s militants and cadres did not play an especially important role. Rather, every organization and institute in Bucharest was assigned a quota and a specific place for fulfilling ceremonial obligations.[38]

In summation, we believe our analysis of the status of pluralism, leadership, ideology, and mobilization under Ceauşescu, especially in the 1974–89 period, merits classifying Romania as a regime that exhibited both strong sultanistic and strong totalitarian qualities.

No one variable ever completely explains complex historical processes. However, an understanding of the nature of a regime that combines totalitarian and sultanistic qualities helps illuminate how and why most of the democratic paths to transition are virtually precluded. It also helps us understand why, even in the aftermath of the transition from sultanism, organized democratic forces are predictably weak and nondemocratic forces who can get credit for destroying the sultan can claim revolutionary credibility.

The Missing Players for a "Pacted Transition"

One of the most common paths away from a nondemocratic to a democratic regime is via a "pacted transition." In this book we have analyzed such pacted transitions from authoritarian regimes in Spain, Brazil, Uruguay, and Poland and even in the mature post-totalitarian regime of Hungary. In essence, pacted transitions are four-player games composed of hard-liners and soft-liners in the regime and moderates and radicals in the opposition. Theoretically and politically, there are two structural preconditions of such a pacted transition to democracy: (1) the existence of organized, nationally known, and nonviolent democratic groups in civil and political society and (2) the existence of soft-liners in the regime who have the desire and autonomy to negotiate a "pacted reform." Neither one of these necessary preconditions is possible in a sultanistic and totalitarian regime. Opposition groups, especially if they are moderate, democratic, and visible, are made to disappear. Within the regime, the sultan does not have room in his personal household staff for soft-liners who negotiate regime change. Thus, the four-player game is not an available transition path because the two most critical players are simply not present.

---

38. For a description of such compulsory mobilization and adulation, see Nelson, *Romania: Politics in the Ceauşescu Era,* 60.

Exits from Sultanism: The Special Role of
Violence and International Influence

Romania's peculiar combination of nationalist sultanism and totalitarianism also helps explain why violence predictably played a major role in the transition and why it was the last country in the Warsaw Pact to have a regime change. In a sultanistic regime there are almost no incentives or vehicles for regime-led democratic transition. The sultanistic erosion of the party's autonomy virtually precluded that a peaceful Bulgarian-type, collective, Politburo decision to remove the maximum leader would be possible. A military-led extrication coup by the "military as organization" was even less likely because not only was there no military as government, but, as Weber indicated, in a sultanistic regime state careers and state organizations lose all their organizational autonomy as they are constantly manipulated in accordance with the sultan's will. Finally, the sultanistic and totalitarian combination virtually precludes a transition in which a democratic and well-organized opposition in civil society brings down the regime without being met by violence. It is precisely this closure of nonviolent paths to regime transition that helps explain why regimes with strongly sultanistic features, probably more than any other type of regime, end in violent or revolutionary upheavals.[39] Cases in point are Somoza's Nicaragua, the Shah's Iran, and Batista's Cuba, as well as Ceauşescu's Romania.

In these circumstances, not only is some form of peaceful regime-led or society-led transition virtually impossible, but external events more than internal events can play an especially important role. Due to the diffusion effect, events in the Soviet Union concerning glasnost and perestroika and the upheavals in Hungary, Poland, East Germany, and even Bulgaria were widely followed throughout Romania via Radio Free Europe and Hungarian and even Bulgarian television.[40]

---

39. There is a growing literature on the propensity of regimes with strong sultanistic qualities to fall by revolutionary upheavals. See Jeff Goodwin and Theda Skocpol, "Explaining Revolutions in the Contemporary Third World," *Politics and Society* 17, no. 4 (1989): 489–509; Richard Snyder, "Combining Structural and Voluntaristic Explanatory Perspectives: Paths Out of Sultanistic Dictatorships," in H. E. Chehabi and Juan J. Linz, eds., *Sultanistic Regimes,* a book-length manuscript in progress; and John Foran and Jeff Goodwin, "Revolutionary Outcomes in Iran and Nicaragua: Coalition Fragmentation, War, and the Limits of Social Transformation," *Theory and Society* 22 (1993): 209–47. Writing months before the violent overthrow of Ceauşescu, Giuseppe di Palma perceptively observed, "Ceauşescu has moved closer to the patrimonial and predatory despotism of Central America. Thus, open repression/open conflict are more likely." See his *To Craft Democracies: An Essay on Democratic Transitions* (Berkeley: University of California Press, 1990), 240.

40. In interview after interview, activists and observers stressed the importance of external events. Even events in the penultimate Warsaw Pact country to fall—Bulgaria—were critical in changing power relations in Romania. Malitza, a former education minister, commented: "From 1988–1989 it was a delight for us to watch Bulgarian television. We got Yugoslavian, Hungarian, Soviet and Bulgarian T.V. To Romanians it was amazing to see such relative freedom. We had always looked down on Bulgaria. In the late 1980s some Romanians began to learn Bulgarian. We knew we could not go any lower. We watched the fall of Zhivkov in Bulgaria. We knew something had to happen here." Interview with Stepan, June 22, 1991, Bucharest. Gabriel Andreescu clearly acknowledged the Bulgarian demonstration effect. "I saw the success of the Bulgarian 'Eco-Glasnost.' I tried to create an ecological group here." Interview, August 26, 1992, Bucharest. Very impor-

Table 18.1. Evaluation of the Most Important Factors Influencing Public Opinion in the Period before the Overthrow of the Ceauşescu Regime

Factor	%
Political change in Eastern Europe	61%
Soviet policy change toward Eastern Europe	53%
Radio Free Europe broadcasts	33%
Romanian dissident activities	28%

Source: Poll administered to 1,500 people in Romania in 1990 by Radio Free Europe and presented by Ronald Linden at the IVth World Congress for Soviet and East European Studies, July 21–26, 1990, Harrogate, England.

The importance of these events and the relative unimportance of domestic dissidence activities is underscored in the results of a poll administered after the overthrow of the Ceauşescu regime (table 18.1). Given the critical importance of such prior events, it is understandable that Romania's sultanistic and totalitarian regime was the last of the Warsaw Pact dominoes to fall.

The "Capture" of the Revolution: Sultanism's Role

Much of the academic and popular literature on the Romanian transition puzzles over the problem of the "captured revolution." The ease with which Ion Iliescu and other neo-Communists were able to assume control of the popular uprising that began in Timisoara has led many commentators to attribute it to Soviet control or to a well-orchestrated prior plot. We are now in a position to advance our claim that sultanism itself is a more powerful explanation.

It was precisely the sultanistic component of Ceauşescu's regime that enabled Iliescu to present Ceauşescu as the embodiment of the system and to imply that he, Iliescu, had changed the political and economic system completely by decapitating the "hydra-headed monster." In no other Warsaw Pact country would this rhetorical trick of focusing moral outrage on a person, not the system, have had such weight. In East Germany, Czechoslovakia, and, to a lesser extent, even Bulgaria, the top leader was removed by the party, but this did virtually nothing to stop the protests against the regimes as such and the demands by the democratic opposition for a change of the entire system.

The extreme personalism and despotism of a regime, however, facilitates the "capture" of a revolution by groups very close to the old regime. The highly personalistic nature of the regime allows new leaders, even if they had close links to the regime, to advance the claim that the sultan was responsible for all of the evil

---

tantly, people felt that peaceful change would not be an option. In the words of the poet Ion Bogdan Lefter, "after 1980 in Poland, after Gorbachev in 1986, and especially after the 1989 dominos, we felt we were an isolated case and that Ceauşescu would never accept peaceful change." Interview, August 27, 1992, Bucharest.

in the country, thereby dissociating themselves from the sultanistic regime by playing a prominent role in his overthrow.

In Romania the radio and television accounts of the new Council of National Salvation emphasized the personalistic nature of the regime. The communiqué talked of the "downfall of the odious dictatorship of the Ceauşescu clan." In fact, this goes a long way to explain why Iliescu's colleagues in the interim regime rapidly eliminated the sultan in a "judicial murder."[41] To understand the new regime and the doubts we have about its liberal democratic character, we cannot but remind the reader of the grotesque nature of the "trial" and "judicial murder" of Nicolae and Elena Ceauşescu, which were totally in contradiction with the principles of rule of law and formal justice. The hurried execution has left many doubts about how it was handled, even though the entire world was shown the trial and the official version of the execution on television. It would seem that the new rulers wanted to exploit the hatred of the Ceauşescu's and at the same time to prevent embarassing accusations of their own past involvement under the sultan. In any case the show trial and summary execution were an inauspicious beginning for the new regime. The success of the revolution was proclaimed to lie in the destruction of the sultan himself, not in the creation of new democratic institutions as such nor in the destruction of the extensive coercive apparatus closely associated with Ceauşescu.[42]

The sultanistic quality of the regime also helps explain why Romania was the only Warsaw Pact country where former high Communist officials won the first elections, not only in the countryside, as in Bulgaria, but in *every* major city.[43] For reasons we have made clear, no democratic leaders or groups with national visibility and organizational resources had emerged in Ceauşescu's Romania. The uprising was too short, spontaneous, and politically manipulated to produce a governing alternative. In this context Iliescu and his allies only had to compete in the elections against two pre–World War II traditional parties, the National Liberal Party, whose leader returned to Romania from many years of exile to run for the presidency after the revolutionary events, the National Peasant Party, and the new Democratic Union of Hungarians in Romania. While the traditional parties had been anti-Communist for decades, they could not make any case that they had

41. On the "squalidness" of the trial, see Almond, *Rise and Fall of Ceauşescu*, 224–36, and Vladimir Tismaneanu, "Romania: Democracy, What Democracy?" *East European Reporter* 4, no. 2 (1990): 30.

42, This follows the logic and dynamics of revolutionary interim regimes that we discussed in chapter 5 and that are analyzed in Yossi Shain and Juan J. Linz, eds., *Between States: Interim Governments and Democratic Transition* (Cambridge: Cambridge University Press, 1995).

43. The only other Warsaw Pact country where there was an electoral triumph by forces closely associated with the Communist regime was Bulgaria. Yet, even there the democratic opposition was strong enough to win in the four largest cities and to win control of the presidency before its victory in the second free elections. In non–Warsaw Pact Albania, the opposition lost the first elections but won every major city. In sharp contrast, no poll ever showed that Iliescu was even behind in Bucharest in the May 1990 elections.

played a role in destroying the sultan, and the Hungarian party was easy prey to nationalist attacks.[44]

In contrast, not only was Ion Iliescu able to take personal credit for eliminating the hydra-headed monster, but he won further credit for almost immediately eliminating many of the most egregious measures personally associated with the sultan. Within weeks of Ceaușescu's death, compulsory gynecological examinations were abolished, condoms became available, the razing of peasant villages was stopped, the schematization plan was scrapped, the typewriter registration law was repealed, and publications proliferated. Under Ceaușescu no one had a personal passport. If a person was given a temporary passport for an officially approved trip abroad, it had to be handed in immediately upon return to get back the individual's indispensable personal identification card. One year after the fall of Ceaușescu, the Foreign Ministry claimed that ten million Romanians had personal passports.[45] Just as importantly, Iliescu was able to use his control of the state apparatus to help himself win the presidency and to help the National Salvation Front (NSF) gain an overwhelming majority in the parliament. Foreign credits were used to bring meat into the stores. The NSF provisional government allocated three million dollars for new printing equipment for the pro-NSF press, while it made newsprint scarce and distribution difficult for the opposition press.[46] While the opposition had some access to the state-controlled television, the NSF had a clear advantage when an analysis is made of what was shown and not shown before the elections.[47] Before we went to Romania, we believed that if the opposition had had more time to campaign they might have possibly won the May 1990 elections. However, two trips to Romania made it clear to us that Iliescu had such personal advantages as the antisultan figure and such structural advantages through his control of the state apparatus that he actually got more popular as the campaign progressed.[48] In this context, major technical fraud on election day was unnecessary, and on May 20, 1990, Iliescu won 85 percent of the presidential vote and the National Salvation Front won 66 percent of the parliamentary vote.[49]

44. For the May 1990 Romanian elections, see Rady, *Romania in Turmoil,* 160–174; Roger East, *Revolutions in Eastern Europe* (London: Pinter Publishers, 1992), 145–46; and Nestor Ratesh, *Romania: The Entangled Revolution,* 142–44.

45. Interview by Stepan with the foreign minister of Romania, Adrian Nastase, Bucharest, June 25, 1992.

46. For example, in the town of Iasi the NSF took over the major Ceaușescu-era newspaper, "which after the revolution changed its name but nothing else." The opposition press in Iasi, however, was regularly denied paper, was intimidated by thirty thugs sent by a former Securitate agent, and was denied access to the city's printing press. See "'24 Hours': An Independent Daily Newspaper Fighting for Survival," *East European Reporter,* 4, no. 2 (1990): 43.

47. See Crisula Stefanescu, "Romanian Radio and Television Coverage of the Election Campaign," *Report on Eastern Europe* 1, no. 23 (1990): 42–45.

48. This point was emphasized to Stepan by a major critic of Iliescu, Pavel Campeanu, who conducted polls during the election campaign. Interview in August 31, 1992, Bucharest.

49. There was some fraud, but the high vote derived from pre-election structural advantage. However, for detailed accounts of electoral irregularities, see Vlad Socor, "National Salvation Front Produces Electoral Landslide," *Report on Eastern Europe* 1, no. 27 (1990): 24–31.

The Nondemocratic Discourse of the Interim Regime

The specific nature of a transition often has an effect on the style of discourse and practices of the successor government. In the case of Romania, the specificity of the transition was that it involved revolutionary uprisings followed by an interim government that never had to have a round table or a pact. In chapter 5 we analyzed how and why interim governments often create a range of problems for the democratic quality of transitions. One of the major predictable (and observable) problems created by interim governments is that they tend to speak and act in the name of revolution and to believe that they are beyond the normal procedural constraints of democracy. Nondemocratic revolutionary discourse and practice will tend to be employed as "normal." If a transition is carried out in the name of revolution rather than democracy, the new power holders, even if they later augment their legitimacy via elections, will tend to govern in a way in which nondemocratic discourse and practice are frequently present.

Even after Iliescu and the National Salvation Front had won an overwhelming electoral victory, they chose to treat their defeated opponents in highly undemocratic ways. In the period between his election and his formal inauguration, Iliescu showed the primacy of revolutionary over democratic discourse and practices when he used vigilante justice against student protesters in Bucharest's University Square. He called upon (and provided elaborate prearranged transportation for) coal miners to come to Bucharest to defend the government and rid the city of the "hooligans." For two days in Bucharest the miners not only brutally beat students, but also seriously damaged the headquarters of the two main opposition parties.[50] One of the defining characteristics of a democratic government is that it meets its obligation to maintain a rule of law and to shape its own actions within the confines of those laws. When the miners left Bucharest, the newly elected president Ion Iliescu went to the train station and publicly addressed them. His discourse was more that of a nondemocratic revolutionary than that of a democratic head of state.

I thank you for everything that you have done these days. I thank you all once again for what you have proved these days: that you are a powerful force, having a high civic and working-class discipline, one can rely on in good and especially in bad times. The whole thing is a part of a bigger and more detailed scenario in the whole of Europe. There has existed a convergent action on behalf of extreme rightist forces that have in mind that in all of Europe extreme rightist forces have to come to power. . . . Everything they have done, all the slogans they have brought forth accusing me and also others that we have confiscated the revolution, as if one could steal away a revolution! But the truth is the extreme right has been trying to turn the Romanian Revolution into the right wing's hands. We have to keep our vigilance awake. . . . We

---

50. See Michael Shafir, "Government Encourages Vigilante Violence in Bucharest," *Report on Eastern Europe* 1, no. 27 (1990): 32–39.

have to maintain a fighting briskness. . . . We know that we can rely on you. We should ask for your help whenever it seems necessary! . . . The very best to you.[51]

Totalitarianism cum Sultanism and Nationalism: The Difficult Legacy

In September and October 1992, Romania again held parliamentary and presidential elections. President Ion Iliescu was re-elected with relative ease. The united democratic opposition (the Democratic Convention) was able to win only 21 percent of the parliamentary vote despite the fact that most international observers did not find too many irregularities.

How can we go about understanding Romanian politics after the parliamentary and presidential elections of September–October 1992? To approach this task we have to go beyond the conceptual framework provided by the scripted uprising, the captured revolution, or neo-Communism. To speak of *scripted* uprisings in Timisoara and Bucharest is to underestimate the importance of the "movements of rage" (to use Ken Jowitt's memorable phrase) in undermining Ceauşescu's coercive power. *Revolution* overestimates the degree to which these movements of rage represented organized opposition groups with their own leaders and programs. *Captured revolution* misses the extemporaneous opportunism and weakness of Iliescu. *Neo-Communism* overstates the principled cohesion of the government that followed Ceauşescu's downfall and in particular does not take into account the profound divisions within the National Salvation Front that emerged in 1991. In fact, in the twelve months before the 1992 elections the anti-Iliescu wing of the National Salvation Front, faced with a crisis of governance in September 1991, formed a coalition government that included some of the traditional liberals, supported the prime minister's courtship of the International Monetary Fund, and, in late March 1992, won control of the party label.[52]

But, as the presidential and parliamentary elections showed, sultanistic rule left behind a flattened political and social landscape.[53] Civil society remained incipi-

---

51. Iliescu's "farewell and thank you" speech to the miners on June 15, 1990, is reprinted in full in Foreign Broadcast Information Service Daily Report, *East Europe,* June 18, 1990, 67–70.

52. See Dan Ionescu, "Romania's Ruling Party Splits after Congress," *RFE/RL Research Report,* 1, no. 16 (1992): 8–12.

53. Gail Kligman correctly stressed that one of the major legacies of Ceauşescu and his demise by uprising was almost the complete lack of what we call *political society.* The "demonstration of public will, in body and voice, was critical in the exhilarating days of the coup/popular revolt, [but] public power may not be best realized through continuous mass street demonstrations. . . . It is one thing to overthrow a dictatorship; it is another to participate in the establishment of a democratic public sphere and of civil society. The current daily events have acquired their own ritualized, theatrical character. They are more exemplary of the inherited legacy of the Ceauşescu years, in which behavior was thoroughly ritualized, than they are of progressive steps on the road to democratic practice. Now there is a need for the institutionalization of interests in formal and informal associations." Gail Kligman, "Reclaiming the Public: A Reflection on Creating Civil Society in Romania," *East European Politics and Societies* 4, no. 3 (1990): 393–437, citation from 410–411.

ent, the rule of law fragile, political coalitions turbulent, and most political tendencies compromised.[54] In this context, the Romanian opposition was not able to mount a principled and united democratic campaign led by a prominent political figure and to carry its message into every corner of the country, as the anti-Pinochet opposition in Chile had been able to do in 1989. The Romanian opposition won only 21 percent of the parliamentary vote, while Emil Constantinescu, the opposition's presidential candidate, won 39 percent of the vote to Iliescu's 61 percent in the second round of the presidential election. The weakness of the opposition, as much as the strength of Iliescu, explained why Iliescu won the presidential run-off in October 1992.[55]

In our analysis of the weakness of the democratic opposition, we have stressed the sultanistic and totalitarian legacy. However, Romania also has a simmering stateness problem, which has been exploited by Ceauşescu's successors. Romania has a minority population of 1.7 million Hungarians, many of whom are concentrated in Transylvania. In an appeal to nationalism, article one of the new Romanian constitution defines Romania as a "unified national state." Article 4 says the state is based on the "unity of the Romanian people." Article 13 says "for Romania, the official language is Romanian."[56] In rejection of this nation-state policy, an important political party, the Hungarian Democratic Alliance, has sometimes stressed its democratic opposition character and sometimes stressed its autonomist character. Both in 1992 and in 1995, the status of the Hungarian Democratic Alliance led to significant splits in the democratic opposition. In this

---

54. Both the National Liberal Party and the Ecological Party split, with one faction of each party joining the government from September 1991 to April 1992. The student leader Marian Munteanu, who had been brutally beaten by the miners in June 1990, was made first chairman of the Havel-like Civic Alliance in November 1990, but by 1991 he had broken with the Civic Alliance and formed a party called Movement for Romania, which deliberately used many of the slogans and symbols of Romania's interwar fascist-inspired Iron Guard. In June 1992, on the 110th anniversary of the birth of Romania's wartime authoritarian and nationalist leader, General Ion Antonescu, almost all members of Parliament stood up and observed a moment of silence in his memory. See Vladimir Tismaneanu, "Endangered Democracy: Emerging Pluralism in Post-Communist Romania" (paper prepared for the Bellagio Conference on New Issues in Democracy, December 1992).

55. The democratic opposition did manage to get eighteen parties together in a coalition called the Democratic Convention. However, the main wing of the National Liberal Party left the convention in April 1992 because it objected to the presence in its ranks of the party representing Romania's Hungarian minority. Subsequently, the convention lost many valuable months deciding on a presidential candidate. The two principal forces in the Democratic Convention were the pre-war National Peasant Party led by Corneliu Coposu, a staunch anti-Communist monarchist octogenarian, and the more modern Civic Alliance Party. Although Pavel Campeanu's polls showed that the Peasant Party had 11 percent of voter support and the Civic Alliance Party had 9 percent, the price of uniting was that the Peasant Party received 55 percent of the slots on the convention's electoral lists, while the Civic Alliance Party received less than 20 percent. In the 1992 electoral campaign there was very poor coordination between the two major wings in the Democratic Convention. As a result, the convention was unable to wage a vigorous campaign in the countryside, which remained under the control of Iliescu and the former Communist nomenklatura, and won only 21 percent of the parliamentary vote. These observations are based on Stepan's pre-electoral visit to Romania and postelectoral conversations with participants.

56. See Aurelian Craiutu, "A Dilemma of Dual Identity: The Democratic Alliance of Hungarians in Romania," in *East European Constitutional Review* 4, no. 2 (1995): pp. 43–49.

context, the Iliescu government, like that of Ceauşescu, has exploited and exaggerated the threat to national integrity. Indeed, in January 1995 stateness problems contributed to the division of the democratic opposition and the temporary agglutination of a sinister "brown-red-sultanistic" four-party ruling coalition. One analyst described this new pro-Iliescu coalition in the following terms:

The chauvinist Greater Romania Party (PRM) and the Socialist Labor Party (PSM), the heir of the defunct Romanian Communist Party, formalized their relationship with the ruling coalition. . . . The fourth signatory to the protocol, the extreme nationalist Party of Romanian National Unity (PUNR), had already joined the government. . . . At the signing of the protocol, Ilie Verdet, a former premier under Ceauşescu and now PSM chairman; Adrian Paunescu, PSM first deputy chairman and a "court poet" of the Ceauşescu family; Corneliu Vadim Tudor, another Ceauşescu "court troubadour" and now the overtly anti-Semitic PRM chairman; and the staunchly anti-Hungarian Funar were immortalized in photographs alongside the PDSR leadership.[57]

This coalition stepped up pressure on opposition mayors, many of them perceived as being too sympathetic to minorities or to the opposition. The constitution watch of the *East European Constitutional Review* noted that, "overall, 133 mayors have been dismissed by government-appointed prefects. . . . Of the 62 mayors who appealed to the Court of Justice only four received redress. Despite the reaction of the parliamentary opposition, international organizations and the electorate, the executive seems determined to carry on its program of purging mayors."[58]

By 1995, Romania seemed to be in a paradoxical position. In contrast to all of the post-Communist East Central European countries we have analyzed thus far (Poland, Hungary, the Czech Republic, and Bulgaria), Romania was the farthest from a consolidated democracy in each of our five arenas. Civil society was still very weak. Political society had not created a robust governing alternative. Rule of law was intermittent, especially in areas concerning local government and the human rights of minorities such as gypsies and Hungarians. The reform of state administration had not been undertaken. Economic society had yet to be crafted. Many of these problems could be directly traced (as in Haiti with its similar problematic configuration) to the legacies of sultanism.

The apparently paradoxical point is that Romania, in poll after poll, emerges as one of the countries where the respondents say that the present regime is a substantial improvement over the former regime.[59] The apparent paradox is ex-

---

57. For a description of the coalition, see Michael Shafir, "Ruling Party Formalizes Relations with Extremists," *Transition*, 1, no. 5 (1995), 42–46, quote from 42.

58. See "Constitution Watch: Romania," in *East European Constitutional Review* 4, no. 2 (1995): 22.

59. For example, in 1993 only 35 percent of those polled viewed the former Communist regime positively, whereas 68 percent viewed the then-current regime positively. This 33 percentage point positive differential is significantly greater than the comparable differentials in Bulgaria, Slovakia, Hungary, and Poland and is slightly higher than that in Slovenia. Only the differential in the Czech Republic was greater.

plained, of course, by the intensity of fear of the sultan and his totalitarian and sultanistic penetration of their private and public lives. Given the terrible memories of the past, some opposition leaders took solace in the fact that, if they were able to strengthen civil and political society, they might do better in the 1996 presidential and parliamentary elections than they had done in 1990 or 1992.

Romania has by now experienced two elections, many of the formal institutional aspects of democracy are in place, and people perceive their new regime as a positive change with respect to the past. However, we cannot refrain from suggesting that Romanian democracy is different from that of all other East Central European countries in this study, as well as from the three Baltic republics, in that, until now, no leaders have gained power who did not have a career in the Communist Party apparatus (not just membership or association with the party). Sociologically, there has been no ruptura. Such continuity is not the same as having ex-Communists leading reformed communist parties (by whatever name) returning to power in free elections. In such polities (Poland, Hungary, and Lithuania), non-Communists were able to create political parties that were able to win elections and oversee a basic ruptura. To date, such a ruptura has only partially happened in Romania.

Why should this have been the case? We argue that the legacy of totalitarian control until the overthrow of Ceauşescu, combined with the legacy of sultanism and the way (as a consequence) that the transition took place, account for that significant difference.

See Richard Rose and Christian Haerpfer, "Adapting to Transformation in Eastern Europe: New Democracies Barometer—II," *Studies in Public Policy* 212 (1993): 47.

19

The Problems of
"Stateness" and Transitions:
The USSR and Russia

THE MOST SEVERE problems of stateness that we consider in this book occurred in the former Soviet Union and in the former Yugoslavia. Stateness problems were also critical, but ultimately less traumatic, in the former Czechoslovakia and, in a unique form, in the former German Democratic Republic. The most difficult problems that must be resolved in Latvia and Estonia before they can become consolidated democracies are not economic but involve citizenship and stateness. From once being neglected in the literature on democratic transitions, stateness problems must increasingly be a central concern of political activists and theorists alike.[1]

As comparativists interested in transitions from nondemocratic regimes, our focus is on what, if anything, can be learned from the disintegration of the Soviet Union and Yugoslavia. All too often, when the horrors of ethnic cleansing in Yugoslavia, the bloody consequences of the Chechen secession struggle, or the interethnic clashes in such former Soviet Republics as Azerbaijan, Moldova, or Georgia are addressed, it has been only too easy to explain the violent conflicts by referring to "primordial identities" and their consequences. Indeed, a growing belief emerged that, in the face of such "irrational emotions," neither international actors such as the European Union, nor statecraft of any sort could do anything to prevent the inevitable clashes of the new age of nationalisms.

However, in our opening discussion of stateness problems we argued that political identities are less primordial and fixed than contingent and changing. They are amenable to being constructed or eroded by political institutions and political choices.[2] In the Spanish case we documented how the choice of electoral sequence

1. For our analysis of why the classical literature on democratic transitions almost completely neglected stateness problems and for an alternative conceptual approach, see chapter 2.

2. With different emphases a variety of works in social science show how history, institutions, and imagination shape and constantly change nations, nationalism, and concepts of citizenship. See Ernest Gellner, *Nations and Nationalisms* (Ithaca: Cornell University Press, 1983); Benedict Anderson, *Imagined Communities: Reflections on the Origin and Spread of Nationalism* (London: Verso, 1991, rev. ed.); and Joseph Rothschild, *Ethnopolitics* (New York: Columbia University Press, 1981). With reference to the Soviet Union, see especially

helped create democratic state power and helped construct multiple and complementary political identities. Even with extremely skillful handling, we acknowledge that the stateness problem in the Soviet Union and Yugoslavia would have been much more difficult than in Spain.[3] However, we want to highlight the consequences of political structures, institutions, incentives, and choices, which we believe do not receive the attention they merit in the new debate about democratization, nationalism, and stateness.

We develop three closely inter-related arguments concerning stateness and transitions in the Soviet Union. First, we argue that the specific institutions and principles of Soviet-type federalism found in the Soviet Union and, with modifications, in Yugoslavia and Czechoslovakia created incentives and resource mobilization opportunities for the politicization of ethnicity. To be sure, in the Soviet Union before Gorbachev, these incentives and opportunities were greatly mitigated by the de facto control by the center of coercive and economic resources and by the fact that the federal constitution remained largely fictive. However, our intention is to call attention to the great *potential* stateness problems these structures engendered.

Second, we argue that, given the above structures, the transition path chosen of perestroika and glasnost, liberalization but not democratization of the early post-totalitarian central power structures, and the electoral sequence of holding the first non-single-party competitive elections at the republican rather than at the all-Union level had severe disintegrative consequences. This path eroded the party-state's ideological, coercive, and economic control capacities; did little to create new democratically legitimated state structures at the center; and directly helped make noninclusive ethnic nationalism the most dynamic force in politics.

Third, we argue that the major successor state of the USSR, Russia, in addition to the normal problems faced by all post-Communist polities, has a highly specific and difficult legacy of stateness and citizenship problems that would have greatly complicated its democratic transition and consolidation no matter what choices were made. However, the privileging of economic restructuring over democratic state restructuring further weakened an already weak state, deprived

---

Ronald Grigor Suny, *The Revenge of the Past: Nationalism, Revolution, and the Collapse of the Soviet Union* (Stanford: Stanford University Press, 1993), and Alexander J. Motyl, ed., *Thinking Theoretically about Soviet Nationalities: History and Comparison in the Study of the USSR* (New York: Columbia University Press, 1992).

3. Indeed, we believe that the problem of the Baltic countries—because of the compounding resentments stemming from their previous status as independent states, their relatively recent and forceful absorption into the USSR, their comparatively greater wealth, and their religious and linguistic differences— was insolvable within the context of the USSR. It could possibly have been better handled by Gorbachev making an announcement that he recognized the illegitimacy of the secret pact between Hitler and Stalin and holding a referendum on the fiftieth anniversary of that pact which asked the population of the Baltic countries whether they wanted to join the Soviet Union voluntarily. Had they voted not to join the Soviet Union (as they probably would have), a peaceful and rapid split might have been arranged with full citizenship rights for all. It is also unlikely that much could have been done to have kept Georgia, and possibly even Moldova, within the USSR.

the original economic reform program of the state the coherence necessary for the creation of an efficacious economic society, and contributed to the mutual delegitimation of the three democratic branches of government.

THE STATE'S CONTRADICTORY STRUCTURING OF NATIONALISMS

One of the reasons for the extraordinary disintegration of the USSR may well be that so many of the major political actors did not really consider that the USSR had the potential for a severe stateness problem. Mikhail Gorbachev, for example, began his famous book, *Perestroika,* with a strong argument that "the country was verging on crisis." There was a "slowing of economic growth," an "erosion of ideological and moral values," and "eulogizing and servility were encouraged." Because of all this, he argued, "Perestroika is our urgent necessity." Delays in reform would mean that the USSR would be "fraught with serious social, economic, and political crises."[4]

Against this threatening backdrop, Gorbachev mentions the nationality policy as an area of almost unqualified success.

The USSR represents a truly unique example in the history of human civilization. These are the fruits of the nationality policy launched by Lenin. The Revolution and socialism have done away with national oppression and inequality, and ensured economic, intellectual and cultural progress for all nations and nationalities.... Every unbiased person is bound to acknowledge the fact that our Party has carried out a tremendous amount of work.... If the nationality problem had not been solved in principle ... our state would not have survived [nor] the republics formed a community based on brotherhood and cooperation, respect and mutual assistance.

Meeting people during my tours of republics and national regions of the Soviet Union, I see for myself over and over again that they appreciate and take pride in the fact that their nations belong to one big international family, that they are part and parcel of a vast and great power which plays such an important role in mankind's progress. This is exactly what Soviet patriotism is all about.[5]

Gorbachev was not alone in this misperception. In separate private conversations with us, both Aleksandr Yakovlev, Gorbachev's key advisor and reform ally, and Yegor Ligachev, a key hard-line opponent in the Politburo, acknowledged that they had not given much attention to potential problems with nationalism when perestroika and glasnost had been launched.[6] This political unawareness was not

---

4. Mikhail Gorbachev, *Perestroika: New Thinking for Our Country and the World* (New York: Harper and Row, 1987), 3–7.

5. Ibid., 104–7.

6. Discussion of Alfred Stepan with Aleksandr Yakovlev in Moscow, October 24, 1989, and of Juan Linz with Yegor Ligachev at Yale University in November 11, 1991. Fedor Burlatskii, a prominent reformer and pro-Gorbachev intellectual, at a lecture given in 1990 at Harvard University, argued that the most important problem the USSR was facing was not ethnic but economic. Indeed, Burlatskii argued that, if economic reforms were accelerated, the national problem would disappear and even the Balts would agree to stay in the union. This line of thought, which emphasized the primacy of economic considerations, was typical of Gorbachev's circle.

confined to party leaders. Writing after the abortive coup of 1991, one of the Soviet Union's leading scholars on ethnicity observed, "The years of perestroika, especially the last two or three years, were marked by an unprecedented upsurge of national movements, national agitation and conflict. . . . These events were completely unexpected by the public, by experts on nationalities, by the press, and by political authorities. Why was this the case?"[7] We will attempt to explain.

One major reason (as in Yugoslavia and in Czechoslovakia) had to do with Soviet leaders' underestimation of the potential for conflict built into Soviet-style federalism. This type of federalism had its origins in history, ideology, and party-state power. The Soviet Union, Europe's last major multiethnic empire, was structured on potentially contradictory principles.[8] Because many of the nations or nationalities had had a prior period of independence, the regime made an effort to win compliance and attain integration by creating a federal system that contained an extraordinarily high degree of dualism. On the one hand, republics were made proto-states, organizations of cultural distinctiveness were legitimized, and there were extensive incentives for elites from the "titular republics" to advance their republic's (and especially their nationality's) specific interests.[9] On the other hand, the republics were members of a regime that espoused a universalistic ideology and was run by a centralizing party-state that not only monopolized important decisions but kept non-Russian nationalities (except for Ukrainians) out of almost all of the key command and control posts in the central party secre-

7. Galina Staravoitova, "Nationality Policies in the Period of Perestroika: Some Comments from a Political Actor," in the extremely informative volume edited by Gail W. Lapidus and Victor Zaslavsky with Philip Goldman, *From Union to Commonwealth: Nationalism and Separatism in the Soviet Republics* (Cambridge: Cambridge University Press, 1992), 114. For a particularly acerbic discussion of the marginalized role of nationality studies in sovietology, see Orest Subtelny, "American Sovietology's Greatest Blunder: The Marginalization of the Nationality Issue," *Nationalities Papers* 22, no. 1 (1994): 141–56.

8. S. N. Eisenstadt, a major theoretician of comparative empires, describes this effort at integrating two principals of legitimation thus: "On the ideological level, the basic mode of legitimation of the new regime—its strong universalistic and participatory orientations—in principle transcended any specific national boundaries. . . . The expression of the cultural heritage of different communities within the overreaching frameworks of the universalistic socialist Fatherland was fully legitimized. . . . It involved also the full scale legitimation of these republics as autonomous, providing them with all the organs of government. . . . Thus, their distinctiveness was fully legitimized, even if in reality these tendencies were overshadowed by the Russian centrist hegemony." He remarked that "the contradictions inherent in these policies could be suppressed by a strong totalitarian regime." See his "Center-Periphery Relations in the Soviet Empire: Some Interpretive Observations," in Motyl, *Thinking Theoretically about Soviet Nationalities*, 220, 205. For a discussion of the concept of *empire* as applied to the USSR, also see Alexander J. Motyl, "From Imperial Decay to Imperial Collapse: The Fall of the Soviet Empire in Comparative Perspective," in Richard Rudolph and David Good, eds., *Nationalism and Empire: The Hapsburg Monarchy and the Soviet Union* (New York: St. Martin's Press, 1991), 15–43. For the idea of the "outer empire," see Alex Pravda, ed., *The End of the Outer Empire: Soviet East-European Relations in Transition 1985–1990* (London: Sage Publications, 1992).

9. For a particularly strong historically anchored comparative analysis of this phenomenon, see Ronald Suny, who argues that, whereas Czarist Russia was called the "prison house of nations," for many groups "the Soviet Union became the incubator of new nations" and that "the story of Soviet nationalities can be characterized as one of a state making nations, but not just as it pleased." See Suny, *Revenge of the Past*, 87, 160.

tariat, the KGB, and the army.[10] Contradiction and conflicts, while in some ways growing, were contained in the Brezhnev period. These contradictory structures remained reasonably effective for managing nationalism as long as the centralized party-state was in overall control of the federation. However, as we shall see when we consider the perestroika period, the same structures can produce different dynamics under different conditions and different policies—especially if such structures harbor as many incentives for the politicization of ethnicity as did those of Soviet-style federalism (exhibit 19.1).[11]

We will conclude this section with a long quotation from an excellent historical study that captures the contradictory aspects of Soviet nationality policy.

Nation-making in the USSR occurred within a unique context: a state that had set out to overcome nationalism and the differences between nations had in fact created a set of institutions and initiated processes that fostered the development of conscious, secular, politically mobilizable nationalities. Despite the stated goals of the Communist party, the processes of nativization, industrialization, urbanization, and state-building in the Soviet Union provided the social and cultural base, first, for ethnic elites to organize low level resistance to rule by Russia and, later, for counterelites to mobilize broad-based nationalist movements. Still, the open challenge to the empire came only after the top party leadership decided to reform radically the political system, only when Communists themselves began a process that delegitimized the Soviet system and allowed a political voice to the nationalist alternative.[12]

In the next section we will explore how, why, and with what consequence Gorbachev began this process of state delegitimization.

Disintegrating the Soviet State: Liberalization without Democratization at the Center

As numerous studies have shown, the Soviet Union under Brezhnev began to experience a series of compounding and interconnecting problems in the late

---

10. For example, writing in 1980, Seweryn Bialer asserted that "not one position in the central party secretariat is occupied by a non-Russian. Only three non-Slavs serve within the central party apparatus, among over 150 top officials." And that "in almost every republic regardless of the degree of its self-administration, three top executive positions are almost invariably occupied by Russians . . . one is the head of the KGB . . . the second is the commander of the military forces stationed within the borders of the republic. The third position, [is] that of second secretary of the republican party organization." See his *Stalin's Successors: Leadership, Stability and Change in the Soviet Union* (New York: Cambridge University Press, 1980), 219, 214.

11. Bialer, in his above-mentioned 1980 book, was exceptionally prescient about the potential dangers these structures presented to the Soviet state. "The concept and reality of Soviet federalism contains a potentially dangerous dualism. . . . In practice it denies any but the slimmest margins of autonomy to the federated nationalities, but at the same time its symbolic institutions and administrative framework provide the base from which the struggle for national autonomy can be waged." (p. 210) "These institutions, . . . which are administered by local indigenous elites . . . provide a ready-made vehicle for those elites to fight for their autonomous national aspirations." (p. 211).

12. Suny, *Revenge of the Past*, 126.

Exhibit 19.1. Preperestroika Soviet Federalism: The Coexistence of Contradictory Structures, Principles, and Incentives

I. Mode of Adhesion to Federation

Theoretically, in any federation there can be three major contrasting modes of adhesion: traditional identification of core units, voluntary petitions to join, and forcible annexation. Traditional identification and voluntary petition present the least potential for conflict over membership. In the USSR, most of the major non-Russian nationalities and republics were brought into the federation by some degree of force. Estonia (1918–40), Latvia (1918–40), and Lithuania (1918–40) had had a significant period of independent statehood and were forcibly annexed as a result of the Molotov-Ribbentrop Pact. Bessarabia seceded from Russia and joined Romania but was annexed by the USSR as the core of the republic of Moldavia. Georgia, Armenia, Azerbaijan, Ukraine, Khiva, and Bukhara had periods of one to four years of independence after World War I. For less than a year Belorussia, the Crimea, Bashkiria, the Volga Tatar region, and the Kazakh-Kirghiz steppe had some degree of independence. Numerous additional nationalities inside the core republic, Russia, claimed autonomy and the right to self-rule. Some of the nationalities that had been a part of the Czarist empire were not members by tradition but had only been annexed in the 19th century after a prior period of political independence.[a]

II. Principle of Federal Unit's Political Identity, Administrative Organization, and Electoral Representation

There can be two contrasting principles of identity and representation in federations: the simple territorial principle or a principle based on ethnicity, language, or religion. The Soviet Union fused these two principles into territorial ethnofederalism. Each of the fifteen republics was explictly based upon and named after a different ethnic nationality. If other ethnic groups in the republics were relatively concentrated, autonomous administrative districts were created for them. In addition to the fifteen union republics, thirty-eight territorial administrations were designated as ethnic homelands: twenty as autonomous republics, eight as autonomous oblasts, and ten as autonomous okrugs. These administrative units in theory were to serve as the basis for electoral representation. In the pre-perestroika era, when elections were not seriously contested and the center controlled politics in the state, these structures did not matter. However, once some degree of electoral competition was introduced, there was a high potential for the mobilization of traditional—and contingently structured—ethnicity.[b]

III. Principle of Individual Citizen's Identity.

In most federations, an individual's primary legal identity is as a citizen of the state. In the Soviet Union, the Communist Party's ideological aspiration (and expectation) was of an ultimate merging (sliyanie) of national ethnic identities into the higher identity of being a member of the Soviet people. However, all internal passports made it obligatory to define oneself as a member of an ethnic nationality. Because the principle of identity was blood, rather than where one lived and worked, one did not acquire a new nationality even if one's family had resided in a different republic for generations. These state-mandated ethnic identities in fact impeded the emergence of multiple complementary political identities.[c]

IV. Principle of Secession

The constitutions of most federations are silent on secession procedures but do have detailed and mandatory mechanisms and courts that regulate federal relationships. Soviet constitutions were unusual in that both the Stalin Constitution of 1936 and the Brezhnev Constitution of 1977 accorded the right of the republics to secede. Article 72 of the 1977 constitution explicitly said that "every union republic shall retain the right of free secession from the USSR." However, the constitution was absolutely silent on how the right of secession could be implemented. Thus, there was inherently a high degree of potential conflict if there was any progress toward the rule of law, if elections became competitive, and if any republic wanted to exercise its constitutional prerogative to secede.

Exhibit 19.1. *(continued)*

V. Principle of International Representation and Foreign Policy Autonomy

Most federations explicitly accord to the center the exclusive right to represent the state internationally and to make treaties. In 1944, the Soviet Constitution accorded the right to the republics to enter into diplomatic relations with other states, to negotiate and sign treaties, and to exchange diplomats and join international organizations. The 1944 amendment was largely motivated by the center's successful effort to get Ukraine and Belorussia admitted to the United Nations as voting members. This amendment was largely fictive but represented a potential for federal conflict and republic resource mobilization if politics became competitive and the center weakened.[d]

VI. Structure of Career Incentives for Republican Political Elites

De jure and de facto in the Soviet Union, the center created a complex system of special incentives and affirmative action policies for the leading titular ethnic group in each republic. In almost all of the republics, the titular nationality was over-represented in universities, party-state posts, and cultural organizations. Ethnic political elites, in return for their privileged position and the extremely long tenure of republican first secretaries, prevented the emergence of ethnic counterelites to the center as long as the center was able to provide critical coercive and economic resources. The conflict potential here was that ethnic political entrepreneurs, with special ethnic constituencies and control over republican institutions, had the capacity and the incentive to act as political entrepreneurs by mobilizing their extensive ethnic political resources if and when their old power base, the centralized party-state, could no longer guarantee their careers.[e]

---

[a]See Alexander J. Motyl, *Sovietology, Rationality, Nationality: Coming to Grips with Nationalism in the USSR* (New York: Columbia University Press, 1990), esp. 30-45, 146–60; Richard Pipes, *The Formation of the Soviet Union: Communism and Nationalism, 1917–23* (Cambridge: Harvard University Press, 1954); and Suny, *Revenge of the Past*, esp. 20–83.
[b]See the excellent article by Philip G. Roeder, who develops a resource mobilization as opposed to a primordial sentiment approach to ethnicity, "Soviet Federalism and Ethnic Mobilization," *World Politics* 43 (Jan. 1991): 196–232.
[c]See Leokadia Drobizheva, "Perestroika and the Ethnic Consciousness of Russians," in Lapidus, Zaslavsky, and Goldman, eds., *From Union to Commonwealth*, 98–114, esp. 98–99, and Suny, *Revenge of the Past* for his discussion of the "territorialization of ethnicity," esp. 110–12. The coexistence of the above principle of the federal units' political identity and the above principle of the individual citizen's political identity involved a potential for contradiction and a legacy of conflict. It meant that a large number of "nationals"—not only Russians—lived in the diaspora in republics or autonomous ethnic homelands other than that of their "titular nationality." One consequence was that, after the independence of the fifteen union republics, many of their residents—citizens—were identified legally as of a nationality that was not the "titular nationality" of the new state. In addition, that nationality—except in the case of mixed marriages—was not the result of a choice of identity nor a result of long-term residence but of descent. Many of the minority problems of the new states are therefore a legacy of Soviet federalism that interacted with and contributed to emerging nationalist identities and sentiments.
[d]A comparative specialist on federations, Stephen Kux, calls these provisions "unique." See his article, "Soviet Federalism," *Problems of Communism* 39 (March–April 1990): 12.
[e]See Roeder, "Soviet Federalism and Ethnic Mobilization," 196–232; Bialer, *Stalin's Successors*, 210–11; and Suny, *Revenge of the Past*, 117–24.

1970s.[13] However, although many of the key ideas and concepts developed by Gorbachev had been aired among intellectuals close to the party before he came to power, Gorbachev was not forced by any group to launch his reforms. Gorbachev and his key advisors made a choice to transform the Soviet system and, in

13. The major work that analyzes the origins and course of perestroika is Archie Brown, *The Gorbachev Factor* (Oxford: Oxford University Press, 1996). Also see the collection of original articles, Archie Brown, ed., *New Thinking in Soviet Politics* (London: Macmillan, 1992). A valuable review of the literature is found in Edward Wilkes Walker, "Structural Pressures, Political Choice, and Institutional Change: Bureaucratic Totalitarianism and the Origins of Perestroika" (Ph.D. diss., Department of Political Science, Columbia University, 1992).

this respect, the Soviet Union clearly falls into our category of a *regime-initiated change*.[14]

However, why did this regime-initiated change lead to an explosion of nationalisms and the disintegration of the Soviet state? Exhibit 19.1 clearly shows that the answer is not just primordial nationalism and irrational emotions. Three of the most important recent bodies of social science literature can be brought to bear in the analysis of Exhibit 19.1: rational choice, resource mobilization, and neo-institutionalism.[15] The existing institutional structures, even before perestroika, provided *rational incentives* for republican elites to play ethnic politics and to build constituencies by creating ethnic agendas. The fact that ethnic regional elites had special control over cultural organizations, universities, and state personnel policies gave them access to *resources they could mobilize*, if politics ever developed in such a way that it was in their interest and within their capacity to do so.[16] In fact, the *institutions* created by the party-state virtually created some nations that had not existed before.[17] The other side of the neo-institutional perspective is, of course, that, in addition to structuring some outcomes, institutions constrain the choices available to decision makers. The existing structures constrained the effective choices Gorbachev could make. He wanted to put pressure on those members of the party-state who were impeding the program of perestroika. The liberalizing policies of glasnost, by allowing a freer press, initially helped mobilize perestroika supporters (especially among intellectuals) and helped shed the glaring light of publicity on practices and groups opposed to perestroika.[18] Eventually, however, Gorbachev, supported by Yakovlev, decided to use elections as part of his regime transformation strategy.

---

14. Gorbachev was at pains in his initial writings to stress that perestroika was a regime choice. A subtitle of his opening chapter of *Perestroika* is called, "What Inspired Us to Launch Perestroika," and he goes on to say that "the perestroika drive started on the Communist Party's initiative, and the Party leads it. . . . Perestroika is not a spontaneous, but a governed process." Gorbachev, *Perestroika*, 41–42. In this book, we have considered two other important cases of regime-initiated change, Spain and Brazil. However, in both cases a complex dialectical process of "regime concession and societal conquest" pushed liberalization to democratization of the center. In the Soviet case, given the interweaving of party and state, a caveat applies. It is difficult to say how much the restructuring was party or state inititated. With this caveat in mind, the restructuring was clearly initiated by the inside, as opposed to the outside, of the regime. But resistance to change could be found both in the official party and in the state apparatus. In addition, given the passivity of society outside some cities, the mobilization of society by the regime initiative—in contrast to the other cases mentioned—was initially limited.

15. A pioneering and convincing use of the rational-choice approach to ethnopolitics in the Soviet Union is Motyl, *Sovietology, Rationality, Nationality,* esp. 30–45, 146–60. For an excellent neo-institutionalist analysis, see Rogers Brubaker, "Nationhood and the National Question in the Soviet Union and Post-Soviet Eurasia: An Institutionalist Account," *Theory and Society* 23 (1994): 47–78.

16. The previously cited article by Roeder, "Soviet Federalism and Ethnic Mobilization," 196–232, is conceptually—and powerfully—driven by the resource mobilization approach.

17. Victor Zaslavsky, as does the previously cited work of Suny, goes as far as to say that these structures "promoted a peculiar process of nation-building." See his "The Evolution of Separatism in Soviet Society under Gorbachev," in Lapidus, Zaslavsky, and Goldman, *From Union to Commonwealth,* 71.

18. This is a classic state-led liberalization tactic used effectively, for example, by Generals Geisel and Golbery in Brazil against their hard-line opponents in the security apparatus. See Alfred Stepan, "State

We do not believe that the role of elections has received the prominence it deserves in the analysis of the disintegration of the Soviet state. The existing structures presented in exhibit 19.1 potentially presented an extraordinarily broad set of incentives and opportunities for the mobilization of ethnicity. Nonetheless, as long as the constitution remained largely fictive and the party-state had sufficient coercive, ideological, and economic resources to maintain control of ethnic elites in the republics, ethnicity, while never disappearing, was not mobilized to a degree that threatened the physical integrity of the USSR.

However, given the structure presented in exhibit 19.1, the regime transformation strategy chosen by Gorbachev directly mobilized the Soviet Union's territorially based titular nationalities against the state. This was due to three interacting phenomena: regime type, the choice of liberalization over democratization, and electoral sequence.

What type of regime did Gorbachev inherit? Let us quote at length from the excellent study of Gorbachev by Archie Brown.

Although there were important differences between the totalitarian dictatorship of Stalin and the highly authoritarian but post-totalitarian Khrushchev and Brezhnev regimes which followed, a great deal of conceptual stretching was involved in any attempt to attach the label, "pluralist," to the Soviet Union at any time earlier than the late 1980s.

Political pluralism implies political organizations independent of the state (or, in the Soviet case, party-state) and to this Soviet leaders from Lenin to Chernenko were implacably opposed. Even a social pluralism encapsulated in the notion of 'civil society' can scarcely be said to have existed prior to the Gorbachev era. . . . In the Soviet Union prior to the second half of the 1980s, the creation of any organization without the sanction and surveillance of the state was impermissible, even if that organization were not overtly political. . . .

. . . in the later Brezhnev years and under Andropov and Chernenko the Soviet dissident movement was at its lowest level of activity in two decades and had, to a large extent, been crushed.[19]

This is not the place to attempt a detailed empirical and historical characterization of the 1917–91 regime in the USSR in terms of our typology. However, the regime that Gorbachev inherited was not just another authoritarian regime, nor was it sultanistic.[20] The real question for this chapter is where the pre-Gorbachev regime stood on the totalitarian–post-totalitarian continuum we discussed in chapter 3. Concerning sociopluralism, the regime was far from being mature post-totalitarian, as the quote from Archie Brown makes absolutely clear.

In comparative terms, detotalitarianization-by-choice in the Soviet Union had certainly not gone nearly as far as in Hungary. There was nothing comparable to

---

Power and the Strength of Civil Society in the Southern Cone of Latin America," in Peter Evans, Dietrich Rueschemeyer, and Theda Skocpol, eds., *Bringing the State Back In* (New York: Cambridge University Press, 1985), 337–38.

19. See Brown, *The Gorbachev Factor*, 16–17 and 8.

20. Some of the long-serving first secretaries of the central Asian republics displayed some patrimonial and indeed at times sultanistic qualities. High Stalinism also had some sultanistic features.

Hungary's 1982 regulations, which created quasi-private property and inaugurated an expanded domain of statewide contractual relations which by 1988 contributed to the emergence of autonomous statewide entrepreneurial and trade union organizations. Most importantly, in Hungary three major opposition political party groupings had emerged before the transition. Nothing remotely similar existed in the Soviet Union.[21]

Indeed, we could even say that the ossification of the apparatus, the gerontocratic leadership, the wooden language of the ideology, the loss of mobilization capacity, and the passivity of the population made the USSR mostly a case of post-totalitarianism by decay.[22] Ironically, it was precisely this decay and degeneration that made the pre-Gorbachev regime *further away* from the totalitarian ideal type than was the German Democratic Republic. In the German Democratic Republic, many top cadres in the mid-1980s still, perhaps because of their constant confrontation with and their need for legitimation against the Federal Republic of Germany, retained a commitment to ideology, which they saw as the necessary justification for the leading role of their party and even a degree of mobilization.[23]

Notwithstanding this decay-induced post-totalitarianism, three factors concerning the uniquely great weight of the totalitarian legacy in the USSR, compared to East-Central Europe, should be stressed. First, for the core population of the USSR, unlike the Central European countries, Leninist and Stalinist versions of totalitarian Communism were domestic creations, not foreign importations. Second, for the people in the core of the USSR, in contrast to those in Central Europe, Communism lasted seventy-five years instead of forty years. Third, some people in Central Europe (the Poles) never lived under fully installed totalitarianism, while others, as in Hungary, lived under totalitarianism for only about fifteen years. Depending on where they lived in the USSR, many citizens lived under conditions that approximated totalitarianism for thirty or forty years.[24]

The fact that the Soviet Union was founded by Lenin after the Civil War in the early twenties as a totalitarian political system and that Soviet citizens lived for decades under Stalin must be stressed. Krushchev's de-stalinization campaign was, of course, important in moving the USSR away from a regime of terror, but it should be remembered that some totalitarian features were reintroduced or in-

21. For further analysis of Hungary, see our discussion in chapter 17. In fact, the USSR before Gorbachev had never advanced even as far on the post-totalitarian criteria as Czechoslovakia had in the Prague Spring in 1968.

22. The distinction between "post-totalitarianism by decay" and "post-totalitarianism by choice" is developed in chapter 3 and especially in chapter 17.

23. As the Friedman survey we discussed in chapter 17 showed, even the GDR coercive elites' belief in the use of force had eroded away from the pure totalitarian pole by the late 1980s.

24. In contrast to Czechoslovakia, we could also say that the USSR virtually had no usable pretotalitarian democratic past and limited advanced capitalist regulatory and/or industrial structures. But in this respect the USSR was not unique. Some other countries in East-Central Europe also had relatively underdeveloped pretotalitarian democratic or advanced capitalist structures.

tensified under Khrushchev, such as the attack on religion, the messianic commitment to "burying the West," and the massive use of force to retotalitarianize Hungary after the successful 1956 revolution. And, as we have seen, the Brezhnev era was more one of detotalitarianization-by-decay than detotalitarianization-by-choice. In summation, we can say that Gorbachev inherited a regime in which entire generations had not experienced any other political system, indeed any other society, than Soviet Communism. The combined influence of the "October Revolution," the Civil War, Stalinism, and the patriotism awakened in the face of the heroic defense against Nazi conquest in World War II understandably had a much greater effect on Soviet society than did the shorter totalitarian period in Central Europe (1948–57 in many countries), which was imposed in the wake of Soviet occupation or "liberation."

In this context liberalization in the USSR and even the dismantling of the party-state that began to occur in the late 1980s after seventy years of Communism could not result in the rapid emergence of a civil society in the Western sense of the term. Too many structures and traditions that managed to survive in the outer empire had, in the USSR, been destroyed or so profoundly distorted (e.g., the Orthodox Church) that their regeneration was a painful task. Thirty-five years of totalitarianism, combined with a totally socialized economy, had shaped the life of all subject-citizens. Practically all those who occupied any positions of social prominence in the early 1980s had been recruited, trained, and formed in the system. Only in some urban centers of the vast Soviet Union did small groups of dissidents develop a "non-Soviet" culture. Even when dismissing, rejecting, and even denouncing the ideology, a distinct Soviet mentality had been shaped by the system.

This helps account for the weakness of the liberal and democratic ways of thinking of the new elites emerging out of Soviet society. In fact, we suspect that in many places the displacement of the top elite who supported Gorbachev or Yeltsin (such as Aleksandr Yakovlev) and who for a variety of reasons had access to other ideas and experiences by second echelon and "provincial" elites who have not had comparable access or experiences has not helped in the transition to "democracy."

The society that had taken shape during almost seventy years of Communism was the one in which Gorbachev came into power and in which those in power in the periphery would try to retain power. Once Gorbachev put into motion actions and policies that began to weaken the ideology and structure of the centralized party-state, republic elites began to look for new sources of power, new sources of ideological legitimacy, and especially new identities. Thus, for the regional republic elites, the ethnofederalism of the USSR and the potential legitimacy to be derived from national cultures, however impoverished, distorted, or invented, became useful. Those in power in the peripheral republics could often most easily attempt to justify themselves by appealing to a specific form of nationalism—that of the "titular nations"—simultaneously against the "minority ethnic" groups in their own territorial domains, as well as against the centralized Soviet state.[25] In this sense the ethnonationalism that emerged during the disintegration of the USSR was a result both of the totalitarian destruction of society and the peculiar instititutions of ethnofederalism of the USSR.[26] We can understand how *independence* came to be privileged over *democratization*. But more about that later, since we have jumped ahead of our story.

Politicians are specialists in the mobilization of hopes and grievances. But what hopes and grievances would be mobilized? And how? And by whom? Gorbachev inherited a "flattened" post-totalitarian social and political landscape. What we mean by a flattened landscape is that many social structures such as churches, business and interest groups, professional associations, and some research institutes (even political parties in Chile and Uruguay) managed to persist with some independence or identity in the authoritarian regimes we analyzed in South America and southern Europe. However, during the totalitarian period in the USSR such organizations had been so penetrated or integrated by the party-state that they could not play a comparable role in the transition in the Soviet Union. This does not mean that with more freedom there could not appear a myriad of groups on the border between "civil society" and an emerging "political society." In fact, despite the flattened landscape a large number of democratic associations, fronts, and clubs managed to spring up during 1987–88. These groups were focused on a diverse set of goals ranging from ecology to the commemoration of the victims of Stalin's terror. These groups were largely composed of people between the ages of thirty and fifty, with higher education, and without experience in the dissident movement. Protopolitical organizations like the Moscow Association of Voters were created in late summer 1989, and their leaders began to plan for the electoral campaign for the Russian Supreme Soviet.

In January 1990 an alliance adopted the name Democratic Russia and ran 5,000 candidates for seats in soviets at all levels in the Russian Soviet Federated Socialist Republic (RSFSR).[27] Democratic Russia was able to organize two large rallies in Moscow, and candidates they supported gained fifty-seven of the sixty-five seats contested in Moscow for the Russian Congress of Peoples Deputies. After the elections Democratic Russia managed to form a parliamentary block in the RSFSR Congress of People's Deputies, but they numbered at best only 30 percent of the total. Although Democratic Russia played a crucial role in supporting re-

---

25. While recognizing the significant degree of elite opportunist utilization of nationalism, we do not want to deny that there were significant groups in each region who genuinely identified with a historic culture. This identification was particularly strong among intellectuals, artists, academics, and, exceptionally, as in Armenia, among members of a church that combined its own tradition *and* external links.

26. Ernest Gellner refers to post-USSR Russia as the "vacuum society." See his "Home of the Unrevolution," *Daedalus* 122, no. 3 (1993): 141–254.

27. See Yitzhak M. Brudny, "The Dynamics of 'Democratic Russia', 1990–1993," *Post-Soviet Affairs* 9 (April-June 1993): 141–70.

form, liberalization, and calls for democratization, they remained more a movement than a political party.

One crucial factor that contributed to the failure of groups like Democratic Russia to become real unionwide parties was the ambivalence, as we shall document in this chapter, of leaders like Gorbachev and Yeltsin, toward the creation of well-organized democratic political parties. Yeltsin benefitted from the support of Democratic Russia in his drive to gain power, but he did not want to lead it as a party or even to help it to become a party. Given such a landscape, if elections were held, the *easiest* hopes, grievances, interests, and identities for politicians to mobilize would predictably be related to ethnicity. In fact, the republics were protostates and the only cleavage that was partially legitimate in the Soviet Union was ethnicity.

This leads us to the question of the constrained choices facing Gorbachev. We are not sufficiently knowledgeable about the Soviet Union to judge whether Gorbachev could have chosen to maintain the status quo or, as China in the 1990s, tried to transform the economic system without transforming the political system. Certainly, many have argued that the party-state at the end of the Brezhnev era was facing a position where it increasingly did not have enough economic and ideological resources to maintain what Peter Hauslohner called its "social contract" with the Soviet citizens.[28] However, since Gorbachev made the choice to realign the system and to use elections as a key part of this restructuring, he fundamentally faced the two classic choices in the transitions literature, to "liberalize" or to "democratize."[29] Here there is a fairly sharp debate among scholars, and much of it depends on one's frame of reference. Some (but by no means all) scholars who were specialists in the Soviet Union and who were inspired by Gorbachev's constant use of the term *democratization* and by the fact that perestroika and glasnost unquestionably set so many liberalizing forces into motion argued that Gorbachev was committed to democracy. In much of the sovietology literature, there was in fact little distinction made between *liberalization* and *democratization*. Often the two processes were equated.[30]

However, as scholars of comparative democratic transitions, we believe that it is important to stress that Gorbachev *never* at any time from 1985 to 1991 unequivocally committed himself, the party-state, or the government of the center to *democratization* in the strict sense. That is, freely contested, all-union, multiparty elections whose winners would form a government at the center and as-

28. Peter Hauslohner, "Gorbachev's Social Contract," in Ferenc Fehér and Andrew Arato, eds., *Gorbachev: The Debate* (Atlantic Highlands, NJ: Humanities Press International, 1989), 61–83.

29. For our discussion of this fundamental distinction, see chapter 1.

30. As we argued in chapter 1, *liberalization* and *democratization* are quite different concepts. Also, empirically, liberalization has often occurred *without* democratization. For a discussion of how different Soviet specialists saw the question of Gorbachev and democracy, see Stephan White, "'Democratization' in the USSR," *Soviet Studies* 42, no. 1 (1990): 3–24 and John Gooding, "Gorbachev and Democracy," *Soviet Studies* 42, no. 2 (1990): 195–231.

sume the management of public policy and the state apparatus were never held or even planned.

Among contemporary theorists of democracy and of democratic transition, there are inevitable differences of emphasis. However, on a number of basic issues there is a consensus, a consensus shared even by the vast majority of Euro-Communists. This consensus includes a clear recognition that, in a democracy, power outcomes are necessarily *contingent* and cannot be guaranteed or fixed by one historical decision,[31] a political *opposition* must have the right to legal existence, internal party democracy is important but never a substitute for free *multiparty elections* for central power, and no degree of social pluralism is a substitute for *political pluralism*. Gorbachev's thought in 1985–89 was hostile or at best ambivalent to all of these positions (exhibit 19.2).

Elections were held in 1989 and 1990 in the USSR.[32] In 1989, the elections to the Congress of People's Deputies in the USSR clearly helped weaken some of the opponents of perestroika. However, in our judgment the elections had fundamental flaws. The 1989 elections to the central legislature were not multiparty. The elections had a mandate to produce a new legislature but not really to produce a government. The legislature never produced a new constitution and without this could not help reconfigure the federation.

The liberalizing elections of 1989 did, even at the center, begin to weaken the centralized party-state in a number of respects. A group of deputies, the Inter-Regional Deputies Group, many of whom wanted to push forward toward real democratization, began to criticize Gorbachev and the party-state for being illegitimate. In turn, a growing hard line in the party began to criticize Gorbachev for allowing the weakening of the party-state. Although the elections of 1989 provided an opportunity in the Baltic republics and the Caucasus for the mobilization of the nationalist-independence movements, in other republics they created the basis for a challenge to the central government under the ambiguous term of *sovereignty*, which cut across ideological lines. This was the case of the Ukraine— where the more independence-minded movement *Rukh* did not win—and in Belarus. The accelerated and irreversible erosion of the party-state and the center, however, came with the campaign for republican elections, which began in late 1989 and were held throughout much of 1990.

Let us look more clearly at elections and particularly at electoral sequences in

31. As Adam Przeworski correctly argued when he discussed the role of uncertainty in the transition to democracy, "Democratic compromise cannot be a substantive compromise; it can only be a contingent institutional compromise. . . . If a peaceful transition to democracy is to be possible, the first problem to be solved is how to institutionalize uncertainty." See his "Some Problems in the Study of the Transition to Democracy," in Guillermo O'Donnell, Philippe Schmitter, and Laurence Whitehead, eds., *Transitions from Authoritarian Rule: Comparative Perspectives* (Baltimore: Johns Hopkins University Press, 1986), 59–60.

32. And, of course, by May and June 1991 important presidential elections were held in Georgia and Russia, respectively.

Exhibit 19.2. Mikhail Gorbachev's Statements on Competitive Democracy: 1987–1991

1. On the Opposition and the Role of the Communist Party: 1987

"Official opposition does not exist in our country. This places even greater responsibility on the Communist Party of the Soviet Union as the ruling party. That is why we regard the further development of intra-party democracy, the strengthening of the principles of collective leadership in work, and broader openness in the party too, as a top priority."[a]

2. On the Noncontingent Nature of Outcomes in the Context of Perestroika and Democratization: 1987–88

"Socialist pluralism, and this is why it is called socialist, is the discussion, the scientific work, that is carried out *within* the boundaries of our socialist choice made by our people once and forever in October 1917."[b]

"We are conducting all our reforms in accordance with the socialist choice. We are looking within socialism, rather than outside it, for the answers to all the questions that arise. . . . Every part of our program of perestroika—and the program as a whole, for that matter, is fully based on the principle of more socialism and more democracy."[c]

3. On the Possibility of a Multiparty System in the Period before the First Multicandidate Semicompetitive Election: February 1989

"There is no basis for discussing it (ie. a multi-party reform) . . . two parties, three parties it is all nonsense. If you have three or four parties you can still have so much tyranny that nobody can open his mouth and speak freely . . . all of this is being foisted upon us by irresponsible people."[d]

4. On the Vanguard Role of the Communist Party: November 26, 1989
(The campaign for the republic elections had begun and the Berlin Wall had fallen.)

"We advocate real democracy . . . A special role in the social organism is played by the Communist Party, which is called upon to be the political vanguard of the Soviet society . . . Developing the masses' independent activity and the processes of the democratization of all social life within the framework of the one-party system is a noble and difficult mission for the Party."[e]

5. On the Communist Party's Role in Developing Pluralism: November 26, 1989

"At the current complex stage, the interests of consolidating society and focusing all its healthy forces on the resolution of the difficult tasks of perestroika dictate the expediency of retaining the one-party system. But the party will nonetheless promote the development of pluralism . . . The Party cannot yield the initiative to populist demagoguery, nationalistic or chauvinistic currents, or unruly group interests."[f]

6. On His Continued Commitment to a Unified Communist Party: Press Conference the Day after the Failed Coup: August 23, 1991

"I am sorry that the forces that should be making a contribution to reform the party are leaving. I see my role in this. I do not intend to give up the positions I have taken."[g]

[a]Mikhail Gorbachev, *Perestroika: New Thinking for Our Country and the World* (New York: Harper and Row, 1987), 23.
[b]Mikhail Gorbachev, "Politika partii, politika obnovleniya," *Kommunist* 4 (1988): 4. Emphasis added. Cited in Neil Robinson, "Gorbachev and the Place of the Party in Soviet Reform, 1985–1991" *Soviet Studies* 44, no. 3 (1992): 423–43.
[c]Gorbachev, *Perestroika*, 23.
[d]Quoted in Victor Yassman, "Gorbachev's Formula for the Second Stage of Perestroika: Full Ahead but Keep Right," *Radio Liberty: Report on the USSR*, March 10, 1989, 19.
[e]Mikhail Gorbachev, "The Socialist Idea and Revolutionary Perestroika," *Pravda*, November 26, 1989, 1–3. English translation in FBIS-Sov-89-226, November 27, 1989, pp. 78–79. On February 5, 1990, however, at a plenum of the Central Committee Gorbachev finally advocated the abandonment of article 6 of the constitution enshrining the leading role of the party and also recommended the creation of the institution of the presidency with sufficient powers to oversee the progress of reform.
[f]Ibid.
[g]Mikhail Gorbachev's Press Conference, English translation in FBIS-Sov-91 164, August 23, 1991, p. 28.

the Soviet Union and at the rather analogous elections in Yugoslavia.[33] In both countries elections were allowed, but in both countries the most democratic and contested elections were for regional power. The point is clearest in Yugoslavia, where competitive all-union elections were simply never held in the post–World War II period. Republic elections were held in Yugoslavia in the summer and fall of 1990 and, not surprisingly, ethnic issues became of paramount concern.

The situation in the Soviet Union was somewhat more complicated. The first elections in the Soviet Union were indeed all-union elections for the Congress of People's Deputies in March 1989. However, these elections were not multiparty, so democratic political society in the real sense could not develop. We should not forget that only in March 1990, just weeks before the elections began in Russia, did the Communist Party of the Soviet Union give up its guaranteed monopoly based on article 6 of the Soviet constitution. Only after article 6 was abrogated could other political parties be registered.[34] Although candidates endorsed by different democratic groups or movements were elected, parliamentary parties—or more exactly caucuses—really emerged only *after* the 1989–90 elections.

We cannot emphasize enough this basic difference from southern Europe, Latin America, and most of Central Europe, where parties had legal existence *before* the first or founding election. One consequence was that, in much of the Soviet Union and especially in Russia, though there were democratizing movements that were expressions of a society in the process of articulation, the transition to political society was delayed. In Russia, Democratic Russia, like Solidarity in Poland, the Civic Forum in Czechoslovakia, the Neues Forum in East Germany, and the Sajudis movement in Lithuania, was an umbrella organization, and its later crisis shows considerable similarities with that of those movements. However, unlike these other umbrella organizations, Democratic Russia *never* coordinated a statewide general election.

The March 1989 elections were extraordinarily important in creating a new spirit of freedom in the Soviet Union. However, from the perspective of creating an autonomous political society or democratic power structures, the elections had some obvious limitations.[35] One-third of the seats in the 2,250-member Con-

---

33. The next few pages draw heavily on our "Political Identities and Electoral Sequences: Spain, the Soviet Union, and Yugoslavia," *Daedalus* 121, no. 2 (1992): 123–40. Permission to cite is gratefully acknowledged.

34. For our subsequent analysis of Russia, it should also be noted that the 1990 elections to the Russian parliament were also not multiparty. In the 1990 Russian elections, Democratic Russia was not in our sense really a political party but an emerging movement on the border of civil society and political society. Because of this state-society context, M. Stephen Fish argues that the 1989–90 political opening was *"too sudden* and *too partial.* It strongly—and negatively—influenced the growth and effectiveness of alternative political parties. The timing of the elections reduced incentives for ambitious radical leaders to join parties and encouraged a highly individualistic form of political entrepreneurship." See his important book, *Democracy from Scratch: Opposition and Regime in the New Russian Revolution* (Princeton: Princeton University Press, 1995), 73. Emphasis in original.

35. For a good discussion of the limits of the 1989 elections, see Victor Sergeyev and Nikolai Biryukov, *Russia's Road to Democracy: Parliament, Communism and Traditional Culture* (Aldershot, England: Edward Elgar, 1993), 101–51.

gress of Peoples' Deputies were set aside for the Communist Party and its affili-ated organizations and did not face popular ratification. Furthermore, the nom-ination process allowed many Communist Party–dominated local electoral com-missions to pack meetings with their supporters and thus control the nominating process. In many districts, all the candidates to emerge from the local electoral commissions were Communist Party supporters. Indeed, in one-quarter of the contests only a single candidate emerged from the local electoral commission. In this context many opposition candidates fell by the wayside.

The highly selective 2,250-member Congress of Peoples' Deputies that emerged from this process became the electoral college for indirect election to the Supreme Soviet. This indirect method of selections further weakened the electoral credi-bility of the upper—and more powerful—house and produced numerous in-equities. For example, Boris Yeltsin won his seat in Moscow with 89 percent of the popular vote but was initially denied a seat in the Supreme Soviet until one mem-ber offered to step down in his favor. Other less prominent deputies were not so lucky. Thus, though the first elections in the Soviet Union *were* all-Union, the proposition holds: the most important and contested elections in both the Soviet Union and Yugoslavia were not at the all-union but at the republic level.

Cognizant of the shortcomings of the all-union electoral law, republic parlia-ments drafted legislation that avoided many of the practices that had helped to discredit the all-union parliament. Election rules varied somewhat across re-publics, but in general they allowed republic-level actors to make a greater claim to legitimacy than their all-union counterparts. Almost all of the republics dis-carded guaranteed seats for the Communist Party and Communist Party–domi-nated public organizations. Inequities did occur in elections to republic parlia-ments, especially in Central Asia and in the area of the rights of ethnic minorities. Yet, on the whole, deputies from republic Supreme Soviets could not only claim to be the defenders of ethnic interests, but also make a stronger claim to legiti-macy than could the USSR Supreme Soviet deputies.

Throughout this book we have argued that elections can create agendas, can create actors, can reconstruct identities, help legitimate and delegitimate claims to obedience, and create power. The regional elections in the USSR and Yu-goslavia did all these things. In Spain the process set in motion by statewide gen-eral elections reconstituted stateness on even firmer grounds. The regional elec-tions in the USSR and Yugoslavia did the opposite. The following series of quotes from reports written by teams of electoral observers with the Helsinki Commis-sion capture the extent to which the process of regional electoral campaigns—in a context of the Soviet multinational state, which had never submitted itself to an all-union election—contributed to the disintegration of the state. It did so by weakening the center and strengthening independence and sovereignty claims by the ruling elites and by mobilizing nationalist sentiments among the titular na-tionalities in the republics.

Moldavia (Election: February 25, 1990)

"The election campaign pointed up the necessity for every movement vying for power in the Republic to develop a program for sovereignty, the minimum demand in Moldavia.... Whether Moscow has to deal directly with a Popular-Front dominated Moldavian Supreme Soviet, or work through Party First Secretary Lucinski is irrelevant, for it will be faced almost immediately with a demand to make good on the republic's demand for sovereignty."[36]

Ukraine (Election: March 18, 1990)

"The Democratic Bloc of opposition groups formed to contest the election successfully focused the campaign on voters' concerns, inducing the Communist Party candidates often to follow suit. High on voters' lists were greater political autonomy, [and] national and cultural issues."[37]

"Increasing demands for the use of Ukrainian language resulted in an important Ukrainian SSR Supreme Soviet decree stipulating that as of January 1, 1990, Ukrainian is the state language of the republic, while Russian is to be used for communication between nationality groups.... Long suppressed national feelings are now sweeping the Ukrainian population."[38]

"It is likely that their will be even greater progress for Ukrainian self-determination leading to independence."[39]

Georgia (Elections: October 28, 1990)

By election day, all contending parties—including the Georgian Communist Party—advocated independence.[40] "In an effort to shore up its nationalist credentials, the Georgian Communist Party platform demands guarantees for Georgia's territorial integrity, the introduction of Georgian citizenship.... Proclaiming that Georgian citizens should only perform military service inside the republic."[41]

The independence and titular nationalist themes of the election exacerbated relations with the center. Nationalist outbidding in Georgia, as in many other republics, worsened relations with minority groups in the republic and eroded a core component of future democratization—full citizenship rights for all inhabitants regardless of ethnicity. The election observer team noted that in Georgia "the eventual winner Gamsakhurdia made many statements that have alarmed non-Geor-

36. *Elections in the Baltic States and the Soviet Republics* (compiled by the Staff of the Commission on Security and Cooperation in Europe, Washington, D.C., December 1990), 89.
37. Ibid., 115.
38. Ibid., 119.
39. Ibid., 135
40. Ibid., 165.
41. Ibid., 170.

gians. In June 1990, for example, he called mixed marriages 'fatal to the Georgian family and the Georgian language.' "[42] "Fearing for their national rights in an independent Georgia, some non-Georgian groups have attempted to protect themselves. . . . the Abkhaz Autonomous Republic and the Southern Ossetian Autonomous Oblast declared sovereignty in August and September, 1990, respectively."[43]

The result of the regional elections in the USSR and Yugoslavia, in the absence of prior freely contested all-union democratic elections, contributed to five interrelated and compounding state-disintegrating dynamics. First, virtually the day after the regional elections, the statewide legitimacy of the central government was damaged because the regional pro-sovereignty forces could make a stronger claim to democratic legitimacy via elections.[44] Nowhere was this more significant than in Russia. The election in the republic of Russia created a new democratically legitimated base for Boris Yeltsin, who was elected chairman of the Russian Parliament in May 1990. From that base he issued Russia's declaration of sovereignty of June 12, 1990. In June 1991 Yeltsin became the directly elected president of Russia. In July 1991, in his first official decree as president, he banned Communist Party organizations from enterprises. Since the Communist Party had no neighborhood organizations but only workplace cells, this decree was effectively a death sentence to the Communist Party in Russia. The coup attempt in August 1991 was thus not only a result of the 9+1 agreement to decentralize the USSR but also of this decree.[45]

Second, in no republic in the Soviet Union did a major new unionwide political organization compete in the elections as an effective counterweight to local nationalism, given the fact that, until article 6 was abrogated in March 1990, the Communist Party of the Soviet Union was the only legal party in the USSR. In Yugoslavia the elections in the republics were also dominated by non-unionwide parties or movements.

Third, in the process of the elections, political identities in the USSR and in Yugoslavia became more narrow, compounding, exclusive, and unsupportive of participation in a potentially all-union democratic entity. In Spain during and after the electoral processes political identities had become more multiple, cross-

---

42. Ibid., 169.

43. Ibid., 165–66.

44. An important indicator of the erosion of stateness is the sharp drop in citizens who answered the unionwide military draft. By the end of 1990 draft, quota fulfillment in Latvia was 39.5 percent, in Lithuania 35.9 percent, Armenia 22.5 percent and in Georgia 18.5 percent. By mid-1991, these figures had declined to 30.8 percent for Latvia, 12.4 percent for Lithuania, 16.4 percent for Armenia, and 8.2 percent for Georgia. Most importantly, by mid-1991 Moscow itself had fulfilled only half its quota for this six-month period. See Steven Foye, "Student Deferments and Military Manpower Shortages," *Report on the USSR* (Aug. 2, 1991): 5–8.

45. The "state" in the Weberian sense had been disintegrating in the Soviet Union even before the failed coup attempt of August 1991, a coup whose trigger was the desperate effort of some elements within the all-union forces of the party, the KGB, and the military to block the implementation of the 9+1 Treaty, which would have given a de jure status to the de facto decentralization of the USSR.

cutting, inclusive, and supportive of participation in a reconstituted Spanish democratic state.

Fourth, in many republics such as Georgia, Azerbaijan, Serbia, and Croatia, the prospect of ethnic warfare led the newly elected presidents to repress dissenting voices within their core ethnic groups and to show greater intolerance toward minority groups.

Fifth, the crisis of stateness and the resulting crises of governability blocked the formulation and implementation of economic policy. The cataclysmic political collapse of any central or coordinating authority in the Soviet Union and Yugoslavia preceded and intensified the economic crisis, not vice versa.[46]

Let us conclude our discussion of the consequences of electoral sequence with the prophetic words of a Soviet social scientist writing before the coup attempt and before the de jure disintegration of the Soviet state. He captured the degree to which regional elections had already contributed to de facto state disintegration: "Local elections contributed to the process of the shift of the rhetoric of nationalist movements from 'civic' to 'ethnic'.... The 'war of laws' and 'parade of sovereignties' followed inevitably after republic and local elections.... The crisis of power in the center of the Union and the process of ungovernability increased enormously."[47]

We will not go into the details of the endgame of the Soviet state because it has been so extensively documented by others. Suffice it to say that the elections in the republics led to the famous "parade of sovereignties" and intensified the "war of laws." This led to a search for a new law of the union, which would feature greater devolution of power to the republics. Gorbachev attempted to shore up the union by holding a referendum on March 17, 1991, on the question, "Do you consider necessary the preservation of the Union of Soviet Socialist Republics as a renewed federation of equal sovereign republics, in which the rights and freedoms of an individual of any nationality will be fully guaranteed?" Of those who voted, 76 percent said yes on this question, so Gorbachev claimed victory. However, a full analysis of the referendum reveals much more equivocal and damaging results. Only three of the union's fifteen republics (Belorussia, Tajikistan, and Turkmenistan) held the referendum exactly the way Gorbachev wanted it to be held. Lithuania, Latvia, Estonia, Georgia, Armenia, and Moldova boycotted Gorbachev's referendum. The remaining six republics, in addition to asking Gorbachev's question, added their own question or questions. The results of the ques-

---

46. In Yugoslavia the federal prime minister, Arte Marković, had been supervising a relatively successful stabilization policy and had reduced the four-digit inflation rate to two digits in the first half of 1990. However, after the stateness crisis exploded, the inflation rate soared to over a trillion by 1993. The Ukraine had positive GNP growth of 4.1 in 1989, but its best performance in 1991–94, after the stateness crisis became full blown, was -12 in 1991. In 1994 Ukrainian GNP growth was -23. Russia, despite all its problems, still had flat growth in industrial production in 1990. For 1992 the figure was -18.8. For 1994, -21. For these economic data see table 21.1.

47. Andranik Migranian, "The End of Perestroika's Romantic Stage" (Moscow, July 1991, unpublished manuscript), 7.

tions framed by the republics gave renewed legitimacy to republic-based decision making. For example, the extra question in Russia successfully turned into a referendum on whether to hold a direct election for a president of Russia. The positive response to this Russian referendum question was another major step in the building of an alternative power center to the union and Gorbachev. A draft treaty was eventually signed with the union and nine republics on April 23, 1991. This in turn set into motion increasing conspiracy activities. The new Union Treaty was due to be signed on August 21, 1991. The coup attempt began on August 18, 1991. The failure of the coup radically accelerated the disintegration of the USSR. All of the major organizations and mechanisms that were holding the USSR together, the Communist Party of the Soviet Union, the KGB, the military, the police, and the office of the presidency, were weakened. In contrast, the position of Boris Yeltsin, who had the legitimacy of having won a directly contested election for the presidency of Russia in June 1991, who had led the resistance against the coup, and who was fighting for more sovereignty for Russia, was greatly strengthened. The red flag came down from the Kremlin on December 25, 1991. The speed and nature of this process of state disintegration left numerous difficult legacies.[48]

The Disintegration of the USSR: Legacies for Democratic Transition and Consolidation

In part 1 we discussed at length the simultaneity problem that all European former Communist countries face. In addition to these problems, the prior nature of the territorially based ethnofederalism in the USSR and the speed and manner of the state's disintegration left additional difficult problems for democratic transition and consolidation. Each of these problems deserves book-length analysis by specialists who are better equipped than we. However, from the perspective of the comparative analysis of democratic theory and practice, let us briefly mention three general problems found in most of the fifteen successor states of the former Soviet Union: the privileging of independence over democratization, the privi-

---

48. For a detailed discussion of the final disintegration of the Soviet state, see John B. Dunlop, *The Rise of Russia and the Fall of the Soviet Empire* (Princeton: Princeton University Press, 1993). For valuable documents see Alexander Dallin and Gail W. Lapidus, eds., *The Soviet System: From Crisis to Collapse*, rev. ed. (Boulder, Colo.: Westview Press, 1995), esp. part 7, "From Coup to Collapse," 565–647. Also see Alexander Dallin, "Causes of the Collapse of the USSR," *Post-Soviet Affairs* 8, no. 4 (1992): 279–302; Suny, *Revenge of the Past*, 145–54; and Graeme Gill, *The Collapse of a Single Party System: The Disintegration of the Communist Party of the Soviet Union* (Cambridge: Cambridge University Press, 1994), esp. 144–85. Virtually all accounts stress that the failed coup attempt weakened further all the statewide institutions that were still holding the USSR together. For invaluable detail on Gorbachev's referendum and how the newly legitimated leaders in the republic made it backfire, see the chapter, "Reports on the Referendum on the Future of the Soviet Union: March 17, 1991," in *Presidential Elections and Independence Referendums in the Baltic States, the Soviet Union and Successor States: A Compendium of Reports, 1991–1992*, compiled by the Staff of the Commission on Security and Cooperation in Europe, Washington, D.C. (August 1992), 15–63. The wording of Gorbachev's question is on p. 20.

leging of collective rights over individual rights, and the privileging of economic restructuring over state restructuring.

The Privileging of Independence over Democratization

In most of the polities that make a completed democratic transition and eventually manage to consolidate democracy, democratic goals are normally a prominent part of the aspiration of important parts of the opposition in the period we call *liberalization*. Also, the oppositional forces, when they come to power, must then proceed to craft democratic practices and institutions so that democracy becomes "the only game in town" even for many groups who initially were ambivalent or even opposed to democracy.

In the Soviet Union the speed and manner in which the state disintegrated foreshortened (or precluded) liberalization, gave a plebiscitary "national liberation" quality to the transition path, and almost pushed matters of democracy crafting off the normative and institutional agenda of politics. In some of the fifteen successor states of the USSR, liberalization, much less democratization, had hardly begun before the failed August 1991 coup led to their independence by January 1992. In many republics, even those whose leaders supported the coup, the unraveling of the USSR led to a hectic search for a new basis of power by incumbents. Anatoly Khazanov, the distinguished anthropologist from the former Soviet Union, has graphically captured this phenomenon: "Ethnic and regional elites, either old ones who only changed their ideological garments, or newly emerged ones, defeated the center-oriented elites. These elites considered *independence* the best guarantee of their positions. However, they are paying only lip service to liberal democratic principles and do not consider them their top priority."[49]

Ronald Grigor Suny likewise underscores how the speed of the disintegration left little time for new democratically structured organizations to acquire political, social, or economic presence, much less power:

> [I]n most republics, nationalism was accompanied by a desperate grab for local power by entrenched native elites. In Uzbekistan, Tajikistan, Turkmenistan and Azerbaijan, the old elites dressed up in national garb to preserve their domination and *suppress democratic* movements. Even in those southern republics, like Armenia, Georgia, Kyrgyzstan, and to a lesser extent, Kazakhstan, where popular democrats were able to remove or reduce the power of the Communists, the deep infrastructure of clan politics remained in place. In Ukraine, Belorussia, and even Russia, former Communists held top political positions and kept their hands firmly on the levers of economic power.[50]

Jonathan Aves, in his review of the new Soviet successor states, makes a similar point.

49. Anatoly Khazanov, "The Collapse of the Soviet Union: Nationalism during Perestroika and Afterwards," *Nationalities Papers* 22, no. 1 (1994), 168. Emphasis added.
50. Suny, *Revenge of the Past*, 156. Emphasis added.

Republican elites were able to adapt to the nationalist agenda not only to free themselves from central control but also to *outmaneuver putative popular movements*. . . . In view of the dramatic nature of these processes, their rapidity and scale, elements of continuity are remarkably numerous. . . . Few of the successor regimes have yet adopted a new constitution and the legislatures of the new states are all recognizably the former Supreme Soviets. . . . The presidents of all the Central Asian republics, with the exception of Askar Akaev in Kyrgyzstan, are former first secretaries of the former republican Supreme Soviets.[51]

The Privileging of Collective Rights over Individual Rights

At the level of both theory and practice, consolidated democracies must respect individual rights. The more inclusive and equal access is to the rights of citizenship, the better the quality of democracy. We argued in chapter 2 that we differ from most liberal theorists of rights, who insist that all rights be individual *and* universal. All rights do not seem to us necessarily to be universal. Theory and practice in consociational democracies in fact accords some form of collective rights (such as linguistic, educational, or religious rights) to groups.[52] However, with all democratic theorists we do accept the injunction that such collective rights—which we believe may be prudentially called for in some multicultural or multinational polities—must *never* violate individual rights or create a category of second-class citizens.

As we have documented, the Soviet Union was one of the world's first ethnoterritorially based federal states. Even before the disintegration of the state, there were frequent tensions in the USSR over special collective privileges given to "titular nationalities" in the republics. Victor Zaslavsky captures these tensions succinctly.

The whole federal political-administrative system served as an elaborate structure of ethnic inequality. It divided ethnic groups into those with recognized territory and certain rank in the hierarchy of the state formations and those without such territory. It organized the former groups into a four-rank hierarchy which determined corresponding amounts of ethnic rights and privileges. Moreover, the borders between ethnic territories were drawn arbitrarily, often in accordance with a divide-and-conquer policy in obvious conflict with historical traditions and existing ethnodemographic conditions. . . . The twin policies of nationality registration in the internal passports and preferential treatment of indigenous nationalities within their administrative units became especially counterproductive. These policies proved to be essentially antimeritocratic. . . . They created strong dissatisfaction among minorities. . . . In many cases it led to the emergence of a potentially explosive ethnic division of labor. . . . The situation be-

51. See his "Assessing the Prospects of the New Soviet Successor States," *Nationalities Papers* 22, no. 1 (1994), 211, 212. Emphasis added.

52. For a review of consociational style group-rights practices that *do not* violate democratic norms, see Arend Lijphart, "Consociational Democracy," *World Politics* 21 (1969): 44–59, and Kenneth D. McRae, ed., *Consociational Democracy: Political Accomodation in Segmented Societies* (Toronto: McCelland and Stewart, 1974).

came particularly tense in republics where titular nationalities had been transformed into numerical minorities.[53]

Obviously, even with most careful democratic political crafting, this legacy of state-structured and state-sanctioned inequality would have been a difficult legacy to transcend. However, as we have just seen, in a situation where independence for the titular nationality was privileged over democratization, independence for most of the leaders of the Soviet successor states meant deepening, codifying, and realizing the collective rights of their "titular" nationality.

In Russia the above problem was exacerbated because Yeltsin, in his struggles against Gorbachev and the Soviet center, frequently told local titular elites in the autonomous republics of Russia to "take all the sovereignty you can swallow."[54] Thus, within months of the Russian republics' declaration of sovereignty, "every one of the autonomous republics within the Russian federation" had followed suit.[55] The situation in Russia was further complicated by the fact that "the titular nationality was a majority in only five of the twenty-one" ethnically defined autonomous republics.[56] The Gorbachev-Yeltsin struggle had two aspects. One aspect was Yeltsin's effort to undermine the union through his insistence on carrying out the Russian Declaration of Sovereignty. Gorbachev, on the other hand, was undermining Yeltsin by encouraging the heads of Russia's autonomous (i.e., non-Russian) regions (who also happened to be very conservative Communists) to negotiate directly with him, Gorbachev, on the New Union Treaty. In fact, Gorbachev insisted that Russian autonomous regions would be a part of the New Union Treaty. Yeltsin resisted Gorbachev's argument on the grounds that it was an attempt to undermine the Russian Federation. Yeltsin's famous statement to the autonomous regions to "take as much sovereignty as you can" ought to be considered in this context.

Ian Bremmer argues that independence, throughout the Soviet Union, came as a "manifestation of nationalism as *liberation*" and of the desire of groups to "claim independence for themselves."[57] He goes on to argue that "the relationship between titular nationalities and lower order titular and non-titular nationalities is one of *domination*. . . . First-order titular nationalities may employ the rhetoric of liberation when dealing with the center, while at the same time rejecting such

53. Victor Zaslavsky, "Success and Collapse: Traditional Soviet Nationality Policy," in Ian Bremmer and Ray Taras, eds., *Nations and Politics in the Soviet Successor States* (Cambridge: Cambridge University Press, 1993), 35, 39.

54. See Gail W. Lapidus and Edward W. Walker, "Nationalism, Regionalism and Federalism: Center-Periphery Relations in Post-Communist Russia," in Gail W. Lapidus, ed., *The New Russia: Troubled Transformation* (Boulder, Colo.: Westview Press, 1995), 83.

55. Ibid.

56. Ibid., 87.

57. Ian Bremmer, "Reassessing Soviet Nationalities Theory," in Bremmer and Taras, *Nations in Soviet Successor States,* 15. Emphasis in the original.

claims (and exerting domination) when they are made by lower order titular or non-titular nationalities within their borders."[58]

This situation, particularly in Russia, often gives rise to two types of actions by the nontitular nationalities which create problems for stateness and/or democratization. The nontitular nationalities are motivated to secede and create their own titular nationality regions. Or they collude with the center to impose forms of nondemocratic direct administrative rule on the titular nationalities.[59]

This problem of collective rights over individual rights acquires added magnitude when we take into consideration the fact that in the Commonwealth of Independent States (CIS) sixty million people are living outside their nation-state or their titular nationality regions. Indeed, after the disintegration of the Soviet state, twenty-five million Russians were living outside of Russia.[60] This new situation has given rise to difficulties in the triadic relationships in the successor states between the elites of the aspirant nation-states, the minorities in these polities, and the homeland states of these minorities.[61] These international tensions in turn present new dangers for would-be consociational democracy crafters because of the fertile soil that is created for nationalists to delegitimize the state for "not protecting their co-nationals abroad" or for authoritarians inside the state, who do not want equal citizenship to be given to "fifth columnist foreigners."[62]

The Privileging of Economic Restructuring over Democratic State Restructuring (the Case of Russia)

A reasonably strong state with a clear hierarchy of laws and the capacity to extract a surplus and to implement the policies of the new democratic government is crucial for democratic consolidation. Indeed, many of the rights of democratic citizenship can only be obtained if there is a coherent state, an enforceable rule of law, and a usable state apparatus. Even market-oriented schemes such as privatization are more effective if done by a state that can formulate and install a clear regulatory framework so that a law-based economic society can emerge.[63] If these

---

58. Ibid., 16–17.

59. See the excellent formal modeling of these relationships of "domination" and "collusion," with numerous empirical referents, in ibid., 11–21.

60. See Khazanov, "Collapse of the Soviet Union," 171.

61. See Rogers Brubaker, "National Minorities, Nationalizing States, and External Homelands in the New Europe," in *Daedalus* (Spring 1995): 107–32. We will explore such a triadic relationship in our next chapter, which examines problems of Russian citizenship in Estonia and Latvia.

62. Would-be democrats are buffered by both these demands. In response to nationalist demands, Russia has military units guarding part of all the CIS "outer borders" in Armenia, Georgia, Kyrgyzstan, and Tajikistan and is trying to negotiate similar arrangements with Azerbaijan, Uzbekistan, and Turkmenistan. Russia has also proposed integration of their troops with the border troops of Ukraine, Belarus, and Kazakhstan. This information was obtained from an interesting paper by Eric Schmelling, "The Near Abroad: Being Too Close" (Central European University, Budapest, January 1995, unpublished paper), based on *Radio Free Europe/Radio Liberty Daily Report,* November 15, 1994, and December 2, 1994.

63. All these arguments are developed in part 1.

capacities do not exist, they must be built by the new democratic forces or democracy cannot be consolidated. This is why we argued that democratization often must begin with the political restructuring of the state so as to give it new consensually and constitutionally based power. This is particularly so where stateness problems exist, as we documented in our analysis of Spain. Statewide elections and the crafting of a consensual constitution are forms of building legitimate state power. Such power can then be brought to bear in the restructuring of federal relations or in restructuring the economy.

In the area of vertical relations within the federation, Russia faced, as we have seen, extraordinary tasks that needed to be addressed before it could become a coherent democratic polity. The implementation of the much needed economic restructuring, in the post–party-state context, also called for the creation of new forms of democratic power. The combination of the old structures of governance and the way the USSR disintegrated also left the state in Russia particularly prone to horizontal power conflicts between the executive and the legislative. Furthermore, the existing Brezhnev era constitution spelled out few conflict regulation devices in the case of legislative/executive disputes over powers. The constitution, for example, did not assign a significant role to the judiciary. As in Czechoslovakia the absence of a framework for democratic government was not a problem when the party-state governed. However, under more democratic conditions in Russia, the absence of democratic procedures for governance led to intrastate impasse and power deflation.

In these circumstances, in our judgment, the first order of business should have been the democratic restructuring of the state so as to create structures of democratic power. What in fact was the first order of business?

Boris Yeltsin's first major policy address to the Congress of People's Deputies and to the citizens of Russia after the coup was on October 28, 1991. He told the congress and the nation that "the present time is one of the most critical moments in Russian history. It is now that the future of Russia and of the country as a whole in the years and decades to come is being decided. We must unreservedly embark on a path of thoroughgoing reforms, in which the support of all strata of the population is needed. The time has come to adopt the main decision and to begin to act."[64]

Thus far we agree, and Yeltsin's appeal to Congress and to the people is similar to the address of Adolfo Suárez to the Cortes and the citizens which we analyzed at length in our chapter on Spain. But Yeltsin's specification of what actions he should privilege contrasted radically with those of Suárez, who emphasized the democratic restructuring of politics and the state as the first priority. In contrast, for Boris Yeltsin "the most important, most decisive actions will have to be taken

64. See Boris Yeltsin, "Speech to the RSFSR Congress of the People's Deputies and to the Citizens of Russia, October 28, 1991," in Dallin and Lapidus, eds., *The Soviet System*, 632.

in the sphere of the economy. The first area is economic stabilization. . . . The second area is privatization and the creation of a healthy mixed economy with a powerful private sector."[65]

Almost in passing, toward the end of the speech Yeltsin mentioned structures of governance.

The time has come to say clearly and precisely that there is one source of power in Russia: the Russian Republic's Congress and Supreme Soviet, the Russian Republic's government, and the Russian Republic's President. A dynamic process of extracting the institutions of power from under the heel of the CPSU is under way. We are not afraid of accusations of being undemocratic, and we will act decisively in this respect . . . In conducting the reforms, the principle burden rests with the Russian government. This burden is too heavy for the government's present make-up and cumbersome structure. It can be borne only by a government of popular confidence, one that people will trust, one that will convince them that its actions are correct.[66]

What is significant is that Yeltsin was absolutely silent about how to create such a government. He did not mention calling new elections for the newly independent state. He did not mention the possibility of a newly elected parliament crafting a new democratic constitution, which would create a framework for the orderly exercise of democratic power.

Yeltsin in October 1991 still commanded great power and prestige. He had been democratically elected in June 1991. He had led the resistence to the coup in August 1991. He was soon to lead Russia to complete independence. In this context (despite the fact that the vast majority of the parliament had been elected with Communist Party support in March 1990), the Congress of People's Deputies voted overwhelmingly to support, by 876 to 16, President Yeltsin's "big bang" free market reforms, his first and second priorities.[67] In November 1991, this same Soviet-era congress voted to give Yeltsin decree power for one year to implement economic reform.

In our judgment, Yeltsin's choice to privilege economic restructuring over democratic state restructuring weakened the state, weakened democracy, and weakened the economy. Timing is crucial in all politics, but especially in democratization processes. Yeltsin and his core advisors in the critical fall months of 1991 took the effort to craft an economic plan and to argue its merits before the parliament and the citizens. We believe he should have made a prior effort to have amplified his party base and, like Adolfo Suárez in Spain, convinced the parliament of the old regime to hold early free elections. Absolutely nothing of this sort was attempted. Let us quote at length from a perceptive eyewitness observer.

65. Ibid.

66. Ibid., 636–37.

67. The vote was taken one week after Yeltsin's address to the Congress and the citizens. For the atmosphere surrounding the vote, see Dunlop, *Rise of Russia and Fall of Soviet Empire*, 265.

[Yeltsin] and his advisors chose not to undertake fundamental political reforms and instead relied on Yeltsin's own personal charisma and authority to sustain the state in carrying out its program of economic transformation.... More striking to contemplate, however, are the decisions and actions Yeltsin did not take. He did not push to adopt a new constitution.... The new regime did little to institutionalize its popular support in society. Yeltsin did not establish a political party; nor did he call for elections to stimulate party development. And despite repeated cries from Democratic Russia, he refused to call new elections in the Fall of 1991.[68]

More research must be done, and historical counterfactuals are never certain. But if Yeltsin, in the immediate aftermath of his anti-coup triumph, with the charismatic aura and authority this gave him, had called in September 1991 for new parliamentary and presidential elections to be held in, say, December 1991, a strong case could be made that he could have convinced the Russian parliament to accede to his proposal. This would have required a lot of politicking, maneuvering, and coalition-building as well as appeals to public opinion. In October 1991 Yeltsin's approval rating was still 61 percent (down from 71 percent in July). His ability to convince parliament to go along with his initiatives in September and October 1991 was still very high, as the overwhelming vote of support this Soviet-era body gave to his economic plan demonstrates.[69] Given the experience Democratic Russia had acquired during Yeltsin's victorious presidential campaign in June 1991, Yeltsin, acting as a leader of Democratic Russia, incorporating in a broad coalition diverse forces, and building a political instrument to support him, might have done well in an election.[70] The self-image of a president above party made such a political strategy unlikely, but if he *had* commited himself to such a strategy, and if elections *had* been held in December 1991, a newly legitimated, in-

68. See the excellent article by Michael McFaul, "State Power, Institutional Change, and the Politics of Privatization in Russia," *World Politics* 47, no. 2 (1995), 226. McFaul was in Moscow in October 1991 and interviewed many Democratic Russia leaders. For a very similar critique by a Russian social scientist, see Lilia Shevtsova, "Russia's Post-Communist Politics: Revolution or Continuity?" in Lapidus, ed., *The New Russia*, 5–37, esp. 8–10. Also see the convincing section entitled "The political mismanagement of economic reform" in Timothy J. Colton, "Boris Yeltsin, Russia's All-Thumbs Democrat," in Timothy J. Colton and Robert C. Tucker, eds., *Patterns in Post-Soviet Leadership* (Boulder: Westview Press, 1995) 49–74, esp. 60–65.

69. On counterfactual analyses see James D. Fearon, "Counterfactuals and Hypothesis Testing in Political Science," *World Politics* 43 (Jan. 1991): 169–95. For Yeltsin's high public opinion ratings in July and October 1991, see the valuable article by Archie Brown, "Political Leadership in Post-Communist Russia," in Amin Saikal and William Maley, eds., *Russia in Search of Its Future* (Cambridge: Cambridge University Press, 1995), 36. Brown also argues that Yeltsin "should have made a serious effort to have a new constitution adoped and a date for fresh elections agreed in late 1991 or early 1992 when his public standing was still sufficiently high for him to have persuaded the Congress of People's Deputies to vote for its own dissolution" (p. 33).

70. McFaul argues that "polling by Democratic Russia indicated that with Yeltsin's backing the organization would win a majority within the Congress of People's Deputies. At the time, Democratic Russia was the only legal party or social movement of national status. Having just organized Yeltsin's electoral victory in June 1991 and then spearheaded the popular resistance to the coup in August, leaders of Democratic Russia were quite certain of victory." See McFaul, "State Power, Institutional Change, and Privatization," 226. Shevtsova argues that, in the fall of 1991, "the only political movement with significant influence at the time was Democratic Russia, the mass-based movement that had helped bring Yeltsin to power in 1990 and 1991." Shevtsova, "Russia's Post-Communist Politics," 18.

dependence-era Russian parliament could have voted support for the economic plan and made some quick but consensual constitutional amendments before undertaking the task of completely rewriting the Soviet-era constitution. This new parliament could have provided the government with a constitutional foundation for political, economic, and social reform. There would have been some short-term costs. The launching of the "big bang" economic reform would possibly have been delayed by a few months. But the long-term gains might have been substantial.

Boris Yeltsin, in his book *The Struggle for Russia,* in retrospect also believes that he missed an opportunity. "I believe the most important opportunity missed after the coup was the radical restructuring of the parliamentary system. I have a sneaking suspicion, though, that society might not have been ready to nominate any decent candidates to a new legislature. The idea of dissolving the Congress and scheduling new elections was in the air (as well as a Constitution for the new country), although we did not take advantage of it."[71] The Yeltsin memoir is particularly revealing in two inter-related respects. First, Yeltsin virtually does not mention the possibility that he could have helped contribute to making Democratic Russia—or any other political party—a powerful instrument of democratic change. Democratic parties were not part of his cognitive or reform world. Second, as the above quote makes clear, Yelstsin was reluctant to take a chance with elections. But, as Adam Przeworski and other democratic theorists insist, democracy building is precisely a process in which political leaders have to accept the risk of the uncertainty of elections. It is the task of democratic politicians and parties to get the voters to support their program by campaigning and coalition building. But Yeltsin's conception of the president as being above parties, rather than the leader of a party or a coalition, and his style of rule would have made such an effort difficult.

In the absence of constitutional restructuring of democratic state power, the Soviet-era legislature and the pro-market, anti-Soviet executive entered into a deadly struggle. This struggle ebbed and flowed but never stopped until Yelstin used armed force to prevail in October 1993. This power struggle hurt the very economic reform in whose name democratic state building had been postponed. The Soviet-era congress that Yeltsin decided to live with actually had interests in the economy and the polity that were distinctly different from those espoused by the "big bang" reformers in Yeltsin's government. In fact, only six months after Gaidar's program had been overwhelmingly approved by the Fifth Congress of the People's Deputies, his program was defeated 632 votes to 231.[72]

---

71. Boris Yeltsin, *The Struggle for Russia* (New York: Times Books, Random House, 1994), 126.

72. A very clear and documented analysis of the multiple conflicts between the legislative power and the executive power in Russia in this period is found in Yitzhak M. Brudny's article, "Ruslan Khasbulatov, Aleksandr Rutskoi and Intra-elite Conflict in Post-Communist Russia, 1991–1994," in Timothy J. Colton and Robert C. Tucker, eds., *Patterns in Post Soviet Leadership* (Boulder, Colo.: Westview Press, 1995), 75–101.

Moreover, the constitution gave the congress an extraordinary number of prerogatives they could call upon to check the executive. A policy conflict between the parliament and the executive was thus predictable. Furthermore, the existing constitutional structures of government were not crafted so as to facilitate and channel democratic contestation.

Yitzhak M. Brudny in a perceptive study makes this clear:

> Features of the Russian constitutional structure made the conflict between the president and the parliament virtually impossible to resolve. First, the Russian presidential system, as it was established in 1991, clearly belonged to the "president-parliamentary" type. In this system both the parliament and the president enjoy some control over the cabinet of ministers but precise division of power between the two is not defined clearly.... The law on the presidency effectively created two competing heads of the state, the president and the chairman of the Supreme Soviet.
>
> Second, the Russian law on the presidency failed to provide a mechanism for resolving potential conflicts between the two branches of government.... The Russian parliamentarians denied the president the right to call referenda or new parliamentary or presidential elections preferring to keep these rights as their exclusive prerogative.[73]

The chairman of the Russian Supreme Soviet, Ruslan Khasbulatov, was able to use his Soviet-era constitutional prerogatives to issue direct orders to government ministries and agencies. His orders often conflicted with decrees issued by Yeltsin. In 1992 Khasbulatov issued 66 such orders. In the first six months of 1993 he issued more than 630.[74]

A core part of the economic reform was dismantled only four months after its initiation. The parliament prevailed in their claim that they had the right to appoint and supervise the president of the central bank. Their nominee followed policies fundamentally at odds with the Yeltsin-Gaidar stabilization policy. The weakness of the government in the congress also meant that state managers, via their allies in the congress, were able to structure legislative outcomes that resulted in "insiders" controlling the vast majority of privatized state enterprises. This same alliance meant that the state continued to give massive subsidies to these structurally unreformed enterprises.[75]

Both parties to the horizontal struggle for state power (the legislature and the executive) claimed democratic legitimacy. Semipresidentialism in Russia manifested even more dangerous tendencies for democracy than it did in the Polish case we have analyzed.[76] Indeed, as the struggle intensified in Russia, both parties

---

73. Ibid., 85–86.
74. Ibid., 86.
75. See the previously cited article by McFaul for documentation. For additional convincing empirical studies of insider control during and after privatization in Russia, see Katherina Pistor, Roman Frydman, and Andrzej Rapaczynski, "Investing in Insider-dominated Firms: A Study of Russian Voucher Privatization Funds," and Joseph R. Blasi, "Corporate Governance in Russia." Both papers were delivered at a joint conference of the World Bank and the Central European University Privatization Project, December 15–16, 1994, Washington, DC.
76. See chapter 16 for our excursus on semipresidentialism and our analysis of it in the Polish context.

claimed prerogatives of the sort not found in any modern consolidated democracy in the world.

During their conflict with the president, the parliament managed to reinsert into the Russian constitution the classic Soviet-era description of the Soviets as the "highest state organs."[77] This phrase and a series of amendments advocated by Khasbulatov implied a form of an "assembly regime" rather than a semipresidential or even a parliamentary regime.[78] That is, the Soviets would directly select, monitor, and even manage the executive and officials of the state apparatus. This assembly regime would also act as judiciary because whenever the Supreme Soviet met they would act as a permanent constituent assembly.[79] From this "all power to the Soviets," Paris Commune perspective, Khasbulatov and the parliament argued their superior legitimacy and periodically tried to impeach Yeltsin. By October 1992 it was also revealed that Khasbulatov had built up a five-thousand-member parliamentary armed guard subordinate through him to the Soviets alone.[80]

Yeltsin for his part appealed to his superior democratic legitimacy based on his direct presidential election. He went further: he frequently made dark warnings that he would appeal directly to the people. In our discussion of Brazil and Argentina, we analyzed the extreme plebiscitary, anti-institutional style of presiden-

---

77. Ibid., 228. This phrase, of course, had roots in Marx's analysis of the Paris Commune in his *The Civil War in France* and Lenin's praise of the Commune in his *State and Revolution*. In a famous section of *State and Revolution* subtitled "The Eradication of Parliamentarianism," Lenin argued that "the Commune replaces the venal and rotten parliamentarianism of bourgeois society." It did this, Lenin argued, by "the conversion of the representative institutions from talking shops into 'working' institutions." The key examples given by Marx and later by Lenin of the Paris Commune as a working institution are those of the commune directly establishing and running the courts and most administration. In this way, direct democracy could lead not only to the eradication of parliamentarianism but eventually to the "withering away of the state." All careful historical studies show, however, that when it actually came to creating structures of power in the Soviet Union, Lenin almost immediately marginalized the "Soviets" or any form of Paris Commune-like direct democracy and built instead the hyperstatism of the centralized party-state. Notwithstanding this historical fact, antiparliamentary, direct democracy discourse of the "all power to the Soviets" sort remained a significant part of post-Soviet political argument. The democratically ambivalent effects of this strand of populist, direct democracy, antiparliamentary legacy of Soviet political culture and philosophy is discussed in the previously cited book by two Russian social scientists, Sergeyev and Biryukov, *Russia's Road to Democracy.*

78. The best discussion of Khasbulatov's program is found in Brudny, "Khasbulatov, Rutskoi and Intra-elite Conflict."

79. The 1977 Constitution [Fundamental Law] of the Union of Soviet Socialist Republics (much of the spirit of which was still in the Russian Constitution in 1991–93) formally gave the Soviets control of virtually all state powers. Article 2 stated "all power in the USSR belongs to the people. The people exercise state power through the Soviets of the People's Deputies, which constitute the political foundation of the USSR. All other state bodies are under the control of, and accountable to, the Soviets of the People's Deputies." Article 108 gave the Soviets control over executive and constitutional power. "The highest body of state authority of the USSR shall be the Supreme Soviet of the USSR. The Supreme Soviet of the USSR is empowered to deal with all matters within the jurisdiction of the Union of Soviet Socialist Republics. The adoption and amendment of the Constitution of the USSR . . . are the exclusive prerogative of the Supreme Soviet of the USSR." See John N. Hazard, ed., *The Union of Soviet Socialist Republics,* in the series edited by Albert P. Blaustein and Gisbert H. Flanz, *Constitutions of the Countries of the World* (Dobbs Ferry, N.Y.: Oceana Publications, Oct. 1990).

80. Brudny, "Khasbulatov, Rutskoi and Intra-elite Conflict."

tialism that Guillermo O'Donnell has called "delegative democracy."[81] Yeltsin in his struggle against parliament approximated O'Donnell's description, with the added twist that he denounced the legitimacy of the legislature because of its Soviet origins. The Russian social scientist, Shevtsova, implicitly agrees. She argues that Yeltsin "embarked on a course of 'revolutionary liberalism' from above," which was characterized by "the use of charisma to personalize the political process, [and] reliance on a vertical system of presidential power to implement his policies."[82]

Dwight Semler, in his review of constitutional developments in Russia in the first six months of 1993, captured graphically how, in the absence of constitutional change, one branch of a potential democracy (the executive) had taken to routinely questioning the legitimacy of another branch of a potential democracy (the legislature). For example, in February 1993,

Yeltsin repeated his contention that the current political situation made Russia impossible to govern. . . . Yeltsin asserted that he was not compelled to adhere to the constitution because it was nothing more than a Soviet-era document repeatedly and opportunistically amended by a short sighted congress. He warned that failure to hammer out a sensible power-sharing agreement would spell either "dictatorship or anarchy for Russia"—the sort of pronouncement that fuelled widespread rumors of 'emergency rule' by Yeltsin. . . .

The tension came to a head on March 20 when Yeltsin made a nationally televised address 'declaring' that Congress had violated the separation of powers and blasting the Constitutional Court for not having stopped them. Yeltsin announced that he had signed a decree establishing a special presidential regime necessary for the preservation of the country. While not attempting to dissolve Congress, Yeltsin made it clear that the new "regime" nullified any legislative acts that ran counter to the President's own directives.[83]

In September and October 1993, the constitutional crisis was resolved by force. Yeltsin unilaterally dissolved the parliament. The icon of August 1991 was Yeltsin on top of a tank defending the White House. The symbol of October 1993 was Yeltsin's tanks shattering the White House.

We reiterate our prior assertion, which we believe we now have documented. Yeltsin's choice in the fall of 1991 to privilege economic restructuring and completely to neglect democratic restructuring of the parliament, the constitution, and the state further weakened an already weak state, deprived the proposed economic reform program of the minimal degree of political and state coherence necessary for its successful implementation, and contributed to the mutual delegitimitation of the three democratic branches of the government.[84]

81. Guillermo O'Donnell, "Delegative Democracy," *Journal of Democracy* 5, no. 1 (Jan. 1994): 55–69, esp. 64.

82. Shevtsova, "Russia's Post-Communist Politics," 9.

83. Dwight Semler, "Special Reports: Crisis in Russia," *East European Constitutional Review* 2, no. 3 (1993): 15–19, quotations from 15 and 17. The March 1993 crisis was defused when Yeltsin softened his written text after strong protests by the Constitutional Court and the legislature.

84. While most of the West supported Yeltsin in his confrontation with the parliament, it should also be noted that the democratic tissue of Russia was hurt in numerous other ways in September 1993. As Archie

Post-Soviet Semipresidentialism: A Concluding Excursus

Soviet and Russian political developments during the transition underscore some of the themes we have stressed in this book. Books can and should be written on the subject of the problems for democracy created by semipresidentialism in the (non-Baltic) post-Soviet and post-Yugoslavian states.[85] As comparativists who have long written on such problems, let us briefly identify some of the features that made semipresidentialism an especially complicated and crisis-prone form of government in Russia and many of the other states of the former Soviet Union.

1. The prolonged cohabitation of a new and vaguely spelled out model of the presidency with the old nondemocratic and partly delegitimated Soviet-era institutions greatly complicated the Russian transition.

2. The creation of a presidency in the case of Russia with Yeltsin democratically legitimated by his election in June 1991, initiated the dynamics of the dual legitimacy of all presidential regimes that coexist with a legislature that is also democratically legitimated and has its own independent mandate. This classic problem of dual legitimacy was further complicated in Russia by the lack of a constitution that defined clearly the powers and roles of the different actors.

3. To the common structural problems of presidential and semipresidential democracies, we have to add the distinctive Soviet "all power to the Soviets" tradition that gave to the legislature and its chairman extraordinary powers, basically incompatible with a model based on a division of powers.

4. To complicate things further, both Gorbachev and Yeltsin supported, for temporary pragmatic reasons, the election of vice presidents who did not share their policy views and who ended by supporting plots against them. This is a pattern well known from crises in other presidential systems.[86]

5. In Matthew S. Shugart's analysis, the most unstable semipresidential variant is one he calls "president-parliamentary." A key aspect of this model is that the assembly may vote no confidence against the cabinet. Shugart argues that, "if the constitution permits [both] the parliamentary majority [and] the president acting unilaterally to dismiss cabinet ministers, there is no institutionally defined au-

---

Brown observes, the violent resolution of the crisis also meant "the suspension of the Constitutional Court, the temporary barring of some twenty newspapers and the tightening of governmental control over, and censorship of, television." See Brown, "Political Leadership in Post-Communist Russia," 33.

For a strong counterfactual analysis that a fall 1991 democratic political strategy by Yeltsin would have contributed to a stronger state and a more successful economic reform in Russia in 1992–93, see McFaul, "State Power, Institutional Change, and Privatization," esp. 238–43.

85. One such book in progress is an edited volume by Ray Taras, tentatively entitled *Presidential Systems in Communist States: A Comparative Analysis.*

86. To cite but a few examples, in Brazil, Vice President João Goulart fundamentally opposed President Janio Quadros' policies. In the Philippines, Vice President Salvador Laurel was at best what we would call "semiloyal" during a major coup attempt against President Corazon Aquino.

thority over the cabinet; executive-legislative conflict is likely. This institutional design has bred instability whenever it has been used . . . most ominously, in Weimar."[87] This precarious model is the norm in the non-Baltic countries of the former Soviet Union. It is true that the removable prime ministers provide a "fuse" protecting the president, but the situation can also lead to constant crises in policy leadership.This affects particularly the economic reform process. Indeed, in the Ukraine in 1991–94 semipresidential institutions led to a triarchy: president, prime minister, and the legislature and its chairman, leading to incertitude and conflict.[88]

6. The availability of the referendum to presumably resolve conflicts between the political actors by turning to the people has been useful in some cases, but it has frequently led to populist mobilization rather than to party politics. It has also led to conflicts about the calling and wording of the referendum, thus complicating the entire bargaining and party-building process that is so crucial to building an institutionalized political society with some degree of autonomy and predictability.

7. Presidentialism and strong semipresidentialism, as we and others have argued elsewhere, in the absence of a long historically structured party system do not encourage the formation of parties. Presidents like to be above party, not to identify with a party, and Yeltsin certainly did not use the opportunity to transform the movement-type formation, Democratic Russia, into a party. This tendency toward presidents being above party politics has been exacerbated by the post-Soviet constitutional practice that presidents, unlike in the French Fifth Republic, cannot lead or even belong to parties.

8. Not all the presidential-parliamentary conflicts in the former USSR have led to such a violent crisis as the shelling of the Parliament by the president in

87. See Matthew S. Shugart, "Of Presidents and Parliaments," *East European Constitutional Review* 2, no. 1 (1993), 30–32. Quotation from p. 30 and p. 32. For the full development of his analytic approach, see Matthew Soberg Shugart and John M. Carey, *Presidents and Assemblies: Constitutional Design and Electoral Dynamics* (Cambridge: Cambridge University Press, 1992).

88. An important study on semipresidentialism in the Ukraine is Andrew Wilson, "Post-Communist Presidents. Ukraine: Two Presidents, but No Settled Powers" (paper presented to the American Association for Advanced Slavic Studies, Philadelphia, November 1994). A revised version will appear in the previously cited edited volume by Ray Taras. Also see the excellent work by a Ukrainian political scientist, Oleg Protsyk, "Do Institutions Matter? Semi-presidentialism in Ukraine and France" (Master's thesis, Central European University, Budapest, June 1995). Post-Soviet presidents caught in this dyarchy or tryarchy constantly try to expand their powers well beyond the already substantial powers of the president in the French Fifth Republic. For example, Shugart and Carey in their *Presidents and Assemblies*, 148–58, develop an index of presidential powers. They give a total score of 7 for the president of the Fifth Republic. In late 1994 a frustrated President Kuchma in the Ukraine proposed a new law of presidential powers. According to Protsyk's estimation, Kuchma's proposal, if implemented, would have yielded an index of presidential power on the Shugart-Carey scale of 19.5, which is even higher than the 14.5 he accords to the "superpresidential" office of the Russian president in the new (1993) Russian constitution. For the Russian presidency, see Stephen Holmes, "Superpresidentialism and Its Problems," *East European Constitutional Review* 2, no. 4 (1993): 123–26.

Russia. But in some post-Soviet republics there is an increasing tendency for non-democratic resolution of presidential/legislative tension. With increasing frequency presidents prorogue parliaments, rule by decree, and call democratically dubious snap referenda to extend their mandates.[89]

Many factors account for the difficulties of democracy in the new states of the former USSR, but one of them, and not the least important, is the lack of early agreement on how to channel institutionally the democratic aspirations of people in decision-making structures. Institutions do matter.

89. In Turkmenistan a truly Soviet-era 99.9 percent of the population voted in a referendum to extend the president's mandate until the year 2000. In Kazakhstan the president, after proroguing the parliament, unilaterally formulated the referendum question and called a quick referendum, the result of which extended his mandate.

20

When Democracy and the Nation-State Are Conflicting Logics: Estonia and Latvia

O U T O F T H E 1991 dissolution of the USSR, fifteen new states emerged. These states were based upon the previous fifteen republics of the Soviet federation. Every one of these new states was named after what had been called in the Soviet federation the "titular nationality" of that republic. However, as we saw in the last chapter, most of these new states in 1991 were demographically multinational.[1] Nonetheless, the elites in charge in most of these newly independent states appealed to the nationalism of the dominant group in each republic as a way to come to and to consolidate power. Once in power most of the elites in charge of these newly independent states followed a strategy of attempting to transform their multinational demos into a "nation-state." In a book devoted to democratization, these realities force us to analyze two central questions. Are there circumstances when *democracy* and *nation-state* are conflicting logics?[2] If so, what can be done to achieve an inclusive democracy?[3] We believe these questions and the complexity of politics in states like the newly independent polities of the former Soviet Union are best explored by an elaboration of the triadic framework of relationships we developed in chapter 2, " 'Stateness,' Nationalism, and Democratization."[4]

1. In addition, the national minorities within them were identified by the nationality registered on their Soviet internal passports. That identification was not subjectively defined but based on origin, irrespective of the individual's personal, linguistic, and cultural identity. We believe that identities are normally socially constructed, multiple and changeable. However, this Soviet bureaucratic routine, to an important degree, fixed singular and unchangeable identities in the USSR. The fact that this was a legal identity based on territoriality is, we believe, unique in multinational, multilinguistic societies. For example, federal systems such as India's or Canada's may put place of birth on the passport or a document, but they would not put ethnic, linguistic, or religious affiliations. Even Yugoslovia's Soviet-style federal system did not stamp ethnic group membership on the passport.

2. This chapter is a substantially revised and expanded version of Alfred Stepan, "When Democracy and the Nation-State Are Competing Logics: Reflections on Estonia," *European Journal of Sociology* 35 (1994): 127–41. Permission to cite from this article is gratefully acknowledged.

3. For the discussion of inclusiveness in modern democracies, see Robert A. Dahl, *Polyarchy: Participation and Opposition* (New Haven: Yale University Press, 1971): 6–7.

4. Once again we want to call attention to the related research in progress by Rogers Brubaker, in which he focuses attention on that aspect of the triadic relationship between elites following nation-state strategies, minorities in states following nation-state policies, and the homeland state of those minorities.

We have decided to explore this implicit triadic relationship in some detail in the Baltic countries of Estonia, Latvia, and Lithuania. We chose these countries for three reasons. First, for reasons having to do with their past experience as democracies, their relatively developed economies, and their potential member-ship in the European Union, these countries have the most supportive conditions for democratization of the fifteen newly independent states of the former Soviet Union. Democratic failure in these countries is in no way overdetermined. Sec-ond, both domestically and internationally, the major problem these countries must resolve before they can become consolidated democracies is precisely the tension between the logic of a nation-state and the logic of a democracy. Russia is a large, unstable, and potentially aggressively nationalistic and self-appointed "homeland" for Russian-speaking minorities in the Baltics. A poor handling of the nation-state minority problem could lead not only to nonconsolidated democ-racies, but also to threats to the integrity of one or more Baltic states. Third, we are fortunate to have a very solid research base to build upon.[5] Let us begin our comparative inquiry with an analysis of the legacy of the Baltic countries' inte-gration into the USSR.

THE BALTICS' DIFFICULT LEGACY

History and the specific legacy of the previous nondemocratic regime are im-portant for all analyses of democratization. There is possibly no area where his-tory is more important than in the Baltics, where the previous nondemocratic regime, the USSR, brutally transformed these polities demographically, cultur-ally, economically, and even ecologically.

Estonia and Latvia had the most substantial prior experience of democratic

---

Brubaker's project is devoted to exploring the "fields of force" between these three components of the tri-adic relationships. Our endeavor is closely related, but we pay special attention to how these evolving rela-tionships affect democratization. For numerous references to Brubaker's work, see our notes in chapter 2.

5. These include on-going major comparative surveys, one under the supervision of Hans-Dieter Klingemann and the other by Richard Rose. David D. Laitin and Rogers Brubaker are also regularly pro-ducing important comparative work on topics such as language and nationalism in the Baltics. Full cita-tions follow in this chapter. Anatol Lieven, *The Baltic Revolution: Estonia, Latvia, Lithuania and the Path to Independence* (New Haven: Yale University Press, 1994, rev. ed.) is the best overall introduction to the key historical and political issues relevant for Baltic democratization. On the interwar years, see George von Rauch, *The Baltic States: The Years of Independence* (Berkeley: University of California Press, 1974), and Tönu Parming, *The Collapse of Liberal Democracy and the Rise of Authoritarianism in Estonia* (London: Sage Publications, 1975). For the Soviet period, see Romuald Misiunas and Rein Taagepera, *The Baltic States: Years of Dependence, 1940–90* (Berkeley: University of California Press, 1993). This is an expanded and re-vised version of the 1983 original. For Estonia, see Rein Taagepera, *Estonia: Return to Independence* (Boul-der, Colo.: Westview Press, 1993). This book contains a nuanced assessment of the nation-state versus Russ-ian minority tensions. For Latvia, see Rasma Karklins, *Ethnopolitics and Transition to Democracy: The Collapse of the USSR and Latvia* (Baltimore: Johns Hopkins University Press, 1994). Unlike Taagepera's book on Estonia, the Karklins book accepts a nation-state strategy as relatively unproblematic for a de facto multinational state.

Table 20.1. Baltic Demography: The 1920s and 1930s versus the 1980s

| | Percentage | | | | | |
| | Estonia | | Latvia | | Lithuania | |
Group	1934	1984	1939	1989	1923	1989
Titular nation	88.8	61.5	75.5	52	69.2	79.6
Russians	8.2	30.3	10.6	34	2.5	9.4
Ukrainians and Byelorussians	NA	4.9	1.4	8.0	NA	NA
Poles	NA	NA	2.5	2.3	15.3	7.0
Jews	NA	NA	4.8	0.9	8.3	0.3
Germans	2.2	0	3.2	0.1	NA	NA
Lithuanians	NA	NA	1.2	1.3	—	—
Other	0.8	3.3	0.8	1.4	4.7*	4.0*

Source: Anatol Lieven, *The Baltic Revolution: Estonia, Latvia, Lithuania and the Path to Independence* (New Haven: Yale University Press, 1994, rev. ed.), 432–34. In Lithuania the stars after *other* refer to Lieven's assessment that most are "mainly byelorussian." Also see Romuald Misiunas and Rein Taagepera, *The Baltic States: Years of Dependence, 1940–90* (Berkeley: University of California Press, 1993), 353, for valuable time series demographic data on the Baltics.
NA, not available.

politics of any of the Soviet republics. These countries, as well as Lithuania, were independent from 1918 to 1940. In the 1920s, they had multiparty elections, and in Estonia constitutional arrangements for cultural minorities were among the most politically responsible in Europe.[6] It is true that democracy broke down in Lithuania in 1927–28 and then in Estonia and Latvia in 1934. Then came secret protocols of the Molotov-Ribbentrop Pact of 1939, which placed the Baltic republics within the Soviet sphere of influence. Soviet troops invaded the countries in June 1940, and they were annexed. The Nazi occupation of 1941–44, and reannexation by the USSR thereafter were obviously devastating setbacks to any democratic evolution. Nonetheless, unlike the other countries of the former Soviet Union, the Balts had a usable democratic past. However, these countries had a radically different demography when they became independent again in 1991. Therein, for Estonia and Latvia, lies the frustration and tension between the goals of being a nation-state *and* a liberal inclusive democracy (table 20.1).

According to the 1989 census, the population of the Estonian Soviet Socialist Republic (ESSR) was 1.6 million, of whom approximately 1 million were ethnic Estonians and 600,000 were non-Estonians. The capital, Tallinn, had just over a 50 percent Russian-speaking population, and Narva, the northeast border town with Russia, was 94 percent Russian speaking. This mix of nationalities, especially the large Russian immigration that had followed the Soviet annexation of 1940,

6. Lijphart singles out Estonia for its pioneering and democratic constitutional procedures for national minorities. See his *Democracies: Patterns of Majoritarian and Consensus Government in Twenty-one Countries* (New Haven: Yale University Press, 1984), 183–84. For a full description of Estonia's 1925 cultural autonomy law, see Karl Aun, "The Cultural Autonomy of National Minorities in Estonia," *Yearbook of the Estonian Learned Society in America* 1 (1951–53): 26–41.

would have created tensions even under the best of circumstances. But, of course, given the historical memory of the Estonians and the other ethnic Balts, the circumstances were not the best but were laden with a sense of loss or even ethnic assault.[7]

But are the russophone minorities in the Baltics actually "transients," as they are often called? Could they ever become loyal citizens in the newly (re)independent Baltic states?[8] In one statistically representative polling sample in 1993, a significant number of the non-Balts in Estonia, 35 percent, said they were born in Estonia. In Latvia the figure was 52 percent. The immense majority of the non-Balts polled said they had lived in the Baltics for more than twenty-one years: 78 percent in Estonia, 86 percent in Latvia, and 81 percent in Lithuania. Of the remainder of the Baltic minority population, 15 percent in Estonia, 9 percent in Latvia, and 10 percent in Lithuania said they had lived as residents in these countries for between eleven and twenty years.[9] The Russians in the Baltics are certainly a peripheral and a difficult legacy, but they are not transients.

After World War II, the population of Latvia, which had dropped from 2 million to 1.4 million during the war, was swollen by 535,000 non-Latvian immigrants. The native population was 75.5 percent in 1939 before the war began and had been reduced to 52 percent in 1989. At independence Latvians were a minority in each of the seven main cities of Latvia, ranging from 47 percent in Jurmala

7. Misiunas and Taagepera, in *The Baltic States*, 354–55, present a table where they make an educated guess as to population losses due to Soviet and Nazi policies in the 1939–45 period. For Estonia alone they estimate that these include Soviet deportations and executions in 1940–41 (15,000), Soviet army mobilization in 1941 and 1944–45 (35,000), evacuations to the USSR in 1941 (30,000), and Soviet executions and deportations in 1944–45 (30,000). They estimate that, for all of the categories, approximately only 20,000 Estonians had returned to Estonia by 1945. The figures they cite for Latvia and Lithuania are even worse. For example, Soviet executions and deportations in 1944–45 in Latvia were 70,000, and in Lithuania were 50,000. During the 1941–45 Nazi occupation, there were 200,000 executions and deportations in Lithuania, 90,000 in Latvia, and 10,000 in Estonia. Of these, it is estimated that, respectively, 180,000, 70,000, and 1,000 were Jews. In the Rose and Maley study of Baltic nationalities, 42 percent of respondents said someone in their family had been deported, imprisoned, or executed. The historical memory of Soviet abuse is much stronger than that of German abuse; eight times more respondents listed the Soviets, as opposed to the Germans, as the source of their suffering (Rose and Maley, question 216). Obviously there are few surviving Jews to remember the Holocaust of Baltic Jews, especially in Lithuania and Latvia. Richard Rose and William Maley, "Nationalities in the Baltic States, a Survey Study," *Studies in Public Policy,* 222 (1994).

8. In the newly (re)independent Baltic states, there is inevitable confusion over the terms *Russians, Russian-speakers,* and *non-Balts.* As table 20.1 shows, at independence Estonia and Latvia had a substantial Ukrainian and Belorussian minority population. Most of these were russophone but not necessarily "Russian." Probably most of the "other" in table 20.1 are also russophones from Soviet republics that are now CIS member states. In this chapter we will call members of the titular nation (e.g., ethnic or cultural Estonians, Latvians, or Lithuanians) *Balts.* We will call the others *non-Balt* or *Baltic minority* populations. Where the survey data specifically indicate "Russian-speaking," as opposed to Russian, we will so identify the data. Since identities are in fact socially constructed and constantly changing, we (building upon the research of David D. Laitin) believe that the russophone population, whether they are from the Ukraine, Belarus, Russia, or some other CIS republic, are actually developing a new diaspora identity of a "Russian-speaking minority."

9. See Rose and Maley, "Nationalities in the Baltic States," 52–53. The data are based upon a September–October 1993 survey that involved 6,136 interviews with statistically representative samples of each of the seven major nationalities in the Baltics.

to only 13 percent in the eastern city of Daugavpils. In Latvia, Russians represent 34 percent of the population, Byelorussians 4.5 percent, and Ukrainians 3.5 percent, although they tend to be Russian-speaking and have lost most of their connection with their original nationality. Russia has, however, offered them citizenship.[10] Riga has been historically a multinational city.[11] The Russian community in Riga is of historic standing, and some of its key leaders supported Latvian independence. To turn Riga into a city with a purely Latvian cultural or political face is at odds with that tradition. Demographically, the most difficult Baltic country in which to reconcile the logic of a nation-state and the logic of a liberal democracy will be Latvia.

Demographically and culturally, the easiest case for a liberal democracy is Lithuania. Lithuania shares the same experience of Soviet annexation and domination, although the Catholic majority kept alive anti-Soviet sentiments. To be sure, the anti-Soviet nationalist mobilization in 1989–91 was as intense or more intense under the leadership of Sajudis and the personality of the nationalist preindependence leader Vytautas Landsbergis as anywhere in the Baltics. However, at independence the Russian minority was only 9 percent of the total population. In addition, there was an important Polish minority of 7 percent that obviously did not consider Russia their homeland. Because there was less demographic "anxiety" in Lithuania among ethnic Baltic political elites, it was psychologically and politically easier to follow an inclusionary citizenship strategy for all residents than it would have been in Latvia or Estonia.[12] As a result of the small proportion of non-Lithuanians and the heterogeneity of the minorities, the Lithuanians never introduced an exclusionary policy on citizenship. Non-Lithuanians enjoy the same political rights as other citizens. All the survey data indicate considerable integration. For purposes of this chapter, therefore, Lithuania does not really have significant tension between the logic of a nation-state and the logic of a liberal democracy.

The three Baltic republics—Estonia, Latvia, and Lithuania—had a tradition of independent statehood and democracy when they regained independence. Unlike most of the other republics in the USSR, they had been part of the Soviet Union only since 1940, not since 1917 or shortly after the civil war. But the Baltic states' integration into the Soviet state and society for nearly fifty years radically differentiates them from the central European states of the "outer empire" in their process of democratization.

The difference between regaining statehood and reconstructing a nation became central to the process of democracy building in the Baltics. The ambiguities of the process were well stated in the slogan painted on the barricades outside the

10. See Lieven, *The Baltic Revolution*, 433–34.

11. For example, Lieven in *The Baltic Revolution* cites data that indicate that in 1867 Germans constituted 42.9 percent of the population of Riga, Russians were 25.1 percent, and Latvians were 23.6 percent.

12. For the granting of inclusive citizenship in Lithuania, see Lieven, *The Baltic Revolution*, 309–10.

parliament in Riga in 1991, taken from the Polish rebellion against the Tsar in 1863: "For our Freedom and Yours." The implicit promise of that slogan was that independence and democracy were to be for all—Balts and other nationalities alike.[13] However, not much time would pass before another discourse emerged concerning citizenship in which belonging to the nation was to be privileged. Large minorities (mainly russophones) were defined as foreign "colonists" or "transients."

Nothing can symbolize better the above set of problems than the fact that at one point there were two democratically elected bodies meeting in Estonia and two in Latvia. One elected body, the Republic Supreme Council, a largely pro-independence Popular Front–dominated parliament, was elected by all residents in the spring of 1990. In another, uniformly pro-independence elected body, called the "Citizens' Congress," the electorate was restricted to *pre-1940 citizens* and their descendants.[14] We could say that the supreme councils were part of the newly emerging multinational democratic state, dominated by the pro-independence popular fronts, while the citizens' congresses were the representation of the nation. In this the Baltics were almost unique in the history of nationalism in that they gave democratic representation to a nation within a state even before independence. This duality was made possible by the ambiguity dominant at the time. This ambiguity was reflected in the fact that there was even some overlap in the membership of both bodies. Significantly, the Constitutional Assembly that drafted the 1992 constitution was formed by thirty members nominated, respectively, by the official Supreme Council and the parallel Congress of Estonia. Let us analyze the complexity of this double transition to independence and to democratic or nondemocratic forms of representation and contestation.

TRANSITION TOWARD INDEPENDENCE AND DEMOCRACY: ELEMENTS OF COMPLEMENTARITY AND TENSION

Active dissidence began to appear in Estonia during the Gorbachev years as protests against ecologically damaging projects or as demands for the restoration of artistic monuments, such as the National Heritage Society in Estonia, which later in January 1989 called for the creation of a Congress elected exclusively by pre-1940 citizens and their descendents. In Latvia, commemorations at the Freedom Monument in Riga in 1987, marking the anniversary of the Stalinist deportations in 1941, gave expression to the national sentiment. Proposals of Latvian economic autonomy in 1987 reflected the frustration with the state of the economy. In the summer of 1989, the Supreme Soviet in Moscow admitted the secret

13. Ibid., 303.
14. For an excellent analysis of the dualism and competition between the Popular Front–dominated parliament of the Estonian Soviet Republic and the ethnic Estonian citizens' committees that eventually created their own parallel Estonian Congress, see Taagepera, *Estonia: Return to Independence,* 170–82.

protocols of the Molotov-Ribbentrop Pact and with it the illegitimacy of Soviet rule. The Baltic Communist parties started splitting between opponents of Gorbachev's reforms and supporters of the Popular Fronts and the Sajudis, whose leaders had found the sympathy of the Moscow reformers like Aleksandr Yakovlev in August 1988. The Popular Front leaders emerged from a variety of backgrounds, mainly from the intelligentsia, both humanistic and technical, many with a Communist Party background. In Estonia the Popular Front was largely founded by the liberal wing of the Communist establishment. In 1989 and 1990 the Lithuanian and Estonian Communist parties, by majority votes, decided to separate from the Soviet Communist party. The Latvian Communist Party split down the middle. The supreme councils passed declarations of sovereignty, new citizenship laws, assertions of control over natural resources and industry, and above all refutations of the legitimacy of the Soviet annexation.

In the elections for the supreme councils in February and March 1990, the right to vote was given to all adult permanent citizens, with the exclusion of the mentally ill.[15] To qualify as a candidate it was necessary to have been a permanent resident of the republic for only ten years. Parties had little time to prepare for the elections and candidates ran as individuals and not as members of a specific party, but frequently they were endorsed by one or several political organizations. The Popular Fronts emerged from these elections as the dominant parliamentary groups.[16] In Estonia, of 105 delegates (4 of whom represented the military), the Popular Front received 46 seats, the Joint Council of Work Collectives (supporting the status of Estonia as a Soviet Republic) with the support of the russophone population won 23 seats, and the Democratic Election Coalition, "Free Estonia," made up of Communists and former Communists favoring independence but with some kind of connection with the USSR, secured 13 mandates. Of the 105 elected deputies in Estonia, approximately 27 were regarded as representatives of the russophone population.

The Latvian Supreme Council consisted of 201 mandates. The Popular Front won 131. The opposition groups opposed to independence, largely led by the Communist Party and its sympathizers, obtained 59 seats. Eight seats went to independents.

Russophone Communists in the Baltics and hard-liners in Moscow joined forces to create Soviet loyalist movements to oppose the reformist and covertly pro-independence forces in the Popular Fronts. In Estonia the pro-Soviet forces were called "the International Movement of Workers in the Estonian SSR," in Latvia, "International Front," and in Lithuania, "Unity." There were also efforts to

---

15. See Jan Åke Dellebrant, "The Reemergence of Multipartism in the Baltic States," in Sten Berglund and Jan Åke Dellebrant, eds., *The New Democracies in Eastern Europe: Party Systems and Political Cleavages* (Aldershot, U.K.: Edward Elgar Publishing, 1991), 71–106.

16. A case can be made that Estonia's and Latvia's "founding elections" were those held in 1990, which were won by the Popular Front. If so, the first postindependence Estonian elections in 1992 represented a significant disenfranchisement of Russians and russophones who had voted in the previous 1990 elections.

mobilize Russian-speaking workers of the "All-Union" factories, sometimes by the official trade unions, by the creation in Estonia and Latvia of the United Council of Work Collectives (OSTK). A general strike called in August 1989 by the Intermovement and OSTK was supported by some 5 to 8 percent of the work force. Similar attempts in May 1990 failed. Most of the workers rejected the corrupt Communist leaders, but only a few were able to distance themselves completely from their Communist past.

In the pro-Soviet wings of the Communist parties, there were also Balts who could not make the transition to support independence—unlike such Communist pro-independence leaders as Algirdas Brazauskas in Lithuania, Anatolijs Gorbunovs in Latvia, and Arnold Rüütel in Estonia. Some of the Communist leaders who did not support independence left the Baltics; others continued active in politics there.

In the Baltic elections of February–March 1990, the Soviet loyalists won most of the votes in Russian-speaking areas. However, in Latvia, the Popular Front gained many votes among the Russian-speaking population in the first round, but Russian minority support for the Popular Front did diminish in the second round after the Lithuanian declaration of independence. The final results were 139 Popular Front candidates elected (including 5 Russian-speaking, 2 Poles, and 2 Jews) and 62 Equal Rights candidates (Inter-front and Communists) elected, 8 of whom were ethnic Latvians.[17]

Certainly, there were some Russian minorities that were not reconciled with independence and the defeat of the Moscow counter-revolution. For example, the Narva Council defied the Estonian constitution, destroyed the border posts, and created a pro-Soviet para-military force, the Workers Detachments. In 1992 the former Communists won victories in local elections in Narva. However, the threat of secession in the border areas seems, in 1995, to be in abeyance.

In the summer of 1990, the three Baltic republics were well on the way to completing a transition to democracy and independence decided by elected representatives. The elections had been competitive, although based on the heterogeneous coalitions of the Popular Fronts and voting for individual candidates, and fair. Subsequent politics would not be a debate about democracy—as we have defined it—but about what kind of democracy: an inclusionary liberal democracy based on citizenship for almost all permanent residents or an exclusionary "ethnic democracy" only for 1940 descendants.[18] A second transition was in the making.

---

17. For an excellent comparative account of the three Baltic elections of 1990, see Lieven, *The Baltic Revolution*, 214–315.

18. For the concept of "ethnic democracy," see Juan J. Linz, "Totalitarian and Authoritarian Regimes," in Fred I. Greenstein and Nelson W. Polsby, eds., *Handbook of Political Science* (Reading, Mass.: Addison-Wesley Publishing, 1975), 3:326–30. In that work Linz characterizes ethnic democracies as polities that are democratic for the dominant group but that exclude, on the basis of ethnicity, other groups from the democratic process. For applications of the concept, see Yoav Peled, "Ethnic Democracy and the Legal Con-

Estonia began its transition under favorable geopolitical circumstances, especially because of its all-important relation with Russia. When the Soviet Union's
"Black Beret" military units (or OMON) attacked and killed nearly twenty Baltic
demonstrators in January 1991, Boris Yeltsin, then the chairman of the Russian
Supreme Soviet, came to Tallinn on the invitation of the Estonian prime minister
to sign immediately a mutual recognition treaty between Russia and all the Baltic
states. Yeltsin appealed to the Russian soldiers not to fire on civilians. The Estonian-
American social scientist (and a presidential candidate in 1992) Rein Taagepera
argues that Yeltsin's support for Estonia pulled the rug from under the self-styled
defenders of Russia who demanded direct imposition of Kremlin rule. Yeltsin's
role was equally critical at the time of the coup attempt against Gorbachev. Soviet
troops moved on Tallinn on August 21, 1991. The next day Estonia declared independence. Two days later, Yeltsin, in the name of Russia, recognized Estonia as an
independent country, before any member of the European Community did so.[19]

To understand the policies in Estonia and Latvia toward the Russian minority,
we should never forget the legacies of the totalitarianism and pre-(re)indepen-
dence periods. Without a reference to that past, it is difficult to understand the
function of the Popular Fronts in Latvia and Estonia or the Sajudis in Lithuania.
They were movements rather than parties. They were coalitions of factions with
different leaders and agendas, more or less united in confronting Moscow and in
the steps toward independence. The components of these umbrella organizations
would end up fighting each other and splitting. But they were historic catalysts.
Given the important reform Communist component of the transition, the fact is
that under the long totalitarian rule almost everybody, even dissidents, had at one
point or another made their career within the regime's organizations. Some did
so in the state, others in the party and in the Komsomol, others in the cultural institutions paying lip service to the regime, and not a few even compromised with
the KGB. This legacy of past involvement with the Soviet regime made the new
pro-independence elites vulnerable to mutually destructive accusations and to
constant attacks by more radical nationalists, especially "provincials" with little
education and standing or emigrés. In that context, many of the politicians who
had originally favored inclusionary politics toward citizenship (called the "Zero
Option" to indicate near automatic citizenship for almost all residents upon independence) shifted to the exclusionary nationalist option. This exclusionary option restricted citizenship only to pre-1940 citizens and their descendants and
thus deprived of citizenship many Russian-speakers who had been born in the
Baltics.

---

struction of Citizenship: Arab Citizens of the Jewish State," *American Political Science Review* 86, no. 2
(1992), 432–43, and Vello Pettai, "Emerging Ethnic Democracy in Estonia and Latvia: The Dynamics of Sovereign Nationalism and Minority Identities" (paper presented at the 14th Conference of the Association for
the Advancement of Baltic Studies, Chicago, Illinois, June 8–11, 1994).

19. Taagepera, *Estonia: Return to Independence*, 202.

Let us give a particularly graphic example of the shift from inclusionary to exclusionary citizenship strategies. On May 6, 1990, two days after the declaration of Latvian sovereignty, the chairman of the Latvian Supreme Council, Anatolijs Gorbunovs, spoke in Russian on Latvian television, promising that *all* those who wanted to be citizens of Latvia could be. He also issued a special note guaranteeing the political and cultural rights of non-Latvians resident in Latvia. He insisted that it was not serious to talk about "second class citizens." However, in the summer of 1992, this same Latvian leader advocated a referendum that would restrict citizenship to pre-1940 citizens and their descendants.[20]

The Baltic Russians: Culturally Unassimilable but Politically Integratable?

The key questions for a democratic multinational state are whether the minorities are or are not *open to multiple and complementary political identities and loyalties* and, if so, whether they will be given citizenship. If minorities' cultural and political freedoms are guaranteed, might they indeed become loyal citizens, or would their primary loyalty remain to their "homeland" state? Obviously, such questions are extremely important in the Estonian and Latvian cases. Fortunately, two different sets of surveys allow us to explore these themes.

A preindependence survey conducted from June to August 1990 and coordinated by the prominent German social scientist Hans-Dieter Klingemann indicated that ethnic Russians, as well as ethnic Estonians and Latvians, had relatively strong identification with their republics and relatively weak identification with the USSR (table 20.2).

There are three key points revealed by table 20.2. First, even when the USSR existed and was still a superpower, the core identification of ethnic Russians in the Baltics with the USSR was relatively weak, although there was somewhat stronger identification in Estonia than in Latvia. Second, in 1992, after the independence of Latvia and Estonia, the disappearance of the Soviet Union, and the emergence of an independent Russia, only 4.2 percent of the Russian speakers in Latvia gave as their first identity Russia, whereas 53.2 percent gave as their first identity the republic in which they resided. Among Russian speakers in Estonia, the proportions were, respectively, 12.0 and 38.3. Third, from our perspective these data indicate that the Russian minority in the Baltics was capable of multiple and complementary identities. That is, objectively and culturally, they were russophone. But, subjectively and politically, they were open to self-identification with the new republics in which they lived.

Another set of questions indicate that the non-Baltic minorities, although with considerably less intensity than the ethnic Balts, felt proud of being residents in

20. Anatol Lieven, *The Baltic Revolution,* 304.

Table 20.2. Identities of Estonians, Latvians, and Non-Estonians and Non-Latvians (Russian Speaking) in the Two Baltic Republics When They Were Part of the USSR (June–August 1990) and after Independence (1992)

Question: "What do you feel yourself in the first place; in the second place?"

		Percentage							
		Estonians		Non-Estonians		Latvians		Non-Latvians	
Answer	Year	1st	2nd	1st	2nd	1st	2nd	1st	2nd
"Of the Republic in which you live"	1990	66.9	30.9	37.3	26.7	72.8	24.5	38.5	39.5
	1992	52.3	34.8	38.3	37.4	63.1	36.6	53.2	35.2
"Of the town, locality in which I live"	1990	30.3	28.3	32.5	28.3	25.6	55.3	41.6	24.5
	1992	44.0	40.4	40.4	21.5	32.9	39.1	37.1	25.2
"Of the USSR"	1990	0.5	2.0	21.5	21.2	0.9	1.7	10.6	17.4
"Of Russia"	1992	—	—	12.0	20.9	0.2	0.2	4.2	15.5
"Some other state"	1992			0.3		0.7	2.1	1.3	6.9
"Of Europe"	1990	1.0	11.5	2.1	4.1	0.5	10.7	0.9	5.7
	1992	2.4	3.5	3.5	5.9	0.9	13.6	0.8	9.0
"Of the whole world"	1990	1.3	3.6	6.6	9.8	0.2	7.8	8.4	13.1
	1992	1.3	2.7	5.6	7.0	2.3	8.5	3.4	8.1
Number of interviews	1990	621		387		449		460	
	1992	629		380		587		481	

Source: Hans-Dieter Klingemann (Berlin) and Mikki Titma (Tallinn), Gesellschaft und Politik in Baltikum, Eine Vergleichende Umfrage in Litauen, Estland und Lettland im Juni–August 1990. The 1992 data are from Hans-Dieter Klingemann, Values and Elections (Preelection Survey) in Estonia, Lithuania and Latvia, machine readable codebook, Zentralarchiv für emprische Sozialforschung an der Universität in Köln, n.d. The question in 1992 was slightly different: Which of these geographic localities would you say you belong to first (show card) and which would you say you belong to second?

their republics. Table 20.3 shows that more than three-quarters of all non-Balts in 1990 felt proud of being residents of their respective republics (table 20.3).

In the same 1990 survey was the question, "What do you wish the future of our Republic to be?" Only 42 percent of the non-Estonians, 30 percent of the non-Latvians, and 28 percent of the non-Lithuanians favored the complete status quo (table 20.4).

Although table 20.4 gives a relatively low percentage of non-Balts who positively favored independence in 1990, data we have for Latvia indicate that non-Latvian loyalties were not fixed but were socially constructed and changeable. Indeed, Rasma Karklin in her study of Latvia shows that in June 1989 only 9 percent of non-Latvians favored independence. In October 1990 26 percent were pro-independence. In March 1991 39 percent were for Latvian independence.[21]

The identity and politics of the russophone diaspora in the former Soviet Union presents some unique characteristics because of the crisis of the Russian identity itself in the Soviet totalitarian state. From 1917 to 1991 Russia was a nation

21. See Karklins, Ethnopolitics and Transition to Democracy, 50.

Table 20.3. "How Much Pride Do You Feel in Being a Resident of the Republic?" Responses of Nationality Groups in the Baltics, 1990

Answer	Percentage					
	Estonians	Non-Estonians	Latvians	Non-Latvians	Lithuanians	Non-Lithuanians
"Very proud"	39.5	11.3	72.7	21.1	45.8	13.1
"Proud"	49.0	65.3	24.9	63.5	43.0	66.4
"Not very proud"	10.4	18.7	1.6	13.5	10.3	15.3
"Not at all proud"	1.2	4.6	.7	1.9	.7	5.1
	(621)	(387)	(449)	(460)	(837)	(163)

Source: The 1990 survey cited in table 20.2.

and a culture that was largely submerged in the Soviet state. The Soviet state itself was involved in its "internationalist" nation building. Exaggerating things, we could say that to be Russian was largely to be Russian speaking. It is no accident that in the diaspora many people identify themselves as "Russian speaking" rather than as "Russians." We need to know much more about the building of a Russian cultural-national identity in the Russian Federal Republic of the USSR and now in newly independent Russia. But, for the time being, there is still evidence of weakness of Russian "nationalism" inside and particularly outside of Russia. Let us not forget that a central element of Russian national-cultural identity, Russian Orthodoxy, was persecuted, destroyed, and "privatized." The mass of the population was significantly dechristianized. Russian history was submerged in Soviet history textbooks. The "Great Patriotic War" was a defense of the "Soviet homeland." Patriotic monuments in Russia were Soviet monuments. All of this past history limits the articulation of minority demands in diaspora more to "linguistic" than to "national" demands. It also places some limits on the willingness of the Russians in the homeland and especially in the "near abroad" to identify with a potential irredenta.[22] What does all of this mean for the future possible identities of the Russian-speaking minority population in the Baltics?

This somewhat decultured working class Russian minority, as long as they see their personal life chances as better in the Baltics than if they return to Russia—a perception reflected in a wealth of survey data—would probably be amenable to accommodation, possibly even in the very long run, to assimilation.[23] Indeed, we

22. In addition, as we discussed in chapter 19, numerous political units within the Russian Federal Republic are non-Russian and include a total of twelve million people.

23. For the Baltic Russians the key thing is whether their and their children's personal life chances would improve by moving to Russia. Studies show that Russians in the Baltics are very skeptical about their chance to obtain jobs and housing in Russia. This makes the exit option risky and not likely. In fact, based on a 1993 survey by David D. Laitin and Jerry Hough of 1,416 respondents in Estonia, Laitin estimates that only 3.1 percent of the Russian-speaking minority indicated serious interest in the exit option. See David D. Laitin, "Identity in Formation: The Russian Speaking Nationality in the Post-Soviet Diaspora" (paper prepared for the 1994 Annual Meeting of the American Political Science Association, New York, September 1–4, 1994), 13.

Table 20.4. Attitudes among Different Nationalities in the Baltics toward a Future Political Relationship with the USSR: July–August 1990

| | Question: "What do you wish the future of your republic to be?" Percentage | | | | | |
| | Estonia | | Latvia | | Lithuania | |
Answer	Estonians	Non-Estonians	Latvians	Non-Latvians	Lithuanians	Non-Lithuanians
An independent state outside of the USSR (independence option)	87	15	84	26	80	27
An independent Republic in the frame of the USSR, which can make treaties with other Republics (confederation option)	11	35	9	32	15	39
An independent Republic in the frame of a Federation of the USSR (status quo option)	1	42	3	30	2	28
Other Answers	1	4	1	1	1	0
Don't Know	0	4	3	11	2	6
Number of Interviews	620	387	449	460	837	163

Source: Hans-Dieter Klingemann and Wolfgang G. Gibowski, "Gesellschaft und Politik im Baltikum" (unpublished manuscript supplied to the authors).

would hypothesize, on the basis of comparative survey work on working class migrants elsewhere, that Russians would want their children to learn a Baltic language simply to improve their repertoire of coping skills.[24] However, prudence would indicate that a requirement to learn Estonian for a middle-aged, only Russian-speaking industrial worker, in order to hold a job or to have access to a vote or to state services, would raise anxiety about his or her job security and *doubts* as to whether the state is for all residents or only for ethnic Estonians.

Language policy for the foreseeable future will be a central concern for the Baltic Russian-speaking minorities. Much of the Russian population have industrial jobs. The linguistic distance between Estonian and Russian is vast. Forty-five percent of the Russians in Estonia and 33 percent in Latvia claim knowledge of a Baltic language. Many of the rest probably only have a moderately serviceable command of Baltic languages. However, an analysis of the 1979 and 1989 census

24. For example, Juan J. Linz, in a survey of youths with two parents who had immigrated to the Basque country (which like Estonia has an extremely difficult language), shows that such youths do not reject the idea that the educational system should teach Basque; 39 percent of respondents wanted the primary schools to teach compulsory Spanish with voluntary Basque, 35 percent wanted Spanish with compulsory Basque, and 18 percent wanted Basque schools with Spanish being obligatory or voluntary. See Juan J. Linz, "Los jóvenes en una España multilingüe y de nacionalidades," in Francisco Andrés Orizo et al., *Juventud española 1984* (Madrid: Ediciones S.M., 1985), 325–436. Data from 384.

Table 20.5. Language Knowledge in the Baltic Republics (Reported in 1992 Interview) by Language Used in the Interview

	Percentage					
	Estonia		Latvia		Lithuania	
Language Knowledge	Estonian	Russian	Latvian	Russian	Lithuanian	Russian
Only Russian (or non-Baltic language)	—	45	—	33	—	22
Only Baltic language	74	1	52	4	64	4
Baltic language and Russian (or other non-Baltic language)	26	54	48	63	36	74

Source: Hans-Dieter Klingemann, Jürgen Lass, and Katrin Mattusch, "Nationalitätenkonflikt und Mechanism politischer Integration im Baltikum" (unpublished manuscript, Wissenschaftszentrum Berlin für Sozialforschung, November 1994). Data supplied to us by Hans-Dieter Klingemann. It should be noted that subjective evaluation of language knowledge in surveys and census data is highly unreliable and particularly subject to social pressures. This said, the above data almost certainly *overstate* knowledge of Baltic languages among the russophone minority.

in Estonia gives estimates that Estonian speakers among the Russian population of the capital of Estonia were only 12 percent in 1979 and 15 percent in 1989 (table 20.5).[25]

In sum, at independence, on linguistic grounds alone the Russian minority population in the Baltics (especially in Estonia) was absolutely *culturally unassimilable* into a democratic nation-state for one or two generations. In contrast, we believe that the Russian minority Baltic population was able to be rapidly *politically integrated* into a democracy. Why? Evidence for this argument is the Russian minorities' low positive identification with the homeland, their tendency to some degree of dual (especially geographic) identity, their strong sense that their (and their children's) life chances would be better in the Baltics than if they returned to their supposed homeland, and, as we shall see, their overall positive evaluation of the political changes that have taken place in their republics. In our judgment a people with these characteristics are potentially loyal citizens to a state that gives them their full political rights and a modicum of cultural protection, especially in areas of language.

Legacies are important for a new democracy, but *choices* made during and shortly after the transition can also decrease or increase the possibilities for democratic consolidation. Let us explore the choices made, especially by ethnic Estonian and ethnic Latvian political elites.

Choices: Inclusionary versus "Othering" Discourses

As the possibility of independence from the Soviet Union grew, Estonian political leaders began to emphasize the logic and rights of the Estonian nation-

25. See Peteris Zvidrins, "Changes of Ethnic Composition in the Baltic States," *Nationalities Papers* 22, no. 2 (1994): 377.

state, instead of independence or democracy per se. A series of legal and political steps were taken to advance these nation-state aspirations. The law on citizenship moved from broad and inclusive definitions of membership in the polity to narrow and exclusive ones as time passed.[26] During the movement for independence, it was proposed at various times that anyone born in Estonia or participating in the independence movement could opt for Estonian citizenship if they so wished. But in the end, for ethnic Estonian nationalists, the urge to identify the independent state with the nation was too strong to withstand. Citizenship was granted outright only to those individuals born in Estonia before the 1940 annexation and to their descendants. This meant, for example, that Canadian or U.S. citizens who had never been to Estonia but were the offspring of Estonians had the right to vote in elections, but the Russians who had been born in Estonia after 1940 and had lived there all their lives were not given citizenship. This exclusion was especially serious because only people who were citizens by 1992 could vote in the September 1992 parliamentary and presidential elections, organize political parties, or be elected to office. In effect, the citizenship law disenfranchised almost 40 percent of the population of Estonia during a key foundational moment of the new would-be democracy.

Language was a particularly sensitive issue, since, as we have seen, a majority of Russians did not speak Estonian. In January 1989, a language law was passed with the support of the Estonian Popular Front, making Estonian the official language of the country. It was expected that, *within two years,* Estonian language requirements would be imposed for all jobs in services or trade. Within four years all official state correspondence had to be in Estonian. For many older, less educated Russians, this law carried the threat that they would lose their jobs, even in the private sector. Also, it could mean that, if they wanted to approach the state to inquire about rights and services, they would have to do so in Estonian. The Estonian polity was beginning to alienate itself from a significant part of the demos living in Estonia.

All of these legislative and political decisions were opposed by some Estonians and non-Estonians in the name of political prudence or political democracy. All were decisively defended, however, on the basis of the logic of the nation-state and the strong supporting body of legal and moral rationales associated with this logic. In the case of language, the presumption was that if the state was an expression of the nation, the only official language that could exist was that of the nation. This belief was intensely felt in Estonia because of the fear that, as a very small country, with a very difficult language, Estonian could easily disappear. The legal and moral right to restrict citizenship to preannexation residents of Estonia and Latvia was based on the analogy of Poland's "right" to expel the Germans in

26. See Peet Kask, "National Radicalization in Estonia: Legislation on Citizenship and Related Issues," *Nationalities Papers* 22, no. 2 (1994): 379–91.

Poznan, including those who Hitler had helped settle there (as well as those living there before). Under international law, occupying forces and their military personnel have no rights of citizenship. Estonian diplomats argued that the Molotov-Ribbentrop Pact of 1939 had led to an illegal usurpation of the state and that the entire 1940–91 period should be classified as a military occupation. On these grounds, all Russians who entered the country after 1940 and their descendants were illegal occupiers with no claim to automatic citizenship.[27]

The argument for restricting voting rights to citizens and for restricting automatic citizenship to those born in the country before annexation was bolstered by reference to the common practice in European countries of excluding guest workers and their children from citizenship in the country in which they work or were even born. Thus, Turkish workers, born in Germany, have no voting rights in the German nation-state, except for representation in local councils.

At this point perhaps we should pause to consider some analytical distinctions between different types of migration. In the case of migrants who come to a foreign country as citizens of another country (or of no country) as tourists, refugees, asylum seekers, or immigrants, it seems to us nonproblematic that the state has the legal right to grant or not to grant them citizenship (normally on the condition of giving up any other citizenship). The same would be true for the children of foreigners born in the country, although there may be reason to facilitate their acquisition of citizenship. Some "immigration countries" like the United States of America have the tradition of automatic citizenship for anyone who is born in the country.

Analytically, migrants who come to a part of their own political unit and where there is "free" circulation of persons within the larger unit would seem to us to belong in a different category than traditional foreign migrants. Normatively, we believe that there is a case to be made for considering that "within-state" migration should be in a special category. The presumption should be that within-state migrants have the right to citizenship unless they prefer another or refuse to apply for it when the subunit becomes independent. Otherwise they would be deprived of a previous status. They did not come to the newly independent country knowing they were foreigners.

Puerto Ricans migrating to New York from the island of Puerto Rico are U.S. citizens, although they are possibly culturally distinctive. They are not resident-aliens. They do not have to apply for an immigration permit. Should Puerto Rico become independent, such Puerto Ricans would continue being, as they had been, U.S. citizens. The United States might, however, ask them to choose Puerto Rican or United States citizenship. The newly independent Puerto Rico might do the same, assuming that neither the United States nor Puerto Rico would allow

27. This is being analyzed and documented in the forthcoming Ph.D. dissertation, by Vello Pettai, Columbia University, Political Science Department.

dual citizenship. However, because they had been U.S. citizens (although Puerto Ricans and possibly even ignorant of English), to deny them United States citizenship would be to deprive them of an acquired right. *Mutatis mutandis,* it would be the same for non–Puerto Rican-American residents in Puerto Rico. To deny them citizenship in the newly independent Puerto Rico—where, until independence, they had been voting citizens—would also be to deny them an acquired right.

The exclusionary definition of citizenship insisted upon by the nationalists in Estonia and Latvia was given support by the silence of the European Community (EC) on this point. An EC official monitoring the September 1992 elections told reporters that the EC would not publicly comment on Estonia's citizenship and language laws.

The argument based on the nation-state in Estonia and Latvia was very powerful because it drew upon the grievances and injustices of the past. The argument addressed cultural and linguistic yearnings that were fully understandable in the light of history. It also had its own logic, as well as legal and political precedents on which to draw.

To argue for a broader definition of political participation, rights, and citizenship is virtually impossible within the logic of a nonassimilationist nation-state. One constantly risks being "trapped in the discourse." To escape one must introduce the value and logic of democracy and the viability and peace of the polity as well. One has, in short, to enrich the terms of the discourse by introducing other important values. Probably one should also, as this chapter is doing, deliberately problematize the tension between the two logics so that national and international actors would make a greater effort to reconcile the goal of national self-affirmation and the goal of democracy and to become more alert to the dangers that could emerge if they fail to do so.

The importance of doing so is all the greater because the logic of the nation-state produces a political language and a set of descriptive terms whose discursive effect is to *create* polar identities and to *work against* the multiple complementary identities that make possible democratic life in a de facto multinational state. For example, the term *colonist* is widely used to describe the Russian component of the population in Estonia and Latvia. The implication of the term is that Russians are an illegitimate presence. But the word *colonist* is descriptively misleading because it excludes far more people from the nation-state than is warranted even by the restrictive law on citizenship. For example, somewhere between 100,000 and 150,000 Russians were resident in Estonia before 1940 and, therefore, they and their descendants are legally Estonian citizens. Yet so powerful and so exclusionary is the language of colonization that many of these legal citizens are beginning to feel that there is no political space for their participation in the nation-state.

Another potentially divisive term is *transient.* Since as many as seven million Russians did indeed come in and out of Estonia, a country of a million and a half, between 1944 and independence in 1991, one can understand the appeal of the term *transient*. These Soviet citizens were mainly military people or construction workers brought in for limited periods of time to build factories. Nonetheless, it too is descriptively misleading, since in addition to the 100,000 to 150,000 pre-1940 Russians, 87,000 of the current Russian population in Estonia were born there after 1940 and have lived all their lives there. If not culturally or linguistically Estonian, they are geographically. The language of the "transient," like that of the "colonist," disguises the fact that many of them consider the Baltic republics their home.

Estonians and Latvians also fear that disloyal Russian immigrants will form a permanent fifth column in their midst. Yet many urban immigrants came as manual workers, who, as numerous studies show, tend to be more concerned about their children's future in society than about joining disloyal political organizations. To be sure, many of the Russian immigrants received material and psychological benefits from being associated with the Soviet empire's power, and many worked in large factories run directly by state ministries in Moscow. However, as power relations between the Baltic states and Russia change and if Estonian and Latvian statehood is secure (and offers a secure home to Russians), Russians may seek out the individual good of a job, instead of the collective good of being a member of a competing nation-state. David D. Laitin hypothesizes, for example, that Russians in Estonia are likely to succumb increasingly to a competitive assimilation logic, in which each family will seek to get ahead by learning Estonian and adapting to the local culture. In a prisoners' dilemma-type game between families, Laitin predicts that each will have a dominant strategy of "defecting" and assimilating.[28]

A last but very powerful part of the nation-state discourse in Estonia concerns the dichotomy drawn between *survival* and *extinction*. Again, this is not an illegitimate concern. There are little more than a million Estonian speakers in the world, and a number of closely related Finno-Ugric languages have disappeared. But since the 1970s all the evidence shows that Estonians are holding their own demographically against non-Estonians.[29] In an independent Estonia, there is little probability that Estonians will become a minority within an independent state, much less become extinct as a people or a culture. But the invocation of the phrase "linguistic extinction" makes it easier to socially construct a politics of Russian exclusion instead of a politics of inclusion.[30]

28. See David D. Laitin, "Language Normalization in Estonia and Catalonia," *Journal of Baltic Studies* 23, no. 2 (1992): 149–66. Instead of Laitin's term *defecting*, we prefer to use the phrase "develop multiple and complementary identities." But for both Laitin and ourselves, the situational logic of building a repertoire of survival skills is essentially the same. For a broader discussion of state rationalization and minorities in the Soviet context, see David D. Laitin, "The National Uprisings in the Soviet Union," *World Politics* 44 (Oct. 1991): 139–77.

29. For example, see Rein Taagepera, "Baltic Population Changes 1950–1980," *Journal of Baltic Studies* 12, no. 1 (1981), 49.

30. If citizenship were granted to those russophones in polls who say they "definitely" would prefer Estonian citizenship, the ethnic Estonians would still have a strong majority of total citizens, but the percentage of noncitizens in the country would be reduced substantially.

Table 20.6. Attitudes toward the System of Government Previously, Now, and in Five Years: Estonians, Latvians, and Non-Balts in 1993

	% of Respondents			
Attitude	Latvians in Latvia	Non-Balts in Latvia	Estonians in Estonia	Non-Balts in Estonia
System of government before independence				
Positive	36	66	32	65
Neutral	14	12	13	14
Negative	50	22	55	21
Present system of government				
Positive	43	43	58	50
Neutral	19	18	15	14
Negative	38	39	26	37
System of government we will have in five years				
Positive	81	71	88	79
Neutral	8	13	6	10
Negative	11	16	5	11

Source: Richard Rose and William Maley, "Nationalities in the Baltic States," Studies in the Public Policy, no. 222 (1994), questions 122–24.

RESPONSES TO "REAL" DEMOCRACY

Despite the shift from an inclusionary to an exclusionary approach to citizenship by the parliaments and governments of newly independent Estonia and Latvia, a reasonably high percentage of russophones (43 percent in Estonia and 50 percent in Latvia) eighteen months after independence felt positive about the "present system of government." An even higher percentage of russophones (79 percent in Estonia and 71 percent in Latvia) held a positive opinion of the political system in five years time. Particularly strong support for our hypothesis that non-Balts are able to be politically integrated comes from the rather astounding finding that, in Latvia, ethnic Latvians and non-Balts alike, while having sharply different assessments of the past, have virtually identical assessments of the present system of government (table 20.6).

In our discussion of Spain, we argued that political attitudes toward the present and especially about the future are more significant than a positive or negative opinion about the nondemocratic past. We believe that table 20.6 underscores this general argument. The non-Baltic population does indeed view the nondemocratic past much more favorably than do the ethnic Estonians and the ethnic Latvians. However, for the possibility of building a democracy, non-Baltic attitudes toward the present and especially the future give grounds for optimism about the possibility of a multinational democracy.[31]

31. Raivo Velik, the head of the Political Science Department at the University of Tartu in Estonia, has been conducting ethnic identity development studies that also give grounds for optimism about the possibility of russophones developing multiple and complementary identities. Using the method developed by

What underlies the generally positive attitude of Balts and non-Balts alike? A key finding is that *all* Baltic residents believe that there has been, on balance, an overall improvement in their political liberties (table 20.7).

However, table 20.7 does call our attention to some warning signs. Russophones in Estonia and Latvia see no improvement in their freedom to live and travel anywhere they want. As we shall see, this relates to their anxieties concerning their rights to live not only as full citizens, but even as resident aliens, in Estonia and Latvia. This insecurity is no doubt based on the reality that harsh laws concerning the status of resident aliens were frequently discussed in both Latvian and Estonian parliaments after independence. Indeed, in June 1993, by a vote of 59 to 3, a Law on Aliens was passed by the Estonian parliament that created such anxiety as to the legal right of noncitizens to remain in Estonia that all twelve governments of the European Community criticized the law. In the face of this diplomatic criticism, President Meri vetoed the law. But the law left a legacy of heightened russophone insecurity. Indeed, a key parliamentary supporter of the law, Kaljo Põldvere, was clear that this was the intention of those who drafted the law. In the parliamentary debate Põldvere said "by means of the present law we have to create a situation where the colonists feel the earth shaking under their feet."[32] More alarming, table 20.7 indicates that, by a margin of 2 to 1 in Estonia and about 4 to 1 in Latvia, Russians believe that the present system of government is worse, rather than better, in protecting the rights of Russians.[33]

Significantly, for our argument that a common political roof can improve minorities' perception of state policies and institutions, in inclusionary Lithuania only 24 percent of the Russians said that the situation regarding protection of rights was worse than in the old regime. In contrast, in exclusionary Latvia, 51 per-

---

Peter Weinreich for "identity structure analysis," he did a pilot study of 266 randomly selected Russian respondents in three Estonian cities. In the pilot study, 72 percent of Russians in April 1993 answered affirmatively to the statement that "at this moment Russians living in Estonia identify themselves with Estonia." Of relevance for our argument that Russians in the diaspora are developing a separate cultural and political identity from that of Russians in Russia is the fact that only 18 percent of the Russians polled in Estonia said they identified more with Russia than with Estonia. However, they estimated that 54 percent of the Russians in Russia would believe that Russians in Estonia identified more with Russia than Estonia. Velik concluded his study with the judgment that "new elements of multiple identities are developing within the Russian community in Estonia while its members are adapting themselves socially to the new sociopolitical environment of their country." See Raivo Velik, "Identity Development and Political Adjustment in Estonia: Research Note," *World Affairs* 157, no. 3 (1995): 148. Also see his "A Strategy for Ethnic Conflict Accommodation" (paper prepared for the XVth World Conference of the International Political Science Association, August 20–25, 1994, Berlin).

    32. For the quote and a description of the debate about the Law on Aliens, see Kask, "National Radicalization in Estonia," 385–88, quote on 386.

    33. In Estonia another worrying indicator is that the Russian minority do not feel that they have a neutral protective state roof over their head. In Estonia 32.8 percent of the minority population answered "not at all" when asked if they had confidence in the police. Only 14.7 percent of ethnic Estonians expressed a similar fear. In Lithuania, in contrast, both non-Lithuanians and ethnic Lithuanians expressed more confidence in the police, and their attitudes were roughly congruent. The data are from question 136 in the 1992 survey conducted by Hans-Dieter Klingemann, cited in table 20.2.

Table 20.7. "Would You Say That Our Current System is Better, Much the Same, or Worse than the Old Soviet System in Allowing People to:"

Answer	Est	Lat	Lit	Avg	EsR	LaR	LiR	Avg
"Say whatever they think"								
Better	95	81	87	**87**	75	71	70	**72**
Much the same	3	12	8	**8**	17	15	18	**17**
Worse	—	2	2	**2**	4	5	2	**4**
Don't know	2	5	3	**3**	4	8	9	**7**
"Travel and choose to live where one wants in the country"								
Better	83	38	64	**62**	35	30	50	**39**
Much the same	8	34	20	**21**	20	23	25	**23**
Worse	6	16	6	**9**	35	32	16	**28**
Don't know	3	12	9	**8**	9	15	9	**11**
"Go abroad or live abroad if one wishes"								
Better	93	83	90	**89**	78	76	83	**79**
Much the same	2	4	3	**3**	8	6	6	**7**
Worse	3	4	1	**3**	7	6	4	**6**
Don't know	2	9	5	**5**	7	12	8	**9**
"Join any organization they want"								
Better	86	72	86	**81**	73	67	72	**71**
Much the same	8	12	7	**9**	10	12	11	**11**
Worse	1	4	1	**2**	5	4	3	**4**
Don't know	6	12	6	**8**	13	17	14	**15**
"Decide whether or not to take part in activities of political parties"								
Better	84	70	83	**79**	59	59	69	**62**
Much the same	9	12	7	**10**	15	13	11	**13**
Worse	1	3	1	**2**	9	5	2	**5**
Don't know	5	14	9	**9**	17	23	18	**19**
"Live without fear of unlawful arrest"								
Better	64	41	57	**54**	39	29	44	**37**
Much the same	14	28	23	**22**	31	31	25	**29**
Worse	11	7	4	**8**	12	9	6	**9**
Don't know	10	23	16	**16**	18	30	25	**24**
"Decide whether or not to believe in God"								
Better	81	76	89	**82**	74	76	80	**76**
Much the same	14	17	7	**13**	19	16	15	**17**
Worse	1	—	1	**1**	1	—	1	**1**
Don't know	3	6	3	**4**	6	8	4	**6**
"Protecting rights of Lithuanians/Latvians/Estonians"								
Better	86	80	84	**84**	79	75	70	**74**
Much the same	8	11	9	**10**	10	8	17	**12**
Worse	1	1	1	**1**	1	1	—	**1**
Don't know	4	7	5	**5**	9	16	13	**13**
"Protecting rights of Russians in this country"								
Better	29	18	43	**30**	24	13	29	**22**
Much the same	29	30	26	**28**	16	17	32	**21**
Worse	21	23	16	**20**	48	51	24	**41**
Don't know	21	28	15	**21**	12	20	15	**16**

Source: Same as for table 20.5, questions 129–137. EsR, Estonian Russians; LaR, Latvian Russians; LiR, Lithuanian Russians.

Table 20.8. "Which of These Statements Best Fits Your Views of Who Should Have the Right to Vote in Elections to Parliament?" Differential Responses of Baltic Nationalities

	% of Respondents					
Answer	Est	EsR	Lat	LaR	Lit	LiR
Pre-1940 citizens and their familes	44	3	49	6	12	2
Everyone born here	31	22	25	24	38	18
Residents of more than ten years	23	37	15	30	25	22
Everyone here at independence	2	19	2	15	11	16
Any former Soviet citizen now living here	1	16	1	12	10	35
Don't know	0	2	7	13	4	6

Souce: Same as for table 20.5, question 120.

cent said the situation was worse. An interesting (and potentially positive finding) is that, in Latvia, ethnic Latvians also believe that the present system is worse vis-à-vis Russian rights than in the previous Soviet system.

The issue that most divides ethnic Balts and the Russian minority in Estonia and Latvia concerns the right to vote in parliamentary elections. Only 3 percent of ethnic Russians in Estonia and 6 percent of ethnic Russians in Latvia believe that the right to vote in such elections should be restricted to pre-1940 citizens and their families. But 44 percent of ethnic Estonians and 49 percent of ethnic Latvians believe in this exclusionary criterion. In inclusionary Lithuania, as we would expect, only 12 percent of the ethnic Lithuanians support the pre-1940 citizenship criterion (table 20.8).

Table 20.8 does contain some positive findings about willingness of the people in the street (as opposed to their political leaders) to accept more inclusionary parliamentary voting rights than current laws allow. For example, if we combine positive answers concerning parliamentary voting rights of "everyone born here," "residents of ten years," and "everyone here at independence," 56 percent of the ethnic Estonians and 42 percent of the ethnic Latvians favored a voting policy that was more inclusionary than the then prevailing statutes.

In September–October 1993, those who responded to a Russian language questionnaire rather than to one in the Baltic language were divided and uncertain about their citizenship. In Estonia, 17 percent defined themselves as Estonian, fully 41 percent as Soviet (a state that had not existed for about two years), only 8 percent as Russian, 4 percent as from another Soviet republic, 6 percent other, and 23 percent as "uncertain, I do not have a passport." In Latvia, 35 percent said Latvian, 20 percent Soviet, 4 percent Russian, 4 percent other Soviet republics, 22 percent other, and 15 percent uncertain. This contrasts with inclusionary Lithuania, where 96 percent said Lithuanian, 2 percent Russian, and 2 percent other. In Lithuania 99 percent of the ethnic Poles said they were "Lithuanian."[34] These data reflected the uncertainty about citizenship of the non-Estonians and non-Latvians resulting from the policies of the newly independent state.

The political consequences of the Estonian citizenship laws (under which the 1992 parliamentary elections and the June 1992 Constitutional Referendum were held) can be illustrated by the fact that, in a population of 1.1 million inhabitants of voting age, the enrolled electorate was only 660,000. In the referendum in a city like Narva on the Russian border, of the 77,000 inhabitants only 6,000 were eligible to vote.

We have centered our discussion of the problem on citizenship, the right to vote in parliamentary elections, and the "inclusiveness" of the demos. This question is different from that of linguistic and cultural assimilation, the level of bilingualism, the rights of the minority to use their language in different arenas, the policy on language in schools and the public support for bilingual education, and the related question of the timing of assimilation. Paradoxically, nation-building of a fully assimilationist inclusionary variant presupposes citizenship, which in a democracy should not exclude the right to vote for parliament.

Liberal values should lead to a more or less generous and nondiscriminatory policy on many of these problems, especially the recognition of some minority rights, a recognition that does not exclude some requirements aimed at a shared culture and language. Not to do so would alienate either the minority or the majority. But these questions are different from the requirement of democratic inclusiveness. We cannot develop here our thinking on the requirements to create a multicultural, partly bilingual society that would allow the minority to assimilate or retain its identity while demanding a minimum of cultural integration. However, we feel that there are solutions which, while not satisfying anyone completely, would be considered by the majority of both ethnic groups as acceptable and even fair and which could contribute to building loyalty to the state and to crafting a stable liberal democratic policy.[35]

Many of the Russians and other immigrants from the USSR are not likely to attain citizenship. In fact, by now, many of those who feel rejected might not even wish it, and those obtaining it are not being considered a minority—with some cultural rights—but as second-class citizens. They, however, in view of the different standards of living in Russia and the Baltics, expectations about the future in

---

34. Rose and Maley, "Nationalities in the Baltic States," question 229. The high number of Russophones who said they were Soviets probably reflects the fact that they did not want to choose to be Russian and that they were not allowed to choose to be Estonian or Latvian. Soviet "citizenship" is thus the only citizenship they have ever held.

35. People in a multilingual-multinational context are often quite willing to make distinctions between situations in which a national language should be required and those where the minority might use its language. The same is true about language and cultural policy in the schools. Ordinary voters and citizens are often more flexible and tolerant on these issues than are ideologues, activists, and governments. For the case of Spanish bilingual regions, see Linz, "Los jóvenes en una España multilingüe," 325–436.

Russia, the lack of family ties, and the lack of any prospects upon returning, are eager to stay. The "exit" option, as we have seen, is considered by only a very few. Significantly, almost half of those who considered the exit option gave as their reason that "my political and human rights are restricted." Also significantly, almost no one (only 2.9 percent of the non-Estonians and 1.5 percent of the non-Latvians) gave as a reason for possible emmigration the statement that "I could not adapt in" Estonia or Latvia.[36]

The Russian minorities in the Baltics are not like the English in India, the French in Algeria, or the Finns of Karelia when it was annexed by the USSR, ready to return to a homeland ready to receive them and help them. Most of them will stay as resident aliens (of a potentially powerful hostile neighbor) in countries where they once believed they were citizens. Or they will stay as citizens of a state engaged in nation-building, demanding assimilation but not particularly eager to help in the assimilation, that is, as second-class citizens.

This is a historical legacy that has no parallel in southern Europe, South America, or even in East Central Europe. It is a legacy that is particular to the former Soviet Union and the former Yugoslavia. There is thus a great burden of history to overcome in the construction of new democracies in Estonia and Latvia. But this legacy has been further exacerbated by some of the decisions made after independence. Unfortunately, the competing logics of nation-state and democracy cannot be forgotten when one thinks about the prospects for democratic consolidation in Estonia or Latvia. Fortunately, it is almost a nonissue in Lithuania. The process of nation-building has also complicated the equally or more necessary process of state-building—the creation of armed forces and a unified police (rather than different organizations, some of them linked to nationalist parties).

The Future: Multinational Democracies or Irredenta

The Baltic republics, like other multiethnic states with a population that can be considered an "irredenta" by a neighbor, particularly a powerful one like Russia, are fearful about a future menace. There is no clear answer to whether a potentially irredentist population will be more loyal to a homeland state that expresses support for their frustrated minority demands or to a state that has granted protection to the cultural and political rights of all the inhabitants in its territory. Can it be argued that citizenship and minority rights encourage disloyalty to the state? Maybe. But our data on Lithuania suggest that the granting of citizenship in Lithuania is associated with a more positive attitude on the part of minorities toward state institutitions.

Denial of rights to a minority is easiest and potentially most effective when that minority has no external homeland sponsor. In many East Central European

36. Question 139 of the 1992 Klingemann survey cited in table 20.2.

countries, this is the situation concerning the gypsies.[37] After the defeat of Germany in World War II, the occupation of Germany by the Allies meant that Czechoslovakia and Poland were able to solve their German problem by expelling almost all of their German minority population. However, Russia's size and current geopolitical situation mean that the forcible expulsion of the Russian residents in the Baltics is simply not an available geopolitical option.

Turning now to the future, we can begin to see that already the logic of the nation-state is producing a politics that is threatening the territorial integrity of the state and perhaps even the democracy of Estonia. If Estonia is too hard on the Russian component of their population, Yeltsin or his potentially more nationalist successors may well feel pressure to come to its defense. In September 1992, the Russian Foreign Minister, Andrei Kozyrev, in an address to the United Nations, indeed attacked Estonia for human rights violations of Russians and raised the question of placing Estonian statehood in receivership via a United Nations trusteeship.[38] By 1995 he explicitly singled out Estonia and Latvia as countries where the use of Russian force to defend the rights of Russian minorities would be justified.[39]

We focus here on the psychological and political effects of the new laws in Estonia, which are much more harmful than the letter of the laws would suggest. Noncitizens were excluded from voting in the presidential and parliamentary elections of September 20, 1992, and from forming political parties. These two provisions meant that the great majority of Russian residents in the territory of Estonia did not have a say in the first election of the newly independent state, did not participate in the creation of the political party system, and did not hold political office on the national level in the parliament of 1992–94. The exclusion of about 40 percent of the population shifted the electoral discourse in this period even further in the direction of nation-state issues. In the 1992 elections, three parties that had advocated strong nation-state positions on citizenship and language won 46 of the 101 seats and were a major force in the first parliament. Since there were no Russian votes to appeal to, even the moderate parties, like the Social Democrats, tilted their discourses in a more nationalist direction. The more consociational Popular Front, which could not get any Russian support, won only sixteen seats. In the 1990–92 parliament, there were twenty-three ethnic Russian deputies. In the 1992–94 parliament, there were none.[40]

Again, none of this was driven by unstoppable primordial nationalism. In fact,

---

37. See Claus Offe, "Ethnische Politik im osteuropäischen Transformationsprozess," in *Der Tunnel am Ende des Lichts, Erkundungen der politischen Transformation im Neuen Osten* (Frankfurt/Main: Campus, 1994), 135–186. See typology on p. 145.

38. *New York Times,* September 23, 1992, 9.

39. See "Meri Dismayed at Kozyrev's Remarks, Latvia Likewise," *Baltic Independent* (April 28–May 4, 1995): 6.

40. See Vello Pettai, "Emerging Ethnic Democracy in Estonia and Latvia" (paper presented at the 14th Association for the Advancement of Baltic Studies Conference, June 8–11, 1994, Chicago).

there was a bitter struggle in the first part of 1992 over whether to allow Russians who had lived in Estonia for twenty years or more to be eligible to vote or at the very least to allow those 5,017 inhabitants who had formally applied for Estonian citizenship to do so. In the latter case, the matter was purely symbolic because this 1 percent of the Russian population was so small and because they were the most pro-independence of the overall Russian population. Nonetheless, it was decided to have a referendum on the issue, during which most of the organized political parties campaigned against allowing the 5,017 Russians to vote; just as important, the president, prime minister, and speaker of Parliament were *silent* on the issue. The referendum was very close: 52 percent of the electorate opposed granting this tiny number of pro-Estonian Russians the vote, and 48 percent supported their right. The point is that political leadership might have made a difference; instead, none of the key figures in the political process helped legitimate the idea of a state made up of multiple complementary identities. The matter was made all the more explosive by allowing, at the last moment, children and grandchildren of pre-1940 citizens to vote in the referendum and the elections, even if they had lived their entire lives abroad.[41]

The language law is also threatening to the idea of a democratic state in which not all its members are alike linguistically or ethnically. Here the impression is much worse than the law because, though Estonian will be required for many jobs in the future, there are many where it will not be (such as in the factories in the predominantly Russian-speaking northeast towns of Narva, Kohtla-Järve, and Sillamäe). But little effort has been made to disseminate this critical information, nor is it clear whether the Estonian state can provide a sufficient number of teachers able and willing to teach Estonian in Russian-language areas. David D. Laitin argues that the high enrollment of Russians in Estonian classes in 1990–91 suggested a greater willingness on the part of the Russians to assimilate than on the part of the Estonians to have them assimilate.[42] Again, all of this is understandable, given the resentment against Russians, who for decades refused to learn even the rudiments of Estonian. Nonetheless, from the point of view of democratic politics, the logic of the nation-state is often quite different from the logic of a democratic state and, in the case of language, the Estonian government has obligations and duties that need to be kept in view.[43]

During 1991–93 in Estonia, the logic, language, and politics of nation-state-building, based on a narrow definition of citizenship, led to a shrinkage of the po-

---

41. These are based on extensive interviews in Estonia by Alfred Stepan in July 1992. Also see Kask, "National Radicalization in Estonia," *Nationalities Papers*, 383–84.

42. Laitin, "National Uprisings in the Soviet Union," 163.

43. While it is true that most Russians in Estonia did not learn Estonian, the key question is whether they or, more likely, their children would be willing to learn Estonian in an independent Estonia. Here the survey data point to a much more positive attitude. Only 37 percent of Russian speakers in Estonia say they are opposed to people like them being made to learn a Baltic language. See Rose and Maley, "Nationalities in the Baltic States," question 206.

litical and social spaces where Estonians and non-Estonians interacted and competed democratically. To date, however, the Russian-speaking minority in the Baltics has opted for passivity, which explains the absence of ethnic violence. In the 1993 survey the non-Estonians and non-Latvians are less likely to participate in a "protest demonstration in the streets about problems facing the government" than are the Balts. A surprisingly high 50 or 51 percent of Russians say that they would "definitely not" engage in a political protest demonstration, compared to 38 and 39 percent among Estonians and Latvians. Even on the question of citizenship and the right to vote, only 38 percent of the Russians in Estonia and 27 percent of the Russians in Latvia said they would possibly consider demonstrating in the streets to advance their rights.[44]

But the events of 1991–94 meant that obstacles to democracy not previously present were, inadvertently or even deliberately, created by politicians caught up in the discourse of nation-state politics and inattentive to the consensual or consociational style of politics. They were inattentive, in short, to a style of politics helpful to the crafting of a consolidated democracy in a multinational state.[45]

We have discussed the cases of Estonia and Latvia in the broader context of the disintegration of the USSR into fifteen new states, but in spite of some basically similar problems in the linkage among the state, multiple nationalities within the state, and democracy, there are significant differences between the Baltic and the CIS states. These differences should not be ignored. In the Baltic countries we are dealing with states that enjoyed independence for a considerable time after 1918. In the other republics of the former Soviet Union, we are dealing with political entities that derived their existence and their boundaries from the Soviet state, although a number of them briefly enjoyed statehood after the disintegration of Czarist rule. The fact that the CIS countries had been part of the empire for a longer time means that the Russian and sometimes other Slavic minorities have been living there as citizen-subjects for many generations. In some of the CIS countries, unlike the Baltics, the Russians are the modernizing group.[46] In contrast, the Balts, due to the large German presence before 1918 and their Lutheran or Catholic culture, were more modernizing or at least more Western than the Russians.

---

44. Rose and Maley, "Nationalities in the Baltic States," 45.

45. For the argument against majoritarian democracy and for more consensual, at times even consociational, practices, see Lijphart, *Democracies.*

46. Indeed, three conditions make potential integration, especially democratic and peaceful integration, between Balts and Russians somewhat easier than the potential democratic integration in the southern CIS states between Moslems and Russians. The first condition is geopolitical. Given the geographic and political proximity of the Baltic countries to the European Union, the Baltics will no doubt be more responsive to European Union criticism concerning violation of citizenship norms than the CIS countries will probably be (and are). The second condition is military. Russia will be more constrained against using its military forces in the Baltics than they would be in the Eurasian near-abroad. The third condition is sociological or cultural. It is probable that there are greater differences between Eurasian Moslems and Russians than between Balts and Russians.

In those political subunits of federal states in which the dominant nationality is different from the dominant nationality of the federal state, the situation is again different. Such is the case of the Russian minorities in Chechnya. Russians in Chechnya are not a diaspora in another state. They are a minority in a federal state. Russia is not their external homeland. The Chechnya tragedy is thus seen by most of the world as an internal rather than an international conflict. In this respect, the Russians in Chechnya are not the same as the Russians in Estonia. An intervention by the Russian state to defend Russians in Estonia would be completely different at the level of international law.[47] Thus, the Russian minorities in the Baltics, in the Eurasian near-abroad, and inside national subunits of the new Russian federation are, analytically and geopolitically, in three quite different and distinct situations.

NATION-BUILDING, STATE-BUILDING, AND DEMOCRACY BUILDING: A TYPOLOGICAL EXCURSUS

Baltic politics allow us to deal somewhat more systematically with the relationship between state-building and nation-building vis-à-vis minorities. There are four basic possibilities with considerable variation within each of them. The typology is based on two dimensions. The first dimension concerns state-building strategies. State policies toward citizenship rights of the minority or minorities can be inclusionary or exclusionary. The second dimension concerns nation-building strategies. National leaders can have an ideology that the demos and the nation should be the same, or ideologically they can accept different minorities and even nations within the demos. The combination of these two dimensions leads to four different types (table 20.9).

Let us first analyze each type as a pure type, although of course empirically in any concrete case there can be considerable within-type variation or even combinations of more than one type. In type I, the elites' ideological identification of demos with nation, combined with their exclusionary strategy toward the citizenship of those defined as alien to the nation, leads to a political system in which the preferred option might be the expulsion of the aliens. At the very least, type I strategies would lead to the encouragement of the exit option of noncitizens via emigration to their presumed homeland as the result of discriminatory policies or, exceptionally, by special payments.

In type II, the elites' acceptance of a differentiation between the demos and the nation and their exclusionary strategy toward citizenship leads to a policy that gives residents who are not part of the nation civil rights as resident aliens, but *not* political rights.

47. David D. Laitin, on the basis of survey data, makes an interesting sociological comparison between the "Russian-speaking nationality" in Estonia and in Bashkortostan but, surprisingly, does not make the distinction we make between a minority in an independent state and a minority in a subunit of a federal state. See Laitin, "Identity in Formation."

Table 20.9. A Typology of State-, Nation-, and Democracy-building Strategies in Multinational Polities

Nation-building Strategies: Ideology toward Demos/Nation Relationship	State-building Strategies: Policies toward Non-national Minority or Minorities	
	Exclusionary Strategy	Inclusionary Strategy
Demos and nation should be the same.	Type I Expel or at least systematically encourage the "exit" option	Type III Make major effort to assimilate minorities into national culture and give no special recognition to minority political or cultural rights
Demos and nation can be different.	Type II Isolate from political process by granting civil liberties but no political rights and thus discouraging "voice" option	Type IV Make major effort to accomodate minorities by crafting a series of political and civil arrangements that recognize minority rights

In type III, an inclusionary strategy toward citizenship combined with an identification in principle between demos and nation will allow the minority or minorities to participate politically *only* if they assimilate into the dominant culture. In type III there is no positive value attached to diversity within the demos or within the polity. Rather, there is a plethora of state-designed assimilation policies. This state-induced assimilation strategy might involve considerable discrimination against and a de facto second-class citizenship for those unable or unwilling to assimilate to the dominant nationality. The result will be a plural but not a pluralistic society.

Finally, in type IV there is an inclusionary strategy concerning citizenship both for the dominant majority and the minority or minorities. Individually, all permanent members of the demos are accepted as full members of the polity with full political rights. Only foreign citizens who have come into the country knowing that they were not citizens are excluded. In addition, the political system grants varying degrees of recognition of group rights to the minority. Of course, to qualify as a liberal democracy, these group rights must never violate any individual rights, whether these individuals are members of the minority or not. These group rights include the political freedom to organize parties representing the minority or possibly bilingualism in education and some public services. That is, type IV shows acceptance of a pluralistic society in which diversity is not considered fully negative.

The range of solutions falling under this fourth type is very great, going from allowing private organization of minority cultural and educational life to various consociational policies. Consociational policies could range from publicly supported communal organizations and public services to official bilingualism at the local or state level. In some cases, federalism might be a solution to the problem of recognizing the fact of the multinational society.

A pure type I strategy is not likely to be "successful" unless the state turns to coercive policies. But, in some cases, coercion might lead to civil war and in others to conflict with the external homeland of the minority. Only under very exceptional circumstances will a type I strategy be compatible with the requirements of a liberal democracy.

A pure type II strategy, if accepted passively by the minority, could possibly create an "ethnic democracy"; that is, a political system in which there are fully democratic political processes for the national majority but only a subject status for the minority. Such an ethnic democracy, of course, would not satisfy the criterion of democratic inclusiveness formulated by Robert A. Dahl in his *Polyarchy*.[48]

Types III and IV represent very different conceptions of democracy. Under certain circumstances assimilation in type III might, in the medium or long run, lead to the building of a democratic nation-state. However, the success of such a policy does not depend only on the aims of the nation-state builders. Success also depends on the readiness of members of the minority to give up their identity, their language, and their culture and to accept the utility of the dominant nationality. Success will also depend upon whether or not there exists a powerful homeland state. If a powerful homeland state exists, this will greatly complicate type III. If type III state-induced assimilation fails, type I could be attempted, but the risks to democracy and possibly even state integrity would rise significantly, especially if a powerful homeland state exists and protests.

For a type III policy to be considered a democracy, even one most committed to pursuing a policy of nation-building cultural assimilation of minorities, it must satisfy certain requirements applicable to cultural minorities: freedoms of expression, assembly, and organization; the formation of parties; presentation of candidates for office, and competition for a share of power by peaceful means. That is, there must be political rights in addition to the normal human rights.

This has two important consequences. First is that the aspirations and grievances of the minority (or minorities) can be expressed or made public. The chance to get representation can, but does not always, attain some specific gains for the individual members of the minorities and its organizations. The fact that (by definition) a linguistic or ethnic minority (unlike an ideologically based minority in the democratic process) cannot for structural reasons ever hope to become a majority makes it less likely in a majoritarian democracy that the minority will make significant gains. Therefore, minority demands will often be articulated to achieve patterns associated with type IV. Even when such consensus or consociational patterns are unattainable, the fact of having political representation may provide an opportunity for the minority to gain a share in power. At the state level minorities can best gain access to power sharing if the national majority is fractioned and needs, either at the time of elections or in the process

48. See Dahl, *Polyarchy: Participation and Opposition*, 5–10.

of forming a government, explicit or implicit coalitions with minorities and/or the support of the minority and/or its representatives. In some cases a minority can exact a heavy price (like the minority parties of the religious Jews in Israel).

The second important consequence of the participation in the democratic process of minorities in type III is that it can lead to highly conflictual patterns. The commitment of the majority to a relentless process of assimilation can lead to the frustration of the minority, to its radicalization, the split between moderates and radicals, and the turn to disloyal behavior by some of its members. Violence by activists is not unlikely and its repression is often difficult and may lead to a spiraling of violence that can be highly destabilizing for democracy and domestic peace. A spiraling of violence can also lead to appeals for foreign intervention, including that of an external homeland. When the intensity of the demands of the minority is great and the unwillingness of the majority to make any accommodation is also great, type III becomes unstable and unviable; if democracy is not to be destroyed, some moves toward type IV are likely to be desirable and even inevitable.

It therefore is evident that a type III inclusionary democratic state has consequences for minority citizens and the polity. The consequences can be positive, facilitating a stable type III polity or some movement toward type IV. But if mismanaged, the consequences can lead to a crisis of democracy and the state.

A democratic polity of type III or of type III ready to move to type IV can isolate the extremists in any ethnic, cultural, or religious national minority but cannot prevent its existence and antidemocratic actions (e.g., the ETA terrorists in Spain). In such a situation democratic leaders can generally count on the support of the peaceful democratic majority of the minority population, thus limiting the influence of the extremists on the polity.[49] Minority and nationalist demands do not need to end in the destruction of democracy, large-scale violence, and civil war, but the absence of extremism is not assured by democracy, just as it does not assure the absence of crime. A democratic polity has the advantage that violent actions (whatever their "idealist" motivations) are likely to be defined in the end as criminal by both the majority and the bulk of the minority. The evolution of the political climate in the Spanish Basque country provides an example of such an evolution (however regrettable, dangerous, and perhaps inevitable the actions of ETA terrorists). They can, if handled well, end by being largely irrelevant for the consolidation and stability of democracy.

However, we should be aware of what democracy can and cannot achieve under certain circumstances and the mistakes, even crimes, that democratic gov-

---

49. See, for example, numerous tables that document the evolution of public opinion against violence by nationalist extemist terrorism under a type IV democracy in the Basque country in Francisco José Llera Ramo, *Los vascos y la política. El proceso político vasco: elecciones, partidos, opinión pública y legitimación en el País Vasco, 1977–1992* (Bilbao: Servicio Editorial de la Universidad del País Vasco, 1994), chap. 4, 97–119.

ernments can commit when confronting ethnic, nationalist, or religious insurgence, as we know from contemporary examples, such as India.[50]

Type IV could either be the original option of the leaders of the state or possibly an option pursued after the failure of a type III attempt.[51] A variety of stable solutions can be found in type IV, which in some cases could lead to a democratic multinational state or at least a democratic state recognizing the cultural and linguistic pluralism of its citizens.

THE TYPOLOGY APPLIED: BALTIC OPTIONS

If one accepts the existence of a nationalist Russia as a homeland state actor vis-à-vis most Baltic minorities and the de facto reality in the 1990s of Estonia, Latvia, and Lithuania as multinational countries, how do they relate to our typology? Lithuania is the easiest to discuss. Lithuania has not gone very far in the consociational direction, but its inclusionary strategy toward citizenship for almost all permanent residents at the start of independence puts Lithuania squarely in type IV. Lithuania could well become a consolidated multinational democracy. We recognize, of course, the fact that the solid demographic majority of ethnic Lithuanians made the selection of type IV easier than it would have been in either Estonia or, especially, Latvia.

Most ethnic Latvian political leaders in 1991–95 explicitly rejected the idea of a type IV polity. Many Latvian leaders might hold out type III assimilation as desirable. However, historically, culturally, and geopolitically, assimilation of Latvian minorities that together constitute a *majority* in all of Latvia's largest cities is a virtual impossibility in the short or even the medium term. For the same reasons type I is a dangerous and difficult option. Type II political isolation of minorities is possibly available if conflict with Russia does not ensue, but the result would not be a liberal democracy but an ethnic democracy. However, if the minorities actively resist this exclusionary strategy, conflict and authoritarianism could be the outcome of a failed type II strategy.

Estonia in terms of elite political strategies is much closer to Latvia than to Lithuania. Most ethnic Estonian political elites reject what we call type IV as a desirable model.[52] Given the Estonian political elites' willingness to allow at least a

50. In a separate publication Linz argues that the instances of most persistent violation of human rights, within an overall context of democracy, have occurred in democracies experiencing a combination of stateness conflict and ethnic, religious, and/or linguistic conflict (e.g., Kashmir). See his "Types of Political Regimes and Respect for Human Rights: Historical and Cross National Perspectives," in Asbjørn Eide and Bernt Hagtvet, eds., *Human Rights in Perspective: A Global Assessment* (Cambridge: Blackwell, 1992), 177–221.

51. As we demonstrated in the case of Spain, when confronted with potential stateness conflicts in Catalonia and the Basque country, Suárez and other leaders of the Spanish transition committed themselves very quickly to a type IV polity.

52. We noted, however, in table 20.8 that ordinary Estonian and Latvian citizens were much more open to Russian minority political participation than were political elites. Given the high degree of factionaliza-

modicum of cultural and political rights to minorities, Estonian political elites in 1992–93 represented themselves to the European Union (and possibly to themselves) as on the road to what we would call a type III polity.[53] However, for the foreseeable future, sociologically and politically, a Type II ethnic democracy is a major competing model in Estonia. A type II ethnic democracy would probably encounter somewhat less resistance in Estonia than in Latvia. Ethnic Estonians are a comparatively larger part of the total population in Estonia than ethnic Latvians are in Latvia; Estonia's economy is also perceived by Russian minorities as somewhat stronger than Latvia's.[54] Latvia's minorities also have a historically stronger tradition of participation in politics than do Estonia's. This said, we should not confuse an economically prosperous and possibly politically stable Estonia, with its passive but alienated Russian population, with a liberal democracy. The hope for liberal democracy in Estonia is that a combination of international pressures from the European Union, Estonian prudence toward a dangerous Russia, and ethnic Estonian and nonethnic Estonian demands for a higher quality democracy together might contribute to an increasingly inclusive Estonian political system.[55]

---

tion in the Estonian party system, even a small russophone party could acquire some weight in a parliament in the government formation period and thus alter the discongruence between Estonia and elite/mass opinions for the better.

53. In the cultural but not in the political area, there was even some accommodation of certain type IV collective Russian demands. A law on cultural autonomy allowed some role for minorities in setting up local councils and educational institutions. The president of Estonia also established "Roundtables of Ethnic Minorities" under his auspices. However, the closing down of Russian television in the spring of 1994 and the 1993 Education Law that prohibited state support for education in the Russian language above the high school level were heavy state-imposed type III policies. See the previously cited paper by Velik, "A Strategy for Ethnic Conflict Accommodation."

54. For example, 64 percent of Russian speakers polled in Estonia agreed with the statement that "this country offers better chances for improving living standards in the future than Russia." Only 44 percent of Russian speakers in Latvia agreed with this statement. See Rose and Maley, "Nationalities in the Baltic States," question 209. However, passivity is not approval. In fact, whereas only 17 percent of the russophones in Lithuania disagreed with the statement, "Would you say that the government treats Russians who live in their country fairly?" 54 percent disagreed in Latvia and 61 percent of the russophones in Estonia disagreed. Ibid., question 159.

55. In 1995 the Estonian political system was still absorbing exclusionary and inclusionary pressures. On the exclusionary side, on January 19, 1995, in one of the last meetings of the 1992–95 parliament, a new citizenship law was passed. The Constitution Watch section of the East European Constitutional Review noted that "the new law extends the residency requirement and application period from three to six years and imposes a new civics exam (in Estonian) for all applicants, on top of the already mandatory language exam. The new exam, which will test knowledge of the constitution as well as the citizenship law, was criticized by leaders of the non-citizen community as harsh and unfair." However, on the inclusionary side, the Constitutional Watch also noted that in the March 5, 1995, elections a russophone party coalition, significantly called "Our Home in Estonia," won 5 seats in the 101-seat parliament. Due to high party fragmentation in the parliament, Our Home in Estonia was able to play some role in the intraparty negotiations that led to an influential opponent of exclusionary policies on the citizenship issues, former Prime Minister Edgar Savisaar, entering into the ruling coalition. In fact, Savisaar became the interior minister, a post that could allow him to play an important role in how state authorities treat non-Baltic minorities. See East European Constitutional Review 4, no. 3 (1995): 11–13.

21

Post-Communist Europe: Concluding Comparative Reflections

GIVEN THE continuing tumultuousness of events in post-Communist Europe, especially in the former Soviet Union and the former Yugoslavia, many readers will no doubt believe that we should conclude this book with reflections on conflict and not on democracy. However, our conceptual approach is concerned with conflicts over power, the state, and citizenship and whether, out of these contestations, democratic practices can become the "only game in town." From this perspective all of the countries of post-Communist Europe can and should be at least briefly compared. To be sure, in some of the twenty-seven post-Communist countries (e.g., Turkmenistan, Uzbekistan, or the Serbian-dominated rump Yugoslavia), a realistic evaluation must lead to the conclusion that the country is currently (1995) nondemocratic and that few weighty actors are even trying to put democracy, as we have defined it, on the agenda.[1] However, in some other countries in post-Communist Europe (e.g., the Czech Republic, Hungary, and possibly even Lithuania), democratic practices are near to becoming the only game in town. Thus, it is indeed relevant to discuss democracy in this conclusion, but we have to develop the critical categories, frames of reference, and evidence that will allow us to attempt comparisons within post-Communist Europe.

1. However, while it is true that rump Yugoslavia (Serbia, Montenegro, and the former province of Kosovo), as presently constituted, is nondemocratic, it is useful to recognize that there are more pressures for democracy in rump Yugoslavia than Western policy makers and public opinion normally recognize. Tibor Varady, the minister of justice in the Milan Panić government in the rump Yugoslavia, says that, when Prime Minister Panić challenged Milošević in the December 1992 presidential election, the West sent fewer than thirty election observers, and most arrived just days before the election. In contrast, in the plebiscite in Chile in 1988 that led to the defeat of Pinochet, the West sent thousands of observers, many of whom were involved months before the election. Why this difference? Commentary in the West in essence assumed that Serbia was univocally for Serbian expansionism and that "primordial nationalism" was so strong that Slobodan Milošević was unbeatable. But, even with the abstention of the Muslims of Kosovo (about 10 percent of the potential electorate), election day technical fraud by Slobodan Milosević of possibly 5–10 percent of the vote, and the lack of election observers and financial and technical support from the West, Panić still won 43 percent of the vote. Our point is that Milošević in December 1992 was not politically unbeatable. Some analysts, when confronted with the Chilean-Serbian comparison, shrug their shoulders and say, "So what, Milošević never would have respected the elections." This again misses the point. Power is always relational. If Milošević had actually lost and then annulled the election, he would have been domestically and internationally weakened in relation to democratic opponents and the myth of univocal support for aggressive nationalism would have been unmasked.

As our contribution to the development of such critical categories, frames of reference, and evidence, we want to develop three points. First, we will discuss what we see as the danger of "inverting the legitimacy pyramid" by activists and analysts who believe that the market will legitimate democracy. We will argue that the history of successful democratization indicates that the reverse normally occurs. Democracy legitimates the market (especially capitalism). Second, many activists and analysts also argue that not only is there the well-known simultaneity problem (which we accept), but also economic and political results must be achieved simultaneously or poor economic results will rapidly derail support for democratization (which we do not accept). We will give empirical data and a theoretical explanation to support our cautiously optimistic hypothesis concerning support for democracy as it relates to East Central Europe and our much less optimistic hypothesis for democratization in the non-Baltic countries of the former Soviet Union. Third, much of the popular press saw the return to power of former Communist political leaders and parties in such vanguard transitions to democracy as Poland, Hungary, and Lithuania as a "return to Communism" and as a major reversal of democracy. We will argue why such an analysis is faulty, both conceptually and politically.

ON THE DANGER OF AN INVERTED LEGITIMACY PYRAMID

In the conclusion to part 2 on southern Europe, we argued that the Spanish sequence of political reform, socioeconomic reform, and then economic reform was probably optimal for the consolidation of democracy in that country. Generally, we are of course reluctant to insist on any sequence because historically quite different sequences have in fact worked.

Most analysts of post-Communist Europe, especially policy advocates, implicitly rejected a Spanish-like sequence as unfeasible because of their perceived need for *simultaneous* economic and political change. Indeed, despite frequent obeisance to this simultaneity imperative, domestic and foreign activists and advisors often *privileged* economic change first. Solid research is just beginning on the question of sequence in post-Communist politics, but on theoretical (and now historical) grounds we believe that more consideration should have been given in the post-Communist cases to the cost of neglecting political reforms, especially state reconstruction. Why?

Theoretically, because, as we argued, the issue for modern democracies is not the creation of a *market*, but the creation of an *economic society*. Further, logic implies that a coherent regulatory environment and a rule of law is required to transform command economies into economic societies. If this is so, then a major priority must be to create democratic regulatory state power.[2] In this respect the two

2. In addition, it is debatable that the privatization of all or most of publicly owned property is necessary for the creation of a functioning market economy. Post–World War II Austria and Italy immediately

empirical extremes presented in this book are Spain and the USSR. Attention to electoral sequence and constitutional change contributed to effective power creation and state reconfiguration in Spain. Inattention to electoral sequence (by Gorbachev) and constitutional change (by Gorbachev *and* Yeltsin) contributed to power erosion and a decomposing state in the USSR and Russia.

Empirically, post hoc studies (as opposed to ex ante doctrinal advocacy) of privatization and structural economic change are just beginning to appear for the region. However, the best studies of the region are confirming a pattern about state power already documented in Latin America, that effective privatization (often mistakenly equated with "state shrinking") is best done by relatively strong states that are able to implement a coherent policy. The essence of a rich body of research on privatization and state restructuring shows that effective privatization entails less state *scope* but greater state *capacity*.[3] In a context of a post-Communist, postcommand economy, a state with rapidly eroding capacity simply cannot manage a process of effective privatization.[4]

---

come to mind as countries that retained a large public sector but were more or less efficient democratic market economies.

3. Four important studies of this phenomenon are Albert Fishlow, "The Latin American State," *Journal of Economic Perspectives* 4, no. 3 (1990): 61–74; Hector Schamis, "Re-forming the State: The Role of Privatization in Chile and Britain" (Ph.D. diss., Columbia University, Department of Political Science, 1994); Peter Evans, "The State as a Problem and Solution: Predation, Embedded Autonomy, and Structural Change," in Stephan Haggard and Robert R. Kaufman, eds., *The Politics of Economic Adjustment: International Constraints, Distributive Conflicts, and the State* (Princeton: Princeton University Press, 1992), 139–81; and Joan M. Nelson, ed., *Intricate Links: Democratization and Market Reforms in Latin America and Eastern Europe* (New Brunswick: Transaction Publishers, 1994), especially the article by Jacek Kochanowicz, "Reforming Weak States and Deficient Bureaucracies," 195–226. China in the first half of the 1990s allowed the emergence of a robust private sector in some areas while maintaining a strong command economy in other sectors and overall near totalitarian practices concerning politics, the media, and even family reproductive decisions.

4. We need more comparative studies of variation in state capacity vis-à-vis privatization and economic restructuring. Such variation could range from significant state reconstruction that increases state capacity and efficacy vis-à-vis privatization, to states that have had modest but unsatisfactory state reconstruction that has led to the creation of new postreform problems and the threat of a low-level equilibrium trap, to the extreme case of near state disintegration and virtually no state capacity for structuring change. East Central Europe and the former Soviet Union provide examples of all of these possible variations. The most popularly supported privatization in Central and Eastern Europe has been in the Czech Republic, which was also the case, despite some corruption, of the greatest transparency and where the freely elected government worked longest at such socioeconomic reforms as job retraining and state restructuring. In contrast, in a country like Romania, where the state has not been reconstructed, some nontransparent privatization has occurred, but there is a danger of a low-level equilibrium trap. In the Ukraine and parts of Russia, a new state had not been constructed, but the old state manifested strong disintegrative tendencies and low capacities in the 1992–93 period. See, for example, the empirically grounded comparative analysis of the Czech Republic and Romania by Olivier Blanchard, Simon Commander, and Fabrizio Coricelli, "Unemployment and Restructuring," World Bank, 1993, mimeo. Also see the chapter on Czechoslovakia in Roman Frydman, Andrzej Rapaczynski, and John Earle, eds., *The Privatization Process in Central Europe* (Budapest: Central European University Press, 1993), 40–94, and Roman Frydman, Andrzej Rapaczynski, and John Earle, eds., *The Privatization Process in Russia, Ukraine and the Baltic States* (Budapest: Central European University Press, 1993). The case studies of Ukraine and Russia underscore the difficulties of orderly, effective, and non-mafia privitization if the state is in disarray. Also see Roman Frydman and Andrzej Rapaczynski, *Privatization in Eastern Europe: Is the State Withering Away?* (Budapest: Central European University Press, 1994).

Note, the key is a strong state and not necessarily a democracy. A strong non-democratic state in Chile privatized reasonably effectively. However, in a post-Communist setting such as Russia, where the old Communist party-state has imploded or is no longer effective, privatization can proceed in an orderly way only after the state has been *reconstructed*. Once the totalitarian or post-totalitarian state, with its extensive command economy, has collapsed, given up, imploded, or disintegrated, state structures must be put in place. But many of the nondemocratic ways of restructuring the state are less available as alternatives than normally thought.

Some people argue (particularly in Russia) that a Pinochet is needed. But in Russia and many other countries of the former Soviet Union, a coherent state and a unified military organization of the sort that supported Pinochet no longer exist.[5] An authoritarian or perhaps a semifascist party-state in Russia is also sometimes held up as a powerful alternative ruling model. However, a single party with ideological legitimacy and the resources to assume and implement nondemocratic power would require the emergence and construction of a state-wide hegemonic semifascist movement, and this also seems unlikely. In our judgment, even an authoritarian or semifascist Russia would still be an example of what Ken Jowitt describes as a polity with a weak state and a weak society.[6] The quiescence of Franco's post–civil war Spain is a less likely outcome of a Russian fascist government than is a series of Chechnyas and Afghanistans. Some people argue for a China-type solution, but the Chinese model, which could possibly have been a pre-perestroika alternative, is also no longer available as an alternative in Russia. Unlike in Russia, the Chinese nondemocratic regime and state never broke down. Indeed, the Chinese regime never initiated or even considered a process of democratization and underwent only a very selective and partial process of liberalization.

Our conclusion is that, for Russia, the cost of a weak democratic state is high, but at the same time many of the nondemocratic solutions either are not available or would probably entail a repressive but still weak state. In Steven Lukes' useful formulation, such a state might have power *over* but not power *to*. For example, a semifascist Russian state might have repressive power over more people but still lack the power to reconstruct a prosperous and peaceful Russia.[7] Thus, in a context where the party-state has imploded and a command economy

5. In Alfred Stepan's frequent visits to Russia in 1991–95, the subject of a Pinochet or a Chinese alternative frequently came up as possible alternatives for Russia in conversations with Russian analysts and policy makers. But in fact, even before the disorderly behavior of the Russian military in Chechnya, only 3 percent of Russian respondents in an April 1994 poll "completely agreed" and only 7 percent "generally agreed" with the statement that "the army should rule" as an alternative political formula for Russia. See Richard Rose and Christian Haerpfer, "New Russian Barometer III: The Results," *Studies in Public Policy* 228 (1994), question 31b.

6. Ken Jowitt, *New World Disorder: The Leninist Extinction* (Berkeley: University of California Press, 1992), esp. 249–331.

7. For this important approach to power, see Steven Lukes, *Power: A Radical View* (London: Macmillan, 1974).

is no longer feasible, the state must be reconstructed. Our argument is that, far from being an irrelevance, some degree of democratic legitimacy can be a way of helping in this state reconstruction.

This leads to our central argument about legitimacy and privatization. In their rush to move away from state-controlled economies, some free market enthusiasts have endorsed privatization as the most important component of the post-1989 process. Privatization, *however it is accomplished,* is often seen as creating the key structural prerequisite for market democracies and the economic foundation for new democracies. We disagree. Repeated surveys in democracies show that at the apex of a hierarchy of democratic legitimacy are the overall democratic processes (e.g., elections, multiple parties, and free speech). At a lower level in the legitimacy hierarchy are incumbents (e.g., parliamentarians). Political institutions related to democracy are normally more legitimate than such economic institutions as market economies—which are always more legitimate than capitalist economies, if they are so labeled in surveys. Furthermore, economic institutions (e.g., market economies) are always more legitimate than economic actors (e.g., capitalists).[8] Thus, on theoretical grounds, the endeavor to legitimate the new post-1989 democracies by the efficacy of the new capitalists and thus by increasing by *whatever means* the number of new capitalists is to invert the legitimacy pyramid.

Such an inverted legitimacy pyramid is especially problematic in those countries, such as Russia, where privatization has been virtually unregulated, highly unequal, and often illegal.[9] In such contexts, the former holders of political power—such as the "red bourgeoisie" in the state enterprises or state financial or trading institutions—have been in a privileged position to transform their former political power into new types of economic power by numerous forms of "spontaneous" privatizations or thefts. Comparative surveys repeatedly show that in most societies some legitimacy is given to earned or inherited private property and to entrepreneurship. However, the new Russian capitalists of the former red bourgeoisie cannot draw upon these principles of legitimation. Indeed, the origins of their new wealth are often condemned as an illegitimate appropriation of public property and may leave a legacy of distrust both of market economies (which will be seen as mafia economies) and of the democracies that tolerated or even created these mafia economies. Much more political, theoretical, and research attention should be given to evaluating the democratic consequences of attempting to build new democratic polities and economic societies on this inverted legitimacy pyramid. The essence of the empirical findings and historical studies of Western democracies has always been that political systems of democ-

---

8. For a detailed analysis and ample documentation of this phenomenon, see Juan J. Linz, "Legitimacy of Democracy and the Socioeconomic System," in Mattei Dogan, ed., *Comparing Pluralist Democracies: Strains on Democracy* (Boulder Colo: Westview Press, 1988), 65–113.

9. See, for example, Stephen Handelman, "The Russian Mafia," *Foreign Affairs* (March–April 1994): 83–96.

racy legitimate market economies, not the reverse. This is so because, as long as a democratic majority does not question private ownership of the means of production when it can do so legally, that property is protected.[10]

On Simultaneity of Results versus the Comparative Politics of Deferred Gratification

The assumption that economic reform—the market and privatization—can legitimate the new democracies is also based on the dubious assumption that economic success and the creation of greater wealth can be achieved simultaneously with the installation and legitimation of democratic institutions. We believe that, for imploded command economies, democratic polities can and must be installed and legitimized by a variety of appeals *before* the possible benefits of a market economy actually materialize fully. Many analysts and political advisors dismiss the argument for prior state restructuring because of their assumption that because of people's demands for material improvements, economic and political gains must not only be pursued, but *occur,* simultaneously. Some even argue that, though simultaneous economic and political reforms are necessary, such simultaneity is impossible.[11] We can call these two perspectives about the relationship between economics and democratization the *tightly coupled* hypothesis and the *loosely coupled* hypothesis.[12]

By loosely coupled we do not mean that there is no relationship between economic and political perceptions, but only that the relationship is not necessarily one to one. For at least a medium range time horizon, people can make independent and even opposite assessments about political and economic trends. We further believe that, if assessments about politics are positive, they can provide a valuable cushion against painful economic restructuring.[13] What evidence do we have

10. See Linz, "Legitimacy of Democracy."

11. The title of a widely disseminated article by Jon Elster captures this perspective, "The Necessity and Impossibility of Simultaneous Economic and Political Reform," in Douglas Greenberg, Stanley N. Katz, Melanie Beth Oliviero, and Steven C. Wheatley, eds., *Constitutionalism and Democracy: Transitions in the Contemporary World* (New York: Oxford University Press, 1993), 267–74. In our own judgment, the reasons for the impossibility of simultaneity are not necessarily those advanced by Elster but may be the fact that the time necessary for successful economic change is inherently longer than the time needed to hold free elections and even draft a democratic constitution. An important survey-based critique of the Elster hypothesis and an argument for the empirical reality of respondents' multiple time horizons and their "political economy of patience" are given by the Hungarian political scientist László Bruszt in "Why on Earth Would East Europeans Support Capitalism?" (paper presented at the XVth World Congress of the International Political Science Association, Berlin, August 21–24, 1994).

12. We presented a preliminary discussion of this relationship under "The Political Economy of Legitimacy and of Coercion" in chapter 5.

13. The voters might, because of negative economic performance, vote incumbents out of office, but the overall economic policies of their successors might well continue to be roughly the same. Poland in 1993–95 and Hungary in 1994–95 (especially after the reform acceleration of 1995) come to mind. Democratic alternation of governing coalitions might in fact give more time to the policies of economic change while at the

Table 21.1. GDP, Industrial Output, and Peak Inflation Rates in Post-Communist Countries: 1989–1995

Country	Measure	1989	1990	1991	1992	1993	1994 (estimated)	1995 (projected)	Industrial Output 1993 (1989=100)	Inflation Rate (at peak year during 1989–93)
Albania	GDP	9.8	-10.0	-27.1	-9.7	11.0	7.0	5.0	52	237 [92]
	Industrial production	5.0	-7.6	-36.9	-44.0	-10.0	na	na		
Armenia	GDP	14.2	-7.4	-11.0	-52.0	-15.0	0	na	na	10900 [93]
Azerbaijan	GDP	na	-11.7	-0.7	-22.6	-13.0	-15.0	-10.0	na	1174 [92]
Belarus	GDP	8.0	-3.0	-1.2	-9.6	-11.6	-26.0	-10	76	2775 [93]
	Industrial production	na	na	-6.8	-10.2	-6.0	na	na		
Bulgaria	GDP	0.5	-9.1	-11.7	-5.6	-4.2	2	4	na	339 [91]
	Industrial production	-1.4	-16.5	-27.3	-22.0	-10.0	4	na		
Croatia	GDP	-1.6	-8.6	-14.4	-9	-3.2	1	6	57	1150 [92]
	Industrial production	na	-11.3	-28.5	-15.0	-6.0	-3.0	6		
Czech Republic	GDP	na	-0.4	-14.2	-7.1	-0.3	3	6	57	52 [91]
	Industrial production	na	-3.5	-22.3	-10.6	-6.3	0	na		
Estonia	GDP	-1.1	-8.1	-11	-14.2	-3.2	5.0	6.0	54	965 [92]
Macedonia	GDP	na	-9.9	-12.1	-14.0	-14.1	-7.2	0	na	1691 [92]
	Industrial production	na	-10.6	-17.2	-16.1	-17.2	na	na		
Georgia	NMP	-4.8	-12.4	-20.8	-43.4	-40.0	-35.0	na	na	na
	Industrial production	-6.9	-29.9	-24.4	-43.4	-21.0	na	na		
Hungary	GDP	0.7	-3.5	-11.9	-4.3	-2.3	3.0	3.0	69	
	Industrial gross output	-1.0	-9.6	-18.2	-9.8	-4.0	9.0	6.0		
Kazakhstan	GDP	-0.4	-0.4	-13.0	-14.0	-12.0	-25.0	na	68	1925 [93]
Kyrgyzstan	GDP	3.8	3.2	-5.0	-25.0	-16.0	-10	1.5	53	1354 [93]
	Industrial production	na	na	0.0	-27.0	-25.0	na	na		
Latvia	GDP	6.8	2.9	-8.3	-33.8	-11.7	3	3	38	958 [91]
	Gross mfg output	na	na	0.4	-48.7	-32.6	na	na		
Lithuania	GDP	1.5	-5.0	-13.1	-37.7	-16.2	4	4	na	1175 [92]
	Industrial production	na	na	na	-50.9	-42.7	na	na		
Moldova	GDP	8.8	-1.5	-11.9	-25.0	-14.0	-20.0	0		837 [93]
Poland	GDP	0.2	-11.6	-7.6	1.5	3.8	4.5	5.0	69	640 [89]
	Industrial production	-1.4	-26.1	-11.9	3.9	5.6	na	na		
Romania	GDP	-5.8	-5.6	-12.9	-13.6	1.0	2.0	3.0	47	296 [93]
	Industrial output	-5.3	-23.7	-22.8	-21.9	1.3	2.0	na		
Russia	GDP	na	na	-13.0	-19.0	-12.0	-15.0	-7.0	60	2138 [92]
	Industrial production	na	-0.1	-8.0	-18.8	-16.0	-21.0	-12.0		

Table 21.1. *(continued)*

Country	Measure	1989	1990	1991	1992	1993	1994 (estimated)	1995 (projected)	Industrial Output 1993 (1989=100)	Inflation Rate (at peak year during 1989–93)
				GDP % change						
Slovakia	GDP	1.4	-0.4	-14.5	-7.0	-4.1	3.5	3.0	55	58 [91]
	Industrial production	-0.7	-3.6	-17.8	-14.0	-10.6	5.5	na		
Slovenia	GDP	-1.8	-4.7	-8.1	-5.4	1.0	5.0	6	46	247 [91]
	Industrial production	-0.1	-10.3	-11.3	-12.0	-2.6	6.6	5.1		
Tajikistan	NMP	-2.9	-1.6	-12.5	-33.7	-28	na	na	56	7344 [93]
	Industrial production	1.9	1.9	-7.4	-35.7	na	na	na		
Turkmenistan	GDP	na	2.0	-4.7	-5.3	-7.6	-10.0	-5.0	90	1875 [93]
Ukraine	GDP	4.1	-3.4	-12	-17.0	-14.0	-23.0	-5.0	79	10155 [93]
	Industrial production	2.8	-0.1	-4.8	-6.5	-8.0	-30.0	na		
Uzbekistan	GDP	3.7	1.6	-0.5	-11.1	-2.4	-2.6	2.0	94	927 [93]
	Industrial output	3.6	1.8	1.8	-12.3	-8.3	na	na		
Yugoslavia	Industrial output	na	na	na	na	na	na	na	35	3.72×10^{13} [93]

Source: The yearly 1989–95 data were supplied by the European Bank for Reconstruction and Development, London, January 1995. The figures for 1994 are estimates; those for 1995 are projections. A common method was used in the data collection. The 1993 industrial output data in relation to a baseline of 100 for 1989 are from Jacek Rostowski, *Macro-economic Instability in Post-Communist Counties* (Oxford: Clarendon Press, Oxford University Press, forthcoming). No data were available for Bosnia. The data on inflation rates are also from Rostowski. The figure for inflation in Yugoslavia (3.72 times 10 to the 13th power) computes to one of the all-time world hyperinflation rates of over 37 trillion.

concerning the relationship between economics and democratization in the first five years of post-Communist Europe? Certainly, if we just look at relatively hard economic data, of the twenty-seven countries in post-Communist Europe, no country (except Poland) experienced positive growth in 1992. Indeed, all post-Communist countries in 1993 were still well below their 1989 industrial output levels (table 21.1).

If we look at the subjective perception of economic well-being in the six East Central European Warsaw Pact countries we have analyzed in this book, the mean positive rating (on a +100 to a –100 scale) among those polled between November 1993 and March 1994 for the Communist economic system was 60.2. But the mean positive rating for the post-Communist economic system was only 37.3, a drop of almost 23 points. The tightly coupled hypothesis would predict that the attitudes toward the political system would drop steeply, even if not the full 23 points. What does the evidence show? In the same survey, the mean positive rank-

same time giving some valuable room for accommodation to the political sentiments or fears of those most hurt by the fundamental socioeconomic changes being undertaken by the new democratic regime.

Table 21.2. Percentages Expressing Positive Attitudes toward Communist versus Post-Communist Economic Systems and Political Systems: Responses from Six East Central European Countries

Question	Country	Percentage of Positive Responses for 1989	Percentage of Positive Responses for 1993–94
"Here is a scale ranking how the *economy* works: the top, plus 100 is the best; the bottom, minus 100 the worst."	Bulgaria	66	15
	Czech	42	66
	Hungary	75	27
	Poland	52	50
	Romania	52	35
	Slovakia	74	31
	Mean	60	35
"Here is a scale ranking how *government* works: the top, plus 100 is the best; the bottom, minus 100 the worst."	Bulgaria	51	59
	Czech	23	78
	Hungary	58	51
	Poland	38	69
	Romania	52	60
	Slovakia	50	52
	Mean	46	62

Source: Richard Rose and Christian Haerfer, "New Democracies Baromester III: Learning from What Is Happening," *Studies in Public Policy* 230 (1994), questions 22–23, 32–33. Percentages are rounded off. The polls were administered in these countries between November 1993 and March 1993.

ing of the Communist political system was 45.7. A one-point drop in political evaluation for every point drop in economic evaluation (a perfectly coupled correlation) would yield a positive evaluation of the political system of only 22.6. However, positive ranking for the post-Communist system did not fall as the tightly coupled hypothesis would expect but *rose* to 61.5, or 38.9 points higher than a perfectly coupled hypothesis would predict, (table 21.2).

How can we explain such incongruence? First of all, human beings are capable of making separate and correct judgments about a basket of economic goods (which may be deteriorating) and a basket of political goods (which may be improving). In fact, in the same survey, in *all* six countries of East Central Europe the citizens polled judged that in important areas directly affected by the democratic political system their life experiences and chances had overwhelmingly improved, even though in the same survey they asserted that their personal household economic situation had worsened (table 21.3).

We do not believe that such incongruence can last forever; however, it indicates that, in a radical transformation such as is occurring in East Central Europe, the deterioration of the economy does not necessarily translate rapidly into erosion of support for the political system.[14] Table 21.2 indicates that the perceived legit-

14. In fact, in a regression model of their data, William Mishler and Richard Rose conclude that "our regression model shows that it takes a four point fall in either current or future economic evaluation to produce a one point fall in evaluations of the [political] regime." Their major explanation of this result is that

Table 21.3. Incongruent Perceptions of the Economic Basket of Goods versus the Political Basket of Goods in the Communist System and the Current System: Six East Central European Countries

Question	Percentage of Respondents answering "better now" versus those answering "worse now"					
	Bulgaria	Czech	Slovakia	Hungary	Poland	Romania
Economic Basket:						
"When you compare your overall household economic situation with five years ago, would you say that in the past it was better, the same, worse?"	16/58	23/49	18/62	6/76	17/62	21/65
Political Basket:						
"Please tell me whether our present political system by comparison with the Communist is [better, the same or worse] in the following areas:"						
"People can join any organization they want."	95/5	90/1	88/3	81/2	79/2	94/1
"Everybody is free to say what he or she thinks."	90/11	84/3	82/4	73/8	83/4	94/2
"People can travel and live wherever they want."	95/5	96/1	87/2	75/4	75/7	90/2
"People can live without fear of unlawful arrest."	88/11	73/4	62/5	59/4	71/5	81/1
"Each person can decide whether or not to take an interest in politics."	97/3	84/0	81/1	n/a	69/5	92/1
"Everybody is free to decide whether or not to practice a religion."	98/2	94/0	96/1	83/1	70/6	95/1

Source: Same as for figure 21.1, questions 26, 35, 36, 37, 39, 40, 42. Where the percentages do not add up to 100 the respondents answered "equal."

imacy of the political system has given democratic institutions in East Central Europe an important degree of insulation from the perceived inefficacy of the new economic system.[15] Indeed, most of the people in East Central Europe in 1993 had a fairly long-time horizon and expressed optimism that by 1998 *both* the

---

East Europeans have a fairly long time horizon. See their "Trajectories of Fear and Hope: The Dynamics of Support for Democracy in Eastern Europe," *Studies in Public Policy* 214 (1993): 27.

15. Some readers might recall that one of us, in a study of the breakdown of democracies—particularly in Europe in the interwar years—posed a more direct relationship between efficacy and legitimacy without data to prove that relationship. In fact, some of the data assembled later showed that the relation was true only for a few countries, particularly for Germany and Austria, but not for Norway and the Netherlands. Why the apparent difference today? We would call attention to the presence in the interwar years of alternative "legitimate" models for the polity: the Soviet-Communist utopia, the new Fascist Italian and later German model, the corporatist-authoritarian-catholic "organic" democracy, the prewar bureaucratic-monarchical authoritarianism, and even (in Spain) the anarchist utopia. They all appealed as alternative answers for inefficacious democracy. Up to now there are no such appealing alternatives to "difficult democracies" today. See Juan J. Linz, *The Breakdown of Democratic Regimes: Crisis, Breakdown, and Reequilibration* (Baltimore: Johns Hopkins University Press, 1978).

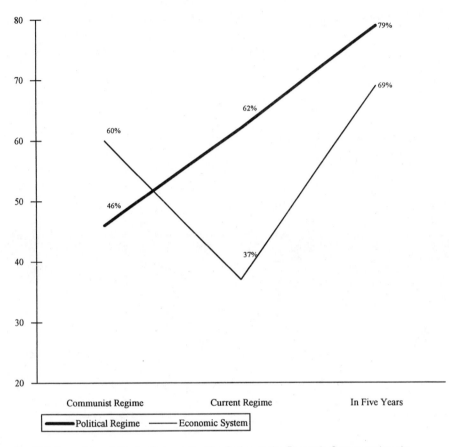

Fig. 21.1. Percentage of People Giving a Positive Rating to the Economic System and to the Political Regime in the Communist System, the Current System, and in Five Years: Six East Central European Countries.
Source: Richard Rose and Christian Haerpfer, "New Russia Barometer III," *Studies in Public Policy* 228 (1994), questions 24 and 34.

performance of the new democracy *and* the performance of the new economic system would improve significantly (figure 21.1).

In East Central Europe the evidence is thus strongly in favor of the argument that deferred gratification and confidence in the future is possible even when there is an acknowledged lag in economic improvements. Simultaneity of rapid political and economic results is indeed normally extremely difficult, but fortunately, as figure 21.1 shows, the citizens of East Central Europe did not perceive such simultaneity as necessary. The overall implication of the tables and figures presented thus far in this chapter seems to us further evidence of the potential danger of policies based on thinking that reflects the inverted legitimacy pyramid.

Before turning to the former Soviet Union, we should note briefly two other factors that help explain the surprisingly high degree of political support for the new political regime (political *regime,* not necessarily political *incumbents*), despite economic hardship. None of the former Warsaw Pact countries of East Central Europe (unlike the former USSR) experienced widespread bloodshed over stateness problems. Also, unlike Russia, there is no ambivalent legacy about the loss of an empire or the disintegration of the USSR.

How do the non-Baltic countries of the former Soviet Union compare with the Warsaw Pact countries of East Central Europe on the same set of dimensions concerning satisfaction with the pre- and post-Communist economies and political systems? Unfortunately, we have data only for Russia, Ukraine, and Belarus, but the differences are striking, especially in the substantially lower ranking accorded to current support for the post-Communist political system (figure 21.2).

A panel of outside observers also notes a set of very different patterns within countries of East Central Europe, in contrast to the former Soviet Union, with respect to their political development. An annual publication of Freedom House has developed a common method to evaluate political rights and civil liberties for almost all of the countries of the world.[16] Freedom House uses a 7-point scale to rank countries concerning political rights and a 7-point scale to rank political liberties. A score of 1 indicates the highest rights and liberties and 7 the lowest. For purposes of our argument about democracy, if a country is ranked no lower than 2 on political rights and no lower than 3 on civil liberties, we will label it as *above* the democratic threshold for that year. If a country is given a 4 or lower on political rights and/or a 5 or lower on civil liberties, we will consider it as *below* the democratic threshold for that year. Countries between the two categories will be labeled as on the *border* of the democratic threshold. In short, the lower the number the better the results for democracy. How does post-Communist Europe rank on this scale? See table 21.4.

To make table 21.4 a bit more useful for a comparative analysis of post-Communist Europe, let us separate these twenty-six countries into three broad categories: East Central Europe, the former Soviet Union, and the former Yugoslavia. Within the former Soviet Union, we will make a further subdivision between those countries that had been a part of the former Soviet Union since the early 1920s and that are now, with Russia, a part of the Commonwealth of Independent States, and those countries that became a part of the Soviet Union only after 1940 (Estonia, Latvia, and Lithuania) and that refused to join the CIS. The classification results are presented in table 21.5.

The implications of the numerous tables and figures we have presented in this chapter, as well as of the qualitative evaluations made in previous chapters, will

16. We discussed the methodology, sources, and panels utilized in this annual Freedom House publication in chapter 3, especially notes 4 and 5.

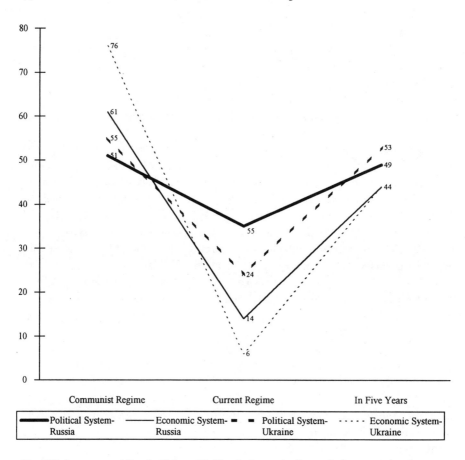

Fig. 21.2. Percentage of People Giving a Positive Rating to the Economic System and to the Political System in the Communist Regime, the Current Regime, and in Five Years: Russia, Ukraine, and Belarus.

Source: For Russia see Richard Rose and Christian Haerpfer, "New Russia Barometer III," *Studies in Public Policy* 228 (1994), questions 15–17 and 27–29. For Ukraine see Rose and Haerpfer, "New Democracies Barometer III," questions 22–24, 32–34. The data for Belarus are roughly similar to those for Ukraine. Positive evaluations of the economic system under communism, in the present, and in five years are 78, 11, and 47, respectively, and positive evaluations for the political systems in these three periods are 64, 28, and 56, respectively. Sources same as cited for Ukraine.

have to be elaborated and analyzed more fully by the new generation of comparativists conducting research into European post-Communist politics. However, we can at least note some patterns.

Respondents in the six former Warsaw Pact countries of East Central Europe gave a mean positive rating of 62 to the post-Communist political system (a *rise* of 16 points over the positive rating they gave to the Communist political system). In sharp contrast, in the three former Soviet Union countries (Russia, Ukraine, and Belarus), a mean of only 29 gave the post-Communist political system a pos-

Table 21.4. Rating of Twenty-six Countries of Post-Communist Europe on the Freedom House Scale of Political Rights and Civil Liberties for the Year 1993

Country	Political Rights	Civil Liberties	Democratic Threshold Rating: "Above," "Below," or "Border"
Armenia	3	4	Border
Azerbaijan	6	6	Below
Belarus	5	4	Below
Bosnia-Herzegovina	6	6	Below
Bulgaria	2	2	Above
Croatia	4	4	Below
Czech Republic	1	2	Above
Estonia	3	2	Border
Georgia	5	5	Below
Hungary	1	2	Above
Kazakhstan	6	4	Below
Kyrgyzstan	5	3	Below
Latvia	3	3	Border
Lithuania	1	3	Above
Macedonia	3	3	Border
Moldova	5	5	Below
Poland	2	2	Above
Romania	4	4	Below
Russia	3	4	Border
Slovakia	3	4	Border
Slovenia	1	2	Above
Tajikistan	7	7	Below
Turkmenistan	7	7	Below
Ukraine	4	4	Border
Uzbekistan	7	7	Below
Yugoslavia (Serbia and Montenegro)	6	6	Below
Summary			6 of 26 Above
			7 of 26 Border
			13 of 26 Below

Source: Raymond D. Gastil, ed., *Freedom in the World: Political Rights and Civil Liberties, 1993–1994* (New York: Freedom House, 1994), 677–678.

itive rating (a *decrease* of 26 points from those who gave the Communist system a positive rating).[17]

Another finding is that *none* of the twelve CIS countries that had been part of the Soviet Union were above the minimal threshold of democratic practices, according to the 1993 annual Freedom House poll. In fact, three of the twelve countries (Turkmenistan, Uzbekistan, and Tajikistan), received the *lowest* possible scores of 7 on political rights and 7 on civil liberties.[18] In contrast, four of the six

17. Even here we should note a partial confirmation of the loosely coupled hypothesis in that the positive evaluation of the current post-Communist political system was 18.7 points higher than the evaluation of the current post-Communist economic system.

18. For the reader to get an idea of how far actual practices are from being democratic in Turkmenistan,

Table 21.5. Comparative Democratic Threshold Rating of Post-Communist Europe: The Countries of East Central Europe, the Former Soviet Union, and the Former Yugoslavia (1993)

Classification	Country	Political Rights	Civil Liberties	Democratic Threshold Rating ("Above," "Border," or "Below")
East Central Europe	Czech Republic	1	2	Above
	Hungary	1	2	Above
	Poland	2	2	Above
	Bulgaria	2	2	Above
	Slovakia	3	4	Border
	Romania	4	4	Below
Summary				4/6 Above
				1/6 Border
				1/6 Below
The former Soviet Union	Lithuania	1	3	Above
(since the 1940s, not CIS members)	Estonia	3	2	Border
	Latvia	3	3	Border
Summary				1/3 Above
				2/3 Border
				0/3 Below
The former Soviet Union	Russia	3	4	Border
(since the 1920s, now CIS members)	Armenia	3	4	Border
	Ukraine	4	4	Border
	Kyrgyzstan	5	3	Below
	Belarus	5	4	Below
	Maldova	5	5	Below
	Kazakhstan	6	4	Below
	Azerbaijan	6	6	Below
	Georgia	6	6	Below
	Tajikistan	7	7	Below
	Turkmenistan	7	7	Below
	Uzbekistan	7	7	Below
Summary				0/12 Above
				3/12 Border
				9/12 Below
The former Yugoslavia	Slovenia	1	2	Above
	Macedonia	3	3	Border
	Croatia	4	4	Below
	Bosnia-Herzegovina	6	6	Below
	Yugoslavia (Serbia and Montenegro)	6	6	Below
Summary				1/5 Above
				1/5 Border
				3/5 Below

Source: Same as Table 21.4 The only country of post-Communist Europe not included is Albania, which did not start its transition until quite late. It also does not fit easily into any of the three geographical-historical categories utilized in the table. In our judgment, Albania as of mid-1995 would score "below" the democratic threshold.

East Central European countries were above the threshold. Romania received the lowest scores of the six former Warsaw Pact countries of East Central Europe, with 4 on political rights and 4 on civil liberties. Thus, it seems accurate to say that both the "ceiling" and the "floor" of democratic practices in East Central Europe were substantially higher in 1993 than in the CIS countries.

We must also note that, in contrast to the six East Central European countries, economic and political judgments are more tightly coupled in the CIS countries. There is thus a much lower propensity for deferred gratification in the non-Baltic parts of the former Soviet Union than in East Central Europe.

What explains such sharp contrasts between East Central Europe and the non-Baltic countries of the former Soviet Union? Let us begin with the question of deferred gratification. No doubt the pattern of difference is partly due to the extreme severity of the drop in positive economic assessments. (In East Central Europe the mean positive evaluation only dropped from 60 to 37, whereas the post-Soviet mean of Russia, Ukraine, and Belarus dropped from 71 to 10.) Timing and perception of the future were also probably important. According to table 21.1 the worst year in East Central Europe in terms of economic decline was 1991. The worst year in Russia, Ukraine, and Belarus was 1994, *after* the poll. The year 1995 will probably be economically somewhat better than 1994, but in late 1993 people might not have seen any light at the end of the tunnel.

We are almost certain, moreover, that economic historians will eventually document the fact that the severity of the stateness problem in the USSR and the subsequent state disintegration and widespread armed conflicts played an independent role in objectively deepening economic disarray. The continuation of such conflicts in 1995 in some CIS countries inevitably also decreased the subjective confidence as to whether deferred gratification was merited. After all, a politics of deferred gratification is rational only if some signs of potential gratification can be discerned. In a context of very weak and contested states, the confidence in the future that was an important ingredient reinforcing the "politics of deferred grat-

Tajikistan, and Uzbekistan, we can say that they are significantly less pluralistic in regard to democratic oppositional electoral activity than in rump Yugoslavia (see the evidence for a degree of pluralism in Yugoslavia we supplied in note 1 of this chapter). In contrast to rump Yugoslavia, where the opposition presidential candidate received 43 percent of the vote in December 1992, open democratic contestation in Turkmenistan, Tajikistan, and Uzbekistan was de facto insignificant in 1994. According to the *Economist*'s useful political synopsis of the twelve members of the Commonwealth of Independent States, Turkmenistan is described as a "one-party state. All members of the parliament, elected in December 1994, were unopposed. In February 1994, 99.99% voted to extend [President] Saparmurat Niyazov's term of office until 1999. Only 212 Turkmen voted No, officially." The *Economist* summarizes politics in Uzbekistan thus: "Main opposition parties banned; media under state control. Ruling party won over 80% of seats in parliamentary elections in December 1994; 99.96% of the electorate voted on March 26, [1995] to extend [President] Islam Karimov's term of office until 2000." The *Economist* notes of Tajikistan: "Imamali Rakhmonov confirmed as president last November [1994] in an election at which most opposition parties were banned. Widespread vote-rigging alleged." See "Less Poor, Less Democratic," *Economist*, April 22–28, 1995, 48. Clearly, no serious theorist should consider that the above three countries are involved in any form of a democratic transition. They are all clear cases of the mere "electoralism" we discussed in chapter 1.

ification" in East Central Europe was understandably weaker in the former Soviet Union and in much of the former Yugoslavia. To be sure, Czechoslovakia had a stateness problem, but because of the orderly and reasonably well-planned velvet divorce, no armed violence was involved and no significant economic downturn occurred in either the Czech Republic or Slovakia.[19]

Stateness problems and not just economic problems critically affect democratic outcomes. This becomes clear when we note that, of the twenty-two independent countries that emerged out of the disintegration of the former Soviet Union and the former Yugoslavia, only two—Lithuania and Slovenia—are *above* the democratic threshold rating (see table 21.5). Both of these countries are exceptions that prove the rule concerning the importance of stateness problems for democratization. As we stressed in the last chapter, Lithuania's economy is not as robust as that of Estonia, but Lithuania was the *only* Baltic country to grant inclusive citizenship to all residents, whether they were ethnic Balts or not. This policy has enabled Lithuania to manage its potential stateness problem in a more democratic fashion than Latvia or Estonia and, thus, Lithuania has, correctly, received a higher score for "political rights" than has Latvia or Estonia.

Of the five countries in the former Yugoslavia, Slovenia is the *only* country not to have a significant stateness problem. Slovenia does not have a significant ethnic minority population, so it has not been embroiled in actual or potential conflicts over a Serbian (or Albanian) irredenta of the sort that have occurred in Croatia, Bosnia-Herzegovenia, and rump Yugoslavia, where armed conflicts have contributed to widespread curtailment of political rights and civil liberties. Macedonia, more than Slovenia, has potentially severe stateness problems (with Albania *and* Serbia and even Bulgaria and Greece), and this has contributed to its less-than-inclusive citizenship and language policies.

Another factor that has no doubt contributed to greater support for the post-Communist regimes in East Central Europe (in contrast to Russia and to some extent Belarus) is that Russian citizens may be happy to be independent but feel nonetheless a sense of geopolitical loss and anger about the way the USSR disintegrated. Among other things, the disintegration of the USSR has left twenty-five million Russians as often beleaguered and sometimes stateless minorities in other countries. Also, unlike the citizens of the Czech Republic, who believe that the velvet divorce improved Czech standards of living, the Russians are convinced that the dissolution of the USSR contributed to the decline of their standard of living (table 21.6).

We can infer that, in contrast to Russian citizens' sense of geopolitical loss over 1991, the citizens of the "outer empire" in countries like Poland no doubt feel a

---

19. In fact, positive GNP growth in the Czech Republic was projected to be 3 percent and 6 percent for 1994 and 1995 and to be 3.5 percent and 3 percent for Slovakia. In contrast, for the same years the Russian figures were -15 percent and -7 percent and the Ukrainian figures were -23 percent and -5 percent. See table 21.1

Table 21.6. Russian Attitudes in 1994 about the Dissolution of the USSR in 1991

Question	% at Age:			
	18–29	30–59	60+	Total
"In December 1991 leaders of Russia, Belorussia and the Ukraine decided to dissolve the USSR and found the CIS. What do you think of that now?"				
It was the right decision.	16	12	8	12
It was the wrong decision.	57	70	75	68
Difficult to answer.	28	18	17	20
"How has the disintegration of the USSR affected Russian living standards?"				
For better.	5	4	3	4
For worse.	68	76	83	76
No change.	11	8	5	8
Difficult to answer.	16	12	9	12

Source: Rose and Haerfper, "New Russian Barometer III," questions 57–59. We believe a similar phenomenon is at work in Belarus as in Russia. The *only* deputy in the Belarus parliament to vote against independence, Aleksandr Lukashenko, was elected president in 1994. In May 1995 he sponsored a referendum in which he argued, "If people call for it, we will also have a political union that is even closer than the Soviet Union was. For the moment I am talking about economic union." See Matthew Kaminski, "Belarussians Seek the Future in the Past," *Financial Times* (May 17, 1995), 3. Lukashenko won support for all questions on the referendum. In the same article the *Financial Times* correspondent noted that "over three-quarters of Belarussian voters in a national referendum chose to bring back Soviet-era national insignia, make Russian the state language, and support economic integration with Russia."

sense of geopolitical gain due to the events of 1989. This is one of the reasons why citizens in Poland had a much stronger preference for the present political system than do those in Russia and thus more willingly accepted the politics of deferred gratification (table 21.7).

We do not want to overstress the preference for the old system in Russia, however. Many people in Spain believe that they lived better under Franco but would not like to return to that political system. The key question in politics is the desired future *alternative*. Russians, in fact, see the political basket of goods we reviewed in table 21.2 as *better* under the new political system, but they feel this by a smaller margin than do respondents in East Central Europe.[20] Thus, despite their sense of ambivalence and loss concerning the dissolution of the USSR, only a small percentage say that they would like to return to Communism and an even smaller percentage prefer military rule as a desired future alternative (table 21.8).

Other important explanatory factors for democratization differences in post-Communist Europe for future researchers to explore are, of course, those related

20. For example, the better/worse ratio concerning freedom to travel was 95/5 in the Czech Republic, 75/7 in Poland, and only 41/28 in Russia. The better/worse ratio for freedom from unlawful arrest was 73/4 in the Czech Republic, 71/5 in Poland, and only 23/15 in Russia. We believe these results, among other things, accurately reflect the stresses for individuals due to the continuing stateness crisis in Russia that we discussed in chapter 19. Data are from table 21.2 in this chapter and Rose and Haerpfer, "New Russia Barometer III," questions 30c and 30e.

Table 21.7. Preferences for Old and New Political Systems in Russia and Poland in January–February 1992

	% at Age:				% Preferring Present
Preference	To 29	30–59	Over 60	Total	System over Old System
In Russia					
Present system better	43	39	21	36	-18
Old system better	45	52	71	54	
Don't know	12	9	8	10	
In Poland					
Present system better				74	+51
Old system better				23	
Don't know				3	

Source: Irina Bolva and Viacheslav Shironin, "Russians between State and Market," *Studies in Public Policy* 205 (1992): 19–22.

Table 21.8. Russian Attitudes toward Restoring the former Communist System: April 1994

Agreement with Statement, "It would be better	% Response at Age:			
to restore the former communist system."	To 29	30–59	60+	Total
Completely agree	5	8	18	9
Generally agree	8	14	19	14
Generally disagree	30	29	23	28
Completely disagree	41	36	22	34
Difficult to answer	16	13	19	15

Source: Rose and Haerfpfer, "New Russia Barometer III," question 31a. In the same poll, only 3% competely agreed and only 7% generally agreed with the statement that "the army should rule." Question 31b. The army is thus clearly not a desired alternative.

to time, prior regime types, and the presence or absence of a usable democratic legacy. The USSR lasted for about seventy-five years, during much of which totalitarian practices predominated. East Central Europe was a part of the Soviet subsystem for only forty years. In Poland for much of this period, authoritarian, not totalitarian, political realities predominated. In Hungary, mature post-totalitarianism evolved. Finally, pre-Communist history must be analyzed comparatively. Czechoslovakia, for example, was democratic from independence in 1919 until the Nazi interventions of 1938. There is virtually no such usable pre-Communist democratic past in the non-Baltic countries of the former Soviet Union. This does not mean that democracy is impossible in these countries; it does mean, however, that there will be longer and more perilous journeys toward constitutionalism and state reconstruction before democracy becomes, if ever, the only game in town.

The astute reader has no doubt noted that we have not built religion into our explanation of the comparatively weaker progress toward democratization in the CIS countries and the former Yugoslavia. We have not done so for two reasons.

First, it is becoming increasingly popular among analysts to make certain religions, *by themselves* (e.g., Orthodox Christianity, Islam, or Confucianism) a major explanation for difficulties in democratization in many parts of the world.[21] The factors we have mentioned in this chapter, *in themselves,* are sufficient to explain the sharply different results of democratization in the non-Baltic countries of the former Soviet Union versus East Central Europe. Second, in an excursus on comparative religion, resistance, and civil society in chapter 16, we have already advanced the argument that religions differ in the range of their autonomously controlled resources and their relationship to the state. We noted that Roman Catholicism as a transnational, hierarchical organization can potentially provide material and doctrinal support to a local Catholic church to help it resist state oppression. To the extent that a Catholic church might resist the state, it could be considered a support for a more robust and autonomous civil society. Empirically, in the resistance stage of democratization we analyze in this book, the Catholic church played a supportive role in Poland and Lithuania, as well as in Chile and Brazil and in the last years of Franco in Spain. Protestantism, with its emphasis on individual conscience and its international networks, can also play a role in supporting civil society's opposition to a repressive state, as in East Germany and Estonia. Concerning civil society and resistance to the state, Orthodox Christianity is often (not always) organizationally and doctrinally in a relatively weak position because of what Max Weber called its "caesaropapist" structure, in which the church is a *national* as opposed to an *transnational* organization. In caesaropapist churches, the national state normally plays a major role in the national church's finances and appointments. Such a national church is not really a relatively autonomous part of civil society because there is a high degree, in Weber's words, of "subordination of priestly to secular power."[22] Having acknowledged this, we do not believe that Orthodox Christianity is an inherently antidemocratic force. That is to say, if the leaders of the state are committed to democracy and follow democratic practices, the caesaropapist structures and incentives should lead to loyal support of democracy by the Orthodox Christian church, as in Greece since 1975. However, if the leaders of the state and political society are antidemocratic, the democratic opposition in civil society will not normally receive substantial or effective support from a national Orthodox church. We hope to develop our thinking on the role of the world's religions and democracy in a future project.[23]

---

21. For an argument concerning the tension or even hostility between Orthodoxy, Confucianism, Islam, and democracy, see Samuel P. Huntington, "The Clash of Civilization," *Foreign Affairs* 72, no. 3 (1993): 22–49. Also see his *The Third Wave: Democratization in the Late Twentieth Century* (Norman: University of Oklahoma Press, 1991), 298–311.

22. For Max Weber's discussion of caesaropapism, see his *Economy and Society,* Guenther Roth and Claus Wittich, eds. (Berkeley: University of California Press, 1978), 2:1159–63, quote from 2:1161.

23. Islam (unlike Confucianism) is an important value system in parts of post-Communist Europe. A complete argument concerning Islam would have to be much more complex than our argument concern-

Democracy and the Return of Communism

Some interpreters have seen the "return of Communists" to power in Poland, Hungary, and Lithuania—countries that played a vanguard role in democratic transitions—as proof that economics and politics are so tightly linked that economic decline means democratic decline. For countries where there has been at least one legitimate victory by democratic electoral forces (and in many countries there has never been such a victory), we believe a more nuanced judgment is appropriate.

By the definitions of democracy we have advanced in this book, the return to power of reformed Communist Party–led coalitions in Lithuania in 1992, in Poland in 1993, and in Hungary in 1994, while a setback for some policies that were deepening democracy (such as local government reform in Poland) was not in itself an example of nondemocratic regime change. We say this because, by almost all reliable accounts as of this writing (July 1995), the reform Communist coalitions accepted the democratic rules of the game in how they contested the election and later in how they ruled. Also, very importantly, they were accepted as legitimate victors and rulers by the parties they defeated. In this sense there was not a *regime change* away from democracy as political scientists normally use the term. Strictly speaking, in comparative terms, the Lithuanian, Polish, and Hungarian elections represented a peaceful democratic alternation of power.

From a long historical perspective, it may even turn out that these elections actually strengthened democracy in Lithuania, Poland, and Hungary in one important respect. They indicated to victors and losers alike that democracy was becoming the only game in town. In fact, precisely because democracy was perceived in 1992–94 as the only game in town, the reformed Communists in Lithuania, Poland, and Hungary were extremely eager to demonstrate that they would govern as democratic parties. Their calculation was that, by so governing, they would be perceived, when they in turn were out of office, as part of the loyal democratic opposition and thus as a legitimate alternative government.[24] To make this point they are holding themselves in some respects to somewhat higher stan-

---

ing Orthodox Christianity. However, we note that the West's fear of fundamentalism has frequently contributed to its shoring up of and even legitimating antidemocratic governments or movements that are seen as bulwarks against the spread of fundamentalism. This is so even when the Islamic parties were elected democratically and had not violated democratic practices. Nowhere was this clearer than in the West's implicit and even explicit endorsement of the military coup in Algeria after Islamic forces had won the first electoral round in 1991. Thus, for geopolitical reasons, authoritarian governments in the former Soviet Union that share borders with Iran and/or Afghanistan (e.g., Turkmenistan, Uzbekistan, and Tajikistan) are to some extent treated by Western policy makers and commentators with a democratic "double standard."

24. This point was stressed in a conversation between Alfred Stepan and Jerzy Wiatr, who chairs an important congressional committee for the former Communists in the Polish parliament. Wiatr stressed that "the most important thing we should accomplish in our government is that we prove we are a legitimate democratic alternative." Conversation in Warsaw, November 5, 1993.

dards of civil liberties than did their predecessors in Hungary and Lithuania, who occasionally violated civil liberties in the name of their nationalist and anti-Communist "mandates." For example, the reform Communists in Hungary are in coalition with the liberal Free Democrats and the coalition's overall policy toward the media has been less flawed than that of the first democratically elected government. In Lithuania, the leader of nationalist independence, Vytautas Landsbergis, pursued his anti-Communist nationalism to such an extent that Anatol Lieven, in his excellent book, referred to him as a "backward-looking, religious-colored nationalist . . . [who] left the nation more divided than when he became its leader."[25] His reform Communist successor, Algirdas Brazauskas, has paid somewhat more attention to providing a "political roof" of individual rights to all citizens and pursuing a politics of inclusion.

Conceptually and politically, what does the phrase "the return of Communists" to power mean and not mean in Central Europe in the mid-1990s? In the full sense of the word, a Communist regime in Central Europe before 1989, even in mature post-totalitarian Hungary or authoritarian Poland, meant a powerful, dependent alliance with a nondemocratic hegemonic world power. In the mid-1990s there is no such alliance, and Russia is not a hegemonic world power. In this new geopolitical context, the reform Communists' best chance for power is to present themselves as—and to be—"social democrats."[26] Even if some of the reformed Communists might not actually have undergone profound changes in their mentality (and many, of course, have not), the external reality to which the reform Communists must respond has changed profoundly. As long as democracy is the only game in town, the incentive structure of those who seek governmental power is derived from the democratic context.

Finally, since voters play a crucial role in weighting the incentive system, what

25. Anatol Lieven, *The Baltic Revolution: Estonia, Latvia, Lithuania and the Path to Independence.* (New Haven: Yale University Press, 1993), 274.

26. In 1989–90 the social democratic political space in post-Communist Europe was not effectively occupied in elections. The historic social democrats were too tarnished and too weak and the neoliberal discourse was too hegemonic. In 1992–94, some reformed Communist parties who were out of power partially restructured themselves to fill this space as the reaction to neoliberalism set in. Also, with the collapse of Communism, the Socialist International sought new allies in post-Communist Europe. The reform Communist parties could gain Socialist International certification and support only if in fact they ruled as democrats. In December 1994, the Council of the Socialist International, meeting in Budapest, recommended that the reform Communist party in Hungary, the Hungarian Socialist Party, be admitted as a full member of the Socialist International. For an astute analysis of the political and structural reasons for the social democratic turn, while out of office, of the Hungarian and Polish post-Communist parties, see Michael Waller, "The Adaptation of the Former Communist Parties of East-Central Europe: A Case of Social Democratization?" (paper prepared for a conference on Political Representation: Parties and Parliamentary Democracy, Central European University, Budapest, June 16–17, 1995). At the same Central European University conference, the president of the Lithuanian Political Science Association, Algis Krupavicius, wrote that, for the Lithuanian post-Communist party that came to power in 1992 (the Democratic Labour Party), "the period in opposition was an extremely favorable opportunity to renew their membership [which dropped from 200,000 in 1989 to 8,000 in 1995], organizational structures, and ideological identity." The quotation is from his conference paper, "Post-Communist Transformation and Political Parties," 12–13.

did they actually want? Did they actually want a return to Communism?[27] The Polish voters, two months after the elections that had supposedly "returned" the former Communists to power, believed, correctly in our judgment, that they had not actually returned the old Communists to power. Polish respondents recognized the fundamental discontinuity in global and national power relations between 1988 and 1993. To the question, "Does the formation of the SLD-PSL [the reform Communist Party and their old Peasant Party ally] government coalition signify the return to power of persons who ruled prior to 1989?", 63 percent answered "no," 13 percent said "difficult to say," and only 24 percent of the population answered "yes."[28] We believe this answer is geopolitically, politically, and historically correct. An observation from the Spanish case may clarify our reasoning. If sometime in the 1990s—as seems probable—the Partido Popular, a party that is perceived by a segment of the electorate as representing a continuity with the right wing that governed with Franco, wins control of the government after an election, their victory in the changed Spanish environment would not signify a "return to francoism" as much as an alternation in power, in which a modern democratic conservative party has won the election with a mandate to rule democratically.[29]

While we are happy to end this book on a somewhat optimistic note concerning the future of democracy in East Central Europe, we want to insist again that

27. In both Poland and Hungary, as we have already discussed, the electoral laws resulted in the reform Communist parties or coalition receiving many more seats than votes. Seats therefore were not a solid indicator of voters' intentions. In Poland in 1993, 35.8 percent of the votes for the reformed Communists and their coalitional peasant allies yielded 65.8 percent of the seats. In Hungary in 1994, the reform Communist party, the Hungarian Socialist Party, received 33 percent of the vote in the first round but an absolute majority of seats after the second round.

28. Poll published by the Polish Public Opinion Service, Centrum Badania Opinii Spolecznej, in November 1993, p. 1. Moreover, in late 1993 and early 1994, when a random sample of the population in Poland and Hungary was asked to comment on the statement, "We should return to Communist rule," 47 percent of those polled in Poland "strongly disagreed" and 35 percent "somewhat disagreed" with this statement. The sum total of respondents in Hungary who disagreed was an identical 82 percent. See Rose and Haerpfer, "New Democracies Barometer III," question 43. The highest percentage of respondents in East Central Europe who "strongly agreed" with the statement was in Bulgaria, with 9 percent. The next highest was Romania, with 4 percent.

29. For many readers the November 1995 victory in Poland of a former communist party leader, Aleksander Kwaśniewski, in the second round of the presidential elections might seem a more clear victory for communism. From the viewpoint of democratic consolidation, the two most important questions for Poland's future are: 1) Will the post-communists (who as a result of the 1993 and 1995 elections had a two-thirds majority in the parliament and controlled the presidency) rule democratically? and 2) Will the anti-communist forces accept the legitimacy of the free election results? While not happy with the November 1995 elections, Timothy Garton Ash was more worried about the second question than the first: "Morally, as well as aesthetically, the triumph of the post-communists in Poland is deeply distasteful, but is it dangerous? Not, I believe, so far as their aims and policies are concerned . . . Kwaśniewski and his friends want desperately to be seen not as eastern post-communists but as regular western social democrats." Concerning the second question, Garton Ash cites a number of post-election declarations by the Polish episcopate and Lech Walesa and concludes that the greatest danger in Poland is "a large right-wing extraparliamentary movement around Lech Walesa, supported by the Church and Solidarity, and simply not accepting President Kwaśniewski as the legitimate head of Poland's Third Republic." See Timothy Garton Ash, "'Neo-Pagan' Poland", *New York Review of Books* (January 11, 1996), 10–14, quotes from 12 and 14.

we do not embrace a geopolitical or philosophical perspective of democratic immanence. It is probable that in some of the countries we have analyzed democracy will never be consolidated. In other countries democracy might become consolidated but will eventually break down. We also unhappily acknowledge that some countries will consolidate democracy but will never *deepen* democracy in the spheres of gender equality, access to critical social services, inclusive citizenship, respect for human rights, and freedom of information. They might, indeed, occasionally violate human rights.

All serious democratic thinkers and activists are now also aware that the much vaunted democratic Third Wave has already produced some dangerous undertows, not only in post-Communist Europe but also in Western Europe.[30] In the United States, influential ideologues of liberty are at times too simplistic and mean spirited for a healthy democratic polity. In this context democratic triumphalism is not only uncalled for but dangerous. Democratic institutions have to be not only created but crafted, nurtured, and developed. We think that we have made abundantly clear that to create an economic society supportive of democracy requires more than just markets and private property. It is time to problematize and transcend "illiberal liberalism" and also to theorize and socially construct integrative identity politics, as opposed to endlessly fragmenting identity politics. Further, to argue that democracy is better than any other form of government once alternatives have been in crisis is not sufficient. Democracy has to be defended on its own merits. Clearly, more research should also be devoted to learning about the great variety of democratic regimes that actually exist in the world. Most important, new *political projects,* as well as research endeavors, must be devoted to improving the *quality* of consolidated democracies.

---

30. Three excellent articles in a special issue of *Daedalus* called "After Communism: What?" (Summer 1994) are devoted to the unexpected crisis Western and Eastern European democrats began to experience after they had lost their legitimating enemy or "other" after the collapse of Communism. Many problems that had long been deferred or denied came on the agenda. For this new and challenging "paradigm lost" situation, see Tony Judt, "Nineteen Eighty-Nine: The End of *Which* European Era," 1–20; Elemér Hankiss, "European Paradigms: East and West, 1945–1994," 115–26; and István Rév, "The Postmortem Victory of Communism," 157–70. Claus Offe, *Der Tunnel am Ende des Lichts: Erkundungen der politischen Transformation im Neuen Osten* (Frankfurt: Campus Verlag, 1994) throughout the book, and particularly in chapter 10, raises similar questions.

Index

266 n, 267, 273, 274; of Portugal, 118, 126; relation to democratic consolidation, 69; of Romania, 345, 349, 351, 355; of Spain, 96, 97; of USSR, 239–43, 371, 380–82, 384, 386
"competitive assimilation game," 32
complementarity of civil and political society, 8
complementary multiple identities, 102
completed transition, requirements for, 107
"condemned to democracy," 221
Connor, Walker, 30 n
Consejo de Fuerzas Políticas de Cataluña, 101 n
consociational democracy, 33, 40, 388, 390; in Chile, 217 n; in multinational polities, 429, 430
consociational pacts, 57
consolidated democracy: attitudinal definition of, 6; behavioral definition of, 5; benefits of parliamentarism in, 141, 142; in Brazil, 166, 172, 187; breakdown in, 6; in Bulgaria, 343; in Chile, 212–15; citizenship policy in, 414; in civilian-led regimes, 69; Communist parties in, 69; conditions necessary for, 7–13; constitutional definition of, 5, 6; constitution-making environments, 81–83; in Czech Republic, 333 n, 434; economic performance in, 77, 80; evaluation of prior regime, 143–47, 171–74; in Greece, 132–38; hierarchical military in, 64; in Hungary, 434; legacies of totalitarian and post-totalitarian regime type, 244–54; legitimacy of territorial unit in, 26, 27; in Lithuania, 432, 434; in multinational settings, 33–37, 424–28; need for market intervention in, 12; nonhierarchical military in, 68; in Poland, 255, 269–92; in Portugal, 124–29; quality of, 137; relation between civil and political society, 8–10; "reserve domains," 67–69, 84, 110, 116, 126, 133; role of parties, 10; role of timing, 37; in Slovakia, 333 n; in South America, 220, 221; in Spain, 108–15; in Uruguay, 159–61; variety of, 6
consolidation tasks, 38, 40, 56; in post-Communist Europe, 253; in post-totalitarian regimes, 295; sequence of, 139
Constantinescu, Emil, 363
constitutionalism, 10, 55; in Argentina, 203; in Brazil, 167; in post-Communist Europe, 248, 249
constitution-making environments, 66, 81–83; in Argentina, 83, 204, 205, 222; in Brazil, 83, 171, 186, 221, 222; in Bulgaria, 341; in Chile, 82, 208–13, 215, 219, 220, 222; consensual constitution-making, 83, 114; constrained constituent assembly, 83, 222; constraints on,

82; control by interim government, 82; in Czechoslovakia, 82, 316; in Estonia, 405; in Greece, 132–35; in Hungary, 311, 312; "paper" constitution, 82; partisan constitution, 83; in Poland, 282–84; in Portugal, 82, 116, 120, 121, 123, 124 126; restoration formulas, 83, 222; in Spain, 83, 98, 102, 116, 117; in Uruguay, 83, 154, 222; in USSR, 82, 381, 396, 398, 399; in Yugoslavia, 82
constrained constituent assembly. *See* constitution-making environments, constrained constituent assembly
constructive vote of no confidence, 115, 310
contestation, inclusiveness of, 96
Contreras, General Manuel, 218, 225 n
Convergència i Unió, 115
COPCON, 122 n
Coposu, Corneliu, 363 n
Coppedge, Michael, 39 n
corporatism, in Brazil, 77
Cortes, role in Spanish transition, 91–96
Costa Pinto, António, 128 n
costs of repression and toleration, 19; in Eastern Europe, 238, 244; in Spanish transition, 98
Council of Europe, norms for democracy, 35
Council of Mutual Economic Assistance (CMEA), 236, 240, 242
Crampton, Richard, 336
Croatia, 385; Serbian irredenta in, 450
Csurka, István, 315, 316
Cuba, 357
Cunhal, Alvaro, 121
Cyprus, invasion by Turkey, 131
Czechoslovakia, xvi, 8, 10 n, 24, 25 n, 111, 142, 235; absence of debt problems, 296, 318; annexation by Germany, 75; antipolitics, 316, 331; atomized non-society, 321; attitudes toward break-up, 329; attitudes toward political and economic systems, 442; behavior of coercive staff, 323; Catholic Church in, 317; Charter of 77, 319, 321, 337; civil society, 327, 337; Communist Party, 317, 318, 320, 326, 332; constituent assembly, 331; constitution-making environment, 82, 316; contrast to Hungary, 318, 321; democracy in interwar period, 76 n, 316, 317, 452; "detotalitarianization by decay," 296; dogmatic Stalinism, 317; elections, 328, 331; events leading to collapse, 325–27; expulsion of German irredenta, 425; "forgetting," 320; founding election, 332; as frozen post-totalitarian regime, 42, 45, 47, 232, 254, 294, 295, 316, 319, 320, 327, 331, 337; Helsinki Ac-

Library of Congress Cataloging-in-Publication Data

Linz, Juan J. (Juan José), 1926–
    Problems of democratic transition and consolidation : southern Europe, South
America, and post-communist Europe / Juan J. Linz and Alfred Stepan.
        p.   cm.
        Includes index.
        ISBN 0-8018-5157-2 (h : alk. paper). —ISBN 0-8018-5158-0 (pbk : alk. paper)
        1. Democracy—History—20th century.   2. Democracy—Europe, Southern.
3. Democracy—South America.   4. Democracy—Europe, Eastern.   I. Stepan,
Alfred C.   II. Title.
JC421.L56   1996
321.8'09'045—dc20   95-43462